de Gruyter Studies in Mathematics 7

Helmut Strasser

Mathematical Theory of Statistics

Statistical Experiments and Asymptotic Decision Theory

W DE G

Walter de Gruyter · Berlin · New York 1985

Author:

Dr. Helmut Strasser
Professor of Mathematics
Universität Bayreuth

For my wife

Library of Congress Cataloging in Publication Data

Strasser, Helmut, 1948–
Mathematical theory of statistics.
(De Gruyter studies in mathematics ; 7)
Bibliography: p.
Includes indexes.
1. Mathematical statistics. 2. Experimental design.
3. Statistical decision. I. Title. II. Series.
QA276.S855 1985 519.5 85–16269
ISBN 0-89925-028-9 (U.S.)

CIP-Kurztitelaufnahme der Deutschen Bibliothek

Strasser, Helmut:
Mathematical theory of statistics : statist. experiments and asymptot. decision theory / Helmut Strasser. –
Berlin ; New York : de Gruyter, 1985.
(De Gruyter studies in mathematics ; 7)
ISBN 3-11-010258-7

NE: GT

Cover design: Rudolf Hübler, Berlin. Typesetting and Printing: Tutte Druckerei GmbH, Salzweg-Passau. Binding: Lüderitz & Bauer, Berlin.

Preface

The present book is neither intended to be a text-book for a course in statistics, nor a monograph on statistical decision theory. It is rather the attempt to connect well-known facts of classical statistics with problems and methods of contemporary research. To justify such a connection, let us recapitulate some modern developments of mathematical statistics.

A considerable amount of statistical research during the last thirty years can be subsumed under the label "asymptotic justification of statistical methods". Already in the first half of this century asymptotic arguments became necessary, as it turned out that the optimization problems of statistics can be solved for finite sample size only in very few particular cases. The starting point of a systematic mathematical approach to asymptotics was the famous paper by Wald [1943]. This early paper contains already many important ideas for the asymptotic treatment of testing hypotheses. Ten years later the thesis of LeCam appeared, which in the meantime has turned out to be leading for asymptotic estimation. Briefly, the situation considered in both papers is as follows. As mathematical model serves a family of probability measures or, for short, an experiment which can be viewed as a finite dimensional differentiable manifold, i.e. a so-called parametric model. By independent replication of the experiment it becomes possible to restrict the analysis to a small subset of the model, i.e. to localize the problem. As the sample size tends to infinity the experiment can locally be approximated by a much simpler one, namely by a Gaussian shift. Essentially, this is due to the smoothness properties of the experiment. Thus, for large sample sizes the statistical analysis of the original experiment can be replaced by the analysis of the approximating Gaussian shift.

It took at least twenty years to understand the structure of the papers of Wald and LeCam in the way described above. Remarkable steps were the papers by LeCam [1960], and by Hajek [1970 and 1972]. Finally, LeCam succeeded in extending his version of decision theory [1955 and 1964] to an asymptotic theory of experiments [1972 and 1979]. It covers the main results of asymptotic statistics obtained so far, thus providing a framework which facilitates the understanding of classical asymptotics considerably. Moreover, for good reasons this theory claims to determine the framework of future developments in asymptotic statistics.

Apart from the above-mentioned papers the asymptotic theory of experiments is presented in Lecture Notes of LeCam, [1969 and 1974] and hopefully soon by a forthcoming monograph of LeCam. The present book is intended to serve as a "missing link" between introductory text-books like those of

Lehmann [1958], Schmetterer [1974], or Witting [1985], and the presentation by LeCam. This goal determines what the book contains as well as the omissions. As to the mathematical prerequisites, we present the asymptotic theory of experiments on a mathematical level corresponding to the usual level of upper graduate courses in probability.

Essentially, there are two sets of problems where the state of the art justifies the attempt of unified presentation. First, there is the general decision-theoretic framework of statistics together with asymptotic decision theory, and second, its application to the case of independent replications of parametric models. The present volume deals mainly with the first complex.

To give a rough outline of the organization of the book, let us discuss briefly the contents. More detailed information is provided by the introductions to the single chapters.

After having collected some more or less well-known facts of probability theory in Chapter 1, we deal in Chapter 2 with basic facts of testing hypotheses. On the one hand, the results of this chapter are needed later, but on the other hand they convey a first idea of handling decision-theoretic concepts. It turns out, that the theory of Neyman-Pearson is the basic tool for the analysis of binary experiments. This gives rise to exemplify the theory of experiments in Chapter 3 by means of these tools only. Solely by the theory of Neyman and Pearson some of the main results of the theory of experiments are proved in an elementary way.

Already classical statistics compares experiments with respect to the information contained. The central role plays the concept of sufficiency. In Chapter 4 we take up this idea and extend it, passing the notion of exhaustivity, to the general concept of randomization of dominated experiments. By relatively simple methods we prove a version of the randomization criterion for dominated experiments. In Chapter 5 we collect the most important applications of sufficiency to exponential experiments and Gaussian shifts.

The testing problems which have been considered up to this point are of dimension one. In Chapter 6 we start with the consideration of higher dimensional testing problems. We begin with Wald's classical complete class theorem and prove the completeness of convex acceptance regions for exponential experiments. Our main interest in this chapter are Gaussian shift experiments of dimension greater than one. At first, some basic facts are proved elementary, i.e. by means of the Neyman-Pearson lemma. The rest of the chapter, however, is devoted to another approach to testing for Gaussian shifts, namely to reduction by invariance. In Chapter 6 we take this opportunity for discussing amenability of groups and for proving the most simple version of the Hunt-Stein theorem. Partly, these results are needed later, but their presentation in Chapter 6 serves mainly as an introduction to the ideas of statistical invariance concepts.

Before we go into the general decision theory we present in Chapter 7 a brief compendium of estimation theory. The power of the Neyman-Pearson theory is illustrated by median unbiased estimates. Sufficiency is applied to mean unbiased estimates. As it becomes clear already in Chapter 3, the natural extension of the Neyman-Pearson lemma to arbitrary experiments leads to the Bayesian calculus which is considered without any regard to "subjectivistic" interpretation. It turns out that invariance-theoretic methods of estimation as well as most proofs of admissibility are, in a technical sense, Bayesian in spirit.

At this point there is plenty of motivation, to introduce the concepts of decision theory in full generality. In Chapter 8 we present the classical results of decision theory, such as the minimax theorem, the complete class theorem and the general Hunt-Stein theorem. Chapter 9 deals with those parts of decision theory which are known under the label of comparison of experiments. The general theorems of asymptotic decision theory are contained in Chapter 10. By means of these results it is possible to carry through our program, namely to reduce asymptotic problems to the analysis of the limit experiments. This is done in the remaining Chapter 11–13.

Let us have a closer look at the program. The asymptotic method consists of three steps corresponding to Chapters 11, 12 and 13. The main idea is to embed a statistical experiment into a convergent sequence of experiments and then to analyse the limit experiment of the sequence instead of the original one. Hence, one major problem is the statistical analysis of the limit experiment. In the present book we confine ourselves to limits which are Gaussian shifts. In Chapter 11 the statistical theory of Gaussian shifts is recapitulated sufficiently general to cover infinite dimensional parameter spaces. A second problem consists in the proof of convergence for certain sequences of experiments. In this context we only consider the case of convergence to Gaussian shifts. This case can be treated by means of stochastic expansions of likelihood processes. By way of example we establish in Chapter 12 the basic expansion for independent replications of a given experiment. As soon as convergence of a sequence against a limit experiment is established the asymptotic decision theory of Chapter 10 may be applied. This synthesis is carried through in Chapter 13 for sequences of experiments converging to Gaussian shifts. In this way, we obtain the main results of classical asymptotics. We show at hand of examples how to treat both parametric as well as nonparametric problems by the tools established so far.

It is clear that the motivation for the development of a general asymptotic decision theory can only be found in classical examples, which are not the main subject of this book. The connoisseur of classical statistics will not mind this lack of discussing the intuitive background of the concepts. But for the beginner we emphasize that this book will completely miss its aim if the reader is not aware of the connection with the origin of the ideas. There is a sufficient number of good textbooks covering classical statistical methods and some asymptotics, which should be used as a permanent reference. Moreover, it is highly recommended to read the original papers quoted in the text.

We do not claim that our presentation is final in any respect but we hope that it will be helpful for some reader.

The author wishes to express his gratitude to H. Bauer, P. Gabriel and W. Schuder for accepting this book for publication. He feels very much indebted to C. Becker and H. Milbrodt who helped during the preparation of the manuscript by working through several versions, filling gaps and correcting numerous mistakes, and to Miss Heike Milbrodt for translating parts of the preface and the introductions into English. Thanks are also due to many collegues for supporting me by valuable hints and remarks, especially I. Bomze, A. Janssen, H. Linhart and J. Pfanzagl. It is a special pleasure to assure Mrs. G. Witzigmann of my most grateful appreciation for the care and skill she displayed in the typing of the manuscript.

Bayreuth, July 1985 Helmut Strasser

Contents

Chapter 5: Exponential Experiments

Chapter 6: More Theory of Testing

Chapter 7: Theory of estimation

Chapter 8: General decision theory

Chapter 9: Comparison of experiments

Chapter 1: Basic Notions on Probability Measures

This chapter contains some mathematical tools that are somehow typical of statistical theory. Strictly speaking, however, their mathematical background has little to do with statistical ideas. We give detailed proofs where the problems have so far hardly been discussed in textbooks on probability theory.

The decomposition of probability measures with the help of likelihood ratios is of particular importance. Here, we base the concept of the likelihood ratio exclusively on the Radon-Nikodym Theorem, because the introduction of a dominating measure seems arbitrary. Section 1 contains fundamental facts and rules on likelihood ratios.

In Section 2 we discuss the variational distance and the Hellinger distance between probability measures. We prove some well-known inequalities which will be useful, later. Section 3 contains brief remarks on topologies of sets of probability measures and in Section 4 we are concerned with separability of those topologies. Separability has important consequences for measurability of the likelihood function. The results are partly due to Pfanzagl [1969] and Nölle [1966].

In Section 5 we occupy ourselves with transforms of measures. Our major concern are the Laplace and the Mellin Transforms of measures. At last, we discuss the Hellinger transform of measures on simplices. For each transform we shall give a uniqueness- and a continuity theorem.

Section 6 contains miscellaneous results needed later and serves mainly for easy reference.

1. Decomposition of probability measures

Let $(\Omega, \mathscr{A})$ be a measurable space and let $P|\mathscr{A}$, $Q|\mathscr{A}$ be probability measures. We begin with existence and uniqueness of Lebesgue decompositions of probability measures.

1.1 Lemma. *There is an $\mathscr{A}$-measurable function $f \geqq 0$ and a set $N \in \mathscr{A}$ such that $P(N) = 0$ and*

$$Q(A) = \int_A f dP + Q(A \cap N), \quad A \in \mathscr{A}.$$

Proof. Since $P \ll P+Q$, $Q \ll P+Q$, there exist the RN-derivatives $\dfrac{dP}{d(P+Q)}$, $\dfrac{dQ}{d(P+Q)}$. If we choose

$$N = \left\{\frac{dP}{d(P+Q)} = 0\right\}, \quad f = \frac{dQ}{d(P+Q)} \bigg/ \frac{dP}{d(P+Q)} \text{ on } \Omega \setminus N,$$

then the assertion is proved. □

1.2 Lemma. *Suppose that f_i, $i = 1, 2$, are $\mathscr{A}$-measurable functions and $N_i \in \mathscr{A}$ are sets such that $P(N_i) = 0$, $i = 1, 2$, and*

$$Q(A) = \int_A f_i dP + Q(A \cap N_i), \quad A \in \mathscr{A}, \quad i = 1, 2.$$

Then $f_1 = f_2$ P-a.e. and $Q(N_1 \triangle N_2) = 0$.

Proof. For every $A \in \mathscr{A}$ we have

$$\int_{A \cap N_1' \cap N_2'} f_1 \, dP = Q(A \cap N_1' \cap N_2') = \int_{A \cap N_1' \cap N_2'} f_2 \, dP$$

which implies that $f_1 = f_2$ P-a.e. on $N_1' \cap N_2'$. Since $P(N_1' \cap N_2') = 1$ we obtain $f_1 = f_2$ P-a.e. Next note that

$$Q(N_1') = \int_{N_1'} f_1 \, dP + Q(N_1' \cap N_1) = \int_{N_1'} f_1 \, dP$$

and

$$Q(N_1') = \int_{N_1'} f_2 \, dP + Q(N_1' \cap N_2).$$

Since $f_1 = f_2$ P-a.e. it follows that $Q(N_1' \cap N_2) = 0$. In a similar way it is shown that $Q(N_2 \cap N_1') = 0$. □

1.3 Definition. Any pair (f, N), where $f \geqq 0$ is an $\mathscr{A}$-measurable function and $N \in \mathscr{A}$ a P-null set such that

$$Q(A) = \int_A f dP + Q(A \cap N), \quad A \in \mathscr{A},$$

is called *Lebesgue-decomposition* of Q with respect to P. The function f is called the *likelihood ratio* of Q and P.

1.4 Example. Let $\nu | \mathscr{A}$ be any σ-finite measure dominating P and Q. Then

$$\frac{dQ}{dP} := \frac{dQ}{d\nu} \bigg/ \frac{dP}{d\nu} \cdot 1_{\left\{\frac{dP}{d\nu} > 0\right\}}, \quad N := \left\{\frac{dP}{d\nu} = 0\right\}$$

defines a Lebesgue decomposition of Q with respect to P.

In the following let $\left(\frac{dQ}{dP}, N\right)$ be a Lebesgue-decomposition of Q with respect to P and $\left(\frac{dP}{dQ}, M\right)$ a Lebesgue-decomposition of P with respect to Q.

1.5 Remark. Let us collect some elementary properties of Lebesgue decompositions.

(1) $\frac{dQ}{dP} = 0$ P-a.e. on M (and therefore also $(P+Q)$-a.e. on M). This follows from

$$0 = Q(M) = \int_M \frac{dQ}{dP}\, dP + Q(M \cap N) = \int_M \frac{dQ}{dP}\, dP.$$

Similarly we have $\frac{dP}{dQ} = 0$ Q-a.e. on N (and therefore $(P+Q)$-a.e. on N).

(2) $P(M \cap N) = Q(M \cap N) = 0$. This is an obvious consequence of $P(N) = 0$ and $Q(M) = 0$. It follows that $P(M' \cup N') = Q(M' \cup N') = 1$.

(3) $P(M \cup N) = P(M)$ and $Q(M \cup N) = Q(N)$. This is obvious too. It follows that $P(M' \cap N') = 1 - P(M)$ and $Q(M' \cap N') = 1 - Q(N)$.

(4) $\frac{dQ}{dP} \cdot \frac{dP}{dQ} = 1$ $(P+Q)$-a.e. on $M' \cap N'$. For every $A \in \mathscr{A}$ we have

$$P(A \cap M' \cap N') = \int_{A \cap M' \cap N'} \frac{dP}{dQ}\, dQ = \int_{A \cap M' \cap N'} \frac{dP}{dQ} \cdot \frac{dQ}{dP}\, dP$$

which proves the equation at least P-a.e. A similar argument shows that it is true also Q-a.e.

(5) $$0 < \frac{dP}{dQ} < \infty \ (P+Q)\text{-a.e. on } M' \cap N', \quad \text{and}$$

$$0 < \frac{dQ}{dP} < \infty \ (P+Q)\text{-a.e. on } M' \cap N'.$$

This is an immediate consequence of (4). It follows that P and Q are equivalent on $M' \cap N'$.

(6) For every $A \in \mathscr{A}$

$$\int_A \frac{dQ}{dP}\, dP = \int_{A \cap M' \cap N'} \frac{dQ}{dP}\, dP, \quad \int_A \frac{dP}{dQ}\, dQ = \int_{A \cap M' \cap N'} \frac{dP}{dQ}\, dQ.$$

The first equation holds since $P(N) = 0$ and $\frac{dQ}{dP} = 0$ P-a.e. on M. The second equation follows immediately.

(7) $\int \frac{dQ}{dP}\, dP = 1 - Q(N), \quad \int \frac{dP}{dQ}\, dQ = 1 - P(M).$

This is obvious from the definition.

(8) $\int f dQ = \int f \frac{dQ}{dP}\, dP + \int\limits_N f dQ$ for every $\mathscr{A}$-measurable function f which is non-negative or Q-integrable.

Property 1.5 (4) suggests a rule of computation which is sometimes useful.

1.6 Lemma. *For every $a \in (0, \infty]$*

$$P\left(\left\{\frac{dP}{dQ} < a\right\} \setminus M\right) = P\left\{\frac{dQ}{dP} > \frac{1}{a}\right\},$$

$$Q\left(\left\{\frac{dQ}{dP} < a\right\} \setminus N\right) = Q\left\{\frac{dP}{dQ} > \frac{1}{a}\right\}.$$

Proof. Using the assertions of 1.5 we obtain

$$P\left(\left\{\frac{dP}{dQ} < a\right\} \setminus M\right) = P\left\{\frac{dP}{dQ} < a\right\} - P\left(M \cap \left\{\frac{dP}{dQ} < a\right\}\right)$$

$$= \int\limits_{\frac{dP}{dQ} < a} \frac{dP}{dQ}\, dQ = \int\limits_{\left\{\frac{dP}{dQ} < a\right\} \cap M' \cap N'} \frac{dP}{dQ}\, dQ = \int\limits_{\left\{\frac{dQ}{dP} > \frac{1}{a}\right\} \cap M' \cap N'} \frac{dP}{dQ}\, dQ$$

$$= \int\limits_{\frac{dQ}{dP} > \frac{1}{a}} \frac{dP}{dQ}\, dQ$$

$$= P\left\{\frac{dQ}{dP} > \frac{1}{a}\right\} - P\left(M \cap \left\{\frac{dQ}{dP} > \frac{1}{a}\right\}\right) = P\left\{\frac{dQ}{dP} > \frac{1}{a}\right\}.$$

The second assertion follows by interchanging P and Q. □

It follows that $P(M) = P\left\{\frac{dQ}{dP} = 0\right\}$ and $Q(N) = Q\left\{\frac{dP}{dQ} = 0\right\}$. We finish the discussion of Lebesgue decompositions by the composition rule for likelihood ratios.

1.7 Lemma. *Suppose that $P|\mathscr{A}$, $Q|\mathscr{A}$ and $R|\mathscr{A}$ are probability measures and $\left(\frac{dQ}{dR}, N_{Q|R}\right)$, $\left(\frac{dQ}{dP}, N_{Q|P}\right)$ and $\left(\frac{dR}{dP}, N_{R|P}\right)$ are the Lebesgue decompositions. Then*

$$\frac{dQ}{dR} \cdot \frac{dR}{dP} = \frac{dQ}{dP} \quad P\text{-a.e. on } \Omega \setminus N_{Q|R}.$$

Proof. Let $A \in \mathscr{A}$. First we observe

$$\begin{aligned}\int_A \frac{dQ}{dP}\,dP &= Q(A) - Q(A \cap N_{Q|P}) \\ &= \int_A \frac{dQ}{dR}\,dR + Q(A \cap N_{Q|R}) - Q(A \cap N_{Q|P}) \\ &= \int_A \frac{dQ}{dR} \cdot \frac{dR}{dP}\,dP + \int_{A \cap N_{R|P}} \frac{dQ}{dR}\,dR \\ &\quad + Q(A \cap N_{Q|R}) - Q(A \cap N_{Q|P}).\end{aligned}$$

We may assume that $A \subseteq \Omega \backslash (N_{R|P} \cup N_{Q|R})$ since $P(N_{R|P}) = 0$ and $P(N_{Q|P}) = 0$. Then we arrive at

$$\int_A \frac{dQ}{dP}\,dP = \int_A \frac{dQ}{dR} \cdot \frac{dR}{dP}\,dP$$

which proves the assertion. □

2. Distances between probability measures

Let $(\Omega, \mathscr{A})$ be a measurable space and let $P|\mathscr{A}$, $Q|\mathscr{A}$ be probability measures. Suppose that $\left(\frac{dQ}{dP}, N\right)$ is a Lebesgue decomposition of Q with respect to P.

2.1 Definition. The *variational distance* between P and Q is defined by

$$d_1(P, Q) = \|P - Q\| = \sup\{|P(A) - Q(A)| : A \in \mathscr{A}\}.$$

2.2 Lemma.

$$\begin{aligned}d_1(P, Q) &= \frac{1}{2} \int \left|\frac{dQ}{dP} - 1\right| dP + \frac{1}{2} Q(N) \\ &= \int \left(\frac{dQ}{dP} - 1\right)^+ dP + Q(N) = \int \left(\frac{dQ}{dP} - 1\right)^- dP \\ &= \sup_{A \in \mathscr{A}} (P(A) - Q(A)).\end{aligned}$$

Proof. First we note that

$$\sup_{A \in \mathscr{A}} (Q(A) - P(A)) = \sup_{A \in \mathscr{A}} \left(\int_A \left(\frac{dQ}{dP} - 1 \right) dP + Q(N \cap A) \right) =$$

$$= \int \left(\frac{dQ}{dP} - 1 \right)^+ dP + Q(N)$$

since the sup is attained for $A = N \cup \left\{ \frac{dQ}{dP} \geqq 1 \right\}$. In a similar way we observe that

$$\sup_{A \in \mathscr{A}} (P(A) - Q(A)) = \sup_{A \in \mathscr{A}} \left(\int_A \left(1 - \frac{dQ}{dP} \right) dP - Q(N \cap A) \right) =$$

$$= \int \left(\frac{dQ}{dP} - 1 \right)^- dP$$

since the sup is attained for $A = \left\{ \frac{dQ}{dP} \leqq 1 \right\} \setminus N$. Substituting A by A', $A \in \mathscr{A}$, we see that

$$\sup_{A \in \mathscr{A}} (Q(A) - P(A)) = \sup_{A \in \mathscr{A}} (P(A) - Q(A)).$$

Hence both expressions are equal to $d_1(P, Q)$ and the same holds for their arithmetic mean. □

2.3 Lemma. *Let* $\mathscr{F} = \mathscr{F}(\Omega, \mathscr{A}) = \{\varphi \in \mathscr{L}(\Omega, \mathscr{A}) \colon 0 \leqq \varphi \leqq 1\}$. *Then*

$$d_1(P, Q) = \sup_{\varphi \in \mathscr{F}} |P\varphi - Q\varphi| = \sup_{\varphi \in \mathscr{F}} (P\varphi - Q\varphi) = \sup_{\varphi \in \mathscr{F}} (Q\varphi - P\varphi).$$

Proof. Substituting φ by $1 - \varphi$ we see that

$$\sup_{\varphi \in \mathscr{F}} (P\varphi - Q\varphi) = \sup_{\varphi \in \mathscr{F}} (Q\varphi - P\varphi).$$

Hence both expressions are equal to $\sup_{\varphi \in \mathscr{F}} |P\varphi - Q\varphi|$. Since $\{1_A \colon A \in \mathscr{A}\} \subseteq \mathscr{F}$ we obtain

$$d_1(P, Q) \leqq \sup_{\varphi \in \mathscr{F}} |P\varphi - Q\varphi|.$$

The reversed inequality follows from

$$(Q\varphi - P\varphi) = \int \varphi \left(\frac{dQ}{dP} - 1 \right) dP + \int_N \varphi \, dQ \leqq$$

$$\leqq \int \left(\frac{dQ}{dP} - 1 \right)^+ dP + Q(N) = d_1(P, Q). \qquad \square$$

2.4 Lemma. *If $\nu|\mathscr{A}$ is any σ-finite measure dominating P and Q, then*

$$d_1(P,Q) = \int\left(\frac{dP}{d\nu} - \frac{dQ}{d\nu}\right)^+ d\nu = \int\left(\frac{dP}{d\nu} - \frac{dQ}{d\nu}\right)^- d\nu$$
$$= \frac{1}{2}\int\left|\frac{dP}{d\nu} - \frac{dQ}{d\nu}\right| d\nu.$$

Proof. It is obvious that

$$\sup_{A\in\mathscr{A}}(P(A) - Q(A)) = \sup_{A\in\mathscr{A}}\int_A\left(\frac{dP}{d\nu} - \frac{dQ}{d\nu}\right)d\nu = \int\left(\frac{dP}{d\nu} - \frac{dQ}{d\nu}\right)^+ d\nu.$$

From

$$0 = \int\left(\frac{dP}{d\nu} - \frac{dQ}{d\nu}\right)^+ d\nu - \int\left(\frac{dP}{d\nu} - \frac{dQ}{d\nu}\right)^- d\nu$$

it follows that

$$\sup_{A\in\mathscr{A}}(P(A) - Q(A)) = \int\left(\frac{dP}{d\nu} - \frac{dQ}{d\nu}\right)^+ d\nu =$$
$$= \int\left(\frac{dP}{d\nu} - \frac{dQ}{d\nu}\right)^- d\nu = \frac{1}{2}\int\left|\frac{dP}{d\nu} - \frac{dQ}{d\nu}\right| d\nu. \qquad \square$$

2.5 Lemma.

(1) $0 \leqq d_1(P,Q) \leqq 1$.
(2) d_1 *is a distance.*
(3) $d_1(P,Q) = 1$ *iff* $P \perp Q$.

Proof. Obvious. $\square$

2.6 Lemma. *Suppose that $(\Omega_i, \mathscr{A}_i)$, $i = 1, 2$, are measurable spaces and $P_1|\mathscr{A}_1$, $P_2|\mathscr{A}_1$, $Q_1|\mathscr{A}_2$, $Q_2|\mathscr{A}_2$ are probability measures. Then*

$$d_1(P_1 \otimes Q_1, P_2 \otimes Q_2) \leqq d_1(P_1, P_2) + d_1(Q_1, Q_2).$$

Proof. Let $\mu_1 = \dfrac{P_1 + Q_1}{2}$, $\mu_2 = \dfrac{P_2 + Q_2}{2}$, and let $f_i = \dfrac{dP_i}{d\mu_i}$, $g_i = \dfrac{dQ_i}{d\mu_i}$, $i = 1, 2$.

Then

$$2d_1(P_1 \otimes Q_1, P_2 \otimes Q_2) = \int|f_1g_1 - f_2g_2|\,d(\mu_1 \otimes \mu_2) \leqq$$
$$\leqq \int|f_1g_1 - f_1g_2|\,d(\mu_1 \otimes \mu_2) + \int|f_1g_2 - f_2g_2|\,d(\mu_1 \otimes \mu_2)$$
$$= 2d_1(Q_1, Q_2) + 2d_1(P_1, P_2). \qquad \square$$

Apart from the variational distance the so-called Hellinger distance is an import tool for statistical purposes.

If $P \ll \nu$, $Q \ll \nu$, where $\nu|\mathscr{A}$ is σ-finite then $\dfrac{dP}{d\nu}$ and $\dfrac{dQ}{d\nu}$ are elements of $L_1(\Omega, \mathscr{A}, \nu)$ and the variational distance satisfies

$$d_1(P,Q) = \frac{1}{2}\left\| \frac{dP}{d\nu} - \frac{dQ}{d\nu} \right\|_1 .$$

Similarly, we may P and Q embed into $L_2(\Omega, \mathscr{A}, \nu)$ and define

$$d_2(P,Q) = \frac{1}{\sqrt{2}}\left\| \left(\frac{dP}{d\nu}\right)^{1/2} - \left(\frac{dQ}{d\nu}\right)^{1/2} \right\|_2 .$$

We have to show that it does not depend on the dominating measure $\nu|\mathscr{A}$. But this is an easy fact the proof of which is left to the reader.

2.7 Definition. If $P \ll \nu$, $Q \ll \nu$, where $\nu|\mathscr{A}$ is σ-finite then

$$d_2(P,Q) = \frac{1}{\sqrt{2}}\left\| \left(\frac{dP}{d\nu}\right)^{1/2} - \left(\frac{dQ}{d\nu}\right)^{1/2} \right\|_2$$

is called *Hellinger distance* between P and Q.

2.8 Definition. If $P \ll \nu$, $Q \ll \nu$, where $\nu|\mathscr{A}$ is σ-finite then

$$a(P,Q) = \int \left(\frac{dP}{d\nu}\right)^{1/2} \cdot \left(\frac{dQ}{d\nu}\right)^{1/2} d\nu$$

is called *affinity* of P and Q.

It is easy to see that the definition of the affinity is independent of the dominating measure $\nu|\mathscr{A}$.

2.9 Lemma. $d_2^2(P,Q) = 1 - a(P,Q)$.

Proof. Obvious. □

2.10 Lemma.

(1) $$a(P,Q) = \int \left(\frac{dQ}{dP}\right)^{1/2} dP.$$

(2) $$d_2^2(P,Q) = \frac{1}{2}\int \left[\left(\frac{dQ}{dP}\right)^{1/2} - 1\right]^2 dP + \frac{1}{2}Q(N).$$

Proof. Suppose that $\left(\frac{dQ}{dP}, N\right)$ is a Lebesgue decomposition of Q with respect to P. We have

$$\int\left(\frac{dQ}{dP}\right)^{1/2} dP = \int\left(\frac{dQ}{dP}\cdot\frac{dP}{d\nu}\right)^{1/2}\left(\frac{dP}{d\nu}\right)^{1/2} d\nu$$

and since Lemma 1.7 implies

$$\frac{dQ}{dP}\cdot\frac{dP}{d\nu} = \frac{dQ}{d\nu} \ \nu\text{-a.e.} \quad \text{on} \quad \Omega\backslash N,$$

$P(N) = 0$ proves (1).

The second relation follows from

$$\begin{aligned} d_2^2(P, Q) = 1 - a(P, Q) &= \frac{1}{2}\left(2 - 2\int\left(\frac{dQ}{dP}\right)^{1/2} dP\right) \\ &= \frac{1}{2}\left(\int\frac{dQ}{dP}\,dP + 1 - 2\int\left(\frac{dQ}{dP}\right)^{1/2} dP\right) + \frac{1}{2}\,Q(N) \\ &= \frac{1}{2}\int\left[\left(\frac{dQ}{dP}\right)^{1/2} - 1\right]^2 dP + \frac{1}{2}\,Q(N). \qquad \square \end{aligned}$$

Assertions 2.11–2.13 are a of a technical nature and are only needed for specific purposes.

2.11 Lemma. *Suppose that $P|\mathscr{A}$, $Q|\mathscr{A}$ and $R|\mathscr{A}$ are probability measures. Let $\left(\frac{dQ}{dP}, N_{Q|P}\right)$ and $\left(\frac{dR}{dP}, N_{R|P}\right)$ be Lebesgue decompositions of Q and R with respect to P. Then*

$$a(Q, R) = \int\left(\frac{dQ}{dP}\right)^{1/2}\cdot\left(\frac{dR}{dP}\right)^{1/2} dP + \beta_P(Q, R)$$

where

$$\beta_P(Q, R) = \int_{N_{R|P}}\left(\frac{dQ}{dR}\right)^{1/2} dR = \int_{N_{Q|P}}\left(\frac{dR}{dQ}\right)^{1/2} dQ.$$

Proof. Note that the expressions for $\beta_P(Q, R)$ are symmetric in Q and R. We need only prove the first one. In view of 1.7 it follows from

$$\begin{aligned} a(Q, R) &= \int\left(\frac{dQ}{dR}\right)^{1/2} dR \\ &= \int\left(\frac{dQ}{dR}\right)^{1/2}\frac{dR}{dP}\,dP + \int_{N_{R|P}}\left(\frac{dQ}{dR}\right)^{1/2} dR \end{aligned}$$

$$= \int \left(\frac{dQ}{dR} \cdot \frac{dR}{dP}\right)^{1/2} \left(\frac{dR}{dP}\right)^{1/2} dP + \int_{N_{R|P}} \left(\frac{dQ}{dR}\right)^{1/2} dR$$

$$= \int \left(\frac{dQ}{dP}\right)^{1/2} \cdot \left(\frac{dR}{dP}\right)^{1/2} dP + \int_{N_{R|P}} \left(\frac{dQ}{dR}\right)^{1/2} dR. \qquad \square$$

2.12 Remarks.

(1) $\beta_P(Q, Q) = Q(N_{Q|P})$.
(2) From 1.7 we obtain that

$$\frac{dQ}{dR} = \frac{dQ}{dP} \cdot \frac{dP}{dR} \quad R\text{-a.e.} \quad \text{on} \quad \Omega \setminus N_{Q|P}.$$

Hence $\frac{dQ}{dR} = 0$ R-a.e. on $N_{R|P} \setminus N_{Q|P}$ and it follows that

$$\beta_P(Q, R) = \int_{N_{R|P} \cap N_{Q|P}} \left(\frac{dQ}{dR}\right)^{1/2} dR.$$

This implies that

$$\beta_P(Q, R) \leqq \sqrt{R(N_{R|P})} \cdot \sqrt{Q(N_{Q|P})}.$$

2.13 Remark. Suppose that $P|\mathscr{A}$, $Q|\mathscr{A}$ and $R|\mathscr{A}$ are probability measures. Let $\left(\frac{dQ}{dP}, N_1\right)$ and $\left(\frac{dR}{dP}, N_2\right)$ be the Lebesgue decompositions of Q and R with respect to P. Later, the functions

$$g_Q = 2\left(\left(\frac{dQ}{dP}\right)^{1/2} - 1\right), \quad g_R = 2\left(\left(\frac{dR}{dP}\right)^{1/2} - 1\right)$$

will be considered. Easy computations show that

$$P(g_Q) = -2 d_2^2(P, Q)$$
$$P(g_Q g_R) = 4[d_2^2(P, Q) + d_2^2(P, R) - d_2^2(Q, R) - \beta_P(Q, R)].$$

2.14 Lemma.

(1) $0 \leqq d_2(P, Q) \leqq 1$.
(2) d_2 *is a distance.*
(3) $d_2(P, Q) = 1$ *iff* $P \perp Q$.
(4) $0 \leqq a(P, Q) \leqq 1$.
(5) $a(P, Q) = 1$ *iff* $P = Q$.
(6) $a(P, Q) = 0$ *iff* $P \perp Q$.

Proof. Obvious. □

The distances d_1 and d_2 are related to each other. We state the main inequalities in the following lemma.

2.15 Lemma.

$$d_2^2(P,Q) \leqq d_1(P,Q) \leqq [d_2^2(P,Q)\cdot(2-d_2^2(P,Q))]^{1/2}.$$

Proof. Let $\{P,Q\} \ll \nu$ and denote $f=\frac{dP}{d\nu}$, $g=\frac{dQ}{d\nu}$. Then

$$d_2^2(P,Q) = \frac{1}{2}\int(\sqrt{f}-\sqrt{g})^2\,d\nu \leqq \frac{1}{2}\int|\sqrt{f}-\sqrt{g}|\cdot|\sqrt{f}+\sqrt{g}|\,d\nu$$
$$= \frac{1}{2}\int|f-g|\,d\nu = d_1(P,Q)$$

and

$$d_1^2(P,Q) = \left(\frac{1}{2}\int|f-g|\,d\nu\right)^2 = \left(\frac{1}{2}\int|\sqrt{f}-\sqrt{g}|\cdot|\sqrt{f}+\sqrt{g}|\,d\nu\right)^2$$
$$\leqq \left(\frac{1}{2}\int|\sqrt{f}-\sqrt{g}|^2\,d\nu\right)\left(\frac{1}{2}\int|\sqrt{f}+\sqrt{g}|^2\,d\nu\right)$$
$$= d_2^2(P,Q)(1+a(P,Q)) = d_2^2(P,Q)(2-d_2^2(P,Q)). \qquad \square$$

For reasons of symmetry we define $\pi(P,Q)=1-d_1(P,Q)$. The statistical significance of π will become clear later (cf. Section 14, Remark 14.5 (4)). We provide a complete tabulation of inequalities between d_1, d_2, a and π in Table 1.

Table 1

	d_1	π	d_2	a
d_1	*	$d_1 = 1-\pi$	$d_1 \geqq d_2^2$ $d_1 \leqq \sqrt{d_2^2(2-d_2^2)}$	$d_1 \geqq 1-a$ $d_1 \leqq \sqrt{1-a^2}$
π	$\pi = 1-d_1$	*	$\pi \geqq 1-\sqrt{d_2^2(2-d_2^2)}$ $\pi \leqq 1-d_2^2$	$\pi \geqq 1-\sqrt{1-a^2}$ $\pi \leqq a$
d_2	$d_2^2 \geqq 1-\sqrt{1-d_1^2}$ $d_2 \leqq \sqrt{d_1}$	$d_2 \geqq 1-\sqrt{\pi(2-\pi)}$ $d_2 \leqq \sqrt{1-\pi}$	*	$d_2 = \sqrt{1-a}$
a	$a \geqq 1-d_1$ $a \leqq \sqrt{1-d_1^2}$	$a \geqq \pi$ $a \leqq \sqrt{\pi(2-\pi)}$	$a = 1-d_2^2$	*

One of the reasons for the importance of the Hellinger distance is its behaviour under multiplication of probability measures.

2.16 Lemma. *Suppose that* $(\Omega_i, \mathscr{A}_i)$, $1 \leqq i \leqq n$, *be measurable spaces and* $P_i|\mathscr{A}_i$, $Q_i|\mathscr{A}_i$, $1 \leqq i \leqq n$, *probability measures. Then*

$$a\left(\bigotimes_{i=1}^{n} P_i, \bigotimes_{i=1}^{n} Q_i\right) = \prod_{i=1}^{n} a(P_i, Q_i).$$

Proof. Obvious. □

2.17 Lemma. *Under the assumptions of Lemma 2.16*

$$1 - \exp\left(-\sum_{i=1}^{n} d_2^2(P_i, Q_i)\right) \leqq d_2^2\left(\bigotimes_{i=1}^{n} P_i, \bigotimes_{i=1}^{n} Q_i\right) \leqq \min\left\{1, \sum_{i=1}^{n} d_2^2(P_i, Q_i)\right\}.$$

Proof. The assertion follows from

$$1 - \exp\left(-\sum_{i=1}^{n} d_2^2(P_i, Q_i)\right) = 1 - \prod_{i=1}^{n} \exp\left(-d_2^2(P_i, Q_i)\right)$$

$$= 1 - \prod_{i=1}^{n} \exp\left(a(P_i, Q_i) - 1\right) \leqq 1 - \prod_{i=1}^{n} a(P_i, Q_i)$$

$$= 1 - a\left(\bigotimes_{i=1}^{n} P_i, \bigotimes_{i=1}^{n} Q_i\right) = d_2^2\left(\bigotimes_{i=1}^{n} P_i, \bigotimes_{i=1}^{n} Q_i\right)$$

$$= 1 - \prod_{i=1}^{n} \left(1 - d_2^2(P_i, Q_i)\right) \leqq 1 - \left(1 - \sum_{i=1}^{n} d_2^2(P_i, Q_i)\right)$$

$$= \sum_{i=1}^{n} d_2^2(P_i, Q_i). \qquad \square$$

Sometimes the right-hand side of the preceding inequality yields an unsatisfactory upper bound. Let us provide a better bound.

2.18 Lemma. *Let* $0 \leqq a_i \leqq 1$, $1 \leqq i \leqq n$. *Then*

$$\prod_{i=1}^{n} a_i \leqq \exp\left(-\sum_{i=1}^{n} (1 - a_i)\right) \leqq \prod_{i=1}^{n} a_i + \frac{1}{2} \max_{1 \leqq i \leqq n} (1 - a_i).$$

Proof. To begin with we note that

$$x \leqq \exp(x - 1) \leqq x + \frac{1}{2}(x - 1)^2 \quad \text{if} \quad 0 \leqq x \leqq 1.$$

The first inequality is obvious and the second follows from

$$\exp(x - 1) - x = \sum_{k=2}^{\infty} (-1)^k \frac{(x - 1)^k}{k!} \leqq \frac{1}{2}(x - 1)^2.$$

Then we obtain

$$
\begin{aligned}
0 &\leqq \exp\Bigl(-\sum_{i=1}^{n}(1-a_i)\Bigr)-\prod_{i=1}^{n}a_i \\
&= \sum_{j=1}^{n}\Bigl(\prod_{i<j}a_i\prod_{i\geqq j}\exp(a_i-1)-\prod_{i\leqq j}a_i\prod_{i>j}\exp(a_i-1)\Bigr) \\
&= \sum_{j=1}^{n}(\exp(a_j-1)-a_j)\prod_{i<j}a_i\prod_{i>j}\exp(a_i-1) \\
&\leqq \sum_{j=1}^{n}(\exp(a_j-1)-a_j)\prod_{i=1}^{n}\exp(a_i-1)\frac{1}{\exp(a_j-1)} \\
&\leqq \frac{1}{2}\sum_{j=1}^{n}|a_j-1|^2\prod_{i=1}^{n}\exp(-|a_i-1|)\cdot e \\
&\leqq \frac{1}{2}e\max_{i\leqq j\leqq n}|a_i-1|\cdot f\Bigl(\sum_{j=1}^{n}|a_j-1|\Bigr)
\end{aligned}
$$

where $f(x)=xe^{-x}$, $x\geqq 0$. Since $f(x)\leqq \frac{1}{e}$, $x\geqq 0$, the assertion follows. □

2.19 Lemma. *Under the assumptions of Lemma 2.16 we have*

$$d_2^2\Bigl(\bigotimes_{i=1}^{n}P_i,\bigotimes_{i=1}^{n}Q_i\Bigr)\leqq 1-\exp\Bigl(-\sum_{i=1}^{n}d_2^2(P_i,Q_i)\Bigr)+\frac{1}{2}\max_{1\leqq i\leqq n}d_2^2(P_i,Q_i).$$

Proof. This is an easy application of Lemma 2.18. □

3. Topologies and σ-fields on sets of probability measures

Let $(\Omega, \mathscr{A})$ be a measure space and $\mathscr{P}$ a set of probability measures on $\mathscr{A}$. The set of all probability measures on $\mathscr{A}$ is denoted by $\mathscr{M}_1(\Omega, \mathscr{A})$.

It follows from Lemma 2.15 that the distances d_1 and d_2 induce the same topology on $\mathscr{P}$. Let us denote this topology by $\mathscr{T}_d$. The uniform structure which is generated by any of the distances d_1 or d_2 is denoted by $\mathscr{U}_d$.

3.1 Remark. Assume that $\mathscr{P}$ is denoted by a σ-finite measure $\nu|\mathscr{A}$. Let $(P_n)\subseteq\mathscr{P}$ and $P\in\mathscr{P}$. It is well-known that

$$d_1(P_n,P)\to 0 \quad\text{iff}\quad \frac{dP_n}{d\nu}\to\frac{dP}{d\nu}\,(\nu).$$

This is usually called "Lemma of Scheffé".

3.2 Theorem (Landers and Rogge [1972]). *Suppose that $\mathscr{P}$ is dominated by a σ-finite measure $\nu|\mathscr{A}$ and ϱ is a distance on $\mathscr{P}$ such that $P \mapsto \frac{dP}{d\nu}$ is ν-continuous. Then the following assertions hold:*

(1) $\mathscr{T}_d \subseteq \mathscr{T}_\varrho$.
(2) *If* $(\mathscr{P}, \mathscr{T}_\varrho)$ *is compact then* $\mathscr{T}_d = \mathscr{T}_\varrho$.
(3) *If* $(\mathscr{P}, \mathscr{T}_\varrho)$ *is locally compact and if* $\lim_{n\to\infty} P_n = \infty\,(\mathscr{T}_\varrho)$ *implies* $\nu\left(\liminf_{n\to\infty} \frac{dP_n}{d\nu}\right) < 1$, *then* $\mathscr{T}_d = \mathscr{T}_\varrho$.

Proof. Assertion (1) follows from Remark 3.1. Then (2) is an immediate consequence since $(\mathscr{P}, \mathscr{T}_d)$ is hausdorff.

(3): Assume that $\lim_{n\to\infty} d_1(P_n, P) = 0$. We have to distinguish between two cases. First, let $\lim_{n\to\infty} P_n = \infty\,(\mathscr{T}_\varrho)$. Choose a subsequence $\mathbb{N}_0 \subseteq \mathbb{N}$ such that $\liminf_{n\in\mathbb{N}_0} \frac{dP_n}{d\nu} = \frac{dP}{d\nu}$ ν-a.e. This implies that $\nu\left(\liminf_{n\in\mathbb{N}_0} \frac{dP_n}{d\nu}\right) = \nu\left(\frac{dP}{d\nu}\right) = 1$ which contradicts the assumption. Therefore the other case happens, i.e. there exists a subsequence $\mathbb{N}_1 \subseteq \mathbb{N}$ such that $\lim_{n\in\mathbb{N}_1} P_n = Q(\mathscr{T}_\varrho)$ for some $Q \in \mathscr{P}$. Since $\mathscr{T}_d$ is hausdorff, it follows that $Q = P$. Thus, we have proved that $\lim_{n\to\infty} P_n = P(\mathscr{T}_d)$ implies $\lim_{n\in\mathbb{N}_1} P_n = P(\mathscr{T}_\varrho)$ for some subsequence $\mathbb{N}_1 \subseteq \mathbb{N}$. This proves the assertion. □

If $\mathscr{P}$ is dominated by $\nu|\mathscr{A}$ then $\mathscr{T}_d$ coincides with the *strong topology* of $\mathscr{P}$ as a subspace of $L_1(\Omega, \mathscr{A}, \nu)$ or $L_2(\Omega, \mathscr{A}, \nu)$. Next we define a topology of $\mathscr{P}$ which corresponds to the weak topology of $L_1(\Omega, \mathscr{A}, \nu)$.

3.3 Remark. By $\mathscr{L}_b(\Omega, \mathscr{A})$ we denote the vector space of all bounded $\mathscr{A}$-measurable functions $f\colon \Omega \to \mathbb{R}$. The elements φ of the convex set $\mathscr{F}(\Omega, \mathscr{A}) = \{\varphi \in \mathscr{L}_b(\Omega, \mathscr{A})\colon 0 \leqq \varphi \leqq 1\}$ are called *tests* or *critical functions*. Every family $\mathscr{H} \subseteq \mathscr{L}_b(\Omega, \mathscr{A})$ defines a uniform structure $\mathscr{U}_{\mathscr{H}}$ on $\mathscr{P}$ by the system of pseudodistances ϱ_J, where $J = \{f_1, \ldots, f_n\} \subseteq \mathscr{H}$, $n \in \mathbb{N}$, and

$$\varrho_J(P, Q) = \max_{1\leqq i\leqq n} |Pf_i - Qf_i|.$$

It is an easy fact that the uniform structures which are defined by $\mathscr{L}_b(\Omega, \mathscr{A})$, $\mathscr{F}(\Omega, \mathscr{A})$ and $\{1_A\colon A \in \mathscr{A}\}$, respectively, coincide.

3.4 Definition. The *uniform structure of* $\mathscr{P}$ which is defined by $\mathscr{L}_b(\Omega, \mathscr{A})$ or $\mathscr{F}(\Omega, \mathscr{A})$ or $\{1_A\colon A \in \mathscr{A}\}$ is denoted by $\mathscr{U}_1$. The topology of $\mathscr{U}_1$ is denoted by $\mathscr{T}_1$.

3.5 Lemma. *$(\mathscr{P}, \mathscr{U}_1)$ is totally bounded.*

Proof. The uniform space $(\mathscr{P}, \mathscr{U}_1)$ is uniformly equivalent to a subset of $[0,1]^{\mathscr{A}}$. □

Let $\mathscr{P}^n = \{P^n: P \in \mathscr{P}\}$, $n \in \mathbb{N}$, and denote by $\mathscr{U}_n$ the uniform structure on $\mathscr{P}$ which is induced by the uniform structure $\mathscr{U}_1(\mathscr{P}^n)$ of $\mathscr{P}^n$. Let $\mathscr{U}_\infty = \bigcup_{n \in \mathbb{N}} \mathscr{U}_n$. The topologies of $\mathscr{U}_n$ and $\mathscr{U}_\infty$ are denoted by $\mathscr{T}_n$ and $\mathscr{T}_\infty$, respectively, $n \in \mathbb{N}$.

3.6 Remark. It is clear that the following relations hold:

(1) $\mathscr{U}_d \supseteq \mathscr{U}_\infty \supseteq \mathscr{U}_n, \quad n \in \mathbb{N}.$

(2) $\mathscr{T}_d \supseteq \mathscr{T}_\infty \supseteq \mathscr{T}_n, \quad n \in \mathbb{N}.$

3.7 Remark. It is a well-known fact (see Dunford-Schwartz [1969: IV, 9]) that $(\mathscr{P}, \mathscr{T}_1)$ is relatively compact in $(\mathscr{M}_1(\Omega, \mathscr{A}), \mathscr{T}_1)$ iff any of the following conditions is satisfied:

(1) If $(A_n) \subseteq \mathscr{A}$, $A_n \downarrow \emptyset$, then $\sup_{P \in \mathscr{P}} P(A_n) \downarrow 0$.

(2) There is a probability measure $P_0|\mathscr{A}$ such that $P \ll P_0$ uniformly for $P \in \mathscr{P}$.

(3) There is a probability measure $P_0|\mathscr{A}$ dominating $\mathscr{P}$ such that the densities dP/dP_0 are uniformly P_0-integrable for $P \in \mathscr{P}$.

3.8 Lemma. *If $(\mathscr{P}, \mathscr{T}_1)$ is relatively compact in $(\mathscr{M}_1(\Omega, \mathscr{A}), \mathscr{T}_1)$ then $\mathscr{T}_1 = \mathscr{T}_\infty$ on $\mathscr{P}$.*

Proof. Let us prove that $\mathscr{T}_1 = \mathscr{T}_n$, $n \in \mathbb{N}$. If $(\mathscr{P}, \mathscr{T}_1)$ is relatively compact then there is a probability measure $P_0|\mathscr{A}$ dominating $\mathscr{P}$ such that $\left\{\frac{dP}{dP_0}: P \in \mathscr{P}\right\}$ is uniformly P_0-integrable. Then also $\left\{\frac{dP^n}{dP_0^n}: P \in \mathscr{P}\right\}$ is uniformly P_0^n-integrable as follows from

$$\int_{\frac{dP^n}{dP_0^n} > a} \frac{dP^n}{dP_0^n}\, dP_0^n \leq n \int_{\frac{dP}{dP_0} > a^{1/n}} \frac{dP}{dP_0}\, dP_0 .$$

Hence, $(\mathscr{P}, \mathscr{T}_n)$ is relatively compact and id: $(\bar{\mathscr{P}}, \mathscr{T}_n) \to (\bar{\mathscr{P}}, \mathscr{T}_1)$ is a homeomorphism. □

Let $\mathscr{C}$ be the σ-field on $\mathscr{P}$ which is generated by the family of function $P \mapsto P(A)$, $A \in \mathscr{A}$. We have $\mathscr{B}(\mathscr{T}_d) \supseteq \mathscr{B}(\mathscr{T}_\infty) \supseteq \ldots \supseteq \mathscr{B}(\mathscr{T}_1) \supseteq \mathscr{C}$. The following example shows that $\mathscr{B}(\mathscr{T}_1) \neq \mathscr{C}$, in general.

3.9 Example. Let $\mathscr{P} = \{\varepsilon_x : x \in \mathbb{R}\}$ and $\mathscr{A} = \mathscr{B}(\mathbb{R})$. Then $\mathscr{T}_1$ is the discrete topology and hence $\mathscr{B}(\mathscr{T}_1) = 2^{\mathbb{R}}$. On the other hand $\mathscr{C}$ is generated by the family of functions $\varepsilon_x \mapsto \varepsilon_x(A) = 1_A(x)$, $x \in \mathbb{R}$, $A \in \mathscr{B}(\mathbb{R})$, und hence $\mathscr{C} = \mathscr{B}(\mathbb{R})$.

In the next section we shall prove that for separable sets $\mathscr{P}$ the σ-fields coincide. At this point we only show that various σ-fields constructed like $\mathscr{C}$ coincide for different $n \in \mathbb{N}$.

3.10 Lemma. *The σ-fields which are generated by the families of functions $P \mapsto P^n(A)$, $A \in \mathscr{A}^n$, for fixed $n \in \mathbb{N}$, and by $P \mapsto P^{\mathbb{N}}(A)$, $A \in \mathscr{A}^{\mathbb{N}}$, respectively, coincide with $\mathscr{C}$.*

Proof. Let $\mathscr{C}_n$ be the initial σ-field of $P \mapsto P^n(A)$, $A \in \mathscr{A}^n$. Obviously, we have $\mathscr{C} \subseteq \mathscr{C}_n$. We show that $P \mapsto P^n(A)$ is $\mathscr{C}$-measurable for every $A \in \mathscr{A}^n$. This is evident if $A \in \mathscr{A}^n$ is a rectangle. Since the system

$$\mathscr{F} = \{A \in \mathscr{A}^n : P \mapsto P^n(A) \text{ is } \mathscr{C}\text{-measurable}\}$$

is a monotone class the assertion follows. If $n \in \mathbb{N}$ is replaced by $\mathbb{N}$ then the proof is similar. □

The σ-field $\mathscr{C}$ has an interesting representation.

3.11 Definition. A subset $A \in \mathscr{A}^{\mathbb{N}}$ is a *0-1-set* if $P^{\mathbb{N}}(A) \in \{0, 1\}$ for all $P \in \mathscr{P}$.

3.12 Theorem (Breiman, LeCam and Schwartz [1964]). *A set $C \subseteq \mathscr{P}$ is in $\mathscr{C}$ iff there is a* 0-1-*set $A \in \mathscr{A}^{\mathbb{N}}$ such that $P^{\mathbb{N}}(A) = 1_C(P)$, $P \in \mathscr{P}$.*

Proof. Let $\mathscr{D}$ be the family of sets $D \subseteq \mathscr{P}$ such that $P^{\mathbb{N}}(A) = 1_D(P)$, $P \in \mathscr{P}$, for some 0-1-set $A \in \mathscr{A}^{\mathbb{N}}$. First, we show that $\mathscr{D}$ is a σ-field. Indeed, $\mathscr{P} \in \mathscr{D}$ and $\mathscr{D}$ is closed under complementation. If $(D_n) \subseteq \mathscr{D}$ and $(A_n) \subseteq \mathscr{A}^{\mathbb{N}}$ are the corresponding 0-1-sets then

$P \in \bigcup_{n \in \mathbb{N}} D_n$ implies $P^{\mathbb{N}}(A_n) = 1$ for some $n \in \mathbb{N}$, hence $P^{\mathbb{N}} \bigcup_{n \in \mathbb{N}} A_n = 1$, and

$P \notin \bigcup_{n \in \mathbb{N}} D_n$ implies $P^{\mathbb{N}}(A_n) = 0$ for every $n \in \mathbb{N}$, hence $P^{\mathbb{N}} \bigcup_{n \in \mathbb{N}} A_n = 0$.

Hence $\bigcup_{n \in \mathbb{N}} D_n \in \mathscr{D}$.

If $D \in \mathscr{D}$ then $D = \{P \in \mathscr{P} : P^{\mathbb{N}}(A) = 1\}$ for some 0-1-set $A \in \mathscr{A}^{\mathbb{N}}$. This implies $D \in \mathscr{C}$. Hence we have $\mathscr{D} \subseteq \mathscr{C}$. To prove the converse we show that $\{P \in \mathscr{P} : P(B) \leq \alpha\} \in \mathscr{D}$ for every $B \in \mathscr{A}$, $0 < \alpha < 1$.

Let $A := \{\liminf_{n \to \infty} \frac{1}{n} \sum_{i=1}^{n} 1_B \circ p_i \leq \alpha\} \in \mathscr{A}^{\mathbb{N}}$. Then

$$P(B) \leqq \alpha \quad \text{implies} \quad P^{\mathbb{N}}(A) = 1,$$
$$P(B) > \alpha \quad \text{implies} \quad P^{\mathbb{N}}(A) = 0.$$

This proves the assertion. □

4. Separable sets of probability measures

Let $(\Omega, \mathscr{A})$ be a measurable space and $\mathscr{P}$ a set of probability measures on $\mathscr{A}$.

4.1 Lemma. *If $\mathscr{P}$ is dominated and $\mathscr{A}$ is countably generated then $(\mathscr{P}, \mathscr{T}_d)$ is separable.*

Proof. Let $\mathscr{P} \ll \nu | \mathscr{A}$. Since the assumptions imply that $L_1(\Omega, \mathscr{A}, \nu)$ is separable it follows that $(\mathscr{P}, \mathscr{T}_d)$ is separable, too. □

4.2 Lemma. *If $(\mathscr{P}, \mathscr{T}_1)$ is separable then $\mathscr{P}$ is dominated.*

Proof. Take as dominating measure a convex combination of a countable, dense subset. □

The preceding lemma will be extended to a full converse of Lemma 4.1 in Section 21. Here we confine ourselves to some consequences of separability.

4.3 Lemma. *If $(\mathscr{P}, \mathscr{T}_1)$ is separable then there exists a countably generated σ-field $\mathscr{A}_0 \subseteq \mathscr{A}$ and a probability measure P_0 dominating $\mathscr{P}$ such that the densities $\frac{dP}{dP_0}$ can be chosen $\mathscr{A}_0$-measurable.*

Proof. Let (P_n) be dense in $(\mathscr{P}, \mathscr{T}_1)$. Then $P_0 := \sum_{n \in \mathbb{N}} \frac{1}{2^n} P_n$ dominates $\mathscr{P}$. Let $\mathscr{A}_0$ be the σ-field which is generated by $\left(\frac{dP_n}{dP_0}\right)_{n \in \mathbb{N}}$. Obviously, $\mathscr{A}_0$ is countably generated. We shall prove that $P_0\left(\frac{dP}{dP_0} | \mathscr{A}_0\right)$ is a version of $\frac{dP}{dP_0}$ for every $P \in \mathscr{P}$. Let $A \in \mathscr{A}$, $\varepsilon > 0$, and choose P_n in such a way that

$$|\int P_0(A|\mathscr{A}_0)\,dP - \int P_0(A|\mathscr{A}_0)\,dP_n| < \frac{\varepsilon}{2}, \quad \text{and}$$

$$|P(A) - P_n(A)| < \frac{\varepsilon}{2}.$$

Then we have

$$\int_A P_0\left(\frac{dP}{dP_0}\,|\,\mathscr{A}_0\right) dP_0 = \int P_0(A\,|\,\mathscr{A}_0)\, P_0\left(\frac{dP}{dP_0}\,|\,\mathscr{A}_0\right) dP_0$$
$$= \int P_0(A\,|\,\mathscr{A}_0)\, dP.$$

On the other hand

$$\int P_0(A\,|\,\mathscr{A}_0)\, dP_n = \int P_0(A\,|\,\mathscr{A}_0)\,\frac{dP_n}{dP_0}\, dP_0$$
$$= \int P_0\left(1_A \frac{dP_n}{dP_0}\,|\,\mathscr{A}_0\right) dP_0 = P_n(A).$$

This implies that

$$\left|\int_A P_0\left(\frac{dP}{dP_0}\,|\,\mathscr{A}_0\right) dP_0 - P(A)\right| < \varepsilon.$$

Since $\varepsilon > 0$ is arbitrary the assertion follows. □

4.4 Theorem. *The following assertions are equivalent:*

(1) $(\mathscr{P}, \mathscr{T}_d)$ *is separable.*
(2) $(\mathscr{P}, \mathscr{T}_\infty)$ *is separable.*
(3) $(\mathscr{P}, \mathscr{T}_1)$ *is separable.*

Proof. It is clear that (1) ⇒ (2) ⇒ (3).

(3) ⇒ (1): Choose $\mathscr{A}_0$ and P_0 according to Lemma 4.3. Lemma 4.1 implies that $(\mathscr{P}\,|\,\mathscr{A}_0, d_1)$ is separable. Since the densities $\frac{dP}{dP_0}$ can be chosen $\mathscr{A}_0$-measurable it follows that

$$d_1(P\,|\,\mathscr{A}_0, Q\,|\,\mathscr{A}_0) = d_1(P, Q), \quad P, Q \in \mathscr{P},$$

which proves that $(\mathscr{P}, d_1)$ is separable, too. □

The preceding result justifies the following definition.

4.5 Definition. The set $\mathscr{P}$ is *separable* if any of the condition 4.4 (1)–(3) is satisfied.

Recall the definition of the σ-field $\mathscr{C}$ on $\mathscr{P}$ in section 3.

4.6 Lemma (Nölle [1966]. *If $\mathscr{P}$ is separable and $\nu\,|\,\mathscr{A}$ is any dominating measure then the densities $\frac{dP}{d\nu}$, $P \in \mathscr{P}$, can be chosen such that $(\omega, P) \mapsto \frac{dP}{d\nu}(\omega)$, $(\omega, P) \in \Omega \times \mathscr{P}$, is $\mathscr{A} \times \mathscr{C}$-measurable.*

Proof. Choose $\mathscr{A}_0$ and P_0 according to Lemma 4.3. Let $(A_i)_{i \in \mathbb{N}}$ be a countable generator of $\mathscr{A}_0$ and $\mathscr{A}_n := \mathscr{A}(A_1, \ldots, A_n)$, $n \in \mathbb{N}$. Let $\{C_1^{(n)}, \ldots, C_{k(n)}^{(n)}\}$ be a finite partition of Ω which generates $\mathscr{A}_n$. Then for every $n \in \mathbb{N}$

$$(\omega, P) \mapsto P_0\left(\frac{dP}{dP_0} \,|\, \mathscr{A}_n\right)(\omega) = \sum_{i=1}^{k(n)} \frac{P(C_k^{(n)})}{P_0(C_k^{(n)})} 1_{C_k^{(n)}}(\omega), \, (\omega, P) \in \Omega \times \mathscr{P}$$

is $\mathscr{A} \times \mathscr{C}$-measurable. Since martingale theorems imply

$$P_0\left(\frac{dP}{dP_0} \,|\, \mathscr{A}_0\right) = \lim_{n \to \infty} P_0\left(\frac{dP}{dP_0} \,|\, \mathscr{A}_n\right) \quad P_0\text{-a.e.}, \quad P \in \mathscr{P},$$

it follows that also

$$(\omega, P) \mapsto P_0\left(\frac{dP}{dP_0} \,|\, \mathscr{A}_0\right)(\omega), \, (\omega, P) \in \Omega \times \mathscr{P}$$

is $\mathscr{A} \times \mathscr{C}$-measurable. In view of the proof of Lemma 4.3 we have

$$\frac{dP}{d\nu} = P_0\left(\frac{dP}{dP_0} \,|\, \mathscr{A}_0\right) \cdot \frac{dP_0}{d\nu} \quad \nu\text{-a.e.}, \quad P \in \mathscr{P},$$

which proves the assertion. □

It will be proved in Section 21 that also the converse of Lemma 4.6 is valid.

4.7 Theorem (Pfanzagl [1969]). *If $\mathscr{P}$ is separable then $\mathscr{C} = \mathscr{B}(\mathscr{T}_1) = \mathscr{B}(\mathscr{T}_\infty)$ $= \mathscr{B}(\mathscr{T}_d)$.*

Proof. Let us show that every d_1-ball is contained in $\mathscr{C}$. This proves $\mathscr{B}(\mathscr{T}_d) \subseteq \mathscr{C}$ since $(\mathscr{P}, \mathscr{T}_d)$ is separable.

Let $\nu | \mathscr{A}$ be σ-finite satisfying $\mathscr{P} \ll \nu$ and let $\frac{dP}{d\nu}$, $P \in \mathscr{P}$, be densities such that $(\omega, P) \mapsto \frac{dP}{d\nu}(\omega)$ is $\mathscr{A} \times \mathscr{C}$-measurable. Then for every $Q \in \mathscr{P}$

$$P \mapsto d_1(P, Q) = \frac{1}{2} \int \left| \frac{dP}{d\nu} - \frac{dQ}{d\nu} \right| d\nu, \quad P \in \mathscr{P},$$

is $\mathscr{C}$-measurable. □

The assertion of Lemma 4.6 can be improved in the following way.

4.8 Theorem. *Assume that $\mathscr{P}$ is separable and $\nu | \mathscr{A}$ is a dominating σ-finite measure. Let $S \subseteq \mathscr{P}$ be countable and dense in $(\mathscr{P}, d_1)$. Then the densities $dP/d\nu$, $P \in \mathscr{P}$, may be chosen such that the random function $(dP/d\nu)_{P \in \mathscr{P}}$ is separable with separant S and $\mathscr{A} \times \mathscr{C}$-measurable.*

Proof. Let $S = (P_n)_{n \in \mathbb{N}}$ be countable and dense in $(\mathscr{P}, d_1)$. Let h_P, $P \in \mathscr{P}$, be arbitrary versions of the densities dP/dv, $P \in \mathscr{P}$. For every $n \in \mathbb{N}$ there exists $\delta_n > 0$ such that

$$d_1(P, Q) < \delta_n \quad \text{implies} \quad v\left\{|h_P - h_Q| > \frac{1}{n}\right\} < \frac{1}{2^n}, \quad P, Q \in \mathscr{P}.$$

Let $A_{ni} = \{Q \in \mathscr{P}: d_1(P_i, Q) < \delta_n\}$, $i \in \mathbb{N}$, $n \in \mathbb{N}$. For every $n \in \mathbb{N}$ define partitions $(C_{ni})_{i \in \mathbb{N}}$ in $\mathscr{C} = \mathscr{B}(\mathscr{T}_d)$ by

$$C_{ni} := A_{ni} \setminus \bigcup_{j=1}^{i-1} C_{nj}, \quad i \in \mathbb{N}.$$

If $\omega \in \Omega$, $Q \in \mathscr{P}$, $n \in \mathbb{N}$, let

$$f_n(\omega, Q) := \sum_{i \in \mathbb{N}} h_{P_i}(\omega) 1_{C_{ni}}(Q)$$

and

$$f(\omega, Q) := \limsup_{n \to \infty} f_n(\omega, Q).$$

For every $P_k \in S$ there exists $n_0 \in \mathbb{N}$ such that $P_k \notin A_{ni}$ if $i < k$ and $n \geqq n_0$. Then $P_k \in C_{nk}$ for $n \geqq n_0$ which implies $h_{P_k} = f(\cdot, P_k)$, $P_k \in S$.

Obviously, $(\omega, P) \mapsto f_n(\omega, P)$ is $\mathscr{A} \otimes \mathscr{C}$-measurable, $n \in \mathbb{N}$, and so is $(\omega, P) \mapsto f(\omega, P)$. Let us prove that $(h_P)_{P \in \mathscr{P}}$ and $(f(\cdot, P))_{P \in \mathscr{P}}$ are equivalent random functions with respect to $v|\mathscr{A}$.

Fix $P \in \mathscr{P}$. For every $n \in \mathbb{N}$ choose $P_{i(n)} \in S$ such that $P \in C_{n, i(n)}$. Then $P \in A_{n, i(n)}$ and $d_1(P_{i(n)}, P) < \delta_n$. It follows that

$$\sum_{n=1}^{\infty} v\left\{|h_P - f_n(.\,, P)| > \frac{1}{n}\right\} = \sum_{n=1}^{\infty} v\left\{|h_P - h_{P_{i(n)}}| > \frac{1}{n}\right\} \leqq \sum_{n=1}^{\infty} \frac{1}{2^n} < \infty$$

which implies

$$h_P = \lim_{n \to \infty} f_n(.\,, P) \quad v\text{-a.e.},$$

and hence $h_P = f(.\,, P)$ v-a.e.

Finally, we have to show that $(f(.\,, P))_{P \in \mathscr{P}}$ is separable with separant S. Let $\omega \in \Omega$. Then

$$f(\omega, P) = \limsup_{n \to \infty} f_n(\omega, P) = \limsup_{n \to \infty} h_{P_{i(n)}}(\omega) = \limsup_{n \to \infty} f(\omega, P_{i(n)}).$$

Since there is a subsequence $\mathbb{N}_0 \subseteq \mathbb{N}$ such that

$$f(\omega, P) = \lim_{n \in \mathbb{N}_0} f(\omega, P_{i(n)}),$$

the assertion is proved. □

5. Transforms of bounded Borel measures

Let $(H, \langle\cdot,\cdot\rangle)$ be a Euclidean space and $\mathscr{B}(H)$ its Borel-σ-field. A *Borel measure* is a measure $\mu|\mathscr{B}(H)$ such that $\mu(K)<\infty$ for every compact $K\subseteq H$. It is bounded if $\mu(H)<\infty$. The Lebesgue measure on H is denoted by λ_H.

We begin with some standard facts on Fourier transforms and two-sided Laplace transforms.

5.1 Definition. Let $\mu|\mathscr{B}(H)$ be a bounded Borel measure. The *Fourier transform* of μ is the mapping

$$\hat{\mu}\colon t\mapsto \int \exp(i\langle t,x\rangle)\,\mu(dx), \quad t\in H.$$

5.2 Examples. (1) Let $\mu|\mathscr{B}(H)$ be a bounded Borel measure and $a\in H$. Then $(\varepsilon_a * \mu)^\wedge(t)=\exp(i\langle t,a\rangle)\,\hat{\mu}(t)$, $t\in H$. If $(H_1,\langle\cdot,\cdot\rangle_1)$ is another Euclidean space and $A\colon H\to H_1$ is a linear mapping then $\hat{\mathscr{L}}(A|\mu)(t)=\hat{\mu}(A^*t)$, $t\in H_1$.

(2) The *standard Gaussian measure* N_H on H is defined by the Lebesgue density $dN_H/d\lambda_H=(2\pi)^{-\dim H/2}\exp\left(-\frac{\|\,.\,\|^2}{2}\right)$. Then the Fourier transform is

$$\hat{N}_H(t)=\exp\left(-\frac{\|t\|^2}{2}\right), \quad t\in H.$$

(3) Let $\mu|\mathscr{B}(H)$ be a bounded Borel measure. It is called *isotropic* if $\mathscr{L}(A|\mu)=\mu$ for all orthogonal mappings $A\in O(H)$. If $\mu\ll\lambda_H$ then μ is isotropic iff $d\mu/d\lambda_H$ is a function of $\|\,.\,\|$. In view of (1) and Lemma 5.3 an arbitrary bounded Borel measure is isotropic iff its Fourier transform is a function of the norm.

(4) Let $\mu|\mathscr{B}(H)$ bounded and isotropic and $\hat{\mu}(t)=\varphi(\|t\|)$, $t\in H$. Then $\hat{\mathscr{L}}(A|\mu)(t)=\varphi(\langle t,St\rangle^{1/2})$, $t\in H$, if $A\colon H\to H$ is linear and $S=A^*A$.

(5) Assume that $S\colon H\to H$ is positive definite and symmetric. Let $N_H(a,S)$ be the *Gaussian measure on H with mean a and covariance S* which is defined by the Lebesgue density

$$(2\pi)^{-\dim H/2}(\det S)^{-1/2}\exp\left(-\frac{1}{2}\langle x-a,S^{-1}(x-a)\rangle\right), \quad x\in H.$$

Since there is a mapping $A\in GL(H)$ such that $A^*A=S$ it follows that

$$N_H(a,S)=\mathscr{L}(A\,\mathrm{id}+a|N_H) \quad\text{and}$$

$$\hat{N}_H(a,S)(t)=\exp\left(i\langle t,a\rangle-\frac{1}{2}\langle t,St\rangle\right), \quad t\in H.$$

(6) The probability measure $\mathscr{L}\left(t\mapsto\frac{t}{\|t\|}\,\middle|\,N_H\right)$ on the unit sphere $S_1=\{t\in H\colon \|t\|=1\}$ is called the *uniform distribution* on S_1.

5.3 Lemma (Feller [1965]). *If $\mu_1|\mathscr{B}(H)$ and $\mu_2|\mathscr{B}(H)$ are bounded Borel measures such that $\hat{\mu}_1 = \hat{\mu}_2$ then $\mu_1 = \mu_2$.*

Proof. For $a > 0$ let $\tau_a = N_H(0, a \cdot \mathrm{id})$. Denote $k = \dim H$. Then easy computations show that

$$\int \exp(-i\langle s, t\rangle) \int \exp(i\langle x, s\rangle)\, \mu_j(dx)\, \tau_a(ds)$$
$$= (2\pi)^{k/2} \frac{d(\mu_j * \tau_a)}{d\lambda_H}(t), \quad j = 1, 2, \quad t \in H.$$

Hence the assumption implies that

$$\mu_1 * \tau_a = \mu_2 * \tau_a \quad \text{for every } a > 0.$$

Now the assertion follows from

$$\mu_1 = \lim_{a\to 0} \mu_1 * \tau_a = \lim_{a\to 0} \mu_2 * \tau_a = \mu_2. \qquad \square$$

5.4 Definition. Let $\mu|\mathscr{B}(H)$ be a Borel measure and let

$$M = \{t \in H: \int \exp\langle t, x\rangle\, \mu(dx) < \infty\} \neq \emptyset.$$

The *Laplace transform* of μ is the function with domain M which is defined by

$$L(\mu): t \mapsto \int \exp\langle t, x\rangle\, \mu(dx), \quad t \in M.$$

5.5 Examples. (1) Let $\mu|\mathscr{B}(H)$ be a Borel measure and $a \in H$. If $L(\mu)$ is defined on M then

$$L(\varepsilon_a * \mu)(t) = \exp\langle t, a\rangle\, L(\mu)(t), \quad t \in M.$$

If $(H_1, \langle\cdot,\cdot\rangle_1)$ is another Euclidean space and $A: H \to H_1$ is a linear mapping then the Laplace transform of $\mathscr{L}(A|\mu)$ is $t \mapsto L(\mu)(A^* t)$, $t \in H_1$.

(2) The Laplace transform of N_H is

$$L(N_H)(t) = \exp\frac{\|t\|^2}{2}, \quad t \in H.$$

It follows that

$$L(N_H(a, S))(t) = \exp(\langle t, a\rangle + \frac{1}{2}\langle t, St\rangle, \quad t \in H,$$

if $a \in H$ and S is a symmetric positive definite mapping.

5.6 Lemma. *Let $\mu|\mathscr{B}(H)$ be a Borel measure. Then the function*

$$z \mapsto \int \exp\langle z, x\rangle\, \mu(dx), \quad z \in M + iH,$$

is analytic on $\mathring{M} + iH$.

Proof. Let $\mathring{M} \neq \emptyset$. We have to show that all directional derivatives exist and are continuous on $\mathring{M} + iH$. For reasons of symmetry we only prove it for the first partial derivative. We denote

$$f(z) = \int \exp\langle z, x\rangle \, \mu(dx), \quad z \in \mathring{M} + iH.$$

Let e be a unit vector. Choosing $z \in \mathring{M} + iH$ and $\delta > 0$ such that $z + h \cdot e \in \mathring{M} + iH$ whenever $|h| < \delta$, we obtain for every $|h| < \delta$

$$\frac{1}{h}(f(z+he) - f(z)) = \int e^{\langle z, x\rangle} \frac{e^{h\langle x, e\rangle} - 1}{h} \mu(dx).$$

The functions under the integral are uniformly dominated by a μ-integrable function, as follows from

$$\left|\frac{e^{h\xi} - 1}{h}\right| = \left|\sum_{n=1}^{\infty} \frac{h^{n-1}\xi^n}{n!}\right| \leqq \sum_{n=1}^{\infty} \frac{\delta^{n-1}|\xi|^n}{n!}$$
$$< \frac{e^{\delta|\xi|}}{\delta} \leqq \frac{e^{\delta\xi} + e^{-\delta\xi}}{\delta}.$$

This implies

$$(Df)(z)(e) = \int \langle x, e\rangle \exp(\langle z, x\rangle) \, \mu(dx), \quad z \in \mathring{M} + iH.$$

It remains to show that the directional derivative is continuous on $\mathring{M} + iH$.

Denote $\dim H = n$ and choose $\delta > 0$ such that $z + h \in \mathring{M} + iH$ whenever $|h| < \sqrt{n}\,\delta$. Let $\{e_1, \ldots, e_n\}$ be an orthonormal basis of H. For $\alpha \subseteq \{1, 2, \ldots, n\}$ we put

$$C_\alpha := \{x \in H : \langle x, e_i\rangle \geqq 0 \quad \text{if} \quad i \in \alpha, \langle x, e_i\rangle < 0 \quad \text{if} \quad i \notin \alpha\}$$

and

$$\delta_\alpha := \delta\Big(\sum_{i\in\alpha} e_i - \sum_{i\notin\alpha} e_i\Big).$$

Since $|\delta_\alpha| = \delta\sqrt{n}$ it follows that $z + \delta_\alpha \in \mathring{M} + iH$. Moreover, for every $h \in H$ such that $|h| \leqq \delta$

$$\begin{aligned}
&|\langle x, e\rangle \exp(\langle z + h, x\rangle)| \\
&= \sum_{\alpha \subseteq \{1, 2, \ldots, n\}} |\langle x, e\rangle \exp(\langle z, x\rangle) 1_{C_\alpha}(x) \exp(\langle h, x\rangle)| \\
&\leqq \sum_{\alpha \subseteq \{1, 2, \ldots, n\}} 1_{C_\alpha}(x) |\langle x, e\rangle \exp(\langle z + \delta_\alpha, x\rangle)|.
\end{aligned}$$

Since the right side is independent of h and μ-integrable we obtain that

$$z \mapsto \int \langle x, e\rangle \exp(\langle z, x\rangle) \, \mu dx)$$

is continuous on $\mathring{M} + iH$. □

5.7 Theorem. *Let $\mu_1|\mathscr{B}(H)$ and $\mu_2|\mathscr{B}(H)$ be Borel measures. If there is an open set $A \neq \emptyset$, $A \subseteq H$ such that $L(\mu_1)(t) = L(\mu_2)(t) < \infty$ for every $t \in A$ then $\mu_1 = \mu_2$.*

Proof. Lemma 5.6 implies that

$$\int \exp\langle z, x\rangle \, \mu_1(dx) = \int \exp\langle z, x\rangle \, \mu_2(dx)$$

for every $z \in A + iH$. If $t_0 \in A$ then it follows that the Fourier transforms of the finite measures $\exp\langle t_0, .\rangle \mu_1$ and $\exp\langle t_0, .\rangle \mu_2$ coincide. Hence we have $\mu_1 = \mu_2$. □

Now, we turn to those transforms which are of particular importance for statistics. The following remark serves as a motivation.

5.8 Remark. Suppose that $P_0, P_1, \ldots, P_k$ are probability measures on a sample space $(\Omega, \mathscr{A})$. The appropriate tool for studying such sets of probability measures is the common distribution of the likelihood ratios dP_i/dP_0, $1 \leqq i \leqq k$, for the denominator P_0. Such distributions are measures on $[0, \infty)^k$ with first moments $\leqq 1$. For their analytic treatment we make use of the Mellin transforms.

Let $T \neq \emptyset$ be a finite set and let $\mu|\mathscr{B}(\mathbb{R}^T)$ be a probability measure which vanishes outside $[0, \infty)^T$ and satisfies $\int x_t \mu(dx) \leqq 1$, $t \in T$. The set of all such probability measures is denoted by $\mathscr{M}(T)$. We introduce the Mellin transforms of the measures $\mu \in \mathscr{M}(T)$. The Mellin transforms are defined on

$$\Delta_T : \{z \in \mathbb{R}^T : 0 \leqq z_t < 1, t \in T, \sum_{t \in T} z_t < 1\}.$$

5.9 Lemma. *For every $\mu \in \mathscr{M}(T)$ and $z \in \Delta_T$*

$$0 \leqq \int \prod_{t \in T} x_t^{z_t} \mu(dx) \leqq 1.$$

Proof. An application of Hölder's inequality yields

$$\int \prod_{t \in T} x_t^{z_t} \mu(dx) \leqq \prod_{t \in T} \left(\int x_t \mu(dx)\right)^{z_t} \left(\int 1 \, \mu(dx)\right)^{1 - \sum_{t \in T} z_t} \leqq 1. \qquad \square$$

5.10 Definition. Suppose that $\mu \in \mathscr{M}(T)$. The *Mellin transform* of μ is the function

$$M(\mu) : \Delta_T \to [0, 1] : z \mapsto \int \prod_{t \in T} x_t^{z_t} \mu(dx).$$

(Define $0^0 := 1$.)

The following example is of importance later. Note that for Gaussian measures $P_0, P_1, \ldots, P_k$ on a Euclidean space $(H, \langle \cdot, \cdot \rangle)$ the logarithms of the likelihood ratio $\log \dfrac{dP_i}{dP_0}$, $1 \leqq i \leqq k$, are Gaussian distributed under P_0.

5.11 Example. Consider a probability space $(\Omega, \mathscr{A}, P)$ and let $(X_t)_{t\in T}$ be a centered Gaussian random vector with covariance function $(s, t) \mapsto K(s, t)$, $(s, t) \in T^2$. Then $P_t = \exp(X_t + a_t) P$, $t \in T$, are probability measures iff $a_t = -\frac{1}{2} P(X_t^2)$, $t \in T$. In this case let us compute the Mellin transform of $\mu = \mathscr{L}\left(\left(\frac{dP_t}{dP}\right)_{t\in T} | P\right)$. If $z \in \Delta_T$ then we get by Example 5.5 (2)

$$\begin{aligned} M(\mu)(z) &= \int \prod_{t\in T} \left(\frac{dP_t}{dP}\right)^{z_t} dP = \int \exp\left(\sum_t z_t(X_t + a_t)\right) dP \\ &= \exp\left(\sum_t z_t a_t + \frac{1}{2} \sum_{s,t} z_s z_t K(s, t)\right) \\ &= \exp\left(\frac{1}{2}\left(\sum_{s,t} z_s z_t K(s, t) - \sum_t z_t K(t, t)\right)\right). \end{aligned}$$

Our next aim is to prove a uniqueness theorem for Mellin transforms. It is natural to rely on the uniqueness theorem for Laplace transforms. However, this is only possible for the interior of Δ_T. On the boundary of Δ_T we have to use the compatibility of the Mellin transforms stated below. In the following $A(T)$ denotes the family of subsets of T. If $\alpha \in A(T)$, $\alpha \neq \emptyset$, then $\mathscr{B}_\alpha$ is the σ-field of cylindrical sets in $\mathscr{B}(\mathbb{R})^T$ with base in $\mathscr{B}(\mathbb{R})^\alpha$. For $\mu \in \mathscr{M}(T)$ we denote $\mu_\alpha := \mathscr{L}(p_\alpha | \mu)$ and $\Delta_\alpha = \{z \in \Delta_T\colon z_t = 0 \text{ if } t \notin \alpha\}$, $\alpha \in A(T)$.

5.12 Remark. Suppose that $\mu \in \mathscr{M}(T)$. If $z \in \Delta_\alpha \cap \Delta_\beta$ then $M(\mu_\alpha)(z) = M(\mu_\beta)(z)$. Since $x^0 := 0$ if $x \geqq 0$, this property follows from

$$\begin{aligned} M(\mu_\alpha)(z) &= \int \prod_{t\in\alpha} x_t^{z_t} \mu_\alpha(dx) = \int \prod_{t\in T} x_t^{z_t} \mu(dx) \\ &= \int \prod_{t\in\beta} x_t^{z_t} \mu_\beta(dx) = M(\mu_\beta)(z). \end{aligned}$$

5.13 Theorem. *Suppose that $\mu_1, \mu_2 \in \mathscr{M}(T)$. If $M(\mu_1) = M(\mu_2)$ then $\mu_1 = \mu_2$.*

Proof. Every set $\mathscr{B}(\mathbb{R})^T \cap ([0, \infty)^T \setminus \{0\}^T)$ can be partitioned into sets of the form $C_\alpha \times \{0\}^{T\setminus\alpha}$, $C_\alpha \in \mathscr{B}^\alpha \cap (0, \infty)^\alpha$, $\alpha \in A(T)$; this is a consequence of the equation

$$[0, \infty)^T = \{0\}^T \cup \bigcup_{\emptyset \neq \alpha \subseteq T} ((0, \infty)^\alpha \times \{0\}^{T\setminus\alpha}).$$

We have to show that for every $\alpha \subseteq T$, $\alpha \neq \emptyset$, and every $C_\alpha \in \mathscr{B}^\alpha \cap (0, \infty)^\alpha$

$$\mu_1(C_\alpha \times \{0\}^{T\setminus\alpha}) = \mu_2(C_\alpha \times \{0\}^{T\setminus\alpha}).$$

Then the assertion follows from

$$\mu_1([0, \infty)^T) = 1 = \mu_2([0, \infty)^T).$$

Let $\alpha \subseteq \beta \subseteq T$, $\alpha \neq \emptyset$. We prove by induction on the cardinality of $\beta \backslash \alpha$ that for every $C_\alpha \in \mathscr{B}^\alpha \cap (0,\infty)^\alpha$

$$\mu_{1,\beta}(C_\alpha \times \{0\}^{\beta\backslash\alpha}) = \mu_{2,\beta}(C_\alpha \times \{0\}^{\beta\backslash\alpha}).$$

First, let $|\beta \backslash \alpha| = 0$, which means $\alpha = \beta$. A simple application of Theorem 5.7 implies that $\mu_{1,\beta} = \mu_{2,\beta}$ on $\mathscr{B}(\mathbb{R})^\beta \cap (0,\infty)^\beta$: Indeed, if $z \in \mathring{\Delta}_\beta$ then we have for $j = 1, 2$

$$M(\mu_j)(z) = M(\mu_{j,\beta})(z), z \in \Delta_\beta,$$

by Remark (5.12). If $z \in \mathring{\Delta}_\beta$ then

$$\begin{aligned} M(\mu_{j,\beta})(z) &= \int_{(0,\infty)^\beta} \prod_{t\in\beta} x_t^{z_t}\, \mu_{j,\beta}(dx) \\ &= \int_{\mathbb{R}^\beta} \exp\big(\sum_{t\in\beta} z_t y_t\big)\, \mathscr{L}(\log|\mu_{j,\beta})(dy), \quad j = 1, 2, \end{aligned}$$

and Theorem 5.7 implies

$$\mathscr{L}(\log|\mu_{1,\beta}) = \mathscr{L}(\log|\mu_{2,\beta}) \quad \text{on} \quad \mathscr{B}(\mathbb{R})^\beta.$$

This settles the case $|\beta \backslash \alpha| = 0$.

Now assume that for some $n \in \mathbb{N}_0$, for $n < |T| - 1$, and for every choice of $\alpha \subseteq \beta \subseteq T$ such that $|\beta \backslash \alpha| \leqq n$ and $C_\alpha \in \mathscr{B}(\mathbb{R})^\alpha \cap (0,\infty)^\alpha$ we have

$$\mu_{1,\beta}(C_\alpha \times \{0\}^{\beta\backslash\alpha}) = \mu_{2,\beta}(C_\alpha \times \{0\}^{\beta\backslash\alpha}).$$

Let $\alpha \subseteq \beta \subseteq T$ such that $|\beta \backslash \alpha| = n + 1$ and $C_\alpha \in \mathscr{B}(\mathbb{R})^\alpha \cap (0,\infty)^\alpha$. Choose $t_0 \in \beta \backslash \alpha$. Then for $i = 1, 2$

$$\begin{aligned} &\mu_{i,\beta}(C_\alpha \times \{0\}^{\beta\backslash\alpha}) \\ &= \mu_{i,\beta}(C_\alpha \times [0,\infty)^{\{t_0\}} \times \{0\}^{\beta\backslash(\{t_0\}\cup\alpha)}) - \mu_{i,\beta}(C_\alpha \times (0,\infty)^{\{t_0\}} \times \{0\}^{\beta\backslash(\{t_0\}\cup\alpha)}) \\ &= \mu_{i,\beta\backslash\{t_0\}}(C_\alpha \times \{0\}^{(\beta\backslash\{t_0\})\backslash\alpha}) - \mu_{i,\beta}((C_\alpha \times (0,\infty)^{\{t_0\}}) \times \{0\}^{\beta\backslash(\{t_0\}\cup\alpha)}). \end{aligned}$$

Sinced $|(\beta \backslash \{t_0\}) \backslash \alpha| = n$ and $|\beta \backslash (\{t_0\} \cup \alpha)| = n$ it follows by assumption that the right hands coincide for $i = 1, 2$ and so do the left hands.

This completes the induction. □

A first application of the uniqueness theorem shows how the likelihood ratio distributions of Example 5.11 are transformed if the denominator is changed.

5.14 Example. Recall the situation of Example 5.11. Let $\alpha \subseteq T$ and $t_0 \in T$. We compute the Mellin transform of $\mu = \mathscr{L}\left(\left(\frac{dP_t}{dP_{t_0}}\right)_{t\in\alpha} \middle| P_{t_0}\right)$. If $z \in \Delta_\alpha$ then we have

$$M(\mu)(z) = \int \prod_{t \in \alpha} \left(\frac{dP_t}{dP_{t_0}} \right)^{z_t} dP_{t_0} =$$
$$= \int \prod_{t \in \alpha} \left(\frac{dP_t}{dP} \right)^{z_t} \left(\frac{dP_{t_0}}{dP} \right)^{1 - \sum_{t \in \alpha} z_t} dP$$
$$= \int \exp\left(\sum z_t (X_t + a_t) + (1 - \sum z_t)(X_{t_0} + a_{t_0})\right) dP.$$

Thus, the Mellin transform can be computed by the formula of Example 5.5 (2). If we denote

$$\bar{K}(s, t) := K(s, t) - K(s, t_0) - K(t_0, t) + K(t_0, t_0), \quad (s, t) \in T^2,$$

then we obtain

$$M(\mu)(z) = \exp\left(\frac{1}{2} \left(\sum_{s, t \in \alpha} z_s z_t \bar{K}(s, t) - \sum_{t \in \alpha} z_t \bar{K}(t, t) \right) \right).$$

It follows that $\left(\log \frac{dP_t}{dP_{t_0}} \right)_{t \in \alpha}$ is a Gaussian random vector on $(\Omega, \mathscr{A}, P_{t_0})$ with covariance $(s, t) \mapsto \bar{K}(s, t)$ and expectation $t \mapsto -\frac{1}{2} \bar{K}(t, t)$.

Now, we turn to continuity properties of the Mellin transform. Compactness of $\mathscr{M}(T)$ makes things much easier.

5.15 Lemma. *The set $\mathscr{M}(T)$ is compact for the weak topology.*

Proof. We prove that $\mathscr{M}(T)$ is weakly closed and uniformly tight. The tightness property follows from

$$\mu\{\max_{t \in T} |x_t| \geqq a\} \leqq \sum_{t \in T} \mu\{|x_t| \geqq a\} \leqq \sum_{t \in T} \frac{1}{a} \int |x_t| \mu(dx)$$
$$\leqq \frac{|T|}{a}, \quad \mu \in \mathscr{M}(T), \ a > 0.$$

It is then clear every vague accumulation point of $\mathscr{M}(T)$ is a probability measure on $[0, \infty)^T$. A simple truncation argument shows that $\mathscr{M}(T)$ is weakly closed. □

5.16 Theorem. *A sequence $(\mu_n)_{n \in \mathbb{N}} \subseteq \mathscr{M}(T)$ converges weakly iff $(M(\mu_n))_{n \in \mathbb{N}}$ converges pointwise on Δ_T. In this case*

$$M(\lim_{n \to \infty} \mu_n) = \lim_{n \to \infty} M(\mu_n).$$

Proof. It is sufficient to show that $\mu_n \to \mu$ weakly, $(\mu_n)_{n \in \mathbb{N}} \subseteq \mathscr{M}(T)$, implies

$M(\mu_n) \to M(\mu)$ pointwise on Δ_T. Then the assertion follows from 5.13 and 5.15 by standard arguments.

Let $z \in \Delta_T$ and $z_0 := 1 - \sum_{t \in T} z_t > 0$. Then for every $\mu \in \mathcal{M}(T)$ and $a > 0$ we have

$$\int_{\bigcup_{t \in T} \{|x_t| > a\}} \prod_{t \in T} x_t^{z_t} \mu(dx) \leqq \sum_{s \in T} \int_{|x_s| > a} \prod_{t \in T} x_t^{z_t} \mu(dx) \leqq \sum_{s \in T} (\mu\{|x_s| > a\})^{1-z_0}$$
$$\leqq \frac{|T|}{a^{1-z_0}}.$$

Assume that $\mu_n \to \mu$ weakly, $(\mu_n)_{n \in \mathbb{N}} \subseteq \mathcal{M}(T)$, and let $a > 0$ be an arbitrary continuity point of $\mathcal{L}(\max_{t \in T} |p_t| | \prod_{t \in T} p_t^{z_t} \mu)$. Then we obtain

$$\begin{aligned}
M(\mu)(z) &\leqq \int_{\max_{t \in T} |x_t| \leqq a} \prod_{t \in T} x_t^{z_t} \mu(dx) + \frac{|T|}{a^{1-z_0}} \\
&= \lim_{n \to \infty} \int_{\max_{t \in T} |x_t| \leqq a} \prod_{t \in T} x_t^{z_t} \mu_n(dx) + \frac{|T|}{a^{1-z_0}} \\
&\leqq \liminf_{n \to \infty} M(\mu_n)(z) + \frac{|T|}{a^{1-z_0}} \leqq \limsup_{n \to \infty} M(\mu_n)(z) + \frac{|T|}{a^{1-z_0}} \\
&\leqq \lim_{n \to \infty} \int_{\max_{t \in T} |x_t| \leqq a} \prod_{t \in T} x_t^{z_t} \mu_n(dx) + \frac{2|T|}{a^{1-z_0}} \\
&= \int_{\max_{t \in T} |x_t| \leqq a} \prod_{t \in T} x_t^{z_t} \mu(dx) + \frac{2|T|}{a^{1-z_0}} \\
&\leqq M(\mu)(z) + \frac{2|T|}{a^{1-z_0}}.
\end{aligned}$$

The assertion follows since $a > 0$ may be chosen arbitrarily large. □

The concept of Mellin transforms is closely related to Hellinger transforms of standard measures.

5.17 Remark. Suppose that $P_0, P_1, \ldots, P_k$ are probability measures on a sample space $(\Omega, \mathcal{A})$. Instead of the distribution of likelihood ratios it is sometimes more convenient to consider the distributions of the densities $dP_i / d \sum_{j=0}^{k} P_j$, $0 \leqq i \leqq k$, under $\sum_{j=0}^{k} P_j$. These distributions are called standard measures. Their support is the standard simplex of $\mathbb{R}^{k+1}$ and they have first moments $= 1$. Hellinger transforms are used for the analytical treatment of standard measures.

If $T \neq \emptyset$ is a finite set then we define the *standard simplex*

$$S_T = \{z \in \mathbb{R}^T : 0 \leqq z_t \leqq 1, \, t \in T, \, \sum_{t \in T} z_t = 1\}.$$

A bounded measure $\sigma | \mathscr{B}(\mathbb{R})^T \cap S_T$ is a *standard measure* if $\int x_t \sigma(dx) = 1$, $t \in T$. The family of all standard measures is denoted by $\mathscr{S}_T$.

5.18 Definiton. Suppose tht $\sigma \in \mathscr{S}_T$ is a standard measure. The *Hellinger transform* of σ is the function

$$H(\sigma): S_T \to [0,1]: z \mapsto \int \prod_{t \in T} x_t^{z_t} \sigma(dx).$$

To show that $H(\sigma)$ actually maps into $[0,1]$ a similar argument is used as for Lemma 5.9.

Now, we prove uniqueness and continuity of Hellinger transforms.

5.19 Theorem. *Suppose that $\sigma_1, \sigma_2 \in \mathscr{S}_T$. If $H(\sigma_1) = H(\sigma_2)$ then $\sigma_1 = \sigma_2$.*

Proof. Let $t_0 \in T$. We will show that $p_{t_0}\sigma_1 = p_{t_0}\sigma_2$ on $\mathscr{B}^T \cap S_T$. Since $t_0 \in T$ may be chosen arbitrarily and $\sum_{t \in T} p_t = 1$ this proves the assertion.

If $T_0 := T \setminus \{t_0\}$ then $\Delta_{T_0} = \{(z_t)_{t \neq t_0}: z \in S_T, z_{t_0} \neq 0\}$. For $z \in S_T$ such that $z_{t_0} \neq 0$ we have

$$\int \prod_{t \in T} x_t^{z_t} \sigma_j(dx) = \int_{x_{t_0} \neq 0} \prod_{t \in T} x_t^{z_t} \sigma_j(dx) = \int \prod_{t \neq t_0} \left(\frac{x_t}{x_{t_0}}\right)^{z_t} x_{t_0} \sigma_j(dx), \quad j = 1, 2,$$

and from Theorem 5.13 it follows that

$$\mathscr{L}\left(\left(\frac{p_t}{p_{t_0}}\right)_{t \neq t_0} \middle| p_{t_0}\sigma_1\right) = \mathscr{L}\left(\left(\frac{p_t}{p_{t_0}}\right)_{t \neq t_0} \middle| p_{t_0}\sigma_2\right)$$

on $\mathscr{B}(\mathbb{R}^{T_0}) \cap [0,\infty)^{T_0}$. Since

$$\left(\frac{p_t}{p_{t_0}}\right)_{t \neq t_0}: \{z \in S_T: z_{t_0} \neq 0\} \to [0,\infty)^{T_0}$$

is a homeomorphism it follows that

$$p_{t_0}\sigma_1 = p_{t_0}\sigma_2 \quad \text{on} \quad \mathscr{B}(\mathbb{R}^{T_0}) \cap \{z \in S_T: z_{t_0} \neq 0\}.$$

Moreover

$$p_{t_0}\sigma_j(\{z \in S_T: z_{t_0} = 0\}) = 0, \quad j = 1, 2,$$

which proves that $p_{t_0}\sigma_1 = p_{t_0}\sigma_2$ on $\mathscr{B}(\mathbb{R})^T \cap S_T$. □

5.20 Lemma. *The set $\mathscr{S}_T$ is compact for the weak topology.*

Proof. Obviously, $\mathscr{S}_T$ is uniformly tight since S_T is compact. Since p_t is continuous and bounded on S_T the functions $\mu \mapsto \int x_t \mu(dx)$ are continuous on $\mathscr{M}^b(S_T, \mathscr{B}(\mathbb{R})^T \cap S_T)$ and $\mathscr{S}_T$ is weakly closed. □

5.21 Theorem. *A sequence $(\sigma_n)_{n\in\mathbb{N}} \subseteq \mathscr{S}_T$ converges weakly iff $(H(\sigma_n))_{n\in\mathbb{N}}$ converges pointwise on S_T. In this case*

$$H(\lim_{n\to\infty} \sigma_n) = \lim_{n\to\infty} H(\sigma_n).$$

Proof. Since $x \mapsto \prod_{t\in T} x_t^{z_t}$, $x \in S_T$, is continuous and bounded for every $z \in S_T$ it follows that $\sigma_n \to \sigma$ weakly, $(\sigma_n)_{n\in\mathbb{N}} \subseteq \mathscr{S}_T$, implies $H(\sigma_n) \to H(\sigma)$ pointwise on S_T. Now the assertion follows from 5.19 and 5.20 by standard arguments. □

6. Miscellaneous results

In this section we collect some well-known facts which are quoted subsequently. For their proof we refer to the literature as far as possible.

6.1 Theorem. *If $C \subseteq \mathbb{R}^k$ is a convex set then $\lambda^k(\partial C) = 0$.*

Proof. See e.g. Gänssler and Stute [1977: Satz 3.1.20]. □

6.2 Theorem (Brunn-Minkowski). *If A and B are subsets of $\mathbb{R}^k$ then $(\lambda^k(A+B))^{1/k} \geqq (\lambda^k(A))^{1/k} + (\lambda^k(B))^{1/k}$.*

Proof. See e.g. Federer [1969: 3.2.41]. □

6.3 Definition. Suppose that D is a locally compact space. A function $f: D \to \mathbb{R}$ is *level compact* if it is bounded from below and if $\{f \leqq a\}$ is compact for every $a < \sup f$.

6.4 Lemma. *Suppose that D is a locally compact space with countable base. Every level compact function $f: D \to \mathbb{R}$ satisfies*

$$f = \sup\{g \in \mathscr{C}_b(D): g \leqq f, g \text{ level compact}\}.$$

Proof. We note that by lower semicontinuity of f we have

$$f = \sup\{g \in \mathscr{C}_b(D): g \leqq f\}.$$

Assume that $\sup f = a < \infty$. We show that for every $\varepsilon > 0$ and every $g \in \mathscr{C}_b(D)$, $g \leqq f$, there is a level compact function $g_1 \in \mathscr{C}_b(D)$ such that $g - \varepsilon \leqq g_1 \leqq f$. Let $b = \inf f$ and $K_1 = \{f \leqq a - \varepsilon\}$. Choose a compact set K, $K_1 \subseteq \mathring{K}$, and define $h \in \mathscr{C}_b(D)$ such that $h = b$ on K_1, $h = a - \varepsilon$ on $D \setminus K$ and $b \leqq h \leqq a - \varepsilon$ elsewhere. Then it is clear that $g_1 = (g - \varepsilon) \cup h$ satisfies $g - \varepsilon \leqq g_1 \leqq h$.

Moreover, g_1 is level compact since $\sup g_1 = a - \varepsilon$ and if $c < a - \varepsilon$ then $\{g_1 \leqq c\} \subseteq \{h \leqq c\} \subseteq K$ is compact. This proves the assertion in case $\sup f < \infty$. If $\sup f = \infty$ the assertion is valid for every $f \cap n$, $n \in \mathbb{N}$, which completes the proof. □

The proof of the following topological lemma is taken from LeCam [1974].

6.5 Definition. Let D be a topological space. A finite set $\{g_0, g_1, \ldots, g_m\} \subseteq \mathscr{C}_b(D)$ is a *partition of the unity* if $g_i \geqq 0$, $0 \leqq i \leqq m$, and $\sum_{i=0}^{m} g_i = 1$.

6.6 Lemma. *Let D be a topological space. Then for any finite set $\{f_1, f_2, \ldots, f_m\} \subseteq \mathscr{C}_b(D)$ and for every $\varepsilon > 0$ there is a finite partition of the unity $\{g_0, g_1, \ldots, g_n\} \subseteq \mathscr{C}_b(D)$ such that the variation of each f_i, $1 \leqq i \leqq m$, is smaller than ε on every set $\{g_j \neq 0\}$, $0 \leqq j \leqq n$.*

Proof. The proof is divided into several steps.

First step: We assume that $m = 1$ and $f := f_1$ is such that $0 \leqq f \leqq 1$. If $\varepsilon > 0$ let $n \in \mathbb{N}$ be such that $\frac{1}{n} < \frac{\varepsilon}{2}$. We define for $k = 1, \ldots, n$

$$h_1 = f \cap \frac{1}{n} = \begin{cases} f & \text{if } 0 \leqq f \leqq \frac{1}{n}, \\ \frac{1}{n} & \text{if } \frac{1}{n} \leqq f \leqq 1, \end{cases}$$

$$h_2 = \left(f \cap \frac{2}{n}\right) - \left(f \cap \frac{1}{n}\right) = \begin{cases} 0 & \text{if } 0 \leqq f \leqq \frac{1}{n}, \\ f - \frac{1}{n} & \text{if } \frac{1}{n} \leqq f \leqq \frac{2}{n}, \\ \frac{1}{n} & \text{if } \frac{2}{n} \leqq f \leqq 1, \end{cases}$$

. . . . .

$$h_k = \left(f \cap \frac{k}{n}\right) - \left(f \cap \frac{k-1}{n}\right) = \begin{cases} 0 & \text{if } 0 \leqq f \leqq \frac{k-1}{n}, \\ f - \frac{k-1}{n} & \text{if } \frac{k-1}{n} \leqq f \leqq \frac{k}{n}, \\ \frac{1}{n} & \text{if } \frac{k}{n} \leqq f \leqq 1. \end{cases}$$

$$h_{k+1} = \left(f \cap \frac{k+1}{n}\right) - \left(f \cap \frac{k}{n}\right) = \begin{cases} 0 & \text{if } 0 \leqq f \leqq \dfrac{k}{n}, \\ f - \dfrac{k}{n} & \text{if } \dfrac{k}{n} \leqq f \leqq \dfrac{k+1}{n}, \\ \dfrac{1}{n} & \text{if } \dfrac{k+1}{n} \leqq f \leqq 1, \end{cases}$$

. . . . .

$$h_n = f - \left(f \cap \frac{n-1}{n}\right) = \begin{cases} 0 & \text{if } 0 \leqq f \leqq \dfrac{n-1}{n}, \\ f - \dfrac{n-1}{n} & \text{if } \dfrac{n-1}{n} \leqq f \leqq 1. \end{cases}$$

Then a partition of the unity is given by

$$g_0 = 1 - nh_1 = \begin{cases} 1 - nf & \text{if } 0 \leqq f \leqq \dfrac{1}{n}, \\ 0 & \text{if } \dfrac{1}{n} \leqq f \leqq 1, \end{cases}$$

$$g_1 = n(h_1 - h_2) = \begin{cases} nf & \text{if } 0 \leqq f \leqq \dfrac{1}{n}, \\ 2 - nf & \text{if } \dfrac{1}{n} \leqq f \leqq \dfrac{2}{n}, \\ 0 & \text{if } \dfrac{2}{n} \leqq f \leqq 1, \end{cases}$$

. . . . .

$$g_k = n(h_k - h_{k+1}) = \begin{cases} 0 & \text{if } 0 \leqq f \leqq \dfrac{k-1}{n}, \\ nf - (k-1) & \text{if } \dfrac{k-1}{n} \leqq f \leqq \dfrac{k}{n}, \\ k+1-nf & \text{if } \dfrac{k}{n} \leqq f \leqq \dfrac{k+1}{n}, \\ 0 & \text{if } \dfrac{k+1}{n} \leqq f \leqq 1, \end{cases}$$

. . . . .

$$g_n = nh_n = \begin{cases} 0 & \text{if } 0 \leqq f \leqq \dfrac{n-1}{n}, \\ nf - (n-1) & \text{if } \dfrac{n-1}{n} \leqq f \leqq 1. \end{cases}$$

It is easy to see that $g_j \geqq 0$, $0 \leqq j \leqq n$, and $\sum_{j=0}^{n} g_j = 1$. Moreover, we observe that $g_j \neq 0$ implies $\left|f - \frac{j}{n}\right| \leqq \frac{1}{n} < \frac{\varepsilon}{2}$ for every $j \in \{0, 1, 2, \ldots, n\}$. This proves the assertion.

Second step: We assume $m = 1$ and $f := f_1 \in \mathscr{C}_b(D)$ arbitrary. Then the assertion is valid for $\bar{f} = \frac{1}{2}\left(1 + \frac{f}{\|f\|_u}\right)$. Hence it is obviously true for f itself.

Third step: We consider the general case. For every single f_i, $1 \leqq i \leqq m$, there is a partition of the unity $\{g_{i0}, g_{i1}, \ldots, g_{in}\}$ with the desired properties. Since

$$1 = \prod_{i=1}^{m} \sum_{j=0}^{n} g_{ij} = \sum_{\{j_1, j_2, \ldots, j_m\}} \prod_{i=1}^{m} g_{ij_i}$$

the set $\{\prod_{i=1}^{m} g_{ij_i} : \{j_1, j_2, \ldots, j_m\} \subseteq \{0, 1, \ldots, n\}^m\}$ solves the problem for the whole set $\{f_1, f_2, \ldots, f_m\}$. □

6.7 Lemma. *Let $(\Omega, \mathscr{A})$ be a measurable space. If $\sigma_i \in ba(\Omega, \mathscr{A})$, $1 \leqq i \leqq n$, then for every $f \in \mathscr{L}_b^+(\Omega, \mathscr{A})$*

$$(\bigcup_{i=1}^{n} \sigma_i)^+(f) = \sup\{\sum_{i=1}^{n} \sigma_i(f_i) : f_i \in \mathscr{L}_b^+(\Omega, \mathscr{A}),\ 1 \leqq i \leqq n,\ \sum_{i=1}^{n} f_i \leqq f\}.$$

Proof. (1) Assume that $\sigma_i \geqq 0$, $1 \leqq i \leqq n$. Then for every $A \in \mathscr{A}$

$$\bigcup_{i=1}^{n} \sigma_i(A) = \sup\{\sum_{i=1}^{n} \sigma_i(A_i) : (A_i)_{1 \leqq i \leqq n}\ \mathscr{A}\text{-measurable partition of } A\}.$$

To see this, let τ be the set function on the right hand. It is easy to see that $\tau \in ba(\Omega, \mathscr{A})$. If $\sigma \geqq \sigma_i$ for every $i \in \{1, 2, \ldots, n\}$ then $\sigma \geqq \tau$. On the other hand we have $\tau \geqq \sigma_i$ for every $i \in \{1, 2, \ldots, n\}$ since taking the partition $A_i = \emptyset$ if $i \neq j$ and $A_j = A$, $A \in \mathscr{A}$, yields $\tau(A) \geqq \sigma_j(A)$.

(2) Still assuming $\sigma_i \geqq 0$, $1 \leqq i \leqq n$, we show that for every $f \in \mathscr{L}_b^+(\Omega, \mathscr{A})$

$$(\bigcup_{i=1}^{n} \sigma_i)(f) = \sup\{\sum_{i=1}^{n} \sigma_i(f_i) : f_i \in \mathscr{L}_b^+(\Omega, A),\ 1 \leqq i \leqq n,\ \sum_{i=1}^{n} f_i \leqq f\}.$$

Since $\bigcup_{i=1}^{n} \sigma_i \geqq 0$ it is clear that

$$\begin{aligned}(\bigcup_{i=1}^{n} \sigma_i)(f) &\geqq \sup\{(\bigcup_{i=1}^{n} \sigma_i)(\sum_{i=1}^{n} f_i) : f_i \in \mathscr{L}_b^+(\Omega, \mathscr{A}),\ \sum_{i=1}^{n} f_i \leqq f\} \\ &\geqq \sup\{\sum_{i=1}^{n} \sigma_i(f_i) : f_i \in \mathscr{L}_b^+(\Omega, \mathscr{A}),\ 1 \leqq i \leqq n,\ \sum_{i=1}^{n} f_i \leqq f\}.\end{aligned}$$

To prove the reversed inequality we note that in view of (1) the assertion is valid for simple functions. Since f may be approximated by simple functions from below the assertion follows.

(3) An immediate consequence of (2) is that for $\sigma_i \geqq 0$, $1 \leqq i \leqq n$, and $f \in \mathscr{L}_b^+(\Omega, \mathscr{A})$

$$\Big(\bigcup_{i=1}^{n} \sigma_i\Big)(f) = \sup\Big\{\sum_{i=1}^{n} \sigma_i(f_i) : f_i \in \mathscr{L}_b^+(\Omega, \mathscr{A}),\ 1 \leqq i \leqq n,\ \sum_{i=1}^{n} f_i = f\Big\}.$$

(4) Now, we prove the asserted equation. Let $\sigma_0 = 0$ and $\tau \geqq 0$ such that $\sigma_i + \tau \geqq 0$ for every $i \in \{1, 2, \ldots, n\}$. Then we obtain

$$\Big(\bigcup_{i=1}^{n} \sigma_i\Big)^+(f) + \tau(f) = \Big(\bigcup_{i=0}^{n} \sigma_i\Big)(f) + \tau(f) = \Big(\bigcup_{i=0}^{n} (\sigma_i + \tau)\Big)(f)$$

$$= \sup\Big\{\tau\Big(f - \sum_{i=1}^{n} f_i\Big) + \sum_{i=1}^{n} (\sigma_i + \tau)(f_i) : f_i \geqq 0,\ \sum_{i=1}^{n} f_i \leqq f\Big\}$$

$$= \sup\Big\{\sum_{i=1}^{n} \sigma_i(f_i) + \tau(f) : f_i \in \mathscr{L}_b^+(\Omega, \mathscr{A}),\ \sum_{i=1}^{n} f_i \leqq f\Big\}. \qquad \square$$

6.8 Definition. Let $(X, \|.\|)$ be a Banach lattice. Then $(X, \|.\|)$ is an *Abstract L-space* if $x \geqq 0$, $y \geqq 0$ imply $\|x + y\| = \|x\| + \|y\|$.

6.9 Theorem (Kakutani). *Every Abstract L-space is isometrically and lattice isomorphic with some $L_1(\Omega, \mathscr{A}, \mu)$ where $(\Omega, \mathscr{A}, \mu)$ is a measure space.*

Proof. See e.g. Schaefer [1974]. $\square$

6.10 Theorem (Landers). *Let $(\Omega, \mathscr{A}, P)$ be a measurable space and (X, d) a σ-compact metric space. Let $h: \Omega \times X \to \bar{\mathbb{R}}$ be a function such that $h(., x)$ is $\mathscr{A}$-measurable for every $x \in X$ and $h(\omega, .)$ is continuous for every $\omega \in \Omega$. If*

$$B(\omega) = \{x \in X : h(\omega, x) = \inf_{y \in X} h(\omega, y)\} \neq \emptyset$$

for P-almost all $\omega \in \Omega$ then there is an $(\mathscr{A}, \mathscr{B}(X))$-measurable function $\varphi: \Omega \to X$ satisfying

$$h(\omega, \varphi(\omega)) = \inf\{h(\omega, y) : y \in X\} \quad P\text{-a.e.}$$

Proof. Landers [1968: Korollar 1.4]. $\square$

6.11 Theorem. *Let $(\Omega, \mathscr{A}, \nu)$ be a σ-finite measure space and $(X, \mathscr{T})$ a locally compact space with countable base. Let $B: L_1(\Omega, \mathscr{A}, \nu) \times \mathscr{C}_{00}(X) \to \mathbb{R}$ be a bilinear function satisfying the following conditions:*

(1) $B(f, g) \geqq 0$ *if* $f \geqq 0, g \geqq 0$.

(2) $B(f, g) \leqq \|f\|_1 \cdot \|g\|_u$ *for all* $f \in L_1(\Omega, \mathscr{A}, \nu)$, $g \in \mathscr{C}_{00}(X)$.

Then there exists a substochastic kernel $\varrho\colon \Omega \times \mathscr{B}(X) \to [0,1]$ *such that*

$$B(f, g) = \int\int g(x)\,\varrho(\omega, dx)\,f(\omega)\,\nu(d\omega)$$

for all $f \in L_1(\Omega, \mathscr{A}, \nu)$ *and* $g \in \mathscr{C}_{00}(X)$.

Proof. The linear function $B(., g)$ is in $L_1(\Omega, \mathscr{A}, \nu)^*$ for every $g \in \mathscr{C}_{00}(X)$. Hence there exists $Tg \in \mathscr{L}_b(\Omega, \mathscr{A})$ such that $\|Tg\|_u \leqq \|g\|_u$ and

$$B(f, g) = \int f \cdot Tg\, d\nu \quad \text{if} \quad f \in L_1(\Omega, \mathscr{A}, \nu).$$

It follows easily that

$$T\Big(\sum_{i=1}^{k} \alpha_i g_i\Big) = \sum_{i=1}^{k} \alpha_i \mathrm{T} g_i \quad \nu\text{-a.e.}$$

for any linear combination in $\mathscr{C}_{00}(X)$.

Let $M \subseteq \mathscr{C}_{00}(X)$ be a countable dense set such that M^+ is dense in $\mathscr{C}_{00}^+(X)$. Let $\mathscr{C}_r$ be the $\mathbb{Q}$-linear hull of M and let $N \in \mathscr{A}$ be the set where

$$L_\omega\colon g \mapsto (Tg)(\omega), \quad g \in \mathscr{C}_r,$$

is not a positive, $\mathbb{Q}$-linear function satisfying $|L_\omega(g)| \leqq \|g\|_u$ if $g \in \mathscr{C}_r$. It follows that $\nu(N) = 0$.

If $\omega \notin N$ then the function L_ω may be extended to a positive, linear function on $\mathscr{C}_{00}(X)$ satisfying $|L_\omega(g)| \leqq \|g\|_u$. For every $\omega \notin N$ there is a Borel measure $\varrho(\omega, .)|\mathscr{B}(X)$ such that

$$L_\omega(g) = \int_X g(x)\,\varrho(\omega, dx) \quad \text{if} \quad g \in \mathscr{C}_{00}(X)$$

and therefore

$$(Tg)(\omega) = \int_X g(x)\,\varrho(\omega, dx) \quad \text{if} \quad g \in \mathscr{C}_r.$$

If $\omega \in N$ then we define $\varrho(\omega, .)$ to be an arbitrary but fixed probability measure $P|\mathscr{B}(X)$.

Let us show that $\omega \mapsto \varrho(\omega, B)$ is $\mathscr{A}$-measurable for every $B \in \mathscr{B}(X)$. If $f \in \mathscr{C}_r$ then

$$\int g(x)\,\varrho(\omega, dx) = (Tg)(\omega) \cdot 1_{\Omega \setminus N}(\omega) + \int g(x)\,P(dx) \cdot 1_N(\omega)$$

for every $\omega \in \Omega$ and therefore $\omega \mapsto \int g(x)\,\varrho(\omega, dx)$ is $\mathscr{A}$-measurable. Hence, the same holds for every $g \in \mathscr{C}_{00}(X)$. This implies that the system of sets $B \in \mathscr{B}(X)$ such that $\omega \mapsto \varrho(\omega, B)$ is $\mathscr{A}$-measurable contains the compacts. Since it is also a Dynkin system it coincides with $\mathscr{B}(X)$. Thus we obtain

$$B(f, g) = \int\int g(x)\,\varrho(\omega, dx)\,f(\omega)\,\nu(d\omega)$$

for every $g \in \mathscr{C}_r$ and $f \in L_1(\Omega, \mathscr{A}, \nu)$. For reasons of continuity this equation is also true for every $g \in \mathscr{C}_{00}(X)$. □

6.12 Lemma. *Let X_n be P_n-integrable random variables on probability spaces $(\Omega, \mathscr{A}_n, P_n)$, $n \in \mathbb{N}$. Assume that*

$$\lim_{n\to\infty} \mathscr{L}(X_n | P_n) = \mu \quad \textit{vaguely},$$

and

$$\lim_{n\to\infty} P(|X_n|) = \int |s| \mu(ds) < \infty.$$

Then the sequence (X_n) is uniformly (P_n)-integrable.

Proof. Let $\varepsilon > 0$ and choose a continuity point $a_\varepsilon > 0$ of μ such that $\int_{|s| > a_\varepsilon} |s| \mu(ds) < \varepsilon$. Then

$$\lim_{n\to\infty} \int_{|X_n| > a_\varepsilon} |X_n| dP_n = \lim_{n\to\infty} \Big(\int |X_n| dP_n - \int_{|X_n| \leqq a_\varepsilon} |X_n| dP_n\Big)$$
$$= \int |s| \mu(ds) - \int_{|s| \leqq a_\varepsilon} |s| \mu(ds) = \int_{|s| > a_\varepsilon} |s| \mu(ds) < \varepsilon.$$

Hence, there exists some $N(\varepsilon) \in \mathbb{N}$ such that

$$\sup_{n \geqq N(\varepsilon)} \int_{|X_n| > a_\varepsilon} |X_n| dP_n < \varepsilon. \qquad \square$$

Chapter 2: Elementary Theory of Testing Hypotheses

This chapter deals with those parts of the theory of testing hypotheses that are exclusively based on the Neyman-Pearson Lemma.

Starting-points will be the concepts of "experiment" and "testing-problem". We adopt the classical point of view where an experiment is described by means of a family of probability measures on a fixed measurable space. In case the family contains exactly two elements we speak of a binary experiment or a dichotomy. A testing problem is a partition of the underlying family of probability measures into two nonempty subsets. One subset is called hypothesis, the other one alternative.

In the simplest case, treated in Section 8, the Neyman-Pearson Lemma contains three statements which render a complete solution of testing problems for binary experiments. More complicated problems sometimes may be reduced to this situation. In this chapter this is done for testing problems which can be described by a one-dimensional parameter. If the underlying family of probability measures has montone likelihood ratios, then, for the most important testing problems, tests are constructed which are simultaneously optimal for all binary subproblems. This property characterizes experiments with monotone likelihood ratios.

Section 9 deals with one-sided testing problems for experiments with monotone likelihood ratios. A special case are exponential experiments of rank 1, as introduced in Section 11. When discussing two-sided testing problems, the set of tests under consideration has to be restricted by more then one linear equation. This requires a generalized version of the Neyman-Perason lemma, as given in Section 10. Since in the following we do not need the existence part of this lemma, we omit it. The interested reader may consult Moussatat [1976], for a modern version of the existence assertion based on Farkas' theorem of linear optimization theory. Sections 12 and 13 present the solutions of the most important two-sided testing problems for exponential experiments of rank 1.

Since the material contained in this chapter is an indispensable part of the theory of hypothesis testing, it is covered by every good text-book on Mathematical Statistics. Therefore we shall not give detailed reference to the original sources where the results have been proved for the first time. As a main source we mention the book by Lehmann [1958]. Another main reference is Schmetterer [1974]. The exposition given by Witting [1985] is much more detailed than ours and gives particular emphasis to examples and applications.

7. Basic definitions

Here we list some basic statistical notions as far as they are of interest for testing. This is continued in Section 33 in a more general setting.

7.1 Definition. Let $\Theta \neq \emptyset$ be an arbitrary set. A *statistical experiment* for the parameter space Θ is a triple $E = (\Omega, \mathscr{A}, \mathscr{P})$ where $(\Omega, \mathscr{A})$ is a sample space and $\mathscr{P} = \{P_\vartheta : \vartheta \in \Theta\}$ is a family of probability measures. The collection of all experiments for the parameter space Θ is denoted by $\mathscr{E}(\Theta)$.

If Θ contains exactly two points, i.e. if $\Theta = \{\vartheta_1, \vartheta_2\}$, then experiments $E \in \mathscr{E}(\Theta)$ are called *binary experiments*. For convenience a binary experiment E can be represented by a sample space $(\Omega, \mathscr{A})$ and a ordered pair (P, Q) of probability measures on $\mathscr{A}$.

An experiment $E = (\Omega, \mathscr{A}, \mathscr{P}) \in \mathscr{E}(\Theta)$ is *dominated* if there is a σ-finite measure $\nu | \mathscr{A}$ such that $P_\vartheta \ll \nu$ for every $\vartheta \in \Theta$. If E is dominated then there exists even a dominating probability measure. An experiment is called *homogeneous* if $P_\sigma \sim P_\tau$ for all $\sigma, \tau \in \Theta$.

Suppose that Θ is a topological space. The experiment is *continuous* if $\vartheta \mapsto P_\vartheta$ is continuous for the variational distance.

7.2 Definition. A *critical function* or a *test* for an experiment with sample space $(\Omega, \mathscr{A})$ is an $\mathscr{A}$-measurable function $\varphi: \Omega \to [0, 1]$. The set of all critical functions is denoted by $\mathscr{F} = \mathscr{F}(\Omega, \mathscr{A})$.

The following assertion is an important technical device for many arguments in testing theory. It is Eberlein's theorem on weak sequential compactness.

7.3 Lemma. *Suppose that* $E = (\Omega, \mathscr{A}, \mathscr{P}) \in \mathscr{E}(\Theta)$ *is a dominated experiment. Then for every sequence* $(\varphi_n)_{n \in \mathbb{N}} \subseteq \mathscr{F}(\Omega, \mathscr{A})$ *there is a subsequence* $\mathbb{N}_0 \subseteq \mathbb{N}$ *such that*

$$\lim_{n \in \mathbb{N}_0} P_\vartheta \varphi_n = P_\vartheta \varphi_0, \quad \vartheta \in \Theta,$$

for some $\varphi_0 \in \mathscr{F}(\Omega, \mathscr{A})$.

Proof. Let $P | \mathscr{A}$ be a dominating, σ-finite measure and let $h_\vartheta := \dfrac{dP_\vartheta}{dP}$, $\vartheta \in \Theta$. The σ-field $\mathscr{A}_0$ which is generated by the sequence $\{\varphi_n : n \in \mathbb{N}\}$ is countably generated. Let $\mathscr{C}$ be a countable field which generates $\mathscr{A}_0$. It is easy to obtain a subsequence $\mathbb{N}_0 \subseteq \mathbb{N}$ such that $\int_A \varphi_n \, dP$, $n \in \mathbb{N}_0$, converges for every $A \in \mathscr{C}$. If we denote

$$\sigma(A) := \lim_{n \in \mathbb{N}_0} \int_A \varphi_n \, dP, \quad A \in \mathscr{C},$$

then $\sigma | \mathscr{C}$ is finitely additive set function. Since

$$A_k \downarrow \emptyset,\ (A_k)_{k\in\mathbb{N}} \subseteq \mathscr{A}_0 \quad \text{implies} \quad \sup_{n\in\mathbb{N}} \int_{A_k} \varphi_n dP \downarrow 0,$$

the set function $\sigma|\mathscr{C}$ may be extended uniquely to a σ-finite set function $\sigma|\mathscr{A}_0$ satisfying

$$\sigma(A) = \lim_{n\in\mathbb{N}_0} \int_A \varphi_n dP$$

for every $A \in \mathscr{A}_0$. It is obvious that $0 \leqq \sigma \leqq P$ and therefore there is $\varphi_0 \in \mathscr{F}(\Omega, \mathscr{A}_0)$ such that

$$\sigma(A) = \int_A \varphi_0 dP, \quad A \in \mathscr{A}_0.$$

It follows that for every $f \in \mathscr{L}_1(\Omega, \mathscr{A}_0, P)$

$$\lim_{n\in\mathbb{N}_0} \int f\varphi_n dP = \int f d\sigma = \int f\varphi_0 dP.$$

For $\vartheta \in \Theta$ we obtain

$$\begin{aligned} P_\vartheta \varphi_0 &= \int \varphi_0 h_\vartheta dP = \int \varphi_0 P(h_\vartheta|\mathscr{A}_0) dP \\ &= \lim_{n\in\mathbb{N}_0} \int \varphi_n P(h_\vartheta|\mathscr{A}_0) dP = \lim_{n\in\mathbb{N}_0} \int \varphi_n h_\vartheta dP \\ &= \lim_{n\in\mathbb{N}_0} P_\vartheta \varphi_n, \end{aligned}$$

which proves the assertion. □

7.4 Definition. Suppose that $E = (\Omega, \mathscr{A}, \{P_\vartheta : \vartheta \in \Theta\})$ is an experiment. A partition (H, K) of Θ is called *testing problem*. The set H is called the *hypothesis* and K is called the *alternative* of the testing problem (H, K).

The value $\varphi(\omega)$ of a critical function is interpreted as the attitude of the statistician in favour of the alternative after having observed $\omega \in \Omega$. This interpretation motivates the following definition.

7.5 Definition. Suppose that $E = (\Omega, \mathscr{A}, P)$ is an experiment in $\mathscr{E}(\Theta)$ and let (H, K) be a testing problem for Θ. A critical function $\varphi \in \mathscr{F}(\Omega, \mathscr{A})$ *is better than* a critical function $\psi \in \mathscr{F}(\Omega, \mathscr{A})$ for (H, K) if

$$\begin{aligned} &P_\vartheta \varphi \leqq P_\vartheta \psi \quad \text{if} \quad \vartheta \in H, \quad \text{and} \\ &P_\vartheta \varphi \geqq P_\vartheta \psi \quad \text{if} \quad \vartheta \in K. \end{aligned}$$

As it is indicated in the preceding definition critical functions $\varphi \in \mathscr{F}(\Omega, \mathscr{A})$ are compared with respect to some experiment $E = (\Omega, \mathscr{A}, \mathscr{P})$ in terms of the functions $\vartheta \mapsto P_\vartheta \varphi$, $\vartheta \in \Theta$. The function $\vartheta \mapsto P_\vartheta \varphi$, $\vartheta \in \Theta$, is called the *power function* of φ. Roughly speaking, a test $\varphi \in \mathscr{F}(\Omega, \mathscr{A})$ has good properties if its power function is small on H and large on K. Tests are *equivalent* if their power functions are equal. In contrast, tests are *equal* if the underlying critical functions are equal P_ϑ-a.e., $\vartheta \in \Theta$.

7.6 Definition. Suppose that $E = (\Omega, \mathscr{A}, \mathscr{P})$ is an experiment in $\mathscr{E}(\Theta)$ and let (H, K) be a testing problem for Θ. If $\mathscr{C} \subseteq \mathscr{F}(\Omega, \mathscr{A})$ then the *envelope power function* of $\mathscr{C}$ with respect to (H, K) is the function

$$g: \vartheta \mapsto \begin{cases} \inf\limits_{\varphi \in \mathscr{C}} P_\vartheta \varphi & \text{if } \vartheta \in H, \\ \sup\limits_{\varphi \in \mathscr{C}} P_\vartheta \varphi & \text{if } \vartheta \in K. \end{cases}$$

A critical function $\varphi^* \in \mathscr{C}$ is *optimal in* $\mathscr{C}$ with respect to (H, K) at the point $\vartheta \in \Theta$ if $P_\vartheta \varphi^* = g(\vartheta)$. It is called *uniformly optimal in* $\mathscr{C}$ if it is optimal at every $\vartheta \in \Theta$.

7.7 Example. If we put $\mathscr{C} = \mathscr{F}(\Omega, \mathscr{A})$ then, obviously, $g = 1_K$. For every $\vartheta \in \Theta$ there is a critical function $\varphi^* \in \mathscr{F}$ which is optimal at ϑ. However, if there exists a test φ^* which is optimal at two different points $\vartheta_1 \in H$ and $\vartheta_2 \in K$ then it follows that $P_{\vartheta_1} \perp P_{\vartheta_2}$. Therefore, the set $\mathscr{C} = \mathscr{F}(\Omega, \mathscr{A})$ contains uniformly optimal tests only in very degenerate cases.

There is more hope to obtain uniformly optimal tests if one considers subsets $\mathscr{C} \subseteq \mathscr{F}(\Omega, \mathscr{A})$ which do not contain "strongly biased" elements.

7.8 Definition. Suppose that $E = (\Omega, \mathscr{A}, \mathscr{P})$ is an experiment in $\mathscr{E}(\Theta)$ and let (H, K) be a testing problem for Θ. A critical function $\varphi \in \mathscr{F}(\Omega, \mathscr{A})$ is *unbiased for* (H, K) if

$$\sup_{\vartheta \in H} P_\vartheta \varphi \leq \inf_{\vartheta \in K} P_\vartheta \varphi.$$

If φ is unbiased for (H, K) then each number $\alpha \in [\sup\limits_{\vartheta \in H} P_\vartheta \varphi, \inf\limits_{\vartheta \in K} P_\vartheta \varphi]$ is called *level of the test* φ and φ is called *unbiased level-α-test* for (H, K). For $\alpha \in [0, 1]$, $\mathscr{F}_\alpha(H, K)$ denotes the set of all unbiased level-α-tests for (H, K).

7.9 Lemma. *Suppose that $E = (\Omega, \mathscr{A}, \mathscr{P})$ is a dominated experiment in $\mathscr{E}(\Theta)$ and let (H, K) be a testing problem for Θ. Let $\alpha \in [0, 1]$. Then for every $\vartheta_0 \in \Theta$ the set $\mathscr{F}_\alpha(H, K)$ contains elements which are optimal at ϑ_0.*

Proof. Let g be the envelope power function and let $(\varphi_n)_{n \in \mathbb{N}} \subseteq \mathscr{F}(\Omega, \mathscr{A})$ be such that

$$\lim_{n \in \mathbb{N}} P_{\vartheta_0} \varphi_n = g(\vartheta_0).$$

According to Lemma 7.3 there is a subsequence $\mathbb{N}_0 \subseteq \mathbb{N}$ and a critical function

$\varphi_0 \in \mathscr{F}(\Omega, \mathscr{A})$ such that

$$P_\vartheta \varphi_0 = \lim_{n \in \mathbb{N}_0} P_\vartheta \varphi_n, \quad \vartheta \in \Theta.$$

It follows that $P_{\vartheta_0} \varphi_0 = g(\vartheta_0)$ and $\varphi_0 \in \mathscr{F}_\alpha(\Omega, \mathscr{A})$, which proves the assertion. □

7.10 Definition. Suppose that $E = (\Omega, \mathscr{A}, \mathscr{P})$ is an experiment in $\mathscr{E}(\Theta)$ and let (H, K) be a testing problem for Θ. Assume that Θ is a topological space. A critical function $\varphi \in \mathscr{F}(\Omega, \mathscr{A})$ is *similar of level* $\alpha \in [0, 1]$ if

$$P_\vartheta \varphi = \alpha \quad \text{for all} \quad \vartheta \in \bar{H} \cap \bar{K}.$$

The set of all similar tests of level $\alpha \in [0, 1]$ is denoted by $\mathscr{F}_\alpha^s(H, K)$.

7.11 Lemma. *Suppose that Θ is a topological space. If $E \in \mathscr{E}(\Theta)$ is continuous then $\mathscr{F}_\alpha(H, K) \subseteq \mathscr{F}_\alpha^s(H, K)$ for every testing problem (H, K).*

Proof. Obvious. □

The notion of similarity is of no direct statistical significance. However, it sometimes turns out that tests which are uniformly optimal in $\mathscr{F}_\alpha(H, K)$ are even uniformly optimal in $\mathscr{F}_\alpha^s(H, K)$.

There are some basic notions which describe the relations between subsets of $\mathscr{F}$.

7.12 Definition. Suppose that $\mathscr{F}_0 \subseteq \mathscr{F}$. A subset $\mathscr{C} \subseteq \mathscr{F}_0$ is called *$\mathscr{F}_0$-complete* for a testing problem (H, K), if for every test $\varphi \in \mathscr{F}_0$ there exists a better test $\psi \in \mathscr{C}$.

An $\mathscr{F}$-complete class $\mathscr{C}$ is simply called *complete*.

7.13 Definition. Suppose that $\mathscr{F}_0 \subseteq \mathscr{F}$. A *function* $g: \Theta \to [0, 1]$ is *$\mathscr{F}_0$-admissible* for a testing problem (H, K) if in $\mathscr{F}_0$ there is no better power function available than g. A *test* $\varphi \in \mathscr{F}(\Omega, \mathscr{A})$ is *$\mathscr{F}_0$-admissible* if its power function is $\mathscr{F}_0$-admissible.

An $\mathscr{F}$-admissible test is simply called *admissible*.

7.14 Definition. A critical function $\varphi \in \mathscr{F}(\Omega, \mathscr{A})$ is *non-randomized* for the experiment $E = (\Omega, \mathscr{A}, \{P_\vartheta: \vartheta \in \Theta\})$ if $\varphi(\omega) \in \{0, 1\}$ P_ϑ-a.e., $\vartheta \in \Theta$.

It is obvious that a critical function φ is non-randomized for E iff $P_\vartheta \varphi = P_\vartheta \varphi^2$, $\vartheta \in \Theta$.

7.15 Lemma. *A non-randomized critical function $\varphi \in \mathscr{F}(\Omega, \mathscr{A})$ is extremal in the following sense: If*

$$\varphi = \frac{1}{2}(\psi_1 + \psi_2) \quad P_\vartheta\text{-a.e.}, \vartheta \in \Theta,$$

for some $\psi_1, \psi_2 \in \mathscr{F}(\Omega, \mathscr{A})$, *then* $\varphi = \psi_1 = \psi_2$ P_ϑ-a.e., $\vartheta \in \Theta$.

Proof. Obvious. □

8. Neyman-Pearson theory for binary experiments

Consider a fixed binary experiment $E = (\Omega, \mathscr{A}, (P, Q))$ and the pertaining Lebesgue decompositions $\left(\frac{dP}{dQ}, M\right)$ and $\left(\frac{dQ}{dP}, N\right)$. We define a class of tests which will turn out to be complete and to contain only admissible tests for $(H, K) = (\{P\}, \{Q\})$.

8.1 Definition. Suppose that $k \in [0, \infty]$ and let $\mathscr{N}_k(P, Q)$ be the family of critical functions $\varphi^* \in \mathscr{F}$ satisfying $(P+Q)$-a.e. the following conditions:

(1) $\varphi^* = 0$ on M,

(2) $\varphi^* = 1$ on N,

(3) $$\varphi^* = \begin{cases} 1 & \text{if } \dfrac{dQ}{dP} > k \\ & \\ 0 & \text{if } \dfrac{dQ}{dP} < k \end{cases} \quad \text{on } (M \cup N)'.$$

Any critical function in $\mathscr{N}(P, Q) := \bigcup_{k \in [0, \infty]} \mathscr{N}_k(P, Q)$ is called *Neyman-Pearson-test* (*NP*-test) for the testing problem $H = \{P\}$, $K = \{Q\}$.

It is clear that the definition of *NP*-tests is independent of the particular choice of the Lebesgue decomposition of P and Q.

8.2 Remark. We have $\varphi^* \in \mathscr{N}_0(P, Q)$ iff $\varphi^* = 1 - 1_M$ $(P+Q)$-a.e., and $\varphi^* \in \mathscr{N}_\infty(P, Q)$ iff $\varphi^* = 1_N$ $(P+Q)$-a.e.

8.3 Lemma. *Suppose that* $k \in [0, \infty]$. *Then* $\varphi^* \in \mathscr{N}_k(P, Q)$ *iff* $1 - \varphi^* \in \mathscr{N}_{1/k}(Q, P)$.

Proof. The assertion is obvious as far as the values of φ^* and $1 - \varphi^*$ on $M \cup N$ are concerned. If $0 < k < \infty$ then the rest follows from 1.5 (4). If $k = 0$ or $k = \infty$ then the assertion follows from Remark 8.2. □

8.4 Remark. (1) Every NP-test φ^* satisfies $Q(N) \leqq Q\varphi^* \leqq 1$ and $0 \leqq P\varphi^* \leqq 1 - P(M)$. This follows from $\varphi^* \geqq 1_N$ and $\varphi^* \leqq 1 - 1_M$.

(2) If $\varphi^* \in \mathcal{N}_0(P, Q)$ then $Q\varphi^* = 1$ and $P\varphi^* = 1 - P(M)$ because $\varphi^* = 1_{\Omega \setminus M}$ $(P+Q)$-a.e.

(3) If $\varphi^* \in \mathcal{N}_\infty(P, Q)$ then $Q\varphi^* = Q(N)$ and $P\varphi^* = 0$ since in this case we have $\varphi^* = 1_N$ $(P+Q)$-a.e.

Now we prove three assertions which contain what usually is called the *Neyman-Pearson-Lemma*. The first assertion states the existence part of the NP-lemma.

8.5 Theorem.

(1) $\{P\varphi^*: \varphi^* \in \mathcal{N}(P, Q)\} = [0, 1 - P(M)]$.

(2) $\{Q\varphi^*: \varphi^* \in \mathcal{N}(P, Q)\} = [Q(N), 1]$.

Proof. The second part follows from (1) by applying 8.3. Let us prove (1). The boundary of $[0, 1 - P(M)]$ is attained by elements of $\mathcal{N}_0(P, Q)$ and $\mathcal{N}_\infty(P, Q)$, respectively. Let $0 < \alpha < 1 - P(M)$. Then there is some $k < \infty$ such that

$$P\left\{\frac{dQ}{dP} > k\right\} \leqq \alpha.$$

If we define

$$k_\alpha = \inf\left\{k < \infty : P\left\{\frac{dQ}{dP} > k\right\} \leqq \alpha\right\}$$

then it is easy to see that

$$P\left\{\frac{dQ}{dP} > k_\alpha\right\} = P \bigcup_{k > k_\alpha} \left\{\frac{dQ}{dP} > k\right\} \leqq \alpha$$

$$\leqq P \bigcap_{k < k_\alpha} \left\{\frac{dQ}{dP} > k\right\} = P\left\{\frac{dQ}{dP} \geqq k_\alpha\right\}.$$

If $P\left\{\frac{dQ}{dP} > k_\alpha\right\} = \alpha$ then we choose $\varphi^* \in \mathcal{N}_{k_\alpha}(P, Q)$ in such a way that $\varphi^* = 0$ on $\left\{\frac{dQ}{dP} = k_\alpha\right\}$ and we obtain $P\varphi^* = \alpha$. If $P\left\{\frac{dQ}{dP} > k_\alpha\right\} < \alpha$ then we have $P\left\{\frac{dQ}{dP} = k_\alpha\right\} > 0$ and we choose $\varphi^* \in \mathcal{N}_{k_\alpha}(P, Q)$ such that

$$\varphi^* = \frac{\alpha - P\left\{\frac{dQ}{dP} > k_\alpha\right\}}{P\left\{\frac{dQ}{dP} = k_\alpha\right\}} \quad \text{on} \quad \left\{\frac{dQ}{dP} = k_\alpha\right\}.$$

Thus we obtain again $P\varphi^* = \alpha$. $\square$

The following property of NP-tests is basic. It is the second part of the NP-lemma.

8.6 Theorem. *For every NP-test $\varphi^* \in \mathcal{N}(P, Q)$ and every $\varphi \in \mathscr{F}$*

(1) *$P\varphi \leqq P\varphi^*$ implies $Q\varphi \leqq Q\varphi^*$,*

(2) *$Q\varphi^* \leqq Q\varphi$ implies $P\varphi^* \leqq P\varphi$.*

Proof. (1): If $\varphi^* \in \mathcal{N}_0(P, Q)$ then $Q\varphi^* = 1$ and the assertion is evident. If $\varphi^* \in \mathcal{N}_\infty(P, Q)$ then $P\varphi^* = 0$ which implies $P\varphi = 0$ and $\varphi = 0$ P-a.e. Hence we obtain $Q\varphi = \int_N \varphi\, dQ \leqq Q(N) \leqq Q\varphi^*$. Before we treat the case $\varphi^* \in \mathcal{N}_k(P, Q)$ with $0 < k < \infty$ we prove two auxiliary assertions:

$$\text{(3)}\quad P\varphi \overset{(}{\leq}{}^{)} P\varphi^* \text{ implies } \int_{M' \cap N'} \varphi\, dP \overset{(}{\leq}{}^{)} \int_{M' \cap N'} \varphi^*\, dP,$$

$$\text{(4)}\quad Q\varphi^* \overset{(}{\leq}{}^{)} Q\varphi \text{ implies } \int_{M' \cap N'} \varphi^* \frac{dQ}{dP}\, dP \overset{(}{\leq}{}^{)} \int_{M' \cap N'} \varphi \frac{dQ}{dP}\, dP.$$

For the proof of (3) we note that

$$P\varphi = \int_M \varphi\, dP + \int_{M'} \varphi\, dP, \quad \text{and}$$

$$P\varphi^* = 0 + \int_{M'} \varphi^*\, dP.$$

For the proof of (4) we note that

$$Q\varphi = \int_{M' \cap N'} \varphi \frac{dQ}{dP}\, dP + \int_{M' \cap N} \varphi\, dQ, \quad \text{and}$$

$$Q\varphi^* = \int_{M' \cap N'} \varphi^* \frac{dQ}{dP}\, dP + \int_{M' \cap N} 1\, dQ.$$

Now we are ready to consider the case where $\varphi^* \in \mathcal{N}_k(P, Q)$ with $0 < k < \infty$. We have

$$(\varphi^* - \varphi)\left(\frac{dQ}{dP} - k\right) \geqq 0 \quad (P + Q)\text{-a.e. on } M' \cap N'.$$

It follows that

$$\int_{M' \cap N'} \varphi^* \frac{dQ}{dP}\, dP - \int_{M' \cap N'} \varphi \frac{dQ}{dP}\, dP \geqq k\Big(\int_{M' \cap N'} \varphi^*\, dP - \int_{M' \cap N'} \varphi\, dP\Big).$$

From $P\varphi \leqq P\varphi^*$, (3) and (4) we obtain $Q\varphi^* \geqq Q\varphi$.

(2): Use (1) and 8.3. □

8.7 Corollary. *For every $\varphi \in \mathscr{F}$ there is a NP-test $\varphi^* \in \mathscr{N}(P, Q)$ which is better than φ for the testing problem $H = \{P\}$, $K = \{Q\}$. Hence $\mathscr{N}(P, Q)$ is a complete class of tests.*

Proof. If $P\varphi \leqq 1 - P(M)$ then we choose $\varphi^* \in \mathscr{N}(P, Q)$ in such a way that $P\varphi = P\varphi^*$. This implies $Q\varphi \leqq Q\varphi^*$. If $P\varphi > 1 - P(M)$ we choose $\varphi^* \in \mathscr{N}_0(P, Q)$. In this case we have $P\varphi^* = 1 - P(M) < P\varphi$ and $Q\varphi^* = 1 \geqq Q\varphi$. □

The last part of the classical NP-lemma is concerned with a uniqueness assertion.

8.8 Theorem. *Suppose that $k \in [0, \infty]$ and $\varphi^* \in \mathscr{N}_k(P, Q)$. If $\varphi \in \mathscr{F}$ is better than φ^* for the testing problem $H = \{P\}$, $K = \{Q\}$ then also $\varphi \in \mathscr{N}_k(P, Q)$ and $P\varphi = P\varphi^*$, $Q\varphi = Q\varphi^*$. Hence, NP-tests are admissible.*

Proof. The equations $P\varphi = P\varphi^*$ and $Q\varphi = Q\varphi^*$ follow immediately from Theorem 8.6. It remains to show that $\varphi \in \mathscr{N}_k(P, Q)$.

(1) The case $0 < k < \infty$: If we recall the auxiliary assertions (3) and (4) of the proof of 8.6 then it follows from

$$(\varphi^* - \varphi)\left(\frac{dQ}{dP} - k\right) \geqq 0 \quad (P + Q)\text{-a.e.} \quad \text{on } M' \cap N',$$

that

$$(\varphi^* - \varphi)\left(\frac{dQ}{dP} - k\right) = 0 \quad (P + Q)\text{-a.e.} \quad \text{on } M' \cap N'.$$

Therefore in all inequalities of the auxiliary assertions (3) and (4) equality holds which implies

$$\int_M \varphi \, dP = 0, \qquad \int_{N \setminus M} (1 - \varphi) \, dQ = 0,$$

whence we obtain

$$\varphi = 0 \quad P\text{-a.e.} \quad \text{on } M, \quad \text{and}$$
$$\varphi = 1 \quad Q\text{-a.e.} \quad \text{on } N.$$

Putting terms together we observe that $\varphi \in \mathscr{N}_k(P, Q)$.

(2) The case $k = 0$: Since $Q\varphi^* = 1$ we have $Q\varphi = 1$ and therefore $\varphi = 1$ Q-a.e. On M' the fact that $P \ll Q$ implies $\varphi = 1$ $(P + Q)$-a.e. on M'. Moreover $P\varphi^* = 1 - P(M)$ implies $P\varphi = 1 - P(M)$. Since $\varphi \geqq 1 - 1_M$ $(P + Q)$-a.e. it follows that $\varphi = 0$ P-a.e. on M. Summing up we have proved that $\varphi = 1 - 1_M$ $(P + Q)$-a.e.

(3) The case $k = \infty$: Note that $1 - \varphi^* \in \mathscr{N}_0(Q, P)$ and apply part (2) of the proof. □

8.9 Remark. Let $\varphi^* \in \mathcal{N}_k(P, Q)$ be a NP-test. Then $k = \infty$ iff $P\varphi^* = 0$ and $k = 0$ iff $Q\varphi^* = 1$. Indeed, if $P\varphi^* = 0$ and if $\varphi^*_\infty \in \mathcal{N}_\infty(P, Q)$ then it follows from 8.4 and 8.6 that $P\varphi^* = P\varphi^*_\infty$ and $Q\varphi^* = Q\varphi^*_\infty$. According to 8.8 it follows that $\varphi^* \in \mathcal{N}_\infty(P, Q)$. A similar argument settles the case when $Q\varphi^* = 1$. The converse is immediate from 8.4.

8.10 Corollary. *Suppose that* $\varphi^* \in \mathcal{N}(P, Q)$. *Then* $P\varphi^* \leqq Q\varphi^*$. *If* $P \neq Q$, *then* $P\varphi^* < 1$ *and* $Q\varphi^* > 0$ *imply* $P\varphi^* < Q\varphi^*$. *In other words:* $P\varphi^* = Q\varphi^*$ *is only possible if the common value is either zero or one.*

Proof. Let $\varphi \in \mathcal{F}$ be the critical function with $\varphi \equiv P\varphi^*$. Then $P\varphi^* = P\varphi$ which implies $Q\varphi \leqq Q\varphi^*$. This proves $P\varphi^* \leqq Q\varphi^*$. If $P\varphi^* = Q\varphi^*$ then φ must be a NP-test. Since any NP-test takes at least one of the values zero or one the second part of the assertion follows. □

8.11 Remark. Let $E = (\Omega, \mathcal{A}, (P, Q))$ be a binary experiment and let $\nu|\mathcal{A}$ be an arbitrary σ-finite measure such that $P \ll \nu$ *and* $Q \ll \nu$. Denote $f_0 := \frac{dP}{d\nu}$ and $f_1 := \frac{dQ}{d\nu}$. Then for the respective Lebesgue decompositions we may choose $M = \{f_1 = 0\}$ and $N = \{f_0 = 0\}$. On $M' \cap N'$ we have

$$\frac{dQ}{dP} = \frac{f_1}{f_0} \quad (P + Q)\text{-a.e.}$$

It is easy to see that $\varphi^* \in \mathcal{N}_k(P, Q)$ with $0 < k < \infty$ iff

$$(1) \qquad \varphi^* = \begin{cases} 1 & \text{if } f_1 > kf_0 \\ 0 & \text{if } f_1 < kf_0 \end{cases} \quad (P + Q)\text{-a.e.}$$

Moreover $\varphi^* \in \mathcal{N}_0(P, Q)$ iff $\varphi^* = 1_{\{f_1 > 0\}}$ $(P + Q)$-a.e. and $\varphi^* \in \mathcal{N}_\infty(P, Q)$ iff $\varphi^* = 1_{\{f_0 = 0\}}$ $(P + Q)$-a.e. It should be noted that in case $P \sim Q$ the representation (1) is valid for every $k \in [0, \infty]$.

We finish this section with an application of the NP-lemma to tests of maximal power.

Consider a fixed binary experiment $E = (\Omega, \mathcal{A}, (P, Q))$. For $0 \leqq \alpha \leqq 1 - P(M)$ let $\mathcal{C}_\alpha = \{\varphi \in \mathcal{F}(\Omega, \mathcal{A}) : P\varphi \leqq \alpha\}$. We characterize those tests in $\mathcal{C}_\alpha$ which are optimal at Q for the testing problem $H = \{P\}$, $K = \{Q\}$.

8.12 Theorem. *A test* $\bar{\varphi} \in \mathcal{C}_\alpha$ *is optimal at* Q *in* $\mathcal{C}_\alpha$ *iff* $\bar{\varphi}$ *is a* NP-*test satisfying* $P\bar{\varphi} = \alpha$.

Proof. Assume that $\bar{\varphi} \in \mathcal{C}_\alpha$ is optimal in $\mathcal{C}_\alpha$. Let $\varphi^* \in \mathcal{N}(P, Q)$ be a NP-test with $P\varphi^* = \alpha$. Then we have $P\bar{\varphi} \leqq P\varphi^*$ and according to 8.6 it follows $Q\bar{\varphi}$

$\leqq Q\varphi^*$. This implies $Q\bar{\varphi} = Q\varphi^*$ and another application of 8.6 yields $P\bar{\varphi} = P\varphi^*$. Thus we obtain $P\bar{\varphi} = \alpha$ and from 8.8 it follows that $\bar{\varphi}$ is a NP-test.

Assume conversely that $\bar{\varphi} \in \mathscr{F}$ is a NP-test with $P\bar{\varphi} = \alpha$. Then for any further test $\varphi \in \mathscr{C}_\alpha$ we have $P\varphi \leqq P\bar{\varphi}$ and hence $Q\varphi = Q\bar{\varphi}$. This proves the assertion. □

8.13 Corollary (Schmetterer [1963]). *The function*

$$h\colon [0,1] \to [0,1]\colon \alpha \mapsto \sup\{Q\varphi\colon \varphi \in \mathscr{C}_\alpha\}$$

has the following properties:

(1) *h is strictly increasing on* $[0, 1 - P(M)]$,
(2) *h is concave,*
(3) *h is continuous,*
(4) $h(0) = Q(N)$, $h(\alpha) = 1$ *for* $\alpha \geqq 1 - P(M)$.

Proof. Assertion (1) follows from Theorem 8.6. Let us prove (2). For every $\alpha \in [0,1]$ let $\bar{\varphi}_\alpha$ be the NP-test in $\mathscr{C}_\alpha$ satisfying

$$Q\bar{\varphi}_\alpha = \sup\{Q\varphi\colon \varphi \in \mathscr{C}_\alpha\}.$$

Let $t \in (0,1)$ and $\alpha_i \in [0,1]$, $i = 1, 2$. Then we have

$$tQ\bar{\varphi}_{\alpha_1} + (1-t)Q\bar{\varphi}_{\alpha_2} \leqq Q(\bar{\varphi}_{t\alpha_1 + (1-t)\alpha_2})$$

since $t\bar{\varphi}_{\alpha_1} + (1-t)\bar{\varphi}_{\alpha_2}$ is a test of level $t\alpha_1 + (1-t)\alpha_2$.

This proves (2) and as a consequence we obtain that h is continuous on $(0,1)$. Assertion (4) is obvious. It remains to show that h is continuous at $\alpha = 0$ and $\alpha = 1$. Since h is concave and increasing it cannot happen that

$$\lim_{\alpha \to 1} h(\alpha) < h(1).$$

This proves continuity at $\alpha = 1$. For proving continuity at $\alpha = 0$ note that $\bar{\varphi}_\alpha | N = 1$ Q-a.e. for $\alpha \leqq 1 - P(M)$. It remains to show that

$$\lim_{\alpha \to 0} \int_{\Omega \setminus N} \bar{\varphi}_\alpha \, dQ = 0.$$

This follows from $\lim_{\alpha \to 0} \int \bar{\varphi}_\alpha \, dP = 0$ and the fact that $Q \ll P$ on $\Omega \setminus N$. □

9. Experiments with monotone likelihood ratios

Let $E = (\Omega, \mathscr{A}, \mathscr{P})$ be a dominated experiment in $\mathscr{E}(\Theta)$ satisfying $P_{\vartheta_1} \neq P_{\vartheta_2}$ if $\vartheta_1 \neq \vartheta_2$. Assume that $\Theta \subseteq \mathbb{R}$. If $\nu | \mathscr{A}$ is a σ-finite measure dominating $\mathscr{P}$ we denote $f_\vartheta := \dfrac{dP_\vartheta}{d\nu}$, $\vartheta \in \Theta$.

9.1 Definition. The experiment E is said to have *monotone likelihood ratios (m.l.r.)* if $\vartheta_1 < \vartheta_2$ implies

$$\frac{f_{\vartheta_2}}{f_{\vartheta_1}} = H_{\vartheta_1,\vartheta_2} \circ S \quad (P_{\vartheta_1} + P_{\vartheta_2})\text{-a.e.},$$

where $S\colon \Omega \to \bar{\mathbb{R}}$ is $\mathscr{A}$-measurable and $H_{\vartheta_1,\vartheta_2}\colon [-\infty, +\infty] \to [0, \infty]$ is increasing.

The importance of the m.l.r.-property is due to the fact that it admits a reduction of the experiment to its binary subexperiments. The terminology of the following definition is taken from Hajek [1969].

9.2 Definition. Suppose that $S\colon \Omega \to \bar{\mathbb{R}}$ is $\mathscr{A}$-measurable. A critical function $\varphi \in \mathscr{F}(\Omega, \mathscr{A})$ is an *upper S-test* if

$$\varphi = \begin{cases} 1 & \text{if } S > t, \\ 0 & \text{if } S < t, \end{cases}$$

where $t \in \bar{\mathbb{R}}$. It is a *lower S-test* if

$$\varphi = \begin{cases} 1 & \text{if } S < t, \\ 0 & \text{if } S > t, \end{cases}$$

where $t \in \bar{\mathbb{R}}$. The function S is called a *test statistic* of φ.

9.3 Lemma. *Suppose that E has monotone likelihood ratios. Every upper S-test $\varphi \in \mathscr{F}$ is a NP-test for each binary experiment $(P_{\vartheta_1}, P_{\vartheta_2})$ which satisfies $\vartheta_1 < \vartheta_2$ and $0 < P_{\vartheta_1}\varphi, P_{\vartheta_2}\varphi < 1$.*

Proof. Let $\vartheta_1 < \vartheta_2$ and let φ be an upper S-test. For convenience we denote $H := H_{\vartheta_1,\vartheta_2}$. Let us show that $0 < H(t) < \infty$. If $H(t) = \infty$ then $\varphi(\omega) > 0$ implies $S(\omega) \geqq t$ and therefore $H(S(\omega)) \geqq H(t) = \infty$. Hence we obtain

$$\{\varphi > 0\} \subseteq \{f_{\vartheta_2} = \infty\} \cup \{f_{\vartheta_1} = 0\}.$$

Since $\nu\{f_{\vartheta_2} = \infty\} = 0$ and $P_{\vartheta_1}\{f_{\vartheta_1} = 0\} = 0$ it follows that $P_{\vartheta_1}\{\varphi > 0\} = 0$ which contradicts $P_{\vartheta_1}\varphi > 0$. If $H(t) = 0$ then $\varphi(\omega) < 1$ implies $S(\omega) \leqq t$ and therefore $H(S(\omega)) \leqq H(t) = 0$. Hence, we obtain

$$\{\varphi < 1\} \subseteq \{f_{\vartheta_2} = 0\} \cup \{f_{\vartheta_1} = \infty\}.$$

Since $\nu\{f_{\vartheta_1} = \infty\} = 0$ and $P_{\vartheta_2}\{f_{\vartheta_2} = 0\} = 0$ it follows that $P_{\vartheta_2}\{\varphi < 1\} = 0$ which contradicts $P_{\vartheta_2}\varphi < 1$.

The assertion is proved if we show that

$$\varphi = \begin{cases} 1 & \text{if } f_{\vartheta_2} > H(t) f_{\vartheta_1}, \\ 0 & \text{if } f_{\vartheta_2} < H(t) f_{\vartheta_1}. \end{cases}$$

Assume that $f_{\vartheta_2}(\omega) > H(t) f_{\vartheta_1}(\omega)$. If $f_{\vartheta_1}(\omega) = 0$ this implies $f_{\vartheta_2}(\omega) > 0$ which only can happen if $H(S(\omega)) = \infty$. Hence $S(\omega) > t$. If $f_{\vartheta_1}(\omega) > 0$ then we obtain $H(S(\omega)) > H(t)$ which implies $S(\omega) > t$. In any case we have $\varphi(\omega) = 1$. Next assume that $f_{\vartheta_2}(\omega) < H(t) f_{\vartheta_1}(\omega)$. Then $f_{\vartheta_1}(\omega) > 0$ and therefore $H(S(\omega)) < H(t)$. This implies $S(\omega) < t$ and $\varphi(\omega) = 0$. □

9.4 Remark. If $P_{\vartheta_1} \sim P_{\vartheta_2}$ then the assertion of Lemma 9.3 holds without the restriction $0 < P_{\vartheta_1}\varphi, P_{\vartheta_2}\varphi < 1$. The reason is that in this case any test φ with $P_{\vartheta_1}\varphi = 0$ is an element of $\mathcal{N}_\infty(P_{\vartheta_1}, P_{\vartheta_2})$ and any test φ with $P_{\vartheta_2}\varphi = 1$ is an element of $\mathcal{N}_0(P_{\vartheta_1}, P_{\vartheta_2})$.

9.5 Lemma. *Suppose that E has monotone likelihood ratios. Every lower S-test $\varphi \in \mathcal{F}$ is a NP-test for each binary experiment $(P_{\vartheta_1}, P_{\vartheta_2})$ which satisfies $\vartheta_1 > \vartheta_2$ and $0 < P_{\vartheta_1}\varphi, P_{\vartheta_2}\varphi < 1$.*

Proof. Apply Lemmas 8.3 and 9.3. □

9.6 Remark. If $P_{\vartheta_2} \sim P_{\vartheta_1}$ then the assertion of Lemma 9.5 holds without the restriction $0 < P_{\vartheta_1}\varphi, P_{\vartheta_2}\varphi < 1$. Confer Remark 9.4.

9.7 Corollary. *Suppose that E has monotone likelihood ratios. Let $\vartheta_0 \in \Theta$.*

(1) *If $\varphi \in \mathcal{F}$ is an upper S-test and $0 < P_{\vartheta_0}\varphi < 1$ then*

$$\vartheta_1 < \vartheta_0 < \vartheta_2 \quad \textit{implies} \quad P_{\vartheta_1}\varphi < P_{\vartheta_0}\varphi < P_{\vartheta_2}\varphi.$$

(2) *If $\varphi \in \mathcal{F}$ is a lower S-test and $0 < P_{\vartheta_0}\varphi < 1$ then*

$$\vartheta_1 < \vartheta_0 < \vartheta_2 \quad \textit{implies} \quad P_{\vartheta_1}\varphi > P_{\vartheta_0}\varphi > P_{\vartheta_2}\varphi.$$

Proof. (1): If φ is an upper S-test then it is a NP-test for $(P_{\vartheta_0}, P_{\vartheta_2})$ or $P_{\vartheta_2}\varphi = 1$. In any case we obtain $P_{\vartheta_0}\varphi < P_{\vartheta_2}\varphi$. On the other hand $1 - \varphi$ is a lower S-test and a NP-test for $(P_{\vartheta_0}, P_{\vartheta_1})$ or $P_{\vartheta_1}(1-\varphi) = 1$. In any case we have $P_{\vartheta_0}(1-\varphi) < P_{\vartheta_1}(1-\varphi)$.

(2): Similarly. □

Similar to the proof of Theorem 8.5 it can be shown that for any $\alpha \in [0, 1]$ and any $\vartheta \in \Theta$ there are upper S-tests φ_1 and lower S-tests φ_2 satisfying $P_\vartheta \varphi_i = \alpha$, $i = 1, 2$.

9.8 Corollary. *Suppose that E has monotone likelihood ratios. Let $\vartheta_0 \in \Theta$ and assume that $\varphi \in \mathcal{F}$ satisfies $0 < P_{\vartheta_0}\varphi < 1$.*

(1) *If φ^* is an upper S-test satisfying $P_{\vartheta_0}\varphi^* = P_{\vartheta_0}\varphi$ then*

$$P_\vartheta \varphi^* \leqq P_\vartheta \varphi \quad \text{if} \quad \vartheta < \vartheta_0,$$
$$P_\vartheta \varphi^* \geqq P_\vartheta \varphi \quad \text{if} \quad \vartheta > \vartheta_0.$$

(2) *If* φ^* *is a lower S-test satisfying* $P_{\vartheta_0}\varphi^* = P_{\vartheta_0}\varphi$ *then*

$$P_\vartheta \varphi^* \geqq P_\vartheta \varphi \quad \text{if} \quad \vartheta < \vartheta_0,$$
$$P_\vartheta \varphi^* \leqq P_\vartheta \varphi \quad \text{if} \quad \vartheta > \vartheta_0.$$

Proof. This is an immediate consequence of 9.3 and 9.5 and Theorem 8.6. □

9.9 Remark. (1) If $P_{\vartheta_0}\varphi = 0$ or $P_{\vartheta_0}\varphi = 1$ then the assertions of Corollary 9.8 are satisfied for all $\vartheta \in \Theta$ with $P_\vartheta \sim P_{\vartheta_0}$.

(2) If the power functions of two upper (lower) S-tests φ_1 and φ_2 coincide at some $\vartheta_0 \in \Theta$ such that $0 < P_{\vartheta_0}\varphi_1 = P_{\vartheta_0}\varphi_2 < 1$ then the power functions coincide on Θ. If $P_{\vartheta_0}\varphi_i = 0$ or $P_{\vartheta_0}\varphi_i = 1$, $i = 1, 2$, then the power functions coincide for all $\vartheta \in \Theta$ with $P_\vartheta \sim P_{\vartheta_0}$.

The preceding results can be applied to the problem of uniformly optimal tests for one-sided testing problems.

9.10 Discussion. Recall that a testing problem is a partition (H, K) of Θ where H is called hypothesis and K alternative. A *one-sided testing problem* is a testing problem where

$$H = \{\vartheta \in \Theta : \vartheta \leqq \vartheta_0\}, \quad K = \{\vartheta \in \Theta : \vartheta > \vartheta_0\},$$

or

$$H = \{\vartheta \in \Theta : \vartheta \geqq \vartheta_0\}, \quad K = \{\vartheta \in \Theta : \vartheta < \vartheta_0\},$$

for some $\vartheta_0 \in \mathbb{R}$. Let $\mathscr{F}_0 = \{\varphi \in \mathscr{F} : P_{\vartheta_0}\varphi \in (0, 1)\}$. Then Corollary 9.8 and Remark 9.9 (2) imply that the set of all upper (lower) S-tests is an $\mathscr{F}_0$-complete class of tests for the first (second) one-sided testing problem. If E is homogeneous then $\mathscr{F}_0$ can be replaced by $\mathscr{F}$.

9.11 Theorem. *Suppose that E is a homogeneous and continuous experiment with m.l.r.*

(1) *The set of upper S-tests is a complete class of admissible tests for the testing problem* $H = \{\vartheta \in \Theta : \vartheta \leqq \vartheta_0\}$, $K = \{\vartheta \in \Theta : \vartheta > \vartheta_0\}$.

(2) *The set of lower S-tests is a complete class of admissible tests for the testing problem* $H = \{\vartheta \in \Theta : \vartheta \geqq \vartheta_0\}$, $K = \{\vartheta \in \Theta : \vartheta < \vartheta_0\}$.

Proof. Completeness follows from 9.10. Let us finish the proof of (1). Suppose that φ^* is an upper S-test and φ is another test which is better than φ^*. Then by Corollary 9.8 there exists an upper S-test $\bar{\varphi}$ which is better than φ and therefore also better than φ^*. It follows from continuity that $P_{\vartheta_0}\bar{\varphi} = P_{\vartheta_0}\varphi^*$ which proves admissibility in view of Remark 9.9 (2). □

Recall that $\mathscr{F}_\alpha(H, K)$ denotes the set of all unbiased tests of level $\alpha \in [0, 1]$ for (H, K), and $\mathscr{F}_\alpha^s(H, K)$ denotes the set of all similar tests of level $\alpha \in [0, 1]$.

9.12 Lemma. *Suppose that E has monotone likelihood ratios. Let* $0 \leqq \alpha \leqq 1$.

(1) *If* $H = \{\vartheta: \vartheta \leqq \vartheta_0\}$, $K = \{\vartheta: \vartheta > \vartheta_0\}$, *then* $\mathscr{F}_\alpha(H, K)$ *contains upper S-tests.*

(2) *If* $H = \{\vartheta: \vartheta \geqq \vartheta_0\}$, $K = \{\vartheta: \vartheta > \vartheta_0\}$, *then* $\mathscr{F}_\alpha(H, K)$ *contains lower S-tests.*

Proof. (1) Choose an upper S-test φ such that $P_{\vartheta_0}\varphi = \alpha$ and apply 9.7 (1).

(2) Choose a lower S-test φ such that $P_{\vartheta_0}\varphi = \alpha$ and apply 9.7 (2). □

9.13 Theorem. *Suppose that* $\Theta \subseteq \mathbb{R}$ *is an intervall, E is continuous and has monotone likelihood ratios. Let* $0 < \alpha < 1$.

(1) *If* $H = \{\vartheta: \vartheta \leqq \vartheta_0\}$, $K = \{\vartheta: \vartheta > \vartheta_0\}$, *then every upper S-test* $\varphi^* \in \mathscr{F}_\alpha(H, K)$ *is uniformly optimal in* $\mathscr{F}_\alpha^s(H, K)$.

(2) *If* $H = \{\vartheta: \vartheta \geqq \vartheta_0\}$, $K = \{\vartheta: \vartheta < \vartheta_0\}$, *then every lower S-test* $\varphi^* \in \mathscr{F}_\alpha(H, K)$ *is uniformly optimal in* $\mathscr{F}_\alpha^s(H, K)$.

Proof. If $\vartheta \mapsto P_\vartheta$ is continuous then every $\varphi \in \mathscr{F}_\alpha(H, K)$ satisfies $P_{\vartheta_0}\varphi = \alpha$. An application of 9.8 proves the assertion. □

9.14 Remark. If the elements of $\mathscr{P}$ are mutually equivalent then the assertion of Theorem 9.13 holds for every $\alpha \in [0, 1]$.

We finish this section showing that the property of having monotone likelihood ratios is even necessary for statements like Lemmas 9.3 or 9.5. Thereby, we restrict ourselves to homogeneous experiments to avoid technicalities.

9.15 Remark. Consider a probability space $(\Omega, \mathscr{A}, P)$. Let $\mathscr{C} \subseteq \mathscr{A}$ be a system of sets such that

(1) $P(A \setminus B) = 0$ or $P(B \setminus A) = 0$ if $A, B \in \mathscr{C}$.

It is very easy to see that property (1) is equivalent with each of the following:

(2) If $A, B \in \mathscr{C}$, $P(A) \leqq P(B)$, then $P(A \setminus B) = 0$.

(3) If $A, B \in \mathscr{C}$, then $P(A \cup B) = \max\{P(A), P(B)\}$.

Moreover, for any finite subsystem $\{B_1, \ldots, B_r\} \subseteq \mathscr{C}$ there is some $i_0 \in \{1, \ldots, r\}$ such that

$$P(\bigcup_{i=1}^{r} B_i \setminus B_{i_0}) = 0.$$

This is proved by induction. It follows that

$$P(\bigcup_{i=1}^{r} B_i) = \max\{P(B_i): 1 \leqq i \leqq r\},$$

which extends immediately to countable subsystems $\mathscr{C}_0 \subseteq \mathscr{C}$ in the way that

$$P(\bigcup \mathscr{C}_0) = \sup\{P(B): B \in \mathscr{C}_0\}.$$

9.16 Lemma (Pfanzagl [1963]). *Consider a probability space $(\Omega, \mathscr{A}, P)$ and a system $\mathscr{C} \subseteq \mathscr{A}$ satisfying 9.15 (1). Then there exists an $\mathscr{A}$-measurable map $S: \Omega \to [0,1]$ satisfying*

$$A = \{S \leqq P(A)\} \quad P\text{-a.e.}, \quad A \in \mathscr{C}.$$

Proof. We may assume that $\Omega \in \mathscr{C}$. We choose a countable subsystem $\mathscr{C}_0 \subseteq \mathscr{C}$ such that $\{P(A): A \in \mathscr{C}_0\}$ is dense in $\{P(A): A \in \mathscr{C}\}$ and define

$$S(\omega) := \inf\{P(B): B \in \mathscr{C}_0, \omega \in B\}, \quad \omega \in \Omega.$$

Clearly, S maps into $[0,1]$ and is $\mathscr{A}$-measurable in view of

$$\{S < \alpha\} = \bigcup \{B \in \mathscr{C}_0: P(B) < \alpha\}, \quad \alpha \in \mathbb{R}.$$

Let $A \in \mathscr{C}$. For A we define

$$B_n := \bigcup \left\{B \in \mathscr{C}_0: P(B) < P(A) + \frac{1}{n}\right\}, \quad n \in \mathbb{N}.$$

Then it follows from Remark (9.15) that

$$P(B_n) = \sup\left\{P(B): B \in \mathscr{C}_0, P(B) < P(A) + \frac{1}{n}\right\} \leqq P(A) + \frac{1}{n}, \quad n \in \mathbb{N},$$

and since (B_n) is decreasing

$$P\left(\bigcap_{n=1}^{\infty} B_n\right) \leqq P(A).$$

On the other hand it is clear that

$$A \subseteq B_n = \left\{S < P(A) + \frac{1}{n}\right\}, \quad n \in \mathbb{N}.$$

This implies

$$A \subseteq \{S \leqq P(A)\} = \bigcap_{n=1}^{\infty} \left\{S < P(A) + \frac{1}{n}\right\} = \bigcap_{n=1}^{\infty} B_n$$

and therefore

$$A = \bigcap_{n=1}^{\infty} B_n = \{S \leqq P(A)\} \quad P\text{-a.e.} \qquad \square$$

Now, we are in the position to prove the announced result.

9.17 Theorem (Pfanzagl [1963]). *Suppose that $E = (\Omega, \mathscr{A}, \{P_\vartheta: \vartheta \in \Theta\})$, $\Theta \subseteq \mathbb{R}$, is an homogeneous experiment with the following property:*

For every $\vartheta_0 \in \Theta$ *and every* $\alpha \in [0,1]$ *there exists a test* $\varphi \in \mathscr{F}(\Omega, \mathscr{A})$ *satisfying* $P_{\vartheta_0}\varphi = \alpha$ *which is in* $\mathscr{N}(P_{\vartheta_1}, P_{\vartheta_2})$ *for every pair* $\vartheta_1 < \vartheta_2$.

Then E has m.l.r.

Proof. Let $P_0|\mathscr{A}$ be any probability measure with $P_0 \sim \mathscr{P}$. We define a system $\mathscr{C}$ of sets

$$\left\{\frac{dP_{\vartheta_2}}{dP_{\vartheta_1}} \geqq k\right\}, \ \vartheta_1 < \vartheta_2, \quad 0 \leqq k \leqq \infty,$$

and show first of all that $\mathscr{C}$ has property 9.15 (1), with $P_0|\mathscr{A}$. For this, let $A_1, A_2 \in \mathscr{C}$, e.g.

$$A_1 = \left\{\frac{dP_{\vartheta_2}}{dP_{\vartheta_1}} \geqq k_1\right\}, \quad A_2 = \left\{\frac{dP_{\sigma_2}}{dP_{\sigma_1}} \geqq k_2\right\}.$$

There exists a test $\varphi \in \mathscr{F}(\Omega, \mathscr{A})$ such that $P_{\vartheta_1}\varphi = P_{\vartheta_1}(A_1)$, which is in $\mathscr{N}(P_{\vartheta_1}, P_{\vartheta_2})$ and in $\mathscr{N}(P_{\sigma_1}, P_{\sigma_2})$.

Since $\varphi \in \mathscr{N}(P_{\vartheta_1}, P_{\vartheta_2})$ it follows that $P_{\vartheta_2}\varphi \geqq P_{\vartheta_2}(A_1)$, and since $1_{A_1} \in \mathscr{N}_{k_1}(P_{\vartheta_1}, P_{\vartheta_2})$ we obtain by Theorem 8.8 that also $\varphi \in \mathscr{N}_{k_1}(P_{\vartheta_1}, P_{\vartheta_2})$, hence $\{\varphi = 1\} \subseteq A_1$ $\mathscr{P}$-a.e. With $P_{\vartheta_1}\varphi = P_{\vartheta_1}(A_1)$ it follows that $\{\varphi = 1\} = A_1$ $\mathscr{P}$-a.e. On the other hand, we have $\varphi \in \mathscr{N}(P_{\sigma_1}, P_{\sigma_2})$ and thus, there is some $k_3 \in [0, \infty]$ such that

$$\left\{\frac{dP_{\sigma_2}}{dP_{\sigma_1}} > k_3\right\} \subseteq \{\varphi = 1\} \subseteq \left\{\frac{dP_{\sigma_2}}{dP_{\sigma_1}} \geqq k_3\right\}.$$

This implies

$$\left\{\frac{dP_{\sigma_2}}{dP_{\sigma_1}} > k_3\right\} \subseteq A_1 \subseteq \left\{\frac{dP_{\sigma_2}}{dP_{\sigma_1}} \geqq k_3\right\} \quad \mathscr{P}\text{-a.e.}$$

which proves that $P_0(A_1 \setminus A_2) = 0$ or $P_0(A_2 \setminus A_1) = 0$.

According to Lemma 9.16 there exists an $\mathscr{A}$-measurable map $S: \Omega \to [0,1]$ satisfying

$$A = \{S \leqq P_0(A)\} \quad P_0\text{-a.e.}, \quad A \in \mathscr{C}.$$

We choose $\vartheta_1 < \vartheta_2$ and fix them. The function

$$f: [0, \infty] \to [0,1]: k \mapsto P_0\left\{\frac{dP_{\vartheta_2}}{dP_{\vartheta_1}} \geqq k\right\}$$

is decreasing and surjective, and

$$g: y \mapsto \sup\{k \in [0, \infty]: f(k) \geqq y\}, \quad y \in [0,1],$$

satisfies

$$y \leqq f(k) \quad \text{iff} \quad g(y) \geqq k, \quad y \in [0,1], \quad k \in [0, \infty].$$

We obtain

$$\left\{\frac{dP_{\vartheta_2}}{dP_{\vartheta_1}} \geqq k\right\} = \left\{S \leqq P_0\left\{\frac{dP_{\vartheta_2}}{dP_{\vartheta_1}} \geqq k\right\}\right\} = \{g \circ S \geqq k\} \quad P_0\text{-a.e.}$$

and therefore

$$\frac{dP_{\vartheta_2}}{dP_{\vartheta_1}} = g \circ S \quad \mathscr{P}\text{-a.e.}$$

It does not matter that g is decreasing. Replacing S by $1/S$ and defining $H_{\vartheta_1,\vartheta_2}$: $t \mapsto g(1/t)$, $t \in [0, \infty]$, leads to Definition 9.1. □

10. The generalized lemma of Neyman-Pearson

Theorem 8.12 can be extended to the case of finitely many linear restrictions. We confine ourselves to some elementary facts which are indispensible for the following but we do without a general discussion of its basis in linear optimization.

10.1 Remark. Suppose that $E = (\Omega, \mathscr{A}, (P, Q))$ is a binary experiment such that $P \sim Q$ with ν-densities f_0, f_1 where ν is a dominating σ-finite measure. Let us consider the problem of maximizing

$$\{\textstyle\int \varphi f_1\, d\nu : \varphi \in \mathscr{F}, \int \varphi f_0\, d\nu = \alpha\},$$

where $0 < \alpha < 1$. We know the solution of this problem from Theorem 8.12. If $\varphi^* \in \mathscr{F}$ is a NP-test such that

$$\textstyle\int \varphi^* f_0\, d\nu = \alpha,$$

then φ^* satisfies

$$\textstyle\int \varphi^* f d\nu = \sup\{\int \varphi f_1\, d\nu : \varphi \in \mathscr{F}, \int \varphi f_0\, d\nu = \alpha\}.$$

Moreover, the solution of the optimization problem is essentially unique.

These facts are now proved for a more general situation. Let $f_1, f_2, \ldots, f_{m+1}$ be ν-integrable functions on $(\Omega, \mathscr{A})$. Let $\mathscr{C}$ be the subfamily of $\mathscr{F}$ which satisfies

$$\textstyle\int \varphi f_i d\nu = c_i, \quad 1 \leqq i \leqq m,$$

where c_i, $1 \leqq i \leqq m$, are given constants. We consider the problem of maximizing

$$\{\textstyle\int \varphi f_{m+1}\, d\nu : \varphi \in \mathscr{C}\}.$$

10.2 Definition. A test $\varphi^* \in \mathscr{F}(\Omega, \mathscr{A})$ is called *generalized NP-test* for $(f_1, f_2, \ldots, f_m; f_{m+1})$ if there are $k_i \in \mathbb{R}$, $1 \leqq i \leqq m$, such that

$$(1) \qquad \varphi^* = \begin{cases} 1 & \text{if } f_{m+1} > \sum_{i=1}^{m} k_i f_i, \\ 0 & \text{if } f_{m+1} < \sum_{i=1}^{m} k_i f_i. \end{cases} \quad \nu\text{-a.e.}$$

We prove generalizations of 8.6 and 8.8. An extension of the existence assertion 8.5 is not straightforward.

10.3 Theorem. *If there exists a generalized NP-test $\varphi^* \in \mathscr{C}$, then*

$$\int \varphi^* f_{m+1}\, d\nu = \sup\{\int \varphi f_{m+1}\, d\nu \colon \varphi \in \mathscr{C}\}.$$

Proof. Assume that φ^* is defined by (1) and let $\varphi \in \mathscr{C}$. Then

$$(\varphi^* - \varphi)\,(f_{m+1} - \sum_{i=1}^{m} k_i f_i) \geqq 0 \quad \nu\text{-a.e.},$$

which proves the assertion. □

10.4 Theorem. *Suppose that there exists a generalized NP-test $\varphi^* \in \mathscr{C}$. If $\bar{\varphi} \in \mathscr{C}$ satisfies*

$$\int \bar{\varphi} f_{m+1}\, d\nu = \sup\{\int \varphi f_{m+1}\, d\nu \colon \varphi \in \mathscr{C}\},$$

then

$$\varphi^* = \bar{\varphi} \quad \nu\text{-a.e.} \quad on \quad \{f_{m+1} \neq \sum_{i=1}^{m} k_i f_i\}.$$

Proof. If φ^* is defined by (1) then we have

$$\int (\varphi^* - \bar{\varphi})\,(f_{m+1} - \sum_{i=1}^{m} k_i f_i)\, d\nu = 0$$

where the integrand is non-negative. This proves the assertion. □

11. Exponential experiments of rank 1

Suppose that $\Theta \subseteq \mathbb{R}$ is an open interval and $E = (\Omega, \mathscr{A}, \{P_\vartheta \colon \vartheta \in \Theta\})$ is a dominated experiment. Let $\{P_\vartheta \colon \vartheta \in \Theta\} \ll \nu | \mathscr{A}$. We shall consider only exponential experiments which are endowed with their natural parameter space. For many wellknown examples a parameter transformation is needed to bring them into such a form.

11.1 Definition. The experiment E is an *exponential experiment (of rank 1)* if

$$f_\vartheta := \frac{dP_\vartheta}{d\nu} = C(\vartheta) h \exp(\vartheta S), \quad \vartheta \in \Theta,$$

where $h: \Omega \to \mathbb{R}$, $S: \Omega \to \mathbb{R}$, are $\mathscr{A}$-measurable functions.

The definition of an exponential experiment is independent of the dominating measure $\nu|\mathscr{A}$. Any exponential experiment is homogeneous. The analysis of one-sided testing problems $H = \{\vartheta: \vartheta \leqq \vartheta_0\}$, $K = \{\vartheta: \vartheta > \vartheta_0\}$, or $H = \{\vartheta: \vartheta \geqq \vartheta_0\}$, $K = \{\vartheta: \vartheta < \vartheta_0\}$ for exponential experiments is contained in Section 9 as follows from the assertion below.

11.2 Lemma. *An exponential experiment of rank 1 has monotone likelihood ratios.*

Proof. It is obvious that for an exponential experiment of rank 1 we have $H_{\vartheta_1,\vartheta_2}(t) = \dfrac{C(\vartheta_2)}{C(\vartheta_1)} \exp((\vartheta_2 - \vartheta_1)t)$, $t \in \mathbb{R}$, which is increasing if $\vartheta_1 < \vartheta_2$. □

A partial converse to Lemma 11.2 is due to Borges and Pfanzagl [1963]. The interested reader may consult Heyer [1982].

It follows that the results of paragraph 9 may be applied to exponential experiments. In addition we obtain the following characterization of NP-tests.

11.3 Corollary. *Suppose that E is an exponential experiment of rank 1. Let $\vartheta_1 < \vartheta_2$.*

(1) *A test $\varphi \in \mathscr{F}$ is a NP-test for $(P_{\vartheta_1}, P_{\vartheta_2})$ iff it is $(h\nu)$-equivalent to an upper S-test.*

(2) *A test $\varphi \in \mathscr{F}$ is a NP-test for $(P_{\vartheta_2}, P_{\vartheta_1})$ iff it is $(h\nu)$-equivalent to a lower S-test.*

Proof. (1) Since $f_{\vartheta_2} \gtrless k f_{\vartheta_1}$ iff

$$\exp((\vartheta_2 - \vartheta_1)S) \gtrless \exp(\log k + \log C(\vartheta_1) - \log C(\vartheta_2)) \quad (h\nu)\text{-a.e.},$$

the assertion is obvious from Remarks 9.4 and 8.11.

(2) Similarly. □

11.4 Corollary. *Suppose that E is an exponential experiment of rank 1. Let (H, K) be a one-sided testing problem with $\bar{H} \cap \bar{K} = \{\vartheta_0\}$. If $\varphi \in \mathscr{F}_\alpha(H, K)$ is optimal in $\mathscr{F}_\alpha(H, K)$ for at least a single point $\vartheta \neq \vartheta_0$, then φ is uniformly optimal in $\mathscr{F}_\alpha^s(H, K)$.*

Proof. We consider only the case where $\vartheta \in H$. If φ is optimal at $\vartheta \neq \vartheta_0$ then it is a *NP*-test for $(P_{\vartheta_0}, P_\vartheta)$ and hence $(h\nu)$-equivalent to an upper or lower *S*-test. □

11.5 Lemma. *Suppose that E is an exponential experiment of rank* 1 *and let* $\varphi \in \mathscr{F}$. *Then* $\vartheta \mapsto P_\vartheta \varphi$, $\vartheta \in \Theta$, *is continuous and differentiable, and*

$$\frac{d}{d\vartheta} P_\vartheta \varphi \bigg|_{\vartheta=\vartheta_0} = P_{\vartheta_0}(S\varphi) - P_{\vartheta_0}(S) \cdot P_{\vartheta_0}(\varphi).$$

Proof. It follows from 5.6 that $\vartheta \mapsto \int e^{\vartheta S} h d\nu$ and $\vartheta \mapsto \int \varphi e^{\vartheta S} h d\nu$, $\vartheta \in \Theta$, are differentiable. The evaluation of the derivative is straightforward. □

Let $\vartheta_0 \in \Theta$, $H = \{\vartheta : \vartheta \leqq \vartheta_0\}$, $K = \{\vartheta : \vartheta > \vartheta_0\}$. We consider the slope of the power function at ϑ_0.

11.6 Theorem. *Suppose that E is an exponential experiment of rank* 1. *Let* $\vartheta_0 \in \Theta$ *and* $\varphi \in \mathscr{F}$.

(1) *If* φ^* *is an upper S-test satisfying* $P_{\vartheta_0}\varphi^* = P_{\vartheta_0}\varphi$ *then*

$$\frac{d}{d\vartheta} P_\vartheta \varphi^* \bigg|_{\vartheta=\vartheta_0} \geqq \frac{d}{d\vartheta} P_\vartheta \varphi \bigg|_{\vartheta=\vartheta_0},$$

or equivalently

$$P_{\vartheta_0}(S\varphi^*) \geqq P_{\vartheta_0}(S\varphi).$$

(2) *If* φ^* *is a lower S-test satisfying* $P_{\vartheta_0}\varphi^* = P_{\vartheta_0}\varphi$ *then*

$$\frac{d}{d\vartheta} P_\vartheta \varphi^* \bigg|_{\vartheta=\vartheta_0} \leqq \frac{d}{d\vartheta} P_\vartheta \varphi \bigg|_{\vartheta=\vartheta_0},$$

or equivalently

$$P_{\vartheta_0}(S\varphi^*) \leqq P_{\vartheta_0}(S\varphi).$$

Proof. This is an immediate consequence of 9.8 and 9.9. □

It follows from the preceding theorem that for every $\alpha \in [0,1]$ and every upper *S*-test φ_α^* such that $P_{\vartheta_0}\varphi_\alpha^* = \alpha$

$$\frac{d}{d\vartheta} P_\vartheta \varphi^* \bigg|_{\vartheta=\vartheta_0} = \sup\left\{\frac{d}{d\vartheta} P_\vartheta \varphi \bigg|_{\vartheta=\vartheta_0} : \varphi \in \mathscr{F}_\alpha^s(H,K)\right\}.$$

11.7 Corollary. *Suppose that E is an exponential experiment of rank* 1. *Let* $\vartheta_0 \in \Theta$ *and* $H = \{\vartheta : \vartheta \leqq \vartheta_0\}$, $K = \{\vartheta : \vartheta > \vartheta_0\}$. *Then*

$$\alpha \mapsto \sup \left\{ \frac{d}{d\vartheta} P_\vartheta \varphi \bigg|_{\vartheta=\vartheta_0} : \varphi \in \mathscr{F}_\alpha^s(H, K) \right\}$$

is concave and continuous on $[0,1]$.

Proof. The proof of concavity and of continuity on $(0,1)$ is almost the same as for Corollary 8.13. If φ_α, $\alpha \in [0,1]$, denote upper S-tests satisfying $P_{\vartheta_0}\varphi_\alpha = \alpha$ then $\varphi_0 = 0$ (hv)-a.e. and $\varphi_1 = 1$ (hv)-a.e. which implies

$$\frac{d}{d\vartheta} P_\vartheta \varphi_0 \bigg|_{\vartheta=\vartheta_0} = \frac{d}{d\vartheta} P_\vartheta \varphi_1 \bigg|_{\vartheta=\vartheta_0} = 0\,.$$

Since

$$\lim_{\alpha \to 0} \varphi_\alpha = 0\,(hv) \quad \text{and} \quad \lim_{\alpha \to 1} \varphi_\alpha = 1\,(hv)$$

we infer from Lemma (11.5) that

$$\lim_{\alpha \to 0} \frac{d}{d\vartheta} P_\vartheta \varphi_\alpha \bigg|_{\vartheta=\vartheta_0} = \lim_{\alpha \to 1} \frac{d}{d\vartheta} P_\vartheta \varphi_\alpha \bigg|_{\vartheta=\vartheta_0} = 0\,.$$

This proves continuity on $[0,1]$. □

12. Two-sided testing for exponential experiments: Part 1

We continue assuming that $\Theta \subseteq \mathbb{R}$ is an open interval and that $E = (\Omega, \mathscr{A}, \mathscr{P})$ is an experiment in $\mathscr{E}(\Theta)$. Now, we turn to the investigation of two-sided testing problems for exponential experiments of rank 1. The first kind of *two-sided testing problems* is of the form

$$H = \{\vartheta\colon \vartheta_1 \leqq \vartheta \leqq \vartheta_2\}, \quad K = \{\vartheta\colon \vartheta < \vartheta_1 \quad \text{or} \quad \vartheta > \vartheta_2\},$$

where $\vartheta_1 < \vartheta_2$.

12.1 Definition. Suppose that E is an exponential experiment of rank 1. A test $\varphi^* \in \mathscr{F}$ is a *two-sided S-test* if

$$\text{(3)} \qquad \varphi^* = \begin{cases} 1 & \text{if} \quad S < t_1 \quad \text{or} \quad S > t_2, \\ 0 & \text{if} \quad t_1 < S < t_2, \end{cases}$$

$t_i \in [-\infty, +\infty]$, $i = 1, 2$, $t_1 \leqq t_2$.

12.2 Lemma. *Suppose that E is an exponential experiment of rank 1. Let $\vartheta_1 < \vartheta_2$. For every test $\varphi \in \mathscr{F}$ there is a two-sided S-test $\varphi^* \in \mathscr{F}$ which satisfies*

$$P_{\vartheta_1}\varphi^* = P_{\vartheta_1}\varphi, \quad P_{\vartheta_2}\varphi^* = P_{\vartheta_2}\varphi\,.$$

Proof. (Ferguson [1967]). Let $\alpha := P_{\vartheta_1}\varphi$, $\beta := P_{\vartheta_2}\varphi$.

For every $\gamma \in [0,1]$ let φ_γ be an upper S-test satisfying $P_{\vartheta_1}\varphi_\gamma = \gamma$. The tests φ_γ, $\gamma \in [0,1]$, can be chosen in such a way that $\gamma_1 \leqq \gamma_2$ implies $\varphi_{\gamma_1} \leqq \varphi_{\gamma_2}$ and $\varphi_0 = 0$, $\varphi_1 = 1$. Let

$$\bar{\varphi}_\gamma := \varphi_\gamma + 1 - \varphi_{1-\alpha+\gamma}, \quad 0 \leqq \gamma \leqq \alpha.$$

Then $\gamma \leqq 1 - \alpha + \gamma$ implies $\varphi_\gamma \leqq \varphi_{1-\alpha+\gamma}$ and hence $\bar{\varphi}_\gamma \in \mathscr{F}$. It is obvious that $\bar{\varphi}_\gamma$, $\gamma \in [0,\alpha]$, are two-sided S-tests. We have

$$P_{\vartheta_1}\bar{\varphi}_\gamma = \alpha \quad \text{whenever} \quad 0 \leqq \gamma \leqq \alpha.$$

Let us show that

$$P_{\vartheta_2}\bar{\varphi}_0 \leqq \beta, \quad P_{\vartheta_2}\bar{\varphi}_\alpha \geqq \beta.$$

Note that $\bar{\varphi}_0 = 1 - \varphi_{1-\alpha}$. The test $\varphi_{1-\alpha}$ is a NP-test for $(P_{\vartheta_1}, P_{\vartheta_2})$ satisfying $P_{\vartheta_1}\varphi_{1-\alpha} = 1 - \alpha = P_{\vartheta_1}(1-\varphi)$. This implies $P_{\vartheta_2}\varphi_{1-\alpha} \geqq P_{\vartheta_2}(1-\varphi)$ and therefore

$$P_{\vartheta_2}\bar{\varphi}_0 = 1 - P_{\vartheta_2}\varphi_{1-\alpha} \leqq \beta.$$

Moreover, note that $\bar{\varphi}_\alpha = \varphi_\alpha$ is also a NP-test for $(P_{\vartheta_1}, P_{\vartheta_2})$ satisfying $P_{\vartheta_1}\varphi_\alpha = \alpha = P_{\vartheta_1}\varphi$ which implies $P_{\vartheta_2}\varphi_\alpha \geqq P_{\vartheta_2}\varphi$ and therefore

$$P_{\vartheta_2}\bar{\varphi}_\alpha \geqq P_{\vartheta_2}\varphi = \beta.$$

We obtain from 8.13 that $\gamma \mapsto P_{\vartheta_2}\varphi_\gamma$ is continuous on $[0,1]$ and therefore $\gamma \mapsto P_{\vartheta_2}\bar{\varphi}_\gamma$ is continuous on $[0,\alpha]$. It follows that there is some $\bar{\gamma} \in [0,\alpha]$ such that $P_{\vartheta_2}\bar{\varphi}_{\bar{\gamma}} = \beta$. This proves the assertion. □

12.3 Remark. In general, for arbitrary pairs $\vartheta_1 < \vartheta_2$ and arbitrary combinations $\alpha, \beta \in [0,1]$ there do not exist tests $\varphi \in \mathscr{F}$ such that $P_{\vartheta_1}\varphi = \alpha$, $P_{\vartheta_2}\varphi = \beta$. Hence there need not exist two-sided S-tests satisfying these conditions. But for every pair $\vartheta_1 < \vartheta_2$ and every $\alpha \in [0,1]$ there are two-sided tests φ^* satisfying

$$P_{\vartheta_1}\varphi^* = \alpha, \quad P_{\vartheta_2}\varphi^* = \alpha.$$

This follows from the preceding lemma choosing $\varphi \equiv \alpha$.

12.4 Lemma. *Suppose that E is an exponential experiment of rank 1. Let $\vartheta_1 < \vartheta < \vartheta_2$ and let φ^* be a two-sided S-test satisfying (3) with $-\infty < t_1 \leqq t_2 < \infty$. Then there are $k_1 > 0$, $k_2 > 0$, such that*

$$\varphi^* = \begin{cases} 1 & \text{if } f_\vartheta < k_1 f_{\vartheta_1} + k_2 f_{\vartheta_2}, \\ 0 & \text{if } f_\vartheta > k_1 f_{\vartheta_1} + k_2 f_{\vartheta_2}. \end{cases} \quad (hv)\text{-a.e.}$$

Proof. We have to show that there are $k_1' > 0$, $k_2' > 0$, such that

$$\varphi^* = \begin{cases} 1 & \text{if } 1 < k_1' e^{b_1 S} + k_2' e^{b_2 S}, \\ 0 & \text{if } 1 > k_1' e^{b_1 S} + k_2' e^{b_2 S}, \end{cases} \quad (h\nu)\text{-a.e.}$$

where $b_1 = \vartheta_1 - \vartheta < 0 < b_2 = \vartheta_2 - \vartheta$.

Case 1: Assume that $t_1 < t_2$. Consider the system of linear equations

$$k_1' e^{b_1 t_1} + k_2' e^{b_2 t_1} = 1,$$
$$k_1' e^{b_1 t_2} + k_2' e^{b_2 t_2} = 1.$$

The system has a unique solution since

$$D := \begin{vmatrix} e^{b_1 t_1} & e^{b_2 t_1} \\ e^{b_1 t_2} & e^{b_2 t_2} \end{vmatrix} = e^{b_1 t_1 + b_2 t_2} - e^{b_1 t_2 + b_2 t_1} > 0.$$

(Note that $b_2(t_2 - t_1) > b_1(t_2 - t_1)$ implies $b_1 t_1 + b_2 t_2 > b_1 t_2 + b_2 t_1$).

The solution is

$$k_1' = \frac{1}{D} \cdot (e^{b_2 t_2} - e^{b_2 t_1}) > 0,$$

$$k_2' = \frac{1}{D} \cdot (e^{b_1 t_1} - e^{b_1 t_2}) > 0.$$

Moreover, we see that

$$t \mapsto k_1' e^{b_1 t} + k_2' e^{b_2 t}, \quad t \in \mathbb{R},$$

is a strictly convex function. Since t_1 and t_2 are exactly the points where the function crosses the level 1 it follows that $1 < k_1' e^{b_1 t} + k_2' e^{b_2 t}$ implies $t < t_1$ or $t > t_2$, and $1 > k_1' e^{b_1 t} + k_2' e^{b_2 t}$ implies $t_1 < t < t_2$. This proves the assertion.

Case 2: Assume that $t_1 = t_2 =: t_0$. Consider the system of linear equations

$$k_1' e^{b_1 t_0} + k_2' e^{b_2 t_0} = 1,$$
$$k_1' b_1 e^{b_1 t_0} + k_2' b_2 e^{b_2 t_0} = 0.$$

The system has a unique solution since

$$D := \begin{vmatrix} e^{b_1 t_0} & e^{b_2 t_0} \\ b_1 e^{b_1 t_0} & b_2 e^{b_2 t_0} \end{vmatrix} = b_2 e^{b_2 t_0 + b_1 t_0} - b_1 e^{b_2 t_0 + b_1 t_0} > 0.$$

The solution is

$$k_1' = \frac{1}{D} \cdot b_2 e^{b_2 t_0} > 0,$$

$$k_2' = -\frac{1}{D} \cdot b_1 e^{b_1 t_0} > 0.$$

Moreover, we see that

$$t \mapsto k_1' e^{b_1 t} + k_2' e^{b_2 t}, \quad t \in \mathbb{R},$$

is a strictly convex function. Since t_0 is exactly the point where the function is tangent to the level 1 it follows that

$$\begin{aligned} 1 &< k_1' e^{b_1 t} + k_2' e^{b_2 t} \quad \text{implies} \quad t \neq t_0, \\ 1 &> k_1' e^{b_1 t} + k_2' e^{b_2 t} \quad \text{for no } t \in \mathbb{R}. \end{aligned}$$

This proves the assertion. □

12.5 Theorem. *Suppose that E is an exponential experiment of rank* 1. *Let* $\vartheta_1 < \vartheta_2$ *and* $\varphi \in \mathscr{F}$. *If* $\varphi^* \in \mathscr{F}$ *is a two-sided S-test satisfying*

$$P_{\vartheta_i} \varphi^* = P_{\vartheta_i} \varphi, \quad i = 1, 2,$$

then

$$\begin{aligned} P_\vartheta \varphi^* &\leqq P_\vartheta \varphi \quad \text{if} \quad \vartheta_1 < \vartheta < \vartheta_2, \\ P_\vartheta \varphi^* &\geqq P_\vartheta \varphi \quad \text{if} \quad \vartheta < \vartheta_1 \quad \text{or} \quad \vartheta > \vartheta_2. \end{aligned}$$

Thus, the set of two-sided S-tests is a complete class of tests for (H, K).

Proof. First assume that φ^* is a two-sided S-test with $t_1 = -\infty$. Then, of course, φ^* is an upper S-test. Therefore it is a NP-test for $(P_{\vartheta_1}, P_{\vartheta_2})$. According to 8.8 φ is also a NP-test of $(P_{\vartheta_1}, P_{\vartheta_2})$, since for this simple testing problem the power functions coincide. Hence φ is $(h\nu)$-equivalent to an upper S-test and from 9.9 (2), it follows that the power functions of φ and φ^* coincide on Θ.

In case $t_2 = +\infty$ the assertion is proved similarly.

Now, let $-\infty < t_1 \leqq t_2 < \infty$. We have to distinguish between $\vartheta < \vartheta_1$, $\vartheta > \vartheta_2$, and $\vartheta_1 < \vartheta < \vartheta_2$.

First case: Consider $\vartheta < \vartheta_1$. Then by Lemma 12.4 there are $k_1 > 0$, $k_2 > 0$, such that

$$\varphi^* = \begin{cases} 1 & \text{if} \quad f_{\vartheta_1} < k_1 f_\vartheta + k_2 f_{\vartheta_2}, \\ 0 & \text{if} \quad f_{\vartheta_1} > k_1 f_\vartheta + k_2 f_{\vartheta_2}, \end{cases} \quad (h\nu)\text{-a.e.}$$

which implies

$$\varphi^* = \begin{cases} 1 & \text{if} \quad f_\vartheta > \dfrac{1}{k_1} f_{\vartheta_1} - \dfrac{k_2}{k_1} f_{\vartheta_2}, \\ 0 & \text{if} \quad f_\vartheta < \dfrac{1}{k_1} f_{\vartheta_1} - \dfrac{k_2}{k_1} f_{\vartheta_2}. \end{cases} \quad (h\nu)\text{-a.e.}$$

From 10.3 we obtain $P_\vartheta \varphi^* \geqq P_\vartheta \varphi$.

Second case: Consider $\vartheta > \vartheta_2$. Then by Lemma 12.4 there are $k_1 > 0$, $k_2 > 0$, such that

$$\varphi^* = \begin{cases} 1 & \text{if} \quad f_{\vartheta_2} < k_1 f_{\vartheta_1} + k_2 f_{\vartheta}, \\ 0 & \text{if} \quad f_{\vartheta_2} > k_1 f_{\vartheta_1} + k_2 f_{\vartheta}, \end{cases} \quad (hv)\text{-a.e.}$$

which implies

$$\varphi^* = \begin{cases} 1 & \text{if} \quad f_{\vartheta} > -\dfrac{k_1}{k_2} f_{\vartheta_1} + \dfrac{1}{k_2} f_{\vartheta_2}, \\ 0 & \text{if} \quad f_{\vartheta} < -\dfrac{k_1}{k_2} f_{\vartheta_1} + \dfrac{1}{k_2} f_{\vartheta_2}. \end{cases} \quad (hv)\text{-a.e.}$$

From 10.3 we obtain $P_\vartheta \varphi^* \geqq P_\vartheta \varphi$.

Third case: Consider $\vartheta_1 < \vartheta < \vartheta_2$. Then by Lemma 12.4 there are $k_1 > 0$, $k_2 > 0$, such that

$$\varphi^* = \begin{cases} 1 & \text{if} \quad f_{\vartheta} < k_1 f_{\vartheta_1} + k_2 f_{\vartheta_2}, \\ 0 & \text{if} \quad f_{\vartheta} > k_1 f_{\vartheta_1} + k_2 f_{\vartheta_2}, \end{cases} \quad (hv)\text{-a.e.}$$

which implies by (10.3) that $P_\vartheta(1-\varphi^*) \geqq P_\vartheta(1-\varphi)$. □

A remarkable consequence is the following

12.6 Corollary. *Suppose that E is an exponential experiment of rank* 1. *If the power functions of two-sided S-tests coincide at two different points of* Θ *then they coincide on* Θ. *Moreover, two-sided S-tests are admissible for* (H, K).

The result of Theorem 12.5 can also be interpreted as an optimum property.

12.7 Corollary. *Suppose that E is an exponential experiment of rank 1. Let* $\alpha \in [0,1]$, $\vartheta_1 < \vartheta_2$ *and* $H = \{\vartheta : \vartheta_1 < \vartheta < \vartheta_2\}$, $K = \Theta \setminus H$. *Assume that* $\varphi^* \in \mathscr{F}_\alpha(H, K)$ *is a two-sided S-test. Then*

$$P_\vartheta \varphi^* = \sup\{P_\vartheta \varphi : \varphi \in \mathscr{F}_\alpha^s(H, K)\} \quad \text{if} \quad \vartheta \in K,$$
$$P_\vartheta \varphi^* = \inf\{P_\vartheta \varphi : \varphi \in \mathscr{F}_\alpha^s(H, K)\} \quad \text{if} \quad \vartheta \in H.$$

Proof. Since every power function $\vartheta \mapsto P_\vartheta \varphi$ is continuous, every $\varphi \in \mathscr{F}_\alpha(H, K)$ satisfies $P_{\vartheta_1}\varphi = P_{\vartheta_2}\varphi = \alpha$. An application of Theorem 12.5 proves the assertion. □

12.8 Corollary. *Suppose that E is an exponential experiment of rank 1. Let* $\alpha \in [0,1]$, $\vartheta_1 < \vartheta_2$ *and* $H = \{\vartheta : \vartheta_1 < \vartheta < \vartheta_2\}$, $K = \Theta \setminus H$. *If a test* $\varphi \in \mathscr{F}_\alpha(H, K)$ *is optimal in* $\mathscr{F}_\alpha(H, K)$ *at a single point* $\vartheta \neq \vartheta_i$, $i = 1, 2$, *then it is uniformly optimal in* $\mathscr{F}_\alpha^s(H, K)$.

Proof. Since E is homogeneous the assertion is trivial in case $\alpha = 0$ or $\alpha = 1$. Let $\alpha \in (0,1)$, $\varphi \in \mathscr{F}_\alpha(H, K)$ and $\vartheta \neq \vartheta_i$, $i = 1, 2$ be the point where φ is optimal. Further let $\varphi^* \in \mathscr{F}_\alpha(H, K)$ be a two-sided S-test, i.e.

$$\varphi^* = \begin{cases} 1 & \text{if} \quad S < t_1 \quad \text{or} \quad S > t_2, \\ 0 & \text{if} \quad t_1 < S < t_2. \end{cases} \quad \nu\text{-a.e.}$$

As $\alpha \in (0,1)$, Lemma 9.7 implies $-\infty < t_1 \leqq t_2 < +\infty$. In case $\vartheta \in K$, Lemma 12.4 gives constants k_1, k_2 such that

$$\varphi^* = \begin{cases} 1 & \text{if} \quad f_\vartheta > k_1 f_{\vartheta_1} + k_2 f_{\vartheta_2}, \\ 0 & \text{if} \quad f_\vartheta < k_1 f_{\vartheta_1} + k_2 f_{\vartheta_2}. \end{cases} \quad \nu\text{-a.e.}$$

Hence, in this case, φ^* is a generalized NP-test for $(f_{\vartheta_1}, f_{\vartheta_2}; f_\vartheta)$, and from the optimality of φ it follows by Theorem (10.4) that φ coincides with φ^* ν-a.e. on $\{f_\vartheta \neq k_1 f_{\vartheta_1} + k_2 f_{\vartheta_2}\}$. According to the proof of Lemma (12.4) the tests φ and φ^* coincide ν-a.e. where $S \neq t_1$ or $S \neq t_2$. Hence, φ is a two-sided S-test and therefore uniformly uniformly optimal in $\mathscr{F}_\alpha^s(H, K)$.

The case $\vartheta \in H$ is treated similarly, the only difference being that $1 - \varphi^*$ is a generalized NP-test for $(f_{\vartheta_1}, f_{\vartheta_2}; f_\vartheta)$. □

13. Two-sided testing for exponential experiments: Part 2

The second kind of *two-sided testing problems* which we consider is of the form $H = \{\vartheta_0\}$, $K = \{\vartheta : \vartheta \neq \vartheta_0\}$, where $\vartheta_0 \in \Theta$.

13.1 Lemma. *Suppose that E is an exponential experiment of rank 1. Let $\vartheta_0 \in \Theta$. For every test $\varphi \in \mathscr{F}$ there is a two-sided S-test $\varphi^* \in \mathscr{F}$ which satisfies*

$$P_{\vartheta_0}\varphi^* = P_{\vartheta_0}\varphi,$$

$$\frac{d}{d\vartheta} P_\vartheta \varphi^* \bigg|_{\vartheta = \vartheta_0} = \frac{d}{d\vartheta} P_\vartheta \varphi \bigg|_{\vartheta = \vartheta_0}.$$

Proof (Ferguson [1967]). Let $\alpha := P_{\vartheta_0}\varphi$, $\beta := \dfrac{d}{d\vartheta} P_\vartheta \varphi \bigg|_{\vartheta = \vartheta_0}$. For every $\gamma \in [0,1]$ let φ_γ be an upper S-test satisfying $P_{\vartheta_0}\varphi_\gamma = \gamma$, $\varphi_0 = 0$, $\varphi_1 = 1$. The tests φ_γ, $\gamma \in [0,1]$, can be chosen such that $\gamma_1 \leqq \gamma_2$ implies $\varphi_{\gamma_1} \leqq \varphi_{\gamma_2}$. Let

$$\bar{\varphi}_\gamma := \varphi_\gamma + 1 - \varphi_{1-\alpha+\gamma}, \quad 0 \leqq \gamma \leqq \alpha.$$

We have $\bar{\varphi}_\gamma \in \mathscr{F}$ and observe that $\bar{\varphi}_\gamma$, $\gamma \in [0, \alpha]$, are two-sided S-tests. Moreover

$$P_{\vartheta_0}\bar{\varphi}_\gamma = \alpha \quad \text{whenever} \quad 0 \leqq \gamma \leqq \alpha.$$

Let us show that

$$\frac{d}{d\vartheta} P_\vartheta \bar{\varphi}_0 \Big|_{\vartheta=\vartheta_0} \leqq \beta \leqq \frac{d}{d\vartheta} P_\vartheta \bar{\varphi}_\alpha \Big|_{\vartheta=\vartheta_0}.$$

Since $\bar{\varphi}_\alpha = \varphi_\alpha$ is an upper S-test it follows from Theorem (11.6) that $\bar{\varphi}_\alpha$ maximizes the slope of the power function at ϑ_0 among all tests $\varphi \in \mathscr{F}$ satisfying $P_{\vartheta_0}\varphi = \alpha$. On the other hand $\bar{\varphi}_0 = 1 - \varphi_{1-\alpha}$ is a lower S-test and it minimizes the slope.

From 11.7 we obtain that

$$\gamma \mapsto \frac{d}{d\vartheta} P_\vartheta \bar{\varphi}_\gamma \Big|_{\vartheta=\vartheta_0}$$

is continuous on $[0, \alpha]$. It follows that there is some $\bar{\gamma} \in [0, \alpha]$ such that

$$\frac{d}{d\vartheta} P_\vartheta \bar{\varphi}_\gamma \Big|_{\vartheta=\vartheta_0} = \beta.$$

This proves the assertion. □

13.2 Remark. Let $\vartheta_0 \in \Theta$. In general, for all $\alpha, \beta \in [0,1]$ there do not exist tests $\varphi \in \mathscr{F}$ such that $P_{\vartheta_0}\varphi = \alpha$, $\frac{d}{d\vartheta} P_\vartheta \varphi \Big|_{\vartheta=\vartheta_0} = \beta$. Hence there need not exist two-sided S-tests satisfying these conditions. But for every $\vartheta_0 \in \Theta$ and every $\alpha \in [0,1]$ there are two-sided S-tests $\varphi^* \in \mathscr{F}$ satisfying

$$P_{\vartheta_0}\varphi^* = \alpha, \quad \frac{d}{d\vartheta} P_\vartheta \varphi^* \Big|_{\vartheta=\vartheta_0} = 0.$$

This follows from the preceding lemma choosing $\varphi \equiv \alpha$.

13.3 Lemma. *Suppose that E is an exponential experiment of rank 1. Let $\vartheta \neq \vartheta_0$ and let φ^* be a two-sided S-test satisfying $-\infty < t_1 \leqq t_2 < \infty$. Then there are $k_1 \in \mathbb{R}$, $k_2 \in \mathbb{R}$, such that*

$$\varphi^* = \begin{cases} 1 & \text{if } f_\vartheta > k_1 f_{\vartheta_0} + k_2 S f_{\vartheta_0}, \\ 0 & \text{if } f_\vartheta < k_1 f_{\vartheta_0} + k_2 S f_{\vartheta_0}. \end{cases} \quad (h\nu)\text{-a.e.}$$

Proof. We have to show that there are $k_1' \in \mathbb{R}$, $k_2' \in \mathbb{R}$, such that

$$\varphi^* = \begin{cases} 1 & \text{if } 1 > k_1' e^{bS} + k_2' S e^{bS}, \\ 0 & \text{if } 1 < k_1' e^{bS} + k_2' S e^{bS}, \end{cases} \quad (h\nu)\text{-a.e.}$$

where $b = \vartheta_0 - \vartheta \neq 0$.

Case 1: Assume that $t_1 < t_2$. Consider the system of linear equations

$$k_1' e^{bt_1} + k_2' t_1 e^{bt_1} = 1,$$
$$k_1' e^{bt_2} + k_2' t_2 e^{bt_2} = 1.$$

The system has a unique solution since

$$D := \begin{vmatrix} e^{bt_1} & t_1 e^{bt_1} \\ e^{bt_2} & t_2 e^{bt_2} \end{vmatrix} = e^{b(t_1+t_2)}(t_2 - t_1) > 0.$$

The solution is

$$k_1' = \frac{1}{D}(t_2 e^{bt_2} - t_1 e^{bt_1}),$$

$$k_2' = \frac{1}{D}(e^{bt_1} - e^{bt_2}).$$

Moreover, we note that $\operatorname{sgn} b \neq \operatorname{sgn} k_2'$. Then, there is no interval where

$$g: t \mapsto k_1' e^{bt} + k_2' t e^{bt}, \quad t \in \mathbb{R},$$

is constant; in addition, the property

$$g'(t)(s-t) \geqq 0 \quad \text{if} \quad g(t) \leqq g(s)$$

implies that g is a quasi-concave function. This implies that $\{g = 1\}$ consists of at most two elements and $\{g > 1\} = (t_1, t_2)$ since $\{t_1, t_2\} \subseteq \{g = 1\}$. Hence

$$1 > k_1' e^{bt} + k_2' t e^{bt} \quad \text{implies} \quad t < t_1 \quad \text{or} \quad t > t_2, \quad \text{and}$$
$$1 < k_1' e^{bt} + k_2' t e^{bt} \quad \text{implies} \quad t_1 < t < t_2.$$

This proves the assertion.

Case 2: Assume that $t_1 = t_2 =: t_0$. Consider the system of linear equations

$$k_1' e^{t_0} + k_2' t_0 e^{bt_0} = 1,$$
$$k_t' b e^{bt_0} + k_2'(bt_0 + 1) e^{bt_0} = 0.$$

The system has a unique solution since

$$D := \begin{vmatrix} e^{bt_0} & t_0 e^{bt_0} \\ b e^{bt_0} & (bt_0 + 1) e^{bt_0} \end{vmatrix} = e^{2bt_0}(bt_0 + 1 - bt_0) > 0.$$

The solution is

$$k_1' = \frac{1}{D}(bt_0 + 1) e^{bt_0},$$

$$k_2' = -\frac{1}{D} b e^{bt_0}.$$

We note that $\operatorname{sgn} b \neq \operatorname{sgn} k_2'$ and argue as in case 1:

$$h: t \mapsto k_1' e^{bt} + k_2' t e^{bt}, \quad t \in \mathbb{R},$$

is a quasi-concave function, and there is no interval where h is constant. Thus a local extremum of h is a strict global maximum, and from $h(t_0) = 1$, $h'(t_0) = 0$ and $h''(t_0) \neq 0$ we get that $1 > k_1 e^{bt} + k_2' t e^{bt}$ is equivalent to $t \neq t_0$. This proves the assertion. □

13.4 Theorem. *Suppose that E is an exponential experiment of rank 1. Let $\vartheta_0 \in \Theta$ and $\varphi \in \mathscr{F}$.* If *$\varphi^* \in \mathscr{F}$ is a two-sided S-test satisfying*

$$P_{\vartheta_0} \varphi^* = P_{\vartheta_0} \varphi,$$

$$\frac{d}{d\vartheta} P_\vartheta \varphi^* \bigg|_{\vartheta = \vartheta_0} = \frac{d}{d\vartheta} P_\vartheta \varphi \bigg|_{\vartheta = \vartheta_0},$$

then

$$P_\vartheta \varphi^* \geqq P_\vartheta \varphi \quad \textit{if} \quad \vartheta \neq \vartheta_0.$$

Thus, the set of all two-sided S-tests is a complete class of tests for (H, K).

Proof. Case 1: Assume that φ^* is a two-sided S-test with $t_1 = -\infty$. Let $f_0 := f_{\vartheta_0}$, $f_1 := S f_{\vartheta_0}$. We observe, that φ^* is an upper S-test and from Theorems (11.6) and (10.4) it follows that φ^* is a generalized NP-test for (f_0, f_1) in the sense of Definition (10.2). The same is true of φ, and φ^* and φ coincide $(h\nu)$-a.e. on $\{f_1 \neq t_2 f_0\}$. Hence φ is $(h\nu)$-equivalent to an upper S-test and from (9.9) (2) it follows that the power functions of φ and φ^* coincide.

Case 2: If $t_2 = +\infty$, then the assertion is proved similarly.

Case 3: Assume that $-\infty < t_1 \leqq t_2 < \infty$. Let $\vartheta \neq \vartheta_0$. By Lemma (13.3) there are $k_1 \in \mathbb{R}$, $k_2 \in \mathbb{R}$, such that

$$\varphi^* = \begin{cases} 1 & \text{if} \quad f_\vartheta > k_1 f_{\vartheta_0} + k_2 S f_{\vartheta_0}, \\ 0 & \text{if} \quad f_\vartheta < k_1 f_{\vartheta_0} + k_2 S f_{\vartheta_0}. \end{cases} \quad (h\nu)\text{-a.e.}$$

From (10.3) we obtain

$$P_\vartheta \varphi^* \geqq P_\vartheta \varphi \quad \text{if} \quad \vartheta \neq \vartheta_0. \qquad \square$$

13.5 Corollary. *Suppose that E is an exponential experiment of rank 1. If value and slope of the power functions of two two-sided S-tests coincide at a point of Θ then they coincide on Θ. Moreover, two-sided S-tests are admissible for (H, K).*

13.6 Corollary. *Suppose that E is an exponential experiment of rank 1. Let $\alpha \in [0, 1]$, $\vartheta_0 \in \Theta$, and $H = \{\vartheta_0\}$, $K = \{\vartheta: \vartheta \neq \vartheta_0\}$. Assume that $\varphi^* \in \mathscr{F}_\alpha(H, K)$ is a two-sided S-test. Then*

$$P_\vartheta \varphi^* = \sup \{P_\vartheta \varphi: \varphi \in \mathscr{F}_\alpha(H, K)\} \quad \textit{if} \quad \vartheta \neq \vartheta_0.$$

Proof. Every $\varphi \in \mathscr{F}_\alpha(H, K)$ satisfies $P_{\vartheta_0}\varphi = \alpha$, $\left.\frac{d}{d\vartheta} P_\vartheta \varphi\right|_{\vartheta = \vartheta_0} = 0$ since the power has a local minimum at ϑ_0. □

13.7 Corollary. *Suppose that E is an exponential experiment of rank 1. Let* $\alpha \in [0, 1]$, $\vartheta_0 \in \Theta$, *and* $H = \{\vartheta_0\}$, $K = \{\vartheta: \vartheta \neq \vartheta_0\}$. *If a test* $\varphi \in \mathscr{F}_\alpha(H, K)$ *is optimal in* $\mathscr{F}_\alpha(H, K)$ *at a single point* $\vartheta \neq \vartheta_0$ *then it is uniformly optimal in* $\mathscr{F}_\alpha(H, K)$.

Proof. Since E is homogeneous the assertion is trivial in case $\alpha = 0$ or $\alpha = 1$. Let $\alpha \in (0, 1)$, $\varphi \in \mathscr{F}_\alpha(H, K)$ and $\vartheta \in K$ be the point where φ is optimal. Further let $\varphi^* \in \mathscr{F}_\alpha(H, K)$ be a two-sided S-test, i.e.

$$\varphi^* = \begin{cases} 1 & \text{if} \quad S < t_1 \quad \text{or} \quad S > t_2, \\ 0 & \text{if} \quad t_1 < S < t_2. \end{cases} \qquad \nu\text{-a.e.}$$

As $\alpha \in (0, 1)$, Lemma 9.7 implies $-\infty < t_1 \leqq t_2 < +\infty$. Hence, Lemma 13.3 gives constants $k_1 \in \mathbb{R}$, $k_2 \in \mathbb{R}$ such that

$$\varphi^* = \begin{cases} 1 & \text{if} \quad f > k_1 f_{\vartheta_0} + k_2 S f_{\vartheta_0} \\ 0 & \text{if} \quad f < k_1 f_{\vartheta_0} + k_2 S f_{\vartheta_0}. \end{cases}$$

This shows that φ^* is a generalized NP-test for $(f_{\vartheta_0}, Sf_{\vartheta_0}; f_\vartheta)$. From the optimality of φ it follows by Theorems 10.4 and 13.4 that φ coincides with φ^* ν-a.e. on $\{f_\vartheta \neq k_1 f_{\vartheta_0} + k_2 S f_{\vartheta_0}\}$. According to the proof of Lemma (13.3) the tests φ and φ^* coincide ν-a.e. where $S \neq t_1$ and $S \neq t_2$. Thus, φ is a two-sided S-test and therefore uniformly optimal in $\mathscr{F}_\alpha(H, K)$. □

Chapter 3: Binary Experiments

The power and simplicity of the lemma of Neyman and Pearson gives rise to the development of a general theory of binary experiments. This theory is a very simple special case of the general decision theory, but its isolation seems to be advantageous in several respects. General decision theory relies on powerful instruments of functional analysis. In contrast, the theory of binary experiments can be based exclusively on the lemma of Neyman and Pearson. A decision-theoretically meaningful distance between experiments, the so-called deficiency, is easy to handle for binary experiments.

In Section 14 we define the error function of a binary experiment. Section 15 contains the discussion of the natural semi-ordering of the class of binary experiments. In particular, we show it can be expressed by the pointwise ordering of error functions. The topological structure is treated similarly. Finally, it is proved that semiordering and convergence of binary experiments can also be expressed by power functions of optimal level-α-tests.

Sections 16 and 17 are concerned with equivalence classes of binary experiments and their characterization. It turns out that besides the error function both the distribution of the likelihood ratio and its Mellin transform determine the equivalence classes uniquely. A consequence is compactness of the space of binary experiments.

It is convenient to introduce at this point the concept of contiguous sequences of probability measures. Essentially, these are sequences of binary experiments whose accumulation points are homogeneous experiments. The essential facts are presented in Section 18.

Practically the whole of chapter 3 is well-known. The concept of contiguity is due to LeCam [1960].

14. The error function

Consider a binary experiment $E = (\Omega, \mathscr{A}, (P, Q))$.

14.1 Definition. The *error function* of the binary experiment E is the function $g\colon [0,1] \to [0,1]$ which is defined by

$$g(\alpha) = \inf_{\varphi \in \mathscr{F}} [(1-\alpha) P\varphi + \alpha Q(1-\varphi)], \quad \alpha \in [0,1].$$

In the following assertion we define for reasons of convenience: $\dfrac{\infty}{1+\infty} = 1$. The

Lebesgue decompositions of P with respect to Q and of Q with respect to P are denoted by $\left(\frac{dP}{dQ}, M\right)$ and $\left(\frac{dQ}{dP}, N\right)$.

14.2 Theorem. *Let g be the error function of E. If $0 \leqq k \leqq \infty$, $0 \leqq \alpha \leqq 1$, and $\varphi^* \in \mathscr{F}$ then the following assertions are equivalent:*

(1) $\varphi^* \in \mathscr{N}_k(P, Q)$ for $k = \frac{1}{\alpha} - 1$.

(2) $g(\alpha) = (1-\alpha)\, P\varphi^* + \alpha Q(1-\varphi^*)$.

Proof. (1) ⇒ (2): If $k = 0$ then $Q\varphi^* = 1$ and therefore

$$\left(\frac{0}{1+0}\right) P\varphi^* + \left(\frac{1}{1+0}\right) Q(1-\varphi^*) = 0.$$

On the other hand we have

$$g\left(\frac{1}{1+0}\right) = g(1) = \inf_{\varphi \in \mathscr{F}} Q(1-\varphi) = 0.$$

If $k = \infty$ then $P\varphi^* = 0$ and therefore

$$\left(\frac{\infty}{1+\infty}\right) P\varphi^* + \left(\frac{1}{1+\infty}\right) Q(1-\varphi^*) = 0.$$

On the other hand we have

$$g\left(\frac{1}{1+\infty}\right) = g(0) = \inf_{\varphi \in \mathscr{F}} P\varphi = 0.$$

Let $0 < k < \infty$ and $\alpha = \frac{1}{1+k}$. For any $\varphi \in \mathscr{F}$ we have

$$\begin{aligned} \alpha \int \frac{dQ}{dP}\, dP + \int_{M' \cap N'} \left[(1-\alpha) - \alpha \frac{dQ}{dP}\right] \varphi\, dP \\ + \alpha \int_N (1-\varphi)\, dQ + (1-\alpha) \int_M \varphi\, dP \\ = (1-\alpha)\, P\varphi + \alpha Q(1-\varphi). \end{aligned}$$

The infimum is attained for $\varphi^* \in \mathscr{F}$ if $\varphi^* = 1$ on N, $\varphi^* = 0$ on M and

$$\varphi^* = \begin{cases} 1 & \text{if } \alpha \frac{dQ}{dP} > 1-\alpha \\ 0 & \text{if } \alpha \frac{dQ}{dP} < 1-\alpha \end{cases} \quad \text{on } M' \cap N'.$$

This is the case for tests of the form

$$\varphi^* = \begin{cases} 1 & \text{if } \dfrac{dQ}{dP} > k \\ 0 & \text{if } \dfrac{dQ}{dP} < k \end{cases} \quad \text{on} \quad M' \cap N',$$

i.e. for tests $\varphi^* \in \mathcal{N}_k$.

(2) $\Rightarrow$ (1): Let $\bar{\varphi} \in \mathcal{F}$ be a NP-test such that $P\bar{\varphi} = P\varphi^*$. Then we have $Q\bar{\varphi} \geqq Q\varphi^*$. On the other hand $\bar{\varphi}$ satisfies $g(\alpha) \leqq (1-\alpha) P\bar{\varphi} + \alpha Q(1-\bar{\varphi})$ which implies $Q\varphi^* \geqq Q\bar{\varphi}$ if $\alpha > 0$. Thus, in this case we obtain $Q\varphi^* = Q\bar{\varphi}$ and therefore φ^* is a NP-test too. Otherwise, if $P\varphi^* = 0$ then $\varphi^* \in \mathcal{N}_\infty(P, Q)$.

Now, let $k = \dfrac{1}{\alpha} - 1$. We have to show that $\varphi^* \in \mathcal{N}_k$. If $\varphi_0^* \in \mathcal{N}_k$ is another test then we know that it satisfies condition (2). Hence we obtain

$$(1-\alpha) P\varphi^* + \alpha Q(1-\varphi^*) = (1-\alpha) P\varphi_0^* + \alpha Q(1-\varphi_0^*)$$

and therefore

$$\alpha \int \frac{dQ}{dP}\, dP + \int_{M' \cap N'} \left[(1-\alpha) - \alpha \frac{dQ}{dP}\right] \varphi^* \, dP$$

$$+ \alpha \int_N (1-\varphi^*)\, dQ + (1-\alpha) \int_M \varphi^* \, dP =$$

$$= \alpha \int \frac{dQ}{dP}\, dP + \int_{M' \cap N'} \left[(1-\alpha) - \alpha \frac{dQ}{dP}\right] \varphi_0^* \, dP$$

$$+ \alpha \int_N (1-\varphi_0^*)\, dQ + (1-\alpha) \int_M \varphi_0^* \, dP.$$

Every NP-test is 1 on N and 0 on M and it follows that

$$\int_{M' \cap N'} \left[(1-\alpha) - \alpha \frac{dQ}{dP}\right] (\varphi^* - \varphi_0^*)\, dP = 0.$$

Since $\varphi_0^* \in \mathcal{N}_k$ and $\dfrac{1}{1+k} = \alpha$ the integrand of this equation is non-negative and therefore vanishes on $M' \cap N'$ P-a.e. This implies that $\varphi^* = \varphi_0^*$ P-a.e. whenever $(1-\alpha) \neq \alpha \dfrac{dQ}{dP}$. Hence $\varphi^* \in \mathcal{N}_k$. □

14.3 Corollary. *The error function g of any binary experiment E is concave and continuous on* $[0, 1]$, *and satisfies* $g(0) = g(1) = 0$.

Proof. Any infimum of a family of affine-linear functions is concave and therefore continuous on $(0,1)$. The values $g(0)=g(1)=0$ are clear from the proof of 14.2. Continuity at $\alpha=0$ and at $\alpha=1$ follows from the inequalities

$$g(\alpha) \leqq (1-\alpha)P1 + \alpha Q(1-1) = 1-\alpha, \quad \text{and}$$
$$g(\alpha) \leqq (1-\alpha)P0 + \alpha Q(1-0) = \alpha. \qquad \square$$

14.4 Corollary. *Let g be the error function of E. Then*

$$g(\alpha) = \alpha \int \frac{dQ}{dP}\,dP - \int \left[(1-\alpha) - \alpha\frac{dQ}{dP}\right]^- dP, \quad 0 \leqq \alpha \leqq 1.$$

Proof. For $\alpha=0$ and $\alpha=1$ the assertion is immediate. For $0<\alpha<1$ it follows from the proof of 14.2. $\square$

14.5 Remark. (1) Every error function g satisfies $|g(\alpha)-g(\beta)| \leqq 2|\alpha-\beta|$ if $0 \leqq \alpha \leqq 1$, $0 \leqq \beta \leqq 1$. The reason is that the function

$$\alpha \mapsto (1-\alpha)P\varphi + \alpha Q(1-\varphi), \quad 0 \leqq \alpha \leqq 1,$$

satisfies this inequality for every $\varphi \in \mathscr{F}$.

(2) The family of all error functions is uniformly equicontinuous on $[0,1]$. Hence, if a sequence of error functions converges pointwise then it converges uniformly. Moreover, any sequence of error functions contains a convergent subsequence.

(3) If g is the error function of $E=(\Omega,\mathscr{A},(P,Q))$ then $\alpha \mapsto g(1-\alpha)$, $0 \leqq \alpha \leqq 1$, is the error function of $\tilde{E} := (\Omega,\mathscr{A},(Q,P))$.

(4) If g is the error function of $E=(\Omega,\mathscr{A},(P,Q))$ then

$$g\left(\frac{1}{2}\right) = \frac{1}{2}(1-d_1(P,Q)) = \frac{1}{2}\pi(P,Q).$$

This follows from 2.3 by elementary computations.

14.6 Lemma. *Let g be the error function of E. Then*

$$\lim_{\alpha\to 0} \frac{g(\alpha)}{\alpha} = \int \frac{dQ}{dP}\,dP = 1 - Q(N),$$

$$\lim_{\alpha\to 1} \frac{g(\alpha)}{1-\alpha} = \int \frac{dP}{dQ}\,dQ = 1 - P(M).$$

Proof. Let us prove the first part of the assertion. Then the second part follows from 14.5 (3). We note that

$$\left[(1-\alpha) - \alpha\frac{dQ}{dP}\right]^- = \max\left\{0, \alpha\left(1+\frac{dQ}{dP}\right) - 1\right\}$$

and therefore

$$\frac{1}{\alpha}\left[(1-\alpha)-\alpha\frac{dQ}{dP}\right]^{-}=\max\left\{0,\left(1+\frac{dQ}{dP}\right)-\frac{1}{\alpha}\right\}.$$

If $\alpha \to 0$ then these functions converge pointwise to 0 and are dominated by a P-integrable function. This implies that their P-integrals converge to zero. Now the assertion follows from 14.4 and 14.5 (3). □

14.7 Examples. (1) Let $E=(P,Q)$ with $P=Q$. Then it follows easily that the error function g is given by

$$g(\alpha)=\begin{cases}1-\alpha & \text{if } \alpha \geqq \frac{1}{2},\\ \alpha & \text{if } \alpha \leqq \frac{1}{2}.\end{cases}$$

(2) Let $E=(P,Q)$ with $P\perp Q$. Then it follows easily that $g=0$ on $[0,1]$.

(3) Let $\Omega=\{0,1\}$ and $p,q\in(0,1)$. Define $P=p\varepsilon_0+(1-p)\varepsilon_1$, $Q=q\varepsilon_0+(1-q)\varepsilon_1$. We consider $E=(P,Q)$ and the n-fold products $E^n=(P^n,Q^n)$. If $S(\omega)$, $\omega\in\Omega^n$, denotes the frequency of 1 in ω, then

$$P^n=\sum_{\omega\in\Omega^n} p^{S(\omega)}(1-p)^{n-S(\omega)}\,\varepsilon_\omega,$$
$$Q^n=\sum_{\omega\in\Omega^n} q^{S(\omega)}(1-q)^{n-S(\omega)}\,\varepsilon_\omega,$$

which implies

$$\frac{dQ^n}{dP^n}:\omega\mapsto\left(\frac{q}{p}\right)^{S(\omega)}\left(\frac{1-q}{1-p}\right)^{n-S(\omega)},\quad \omega\in\Omega^n.$$

With

$$r(m):=1\Bigg/\left(1+\left(\frac{q}{p}\right)^{m}\left(\frac{1-q}{1-p}\right)^{n-m}\right),\quad 0\leqq m\leqq n,$$

we have

$$\frac{dQ^n}{dP^n}(\omega)<\frac{1-\alpha}{\alpha}\quad\text{iff}\quad r(S(\omega))>\alpha,\quad \alpha\in[0,1].$$

Thus, we arrive at the error function of E^n

$$g_n(\alpha)=\alpha\int_{\frac{dQ^n}{dP^n}<\frac{1-\alpha}{\alpha}}\frac{dQ^n}{dP^n}\,dP^n+(1-\alpha)\,P^n\left\{\frac{dQ^n}{dP^n}\geq\frac{1-\alpha}{\alpha}\right\}$$
$$=\alpha\sum_{m:\,r(m)>\alpha}\binom{n}{m}q^m(1-q)^{n-m}$$
$$+(1-\alpha)\sum_{m:\,r(m)\leqq\alpha}\binom{n}{m}p^m(1-p)^{n-m},\quad \alpha\in[0,1].$$

(4) Let $\Omega = \{0, 1, 2, \ldots, n\}$ and $P_n = \sum_{m=0}^{n} \binom{n}{m} p^m (1-p)^{n-m} \varepsilon_m$, $Q_n = \sum_{m=0}^{n} \binom{n}{m} q^m (1-q)^{n-m} \varepsilon_m$, where $p, q \in (0,1)$. Then $E_n = (P_n, Q_n)$ has the same error function as $E^n = (P^n, Q^n)$ in the preceding example.

(5) Let $\Omega = \mathbb{N}_0$ and $p, q \in (0,1)$. Define $P = \sum_{k=0}^{\infty} p(1-p)^k \varepsilon_k$, $Q = \sum_{k=0}^{\infty} q(1-q)^k \varepsilon_k$. Then similar computations as for (3) yield the error function of $E = (P, Q)$

$$g(\alpha) = \alpha(1-(1-q)^{k_\alpha}) + (1-\alpha)(1-p)^{k_\alpha} \quad \text{if} \quad r(k_\alpha) \leqq \alpha < r(k_\alpha - 1), \quad \alpha \in [0,1],$$

where

$$r(k) = 1 \Big/ \left(1 + \frac{q}{p}\left(\frac{1-q}{1-p}\right)^k\right), \quad k \in \mathbb{N}_0.$$

(6) Let $\Omega = \mathbb{N}_0$, $\lambda, \mu \in (0, \infty)$, and define

$$P = e^{-\lambda} \sum_{k=0}^{\infty} \frac{\lambda^k}{k!} \varepsilon_k \quad \text{and} \quad Q = e^{-\mu} \sum_{k=0}^{\infty} \frac{\mu^k}{k!} \varepsilon_k.$$

Then with the notation

$$r(k) = 1 \Big/ \left(1 + e^{\lambda - \mu}\left(\frac{\mu}{\lambda}\right)^k\right), \quad k \in \mathbb{N}_0,$$

the error function of $E = (P, Q)$ is

$$g(\alpha) = \alpha e^{-\mu} \sum_{r(k) > \alpha} \frac{\mu^k}{k!} + (1-\alpha) e^{-\lambda} \sum_{r(k) \leqq \alpha} \frac{\lambda^k}{k!}, \quad \alpha \in [0,1].$$

(7) Let $\Omega = \mathbb{R}_+^n$ and $a > 0$, $b > 0$. Define P and Q by

$$\frac{dP}{d\lambda^n}(x) = a^n \exp\left(-a \sum_{i=1}^{n} x_i\right),$$

$$\frac{dQ}{d\lambda^n}(x) = b^n \exp\left(-b \sum_{i=1}^{n} x_i\right), \quad x \in \mathbb{R}_+^n.$$

Put $S(x) := \sum_{i=1}^{n} x_i$, $x \in \mathbb{R}_+^n$, and assume that $a > b$. Then the error function of $E = (P, Q)$ is

$$g(\alpha) = \alpha \Gamma_{b,n}\left(\frac{1}{a-b}\log\left(\frac{1-\alpha}{\alpha}\left(\frac{a}{b}\right)^n\right)\right)$$
$$+ (1-\alpha)\left(1-\Gamma_{a,n}\left(\frac{1}{a-b}\log\left(\frac{1-\alpha}{\alpha}\left(\frac{a}{b}\right)^n\right)\right)\right), \quad \alpha \in [0,1].$$

(8) If $\Omega = \mathbb{R}_+$ and $P = \Gamma_{a,n}$, $Q = \Gamma_{b,n}$, $a > 0$, $b > 0$, then $E = (P, Q)$ has the same error function as the preceding example.

(9) Let $\Omega = \mathbb{R}$ and $P = \nu_{0,\sigma^2}$, $Q = \nu_{t,\sigma^2}$, $\sigma^2 > 0$, $t \neq 0$. Then easy computations yield the error function of $E = (P, Q)$ as

$$g(\alpha) = \alpha \Phi\left(-\frac{|t|}{2\sigma} + \frac{\sigma}{|t|}\log\frac{1-\alpha}{\alpha}\right)$$
$$+ (1-\alpha)\,\Phi\left(-\frac{|t|}{2\sigma} - \frac{\sigma}{|t|}\log\frac{1-\alpha}{\alpha}\right), \quad \alpha \in [0,1].$$

15. Comparison of binary experiments

In this section we shall compare binary experiments in terms of power functions. The formal definition of this idea is straightforward.

15.1 Definition. Assume that $(\Omega_1, \mathscr{A}_1)$ and $(\Omega_2, \mathscr{A}_2)$ are measurable spaces and that $E_1 = (\Omega_1, \mathscr{A}_1, (P_1, Q_1))$ and $E_2 = (\Omega_2, \mathscr{A}_2, (P_2, Q_2))$ are (binary) experiments. Let $\varepsilon \geqq 0$. Then E_1 is called *ε-deficient* with respect to E_2 (i.e. $E_1 \underset{2}{\overset{\varepsilon}{\supseteq}} E_2$) if for every $\varphi_2 \in \mathscr{F}(\Omega_2, \mathscr{A}_2)$ there is some $\varphi_1 \in \mathscr{F}(\Omega_1, \mathscr{A}_1)$ such that

$$P_1\varphi_1 \leqq P_2\varphi_2 + \frac{\varepsilon}{2}, \quad \text{and}$$

$$Q_1\varphi_1 \geqq Q_2\varphi_2 - \frac{\varepsilon}{2}.$$

15.2 Remark. (1) If E_1 is 0-deficient with respect to E_2 then E_1 is called *more informative* than E_2 (i.e. $E_1 \underset{2}{\supseteq} E_2$).

(2) If $E_1 \underset{2}{\overset{\varepsilon}{\supseteq}} E_2$ for every $\varepsilon > 0$ then E_1 is more informative than E_2. The proof follows from Lemma 7.3.

(3) The relation „$\underset{2}{\supseteq}$“ is an order relation on the family of all experiments. If $E_1 \underset{2}{\supseteq} E_2$ and $E_2 \underset{2}{\supseteq} E_1$ then E_1 and E_2 are called *equivalent* (i.e. $E_1 \underset{2}{\sim} E_2$). An equivalence class of experiments is called *experiment type*.

(4) Let $\delta_2(E_1, E_2) = \inf\{\varepsilon > 0 \colon E_1 \underset{2}{\overset{\varepsilon}{\supseteq}} E_2\}$. It follows by the same argument as in (2) that E_1 is $\delta_2(E_1, E_2)$-deficient with respect to E_2.

15.3 Definition. The *deficiency* between two experiments E_1 and E_2 is given by

$$\Delta_2(E_1, E_2) := \max\{\delta_2(E_1, E_2), \delta_2(E_2, E_1)\}.$$

15.4 Lemma. *The deficiency Δ_2 is a pseudo-distance on the family of all experiments.*

Proof. It is sufficient to show that δ_2 satisfies a triangle inequality. This follows easily. □

15.5 Lemma. *Two experiments E_1 and E_2 are equivalent iff $\Delta_2(E_1, E_2) = 0$.*

Proof. Obvious. □

Let $\mathscr{E}_2/\sim$ be the family of all experiment types. The equivalence class of $E \in \mathscr{E}_2$ in $\mathscr{E}_2/\sim$ is denoted by $\dot{E}$. Then we may define a distance Δ_2 on $\mathscr{E}_2/\sim$ by

$$\Delta_2(\dot{E}_1, \dot{E}_2) := \Delta_2(E_1, E_2) \quad \text{if} \quad E_1 \in \dot{E}_1,\ E_2 \in \dot{E}_2.$$

It follows from 15.5 that this is well defined. Hence $(\mathscr{E}_2/\sim, \Delta_2)$ is a metric space.

15.6 Theorem. *Let E_1 be an experiment with error function g_1 and E_2 an experiment with error function g_2. Then for every $\varepsilon \geqq 0$*

$$E_1 \underset{2}{\overset{\varepsilon}{\supseteq}} E_2 \quad \textit{iff} \quad g_1(\alpha) \leqq g_2(\alpha) + \frac{\varepsilon}{2}, \quad 0 \leqq \alpha \leqq 1.$$

Proof. (1) Assume that $E_1 \underset{2}{\overset{\varepsilon}{\supseteq}} E_2$. Let $\varphi_2 \in \mathscr{F}(\Omega_2, \mathscr{A}_2)$ and $0 \leqq \alpha \leqq 1$. Then there is some $\varphi_1 \in \mathscr{F}(\Omega_1, \mathscr{A}_1)$ such that

$$P_1\varphi_1 \leqq P_2\varphi_2 + \frac{\varepsilon}{2} \quad \text{and}$$

$$Q_1\varphi_1 \geqq Q_2\varphi_2 - \frac{\varepsilon}{2}.$$

This implies

$$\begin{aligned} g_1(\alpha) &\leqq (1-\alpha)P_1\varphi_1 + \alpha Q_1(1-\varphi_1) \\ &\leqq (1-\alpha)\left(P_2\varphi_2 + \frac{\varepsilon}{2}\right) + \alpha\left(Q_2(1-\varphi_2) + \frac{\varepsilon}{2}\right) \\ &= (1-\alpha)P_2\varphi_2 + \alpha Q_2(1-\varphi_2) + (1-\alpha)\frac{\varepsilon}{2} + \alpha\frac{\varepsilon}{2} \\ &= (1-\alpha)P_2\varphi_2 + \alpha Q_2(1-\varphi_2) + \frac{\varepsilon}{2}. \end{aligned}$$

Since $\varphi_2 \in \mathscr{F}(\Omega_2, \mathscr{A}_2)$ has been chosen arbitrarily it follows that $g_1 \leqq g_2 + \frac{\varepsilon}{2}$.

(2) Assume conversely that $g_1 \leqq g_2 + \frac{\varepsilon}{2}$. Let $\varphi_2 \in \mathscr{F}(\Omega_2, \mathscr{A}_2)$. We have to distinguish between two cases. First, we assume that $P_2\varphi_2 + \frac{\varepsilon}{2} \leqq 1 - P_1(M_1)$ (where M_1 denotes the set of singularity in a Lebesgue decomposition of P_1 with respect to Q_1). Then there is a test $\varphi_1 \in \mathscr{N}(P_1, Q_1)$ such that

$$P_1\varphi_1 = P_2\varphi_2 + \frac{\varepsilon}{2}.$$

Let k be such that $\varphi_1 \in \mathscr{N}_k(P_1, Q_1)$. Then we obtain

$$\begin{aligned}\left(\frac{k}{1+k}\right)P_1\varphi_1 + \left(\frac{1}{1+k}\right)Q_1(1-\varphi_1) &= g_1\left(\frac{1}{1+k}\right) \leqq g_2\left(\frac{1}{1+k}\right) + \frac{\varepsilon}{2} \\ &\leqq \left(\frac{k}{1+k}\right)P_2\varphi_2 + \left(\frac{1}{1+k}\right)Q_2(1-\varphi_2) + \frac{\varepsilon}{2}\end{aligned}$$

which implies

$$Q_1\varphi_1 \geqq Q_2\varphi_2 - \frac{\varepsilon}{2}.$$

This proves the assertion for the first case.

Secondly, we assume that $P_2\varphi_2 + \frac{\varepsilon}{2} > 1 - P_1(M_1)$. Then we choose $\varphi_1 \in \mathscr{N}_0(P_1, Q_1)$ and obtain

$$P_1\varphi_1 = 1 - P_1(M_1) < P_2\varphi_2 + \frac{\varepsilon}{2}, \quad \text{and}$$

$$Q_1\varphi_1 = 1 \geqq Q_2\varphi_2 \geqq Q_2\varphi_2 - \frac{\varepsilon}{2}. \qquad \square$$

15.7 Corollary. *Let E_i be an experiment with error function g_i, $i = 1, 2$. The the following assertions hold:*

(1) $\frac{1}{2}\delta_2(E_1, E_2) = \sup\limits_{0 \leqq \alpha \leqq 1} (g_1(\alpha) - g_2(\alpha))$.

(2) $\frac{1}{2}\Delta_2(E_1, E_2) = \sup\limits_{0 \leqq \alpha \leqq 1} |g_1(\alpha) - g_1(\alpha)|$.

(3) $E_1 \supseteq E_2$ *iff* $g_1 \leqq g_2$.

(4) $E_1 \sim E_2$ *iff* $g_1 = g_2$.

Proof. The assertions are obvious consequences of Theorem 15.6. $\square$

The experiments of Examples 14.7 (3) and (4), and of 14.7 (7) and (8) are equivalent.

15.8 Remark. It follows from 15.7 that convergence of experiment types in $(\mathscr{E}_2/\sim, \Delta_2)$ is equivalent to uniform convergence of their respective error functions.

15.9 Remark. If $E_1 \overset{\varepsilon}{\underset{2}{\supseteq}} E_2$ then $g_1\left(\frac{1}{2}\right) \leqq g_2\left(\frac{1}{2}\right) + \frac{\varepsilon}{2}$ which implies that $d_1(P_1, Q_1) \geqq d_1(P_2, Q_2) - \varepsilon$. Hence $E_1 \underset{2}{\supseteq} E_2$ implies $d_1(P_1, Q_1) \geqq d_1(P_2, Q_2)$.

It is interesting to note that binary experiments can also be compared in terms of power functions.

15.10 Theorem. *Suppose that* $E_1 = (\Omega_1, \mathscr{A}_1, (P_1, Q_1))$ *and* $E_2 = (\Omega_2, \mathscr{A}_2, (P_2, Q_2))$ *are binary experiments. Let* $\varepsilon \geqq 0$. *Then the following assertions are equivalent:*

(1) $E_1 \overset{\varepsilon}{\underset{2}{\supseteq}} E_2$.

(2) *For every* $\alpha \in [0, 1]$

$$\sup\{Q_1\varphi_1: P_1\varphi_1 \leqq \alpha, \varphi_1 \in \mathscr{F}(\Omega_1, \mathscr{A}_1\}$$
$$\geqq \sup\{Q_2\varphi_2: P_2\varphi_2 \leqq \alpha - \frac{\varepsilon}{2}, \varphi_2 \in \mathscr{F}(\Omega_2, \mathscr{A}_2)\} - \frac{\varepsilon}{2}.$$

(3) *For every* $\beta \in [0, 1]$

$$\inf\{P_1\varphi_1: Q_1\varphi_1 \geqq \beta, \varphi_1 \in \mathscr{F}(\Omega_1, \mathscr{A}_1)\}$$
$$\leqq \inf\{P_2\varphi_2: Q_2\varphi_2 \geqq \beta + \frac{\varepsilon}{2}, \varphi_2 \in \mathscr{F}(\Omega_2, \mathscr{A}_2)\} + \frac{\varepsilon}{2}.$$

Proof. The equivalence (2) $\Leftrightarrow$ (3) is immediate for reasons of symmetry.

(1) $\Rightarrow$ (2): Let $\varphi_2 \in \mathscr{F}(\Omega_2, \mathscr{A}_2)$ be such that $P_2\varphi_2 \leqq \alpha - \frac{\varepsilon}{2}$. Then $E_1 \overset{\varepsilon}{\underset{2}{\supseteq}} E_2$ implies the existence of a test $\varphi_1 \in \mathscr{F}(\Omega_1, \mathscr{A}_1)$ satisfying $P_1\varphi_1 \leqq P_2\varphi_2 + \frac{\varepsilon}{2} \leqq \alpha$ and $Q_1\varphi_1 \geqq Q_2\varphi_2 - \frac{\varepsilon}{2}$. This proves the assertion.

(2) $\Rightarrow$ (1): Let $\varphi_2 \in \mathscr{F}(\Omega_2, \mathscr{A}_2)$. We have to distinguish between two cases. If $P_2\varphi_2 > 1 - P_1(M) - \frac{\varepsilon}{2}$ then choosing $\varphi_1 \in \mathscr{N}_0(P_1, Q_1)$ yields $Q_1\varphi_1 \geqq Q_2\varphi_2 - \frac{\varepsilon}{2}$ and $P_1\varphi_1 \leqq P_2\varphi_2 + \frac{\varepsilon}{2}$. If $P_2\varphi_2 \leqq 1 - P_1(M) - \frac{\varepsilon}{2}$, let α be such that $P_2\varphi_2 = \alpha - \frac{\varepsilon}{2}$ and choose a NP-test $\varphi_1 \in \mathscr{F}(\Omega_1, \mathscr{A}_1)$ with $P_1\varphi_1 = \alpha$. Then

$P_1\varphi_1 = P_2\varphi_2 + \frac{\varepsilon}{2}$ and it follows from (2) that $Q_1\varphi_1 \geqq Q_2\varphi_2 - \frac{\varepsilon}{2}$. This proves the assertion. □

15.11 Corollary. *Let $E_n = (\Omega_n, \mathscr{A}_n, (P_n, Q_n))$, $n \in \mathbb{N}$, and $E = (\Omega, \mathscr{A}, (P, Q))$ be binary experiments. Suppose that $\Delta_2(E_n, E) \to 0$. If $(\varphi_n)_{n\in\mathbb{N}}$ is a sequence of NP-tests, $\varphi_n \in \mathscr{F}(\Omega_n, \mathscr{A}_n)$, $n \in \mathbb{N}$, such that $P_n\varphi_n \to \alpha$, then it follows that $Q_n\varphi_n \to \sup\{Q\varphi\colon P\varphi \leqq \alpha, \varphi \in \mathscr{F}(\Omega, \mathscr{A})\}$.*

Proof. Let $h(\alpha) = \sup\{Q\varphi\colon P\varphi \leqq \alpha, \varphi \in \mathscr{F}(\Omega, \mathscr{A})\}$, $\alpha \in [0, 1]$, and recall from Corollary (8.13) that h is continuous. From Theorem (15.10) we obtain

$$h\left(P_n\varphi_n - \frac{1}{2}\Delta_2(E_n, E)\right) - \frac{1}{2}\Delta_2(E_n, E)$$
$$\leqq Q_n\varphi_n \leqq h\left(P_n\varphi_n + \frac{1}{2}\Delta_2(E_n, E)\right) + \frac{1}{2}\Delta_2(E_n, E).$$

This proves the assertion. □

16. Representation of experiment types

Suppose that $E = (\Omega, \mathscr{A}, (P, Q))$ is a binary experiment. The distribution $\mu_E = \mathscr{L}\left(\frac{dQ}{dP}\middle| P\right)$ of the likelihood ratio is a Borel measure on $[0, \infty)$ satisfying $\int x\,\mu_E(dx) \leqq 1$.

Let $\mathscr{M}$ be the family of all probability measures μ on $[0, \infty)$ satisfying $\int x\,\mu(dx) \leqq 1$ (cf. section 5) and let $\mathscr{T}$ be the weak topology of $\mathscr{M}$. In the present paragraph we show that $(\mathscr{E}_2/\sim, \Delta_2)$ and $(\mathscr{M}, \mathscr{T})$ are topologically equivalent.

16.1 Remark. Let $E = (\Omega, \mathscr{A}, (P, Q))$ be an experiment and let $\mu = \mathscr{L}\left(\frac{dQ}{dP}\middle| P\right)$. Then it follows from 14.4 that the error function of E is given by

$$g(\alpha) = \alpha\int x\,\mu(dx) - \int (1 - \alpha(1 + x))^-\,\mu(dx), \quad 0 \leqq \alpha \leqq 1.$$

For convenience we define

$$\psi_\alpha\colon x \mapsto \alpha x - (1 - \alpha(1 + x))^-, \quad x \geqq 0.$$

Then we have $g(\alpha) = \int \psi_\alpha\,d\mu$, $0 \leqq \alpha \leqq 1$. It is easy to see that $\psi_0 = 0$ and $\psi_1 = 0$ which implies that $g(0) = g(1) = 0$.

16.2 Definition. If $\mu \in \mathscr{M}$ define $\tilde{\mu}\colon [0, 1] \to [0, 1]$ by $\tilde{\mu}(\alpha) := \int \psi_\alpha\,d\mu$, $0 \leqq \alpha \leqq 1$.

16.3 Lemma. *Suppose that $\mu \in \mathcal{M}$ and let $M(x) = \mu([0, x))$, $x \geqq 0$. Then*

$$\tilde{\mu}(\alpha) = (1-\alpha) - \alpha \int_0^{\frac{1-\alpha}{\alpha}} M(\alpha)\,dx, \quad 0 \leqq \alpha \leqq 1.$$

Proof. Integration by parts yields for every $a > 0$

$$\int_0^a \psi_\alpha\,d\mu = \psi_\alpha(a)\,M(a) - \psi_a(0)\,M(0) - \int_0^a \psi'_\alpha(x)\,M(x)\,dx.$$

Letting $a \to \infty$ we obtain

$$\int_0^\infty \psi_\alpha\,d\mu = (1-\alpha) - 0 - \alpha \int_0^{\frac{1-\alpha}{\alpha}} M(x)\,dx. \quad \square$$

16.4 Theorem. *Suppose that $\mu_1, \mu_2 \in \mathcal{M}$. Then $\mu_1 = \mu_2$ iff $\tilde{\mu}_1 = \tilde{\mu}_2$.*

Proof. Assume that $\tilde{\mu}_1 = \tilde{\mu}_2$. This implies that

$$\int_0^z M_1(x)\,dx = \int_0^z M_2(x)\,dx, \quad 0 < z < \infty.$$

Hence M_1 and M_2 coincide on the set of all points where both M_1 and M_2 are continuous. This set is dense in $(0, \infty)$ and therefore all one-sided limits of M_1 and M_2 are equal. It follows that for every interval $(a, b) \subseteq (0, \infty)$ we have

$$\begin{aligned}\mu_1((a, b)) &= M_1(b-) - M_1(a+) = M_2(b-) - M_2(a+)\\ &= \mu_2((a, b)).\end{aligned}$$

Hence we obtain $\mu_1 = \mu_2$. $\square$

16.5 Corollary. *Let $E_1 = (\Omega, \mathcal{A}_1, (P_1, Q_1))$ and $E_2 = (\Omega_2, \mathcal{A}_2, (P_2, Q_2))$ be experiments. Then*

$$E_1 \underset{2}{\sim} E_2 \quad \text{iff} \quad \mathcal{L}\left(\frac{dQ_1}{dP_1}\middle| P_1\right) = \mathcal{L}\left(\frac{dQ_2}{dP_2}\middle| P_2\right).$$

Proof. Apply 16.4 and 15.7 (4). $\square$

If $\dot{E}$ is an experiment type then there is a uniquely determined $T(\dot{E}) \in \mathcal{M}$ which satisfies

$$T(\dot{E}) = \mu_E = \mathcal{L}\left(\frac{dQ}{dP}\middle| P\right) \quad \text{if} \quad (P, Q) \in \dot{E}.$$

Let us show that T: $(\mathcal{E}_2/\sim, \Delta_2) \to (\mathcal{M}, \mathcal{T})$ is a homeomorphism.

16.6 Lemma. *The mapping T: $(\mathcal{E}_2/\sim, \Delta_2) \to (\mathcal{M}, \mathcal{T})$ is a bijection.*

Proof. (1) Let us show that T is injective. If $T(\dot{E}_1) = T(\dot{E}_2)$ and if $E_1 \in \dot{E}_1$ and $E_2 \in \dot{E}_2$, then the distributions of the likelihood ratios of E_1 and E_2 coincide which implies by 16.5 that $E_1 \underset{2}{\sim} E_2$. Hence $\dot{E}_1 = \dot{E}_2$.

(2) Next we prove that T is surjective. Let $\mu \in \mathscr{M}$ and $\Omega = [0, \infty]$. If we define $P = \mu$ and $Q = \mathrm{id}\,\mu + (1 - \int x\,d\mu)\,\varepsilon_\infty$ then we have

$$\mathscr{L}\left(\frac{dQ}{dP}\middle| P\right) = \mu.$$

Hence $E = (P, Q)$ satisfies $T(\dot{E}) = \mu$. □

16.7 Lemma. *$(\mathscr{M}, \mathscr{T})$ is compact.*

Proof. This is a particular case of 5.15. □

16.8 Theorem. *$T: (\mathscr{E}_2/\sim, \Delta_2) \to (\mathscr{M}, \mathscr{T})$ is a homeomorphism.*

Proof. Since $(\mathscr{M}, \mathscr{T})$ is compact it is sufficient to prove that T^{-1} is continuous. Let $\mu_n \to \mu$ weakly and let $T(\dot{E}_n) = \mu_n$, $n \in \mathbb{N}$, and $T(\dot{E}) = \mu$. Since $\psi_\alpha \in \mathscr{C}_b([0, \infty))$ if $0 \leqq \alpha \leqq 1$ it follows that $\tilde{\mu}_n \to \tilde{\mu}$ which means that the error functions of $E_n \in \dot{E}_n$ converge to the error function of $E \in \dot{E}$. Now 15.8 proves that $\Delta_2(\dot{E}_n, \dot{E}) \to 0$. □

16.9 Corollary. *The metric space $(\mathscr{E}_2/\sim, \Delta_2)$ is compact.*

Convergence of binary experiments can also be expressed in terms of pointwise convergence of power functions.

16.10 Theorem. *Let $E_n = (\Omega_n, \mathscr{A}_n, (P_n, Q_n))$, $n \in \mathbb{N}$, be a sequence of experiments. Then $(E_n)_{n \in \mathbb{N}}$ converges to $E = (\Omega, \mathscr{A}, (P, Q))$ iff any of the following conditions is satisfied:*

$$(1) \quad \lim_{n\to\infty} \sup\{Q_n\varphi_n : P_n\varphi_n \leqq \alpha, \varphi_n \in \mathscr{F}(\Omega_n, \mathscr{A}_n)\} = \sup\{Q\varphi : P\varphi \leqq \alpha, \varphi \in \mathscr{F}(\Omega, \mathscr{A})\}$$

for every $\alpha \in [0, 1]$.

$$(2) \quad \lim_{n\to\infty} \inf\{P_n\varphi_n : Q_n\varphi_n \geqq \beta, \varphi_n \in \mathscr{F}(\Omega_n, \mathscr{A}_n)\} = \inf\{P\varphi : P\varphi \geqq \beta, \varphi \in \mathscr{F}(\Omega, \mathscr{A})\}.$$

Proof. It is clear that the assertions (1) and (2) are equivalent. To show that $E_n \to E$ implies (1) we need only refer to Theorem 15.10 and Corollary 8.13.

The converse is proved by a topological argument. If we endow $\mathscr{E}_2/\sim$ with the topology $\mathscr{T}_0$ of pointwise convergence of the functions

$$\alpha \mapsto \sup\{Q_n\varphi_n\colon P_n\varphi_n \leqq \alpha,\ \varphi_n \in \mathscr{F}(\Omega_n, \mathscr{A}_n)\},$$

then Theorem (15.10) shows that $(\mathscr{E}_2/\sim, \mathscr{T}_0)$ is a Hausdorff space. The first part of the present proof implies that id: $(\mathscr{E}_2/\sim, \Delta_2) \to (\mathscr{E}_2/\sim, \mathscr{T}_0)$ is continuous and therefore is a homeomorphism. □

17. Concave function and Mellin transforms

Suppose that $E=(\Omega_1, \mathscr{A}_1, (P_1, Q_1))$ and $F=(\Omega_2, \mathscr{A}_2, (P_2, Q_2))$ are binary experiments. Then the fact $E \overset{\varepsilon}{\underset{2}{\supseteq}} F$, $\varepsilon \geqq 0$, can be characterized by the integrals of μ_E and μ_F over certain concave functions.

17.1 Theorem. *Let $\varepsilon \geqq 0$. Then the following assertions are equivalent:*

(1) $E \overset{\varepsilon}{\underset{2}{\supseteq}} F$.

(2) $\int f\,d\mu_E \leqq \int f\,d\mu_F + \frac{\varepsilon}{2}(f'(0)+f(\infty))$ *for every increasing concave function $f\colon [0,\infty) \to [0,\infty)$ which satisfies $f(0)=0$.*

Proof. For every $\alpha \in [0,1]$ the function $\psi_\alpha\colon [0,\infty) \to [0,\infty)$ is increasing, concave and satisfies $\psi_\alpha(0)=0$. Moreover, we have $\psi'_\alpha(0)=\alpha$ and $\psi_\alpha(\infty)=1-\alpha$. Hence the implication (2) ⇒ (1) follows immediately from Theorem (15.6) and Remark 16.1.

Conversely, (1) implies the inequality under (2) at least for $f=\psi_\alpha$, $0 \leqq \alpha \leqq 1$. Let C be the set of all increasing concave functions $f\colon [0,\infty) \to [0,\infty)$ which satisfy $f(0)=0$ and the inequality under (2). Then C is a convex cone which contains the limits of increasing sequences in C. Let us show that C contains all increasing concave functions $f\colon [0,\infty) \to [0,\infty)$, whenever C contains every ψ_α, $0 \leqq \alpha \leqq 1$.

Let $f\colon [0,\infty) \to [0,\infty)$ be an arbitrary increasing concave function. We show that $f \in C$. For every $x \geqq 0$ and $k \geqq 0$ let

$$\varphi_{k,x}\colon t \mapsto \begin{cases} kt & \text{if } 0 \leqq t \leqq x, \\ kx & \text{if } t > x. \end{cases}$$

Note that $\psi_\alpha = \varphi_{\alpha, \frac{1-\alpha}{\alpha}}$. For every pair $k \geqq 0$, $x \geqq 0$, we have $\varphi_{k,x} \in C$ since $\varphi_{k,x} = \frac{k}{\alpha}\varphi_{\alpha,\frac{1-\alpha}{\alpha}}$ for $\alpha = \frac{1}{1+x}$. Next, let $n \in \mathbb{N}$ and let $f_n\colon [0,\infty) \to [0,\infty)$ be the continuous function which coincides with f at the points $x_j = \frac{j}{n}$, $0 \leqq j \leqq n^2$, which is linear on the intervals (x_j, x_{j+1}), $0 \leqq j \leqq n^2-1$, and is constant on

$[n, \infty)$. It is easy to see that $f_n \uparrow f$ and therefore the assertion is proved if we show that $f_n \in C$, $n \in \mathbb{N}$.

We prove that $f_n \in C$ by constructing numbers $k_1, k_2, \ldots, k_{n^2}$ such that

$$f_n(t) = \sum_{j=1}^{n^2} \varphi_{k_j, x_j}.$$

We choose $k_1, k_2, \ldots, k_{n^2}$ in such a way that

$$\begin{aligned} k_1 + k_2 + \ldots + k_{n^2} &= n(f(x_1) - f(0)), \\ k_2 + \ldots + k_{n^2} &= n(f(x_2) - f(x_1)), \\ &\ldots \\ k_{n^2} &= n(f(x_{n^2}) - f(x_{n^2-1})). \end{aligned}$$

From the fact that f is increasing and concave it follows that $k_1 \geqq 0$, $k_2 \geqq 0, \ldots, k_{n^2} \geqq 0$. It is clear that the function

$$\sum_{j=1}^{n^2} \varphi_{k_j, x_j}$$

is continuous, linear on the intervalls (x_j, x_{j+1}), $0 \leqq j \leqq n^2 - 1$, and constant on (n, ∞). Thus it remains to show that it coincides with f at every x_j, $0 \leqq j \leqq n^2$. This property follows from

$$\begin{aligned} \sum_{i=1}^{n^2} \varphi_{k_i, x_i}(x_j) &= \sum_{i=1}^{j} k_i x_i + \sum_{i=j+1}^{n^2} k_i x_j \\ &= \sum_{i=1}^{j} i \frac{k_i}{n} + \sum_{i=j+1}^{n^2} j \frac{k_i}{n} \\ &= \frac{1}{n} \sum_{i=1}^{j} \sum_{l=i}^{n^2} k_l \\ &= \sum_{i=1}^{j} (f(x_i) - f(x_{i-1})) = f(x_j). \end{aligned}$$ □

Let $\mu \in \mathscr{M}$ where $\mathscr{M}$ is defined as in section 16. Recall that the Mellin transform of μ is given by $M(\mu)(s) = \int_{[0,\infty)} x^s \mu(dx)$, $0 < s < 1$. The Mellin transform can continuously be extended to $s \in [0, 1]$ by

$$M(\mu)(0) = \lim_{s \to 0} M(\mu)(s) = 1 - \mu\{0\} \quad \text{and}$$

$$M(\mu)(1) = \lim_{s \to 1} M(\mu)(s) = \int_{[0,\infty)} x \mu(ds).$$

From 5.13 it follows that the measures $\mu \in \mathscr{M}$ are uniquely determined by their

Mellin transforms. Weak convergence in $\mathcal{M}$ is equivalent with pointwise convergence of the Mellin transforms on $(0,1)$, (Theorem 5.16).

17.2 Definition. Suppose that $E = (\Omega, \mathcal{A}, (P, Q))$ is a binary experiment. The Mellin transform $M(\mu_E)$ of $\mu_E = \mathcal{L}\left(\frac{dQ}{dP}\middle| P\right)$ is called the *Mellin transform of E*.

Let $E_1 \in \mathcal{E}_2$ and $E_2 \in \mathcal{E}_2$. Since $E_1 \underset{2}{\sim} E_2$ iff $\mu_{E_1} = \mu_{E_2}$ and since $\mu_{E_1} = \mu_{E_2}$ iff $M(\mu_{E_1}) = M(\mu_{E_2})$, the Mellin transforms characterize experiment types. Moreover, convergence of experiments may be described in terms of convergence of the Mellin transforms. This follows from 15.15, 5.16 and 16.8.

17.3 Corollary. *Let $E_i = (\Omega_i, \mathcal{A}_i, (P_i, Q_i)) \in \mathcal{E}_2$, $i = 1, 2$. Then $E_1 \underset{2}{\supseteq} E_2$ implies $M(\mu_{E_1}) \leqq M(\mu_{E_2})$ and $d_2(P_1, Q_1) \geqq d_2(P_2, Q_2)$.*

Proof. From Theorem 17.1 it follows that $M(\mu_{E_1}) \leqq M(\mu_{E_2})$. The rest follows from $M(\mu_{E_i})\left(\frac{1}{2}\right) = 1 - d_2^2(P_i, Q_i)$, $i = 1, 2$. □

17.4 Corollary. *Let $E_n = (\Omega_n, \mathcal{A}_n, (P_n, Q_n))$, $n \in \mathbb{N}$, be a sequence of binary experiments which converges to $E = (\Omega, \mathcal{A}, (P, Q))$. Then*

$$\lim_{n\to\infty} d_2(P_n, Q_n) = d_2(P, Q).$$

In particular:

$$\lim_{n\to\infty} d_2(P_n, Q_n) = 1 \quad \textit{iff} \quad P \perp Q,$$

$$\lim_{n\to\infty} d_2(P_n, Q_n) = 0 \quad \textit{iff} \quad P = Q.$$

Proof. Obvious. □

17.5 Examples. (1) If $E = (P, Q)$ with $P = Q$ then $M(\mu_E) \equiv 1$.

(2) If $E = (P, Q)$ with $P \perp Q$ then $M(\mu_E) \equiv 0$.

(3) Let $\Omega = \mathbb{R}$ and $P = \nu_{0,\sigma^2}$, $Q = \nu_{t,\sigma^2}$, $\sigma^2 > 0$, $t \neq 0$. Define $E = (P, Q)$. Then the Mellin transform of E is

$$M(\mu_E)\colon s \mapsto \exp\left(-\frac{t^2}{2\sigma^2} s(1-s)\right), \quad 0 < s < 1.$$

As a consequence it follows that $d_2^2(P, Q) = 1 - \exp\left(-\frac{t^2}{8\sigma^2}\right)$.

(4) Let $\Omega = \mathbb{N}_0$, $\lambda, \mu \in (0, \infty)$, and define

$$P = e^{-\lambda} \sum_{k=0}^{\infty} \frac{\lambda^k}{k!} \varepsilon_k \quad \text{and} \quad Q = e^{-\mu} \sum_{k=0}^{\infty} \frac{\mu^k}{k!} \varepsilon_k .$$

Then the Mellin transform of $E = (P, Q)$ is

$$M(\mu_E): s \mapsto \exp(-\mu s - \lambda(1-s) + \mu^s \lambda^{1-s}), \quad 0 < s < 1 .$$

(5) Consider the experiment of Example 14.7 (3). Then it is easy to see that its Mellin transform is

$$M(\mu_{E^n}): s \mapsto (q^s p^{1-s} + (1-q)^s (1-p)^{1-s})^n, \quad 0 < s < 1 .$$

(The case $n = 1$ is immediate and the formula $M(\mu_{E^n}) = M^n(\mu_E)$ is obvious). It is clear, that this is also the Mellin transform of the experiment considered in Example 14.7 (4).

We finish this section with some examples of convergent sequences of binary experiments.

17.6 Examples. (1) Let $E = (P, Q)$ be a binary experiment with $P \neq Q$. Then the Mellin transform satisfies $M(\mu_E) < 1$ on $(0, 1)$ and therefore

$$\lim_{n \to \infty} M(\mu_{E^n}) = \lim_{n \to \infty} M^n(\mu_E) = 0 \quad \text{on} \quad (0, 1) .$$

It follows that (E^n) converges to binary experiments of singular type.

(2) Let $\Omega_n = \{0, 1, 2, \ldots, n\}$, $p \in (0, 1)$ and $q_n = p + t/\sqrt{n}$, $t \neq 0$, $n \in \mathbb{N}$. Define

$$P_n = \sum_{m=0}^{n} \binom{n}{m} p^m (1-p)^{n-m} \varepsilon_m, \quad n \in \mathbb{N},$$

$$Q_n = \sum_{m=0}^{n} \binom{n}{m} q_n^m (1-q_n)^{n-m} \varepsilon_m, \quad n \in \mathbb{N} .$$

We consider the asymptotic behaviour of the sequence $E_n = (P_n, Q_n)$, $n \in \mathbb{N}$.

For this, we expand the Mellin transforms by the binomial series obtaining

$$M(\mu_{E_n})(s) = \left(\left(p + \frac{t}{\sqrt{n}} \right)^s p^{1-s} + \left(1 - p - \frac{t}{\sqrt{n}} \right)^s (1-p)^{1-s} \right)^n$$

$$= \left(\left(1 + \frac{t}{\sqrt{np}} \right)^s p + \left(1 - \frac{t}{\sqrt{n}(1-p)} \right)^s (1-p) \right)^n$$

$$= \left(1 + \binom{s}{2} \frac{t^2}{np(1-p)} + \ldots \right)^n, \quad 0 < s < 1 .$$

It follows that

$$\lim_{n\to\infty} M(\mu_{E_n})(s) = \exp\left(-\frac{s(1-s)}{2}\cdot\frac{t^2}{p(1-p)}\right), \quad 0<s<1,$$

which shows that the sequence converges to the experiment considered in Example 17.5 (3), with $\sigma^2 = p(1-p)$.

(3) Now we change the preceding example replacing p_n by $p_n = \frac{\lambda}{n}$ and q_n by $q_n = \frac{\mu}{n}$ where $\lambda > 0$, $\mu > 0$. Again, we are interested in the asymptotic behaviour of the sequence $E_n = (P_n, Q_n)$, $n \in \mathbb{N}$, and for this expand the Mellin transforms obtaining

$$\begin{aligned} M(\mu_{E_n})(s) &= \left(\frac{\mu^s\lambda^{1-s}}{n} + \left(1-\frac{\mu}{n}\right)^s\left(1-\frac{\lambda}{n}\right)^{1-s}\right)^n \\ &= \left(1 - \frac{s\mu}{n} - (1-s)\frac{\lambda}{n} + \frac{\mu^s\lambda^{1-s}}{n} + o\left(\frac{1}{n}\right)\right)^n. \end{aligned}$$

It follows that

$$\lim_{n\to\infty} M(\mu_{E_n})(s) = \exp(-s\mu - (1-s)\lambda + \mu^s\lambda^{1-s}), \quad 0<s<1,$$

which shows that the sequence converges to the experiment considered in Example 17.5 (5).

18. Contiguity of probability measures

Suppose that $E_n = (\Omega_n, \mathscr{A}_n, (P_n, Q_n))$, $n \in \mathbb{N}$, is a sequence of binary experiments. Assume that $(E_n)_{n\in\mathbb{N}}$ converges to an experiment $E = (\Omega, \mathscr{A}, (P, Q))$. We will give necessary and sufficient conditions for $P \ll Q$ and $Q \ll P$ in terms of the sequences $(P_n)_{n\in\mathbb{N}}$ and $(Q_n)_{n\in\mathbb{N}}$.

Recall the characterization of absolute continuity in terms of μ_E: Since $\mu_E = \mathscr{L}\left(\frac{dQ}{dP}\middle| P\right)$ we have

$$P \ll Q \quad \text{iff} \quad \mu_E\{0\} = 0, \quad \text{and}$$

$$Q \ll P \quad \text{iff} \quad \int_{[0,\infty)} x\,\mu_E(dx) = 1.$$

18.1 Lemma. *Assume that* $P_n \sim Q_n$, $n \in \mathbb{N}$, *and* $E_n \to E$. *Then* $\mathscr{L}\left(\frac{dQ_n}{dP_n}\middle| Q_n\right)$, $n \in \mathbb{N}$, *converges vaguely to the measure*

$$B \mapsto \int_B x\,\mu_E(dx), \quad B \in \mathscr{B}.$$

Proof. Let $f \in \mathscr{C}_{00}$. Then $x \mapsto xf(x)$ is continuous and bounded and we have

$$\lim_{n\to\infty} \int f\left(\frac{dQ_n}{dP_n}\right) dQ_n = \lim_{n\to\infty} \int xf(x)\,\mu_n(dx)$$
$$= \int xf(x)\,\mu(dx). \qquad \square$$

It should be noted that the limit of $\mathscr{L}\left(\frac{dQ_n}{dP_n}\middle| Q_n\right)$, $n \in \mathbb{N}$, need not be a probability measure.

18.2 Definition. The sequence (Q_n) is *contiguous* to the sequence (P_n) (briefly $(Q_n) \ll (P_n)$) if

$$P_n(A_n) \to 0,\ A_n \in \mathscr{A}_n, \quad \text{implies} \quad Q_n(A_n) \to 0.$$

18.3 Remark. The following facts are immediate.

(1) If $d_2(P_n, Q_n) \to 0$, then $(Q_n) \ll (P_n)$ and $(P_n) \ll (Q_n)$.

(2) If $(Q_n) \ll (P_n)$ or $(P_n) \ll (Q_n)$, then $\limsup_{n\to\infty} d_2(P_n, Q_n) < 1$.

We continue with a few basic lemmas on contiguity.

18.4 Lemma. $(Q_n) \ll (P_n)$ *iff for every sequence of* $\mathscr{A}_n$*-measurable functions* $f_n\colon \Omega_n \to \mathbb{R}$, $n \in \mathbb{N}$,

$$f_n \to 0\,(P_n) \quad \textit{implies} \quad f_n \to 0\,(Q_n).$$

Proof. Obvious. $\square$

18.5 Lemma. *If* $(Q_n)_{n\in\mathbb{N}} \ll (P_n)_{n\in\mathbb{N}}$ *then for every infinite subsequence* $\mathbb{N}_0 \subseteq \mathbb{N}$ *also* $(Q_n)_{n\in\mathbb{N}_0} \ll (P_n)_{n\in\mathbb{N}_0}$.

Proof. If $\mathbb{N}_0 \subseteq \mathbb{N}$ and $(A_n)_{n\in\mathbb{N}_0}$ is such that $\lim_{n\in\mathbb{N}_0} P_n(A_n) = 0$, then consider the sequence

$$B_n = \begin{cases} A_n & \text{if } n \in \mathbb{N}_0 \\ \emptyset & \text{otherwise}, \end{cases}$$

and apply $(Q_n)_{n\in\mathbb{N}} \ll (P_n)_{n\in\mathbb{N}}$. $\square$

18.6 Lemma. $(Q_n) \ll (P_n)$ *iff for every* $\varepsilon > 0$ *there are* $\delta(\varepsilon) > 0$, $N(\varepsilon) \in \mathbb{N}$, *such that for* $n > N(\varepsilon)$

$$P_n(A_n) < \delta(\varepsilon),\ A_n \in \mathscr{A}_n, \quad \textit{implies} \quad Q_n(A_n) < \varepsilon.$$

Proof. It is obvious that the condition is sufficient for contiguity. If it were not necessary then there would exist $\varepsilon > 0$ and sequences $(n_k) \subseteq \mathbb{N}$, $n_k \uparrow \infty$, and $A_{n_k} \in \mathscr{A}_{n_k}$, $k \in \mathbb{N}$, such that

$$P_{n_k}(A_{n_k}) < \frac{1}{k}, \; Q_{n_k}(A_{n_k}) \geqq \varepsilon, \quad k \in \mathbb{N}.$$

According to Lemma (18.5) this contradicts $(Q_n) \ll (P_n)$. □

18.7 Lemma. $(Q_n) \ll (P_n)$ *iff every infinite subsequence* $\mathbb{N}_1 \subseteq \mathbb{N}$ *contains another subsequence* $\mathbb{N}_2 \subseteq \mathbb{N}_1$ *such that* $(Q_n)_{n \in \mathbb{N}_2} \ll (P_n)_{n \in \mathbb{N}_2}$.

Proof. If $(Q_n) \ll (P_n)$ then the condition is valid according to Lemma 18.5. Assume conversely that the condition is satisfied. If $(Q_n) \not\ll (P_n)$ then there exists a sequence of sets $A_n \in \mathscr{A}_n$, $n \in \mathbb{N}$, and a subsequence $\mathbb{N}_1 \subseteq \mathbb{N}$ such that for some $\varepsilon > 0$

$$P_n(A_n) \to 0, \quad \text{but} \quad Q_n(A_n) \geqq \varepsilon \quad \text{if} \quad n \in \mathbb{N}_1.$$

Taking a subsequence $\mathbb{N}_2 \subseteq \mathbb{N}_1$ such that $(Q_n)_{n \in \mathbb{N}_2} \ll (P_n)_{n \in \mathbb{N}_2}$ we obtain a contradiction. □

The following theorems give necessary and sufficient conditions for contiguity in terms of likelihood ratios. Let $\left(\frac{dQ_n}{dP_n}, N_n\right)$ be a Lebesgue decomposition of Q_n w.r.t. P_n, $n \in \mathbb{N}$.

18.8 Remark. A basic condition will be that any versions of the distributions $\mathscr{L}\left(\frac{dQ_n}{dP_n} 1_{\Omega_n \setminus N_n} \middle| Q_n\right)$, $n \in \mathbb{N}$, are uniformly tight. This condition can be expressed in two equivalent manners stated below:

(1) For every sequence $c_n \to \infty$, $0 < c_n < \infty$, $n \in \mathbb{N}$,

$$\lim_{n \in \mathbb{N}} Q_n \left\{\frac{dQ_n}{dP_n} > c_n\right\} \setminus N_n = 0.$$

(2) For every $\varepsilon > 0$ there is $0 < c_\varepsilon < \infty$ such that

$$Q_n \left\{\frac{dQ_n}{dP_n} > c_\varepsilon\right\} \setminus N_n < \varepsilon \quad \text{if} \quad n \in \mathbb{N}.$$

18.9 Theorem. $(Q_n) \ll (P_n)$ *iff the measures* $\mathscr{L}\left(\frac{dQ_n}{dP_n} 1_{\Omega_n \setminus N_n} \middle| Q_n\right)$, $n \in \mathbb{N}$, *are uniformly tight and* $Q_n(N_n) \to 0$.

Proof. Assume that $(Q_n) \ll (P_n)$ and let $c_n \to \infty$, $0 < c_n < \infty$. We have $P_n(N_n) = 0$

which implies $Q_n(N_n) \to 0$. Moreover, we have

$$\lim_{n\in\mathbb{N}} P_n\left\{\frac{dQ_n}{dP_n} > c_n\right\} \leqq \lim_{n\in\mathbb{N}} \frac{1}{c_n} = 0$$

which implies

$$\lim_{n\in\mathbb{N}} Q_n\left\{\frac{dQ_n}{dP_n} > c_n\right\} \setminus N_n = 0.$$

Hence the condition holds.

Assume conversely that the conditions are valid. Let $\varepsilon > 0$. Then there is $0 < c_\varepsilon < \infty$ and $N(\varepsilon) \in \mathbb{N}$ such that

$$Q_n\left(N_n \cup \left\{\frac{dQ_n}{dP_n} > c_\varepsilon\right\}\right) < \varepsilon \quad \text{if} \quad n \geqq N(\varepsilon).$$

Assume that $P_n(A_n) \to 0$. Then

$$Q_n(A_n) \leqq Q_n\left(N_n \cup \left\{\frac{dQ_n}{dP_n} > c_\varepsilon\right\}\right) + \int\limits_{A_n \cap \left\{\frac{dQ_n}{dP_n} \leqq c_\varepsilon\right\}} \frac{dQ_n}{dP_n}\, dP_n$$

implies

$$\limsup_{n\in\mathbb{N}} Q_n(A_n) \leqq \varepsilon. \qquad \square$$

The next theorem is a counter part of the preceding one. It gives a criterion for $(P_n) \ll (Q_n)$ in terms of $\frac{dQ_n}{dP_n}$, $n \in \mathbb{N}$.

18.10 Theorem. $(P_n) \ll (Q_n)$ *iff any of the following conditions is valid:*

(1) *For every sequence* $c_n \to 0$, $0 < c_n < \infty$, $n \in \mathbb{N}$,

$$\lim_{n\in\mathbb{N}} P_n\left\{\frac{dQ_n}{dP_n} < c_n\right\} = 0.$$

(2) *For every* $\varepsilon > 0$ *there are* $0 < c_\varepsilon < \infty$, $N(\varepsilon) \in \mathbb{N}$, *such that*

$$P_n\left\{\frac{dQ_n}{dP_n} < c_\varepsilon\right\} < \varepsilon \quad \text{if} \quad n \geqq N(\varepsilon).$$

Proof. It is obvious that (1) $\Leftrightarrow$ (2). Assume that $(P_n) \ll (Q_n)$. Let $c_n \to 0$, $0 < c_n < \infty$. Then

$$Q_n\left(N_n' \cap \left\{\frac{dQ_n}{dP_n} < c_n\right\}\right) = \int\limits_{\frac{dQ_n}{dP_n} < c_n} \frac{dQ_n}{dP_n}\, dP_n < c_n$$

implies

$$\lim_{n \in \mathbb{N}} P_n \left\{ \frac{dQ_n}{dP_n} < c_n \right\} = 0 .$$

This proves (1). Assume conversely that (2) is true. Let $Q_n(A_n) \to 0$, $\varepsilon > 0$, and choose $0 < c_\varepsilon < \infty$, $N(\varepsilon) \in \mathbb{N}$, according to (2). Then

$$\begin{aligned} P_n(A_n) &\leqq P_n \left(A_n \cap \left\{ \frac{dQ_n}{dP_n} \geqq c_\varepsilon \right\} \right) + P_n \left\{ \frac{dQ_n}{dP_n} < c_\varepsilon \right\} \\ &\leqq \frac{1}{c_\varepsilon} \int_{A_n} \frac{dQ_n}{dP_n} \, dP_n + \varepsilon \leqq \frac{1}{c_\varepsilon} Q_n(A_n) + \varepsilon \end{aligned}$$

implies

$$\limsup_{n \in \mathbb{N}} P_n(A_n) \leqq \varepsilon . \qquad \square$$

If $\mathscr{L}\left(\frac{dQ_n}{dP_n} \middle| P_n \right) \to \mu$ weakly, then we can characterize contiguity in terms of μ. But, since μ corresponds to a binary experiment E we prefer an equivalent formulation in terms of E.

18.11 Theorem. *Suppose that $E_n = (P_n, Q_n) \to E = (P, Q)$. Then $(Q_n) \ll (P_n)$ iff $Q \ll P$.*

Proof. Assume that $(Q_n) \ll (P_n)$. For every $\delta > 0$ there is a continuity point $C_\delta < \infty$ of μ_E such that $\mu_E([0, C_\delta]) > 1 - \delta$. Fix $\varepsilon > 0$ and choose $\delta = \delta(\varepsilon) > 0$, $N(\varepsilon) \in \mathbb{N}$, according to Lemma 18.6. Then

$$\lim_{n \in \mathbb{N}} P_n \left\{ \frac{dQ_n}{dP_n} \leqq C_\delta \right\} = \mu_E([0, C_\delta]) > 1 - \delta$$

implies

$$\lim_{n \in \mathbb{N}} Q_n \left\{ \frac{dQ_n}{dP_n} \leqq C_\delta \right\} \geqq 1 - \varepsilon .$$

This gives

$$\begin{aligned} \int_{[0, C_\delta]} x \, \mu_E(dx) &= \lim_{n \in \mathbb{N}} \int_{\frac{dQ_n}{dP_n} \leqq C_\delta} \frac{dQ_n}{dP_n} \, dP_n \\ &\geqq \lim_{n \in \mathbb{N}} Q_n \left\{ \frac{dQ_n}{dP_n} \leqq C_\delta \right\} - \lim_{n \in \mathbb{N}} Q_n(N_n) \geqq 1 - \varepsilon . \end{aligned}$$

It follows that $\int x \, \mu_E(dx) = 1$, hence $Q \ll P$.

Assume conversely that μ_E satisfies $\int x \, \mu_E(dx) = 1$. For every $\varepsilon > 0$ there is a continuity point $C_\varepsilon < \infty$ of μ_E such that

$$\int_{[0,C_\varepsilon]} x\,\mu_E(dx) > 1 - \varepsilon .$$

Fix $\varepsilon > 0$ and choose $A_n \in \mathscr{A}_n$, $n \in \mathbb{N}$. Then we have

$$\begin{aligned} Q_n(A_n) &\leqq \int_{A_n} \frac{dQ_n}{dP_n}\, dP_n + Q_n(N_n) \\ &\leqq \int_{A_n \cap \left\{\frac{dQ_n}{dP_n} \leqq C_\varepsilon\right\}} \frac{dQ_n}{dP_n}\, dP_n + \int_{\frac{dQ_n}{dP_n} > C_\varepsilon} \frac{dQ_n}{dP_n}\, dP_n + Q_n(N_n) \\ &\leqq C_\varepsilon P_n(A_n) + 1 - \int_{\frac{dQ_n}{dP_n} > C_\varepsilon} \frac{dQ_n}{dP_n}\, dP_n \end{aligned}$$

which implies

$$\limsup_{n \in \mathbb{N}} Q_n(A_n) \leqq C_\varepsilon \limsup_{n \in \mathbb{N}} P_n(A_n) + 1 - (1 - \varepsilon) .$$

It is then clear that $(Q_n) \ll (P_n)$. □

18.12 Corollary. *Let $(E_n)_{n \in \mathbb{N}}$ be an arbitrary sequence in $\mathscr{E}_2$. Then $(Q_n) \ll P_n)$ iff every accumulation point $E = (P, Q)$ of $(E_n)_{n \in \mathbb{N}}$ satisfies $Q \ll P$.*

Chapter 4: Sufficiency, Exhaustivity and Randomizations

Sufficient maps and sufficient σ-fields have been playing an important part in statistical methodology for a long time. But not before 1964 the theory succeeded in clarifying the relations between sufficiency and decision theory. This has been done by LeCam [1964] who took up ideas of Blackwell [1951 and 1953] and solved the problem by proving the randomization criterion.

The present Chapter 4 is a first introduction into these ideas. We prove some classical facts and introduce the most suitable generalization of sufficiency based on the concept of randomization.

In Section 19 sufficient σ-fields are introduced at hand of binary experiments. In this case, the relation between sufficiency and decision theory can be treated elementary, i.e. by means of the Neyman-Pearson lemma. Section 20 is classical. A converse of the main theorem of section 4 is proved in Section 21. In Section 22 we translate the results of 19 and 20 into the terms of decision theory.

There have been many attempts to generalize the idea of sufficiency coming off from restricting the σ-field of an experiment, aiming at a satisfactory theory for the comparison of arbitrary experiments. Thereby, the concept of exhaustivity is of historical interest and is discussed in Section 23. However, it turned out that exhaustivity depends too much on regularity conditions which have nothing to do with the nature of the problem. For this reason, the kernels on which the concept of exhaustivity is based should be replaced by linear operators. This leads to the idea of randomization which is considered in Section 24. In Section 25 we prove the randomization criterion for dominated experiments.

The introduction of sufficiency by means of the Neyman Pearson lemma is due to Pfanzagl [1974]. A highly important paper on sufficiency is Halmos and Savage [1949]. Most text-books rely on this paper. Our presentation is restricted to a few basic facts which are needed later. More information is provided by Bahadur [1954], and the related papers of Landers [1972], and Rogge [1972]. The content of Section 21 is due to Pfanzagl [1969]. The randomization criterion of Section 25 is proved combining the finite case of Blackwell [1953] with Theorem 22.5, going back to Torgersen [1970].

At this point we note that the concept of sufficient σ-fields only leads to satisfactory results if one is dealing with dominated experiments. The case of undominated experiments is treated by Burkholder [1961], and by Landers [1972], and Rogge [1972].

19. The idea of sufficiency

Suppose that $E=(\Omega, \mathscr{A}, (P,Q))$ is a binary experiment and let $\mathscr{A}_0 \subseteq \mathscr{A}$ be a sub-σ-field. Let $E|\mathscr{A}_0 := (\Omega, \mathscr{A}_0, (P|\mathscr{A}_0, Q|\mathscr{A}_0))$. It is obvious that $E \underset{2}{\supseteq} E|\mathscr{A}_0$. This means that a reduction of data in general leads to a loss of information. A sub-σ-field $\mathscr{A}_0 \subseteq \mathscr{A}$ contains the same information as $\mathscr{A}$ if $E \underset{2}{\sim} E|\mathscr{A}_0$.

19.1 Theorem (Pfanzagl [1974]). *Suppose that $E=(\Omega, \mathscr{A}, (P,Q))$ is a binary experiment and let $\mathscr{A}_0 \subseteq \mathscr{A}$ be a sub-σ-field. Then the following assertions are equivalent:*

(1) $E \underset{2}{\sim} E|\mathscr{A}_0$.

(2) *For every $A \in \mathscr{A}$ there is a $\mathscr{A}_0$-measurable function f_A such that $f_A = P(A|\mathscr{A}_0)$ P-a.e. and $f_A = Q(A|\mathscr{A}_0)$ Q-a.e.*

(3) *There exists a Lebesgue decomposition $\left(\frac{dQ}{dP}, N\right)$ of $Q|\mathscr{A}$ with respect to $P|\mathscr{A}$ where $\frac{dQ}{dP}$ is $\mathscr{A}_0$-measurable and $N \in \mathscr{A}_0$.*

Proof. (1) $\Rightarrow$ (2): The assumption implies that for every critical function $\varphi \in \mathscr{F}(\Omega, \mathscr{A})$ there is a critical function $\varphi_0 \in \mathscr{F}(\Omega, \mathscr{A}_0)$ such that

$$P\varphi_0 \leqq P\varphi \quad \text{and} \quad Q\varphi_0 \geqq Q\varphi.$$

Let $f = dQ/d(P+Q)$ and let $k \in (0,\infty)$. If we define

$$\varphi = \begin{cases} 1 & \text{if } f \geqq k(1-f) \\ 0 & \text{if } f < k(1-f) \end{cases}$$

then $\varphi \in \mathscr{N}_k(P,Q)$ and it follows from Theorem 8.8 that $\varphi_0 \in \mathscr{N}_k(P,Q)$, too. Moreover, we have $P\varphi_0 = P\varphi$ and $Q\varphi_0 = Q\varphi$. The specific choice of φ implies that $\varphi_0 \leqq \varphi$ $(P+Q)$-a.e. whence we obtain $\varphi_0 = \varphi$ $(P+Q)$-a.e. Since $k \in (0,\infty)$ was arbitrary it follows that f is $\mathscr{A}_0$-measurable (mod $(P+Q)$).

Let $A \in \mathscr{A}$ and $B \in \mathscr{A}_0$. Define $f_A = \left(\frac{P+Q}{2}\right)(A|\mathscr{A}_0)$. Then we have

$$\int_B Q(A|\mathscr{A}_0)\,dQ = 2\int_B 1_A f\, d\left(\frac{P+Q}{2}\right) = 2\int_B f_A f\, d\left(\frac{P+Q}{2}\right) = \int_B f_A\, dQ$$

which implies $f_A = Q(A|\mathscr{A}_0)$ Q-a.e. In a similar way one proves that $f_A = P(A|\mathscr{A}_0)$ P-a.e.

(2) $\Rightarrow$ (3): From the proof of (2) we see that $f = \dfrac{dQ}{d(P+Q)}$ can be chosen $\mathscr{A}_0$-measurable. Defining $N = \{f=1\}$ and $\dfrac{dQ}{dP} = \dfrac{f}{1-f} \cdot 1_{\Omega \setminus N}$ proves (3).

(3) $\Rightarrow$ (1): From (3) it follows that every NP-test for E can be chosen $\mathscr{A}_0$-measurable. Hence (1) is obvious. □

The idea of the following is simple enough: Let $E = (\Omega, \mathscr{A}, \{P_\vartheta : \vartheta \in \Theta\})$ be an arbitrary experiment and call a sub-σ-field $\mathscr{A}_0 \subseteq \mathscr{A}$ E-sufficient if $E \underset{2}{\sim} E|\mathscr{A}_0$ (see Definition 22.1). Then the problem is to generalize the assertion of Theorem 19.1 in order to obtain conditions for sufficiency which are simple to check. However, for reasons of history, the term sufficiency is connected with part (2) of Theorem 19.1 instead of part (1).

19.2 Definition. Let $(\Omega, \mathscr{A})$ be a measurable space and $\mathscr{P} = \{P|\mathscr{A}\}$ a set of probability measures. A σ-field $\mathscr{A}_0 \subseteq \mathscr{A}$ is *$\mathscr{P}$-sufficient* if for every $A \in \mathscr{A}$ there is an $\mathscr{A}_0$-measurable function f_A such that $f_A = P(A|\mathscr{A}_0)$ P-a.e. for every $P \in \mathscr{P}$.

Let $E = (\Omega, \mathscr{A}, \mathscr{P})$ be an experiment. For convenience we call a σ-field $\mathscr{A}_0 \subseteq \mathscr{A}$ *E-sufficient* if $\mathscr{A}_0$ is $\mathscr{P}$-sufficient.

Let us finish this section with an important lemma.

19.3 Lemma. *Let $\mathscr{P} = \{P|\mathscr{A}\}$ be a set of probability measures on $(\Omega, \mathscr{A})$ and assume that $\mathscr{P} \ll P_0|\mathscr{A}$. If $\mathscr{A}_0$ is $\{P, P_0\}$-sufficient for every $P \in \mathscr{P}$ then $\mathscr{A}_0$ is $\mathscr{P}$-sufficient and $f_A = P_0(A|\mathscr{A}_0)$ P-a.e. for every $P \in \mathscr{P}$ and $A \in \mathscr{A}$.*

Proof. Since $\mathscr{A}_0$ is $\{P, P_0\}$-sufficient there exists an $\mathscr{A}_0$-measurable function $f_A^{(P)}$ such that

$$P(A \cap B) = \int_B f_A^{(P)} dP, \quad A \in \mathscr{A}, \; B \in \mathscr{A}_0, \quad \text{and}$$

$$P_0(A \cap B) = \int_B f_A^{(P)} dP_0, \quad A \in \mathscr{A}, \; B \in \mathscr{A}_0.$$

Since $f_A^{(P)} = P_0(A|\mathscr{A}_0)$ P_0-a.e. and $P \ll P_0$ it follows that $f_A^{(P)} = P_0(A|\mathscr{A}_0)$ P-a.e. Hence we obtain

$$P(A \cap B) = \int_B P_0(A|\mathscr{A}_0) dP, \quad A \in \mathscr{A}, \; B \in \mathscr{A}_0,$$

which proves the assertion. □

20. Pairwise sufficiency and the factorization theorem

Let $E = (\Omega, \mathscr{A}, \mathscr{P})$ be an experiment where $\mathscr{P} = \{P_\vartheta : \vartheta \in \Theta\}$. Then we define the set $C(\mathscr{P})$ to be the set of all probability measures

$$Q = \sum_{n=1}^{\infty} \alpha_n P_n$$

where $P_n \in \mathscr{P}$, $\alpha_n \geqq 0$, $n \in \mathbb{N}$, $\sum_{n=1}^{\infty} \alpha_n = 1$.

Our first lemma is almost trivial.

20.1 Lemma. *Suppose that $\mathscr{A}_0 \subseteq \mathscr{A}$ is $\mathscr{P}$-sufficient. Then $\mathscr{A}_0$ is $C(\mathscr{P})$-sufficient.*

Proof. Let $A \in \mathscr{A}$ and $Q = \sum_{n=1}^{\infty} \alpha_n P_n$. Then for every $B \in \mathscr{A}_0$ we have

$$Q(A \cap B) = \sum_{n=1}^{\infty} \alpha_n P_n(A \cap B) = \sum_{n=1}^{\infty} \alpha_n \int_B f_A \, dP_n = \int_B f_A \, dQ$$

where $f_A = P(A|\mathscr{A}_0)$ P-a.e. for every $P \in \mathscr{P}$. □

The next lemma is basic.

20.2 Lemma. *Suppose that $E = (\Omega, \mathscr{A}, \mathscr{P})$ is an experiment. Let $P \in \mathscr{P}$. If $\mathscr{A}_0$ is $\{Q, P\}$-sufficient for every $Q \in \mathscr{P}$ then $\mathscr{A}_0$ is $\{Q, P\}$-sufficient for every $Q \in C(\mathscr{P})$.*

Proof. Let $Q = \sum_{n \in \mathbb{N}} \alpha_n P_n \in C(\mathscr{P})$. For every $n \in \mathbb{N}$ let $\left(\frac{dP_n}{dP}, N_n\right)$ be a Lebesgue decomposition of $P_n|\mathscr{A}$ with respect to $P|\mathscr{A}$ such that $\frac{dP_n}{dP}$ is $\mathscr{A}_0$-measurable and $N_n \in \mathscr{A}_0$. Let $N = \bigcup_{n \in \mathbb{N}} N_n$. It follows that for every $A \in \mathscr{A}$ and $n \in \mathbb{N}$

$$P_n(A) = \int_A \frac{dP_n}{dP} \, dP + P_n(N \cap A).$$

Hence,

$$\left(\sum_{n \in \mathbb{N}} \alpha_n \frac{dP_n}{dP}, N\right)$$

is a Lebesgue decomposition of $Q|\mathscr{A}$ with respect to $P|\mathscr{A}$ which is $\mathscr{A}_0$-measurable. This proves the assertion. □

20.3 Lemma (Halmos and Savage [1949]). *If $E = (\Omega, \mathscr{A}, \mathscr{P})$ is dominated, then there exists $P_0 \in C(\mathscr{P})$ such that $\mathscr{P} \sim P_0$.*

Proof. Let $\nu|\mathscr{A}$ be finite such that $\mathscr{P} \ll \nu$. For every $P \in \mathscr{P}$ let $S_P = \left\{\frac{dP}{d\nu} > 0\right\}$ and $\mathscr{M} = \left\{\bigcup_{n=1}^{\infty} S_{P_n} : (P_n) \subseteq \mathscr{P}\right\}$. Define

$$s := \sup\{\nu(M) : M \in \mathscr{M}\}.$$

Then an easy argument shows the existence of some $M_0 \in \mathscr{M}$ such that $s = \nu(M_0)$. Define

$$P_0 = \sum_{n=1}^{\infty} 2^{-n} P_n \quad \text{if} \quad M_0 = \bigcup_{n=1}^{\infty} S_{P_n}.$$

Then $P_0 \in C(\mathscr{P})$. If $P(A) = 0$ for every $P \in \mathscr{P}$ then $P_0(A) = 0$.

Let us prove the converse. Assume that $P_0(N) = 0$ and let $P \in \mathscr{P}$. It is sufficient to prove $P(N \cap S_P) = 0$. To this end we will show that

$$\nu(N \cap S_P) = \nu(N \cap S_P \cap M_0) + \nu((N \cap S_P) \setminus M_0) = 0 .$$

First we note that

$$\begin{aligned} \nu((N \cap S_P) \setminus M_0) &= \nu(M_0 \cup (N \cap S_P)) - \nu(M_0) \\ &\leqq \nu(M_0 \cup S_P) - \nu(M_0) = s - s = 0 . \end{aligned}$$

Moreover we have

$$\nu(N \cap S_P \cap M_0) \leqq \sum_{n=1}^{\infty} \nu(N \cap S_{P_n}) .$$

Since $P_0(N) = 0$ implies $P_n(N) = 0$, $n \in \mathbb{N}$, it follows that

$$\begin{aligned} \nu\left(N \cap \left\{\frac{dP_n}{d\nu} > \varepsilon\right\}\right) &\leqq \frac{1}{\varepsilon} \int_{N \cap \left\{\frac{dP_n}{d\nu} > \varepsilon\right\}} \frac{dP_n}{d\nu}\, d\nu \\ &\leqq \frac{1}{\varepsilon}\, P_n(N) = 0, \quad n \in \mathbb{N}, \end{aligned}$$

which implies $\nu(N \cap S_{P_n}) = 0$, $n \in \mathbb{N}$. □

20.4 Theorem (Halmos and Savage [1949]). *Suppose that $E = (\Omega, \mathscr{A}, \mathscr{P})$ is a dominated experiment. If $\mathscr{A}_0 \subseteq \mathscr{A}$ is $\{P_1, P_2\}$-sufficient for every set $\{P_1, P_2\} \subseteq \mathscr{P}$ then $\mathscr{A}_0$ is $\mathscr{P}$-sufficient.*

Proof. According to Theorem 20.3 there exists $P_0 = \sum_{n \in \mathbb{N}} \alpha_n P_n \in C(\mathscr{P})$ such that $\mathscr{P} \ll P_0$. For every $P \in \mathscr{P}$ and every $n \in \mathbb{N}$ the σ-field $\mathscr{A}_0$ is $\{P_n, P\}$-sufficient. Lemma 20.2 implies that $\mathscr{A}_0$ is $\{P_0, P\}$-sufficient for all $P \in \mathscr{P}$. Since $\mathscr{P} \ll P_0$ we obtain from Lemma 19.3 that $\mathscr{A}_0$ is $\mathscr{P}$-sufficient. □

20.5 Corollary. *Suppose that $E = (\Omega, \mathscr{A}, \mathscr{P})$ is a dominated experiment and that $\mathscr{A}_0 \subseteq \mathscr{A}$ is an E-sufficient sub-σ-field. Let $P_0|\mathscr{A}$ be such that $\mathscr{P} \ll P_0$ and $P_0 \in C(\mathscr{P})$. Then for every $A \in \mathscr{A}$*

$$P_0(A|\mathscr{A}_0) = P(A|\mathscr{A}_0)\ P\text{-a.e.}, \quad P \in \mathscr{P} .$$

Proof. Apply Lemma 19.3. □

Sufficiency can be characterized in terms of measurability properties of densities.

20.6 Lemma. *Let $E = (\Omega, \mathscr{A}, \mathscr{P})$ be a dominated experiment. Assume that $\mathscr{A}_0 \subseteq \mathscr{A}$ is a σ-field.*

(1) *If there exists a probability measure $P_0|\mathscr{A}$ such that $\mathscr{P} \ll P_0$ and $\dfrac{dP|\mathscr{A}}{dP_0|\mathscr{A}}$ can be chosen $\mathscr{A}_0$-measurable for every $P \in \mathscr{P}$ then $\mathscr{A}_0$ is E-sufficient.*

(2) *If $\mathscr{A}_0$ is E-sufficient then for every $P_0 \in C(\mathscr{P})$ such that $\mathscr{P} \ll P_0$ the density $\dfrac{dP}{dP_0}$ can be chosen $\mathscr{A}_0$-measurable for every $P \in \mathscr{P}$.*

Proof. (1) Combine Theorem 19.1 and Lemma 19.3.

(2) Combine Lemma 20.1 and Theorem 19.1. □

20.7 Theorem (Halmos and Savage [1949]). *Let $E = (\Omega, \mathscr{A}, \mathscr{P})$ be a dominated experiment and $\mathscr{P} \ll \nu$ where $\nu|\mathscr{A}$ is σ-finite. For every σ-field $\mathscr{A}_0 \subseteq \mathscr{A}$ the following assertions are equivalent.*

(1) *$\mathscr{A}_0$ is E-sufficient.*

(2) *There are an $\mathscr{A}$-measurable function h and for every $P \in \mathscr{P}$ an $\mathscr{A}_0$-measurable function g_P such that*

$$\frac{dP}{d\nu} = g_P h \quad \nu\text{-a.e.}$$

Proof. (1) ⇒ (2): Let $P_0 \in C(\mathscr{P})$ such that $\mathscr{P} \sim P_0$. According to Lemma 20.6, (2), $\dfrac{dP}{dP_0}$ can be chosen $\mathscr{A}_0$-measurable for every $P \in \mathscr{P}$. For every $P \in \mathscr{P}$ let g_P be an $\mathscr{A}_0$-measurable function satisfying $g_P = \dfrac{dP}{dP_0}$ P_0-a.e. Then for every $A \in \mathscr{A}$ and $P \in \mathscr{P}$

$$P(A) = \int_A g_P \, dP_0 = \int_A g_P \frac{dP_0}{d\nu} \, d\nu .$$

(2) ⇒ (1): According to the proof of Theorem (20.1) there is $P_0 \in C(\mathscr{P})$, $P_0 = \sum_{n=1}^{\infty} 2^{-n} P_n$, $(P_n) \subseteq \mathscr{P}$, such that $\mathscr{P} \sim P_0$. It follows that

$$\frac{dP_0}{d\nu} = h \sum_{n=1}^{\infty} 2^{-n} g_{P_n} \quad \nu\text{-a.e.}$$

which implies

$$\frac{dP}{dP_0} = g_P \Big(\sum_{n=1}^{\infty} 2^{-n} g_{P_n} \Big)^{-1} \quad P_0\text{-a.e.} \quad \text{if} \quad P \in \mathscr{P} .$$

This proves the assertion according to Lemma 20.6 (1). □

20.8 Definition. Let $E = (\Omega, \mathscr{A}, \mathscr{P})$ be an experiment. A measurable mapping $T: (\Omega, \mathscr{A}) \to (\Omega_1, \mathscr{A}_1)$ is called *E-sufficient* if the σ-field $T^{-1}(\mathscr{A}_1)$ is E-sufficient.

20.9 Theorem. *Suppose that $E = (\Omega, \mathscr{A}, \mathscr{P})$ is a dominated experiment and $\mathscr{P} \ll \nu$ where $\nu|\mathscr{A}$ is σ-finite. Let T: $(\Omega, \mathscr{A}) \to (\Omega_1, \mathscr{A}_1)$ be a measurable mapping. Then the following assertions are equivalent:*

(1) *T is E-sufficient.*

(2) *There are an $\mathscr{A}$-measurable function $h: \Omega \to \mathbb{R}$ and for every $P \in \mathscr{P}$ an $\mathscr{A}_1$-measurable function $g_P: \Omega_1 \to \mathbb{R}$ such that*

$$\frac{dP}{d\nu} = (g_P \circ T)h \quad \nu\text{-a.e.}, \quad P \in \mathscr{P}.$$

Proof. This is an immediate consequence of Theorem 20.7. □

21. Sufficiency and topology

Using the notion of sufficiency some results of sections 3 and 4 can be clearly arranged. Let $(\Omega, \mathscr{A})$ be a measurable space and $\mathscr{P}$ a set of probability measures on $\mathscr{A}$. The symbol $\mathscr{M}_1(\Omega, \mathscr{A})$ denotes the set of all probability measures on $(\Omega, \mathscr{A})$.

21.1 Lemma. *Suppose that $\mathscr{A}_0 \subseteq \mathscr{A}$ is a $\mathscr{P}$-sufficient σ-field. Then $\mathscr{A}_0$ is sufficient for the $\mathscr{T}_1$-closed hull of $\mathscr{P}$ in $\mathscr{M}_1(\Omega, \mathscr{A})$.*

Proof. Let Q be a $\mathscr{T}_1$-accumulation point of $\mathscr{P}$. Let $A \in \mathscr{A}$, $B \in \mathscr{A}_0$, and $f_A \in P(A|\mathscr{A}_0)$, $P \in \mathscr{P}$. For every $\varepsilon > 0$ there exists $P \in \mathscr{P}$ such that

$$|Q(A \cap B) - P(A \cap B)| < \frac{\varepsilon}{2},$$

$$\left|\int_B f_A \, dQ - \int_B f_A \, dP\right| < \frac{\varepsilon}{2},$$

which implies

$$\left|Q(A \cap B) - \int_B f_A \, dQ\right| < \varepsilon.$$

Choosing $\varepsilon > 0$ arbitrarily small proves the assertion. □

21.2 Lemma. *Suppose that $\mathscr{A}_0 \subseteq \mathscr{A}$ is a $\mathscr{P}$-sufficient σ-field. Then the families $\mathscr{P}$ and $\mathscr{P}|\mathscr{A}_0$ have the same topology $\mathscr{T}_1$, the same uniform structure $\mathscr{U}_1$, the same distances d_1 and d_2, and the same σ-field $\mathscr{C}$ (recall the definition of $\mathscr{C}$ below Lemma 3.8).*

Proof. For every $A \in \mathscr{A}$ let $f_A = P(A|\mathscr{A}_0)$ P-a.e., $P \in \mathscr{P}$. Then $|P(A) - Q(A)| = |P(f_A) - Q(f_A)|$, $P, Q \in \mathscr{P}$. This implies that the topologies $\mathscr{T}_1$ and the uniformities $\mathscr{U}_1$ coincide for $\mathscr{P}$ and $\mathscr{P}|\mathscr{A}_0$. The assertion concerning d_1 and d_2 follows from Lemma (20.6). To prove the last assertion denote the respective σ-fields by $\mathscr{C}(\mathscr{A})$ and $\mathscr{C}(\mathscr{A}_0)$. Obviously, $\mathscr{C}(\mathscr{A}) \supseteq \mathscr{C}(\mathscr{A}_0)$. Since $P(A) = P(f_A)$, $A \in \mathscr{P}$, it follows that $P \mapsto P(A)$, $P \in \mathscr{P}$, is $\mathscr{C}(\mathscr{A}_0)$-measurable for every $A \in \mathscr{A}$. Hence $\mathscr{C}(\mathscr{A}) \subseteq \mathscr{C}(\mathscr{A}_0)$. □

21.3 Theorem (Berger, 1951, Pfanzagl, 1969). *The set $\mathscr{P}$ is separable (cf. Definition 4.5) iff it is dominated and if there exists a countably generated, $\mathscr{P}$-sufficient σ-field.*

Proof. If $\mathscr{P}$ is separable then one part of the assertion follows from Lemma (4.3) and Lemma (20.6). Conversely, if $\mathscr{P}$ is dominated and $\mathscr{A}_0$ is a countably generated σ-field, then $\mathscr{P}|\mathscr{A}_0$ is separable by Lemma 4.1. If $\mathscr{A}_0$ is $\mathscr{P}$-sufficient then Lemma 21.2 implies that $\mathscr{P}$ is separable, too. □

21.4 Corollary (Pfanzagl [1969]). *The set $\mathscr{P}$ is separable iff any of the following equivalent conditions is satisfied:*

(1) *$\mathscr{P}$ is dominated and for every σ-finite measure $\nu|\mathscr{A}$ such that $\mathscr{P} \ll \nu$ there are densities $\frac{dP}{d\nu}$, $P \in \mathscr{P}$, such that $(\omega, P) \mapsto \frac{dP}{d\nu}(\omega)$ is $\mathscr{A} \otimes \mathscr{C}$-measurable.*

(2) *There exists a σ-finite measure $\nu|\mathscr{A}$ dominating $\mathscr{P}$ such that there are densities $\frac{dP}{d\nu}$, $P \in \mathscr{P}$, with $(\omega, P) \mapsto \frac{dP}{d\nu}(\omega)$ being $\mathscr{A} \otimes \mathscr{C}$-measurable.*

Proof. If $\mathscr{P}$ is separable then Lemma 4.6 implies (1) and obviously (1) implies (2). Assume that (2) is satisfied. Since $\mathscr{B}(\mathbb{R})$ is countably generated there exist countably generated σ-fields $\mathscr{A}_0 \subseteq \mathscr{A}$ and $\mathscr{C}_0 \subseteq \mathscr{C}$ such that $(\omega, P) \mapsto \frac{dP}{d\nu}(\omega)$ is $\mathscr{A}_0 \otimes \mathscr{C}_0$-measurable. From Lemma 20.6 we obtain that $\mathscr{A}_0$ is $\mathscr{P}$-sufficient. This implies by Theorem 21.3 that $\mathscr{P}$ is separable. □

22. Comparison of dominated experiments by testing problems

22.1 Definition. Let $\Theta \neq \emptyset$ be an arbitrary set and let $E_i = (\Omega_i, \mathscr{A}_i, \{P_{i,\vartheta}: \vartheta \in \Theta\})$, $i = 1, 2$, be dominated experiments. Then E_1 is called *more informative than E_2 for testing problems* ($E_1 \underset{2}{\supseteq} E_2$) if for every testing problem (H, K) and every critical function $\varphi_2 \in \mathscr{F}(\Omega_2, \mathscr{A}_2)$ there exists a critical function $\varphi_1 \in \mathscr{F}(\Omega_1, \mathscr{A}_1)$ such that

$$P_{1,\vartheta}\varphi_1 \leqq P_{2,\vartheta}\varphi_2 \quad \text{if} \quad \vartheta \in H, \quad \text{and}$$
$$P_{1,\vartheta}\varphi_1 \geqq P_{2,\vartheta}\varphi_2 \quad \text{if} \quad \vartheta \in K.$$

This concept of informativity will later be generalized in the framework of decision theory. At the moment we only note that „$\underset{2}{\supseteq}$" defines an order relation on the set of all dominated experiments with fixed parameter space $\Theta \neq \emptyset$. Two experiments E_1 and E_2 are called *equivalent for testing problems* ($E_1 \underset{2}{\sim} E_2$) if $E_1 \underset{2}{\supseteq} E_2$ and $E_2 \underset{2}{\supseteq} E_1$.

Let $E = (\Omega, \mathscr{A}, \{P_\vartheta: \vartheta \in \Theta\})$ be an experiment. If $\mathscr{A}_0 \subseteq \mathscr{A}$ is a sub-σ-field then we define $E|\mathscr{A}_0 = (\Omega, \mathscr{A}_0, \{P_\vartheta|\mathscr{A}_0: \vartheta \in \Theta\})$. If $T: (\Omega, \mathscr{A}) \to (\Omega_1, \mathscr{A}_1)$ is a measurable mapping then the image of E unter T is defined to be

$$T_* E = (\Omega_1, \mathscr{A}_1, \{P_\vartheta \circ T^{-1}: \vartheta \in \Theta\}).$$

We note the obvious facts that $E \underset{2}{\supseteq} E|\mathscr{A}_0$ and $E \underset{2}{\supseteq} T_* E$. If E is dominated then $T_* E$ is dominated, too.

22.2 Theorem. *Suppose that $E = (\Omega, \mathscr{A}, \{P_\vartheta: \vartheta \in \Theta\})$ is a dominated experiment and $\mathscr{A}_0 \subseteq \mathscr{A}$ is a sub-σ-field. The assertions*

(1) *$\mathscr{A}_0$ is E-sufficient,*

(2) *$E \underset{2}{\sim} E|\mathscr{A}_0$,*

are equivalent.

Proof. (1) ⇒ (2): For every $\varphi \in \mathscr{F}(\Omega, \mathscr{A})$ there exists some $\varphi_0 \in \mathscr{F}(\Omega, \mathscr{A}_0)$ such that

$$\varphi_0 = P_\vartheta(\varphi|\mathscr{A}_0)\ P_\vartheta\text{-a.e.} \quad \text{if} \quad \vartheta \in \Theta.$$

Then $P_\vartheta \varphi_0 = P_\vartheta \varphi$ if $\vartheta \in \Theta$.

(2) ⇒ (1): This is an immediated consequence of Theorems 19.1 and 20.4. □

22.3 Lemma. *Let $E = (\Omega, \mathscr{A}, \{P_\vartheta: \vartheta \in \Theta\})$ be a dominated experiment and let T: $(\Omega, \mathscr{A}) \to (\Omega_1, \mathscr{A}_1)$ be a measurable mapping. Then $T_* E \underset{2}{\sim} E|T^{-1}(\mathscr{A}_1)$.*

Proof. Let $\varphi_2 \in \mathscr{F}(\Omega_1, \mathscr{A}_1)$. Then $\varphi_1 = \varphi_2 \circ T \in \mathscr{F}(\Omega, T^{-1}(\mathscr{A}_1))$ and satisfies

$$P_\vartheta \varphi_1 = (P_\vartheta \circ T^{-1})\varphi_2 \quad \text{if} \quad \vartheta \in \Theta.$$

This proves $E|T^{-1}(\mathscr{A}_1) \underset{2}{\supseteq} T_* E$. Let conversely $\varphi_1 \in \mathscr{F}(\Omega, T^{-1}(\mathscr{A}_1))$. Then there exists $\varphi_2 \in \mathscr{F}(\Omega_1, \mathscr{A}_1)$ such that $\varphi_1 = \varphi_2 \circ T$ and we have

$$P_\vartheta \varphi_1 = (P_\vartheta \circ T^{-1})\varphi_2 \quad \text{if} \quad \vartheta \in \Theta.$$

This proves $T_* E \underset{2}{\supseteq} E|T^{-1}(\mathscr{A}_1)$. □

22.4 Corollary. *Let $(\Omega, \mathscr{A}, \mathscr{P})$ be an experiment and let T: $(\Omega, \mathscr{A}) \to (\Omega_1, \mathscr{A}_1)$*

be a measurable mapping. Then the assertions

(1) *T is E-sufficient,*

(2) $E \underset{2}{\sim} T_* E$,

are equivalent.

Proof. Combine 22.2 and 22.3. □

Statistical consequences of Corollary 22.4 are illustrated by the study of exponential experiments in Chapter 5.

Now, we turn to the comparison of arbitrary dominated experiments. Recall that $A(\Theta)$ denotes the system of finite subsets of Θ.

22.5 Theorem (Torgersen [1970]). *Suppose that $E = (\Omega_1, \mathscr{A}_1, \{P_\vartheta: \vartheta \in \Theta\})$ and $F = (\Omega_2, \mathscr{A}_2, \{Q_\vartheta: \vartheta \in \Theta\})$ are dominated experiments. Then $E \underset{2}{\supseteq} F$ iff*

$$\|\sum_{\sigma\in\alpha} a_\sigma P_\sigma\| \geqq \|\sum_{\sigma\in\alpha} a_\sigma Q_\sigma\|$$

for every $\alpha \in A(\Theta)$ and every $(a_\sigma)_{\sigma\in\alpha} \in \mathbb{R}^\alpha$.

Proof. (1) Suppose that $E \underset{2}{\supseteq} F$. Let $(a_\sigma)_{\sigma\in\alpha} \in \mathbb{R}^\alpha$. W.l.g. we assume that $a_\sigma \neq 0$, $\sigma \in \alpha$, and we denote $\alpha^+ = \{\sigma \in \alpha: a_\sigma > 0\}$, $\alpha^- = \{\sigma \in \alpha: a_\sigma < 0\}$. Let $\psi \in \mathscr{F}(\Omega_2, \mathscr{A}_2)$. Then there exists $\varphi \in \mathscr{F}(\Omega_1, \mathscr{A}_1)$ such that

$$\begin{aligned} P_\sigma\varphi &\leqq Q_\sigma\psi \quad \text{if} \quad \sigma\in\alpha^-, \\ P_\sigma\varphi &\geqq Q_\sigma\psi \quad \text{if} \quad \sigma\in\alpha^+. \end{aligned}$$

This implies

$$\sum_{\sigma\in\alpha} a_\sigma P_\sigma\varphi \geqq \sum_{\sigma\in\alpha} a_\sigma Q_\sigma\psi.$$

It follows that

$$\begin{aligned} \Big(\sum_{\sigma\in\alpha} a_\sigma P_\sigma\Big)^+(1) &= \sup_{\varphi\in\mathscr{F}(\Omega_1,\mathscr{A}_1)} \sum_{\sigma\in\alpha} a_\sigma P_\sigma\varphi \\ &\geqq \sup_{\psi\in\mathscr{F}(\Omega_2,\mathscr{A}_2)} \sum_{\sigma\in\alpha} a_\sigma Q_\sigma\psi = \Big(\sum_{\sigma\in\alpha} a_\sigma Q_\sigma\Big)^+(1). \end{aligned}$$

Replacing $(a_\sigma)_{\sigma\in\alpha}$ by $(-a_\sigma)_{\sigma\in\alpha}$ leads to

$$\Big(\sum_{\sigma\in\alpha} a_\sigma P_\sigma\Big)^-(1) \geqq \Big(\sum_{\sigma\in\alpha} a_\sigma Q_\sigma\Big)^-(1),$$

which proves one part of the assertion.

(2) Assume conversely that the condition is satisfied. Let $\psi \in \mathscr{F}(\Omega_2, \mathscr{A}_2)$ and define $\psi_1 = 2\left(\psi - \frac{1}{2}\right)$. We define a linear function L: span $\{P_\vartheta: \vartheta \in \Theta\} \to \mathbb{R}$ by

$$L(\sum_{\sigma\in\alpha} a_\sigma P_\sigma) := \sum_{\sigma\in\alpha} a_\sigma Q_\sigma \psi_1 .$$

where $(a_\sigma)_{\sigma\in\alpha} \in \mathbb{R}^\alpha$, $\alpha \in A(\Theta)$. This is well-defined since $\sum_{\sigma\in\alpha} a_\sigma P_\sigma = \sum_{\tau\in\beta} b_\tau P_\tau$ implies

$$0 = \| \sum_{\sigma\in\alpha} a_\sigma P_\sigma - \sum_{\tau\in\beta} b_\tau P_\tau \| \geqq \| \sum_{\sigma\in\alpha} a_\sigma Q_\sigma - \sum_{\tau\in\beta} b_\tau Q_\tau \| .$$

The linear function L satisfies on span $\{P_\vartheta: \vartheta \in \Theta\}$

$$|L(\sigma) \leqq \|\sigma\|$$

and by the Hahn-Banach theorem it can be extended to $L_1(\Omega_1, \mathscr{A}_1, \nu_1)$ where $\nu_1|\mathscr{A}_1$ is some σ-finite measure dominating $\{P_\vartheta: \vartheta \in \Theta\}$. It follows that there is some $\varphi_1 \in \mathscr{L}_b(\Omega_1, \mathscr{A}_1)$, $\|\varphi_1\|_u \leqq 1$, such that $P_\vartheta \varphi_1 = Q_\vartheta \psi_1$, $\vartheta \in \Theta$. Defining $\varphi = \frac{1}{2}(1+\varphi_1) \in \mathscr{F}(\Omega_1, \mathscr{A}_1)$ we obtain $P_\vartheta \varphi = Q_\vartheta \psi$, $\vartheta \in \Theta$. This proves $E \underset{2}{\supseteq} F$. □

22.6 Corollary. *Suppose that* $E = (\Omega_1, \mathscr{A}_1, \{P_\vartheta: \vartheta \in \Theta\})$ *and* $F = (\Omega_2, \mathscr{A}_2, \{Q_\vartheta: \vartheta \in \Theta\})$ *are dominated experiments. If* $E \underset{2}{\supseteq} F$, *then for every* $\psi \in \mathscr{F}(\Omega_2, \mathscr{A}_2)$ *there exists* $\varphi \in \mathscr{F}(\Omega_1, \mathscr{A}_1)$ *such that* $P_\vartheta \varphi = Q_\vartheta \psi$, $\vartheta \in \Theta$.

Proof. Look at part (2) of the preceding proof. □

22.7 Remark. Consider the situation of the last corollary. Then for every $A \in \mathscr{A}_2$ there is a critical function $\varphi_A \in \mathscr{F}(\Omega_1, \mathscr{A}_1)$ such that $P_\vartheta \varphi_A = Q_\vartheta(A)$, $\vartheta \in \Theta$. This suggests to consider the problem whether the functions φ_A, $A \in \mathscr{A}_2$, can be put together to a kernel $K: \Omega_1 \times \mathscr{A}_2 \to [0,1]$ satisfying

$$Q_\vartheta(A) = \int K(\omega_1, A) P_\vartheta(d\omega_1), \vartheta \in \Theta, \quad A \in \mathscr{A}_2 .$$

This idea is briefly discussed in the next section.

23. Exhaustivity

Suppose that $E = (\Omega, \mathscr{A}, \{P_\vartheta: \vartheta \in \Theta\})$ is an experiment and $\mathscr{A}_0 \subseteq \mathscr{A}$ a sub-σ-field.

23.1 Remark. Assume that $\mathscr{A}_0$ is E-sufficient and every probability measure $P|\mathscr{A}$ admits a regular conditional probability given $\mathscr{A}_0$. If $Q \in C(\mathscr{P})$ and $\mathscr{P} \ll Q$ then a regular conditional probability $K: \Omega \times \mathscr{A} \to [0,1]$ of Q given $\mathscr{A}_0$ satisfies for every $A \in \mathscr{A}$

$$K(.,A) = P_\vartheta(A|\mathscr{A}_0)\ P_\vartheta\text{-a.e.}, \quad \vartheta \in \Theta .$$

This is a consequence of Corollary 20.5. It follows that

$$P_\vartheta(A) = \int K(\omega, A)\,(P_\vartheta|\mathscr{A}_0)\,(d\omega),\ \vartheta \in \Theta,\ A \in \mathscr{A}.$$

Hence the probability measures of E may be recovered from the probability measures of $E|\mathscr{A}_0$ by a randomization which is independent of $\vartheta \in \Theta$.

23.2 Definition. Let $(\Omega, \mathscr{A})$ and $(\Omega_1, \mathscr{A}_1)$ be measurable spaces. A (*stochastic or Markov*) *kernel* from $(\Omega, \mathscr{A})$ to $(\Omega_1, \mathscr{A}_1)$ is a function $K: \Omega \times \mathscr{A}_1 \to [0,1]$ such that:

(1) $\omega \mapsto K(\omega, A)$, $\omega \in \Omega$, is $\mathscr{A}$-measurable for every $A \in \mathscr{A}_1$,

(2) $A \mapsto K(\omega, A)$, $A \in \mathscr{A}_1$, is a probability measure for every $\omega \in \Omega$.

23.3 Definition. Let $E_i = (\Omega_i, \mathscr{A}_i, \{P_{i,\vartheta}: \vartheta \in \Theta\})$, $i = 1, 2$, be experiments. Then E_1 is called *exhaustive* (or *Blackwell-sufficient*) for E_2 if there is a kernel K from $(\Omega_1, \mathscr{A}_1)$ to $(\Omega_2, \mathscr{A}_2)$ such that

$$P_{2,\vartheta}(A_2) = \int K(\omega_1, A_2)\,P_{1,\vartheta}(d\omega_1)$$

for every $\vartheta \in \Theta$ and every $A_2 \in \mathscr{A}_2$.

23.4 Examples. (1) Let $E = (\Omega, \mathscr{A}, \{P_\vartheta: \vartheta \in \Theta\})$ be an experiment and $\mathscr{A}_0 \subseteq \mathscr{A}$ a sub-σ-field. Then E is exhaustive for $E|\mathscr{A}_0$. To prove it define $K(\omega, A) = 1_A(\omega)$ if $A \in \mathscr{A}_0$ and $\omega \in \Omega$.

(2) Let $E = (\Omega, \mathscr{A}, \{P_\vartheta: \vartheta \in \Theta\})$ be an experiment and $\mathscr{A}_0 \subseteq \mathscr{A}$ a sub-σ-field. If the assumptions of Remark 23.1 are satisfied then also the converse of (1) is true, namely $E|\mathscr{A}_0$ is exhaustive for E.

(3) Let $E = (\Omega, \mathscr{A}, \{P_\vartheta: \vartheta \in \Theta\})$ be an experiment and $T: (\Omega, \mathscr{A}) \to (\Omega_1, \mathscr{A}_1)$ a measurable mapping. Then E is exhaustive for $T_* E$. To prove it define $K(\omega, A) = (1_A \circ T)(\omega)$ if $A \in \mathscr{A}_1$, $\omega \in \Omega$.

(4) The question whether a converse of (3) holds for E-sufficient mappings depends on regularity assumptions similar to (2).

23.5 Lemma. *Suppose that* $E = (\Omega, \mathscr{A}, \{P_\vartheta: \vartheta \in \Theta\})$ *is an experiment and* $T: (\Omega, \mathscr{A}) \to (\Omega_1, \mathscr{A}_1)$ *is a measurable mapping. Then the experiments* $T_* E$ *and* $E|T^{-1}(\mathscr{A}_1)$ *are mutually exhaustive.*

Proof. It is clear that $T_* E = T_*(E|T^{-1}(\mathscr{A}_1))$. This implies that $E|T^{-1}(\mathscr{A}_1)$ is exhaustive for $T_* E$. To prove the converse define

$$K(A, \omega_1) = 1_{T(A)}(\omega_1) \quad \text{if} \quad A \in T^{-1}(\mathscr{A}_1), \quad \omega_1 \in \Omega_1.$$

Note that $A = T^{-1}(A_1)$ implies $T^{-1}(T(A)) = T^{-1}(A_1)$. It follows that

$$\begin{aligned} P_\vartheta(A) &= P_\vartheta(T^{-1}(A_1)) = \int 1_{T^{-1}(A_1)}(\omega)\,P_\vartheta(d\omega) \\ &= \int 1_{T^{-1}(T(A))}(\omega)\,P_\vartheta(d\omega) = \int 1_{T(A)}(\omega_1)\,(P_\vartheta \circ T^{-1})\,(d\omega_1). \qquad \square \end{aligned}$$

Let us consider some statistical implications of exhaustivity.

23.6 Lemma. *Suppose that* $E_i \in \mathscr{E}(\Theta)$, $i = 1, 2$. *If* E_1 *is exhaustive for* E_2 *then* $E_1 \underset{2}{\supseteq} E_2$.

Proof. If we use the notations of Definition 23.3 then for every $\varphi_2 \in \mathscr{F}(\Omega_2, \mathscr{A}_2)$ the critical function

$$\varphi_1 : \omega_1 \mapsto \int \varphi_2(\omega_2)\, K(\omega_1, d\omega_2),\ \omega_1 \in \Omega_1,$$

is in $\mathscr{F}(\Omega_1, \mathscr{A}_1)$ and satisfies $P_{1,\vartheta}\varphi_1 = P_{2,\vartheta}\varphi_2$ for every $\vartheta \in \Theta$. □

23.7 Corollary. *Suppose that* $E = (\Omega, \mathscr{A}, \mathscr{P})$ *is a dominated experiment and* $\mathscr{A}_0 \subseteq \mathscr{A}$ *a sub-σ-field. If* $E|\mathscr{A}_0$ *is exhaustive for* E *then* $\mathscr{A}_0$ *is E-sufficient.*

Proof. Combine Lemma 23.6 and Theorem 22.2. □

23.8 Corollary (Bahadur [1955]; Sacksteder [1967]; Heyer [1972]). *Suppose that* $E = (\Omega, \mathscr{A}, \mathscr{P})$ *is a dominated experiment and* $T: (\Omega, \mathscr{A}) \to (\Omega_1, \mathscr{A}_1)$ *is a measurable mapping. If* $T_* E$ *is exhaustive for* E *then* T *is E-sufficient.*

Proof. (Pfanzagl [1974]). Combine Lemma 23.6 and Corollary 22.4. □

The converse assertions of Corollaries 23.7 and 23.8 (Example 23.4 (2) and (4)) depend on regularity properties of the underlying measure spaces. This is the reason why the concept of exhaustivity has been considered as unsatisfactory. In the next two paragraphs we deal with a generalization of exhaustivity which does not rely on kernels but on linear operators.

We finish this section discussing the problem of determining critical functions by power functions.

Corollary 22.6 shows that if a power function is available for an experiment $F \in \mathscr{E}(\Theta)$ then it is also available for every experiment $E \in \mathscr{E}(\Theta)$ which is more informative than F. It may happen that in E the power function determines the underlying critical function uniquely. Does this property carry over to the experiment F? For an application see Corollary 26.5.

23.9 Theorem. *Suppose that* $E = (\Omega, \mathscr{A}, \{P_\vartheta : \vartheta \in \Theta\})$ *is a dominated experiment and is exhaustive for* $F = (\Omega_1, \mathscr{A}_1, \{Q_\vartheta : \vartheta \in \Theta\})$. *Let* $\varphi \in \mathscr{F}(\Omega, \mathscr{A})$ *and* $\psi \in \mathscr{F}(\Omega_1, \mathscr{A}_1)$ *be critical functions such that* $P_\vartheta \varphi = Q_\vartheta \psi$, $\vartheta \in \Theta$. *If* φ *is nonrandomized and uniquely determined by its power function then* ψ *is also nonrandomized and uniquely determined by its power function.*

Proof. Suppose that $\psi_1, \psi_2 \in \mathscr{F}(\Omega_1, \mathscr{A}_1)$ are such that $Q_\vartheta \psi_1 = Q_\vartheta \psi_2 = P_\vartheta \varphi$, $\vartheta \in \Theta$. Define $\psi := \frac{1}{2}(\psi_1 + \psi_2)$. Then also ψ has the same power function as φ.

If ψ is non-randomized then the assertion follows from Lemma 7.15. Let us prove that ψ is non-randomized.

Let $K: \Omega \times \mathscr{A}_1 \to [0,1]$ be a stochastic kernel such that $Q_\vartheta = KP_\vartheta$, $\vartheta \in \Theta$. Then $\tilde{\varphi} := \psi K$ is a critical function in $\mathscr{F}(\Omega, \mathscr{A})$ which has the same power function as φ. Hence it follows that $\varphi = \psi K$ P_ϑ-a.e., $\vartheta \in \Theta$. Now,

$$\begin{aligned}\int (\psi - \psi^2)\, dQ_\vartheta &= \int (\psi K)\, dP_\vartheta - \int \psi^2 K\, dP_\vartheta \\ &\leqq \int \varphi\, dP_\vartheta - \int \varphi^2\, dP_\vartheta = 0, \ \vartheta \in \Theta,\end{aligned}$$

since φ is non-randomized. Hence the assertion. □

The condition that φ is non-randomized cannot be dispensed with as the following theorem shows. It is the most simple special case of a general result of LeCam [1979] (see Theorem 63.6).

23.10 Theorem. *Suppose that $E = (\Omega, \mathscr{A}, \{P_\vartheta: \vartheta \in \Theta\})$ is a dominated experiment and $\varphi \in \mathscr{F}(\Omega, \mathscr{A})$. Assume that the following is valid: Whenever E is exhaustive for an experiment $F = (\Omega_1, \mathscr{A}_1, \{Q_\vartheta: \vartheta \in \Theta\})$ and $\psi \in \mathscr{F}(\Omega_1, \mathscr{A}_1)$ satisfies $P_\vartheta \varphi = Q_\vartheta \psi$, $\vartheta \in \Theta$, then ψ is uniquely determined by its power function. Then φ is non-randomized.*

Proof. Let $F = (\{0,1\} \times \Omega, 2^{\{0,1\}} \otimes \mathscr{A}, \{Q_\vartheta: \vartheta \in \Theta\})$ be such that

$$Q_\vartheta(\{0\} \times A) = \int_A (1 - \varphi)\, dP_\vartheta,$$

$$Q_\vartheta(\{1\} \times A) = \int_A \varphi\, dP_\vartheta,$$

$A \in \mathscr{A}$, $\vartheta \in \Theta$. Then E is exhaustive for F since

$$K(\omega, \{0\} \times A) := (1 - \varphi(\omega))\, 1_A(\omega),$$
$$K(\omega, \{1\} \times A) := \varphi(\omega)\, 1_A(\omega),$$

$\omega \in \Omega$, $A \in \mathscr{A}$, defines a stochastic kernel satisfying

$$Q_\vartheta(B \times A) = \int K(\omega, B \times A)\, P_\vartheta(d\omega)$$

for $\vartheta \in \Theta$, $B \subseteq \{0,1\}$, $A \in \mathscr{A}$. For the experiment F there exists a critical function ψ with power function $\vartheta \mapsto P_\vartheta \varphi$, $\vartheta \in \Theta$, namely

$$\psi(x, \omega) := x, \ x \in \{0,1\}, \ \omega \in \Omega.$$

By assumption, ψ is uniquely determined by its power function. Moreover, ψ is non-randomized. Since F is exhaustive for E, we may apply Theorem 23.9 with E and F interchanged. This implies that φ is non-randomized. □

24. Randomization of experiments

Let us begin with some general remarks. Let $(\Omega_i, \mathscr{A}_i, \nu_i)$, $i = 1, 2$, be σ-finite measure spaces.

24.1 Definition. A positive, linear operator
$M_1: L_1(\Omega_1, \mathscr{A}_1, \nu_1) \to L_1(\Omega_2, \mathscr{A}_2, \nu_2)$ is a *stochastic operator* or a *transition* if $\|M_1 g\|_1 = \|g\|_1$ for every $g \in L_1^+(\Omega_1)$.

It follows by definition that any stochastic operator is continuous.

24.2 Definition. A positive, linear operator
$M_2: L_\infty(\Omega_2, \mathscr{A}_2, \nu_2) \to L_\infty(\Omega_1, \mathscr{A}_1, \nu_1)$ is a *Markov operator* if $M_2 1 = 1$ and if $f_n \downarrow 0$, $(f_n)_{n \in \mathbb{N}} \subseteq L_\infty(\Omega_2)$, imply $M_2 f_n \downarrow 0$.

Again, it follows by definition that every Markov operator is continuous.

24.3 Definition. Let $M_1: L_1(\Omega_1) \to L_1(\Omega_2)$ and $M_2: L_\infty(\Omega_2) \to L_\infty(\Omega_1)$ be continuous linear operators. Then (M_1, M_2) is a *dual pair* if

$$\int f(M_1 g)\, d\nu_2 = \int (M_2 f) g\, d\nu_1$$

for all $g \in L_1(\Omega_1)$, $f \in L_\infty(\Omega_2)$.

24.4 Theorem. *For every stochastic operator $M_1: L_1(\Omega_1) \to L_1(\Omega_2)$ there is a uniquely determined continuous linear operator $M_2: L_\infty(\Omega_2) \to L_\infty(\Omega_1)$ which is dual to M_1. M_2 is a Markov operator.*

Proof. For every $f \in L_\infty(\Omega_2)$ we define a linear function

$$L_f: g \mapsto \int f(M_1 g)\, d\nu_2, \quad g \in L_1(\Omega_1).$$

Since

$$|L_f(g)| \leqq \|M_1 g\|_1 \|f\|_\infty = \|g\|_1 \|f\|_\infty, \quad g \in L_1(\Omega_1),$$

it follows that $L_f \in (L_1(\Omega_1))^*$. Hence there is $M_2 f \in L_\infty(\Omega_1)$ such that

$$L_f(g) = \int g(M_2 f)\, d\nu_1 \quad \text{if} \quad g \in L_1(\Omega_1).$$

It is obvious that $M_2: L_\infty(\Omega_2) \to L_\infty(\Omega_1)$ is a linear operator. It is positive since $f \geqq 0$ and $M_1 \geqq 0$ imply $L_f \geqq 0$. It is a Markov operator since

$$\begin{aligned} \int (M_2 1) g\, d\nu_1 &= \int 1(M_1 g)\, d\nu_2 = \|M_1 g\|_1 = \|g\|_1 \\ &= \int g\, d\nu_1, \quad g \in L_1^+(\Omega_1), \end{aligned}$$

implies $M_2 1 = 1$, and because $f_n \downarrow 0$, $(f_n) \subseteq L_\infty(\Omega_2)$, implies

$$\begin{aligned} \int (\lim M_2 f_n) g\, d\nu_1 &= \lim \int (M_2 f_n) g\, d\nu_1 \\ &= \int f_n(M_1 g)\, d\nu_2 = 0. \qquad \square \end{aligned}$$

24.5 Theorem. *For every Markov operator $M_2: L_\infty(\Omega_2) \to L_\infty(\Omega_1)$ there is a uniquely determined continuous linear operator $M_1: L_1(\Omega_1) \to L_1(\Omega_2)$ which is dual to M_2. M_1 is a stochastic operator.*

Proof. For every $g \in L_1(\Omega_1)$ define a linear function

$$L_g: f \mapsto \int (M_2 f) g\, dv, \quad f \in L_\infty(\Omega_2).$$

If $f_n \downarrow 0$, $(f_n) \subseteq L_\infty(\Omega_2)$, then we have $M_2 f_n \downarrow 0$ which implies $L_g(f_n) \to 0$. Hence, there is $M_1 g \in L_1(\Omega_2)$ such that

$$L_g(f) = \int f(M_1 g)\, dv_2 \quad \text{if} \quad f \in L_\infty(\Omega_2).$$

Obviously, $M_1: L_1(\Omega_1) \to L_1(\Omega_1)$ is a positive operator. It is a stochastic operator since

$$\begin{aligned} \|M_1 g\|_1 = \int (M_1 g)\, dv_2 &= \int (M_2 1) g\, dv_1 = \int g\, dv_1 \\ &= \|g\|_1, \quad g \in L_1^+(\Omega_1). \quad \square \end{aligned}$$

Now, we return to statistical questions. We begin with the definition of two characteristic Banach spaces of an experiment E. More on this subject is contained in sections 41 and 57.

24.6 Definition. Let $E = (\Omega, \mathscr{A}, \mathscr{P})$ be a dominated experiment and let $\mathscr{P} \sim v$ where $v|\mathscr{A}$ is σ-finite. Then the Banach space $L_1(\Omega, \mathscr{A}, v)$ is called *L-space of E* and is denoted by $L(E)$.

24.7 Remark. Any two L-spaces of a dominated experiment are isometrically isomorphic (relative to linear and order structure) to each other. Indeed, let $\mathscr{P} \sim v_1$ and $\mathscr{P} \sim v_2$. If $f \in L_1(\Omega, \mathscr{A}, v_1)$ then $f \dfrac{dv_1}{dv_2} \in L_1(\Omega, \mathscr{A}, v_2)$ and $\|f\|_{1, v_1} = \left\| f \dfrac{dv_1}{dv_2} \right\|_{1, v_2}$. Moreover, the L-space can be identified with the space of signed measures $\sigma \ll v_i$, $i = 1, 2$.

24.8 Definition. Let $E = (\Omega, \mathscr{A}, \mathscr{P})$ be a dominated experiment and $\mathscr{P} \sim v$ where $v|\mathscr{A}$ is σ-finite. Then the Banach space $L_\infty(\Omega, \mathscr{A}, v)$ is called *M-space of E* and is denoted by $M(E)$.

24.9 Remark. Any two M-spaces of a dominated experiment are isometrically isomorphic (relative to linear and order structure) to each other. This follows immediately from the fact that $v_1 \sim v_2$ implies $L_\infty(\Omega, \mathscr{A}, v_1) = L_\infty(\Omega, \mathscr{A}, v_2)$.

24.10 Definition. Let $E_i = (\Omega_i, \mathscr{A}_i, \{P_{i,\vartheta}: \vartheta \in \Theta\})$ be dominated experiments and $L(E_i) = L_1(\Omega_i, \mathscr{A}_i, v_i)$, $i = 1, 2$. The experiment E_2 is a *randomization* of E_1

if any of the following two equivalent conditions is satisfied:

(1) There is a stochastic operator $M_1: L(E_1) \to L(E_2)$ such that $\frac{dP_{2,\vartheta}}{d\nu_2} = M_1\left(\frac{dP_{1,\vartheta}}{d\nu_1}\right)$ for every $\vartheta \in \Theta$.

(2) There is a Markov operator $M_2: M(E_2) \to M(E_1)$ such that $P_{1,\vartheta} \circ M_2 = P_{2,\vartheta}$ for every $\vartheta \in \Theta$.

First we show that randomization is a weaker concept then exhaustivity.

24.11 Theorem. *Suppose that $E_i = (\Omega_i, \mathscr{A}_i, \{P_{i,\vartheta}: \vartheta \in \Theta)$, $i = 1, 2$, are dominated experiments. If E_1 is exhaustive for E_2 then E_2 is a randomization of E_1.*

Proof. Let $K: \Omega_1 \times \mathscr{A}_2 \to [0, 1]$ be a kernel which satisfies

$$P_{2,\vartheta}(A_2) = \int K(\omega_1, A_2) P_{1,\vartheta}(d\omega_1)$$

for every $A_2 \in \mathscr{A}_2$, $\vartheta \in \Theta$. For every $g \in M(E_2)$ define

$$M_2 g: \omega_1 \mapsto \int g(\omega_2) K(\omega_1, d\omega_2), \quad \omega_1 \in \Omega_1.$$

Then $M_2: M(E_2) \to M(E_1)$ is a Markov operator which satisfies $P_{1,\vartheta} \circ M_2 = P_{2,\vartheta}$, $\vartheta \in \Theta$. □

Now, it follows that $E|\mathscr{A}_0$ and $T_* E$ are randomizations of E whenever $E = (\Omega, \mathscr{A}, \mathscr{P})$ is a dominated experiment, $\mathscr{A}_0 \subseteq \mathscr{A}$ a sub-σ-field and $T: (\Omega, \mathscr{A}) \to (\Omega_1, \mathscr{A}_1)$ a measurable mapping.

For the converse of Theorem 24.11 additional regularity conditions are needed.

24.12 Theorem. *Suppose that $E_i = (\Omega_i, \mathscr{A}_i, \{P_{i,\vartheta}: \vartheta \in \Theta\})$, $i = 1, 2$, are dominated experiments. Assume that Ω_2 is a locally compact space with countable base and $\mathscr{A}_2$ is its Borel σ-field. If E_2 is a randomization of E_1 then E_1 is exhaustive for E_2.*

Proof. Essentially, this is Theorem 6.11. Details are left to the reader. □

It turns out that the concept of randomization is a proper generalization of sufficiency.

24.13 Theorem. *Suppose that $E = (\Omega, \mathscr{A}, \{P_\vartheta: \vartheta \in \Theta\})$ is a dominated experiment and $\mathscr{A}_0 \subseteq \mathscr{A}$ is a sub-σ-field. Then the following assertions are equivalent:*

(1) *$\mathscr{A}_0$ is E-sufficient.*

(2) *$E|\mathscr{A}_0 \underset{2}{\sim} E$.*

(3) *E is a randomization of $E|\mathscr{A}_0$.*

Proof. The equivalence (1) $\Leftrightarrow$ (2) has been proved in Theorem 22.2.

(3) $\Rightarrow$ (2): Let $\varphi \in \mathscr{F}(\Omega, \mathscr{A})$ and M_2 be a Markov operator satisfying 24.10 (2). If $\tilde{\varphi}$ denotes the element of $M(E)$ which contains φ then $M_2\tilde{\varphi} \in M(E|\mathscr{A}_0)$ contains a critical function $\varphi_0 \in \mathscr{F}(\Omega, \mathscr{A}_0)$. From $(P_\vartheta|\mathscr{A}_0)(M_2\tilde{\varphi}) = P_\vartheta\tilde{\varphi}$ it follows that

$$(P_\vartheta|\mathscr{A}_0)(\varphi_0) = P_\vartheta\varphi$$

for every $\vartheta \in \Theta$. This proves (2).

(1) $\Rightarrow$ (3): Denote $\mathscr{P} = \{P_\vartheta\colon \vartheta \in \Theta\}$. Let $Q_0 \in C(\mathscr{P})$ be such that $Q_0 \sim \mathscr{P}$. We may choose $L(E) = L_1(\Omega, \mathscr{A}, Q_0)$ and $L(E|\mathscr{A}_0) = L_1(\Omega, \mathscr{A}_0, Q_0)$. Let $M_1\colon L_1(\Omega, \mathscr{A}_0, Q_0) \to L_1(\Omega, \mathscr{A}, Q_0)$ be the operator such that for every Q_0-equivalence class $f \in L_1(\Omega, \mathscr{A}_0, Q_0)$ the value $M_1 f$ is the corresponding equivalence class in $L_1(\Omega, \mathscr{A}, Q_0)$. Note that the functions in $M_1 f$ are $\bar{\mathscr{A}}_0$-measurable where $\bar{\mathscr{A}}_0$ denotes the Q_0-completion of $\mathscr{A}_0$ in $\mathscr{A}$. It is obvious that M_1 is a stochastic operator. It remains to show that $M_1\left(\frac{dP_\vartheta|\mathscr{A}_0}{dQ_0|\mathscr{A}_0}\right) = \frac{dP_\vartheta|\mathscr{A}}{dQ_0|\mathscr{A}}$ for every $\vartheta \in \Theta$. This follows from 20.6 where it is shown that $\frac{dP_\vartheta|\mathscr{A}}{dQ_0|\mathscr{A}}$ is $\bar{\mathscr{A}}_0$-measurable for every $\vartheta \in \Theta$. □

24.14 Remark. Suppose that $E = (\Omega, \mathscr{A}, \mathscr{P})$ is a dominated experiment and let $\bar{\mathscr{A}}$ be the $\mathscr{P}$-completion of $\mathscr{A}$. Define $\bar{E} = (\Omega, \bar{\mathscr{A}}, \mathscr{P})$. Then it is obvious that $\bar{E}|\mathscr{A} = E$ and hence E is a randomization of $\bar{E}$. On the other hand we note that $\mathscr{A}$ is $\bar{E}$-sufficient. Hence Theorem 24.13 implies that $\bar{E}$ is a randomization of E.

24.15 Theorem. *Suppose that $E = (\Omega, \mathscr{A}, \{P_\vartheta\colon \vartheta \in \Theta\})$ is a dominated experiment and $T\colon (\Omega, \mathscr{A}) \to (\Omega_1, \mathscr{A}_1)$ is a measurable mapping. Then the following assertions are equivalent:*

(1) *T is E-sufficient.*
(2) *$E \underset{2}{\sim} T_* E$.*
(3) *E is a randomization of $T_* E$.*

Proof. The equivalence (1) $\Leftrightarrow$ (2) follows from 22.4. The further arguments rely on Lemma 23.5 which implies that $T_* E$ and $E|T^{-1}(\mathscr{A}_1)$ are mutual randomizations of each other. From Theorem 24.13 we obtain that (1) is equivalent with the fact that E is a randomization of $E|T^{-1}(\mathscr{A}_1)$. Since the relation of being a randomization is transitive it follows that E is a randomization of $T_* E$. Conversely, another application of transitivity shows that E is a randomization of $E|T^{-1}(\mathscr{A}_1)$ if it is a randomization of $T_* E$. This implies (1). □

The implication (3) $\Rightarrow$ (2) of Theorem 24.13 has an immediate generalization to arbitrary pairs of dominated experiments.

24.16 Theorem. *If a dominated experiment $F \in \mathscr{E}(\Theta)$ is a randomization of a dominated experiment $E \in \mathscr{E}(\Theta)$ then $E \underset{2}{\supseteq} F$.*

Proof. Denote $E = (\Omega_1, \mathscr{A}_1, \{P_\vartheta: \vartheta \in \Theta\})$ and $F = (\Omega_2, \mathscr{A}_2, \{Q_\vartheta: \vartheta \in \Theta\})$. Let $M_1: L(E) \to L(F)$ be a transition such that $M_1 P_\vartheta = Q_\vartheta, \vartheta \in \Theta$. If $\varphi \in \mathscr{F}(\Omega_2, \mathscr{A}_2)$ let $\bar{\varphi}$ be the corresponding class in $M(F)$. Let M_2 be the Markov operator which is dual to M_1. Then for $\psi \in M_2 \bar{\varphi}$, $0 \leqq \psi \leqq 1$, we have $P_\vartheta \psi = P_\vartheta(M_2 \bar{\varphi}) = (M_1 P_\vartheta)(\bar{\varphi}) = Q_\vartheta \bar{\varphi} = Q_\vartheta \varphi$, $\vartheta \in \Theta$. □

The converse of the preceding assertion is not valid. The order structure which is defined by the relation "is a randomization of" does not coincide with the order structure $\underset{2}{\subseteq}$. A decision theoretic interpretation of the former order structure is possible and is established in Chapter 9. However, both order structures induce the same equivalence relation. This is proved for dominated experiments in the following section.

24.17 Remark. Finally, we note that Theorem (23.9) remains valid if the assumption of exhaustivity is replaced by the assumption that F is a randomization of E. For proving this, repeat the proof of Theorem (23.9) using a pair of operators instead of the kernel K.

25. Statistical isomorphism

25.1 Definition. Two dominated experiments in $\mathscr{E}(\Theta)$ are *statistically isomorphic* if each is a randomization of the other.

25.2 Example. If $E = (\Omega, \mathscr{A}, \{P_\vartheta: \vartheta \in \Theta\})$ is an experiment and $\mathscr{A}_0 \subseteq \mathscr{A}$ is a sub-σ-field then E and $E|\mathscr{A}_0$ are statistically isomorphic iff $E \underset{2}{\sim} E|\mathscr{A}_0$. This is a consequence of Theorem 24.13.

We shall prove in this section that two dominated experiments E and F are statistically isomorphic iff $E \underset{2}{\sim} F$. This result is a particular case of the randomization criterion which is proved in full generality in section 55. First, we consider finite experiments.

25.3 Definition (Blackwell [1951]). Let Θ be a finite set and $E = (\Omega, \mathscr{A}, \{P_\vartheta: \vartheta \in \Theta\})$ an experiment. Then

$$\sigma_E := \mathscr{L}\left(\left(\frac{dP_\vartheta}{d \sum\limits_{\sigma \in \Theta} P_\sigma}\right)_{\vartheta \in \Theta} \Bigg| \sum_{\sigma \in \Theta} P_\sigma\right)$$

is the *standard measure* of E.

25.4 Theorem (Blackwell [1951]). *Let Θ be a finite set and $E, F \in \mathscr{E}(\Theta)$. Then F is a randomization of E iff there exists a stochastic kernel $K: S_\Theta \times \mathscr{B}(S_\Theta) \to [0,1]$ satisfying the following conditions:*

(1) $\int p_\vartheta(y) K(x, dy) = p_\vartheta(x), \quad x \in S_\Theta, \vartheta \in \Theta.$

(2) $\sigma_E(A) = \int K(x, A)\, \sigma_F(dx), \quad A \in \mathscr{B}(S_\Theta).$

Proof. Assume that $F = (\Omega_2, \mathscr{A}_2, \{Q_\vartheta: \vartheta \in \Theta\})$ is a randomization of $E = (\Omega_1, \mathscr{A}_1, \{P_\vartheta: \vartheta \in \Theta\})$. For E and F we define the so-called standard experiments

$$E_s := (S_\Theta, \mathscr{B}(S_\Theta), \{p_\vartheta \sigma_E: \vartheta \in \Theta\}), \quad \text{and}$$
$$F_s := (S_\Theta, \mathscr{B}(S_\Theta), \{p_\vartheta \sigma_F: \vartheta \in \Theta\}).$$

Let

$$T_1: \omega_1 \mapsto \left(\frac{dP_\vartheta}{d \sum_{\sigma \in \Theta} P_\sigma} (\omega_1) \right)_{\vartheta \in \Theta}, \quad \omega_1 \in \Omega_1,$$

$$T_2: \omega_2 \mapsto \left(\frac{dQ_\vartheta}{d \sum_{\sigma \in \Theta} Q_\sigma} (\omega_2) \right)_{\vartheta \in \Theta}, \quad \omega_2 \in \Omega_2.$$

Then T_1 is E-sufficient, T_2 is F-sufficient and $E_s = T_{1,*}E$, $F_s = T_{2,*}F$. It follows from Theorem 24.15 that E is a randomization of E_s. By assumption F is a randomization E, and by Example 23.4 (3) and Theorem 24.11, F_s is a randomization of F. It follows that F_s is a randomization of E_s and Theorem 24.12 implies, that E_s is even exhaustive for F_s. Hence, there exists a stochastic kernel $M: S_\Theta \times \mathscr{B}(S_\Theta) \to [0,1]$ such that

$$\int_A p_\vartheta \, d\sigma_F = \int M(.,A) p_\vartheta \, d\sigma_E, \; A \in \mathscr{B}(S_\Theta), \quad \vartheta \in \Theta.$$

Let $\mu | \mathscr{B}(S_\Theta) \times \mathscr{B}(S_\Theta)$ be the probability measure which is defined by

$$\mu(A_1 \times A_2) = \int_{A_1} M(x, A_2)\, \sigma_E(dx), \; A_i \in \mathscr{B}(S_\Theta), \quad i = 1, 2.$$

Let $K: S_\Theta \times \mathscr{B}(S_\Theta) \to [0,1]$ be a stochastic kernel such that

$$\begin{aligned} \mu(A_1 \times A_2) &= \int_{A_2} K(x, A_1)\, \mu(dx, S_\Theta) \\ &= \int_{A_2} K(x, A_1)\, \sigma_F(dx), \; A_i \in \mathscr{B}(S_\Theta), \quad i = 1, 2. \end{aligned}$$

It is obvious that K satisfies condition (2). Moreover, we have

$$\begin{aligned} \int_A p_\vartheta \, d\sigma_F &= \int M(.,A) p_\vartheta \, d\sigma_E = \int_A p_\vartheta \, d\mu \\ &= \int_A \int p_\vartheta(y) K(., dy)\, d\sigma_F \end{aligned}$$

for $\vartheta \in \Theta$ and every $A_2 \in \mathscr{B}(S_\Theta)$. Eventually improving K on a set of σ_F-measure zero yields a kernel satisfying condition (1).

Repeating this proof in reversed order yields the proof of the converse. □

Using the terminology of potential theory we have obtained that F is a randomization of E iff σ_E is a *dilation* of σ_F.

25.5 Corollary. *Let Θ be a finite set and $E, F \in \mathscr{E}(\Theta)$. Then E and F are statistically isomorphic iff $\sigma_E = \sigma_F$.*

Proof. Assume that E and F are statistically isomorphic. Let us apply Theorem (5.19). For $z \in S_T$ the function

$$\psi_z\colon (x_t)_{t\in T} \mapsto \prod_{t\in T} x_t^{z_t},\ (x_t)_{t\in T} \in S_T,$$

is concave. Since σ_E is a dilation of σ_F we have

$$\begin{aligned} H(\sigma_E) &= \int \psi_z\, d\sigma_E = \int\int \psi_z(y)\, K(x, dy)\, \sigma_F(dx) \\ &\leqq \int \psi_z\left(\int y\, K(x, dy)\right) \sigma_F(dx) \\ &= \int \psi_z\, d\sigma_F = H(\sigma_F). \end{aligned}$$

Since also σ_F is a dilation of σ_E we have $H(\sigma_F) \leqq H(\sigma_E)$ which implies $H(\sigma_E) = H(\sigma_F)$.

Assume conversely, that $\sigma_E = \sigma_F$. Then with the notation of the proof of Theorem 25.4 we have $E_s = F_s$. Since both E and E_s, and F and F_s are statistically isomorphic it follows that E and F are statistically isomorphic, too. □

Statistical isomorphism can be expressed in terms of the likelihood processes. Let $E = (\Omega_1, \mathscr{A}_1, \{P_\vartheta \in \Theta\})$ and $F = (\Omega_2, \mathscr{A}_2, \{Q_\vartheta\colon \vartheta \in \Theta\})$. Then $\left(\dfrac{dP_\sigma}{dP_\vartheta}\right)_{\sigma\in\Theta}$ and $\left(\dfrac{dQ_\sigma}{dQ_\vartheta}\right)_{\sigma\in\Theta}$ are the likelihood processes of E and F with base ϑ.

25.6 Corollary. *Let Θ be a finite set and $E, F \in \mathscr{E}(\Theta)$. Then E and F are statistically isomorphic iff*

$$\mathscr{L}\left(\left(\frac{dP_\sigma}{dP_\vartheta}\right)_{\sigma\in\Theta} \middle| P_\vartheta\right) = \mathscr{L}\left(\left(\frac{dQ_\sigma}{dQ_\vartheta}\right)_{\vartheta\in\Theta} \middle| Q_\vartheta\right)$$

for every $\vartheta \in \Theta$.

Proof. Assume that E and F are statistically isomorphic. Then we have $\sigma_E = \sigma_F$. Let $\vartheta \in \Theta$ and $z \in S_\Theta$ such that $z_\vartheta \neq 0$. Easy computations yield

$$\int \prod_{\sigma \neq \vartheta} \left(\frac{dP_\sigma}{dP_\vartheta}\right)^{z_\sigma} dP_\vartheta = H(\sigma_E)(z) = H(\sigma_F)(z) = \int \prod_{\sigma \neq \vartheta} \left(\frac{dQ_\sigma}{dQ_\vartheta}\right)^{z_\sigma} dQ_\vartheta .$$

An application of Theorem 5.13 proves one part of the assertion. For the other part we note that

$$\frac{dP_\sigma}{d \sum_{\tau \in \Theta} P_\tau} = \frac{\dfrac{dP_\sigma}{dP_\vartheta}}{1 + \sum_{\tau \neq \sigma} \dfrac{dP_\tau}{dP_\vartheta}} \quad P_\vartheta\text{-a.e.} \quad \text{if} \quad \sigma \neq \vartheta,$$

and

$$\frac{dP_\vartheta}{d \sum_{\tau \in \Theta} P_\tau} = \frac{1}{1 + \sum_{\tau \neq \vartheta} \dfrac{dP_\tau}{dP_\vartheta}} \quad P_\vartheta\text{-a.e.}$$

Since a similar relation holds with P replaced by Q, it follows from the assumption, that

$$\mathscr{L}\left(\left(\frac{dP_\sigma}{d \sum_{\tau \in \Theta} P_\tau}\right)_{\sigma \in \Theta} \middle| P_\vartheta\right) = \mathscr{L}\left(\left(\frac{dQ_\sigma}{d \sum_{\tau \in \Theta} Q_\tau}\right)_{\sigma \in \Theta} \middle| Q_\vartheta\right)$$

for every $\vartheta \in \Theta$. Adding these equalities for all $\vartheta \in \Theta$ the assertion $\sigma_E = \sigma_F$ follows. □

Now, we are in the position to prove the randomization criterion for finite experiments.

25.7 Theorem. *Let Θ be a finite set and $E, F \in \mathscr{E}(\Theta)$. Then E and F are statistically isomorphic iff $E \underset{2}{\sim} F$.*

Proof. One part of the assertion is a consequence of Theorem 24.16. Assume conversely that $E \underset{2}{\sim} F$. Let $m \in S_\Theta$. Theorem 22.5 implies that

$$\left\| \frac{a}{|\Theta|} \sum_{\sigma \in \Theta} P_\sigma + b \sum_{\sigma \in \Theta} m_\sigma P_\sigma \right\| = \left\| \frac{a}{|\Theta|} \sum_{\sigma \in \Theta} Q_\sigma + b \sum_{\sigma \in \Theta} m_\sigma Q_\sigma \right\|$$

for all $a, b \in \mathbb{R}$. Let $P_0 = \frac{1}{|\Theta|} \sum_{\sigma \in \Theta} P_\sigma$, $P_1 = \sum_{\sigma \in \Theta} m_\sigma P_\sigma$, $Q_0 = \frac{1}{|\Theta|} \sum_{\sigma \in \Theta} Q_\sigma$, $Q_1 = \sum_{\sigma \in \Theta} m_\sigma Q_\sigma$. Another application of Theorem (22.5) yields $(P_0, P_1) \underset{2}{\sim} (Q_0, Q_1)$.

From Corollary 16.5 we obtain

$$\mathscr{L}\left(\frac{dP_1}{dP_0} \middle| P_0\right) = \mathscr{L}\left(\frac{dQ_1}{dQ_0} \middle| Q_0\right)$$

which implies

$$\mathscr{L}\left(\sum_{\vartheta\in\Theta} m_\vartheta \frac{dP_\vartheta}{d\sum\limits_{\sigma\in\Theta} P_\sigma} \,\middle|\, \frac{1}{|\Theta|}\sum_{\sigma\in\Theta} P_\sigma\right)$$

$$= \mathscr{L}\left(\sum_{\vartheta\in\Theta} m_\vartheta \frac{dQ_\vartheta}{d\sum\limits_{\sigma\in\Theta} Q_\sigma} \,\middle|\, \frac{1}{|\Theta|}\sum_{\sigma\in\Theta} Q_\sigma\right).$$

This is valid for every $m \in S_\Theta$ and therefore it follows easily that $\sigma_E = \sigma_F$. This proves the assertion by Corollary 25.5. □

The case of arbitrary dominated experiments is a little bit more involved.

25.8 Theorem. *Suppose that $E, F \in \mathscr{E}(\Theta)$ are dominated experiments. Then E and F are statistically isomorphic iff $E \underset{2}{\sim} F$.*

Proof. Again, one part of the assertion is a consequence of Theorem 24.16. Assuming that $E \underset{2}{\sim} F$ it follows from Theorem 22.5 that the mapping $P_\vartheta \mapsto Q_\vartheta$ defines a linear isometry between span $\{P_\vartheta: \vartheta \in \Theta\}$ and span $\{Q_\vartheta: \vartheta \in \Theta\}$. It can therefore be extended to a linear isometry between $\overline{\text{span}}\,\{P_\vartheta: \vartheta \in \Theta\}$ and $\overline{\text{span}}$ $\{Q_\vartheta: \vartheta \in \Theta\}$. Let $P_0 \in C(\mathscr{P})$ such that $P_0 \sim \{P_\vartheta: \vartheta \in \Theta\}$ and let Q_0 be the image of P_0 under the isometry defined above. Another application of Theorem 22.5 implies that

$$(\Omega_1, \mathscr{A}_1, \{P_\vartheta: \vartheta \in \Theta \cup \{0\}\}) \underset{2}{\sim} (\Omega_2, \mathscr{A}_2, \{Q_\vartheta: \vartheta \in \Theta \cup \{0\}\}).$$

We obtain from Corollary 25.6 that

$$\mathscr{L}\left(\left(\frac{dP_\vartheta}{dP_0}\right)_{\vartheta\in\alpha} \,\middle|\, P_0\right) = \mathscr{L}\left(\left(\frac{dQ_\vartheta}{dQ_0}\right)_{\vartheta\in\alpha} \,\middle|\, Q_0\right)$$

for every $\alpha \in A(\Theta)$ and hence even for $\alpha = \Theta$. Denote this distribution on $\bigotimes_{\vartheta\in\Theta} \mathscr{B}(\mathbb{R}_+)$ by μ. In particular it follows that $Q_0 \sim \{Q_\vartheta: \vartheta \in \Theta\}$. Now, we define the experiment

$$G = (\mathbb{R}_+^\Theta, \bigotimes_{\vartheta\in\Theta} \mathscr{B}(\mathbb{R}_+), \{p_\vartheta \mu: \vartheta \in \Theta\}).$$

Let

$$T_1: \omega_1 \mapsto \left(\frac{dP_\vartheta}{dP_0}(\omega_1)\right)_{\vartheta\in\Theta}, \quad \omega_1 \in \Omega_1,$$

$$T_2: \omega_2 \mapsto \left(\frac{dQ_\vartheta}{dQ_0}(\omega_2)\right)_{\vartheta\in\Theta}, \quad \omega_2 \in \Omega_2.$$

Then we have $T_{1,*}E = G = T_{2,*}F$. Moreover, by Lemma 20.6 the mappings T_1 and T_2 are E- and F-sufficient. Hence, by Theorem 24.15 E and $T_{1,*}E = G$ are statistically isomorphic, and also F and $T_{2,*}F = G$ are statistically isomorphic. This proves that E and F are statistically isomorphic. □

25.9 Corollary. *Two dominated experiments $E = (\Omega_1, \mathscr{A}_1, \{P_\vartheta: \vartheta \in \Theta\})$ and $F = (\Omega_2, \mathscr{A}_2, \{Q_\vartheta: \vartheta \in \Theta\})$ are statistically isomorphic iff*

$$\mathscr{L}\left(\left(\frac{dP_\sigma}{dP_\vartheta}\right)_{\sigma \in \Theta} \middle| P_\vartheta\right) = \mathscr{L}\left(\left(\frac{dQ_\sigma}{dQ_\vartheta}\right)_{\sigma \in \Theta} \middle| Q_\vartheta\right), \quad \vartheta \in \Theta.$$

Proof. Assume that E and F are statistically isomorphic. Then Corollary 25.6 implies that

$$\mathscr{L}\left(\left(\frac{dP_\sigma}{dP_\vartheta}\right)_{\sigma \in \alpha} \middle| P_\vartheta\right) = \mathscr{L}\left(\left(\frac{dQ_\sigma}{dQ_\vartheta}\right)_{\sigma \in \alpha} \middle| Q_\vartheta\right), \quad \vartheta \in \Theta,$$

for every $\alpha \in A(\Theta)$ and hence even for $\alpha = \Theta$.

If conversely the condition is satisfied then it follows from Corollary 25.6 that all finite subexperiments are statistically isomorphic. A glance at Theorems 25.8 and 22.5 shows that in this case even E and F are isomorphic. □

The method of the proof of Theorem 25.8 is restricted to dominated experiments since it rests on a particular construction of a "standard experiment" on $\mathbb{R}_+^\Theta$. For arbitrary experiments this construction is not possible and rather different methods have to be developed to prove similar results. This is done in Chapters 8 and 9.

Chapter 5: Exponential Experiments

The object of the present chapter is to provide the most important facts concerning the testing of linear functions on Gaussian shift experiments. Admittedly, for one-sided testing problems it is possible to give elementary proofs of the basic facts, using only the Neyman-Pearson lemma. But for two-sided testing problems the most convenient way runs over the theory of conditional tests for exponential experiments. However, we discuss exponential experiments only to that extent as is indispensable for our purposes.

Section 26 contains the basic facts on exponential experiments such as reduction by sufficiency and decomposition with respect to a one-dimensional parameter into a mixture of exponential experiments of rank 1. In Section 27 this decomposition is used to develop some theory of conditional tests. The results obtained there are applied to Gaussian shift experiments in Section 28.

The content of Chapter 5 is a purely classical one and its presentation goes back to the book of Lehmann [1959]. A much more detailed discussion of the theory of conditional tests and its applications is offered by Witting [1985].

26. Basic facts

26.1 Definition. Let $(\Omega, \mathscr{A}, \nu)$ be a σ-finite measure space and let $\Theta \subseteq \mathbb{R}^k$ be open and convex. An experiment $E = (\Omega, \mathscr{A}, \{P_\vartheta | \mathscr{A} : \vartheta \in \Theta\})$ is an *exponential experiment* if

$$\frac{dP_\vartheta}{d\nu} = C(\vartheta) h \exp(\langle \vartheta, S \rangle), \quad \vartheta \in \Theta,$$

where $h: \Omega \to \mathbb{R}$ and $S: \Omega \to \mathbb{R}^k$ are $\mathscr{A}$-measurable functions.

By definition every exponential experiment is homogeneous. From Theorem 20.9 it follows that the mapping S is E-sufficient. Hence, by Corollary 22.4, we have $S_* E \underset{2}{\sim} E$. For the analysis of testing problems it is therefore sufficient to consider $S_* E$ instead of E.

26.2 Remark. Suppose that $E = (\Omega, \mathscr{A}, \{P_\vartheta : \vartheta \in \Theta\})$ is an exponential experiment. Let $\mathscr{A}_0 \subseteq \mathscr{A}$ be the σ-field which is induced by S. Since $\mathscr{A}_0$ is E-sufficient there exists a Borel function $h_1: \mathbb{R}^k \to \mathbb{R}$ such that

$$\frac{dP_\vartheta|\mathscr{A}_0}{d\nu|\mathscr{A}_0} = C(\vartheta)\, h_1 \circ S \exp(\langle\vartheta, S\rangle), \quad \vartheta \in \Theta.$$

If we denote $\mu := h_1 \cdot \nu \circ S^{-1}$ then we obtain

$$\frac{d\mathscr{L}(S|P_\vartheta)}{d\mu}(t) = C(\vartheta) \exp(\langle\vartheta, t\rangle), \quad t \in \mathbb{R}^k, \vartheta \in \Theta.$$

Hence $S_* E = (\mathbb{R}^k, \mathscr{B}^k, \{\mathscr{L}(S|P_\vartheta): \vartheta \in \Theta\})$ is an exponential experiment.

26.3 Definition. An exponential experiment $E = (\mathbb{R}^k, \mathscr{B}^k, \{P_\vartheta: \vartheta \in \Theta\})$ is *reduced* if

$$\frac{dP_\vartheta}{d\nu}(t) = C(\vartheta) \exp(\langle\vartheta, t\rangle), \; t \in \mathbb{R}^k, \vartheta \in \Theta.$$

26.4 Theorem. *A reduced exponential experiment $(\mathbb{R}^k, \mathscr{B}^k, \{P_\vartheta: \vartheta \in \Theta\})$ is complete, i.e.: If $g: \mathbb{R}^k \to \mathbb{R}$ is a Borel function satisfying $P_\vartheta|g| < \infty$ and $P_\vartheta g = 0$ for every $\vartheta \in \Theta$, then $g = 0$ ν-a.e.*

Proof. The assertion follows from Theorem 5.7. □

26.5 Corollary. *If E is an arbitrary exponential experiment of the form of 26.1 then every non-randomized critical function which only depends on S is uniquely determined by its power function.*

Proof. The reduced experiment $S_* E$ is complete and therefore every critical function for $S_* E$ is uniquely determined by its power function. From Theorem 24.15 it follows that E is a randomization of $S_* E$. If $\psi = \varphi \circ S \in \mathscr{F}(\Omega, \mathscr{A})$ is non-randomized then $\varphi \in \mathscr{F}(\mathbb{R}^k, \mathscr{B}^k)$ is non-randomized and has the same power function for $S_* E$ as ψ has for E. By Remark 24.17 ψ is uniquely determined by its power function. □

Since we consider only testing problems which involve one single coordinate of $\vartheta \in \Theta$ and treat the other coordinates as nuisance parameters it will be convenient to change our notation. In the following we write the elements of Θ as pairs (ϑ, τ) where $\vartheta \in \mathbb{R}$ and $\tau \in \mathbb{R}^{k-1}$. Let us call the first coordinate ϑ of $(\vartheta, \tau) \in \Theta$ the *structural parameter* and the second coordinate τ the *nuisance parameter*. With this notation the densities of a reduced exponential experiment can be written as

$$\frac{dP_{\vartheta,\tau}}{d\nu}(x, y) = C(\vartheta, \tau)\, e^{\vartheta x} e^{\langle\tau, y\rangle}, \; (x, y) \in \mathbb{R} \times \mathbb{R}^{k-1}, \; (\vartheta, \tau) \in \Theta.$$

The following is the basic decomposition theorem for exponential experiments.

26.6 Theorem. *Suppose that* $E = (\mathbb{R}^k, \mathscr{B}^k, \{P_{\vartheta,\tau}: (\vartheta, \tau) \in \Theta\})$ *is a reduced exponential experiment. Then* $\mathscr{P} = \{P_{\vartheta,\tau}: (\vartheta, \tau) \in \Theta\}$ *can be decomposed in the following way:*
There are Markov kernels $F_\vartheta | \mathscr{B} \times \mathbb{R}^{k-1}$, $\vartheta \in \mathrm{pr}_1(\Theta)$, *and probability measures* $G_{\vartheta,\tau} | \mathscr{B}^{k-1}$, $(\vartheta, \tau) \in \Theta$, *satisfying the relation*

$$P_{\vartheta,\tau}(A) = \int F_\vartheta(A^y, y)\, G_{\vartheta,\tau}(dy),$$

for every $A \in \mathscr{B}^k$, $(\vartheta, \tau) \in \Theta$, *such that*

(1) *for every* $y \in \mathbb{R}^{k-1}$ *the experiment* $(\mathbb{R}, \mathscr{B}, \{F_\vartheta(.\,, y): \vartheta \in \mathrm{pr}_1(\Theta)\})$ *is a reduced exponential experiment of rank 1, and*

(2) *for every* $\vartheta \in \Theta$ *the experiment* $(\mathbb{R}^{k-1}, \mathscr{B}^{k-1}, \{G_{\vartheta,\tau}: \tau \in \Theta^\vartheta\})$ *is a reduced exponential experiment.*

Proof. There is a probability measure $P | \mathscr{B}^k$ and a $\mathscr{B}^k$-measurable function $h: \mathbb{R} \times \mathbb{R}^{k-1} \to \mathbb{R}_+$ such that

$$P_{\vartheta,\tau}(A) = C(\vartheta, \tau) \int_A e^{\vartheta x + \langle \tau, y \rangle} h(x, y)\, P(dx, dy)$$

for $A \in \mathscr{B}^k$, $(\vartheta, \tau) \in \Theta$. Take for example some $(\vartheta_0, \tau_0) \in \Theta$ and define $P := P_{\vartheta_0, \tau_0}$. The probability measure $P | \mathscr{B}^k$ can be decomposed by a regular conditional probability $Q | \mathbb{R}^{k-1} \times \mathscr{B}$ such that

$$P(A) = \int Q(y, A^y)\, P_0(dy), \quad A \in \mathscr{B}^k,$$

where $P_0 = P | \mathscr{B}^{k-1} \times \mathbb{R}$. It follows that for every $A \in \mathscr{B}^k$ and every $(\vartheta, \tau) \in \Theta$

$$P_{\vartheta,\tau}(A) = C(\vartheta, \tau) \int_{\mathbb{R}^{k-1}} \int_{A^y} e^{\vartheta x} e^{\langle \tau, y \rangle} h(x, y)\, Q(y, dx)\, P_0(dy).$$

Let us define

$$k(y, \vartheta) := \int_{\mathbb{R}} e^{\vartheta x} h(x, y)\, Q(y, dx), \; (y, \vartheta) \in \mathbb{R}^{k-1} \times \mathrm{pr}_1(\Theta).$$

It is obvious that for every $\vartheta \in \mathrm{pr}_1(\Theta)$ we have $P_0\{y \in \mathbb{R}^{k-1}: k(y, \vartheta) = \infty\} = 0$. This implies that $\lambda\{\vartheta \in \mathrm{pr}_1(\Theta): k(y, \vartheta) = \infty\} = 0$ for P_0-almost every $y \in \mathbb{R}^{k-1}$. However, $\mathrm{pr}_1(\Theta)$ is an open interval and $\{\vartheta \in \mathrm{pr}_1(\Theta): k(y, \vartheta) < \infty\}$ is an interval for every $y \in \mathbb{R}^{k-1}$. This implies that for P_0-almost every $y \in \mathbb{R}^{k-1}$ the set $\{\vartheta \in \mathrm{pr}_1(\Theta): k(y, \vartheta) = \infty\} = \emptyset$. We may therefore change the kernel Q in such a way that $k(y, \vartheta) < \infty$ for every $y \in \mathbb{R}^{k-1}$ and every $\vartheta \in pr_1(\Theta)$.

Let $y \in \mathbb{R}^{k-1}$ be fixed and assume that $k(y, \vartheta_1) = 0$ for some $\vartheta_1 \in \mathrm{pr}_1(\Theta)$. It follows that $h(.\,, y) = 0$ $Q(y, .)$-a.e. and therefore $k(y, \vartheta) = 0$ for every $\vartheta \in \mathrm{pr}_1(\Theta)$. Hence we obtain that for every $y \in \mathbb{R}^{k-1}$ the function $\vartheta \mapsto k(y, \vartheta)$ either is positive or vanishes identically.

Let $M = \{y \in \mathbb{R}^{k-1}: k(y, .) = 0\}$. It is clear that $M \in \mathscr{B}^{k-1}$. We define for $\vartheta \in \mathrm{pr}_1(\Theta)$ and $B \in \mathscr{B}$

$$F_\vartheta(B, y) := \frac{1}{k(y, \vartheta)} \int_B e^{\vartheta x} h(x, y)\, Q(y, dx), \quad y \notin M,$$

and $F_\vartheta(B, y) = F_\vartheta(B, y_0)$ for some fixed $y_0 \notin M$ if $y \in M$. Then $F_\vartheta | \mathscr{B} \times \mathbb{R}^{k-1}$, $\vartheta \in \mathrm{pr}_1(\Theta)$, satisfies (1). For $(\vartheta, \tau) \in \Theta$ and $B \in \mathscr{B}^{k-1}$ we define

$$G_{\vartheta,\tau}(B) = C(\vartheta, \tau) \int_{\mathbb{R} \times B} e^{\vartheta x} e^{\langle \tau, y \rangle} h(x, y)\, P(dx, dy).$$

Obviously, $G_{\vartheta,\tau} | \mathscr{B}^{k-1}$, $(\vartheta, \tau) \in \Theta$, satisfies (2).

The remaining assertion follows from

$$\begin{aligned}
P_{\vartheta,\tau}(A) &= C(\vartheta, \tau) \int_A e^{\vartheta x} e^{\langle \tau, y \rangle} h(x, y)\, P(dx, dy) \\
&= C(\vartheta, \tau) \int_{\mathbb{R}^{k-1}} \int_{A^y} e^{\vartheta x} e^{\langle \tau, y \rangle} h(x, y)\, Q(y, dx)\, P_0(dy) \\
&= C(\vartheta, \tau) \int_{M'} F_\vartheta(A^y, y)\, k(y, \vartheta)\, e^{\langle \tau, y \rangle} P_0(dy) \\
&= C(\vartheta, \tau) \int F_\vartheta(A^y, y)\, k(y, \vartheta)\, e^{\langle \tau, y \rangle} P_0(dy) \\
&= C(\vartheta, \tau) \int F_\vartheta(A^y, y) \int_{\mathbb{R}} e^{\vartheta x} h(x, y)\, Q(y, dx)\, e^{\langle \tau, y \rangle} P_0(dy) \\
&= C(\vartheta, \tau) \int F_\vartheta(A^y, y)\, e^{\vartheta x} e^{\langle \tau, y \rangle} h(x, y)\, P(dx, dy) \\
&= \int F_\vartheta(A^y, y)\, G_{\vartheta,\tau}(dy), \quad A \in \mathscr{B}^k,\ (\vartheta, \tau) \in \Theta. \qquad \square
\end{aligned}$$

It is important to note that the measures $G_{\vartheta,\tau}$, $(\vartheta, \tau) \in \Theta$, are necessarily pairwise equivalent.

Given a decomposition of the kind proved in Theorem 26.6 it is immediate that $G_{\vartheta,\tau} | \mathscr{B}^{k-1} = P_{\vartheta,\tau} | \mathbb{R} \times \mathscr{B}^{k-1}$ and that $y \mapsto F_\vartheta(A^y, y)$, $y \in \mathbb{R}^{k-1}$, is a version of the conditional probability of $P_{\vartheta,\tau}$ given $\mathscr{B}^{k-1}$. It is essential that this conditional probability is independent of the nuisance parameter τ.

26.7 Remark. Suppose that $E = (\Omega, \mathscr{A}, \{P_{\vartheta,\tau} : (\vartheta, \tau) \in \Theta\})$ is an exponential experiment. Then $S_* E$ is a reduced exponential experiment. If we denote $S_* E = (\mathbb{R}^k, \mathscr{B}^k, \{Q_{\vartheta,\tau} : (\vartheta, \tau) \in \Theta\})$ then Theorem 26.6 implies for every $A \in \mathscr{B}^k$

$$Q_{\vartheta,\tau}(A) = \int F_\vartheta(A^y, y)\, G_{\vartheta,\tau}(dy), \ (\vartheta, \tau) \in \Theta,$$

which means in terms of E that

$$P_{\vartheta,\tau}\{S \in A\} = \int_{\mathbb{R}^k} F_\vartheta(A^y, y)\, \mathscr{L}(S | P_{\vartheta,\tau})(dx, dy).$$

It follows that

$$P_{\vartheta,\tau}(S \in A | S_2, \ldots, S_k) = F_\vartheta(A^{S_2, \ldots, S_k}, (S_2, \ldots, S_k))$$

which does not depend on the nuisance parameter τ.

26.8 Lemma. *Suppose that E is an exponential experiment and let* $\varphi \in \mathscr{F}(\Omega, \mathscr{A})$. *Then E is continuous and for every* $\tau \in \mathrm{pr}_2(\Theta)$ *the function* $\vartheta \mapsto P_{\vartheta,\tau}\varphi$ *is differentiable on* Θ^τ *with derivative*

$$\frac{\partial}{\partial \vartheta} P_{\vartheta,\tau}\varphi \Big|_{\vartheta=\vartheta_0} = P_{\vartheta_0,\tau}(S_1\varphi) - P_{\vartheta_0,\tau}(S_1)\,P_{\vartheta_0,\tau}(\varphi).$$

Proof. The assertion follows from Lemmas 5.6 and 11.5. □

26.9 Corollary. *Suppose that E is a reduced exponential experiment and let* $\varphi \in \mathscr{F}(\mathbb{R}^k, \mathscr{B}^k)$. *If* $\tau \mapsto P_{\vartheta_0,\tau}\varphi$ *is constant on* Θ^{ϑ_0} *then*

$$\frac{\partial}{\partial \vartheta} P_{\vartheta,\tau}\varphi \Big|_{\vartheta=\vartheta_0} = \int \frac{\partial}{\partial \vartheta} F_\vartheta(\varphi, y)\Big|_{\vartheta=\vartheta_0} G_{\vartheta_0,\tau}(dy).$$

Proof. Let $P_{\vartheta_0,\tau}\varphi = \alpha$, $\tau \in \Theta^{\vartheta_0}$. Then it follows that $F_{\vartheta_0}(\varphi\,|\,y) = \alpha$, $G_{\vartheta_0,\tau}$-a.e., $(\vartheta_0, \tau) \in \Theta$. We obtain that

$$\begin{aligned}
&\int \frac{\partial}{\partial \vartheta} F_\vartheta(\varphi, y)\Big|_{\vartheta=\vartheta_0} G_{\vartheta_0,\tau}(dy)\\
&= \int F_{\vartheta_0}(\varphi\,\mathrm{id}, y)\, G_{\vartheta_0,\tau}(dy) - \alpha \int F_{\vartheta_0}(\mathrm{id}, y)\, G_{\vartheta_0,\tau}(dy)\\
&= P_{\vartheta_0,\tau}(\varphi\,\mathrm{id}) - \alpha P_{\vartheta_0,\tau}(\mathrm{id}).
\end{aligned}$$

This proves the assertion. □

27. Conditional tests

Suppose that $E = (\mathbb{R}^k, \mathscr{B}^k, \{P_{\vartheta,\tau}: (\vartheta,\tau) \in \Theta\})$ is a reduced exponential experiment. Let $\vartheta_0 \in \mathrm{pr}_1(\Theta)$. We will consider two kinds of testing problems: One-sided testing problems, which are of the form

$$\begin{aligned}
H &= \{(\vartheta,\tau) \in \Theta: \vartheta \leqq \vartheta_0, \tau \text{ arbitrary}),\\
K &= \{(\vartheta,\tau) \in \Theta: \vartheta > \vartheta_0, \tau \text{ arbitrary}\},
\end{aligned}$$

and two-sided testing problems of the form

$$\begin{aligned}
H &= \{(\vartheta,\tau) \in \Theta: \vartheta = \vartheta_0, \tau \text{ arbitrary}\},\\
K &= \{(\vartheta,\tau) \in \Theta: \vartheta \neq \vartheta_0, \tau \text{ arbitrary}\}.
\end{aligned}$$

27.1 Definition. A test $\varphi \in \mathscr{F}(\mathbb{R}^k, \mathscr{B}^k)$ is a *conditional upper test* if

$$\varphi(x,y) = \begin{cases} 1 & \text{if } x > t(y),\\ 0 & \text{if } x < t(y),\end{cases}$$

where $t: \mathbb{R}^{k-1} \to \bar{\mathbb{R}}$ is a Borel function.

As we shall see, conditional upper tests are proper candidates for optimal tests of one-sided testing problems (H, K).

27.2 Lemma. *Suppose that (H, K) is a one sided testing problem. A conditional upper test $\varphi \in \mathscr{F}(\mathbb{R}^k, \mathscr{B}^k)$ is in $\mathscr{F}_\alpha^s(H, K)$ respectively in $\mathscr{F}_\alpha(H, K)$ iff it satisfies*

$$F_{\vartheta_0}(\varphi(.,y), y) = \alpha \quad G_{\vartheta_0,\tau}\text{-a.e., } \tau \in \Theta^{\vartheta_0}.$$

Proof. Assume that $\varphi \in \mathscr{F}_\alpha^s(H, K)$. Then $P_{\vartheta_0,\tau}\varphi = \alpha$, $\tau \in \Theta^{\vartheta_0}$. Then one part of the assertion follows from Theorems 26.6 and 26.4. Assuming conversely that the condition is satisfied we choose $\psi(x, y) = \alpha$, $(x, y) \in \mathbb{R}^k$. Then Corollary 9.8 implies that

$$\begin{aligned} F_\vartheta(\varphi(.,y), y) &\leqq \alpha \quad \text{if} \quad \vartheta \leqq \vartheta_0, \\ F_\vartheta(\varphi(.,y), y) &\geqq \alpha \quad \text{if} \quad \vartheta > \vartheta_0, \end{aligned} \quad G_{\vartheta_0,\tau}\text{-a.e., } \tau \in \Theta^{\vartheta_0},$$

which proves the assertion. □

27.3 Lemma. *Suppose that (H, K) is a one-sided testing problem. Then for every $\alpha \in [0, 1]$ there is a conditional upper test $\varphi \in \mathscr{F}_\alpha(H, K)$.*

Proof. Recall the decomposition of Theorem 26.6. Let $(t_n)_{n \in \mathbb{R}} \subseteq \mathbb{R}$ be dense and define

$$t(y) := \inf\{t_n \colon F_{\vartheta_0}((t_n, \infty), y) \leqq \alpha,\ n \in \mathbb{N}\},\ y \in \mathbb{R}^{k-1}.$$

It is obvious that $t\colon \mathbb{R}^{k-1} \to \bar{\mathbb{R}}$ is a Borel function. Moreover, it is easily seen that $F_{\vartheta_0}((t(y), \infty), y) \leqq \alpha$ and $F_{\vartheta_0}([t(y), \infty), y) \geqq \alpha$. Now standard reasoning shows that the test

$$\varphi_\alpha(x, y) = \begin{cases} 1 & \text{if} \quad x > t(y), \\ 0 & \text{if} \quad x < t(y), \end{cases} \quad (x, y) \in \mathbb{R}^k,$$

can be chosen to be in $\mathscr{F}_\alpha(H, K)$. □

27.4 Theorem. *Suppose that (H, K) is a one-sided testing problem. If $\varphi^* \in \mathscr{F}_\alpha(H, K)$ is a conditional upper test then φ^* is uniformly optimal in $\mathscr{F}_\alpha^s(H, K)$.*

Proof. Let $\varphi \in \mathscr{F}_\alpha^s(H, K)$ be arbitrary. Then $P_{\vartheta_0,\tau}\varphi = \alpha$ for every $(\vartheta_0, \tau) \in \Theta$. Combining Theorems 26.4 and 26.6 we obtain

$$\int \varphi(x, y)\, F_{\vartheta_0}(dx|y) = \alpha \quad G_{\vartheta_0,\tau}\text{-a.e.,} \quad \tau \in \Theta^{\vartheta_0}.$$

The same assertion holds for φ^*. Hence there is $M \subseteq \mathbb{R}^{k-1}$ such that $G_{\vartheta_0,\tau}(M) = 1$, $\tau \in \Theta^{\vartheta_0}$, and

$$\int \varphi^*(x, y) F_{\vartheta_0}(dx, y) = \int \varphi(x, y) F_{\vartheta_0}(dx, y) = \alpha \quad \text{on } M.$$

Since $\varphi^*(., y)$ is an upper id-test for every fixed $y \in \mathbb{R}^{k-1}$ it follows from Corollary 9.8 and Remark 9.9 that

$$\int \varphi^*(x, y) F_\vartheta(dx, y) \gtreqless \int \varphi(x, y) F_\vartheta(dx, y) \quad \text{if} \quad \vartheta \gtreqless \vartheta_0, \quad y \in M.$$

This implies

$$P_{\vartheta,\tau}\varphi^* \gtreqless P_{\vartheta,\tau}\varphi \quad \text{if} \quad \vartheta \gtreqless \vartheta_0, \quad (\vartheta, \tau) \in \Theta. \qquad \square$$

27.5 Corollary. *Suppose that (H, K) is a one-sided testing problem. If $\varphi \in \mathscr{F}_\alpha^s(H, K)$ is optimal in $\mathscr{F}_\alpha(H, K)$ for at least one point $(\vartheta_1, \tau_1) \in \Theta$, $\vartheta_1 \neq \vartheta_0$, then φ is uniformly optimal in $\mathscr{F}_\alpha^s(H, K)$.*

Proof. Let $\varphi^* \in \mathscr{F}_\alpha(H, K)$ be a conditional upper test. Combining Theorems 26.4, 26.6 and 27.4 we obtain

$$\int \varphi(x, y) F_{\vartheta_0}(dx, y) = \int \varphi^*(x, y) F_{\vartheta_0}(dx, y) = \alpha$$

$G_{\vartheta,\tau}$-a.e. for every $(\vartheta, \tau) \in \Theta$, and employing the optimality of φ at (ϑ_1, τ_1) we obtain

$$\int \left(\int \varphi(x, y) F_{\vartheta_1}(dx, y) - \int \varphi^*(x, y) F_{\vartheta_1}(dx, y)\right) G_{\vartheta_1,\tau_1}(dy) = 0.$$

Let M be the set of y where the first equations hold. For $y \in M$ consider the experiments $E_y := \{F_\vartheta(., y): \vartheta \in \mathrm{pr}_1(\Theta)\}$ and the testing problem $(\tilde{H}, \tilde{K})$, where $\tilde{H} = \{\vartheta \in \mathrm{pr}_1(\Theta): \vartheta \leqq \vartheta_0\}$ and $\tilde{K} := \mathrm{pr}_1(\Theta) \setminus \tilde{H}$. By the proof of Theorem (27.4), $\varphi^*(., y)$ is uniformly optimal in $\mathscr{F}_\alpha^s(\tilde{H}, \tilde{K})$ for E_y, $y \in M$. Therefore, if $\vartheta_1 \leqq \vartheta_0$ we have

$$\int \varphi(x, y) F_{\vartheta_1}(dx, y) \geqq \int \varphi^*(x, y) F_{\vartheta_1}(dx, y), \quad y \in M,$$

and if $\vartheta_1 > \vartheta_0$

$$\int \varphi(x, y) F_{\vartheta_1}(dx, y) \leqq \int \varphi^*(x, y) F_{\vartheta_1}(dx, y), \quad y \in M.$$

In any case, we obtain

$$\int \varphi(x, y) F_{\vartheta_1}(dx, y) = \int \varphi^*(x, y) F_{\vartheta_1}(dx, y)$$

G_{ϑ_1,τ_1}-a.e. and hence, $G_{\vartheta,\tau}$-a.e. for every $(\vartheta, \tau) \in \Theta$. Now, restrict M to those points y where the last equation holds. Since then for $y \in M$ the power functions of $\varphi(., y)$ and $\varphi^*(., y)$ coincide at ϑ_0 and ϑ_1, Corollary 11.4 shows that $\varphi(., y)$ is uniformly optimal in $\mathscr{F}_\alpha^s(\tilde{H}, \tilde{K})$. It follows that

$$\int \varphi(x, y) F_\vartheta(dx, y) = \int \varphi^*(x, y) F_\vartheta(dx, y), \ \vartheta \in \mathrm{pr}_1(\Theta),$$

and hence the assertion. $\square$

As another consequence we observe that the test φ^* of Theorem 27.4 is admissible. In fact, any better test is in $\mathscr{F}_\alpha(H, K)$ and therefore should be optimal in $\mathscr{F}_\alpha(H, K)$. Hence, it coincides with φ^*.

27.6 Definition. A test $\varphi \in \mathscr{F}(\mathbb{R}^k, \mathscr{B}^k)$ is a *conditional two-sided test* if

$$\varphi(x, y) = \begin{cases} 1 & \text{if} \quad x < t_1(y) \quad \text{or} \quad x > t_2(y), \\ 0 & \text{if} \quad t_1(y) < x < t_2(y), \end{cases}$$

where t_i: $\mathbb{R}^{k-1} \to \bar{\mathbb{R}}$, $i = 1, 2$, are Borel functions.

27.7 Lemma. *Suppose that (H, K) is a two-sided testing problem. A conditional two-sided test $\varphi \in \mathscr{F}(\mathbb{R}^k, \mathscr{B}^k)$ is in $\mathscr{F}_\alpha(H, K)$ iff it satisfies*

(1) $F_{\vartheta_0}(\varphi(., y), y) = \alpha \quad G_{\vartheta_0,\tau}$*-a.e.*, $\tau \in \Theta^{\vartheta_0}$,

(2) $\left.\dfrac{d}{d\vartheta} F_\vartheta(\varphi(., y), y)\right|_{\vartheta = \vartheta_0} = 0 \quad G_{\vartheta_0,\tau}$*-a.e.*, $\tau \in \Theta^{\vartheta_0}$.

Proof. Assume that $\varphi \in \mathscr{F}_\alpha(H, K)$. Then $P_{\vartheta_0,\tau}\varphi = \alpha$ for every $\tau \in \Theta^{\vartheta_0}$. This implies (1) by Theorem 26.6. Moreover, for every $\tau \in \Theta^{\vartheta_0}$ the function $\vartheta \mapsto P_{\vartheta,\tau}\varphi$ has a global minimum at $\vartheta = \vartheta_0$ which implies that

$$\left.\frac{d}{d\vartheta} P_{\vartheta,\tau}\varphi\right|_{\vartheta = \vartheta_0} = 0, \quad \tau \in \Theta^{\vartheta_0}.$$

Now, (2) follows from Corollary 26.9. Assume conversely that φ satisfies conditions (1) and (2). Let $\psi(x, y) = \alpha$, $(x, y) \in \mathbb{R}^k$. Then Theorem (13.4) implies that $F_\vartheta(\varphi(., y), y) \geqq \alpha$ if $\vartheta \neq \vartheta_0$, $G_{\vartheta_0,\tau}$-a.e., $\tau \in \Theta^{\vartheta_0}$. It is then clear that $\varphi \in \mathscr{F}_\alpha(H, K)$. □

27.8 Remark. We will indicate how to construct a conditional two-sided test $\varphi^* \in \mathscr{F}_\alpha(H, K)$, $\alpha \in [0,1]$. For every $\gamma \in [0,1]$ let $\varphi_\gamma \in \mathscr{F}(\mathbb{R}^k, \mathscr{B}^k)$ be a conditional upper test for the one-sided testing problem centered at ϑ_0 such that $\varphi_0 = 0$, $\varphi_1 = 1$ and $\gamma_1 \leqq \gamma_2$ implies $\varphi_{\gamma_1} \leqq \varphi_{\gamma_2}$. Then $\bar{\varphi}_\gamma := \varphi_\gamma + 1 - \varphi_{1-\alpha+\gamma}$, $0 \leqq \gamma \leqq \alpha$, is a conditional two-sided test satisfying $P_{\vartheta_0,\tau}\bar{\varphi}_\gamma = \alpha$ if $0 \leqq \gamma \leqq \alpha$. Similarly as in the proof of Lemma (13.1) it follows that

$$\left.\frac{d}{d\vartheta} F_\vartheta(\bar{\varphi}_0, y)\right|_{\vartheta = \vartheta_0} \leqq 0 \leqq \left.\frac{d}{d\vartheta} F_\vartheta(\bar{\varphi}_\alpha, y)\right|_{\vartheta = \vartheta_0}$$

for $G_{\vartheta_0,\tau}$-almost every $y \in \mathbb{R}^{k-1}$. Hence, we may find a function γ: $\mathbb{R}^{k-1} \to [0, \alpha]$ such that

$$\left.\frac{d}{d\vartheta} F_\vartheta(\bar{\varphi}_{\gamma(y)}, y)\right|_{\vartheta = \vartheta_0} = 0 \quad G_{\vartheta_0,\tau}\text{-a.e.}$$

The problem is whether γ can be chosen in such a way that $(x, y) \mapsto \bar{\varphi}_{\gamma(y)}(x, y)$ is $\mathscr{B}^k$-measurable. However, this is only a theoretical problem which can be answered positively as in Lemma 27.3. For practical purposes the conditional tests have to be constructed explicitely which solves the problem of measurability as a by-product.

27.9 Theorem. *Suppose that (H, K) is a two-sided testing problem. If $\varphi^* \in \mathscr{F}_\alpha(H, K)$ is a conditional two-sided test then φ^* is uniformly optimal in $\mathscr{F}_\alpha(H, K)$.*

Proof. Let $\varphi \in \mathscr{F}_\alpha(H, K)$ be arbitrary. Then it follows that $P_{\vartheta_0,\tau}\varphi = \alpha$ and $\left.\frac{d}{d\vartheta} P_{\vartheta,\tau}\varphi\right|_{\vartheta=\vartheta_0} = 0$ for every $\tau \in \Theta^{\vartheta_0}$. Combining Theorems 26.6 and 26.4 and Corollary 26.9 we obtain

$$F_{\vartheta_0}(\varphi(.\,, y), y) = \alpha \quad G_{\vartheta_0,\tau}\text{-a.e.}, \ \tau \in \Theta^{\vartheta_0},$$

$$\left.\frac{d}{d\vartheta} F_\vartheta(\varphi(.\,, y), y)\right|_{\vartheta=\vartheta_0} = 0 \quad G_{\vartheta_0,\tau}\text{-a.e.}, \ \tau \in \Theta^{\vartheta_0}.$$

The same assertions are true of φ^*. Hence there is $M \subseteq \mathbb{R}^{k-1}$ such that $G_{\vartheta_0,\tau}(M) = 1$, $\tau \in \Theta^{\vartheta_0}$, and

$$F_{\vartheta_0}(\varphi(.\,, y), y) = F_{\vartheta_0}(\varphi^*(.\,, y), y),$$

$$\left.\frac{d}{d\vartheta} F_\vartheta(\varphi(.\,, y), y)\right|_{\vartheta=\vartheta_0} = \left.\frac{d}{d\vartheta} F_\vartheta(\varphi^*(.\,, y), y)\right|_{\vartheta=\vartheta_0},$$

on M. Since $\varphi^*(.\,, y)$ is a conditional upper test for every $y \in \mathbb{R}^{k-1}$ it follows from Theorem 13.4 that

$$F_\vartheta(\varphi^*(.\,, y), y) \geqq F_\vartheta(\varphi(.\,, y), y) \quad \text{if} \quad \vartheta \neq \vartheta_0, \quad y \in M.$$

This proves the assertion. □

27.10 Corollary. *Suppose that (H, K) is a two-sided testing problem. If $\varphi \in \mathscr{F}_\alpha(H, K)$ is optimal in $\mathscr{F}_\alpha(H, K)$ for at least one point $(\vartheta_1, \tau_1) \in \Theta$, $\vartheta_1 \neq \vartheta_0$, then φ is uniformly optimal in $\mathscr{F}_\alpha(H, K)$.*

Proof. Let $\varphi^* \in \mathscr{F}_\alpha(H, K)$ be a conditional two-sided test. Combining Theorems 26.4, 26.6 and 27.9 we obtain

$$\int \varphi(x, y)\, F_{\vartheta_0}(dx, y) = \int \varphi^*(x, y)\, F_{\vartheta_0}(dx, y) = \alpha,$$

$$\left.\frac{d}{d\vartheta} \int \varphi(x, y)\, F_\vartheta(dx, y)\right|_{\vartheta=\vartheta_0} = \left.\frac{d}{d\vartheta} \int \varphi^*(x, y)\, F_\vartheta(dx, y)\right|_{\vartheta=\vartheta_0} = 0$$

$G_{\vartheta_0,\tau}$-a.e. for every $(\vartheta, \tau) \in \Theta$, and employing the optimality of φ at (ϑ_1, τ_1)

$$\int (\int \varphi(x, y) F_{\vartheta_1}(dx, y) - \int \varphi^*(x, y) F_{\vartheta_1}(dx, y)) G_{\vartheta_1,\tau_1}(dy) = 0 .$$

Let M be the set of y where the first equations hold. For $y \in M$ consider the experiments $E_y := \{F_\vartheta(., y): \vartheta \in \mathrm{pr}_1(\Theta)\}$ and the testing problem $(\tilde{H}, \tilde{K})$, where $\tilde{H} := \{\vartheta_0\}$ and $\tilde{K} := \mathrm{pr}_1(\Theta) \setminus \tilde{H}$. By the proof of Theorem 27.9, $\varphi^*(., y)$ is uniformly optimal in $\mathscr{F}_\alpha^s(\tilde{H}, \tilde{K})$ for E_y, $y \in M$. Therefore, we have

$$\int \varphi(x, y) F_{\vartheta_1}(dx, y) \leqq \int \varphi^*(x, y) F_{\vartheta_1}(dx, y), \quad y \in M,$$

and obtain

$$\int \varphi(x, y) F_{\vartheta_1}(dx, y) = \int \varphi^*(x, y) F_{\vartheta_1}(dx, y)$$

G_{ϑ_1,τ_1}-a.e. and hence, $G_{\vartheta,\tau}$-a.e. for every $(\vartheta, \tau) \in \Theta$. Now, restrict M to those points y where the last equation holds. Since then for $y \in M$ the power functions of $\varphi(., y)$ and $\varphi^*(., y)$ coincide at ϑ_0 and ϑ_1, Corollary 13.7 shows that $\varphi(., y)$ is uniformly optimal in $\mathscr{F}_\alpha(\tilde{H}, \tilde{K})$. It follows that

$$\int \varphi(x, y) F_\vartheta(dx, y) = \int \varphi^*(x, y) F_\vartheta(dx, y), \; \vartheta \in \mathrm{pr}_1(\Theta),$$

and hence the assertion. □

Again, we obtain that the test φ^* of Theorem 27.9 is admissible. The argument is the same as below Corollary 27.5.

28. Gaussian shifts with nuisance parameters

Suppose that $(H, \langle \cdot, \cdot \rangle)$ is a Euclidean space, $\mathscr{B}(H)$ the Borel σ-field of H and $N_H | \mathscr{B}(H)$ the standard Gaussian measure of H. We consider the *Gaussian shift experiment* $E = (H, \mathscr{B}(H), \{\varepsilon_a * N_H: a \in L\})$ where $L \subseteq H$ is a linear subspace. For simplicity we denote $P_a := \varepsilon_a * N_H$.

The testing problem under consideration is supposed to be defined by a linear function $f: L \to \mathbb{R}$. We distinguish one-sided testing problems of the kind

$$H_1 = \{a \in L: f(a) \leqq 0\},$$
$$K_1 = \{a \in L: f(a) > 0\},$$

and two-sided testing problems of the form

$$H_2 = \{a \in L: f(a) = 0\},$$
$$K_2 = \{a \in L: f(a) \neq 0\}.$$

Let us begin with a direct analysis of the one-sided problem.

28.1 Lemma. *Suppose that* $\varphi \in \mathscr{F}(H, \mathscr{B}(H))$ *and* $\alpha \in [0,1]$. *For all pairs* $a, b \in L$ *the following holds true:*

(1) *If* $P_a\varphi \leqq \alpha$, *then* $P_b\varphi \leqq \Phi(N_\alpha + \|b-a\|)$

(2) *If* $P_a\varphi \geqq \alpha$, *then* $P_b\varphi \geqq \Phi(N_\alpha - \|b-a\|)$.

Proof. This is an easy consequence of the Neyman-Pearson lemma. Let us indicate the proof of (1). Let φ^* be an *NP*-test satisfying $P_a\varphi^* = \alpha$. Then $P_a\varphi \leqq P_a\varphi^*$ implies $P_b\varphi \leqq P_b\varphi^*$. To compute $P_b\varphi^*$ we note first that

$$\frac{dP_b}{dP_a} > k \quad \text{iff} \quad \langle b-a, \mathrm{id}_H\rangle > c(k),$$

and therefore

$$\varphi^* = \begin{cases} 1 & \qquad > \\ & \text{if} \quad \langle b-a, \mathrm{id}_H\rangle \qquad \langle b-a, a\rangle + N_{1-\alpha}\|b-a\| \\ 0 & \qquad < \end{cases}$$

is an *NP*-test with $P_a\varphi^* = \alpha$. Now easy computations yield $P_b\varphi^* = \Phi(N_\alpha + \|b-a\|)$. □

In the following let $e \in L$ be the unit vector with $e \perp \ker f$ and $f(e) > 0$. Then $\|f\| = f(e)$ and $f \circ p_L = \langle\cdot,\cdot\rangle\|f\|$ where p_L denotes the orthogonal projection of H onto L.

28.2 Corollary. *Every test* $\varphi \in \mathscr{F}_\alpha^s(H_1, K_1)$ *satisfies*

$$P_a\varphi \geqq \Phi(N_\alpha + f(a)/\|f\|) \quad \textit{if} \quad a \in H_1,$$
$$P_a\varphi \leqq \Phi(N_\alpha + f(a)/\|f\|) \quad \textit{if} \quad a \in K_1.$$

Proof. Every $a \in L$ is of the form $a = \langle a, e\rangle e + s$ where $s \in \ker f$ and $\langle a, e\rangle = f(a)/f(e)$. If $\varphi \in \mathscr{F}_\alpha^s(H_1, K_1)$ then $P_s\varphi = \alpha$ by continuity of E and it follows from Lemma 28.1 that

$$\Phi(N_\alpha - |\langle a, e\rangle|) \leqq P_a\varphi \leqq \Phi(N_\alpha + |\langle a, e\rangle|), \quad a \in L.$$

This proves the assertion. □

28.3 Theorem. *The test*

$$\varphi^*(x) = \begin{cases} 1 & \textit{if} \quad f(p_L(x)) > N_{1-\alpha}\|f\|, \\ 0 & \textit{if} \quad f(p_L(x)) < N_{1-\alpha}\|f\|, \end{cases} \qquad x \in H,$$

is uniformly optimal in $\mathscr{F}_\alpha^s(H_1, K_1)$.

Proof. The power of φ^* at $a \in L$ is

$$P_a\varphi^* = \Phi(N_\alpha + \langle a, e\rangle).$$

Hence, if $f(a) = 0$ then $P_a \varphi^* = \alpha$. Moreover, we obtain from Corollary 28.2 that $P_a \varphi^*$ attains the envelope power function for every $a \in L$. □

To deal with the two-sided problem we have to apply the theory developed in sections 26 and 27.

The problem may be phrased in terms of exponential experiments. Let $k = \dim L$ and $n = \dim H$. The point $e_1 := e$ can be extended to an orthonormal base $e_1, \ldots, e_n$ of H in such a way that $e_1, \ldots, e_k$ is a base of L. If we denote $x_i = \langle x, e_i \rangle$, $1 \leqq i \leqq n$, $x \in H$, then we have

$$P_a(B) = (2\pi)^{-n/2} \exp\left(-\frac{1}{2}\|a\|^2\right) \int_B \exp\left(\sum_{i=1}^k x_i a_i\right) \exp\left(-\frac{1}{2}\|x\|^2\right) dx,$$

$$B \in \mathscr{B}(H),\ a \in L.$$

Substituting $\vartheta = a_1$, $\tau = (a_2, \ldots, a_k)$, we see that E is a exponential family. We may apply the results of section 27.

The point is, however, that in this situation there are even unconditional tests which are uniformly optimal in $\mathscr{F}_\alpha(H, K)$. The technical key is the following assertion. We use the notation of section 26.

28.4 Theorem. *Suppose that* $E = (\mathbb{R}^k, \mathscr{B}^k, \{P_{\vartheta,\tau}: (\vartheta, \tau) \in \Theta\})$ *is a reduced exponential experiment and let* $\vartheta_0 \in \mathrm{pr}_1(\Theta)$. *If for a measurable map* $h: \mathbb{R}^k \to \mathbb{R}$ *the distributions* $\mathscr{L}(h|P_{\vartheta_0,\tau})$ *do not depend on* $\tau \in \Theta^{\vartheta_0}$ *then* h *and* $(x, y) \mapsto y$, $(x, y) \in \mathbb{R} \times \mathbb{R}^{k-1}$, *are stochastically independent for every* $P_{\vartheta_0,\tau}$, $\tau \in \Theta^{\vartheta_0}$.

Proof. Let $P_{\vartheta_0,\tau}\{h \in B\} =: \mu(B)$, $B \in \mathscr{B}^1$, $\tau \in \Theta^{\vartheta_0}$. It follows that

$$\int (F_{\vartheta_0}(\{h(.\,, y) \in B\}, y) - \mu(B))\, G_{\vartheta_0,\tau}(dy) = 0, \quad \tau \in \Theta^{\vartheta_0},$$

and from Theorem (26.6), (2), and (26.4) we obtain that

$$F_{\vartheta_0}(\{h(.\,, y) \in B\}, y) = \mu(B) \quad G_{\vartheta_0,\tau}\text{-a.e.}, \quad \tau \in \Theta^{\vartheta_0}.$$

If $B \in \mathscr{B}^1$ and $C \in \mathscr{B}^{k-1}$ then we have for $\tau \in \Theta^{\vartheta_0}$

$$\begin{aligned} &F_{\vartheta_0}\{(x, y) \in \mathbb{R}^k: h(x, y) \in B, y \in C\} \\ &= \int_C F_{\vartheta_0}(\{h(.\,, y) \in B\}, y)\, G_{\vartheta_0,\tau}(dy) \\ &= \mu(B)\, G_{\vartheta_0,\tau}(C) \\ &= P_{\vartheta_0,\tau}\{h \in B\} \cdot P_{\vartheta_0,\tau}\{(x, y) \in \mathbb{R}^k: y \in C\}. \end{aligned}$$

This proves the assertion. □

28.5 Lemma. *For every* $a \in L$ *with* $f(a) = 0$ *the equality* $\mathscr{L}(f \circ p_L / \|f\| \,|\, P_a) = \nu_{0,1}$ *holds true.*

Proof. It is clear that $\mathscr{L}(\langle ., e_1 \rangle | P_a) = \nu_{a_1, 1}$ whenever $a \in L$. Since $f(a) = 0$ iff $a_1 = 0$ the assertion follows. □

Now, we are ready to establish uniformly optimal tests for the experiment E. By way of illustration we show how to derive the optimal test of Theorem 28.3 by means of Theorem 28.4.

28.6 Theorem. *A critical function* $\varphi^* \in \mathscr{F}(H, \mathscr{B}(H))$ *is uniformly optimal in* $\mathscr{F}_\alpha^s(H_1, K_1)$ *iff*

$$\varphi^*(x) = \begin{cases} 1 & \text{if } \; f(p_L(x)) > N_{1-\alpha}\|f\|, \\ 0 & \text{if } \; f(p_L(x)) < N_{1-\alpha}\|f\|. \end{cases} \quad \lambda\text{-a.e.}$$

Proof. Uniqueness follows from Corollary 26.5. Let us prove optimality. Since $f \circ p_L / \|f\| = \langle ., e_1 \rangle$ and because an unconditional test is a conditional test in a trivial sense it follows that φ^* is a conditional upper test. By Theorem 27.4 it is sufficient to show that $\varphi^* \in \mathscr{F}_\alpha(H_1, K_1)$. For this, we have to verify the condition of Lemma 27.2 which is equivalent with $P_a(\varphi^*) = \alpha$ for all $a \in L$ with $f(a) = 0$. The latter follows from Lemma 28.5 and hence, Theorem 28.4 proves the condition.

It is clear that φ^* is admissible for (H_1, K_1).

28.7 Corollary. *If* $\varphi \in \mathscr{F}_\alpha^s(H_1, K_1)$ *is optimal in* $\mathscr{F}_\alpha^s(H_1, K_1)$ *for some* $a \in L$ *with* $f(a) \neq 0$, *then* φ *is uniformly optimal in* $\mathscr{F}_\alpha^s(H_1, K_1)$.

Proof. This is a consequence of Corollary 27.5. □

Now we turn to two-sided testing problems.

28.8 Theorem. *A critical function* $\varphi^* \in \mathscr{F}(H, \mathscr{B}(H))$ *is uniformly optimal in* $\mathscr{F}_\alpha(H_2, K_2)$ *iff*

$$\varphi^*(x) = \begin{cases} 1 & \textit{if } \; |f(p_L(x))| > N_{1-\alpha/2}\|f\|, \\ 0 & \textit{if } \; |f(p_L(x))| < N_{1-\alpha/2}\|f\|. \end{cases} \quad \lambda\textit{-a.e.}$$

Proof. Uniqueness follows from Corollary 26.5. Let us prove optimality. We observe that φ^* is a conditional two-sided test and have to show that $\varphi^* \in \mathscr{F}_\alpha(H_2, K_2)$ (Theorem 27.9). To verify the condition of Lemma 27.7 we apply Lemma 28.5 and Theorem 28.4 to obtain that φ^* is independent of $(x, y) \mapsto y$. Hence

$$F_0(\varphi^*(.,y),y) = P_{0,\tau}(\varphi^*) = P_a(\varphi^*) = \alpha,$$

whenever $f(a) = 0$, and

$$\frac{d}{d\vartheta} F_\vartheta(\varphi^*(.,y),y)\bigg|_{\vartheta=0} = \frac{d}{d\vartheta} P_{\vartheta,\tau}(\varphi^*)\bigg|_{\vartheta=0} = \frac{\partial}{\partial a_1} P_a(\varphi^*)\bigg|_{a_1=0} = 0.$$

This proves the assertion. □

It is clear that φ^* is admissible for (H_2, K_2).

28.9 Corollary. *If $\varphi \in \mathscr{F}_\alpha(H_2, K_2)$ is optimal in $\mathscr{F}_\alpha(H_2, K_2)$ for some $a \in L$ with $f(a) \neq 0$, then φ is uniformly optimal in $\mathscr{F}_\alpha(H_2, K_2)$.*

Proof. This is a consequence of Lemma 27.10. □

Next, we extend the problem to obtain a more general situation. For $a \in L$ and $\sigma > 0$ let $P_{a,\sigma}\colon B \mapsto N_H\{x \in H\colon \sigma x + a \in B\}$, $B \in \mathscr{B}(H)$. In the following we consider the experiment $F = (H, \mathscr{B}(H), \{P_{a,\sigma}\colon a \in L, \sigma > 0\})$. The testing problems (H_1, K_1) and (H_2, K_2) are defined in an analogous way as for the experiment E. Keeping our previous notation we have

$$P_{a,\sigma}(B) =$$
$$(2\pi\sigma^2)^{-n/2} \exp\left(-\frac{1}{2\sigma^2}\|a\|^2\right) \int_B \exp\left(\sum_{i=1}^k x_i \frac{a_i}{\sigma^2}\right) \exp\left(-\frac{1}{2\sigma^2}\|x\|^2\right) dx,$$
$$B \in \mathscr{B}(H),\ a \in L.$$

Substituting $\vartheta = \dfrac{a_1}{\sigma^2}$, $\tau = \left(\dfrac{a_2}{\sigma^2}, \ldots, \dfrac{a_k}{\sigma^2}, -\dfrac{1}{2\sigma^2}\right)$ we see that E is an exponential experiment. By the mapping $S(x) = (x_1, \ldots, x_k, \|x\|^2)$, $x \in H$, we obtain a reduced exponential experiment $S_*(E)$ which satisfies $S_*(E) \underset{2}{\sim} E$.

28.10 Lemma. *The distribution $\mathscr{L}(h|P_{a,\sigma})$ of*

$$h(x) = \frac{f(p_L(x))}{\|f\|\,\|x - p_L(x)\|}, \quad x \in H,$$

does not depend on $(a,\sigma) \in L \times \mathbb{R}^+$ whenever $f(a) = 0$, $a \in L$.

Proof. Let $h_1\colon x \mapsto x_1$ and $h_2\colon x \mapsto \|x - p_L(x)\|$, $x \in H$. Then it is clear that $\mathscr{L}\left(\frac{1}{\sigma}h_1, \frac{1}{\sigma}h_2 \,\middle|\, P_{a,\sigma}\right)$ does not depend on $(a,\sigma) \in L \times \mathbb{R}^+$ whenever $f(a) = 0$. Since $h = h_1/h_2 = \frac{1}{\sigma}h_1 \big/ \frac{1}{\sigma}h_2$ the assertion follows. □

28.11 Theorem. *A critical function* $\varphi^* \in \mathscr{F}(H, \mathscr{B}(H))$ *is uniformly optimal in* $\mathscr{F}_\alpha^s(H_1, K_1)$ *iff*

$$\varphi^*(x) = \begin{cases} 1 & \text{if } \dfrac{f(p_L(x))}{\|x - p_L(x)\|} > \kappa_\alpha, \\ 0 & \text{if } \dfrac{f(p_L(x))}{\|x - p_L(x)\|} < \kappa_\alpha, \end{cases} \quad \lambda\text{-a.e.},$$

where κ_α *is such that* $P_{a,\sigma}(\varphi^*) = \alpha$ *for* $f(a) = 0$, $\sigma > 0$.

Proof. Uniqueness follows from Corollary 26.5. The proof of optimality is similar to the proof of Theorem 28.6. □

28.12 Corollary. *If* $\varphi \in \mathscr{F}_\alpha^s(H_1, K_1)$ *is optimal in* $\mathscr{F}_\alpha^s(H_1, K_1)$ *for some* $(a, \sigma) \in L \times \mathbb{R}^+$ *with* $f(a) \neq 0$, *then* φ *is uniformly optimal in* $\mathscr{F}_\alpha^s(H_1, K_1)$.

Proof. Apply Corollary 27.5.

28.13 Theorem. *A critical function* $\varphi^* \in \mathscr{F}(H, \mathscr{B}(H))$ *is uniformly optimal in* $\mathscr{F}_\alpha(H_2, K_2)$ *iff*

$$\varphi^*(x) = \begin{cases} 1 & \text{if } \dfrac{|f(p_L(x))|}{\|x - p_L(x)\|} > \kappa_\alpha, \\ 0 & \text{if } \dfrac{|f(p_L(x))|}{\|x - p_L(x)\|} < \kappa_\alpha, \end{cases} \quad \lambda\text{-a.e.},$$

where κ_α *is such that* $P_{a,\sigma}(\varphi^*) = \alpha$ *for* $f(a) = 0$, $\sigma > 0$.

Proof. Uniqueness follows from Corollary 26.5. The proof of optimality is similar to the proof of Theorem 28.6. □

28.14 Corollary. *If* $\varphi \in \mathscr{F}_\alpha(H_2, K_2)$ *is optimal in* $\mathscr{F}_\alpha(H_2, K_2)$ *for some* $(a, \sigma) \in L \times \mathbb{R}^+$ *with* $f(a) \neq 0$, *then* φ *is uniformly optimal in* $\mathscr{F}_\alpha(H_2, K_2)$.

Proof. Apply Lemma 27.10. □

Chapter 6: More Theory of Testing

The theory of testing presented in Sections 9, 11–13, and 26–28, relies mainly on the linear ordering of the parameter space. Thus, the applicability of this theory is naturally restricted to one-dimensional problems. If a parameter of higher dimension is subject of testing, further ideas are needed to simplify the analysis.

In Section 29 we begin with a direct proof of Wald's complete class theorem and apply it to show that convex acceptance regions form a complete class for exponential experiments. Results of this kind have been proved several times, beginning with Birnbaum [1955], followed by Chibisov [1967], and Roussas [1972]. Our proof follows Moussatat [1976].

Section 30 deals with testing linear problems for Gaussian shifts. We begin with a basic lemma whose idea goes back to Wald [1947]. This yields a complete solution of the problem of testing a point against a surrounding sphere. Additional results are obtained by the application of Section 29.

In the remaining sections we consider invariance properties of the experiment under a group of transformations. If invariance is at hand, one can try to facilitate the choice of a suitable test by considering only tests which are invariant under the group of transformations. In general, such a reduction does not preserve the amount of information of the experiment. However, if the information of an experiment is not measured by the values of the available power functions as is done in Definition 22.1 but in terms of the least favorable values of the power functions on the orbits of the transformation group, then, in some cases, reduction by invariance preserves this modified amount of information. Apparently, this preservation depends on amenability of the transformation group.

In Sections 31 and 32 the reduction by invariance is carried through for testing problems and applied to Gaussian shift experiments. This process is a special case of a decision-theoretic method which will be discussed much more thoroughly in subsequent sections.

Section 31 deals with the transition from the original invariant experiment to that experiment which admits only invariant tests. By way of illustration we discuss this transition by Euclidean shift experiments which are generated by isotropic probability measures.

If the transformation group is amenable, reduction by invariance preserves the modified amount of information. This is the content of the famous result of Hunt and Stein which is presented in Section 32. Finally, we apply the results obtained so far to construct maximin tests for Gaussian shift experiments and testing problems of dimension greater than 1.

Again the content of Sections 31 and 32 is well-known. Its presentation follows Lehmann [1958]. Many applications to regression and analysis of variance are contained in Witting and Noelle [1970]. Much more information on applications of invariance theory to multivariate analysis can be found in Giri [1976] and Farrell [1985].

29. Complete classes of tests

We begin this section with a general version of the complete class theorem for testing, and then specify to the case of exponential experiments.

29.1 Theorem (Wald). *Let* $\Theta \neq \emptyset$ *be a finite set and* $E \in \mathscr{E}(\Theta)$. *Consider a testing problem* (H, K) *and let* $\operatorname{co} H := \operatorname{co}\{P_\vartheta : \vartheta \in H\}$, $\operatorname{co} K := \operatorname{co}\{P_\vartheta : \vartheta \in K\}$. *Then*

$$\mathscr{N} := \bigcup \{\mathscr{N}(P, Q): P \in \operatorname{co} H,\ Q \in \operatorname{co} K\}$$

is a complete class of tests for (H, K).

Proof. Let us introduce some notations. For $\alpha \in [0,1]$, $m_1 \in S_H$ and $m_2 \in S_K$, and for any $\varphi \in \mathscr{F}(\Omega, \mathscr{A})$ define

$$g(\alpha, m_1, m_2)(\varphi) = (1-\alpha) \int P_\sigma \varphi\, m_1(d\sigma) + \alpha \int P_\tau (1-\varphi) m_2(d\tau).$$

Let

$$\psi(\alpha, m_1, m_2) := \inf\{g(\alpha, m_1, m_2)(\varphi): \varphi \in \mathscr{F}(\Omega, \mathscr{A})\}.$$

Moreover, let $M \subseteq \mathbb{R}^\Theta$ be the set of all vectors $(x_\vartheta)_{\vartheta \in \Theta}$ such that there exists some $\varphi \in \mathscr{F}(\Omega, \mathscr{A})$ satisfying

$$x_\sigma \geqq P_\sigma \varphi \quad \text{if} \quad \sigma \in H, \quad \text{and}$$
$$x_\tau \leqq P_\tau \varphi \quad \text{if} \quad \tau \in K.$$

Then M is a closed convex subset of $\mathbb{R}^\Theta$.

Let $\varphi_0 \in \mathscr{F}(\Omega, \mathscr{A})$ be an arbitrary critical function. Then define

$$\varepsilon := \inf\{g(\alpha, m_1, m_2)(\varphi_0) - \psi(\alpha, m_1, m_2):$$
$$\alpha \in [0,1],\ m_1 \in S_H,\ m_2 \in S_K\}.$$

This implies that for all $\alpha \in [0,1]$, $m_1 \in S_H$ and $m_2 \in S_K$,

(1) $$g(\alpha, m_1, m_2)(\varphi_0) - \varepsilon \geqq \psi(\alpha, m_1, m_2).$$

Consider $x_0 := (P_\vartheta \varphi_0 - \varepsilon)_{\vartheta \in \Theta} \in \mathbb{R}^\Theta$. We claim that $x_0 \in M$. If this is not the case then there is $(c_\vartheta)_{\vartheta \in \Theta} \in \mathbb{R}^\Theta$ such that

$$(2) \qquad \sum_{\vartheta \in \Theta} c_\vartheta (P_\vartheta \varphi_0 - \varepsilon) < \inf_{x \in M} \sum_{\vartheta \in \Theta} c_\vartheta x_\vartheta .$$

From the structure of M it is clear that $c_\sigma \geqq 0, \sigma \in H$, and $c_\tau \leqq 0, \tau \in K$. Moreover, it is easy to see that there exist $h \geqq 0$, $k \leqq 0$, $(h,k) \neq (0,0)$, and $m_1 \in S_H$, $m_2 \in S_K$, satisfying $c_\sigma = h \cdot m_1(\sigma)$, $\sigma \in H$, $c_\tau = k \cdot m_2(\tau)$, $\tau \in K$. Normalizing (2) by $1/(h-k)$ yields a contradiction to (1).

Thus, having proved that $x_0 \in M$, there exists $\varphi_1 \in \mathscr{F}(\Omega, \mathscr{A})$ satisfying $P_\sigma \varphi_1 \leqq P_\sigma \varphi_0 - \varepsilon$, $\sigma \in H$, and $P_\tau \varphi_1 \geqq P_\tau \varphi_0 - \varepsilon$, $\tau \in K$. It follows that for all $\alpha \in [0,1]$, $m_1 \in S_H$, $m_2 \in S_K$,

$$\begin{aligned} &g(\alpha, m_1, m_2)(\varphi_1) - \psi(\alpha, m_1, m_2) \\ &\quad \leqq g(\alpha, m_1, m_2)(\varphi_0) - \psi(\alpha, m_1, m_2) - \varepsilon . \end{aligned}$$

By definition of ε we obtain that

$$\begin{aligned} &\inf \{ g(\alpha, m_1, m_2)(\varphi_1) - \psi(\alpha, m_1, m_2): \\ &\quad \alpha \in [0,1],\ m_1 \in S_H,\ m_2 \in S_K \} = 0 . \end{aligned}$$

By lower semicontinuity the infimum is attained for some tripel $\alpha \in [0,1]$, $m_1 \in S_H$, $m_2 \in S_K$. Hence, the test φ_1 minimizes the error function of the binary experiment $(\int_H P_\sigma m_1(d\sigma), \int_K P_\tau m_2(d\tau))$ at the point α. An application of Theorem (14.2) proves that $\varphi_1 \in \mathscr{N}$. □

29.2 Corollary. (Wald). *Let $\Theta \neq \emptyset$ be an arbitrary set and $E \in \mathscr{E}(\Theta)$ a dominated experiment. Consider a testing problem (H, K) and let $\operatorname{co} H := \{\int P_\sigma m(d\sigma): m \in S_H\}$, $\operatorname{co} K := \{\int P_\tau m(d\tau): m \in S_K\}$. Then the weak hull $\bar{\mathscr{N}}$ in $M(E)$ of*

$$\mathscr{N} := \bigcup \{ \mathscr{N}(P, Q): P \in \operatorname{co} H,\ Q \in \operatorname{co} K \}$$

is a complete class of tests for (H, K).

Proof. Let $\varphi \in \mathscr{F}(\Omega, \mathscr{A})$. If $\alpha \in A(H)$ and $\beta \in A(K)$ then $F_{\alpha,\beta} := \{\psi \in \bar{\mathscr{N}}: \psi$ is better than φ for $(\alpha, \beta)\} \neq \emptyset$ by the preceding theorem. The sets $F_{\alpha,\beta}$, $\alpha \in A(H)$, $\beta \in A(K)$, are closed in $M(E)$ and directed from below. Since $\mathscr{F}(\Omega, \mathscr{A})$ is weakly compact in $M(E)$ it follows that

$$\bigcap_{\alpha \in A(H)} \bigcap_{\beta \in A(K)} F_{\alpha,\beta} \neq \emptyset . \qquad \square$$

29.3 Discussion. Suppose that $\Theta \subseteq \mathbb{R}^k$ is a convex set and $E \in \mathscr{E}(\Theta)$ is a reduced exponential experiment. Let $\vartheta_0 \in \Theta$ and consider the testing problem

$H = \{\vartheta_0\}$, $K = \Theta \setminus \{\vartheta_0\}$. Then the tests in $\mathcal{N}$ are of the form

$$\varphi(x) = \begin{cases} 1 \\ 0 \end{cases} \text{if } \int \frac{C(\vartheta)}{C(\vartheta_0)} \exp\langle \vartheta - \vartheta_0, x\rangle\, m(d\vartheta) \gtrless c$$

for some $m \in S_K$ and $c \in \bar{\mathbb{R}}$. Let

$$C := \{x \in \mathbb{R}^k : \int \frac{C(\vartheta)}{C(\vartheta_0)} \exp\langle \vartheta - \vartheta_0, x\rangle\, m(d\vartheta) \leqq c\}.$$

Obviously, $C \subseteq \mathbb{R}^k$ is a closed and convex subset and

$$\mathring{C} := \{x \in \mathbb{R}^k : \int \frac{C(\vartheta)}{C(\vartheta_0)} \exp\langle \vartheta - \vartheta_0, x\rangle\, m(d\vartheta) < c\}.$$

Hence, the tests $\varphi \in \mathcal{N}$ are of the form

$$\varphi(x) = \begin{cases} 1 & \text{if } x \notin C, \\ 0 & \text{if } x \in \mathring{C}, \end{cases}$$

where $C \subseteq \mathbb{R}^k$ is some closed, convex set.

29.4 Theorem (Birnbaum [1955]). *Suppose that $\Theta \subseteq \mathbb{R}^k$ is a convex set and $E \in \mathscr{E}(\Theta)$ is a reduced exponential experiment. Let $\vartheta_0 \in \Theta$. Then the family of critical functions*

$$\varphi(x) = \begin{cases} 1 & \textit{if } x \notin C, \\ 0 & \textit{if } x \in \mathring{C}, \end{cases}$$

where $C \subseteq \mathbb{R}^k$ is closed and convex, is a complete class of tests for the testing problem $H = \{\vartheta_0\}$, $K = \Theta \setminus \{\vartheta_0\}$.

Proof. Let $\mathscr{C} \subseteq \mathscr{F}(\mathbb{R}^k, \mathscr{B}^k)$ be the class of critical functions

$$\varphi(x) = \begin{cases} 1 & \text{if } x \notin C, \\ 0 & \text{if } x \in \mathring{C}, \end{cases}$$

where $C \subseteq \mathbb{R}^k$ is closed and convex. By Corollary 29.2 and Discussion 29.3 we have to show that $\mathscr{C}$ is weakly closed in $M(E)$.

Let $\nu | \mathscr{B}^k$ be a dominating σ-finite measure, equivalent with $\{P_\vartheta : \vartheta \in \Theta\}$. Then $M(E) = L_\infty(\mathbb{R}^k, \mathscr{B}^k, \nu)$. Since $L_1(\mathbb{R}^k, \mathscr{B}^k, \nu)$ is separable, the weak topology of the unit sphere in $L_\infty(\mathbb{R}^k, \mathscr{B}^k, \nu)$ is metrizable. It suffices therefore to show that the weak limit of any sequence in $\mathscr{C}$ is in $\mathscr{C}$, too.

Let $(\varphi_n) \subseteq \mathscr{C}$ be a weakly convergent sequence of tests. For every φ_n there is a closed convex set $C_n \subseteq \mathbb{R}^k$ such that

$$\varphi_n(x) = \begin{cases} 1 & \text{if} \quad x \notin C_n, \\ 0 & \text{if} \quad x \in \mathring{C}_n. \end{cases}$$

Let $\varphi \in \mathscr{F}(\mathbb{R}^k, \mathscr{B}^k)$ be a weak limit of (φ_n). We shall construct a closed, convex subset $C \subseteq \mathbb{R}^n$ such that

$$\varphi(x) = \begin{cases} 1 & \text{if} \quad x \notin C, \\ 0 & \text{if} \quad x \in \mathring{C}. \end{cases} \quad \nu\text{-a.e.},$$

For this, let $f_n(x) := \operatorname{dist}(x, C_n)$, $x \in \mathbb{R}^k$, $n \in \mathbb{N}$. The functions f_n, $n \in \mathbb{N}$, are convex and Lipschitz-continuous with $\operatorname{Lip}(f_n) = 1$, $n \in \mathbb{N}$. Hence, the sequence (f_n) is equicontinuous. Now, we have to distinguish between two cases. If $\limsup C_n = \emptyset$, then $\varphi \equiv 1$ ν-a.e. and we may take $C = \emptyset$. On the other hand, if $\limsup C_n \neq \emptyset$, then $(f_n(0))_{n \in \mathbb{N}}$ has limit points in $\mathbb{R}$. Hence, there exists a subsequence $\mathbb{N}_1 \subseteq \mathbb{N}$ such that $(f_n(0))_{n \in \mathbb{N}_1}$ is bounded. Then, by Arzela-Ascoli's theorem, $(f_n)_{n \in \mathbb{N}_1}$ contains a subsequence $\mathbb{N}_0$ which converges uniformly on compacts. Let $f = \lim\limits_{n \in \mathbb{N}_0} f_n$. Since f is convex and continuous, the set $C := \{f = 0\}$ is closed and convex. Let us show that $\mathring{C} \subseteq \liminf\limits_{n \in \mathbb{N}_0} \mathring{C}_n \subseteq \limsup\limits_{n \in \mathbb{N}_0} C_n \subseteq C$. The inequality $\limsup\limits_{n \in \mathbb{N}_0} C_n \subseteq C$ is easy, since $x \in \limsup\limits_{n \in \mathbb{N}_0} C_n$ implies $f_n(x) = 0$ infinitely often, $n \in \mathbb{N}_0$, and hence $f(x) = 0$. In order to prove $\mathring{C} \subseteq \liminf\limits_{n \in \mathbb{N}_0} \mathring{C}_n$ let $x \in \mathring{C}$. Then there exists $\delta > 0$ such that $\bar{B}(x, \delta) \subseteq \mathring{C}$. Since $f_n \to f$ uniformly on compacts, there is $n_0 \in \mathbb{N}$ with

(1) $$\sup_{z \in B(x, \delta)} |f_n(z) - f(z)| < \delta \quad \text{if} \quad n \geqq n_0, \quad n \in \mathbb{N}_0.$$

Since $x \in C$, we have $f_n(x) < \delta$ and $\operatorname{dist}(x, C_n) < \delta$ if $n \geqq n_0$, $n \in \mathbb{N}_0$. We show that $x \in \mathring{C}_n$ for $n \geqq n_0$, $n \in \mathbb{N}_0$. Suppose that $x \notin \mathring{C}_n$. Then, by convexity of C_n, the ball $\bar{B}(x, \delta)$ contains some point z_0 such that $\operatorname{dist}(z_0, C_n) \geqq \delta$. But (1) implies $f_n(z_0) = \operatorname{dist}(z_0, C_n) < \delta$ which is a contradiction.

Now, it is not difficult to complete the proof. Let $A \in \mathscr{B}^k$ an arbitrary ν-integrable set. Then

$$\limsup_{n \in \mathbb{N}_0} C_n \subseteq C \quad \text{implies} \quad \limsup_{n \in \mathbb{N}_0} \int_A 1_{C_n} d\nu \leqq \int_A 1_C d\nu$$

and

$$\mathring{C} \subseteq \liminf_{n \in \mathbb{N}_0} \mathring{C}_n \quad \text{implies} \quad \int_A 1_{\mathring{C}} d\nu \leqq \liminf_{n \in \mathbb{N}_0} \int_A 1_{\mathring{C}_n} d\nu.$$

We obtain

$$\begin{aligned} \int_A (\varphi - 1_{C'}) d\nu &= \int_A (\varphi - 1) d\nu + \int_A 1_C d\nu \\ &\geqq \lim_{n \in \mathbb{N}_0} \int_A (\varphi_n - 1) d\nu + \limsup_{n \in \mathbb{N}_0} \int_A 1_{C_n} d\nu \\ &= \limsup_{n \in \mathbb{N}_0} \int_A (\varphi_n - 1_{C_n'}) d\nu \geqq 0, \end{aligned}$$

and

$$\int_A (1 - 1_{\mathring{C}} - \varphi)\,d\nu \geqq \lim_{n\in\mathbb{N}_0} \int_A (1 - \varphi_n)\,d\nu - \liminf_{n\in\mathbb{N}_0} \int_A 1_{\mathring{C}_n}\,d\nu$$
$$= \limsup_{n\in\mathbb{N}_0} \int_A (1 - 1_{\mathring{C}_n} - \varphi_n)\,d\nu \geqq 0\,.$$

This proves that φ and C are related as we have claimed at the beginning of the proof. □

29.5 Corollary. *Suppose that $\Theta \subseteq \mathbb{R}^k$ is a convex set and $E \in \mathscr{E}(\Theta)$ is a reduced exponential experiment which is dominated by the Lebesgue measure. Let $\vartheta_0 \in \Theta$. Then the family of critical functions*

$$\varphi(x) = \begin{cases} 1 & \text{if} \quad x \notin C, \\ 0 & \text{if} \quad x \in C, \end{cases}$$

where $C \subseteq \mathbb{R}^k$ is closed and convex, is a complete class of tests for the testing problem $H = \{\vartheta_0\}$, $K = \Theta \setminus \{\vartheta_0\}$.

Proof. This follows from the preceding theorem since the boundary of closed, convex sets in $\mathbb{R}^k$ is of Lebesgue measure zero (see Theorem 6.1). □

30. Testing for Gaussian shifts

Let $(H, \langle .,. \rangle)$ be a Euclidean space, $\mathscr{B}(H)$ the Borel-σ-field of H and $N_H|\mathscr{B}(H)$ the standard Gaussian measure on H. Consider the Gaussian shift experiment $E = (H, \mathscr{B}(H), \{P_a: a \in L\})$ where $P_a = \varepsilon_a * N_H$ and $L \subseteq H$ is a linear subspace.

We begin with the analysis of the simplest testing problem $\{0\}$, $\{a \in L: a \neq 0\}$. For every $c > 0$ let B_c be the sphere $B_c = \{a \in L: \|a\| = c\}$. The uniform distribution on the sphere B_c is denoted by λ_c, $c > 0$. Let p_L be the orthogonal projection of H onto L.

30.1 Lemma. *Let $k \in [0, \infty]$. Then the test*

$$\varphi^*(x) = \begin{cases} 1 & \text{if} \quad \|p_L(x)\| > k, \\ 0 & \text{if} \quad \|p_L(x)\| \leqq k, \end{cases} \qquad x \in H,$$

is an NP-test for each binary experiment $(P_0, \int_{B_c} P_a \lambda_c(da))$, $c > 0$.

Proof. Let $\varphi \in \mathscr{N}(P_0, \int_{B_c} P_a \lambda_c(da))$ be such that $P_0\varphi = P_0\varphi^*$. We show that

$$\int_{B_c} P_a\varphi^* \lambda_c(da) = \int_{B_c} P_a\varphi \lambda_c(da), \quad c>0.$$

For this we observe that

$$\begin{aligned}
&\int_{B_c} \frac{dP_a}{dP_0}(x)\lambda_c(da)\\
&\qquad = \int_{B_c} \exp\left(\langle p_L(x), a\rangle - \frac{1}{2}\|a\|^2\right)\lambda_c(da)\\
&\qquad = e^{-c^2/2}\int_{B_c} \exp\left(c\|p_L(x)\|\cos(p_L(x), a)\right)\lambda_c(da)\\
&\qquad = e^{-c^2/2}\int_{B_c} \exp\left(c\|p_L(x)\|\cos(e_1, a)\right)\lambda_c(da)\\
&\qquad = e^{-c^2/2}\int_{B_c} \exp\left(\|p_L(x)\|\langle e_1, a\rangle\right)\lambda_c(da) =: f_c(\|p_L(a)\|)
\end{aligned}$$

where f_c is strictly increasing. This proves that

$$\varphi(x) = \begin{cases} 1 & \text{if} \quad \|p_L(x)\| > f_c^{-1}(k_1) \\ 0 & \text{if} \quad \|p_L(x)\| < f_c^{-1}(k_1) \end{cases}$$

for some $k_1 \in [0, \infty]$. Since $P_0\varphi = P_0\varphi^*$ it follows that $f_c^{-1}(k_1) = k$ for every $c > 0$. This proves the assertion. □

30.2 Theorem. *For* $\alpha \in [0, 1]$ *let* k_α *be such that* $P_0\{\|p_L(.)\| > k_\alpha\} = \alpha$. *Then*

$$\varphi^*(x) = \begin{cases} 1 & \textit{if} \quad \|p_L(x)\| > k_\alpha, \\ 0 & \textit{if} \quad \|p_L(x)\| < k_\alpha, \end{cases} \qquad x \in H,$$

satisfies

$$\inf_{a\in B_c} P_a\varphi^* \geqq \inf_{a\in B_c} P_a\varphi$$

for all $\varphi \in \mathscr{F}(H, \mathscr{B}(H))$ *with* $P_0\varphi \leqq \alpha$ *and all* $c > 0$.

Proof. From the preceding lemma it follows that

$$\begin{aligned}
\inf_{a\in B_c} P_a\varphi &\leqq \int_{B_c} P_a\varphi\lambda_c(da)\\
&\leqq \int_{B_c} P_a\varphi^*\lambda_c(da).
\end{aligned}$$

Since $a \mapsto P_a\varphi^*$ is constant on B_c, $c > 0$, the assertion follows. □

Tests with such an optimum property as φ^* are sometimes called *maximin tests.*

30.3 Corollary. *Let* φ^* *be the test of Theorem 30.2 for some* $\alpha \in [0, 1]$. *Let*

$c > 0$. *If* $\varphi \in \mathscr{F}(H, \mathscr{B}(H))$ *is such that*

$$P_0\varphi \leqq \alpha,$$
$$P_a\varphi \geqq P_a\varphi^* \quad \textit{whenever} \quad a \in B_c$$

then $\varphi = \varphi^*$ P_0-a.e. *Hence* φ^* *is admissible for every testing problem* $(\{0\}, B_c)$, $c > 0$, *and is uniquely determined by its power function on* $\{0\} \cup B_c$.

Proof. Let $c > 0$ and assume that $\varphi \in \mathscr{F}(H, \mathscr{B}(H))$ is such that $P_0\varphi \leqq P_0\varphi^*$ and $P_a\varphi \geqq P_a\varphi^*$ for $a \in B_c$. Then it follows that

$$\int_{B_c} P_a\varphi\,\lambda_c(da) \geqq \int_{B_c} P_a\varphi^*\,\lambda_c(da).$$

Since φ^* is an NP-test for $(P_0, \int_{B_c} P_a\lambda_c(da))$ we obtain from Theorem 8.8 that $\varphi = \varphi^*$ P_0-a.e. which proves the assertion. □

In particular, it follows that the tests φ^* are admissible for the testing problem $(\{0\}, \{a \in L: a \neq 0\})$. But this is a particular case of a more general result.

30.4 Theorem (Birnbaum [1955]). *Let* $C \subseteq L$ *be a closed convex subset. Then*

$$\varphi^*(x) = \begin{cases} 1 & \textit{if} \quad p_L(x) \notin C, \\ 0 & \textit{if} \quad p_L(x) \in C, \end{cases} \qquad x \in H,$$

is an admissible test for the testing problem $(\{0\}, \{a \in L: a \neq 0\})$ *and is uniquely determined by its power function.*

Proof. If $C = L$ then the assertion is trivial. Suppose that $C \neq L$. Assume that there exists a critical function $\varphi \in \mathscr{F}(H, \mathscr{B}(H))$ such that $P_0\varphi \leqq P_0\varphi^*$, $P_h\varphi \geqq P_h\varphi^*$ if $h \neq 0$, with strict inequality at least for one $h \in H$. Then $P_0\{\varphi \neq \varphi^*\} > 0$, and since $P_0\varphi \leqq P_0\varphi^*$ we have $P_0\{\varphi^* > \varphi\} > 0$. From $\varphi^* = 1 - 1_C \circ p_L$ it follows that

$$\{\varphi^* > \varphi\} = \{p_L \notin C\} \cap \{\varphi < 1\}.$$

It follows from standard facts on separation of convex sets that

$$C = \bigcap_{n=1}^{\infty} \{x \in L: \langle y_n, x\rangle \leqq r_n\}$$

where $(y_n)_{n\in\mathbb{N}} \subseteq L$ and $r_n \in \mathbb{R}$, $n \in \mathbb{N}$. Then

$$C' = \bigcup_{n=1}^{\infty} \{x \in L: \langle y_n, x\rangle > r_n\}$$

and from $P_0(\{p_L \notin C\} \cap \{\varphi < 1\}) > 0$ it follows that there exists $n \in \mathbb{N}$ such that

$$P_0(\{\langle y_n, p_L(.)\rangle > r_n\} \cap \{\varphi < 1\}) > 0.$$

Fix $n \in \mathbb{N}$ and let $\lambda > 0$ be arbitrary. Since

$$P_{\lambda y_n}\varphi^* \leqq P_{\lambda y_n}\varphi$$

we obtain

$$\begin{aligned}
0 &\geqq \int (1_{C'} - \varphi)\, dP_{\lambda y_n} \\
&= \int (1_{C'} - \varphi) \exp(\lambda \langle y_n, p_L(.)\rangle - \frac{1}{2}\|\lambda y_n\|^2)\, dP_0 \\
&= \exp(-\frac{1}{2}\|\lambda y_n\|^2 + \lambda r_n) \int (1_{C'} - \varphi) \exp(\lambda(\langle y_n, p_L(.)\rangle - r_n))\, dP_0 \\
&= \exp(-\frac{1}{2}\|\lambda y_n\|^2 + \lambda r_n) \\
&\quad \Bigg(\int\limits_{\langle y_n, p_L(.)\rangle - r_n > 0} (1_{C'} - \varphi) \exp(\lambda(\langle y_n, p_L(.)\rangle - r_n)\, dP_0 \\
&\quad + \int\limits_{\langle y_n, p_L(.)\rangle - r_n \leqq 0} (1_{C'} - \varphi) \exp(\lambda(\langle y_n, p_L(.)\rangle - r_n))\, dP_0 \Bigg).
\end{aligned}$$

Since $\lambda \to \infty$ the second integral is bounded and the first integral tends to infinity we arrive at a contradiction for sufficiently large $\lambda > 0$. □

Completeness of the class of tests under consideration follows from Corollary 29.5.

Now, we extend the preceding results to linear testing problems $(L_0, L \setminus L_0)$ where $L_0 \subseteq L$ is a linear subspace. For every $c > 0$ we denote $B_c = \{a \in L: \|a - p_{L_0}(a)\| = c\}$.

30.5 Theorem. *For $\alpha \in [0,1]$ let k_α be such that $P_0\{\|p_L(.) - p_{L_0}(.)\| > k_\alpha\} = \alpha$. Then*

$$\varphi^*(x) = \begin{cases} 1 & \text{if } \|p_L(x) - p_{L_0}(x)\| > k_\alpha, \\ 0 & \text{if } \|p_L(x) - p_{L_0}(x)\| < k_\alpha, \end{cases} \quad x \in H,$$

satisfies

$$\inf_{a \in B_c} P_a\varphi^* \geqq \inf_{a \in B_c} P_a\varphi$$

for all $\varphi \in \mathscr{F}(H, \mathscr{B}(H))$ with $P_a\varphi \leqq \alpha$, $a \in L_0$, and all $c > 0$.

Proof. Let $L_0^\perp$ be the orthogonal complement of L_0 in L. Then it follows from Theorem (30.2), considering the experiment $E|_{L_0^\perp}$, that the test φ^* satisfies

$$\inf_{a \in B_c \cap L_0^\perp} P_a\varphi^* \geqq \inf_{a \in B_c \cap L_0^\perp} P_a\varphi$$

for all $\varphi \in \mathscr{F}(H, \mathscr{B}(H))$ with $P_0 \varphi \leqq \alpha$ and all $c > 0$. Since

$$P_a \varphi^* = P_b \varphi^*$$

whenever $p_L(a) - p_{L_0}(a) = p_L(b) - p_{L_0}(b)$, the assertion follows. □

30.6 Corollary. *Let φ^* be the test of Theorem 30.5 for some $\alpha \in [0,1]$. Let $c > 0$. If $\varphi \in \mathscr{F}(H, \mathscr{B}(H))$ is such that*

$$P_0 \varphi \leqq \alpha,$$
$$P_a \varphi \geqq P_a \varphi^* \quad \textit{whenever} \quad a \in B_c,\ a \perp L_0,$$

then $\varphi = \varphi^*$ P_0-a.e. Hence φ^* is admissible for every testing problem $(\{0\}, B_c \cap L_0^\perp)$ and is uniquely determined by its power function on $\{0\} \cup (B_c \cap L_0^\perp)$, $c > 0$.

Proof. Let $c > 0$ and assume that $\varphi \in \mathscr{F}(H, \mathscr{B}(H))$ is such that $P_0 \varphi \leqq \alpha$, $P_a \varphi \geqq P_a \varphi^*$ for $a \in B_c$, $a \perp L_0$. Note, that for the experiment restricted to $\{a \in L: a \perp L_0\}$ the test coincides with that of Theorem 30.2. Hence, by Corollary 30.3 $\varphi = \varphi^*$ P_0-a.e. which proves the assertion. □

30.7 Theorem. *Let $C \subseteq L_0^\perp$ be a closed convex subset. Then*

$$\varphi^*(x) = \begin{cases} 1 & \text{if} \quad p_L(x) - p_{L_0}(x) \notin C, \\ 0 & \text{if} \quad p_L(x) - p_{L_0}(x) \in C, \end{cases} \qquad x \in H,$$

is an admissible test for the testing problem $(L_0, L \setminus L_0)$ and is uniquely determined by its power function.

Proof. Apply Theorem 30.4 to $E|_{L_0^\perp}$ and to the testing problem $(\{0\}, L_0^\perp \setminus \{0\})$. □

Finally, let us discuss briefly the problem of testing a linear function $f: L \to \mathbb{R}^k$. W.l.g., assume that $\operatorname{im}(f) = \mathbb{R}^k$. Consider the testing problem $(\{f = 0\}, \{f \neq 0\})$.

30.8 Discussion. Let $L_0 = \ker f$. Then the testing problem can be written as $(L_0, L \setminus L_0)$ and its solution is given in Theorem 30.5 and Corollary 30.6. Let us express the optimal test φ^* in terms of f. It is easy to see that

$$p_L - p_{L_0} = f^* \circ (f \circ f^*)^{-1} \circ f \circ p_L.$$

The test φ^* depends on $\|p_L(x) - p_{L_0}(x)\|$, $x \in H$, which is of the form

$$\|p_L(x) - p_{L_0}(x)\|^2 = (f \circ p_L(x))^* \Gamma (f \circ p_L(x)), \quad x \in H,$$

where Γ is the matrix of $(f \circ f^*)^{-1}: \mathbb{R}^k \to \mathbb{R}^k$. Hence, we arrive at

$$\varphi^* = \begin{cases} 1 & \text{if } f \circ p_L \notin C, \\ 0 & \text{if } f \circ p_L \in C, \end{cases}$$

where $C = \{z \in \mathbb{R}^k : z^* \Gamma z \leqq k\}$ for some $k \in [0, \infty]$. It follows from Theorem (30.7) that replacing C by an arbitrary closed convex set in $\mathbb{R}^k$, the test remains to be admissible. This is especially true, if Γ is replaced by any positive semidefinite symmetric (k,k)-matrix.

31. Reduction of testing problems by invariance

Let $E = (\Omega, \mathscr{A}, \{P_\vartheta : \vartheta \in \Theta\})$ be an experiment and denote $\mathscr{P} := \{P_\vartheta : \vartheta \in \Theta\}$. Suppose that there is a locally compact group G with countable base for its topology consisting of measurable transformations $g: \Omega \to \Omega$. The Borel-σ-field of G is denoted by $\mathscr{B}(G)$. We assume that the operation $(g, \omega) \mapsto g\omega$ is $\mathscr{B}(G) \otimes \mathscr{A}$-measurable.

31.1 Definition. The *experiment* E is *G-invariant* if $P_\vartheta \circ g^{-1} \in \mathscr{P}$ for all $g \in G$ and $\vartheta \in \Theta$. A *testing problem* (H, K) is *G-invariant* if for all $g \in G$

$$P_\vartheta \circ g^{-1} \in \begin{cases} \{P_\sigma : \sigma \in H\} & \text{if } \vartheta \in H. \\ \{P_\sigma : \sigma \in K\} & \text{if } \vartheta \in K. \end{cases}$$

For the present section we assume that E is G-invariant. For every $\omega \in \Omega$ the *orbit* of ω under G is the set $G\omega := \{g\omega : g \in G\}$. Two points of Ω are called *connected* if they belong to the same orbit.

31.2 Definition. A map S defined on Ω is called *G-invariant* if it is constant on orbits. It is called *maximal G-invariant* if it is G-invariant and has different values on different orbits.

Let us call a *critical function* $\varphi \in \mathscr{F}(\Omega, \mathscr{A})$ *G-invariant* if it is a G-invariant map. The indicator of a set $A \in \mathscr{A}$ is G-invariant iff $g^{-1}A = A$ for every $g \in G$. It is easy to see that

$$\mathscr{A}_i := \{A \in \mathscr{A} : g^{-1}A = A \quad \text{for every } g \in G\}$$

is a σ-field and that a critical function is G-invariant iff it is $\mathscr{A}_i$-measurable.

31.3 Remark. Let $S: \Omega \to \mathbb{R}^k$ be $(\mathscr{A}, \mathscr{B}^k)$-measurable and maximal G-invariant. Then it is clear that every critical function $\psi \in \mathscr{F}(\mathbb{R}^k, \mathscr{B}^k)$ yields a G-invariant critical function $\varphi = \psi \circ S$ in $\mathscr{F}(\Omega, \mathscr{A})$. For the converse we need additional assumptions. Consider the diagram:

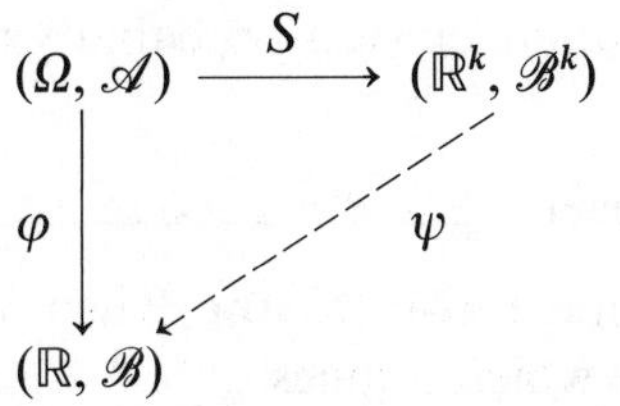

It is well-known that there exists a Borel function $\psi: \mathbb{R}^k \to \mathbb{R}$ such that $\varphi = \psi \circ S$ iff $\varphi^{-1}(\mathscr{B}) \subseteq S^{-1}(\mathscr{B}^k)$. In general, one can only show that ψ is $\mathscr{B}_S$-measurable where $\mathscr{B}_S = \{B \subseteq \mathbb{R}^k: S^{-1}(B) \in \mathscr{A}\}$.

If $(\Omega, \mathscr{A}, \nu)$ is a perfect measure space then we have $\mathscr{B}^k = \mathscr{B}_S$ (mod $\mathscr{L}(S|\nu)$) and we may find a Borel function $\bar{\psi}: \mathbb{R}^k \to \mathbb{R}$ such that $\varphi = \bar{\psi} \circ S$ ν-a.e. Then we obtain the following result.

31.4 Lemma. *Suppose that $(\Omega, \mathscr{A}, \nu)$ is a perfect measure space. Suppose further that there is an $(\mathscr{A}, \mathscr{B}^k)$-measurable, maximal G-invariant function $S: \Omega \to \mathbb{R}^k$. Then for every G-invariant critical function $\varphi \in \mathscr{F}(\Omega, \mathscr{A})$ there exists a critical function $\psi \in \mathscr{F}(\mathbb{R}^k, \mathscr{B}^k)$ such that $\varphi = \psi \circ S$ ν-a.e.*

The preceding assertion can be put into statistical terms.

31.5 Corollary. *Suppose that $E = (\Omega, \mathscr{A}, \{P_\vartheta: \vartheta \in \Theta\})$ is an experiment and $\nu|\mathscr{A}$ a dominating σ-finite measure. Let $E_i = (\Omega, \mathscr{A}_i, \{P_\vartheta: \vartheta \in \Theta\})$ be the restriction of E to the G-invariant σ-field. Under the assumption of Lemma 31.4 it follows that $E_i \underset{2}{\sim} S_*(E)$.*

Now, we turn to a slightly more general notion of invariance.

31.6 Definition. A critical function $\varphi \in \mathscr{F}(\Omega, \mathscr{A})$ is *$\mathscr{P}$-almost G-invariant* if $\varphi \circ g = \varphi$ P_ϑ-a.e. for all $g \in G$ and $\vartheta \in \Theta$.

The indicator of a set $A \in \mathscr{A}$ is $\mathscr{P}$-almost G-invariant iff $P_\vartheta(A \triangle g^{-1}A) = 0$ for all $g \in G$ and $\vartheta \in \Theta$. It is easy to see that

$$\bar{\mathscr{A}}_i := \{A \in \mathscr{A}: P_\vartheta(A \triangle g^{-1}A) = 0 \text{ for all } g \in G \text{ and } \vartheta \in \Theta\}$$

is a σ-field and that a critical function is $\mathscr{P}$-almost G-invariant iff it is $\bar{\mathscr{A}}_i$-measurable.

Let $F_i = (\Omega, \bar{\mathscr{A}}_i, \{P_\vartheta: \vartheta \in \Theta\})$ be the restriction of E to the σ-field $\bar{\mathscr{A}}_i$. Then $\mathscr{A}_i \subseteq \bar{\mathscr{A}}_i \subseteq \mathscr{A}$ implies $E \underset{2}{\supseteq} F_i \underset{2}{\supseteq} E_i$.

The second inequality, however, can be improved to be an equivalence.

31.7 Theorem. *Suppose that E is dominated. Then for every $\mathscr{P}$-almost G-invariant critical function φ there exists a G-invariant critical function ψ such that $\varphi = \psi$ P_ϑ-a.e. for all $\vartheta \in \Theta$.*

Proof. Assume that $\nu|\mathscr{A}$ is a σ-finite measure being equivalent to $\mathscr{P}$ and let λ be a right Haar measure of G. Since λ is σ-finite there exists a probability measure $\lambda_0|\mathscr{B}$ which is equivalent to λ. This implies

$$\lambda_0(B) = 0 \quad \text{iff} \quad \lambda_0(Bg) = 0 \quad \text{whenever} \quad B \in \mathscr{B}, \quad g \in G.$$

Let φ be a critical function which is $\mathscr{P}$-almost G-invariant. Then we have $v\{\omega \in \Omega: \varphi(g\omega) \neq \varphi(\omega)\} = 0$ for every $g \in G$ which implies

$$(v \otimes \lambda_0)\{(\omega, g) \in \Omega \times G: \varphi(g\omega) \neq \varphi(\omega)\} = 0.$$

Hence we obtain

$$\lambda_0\{g \in G: \varphi(g\omega) \neq \varphi(\omega)\} = 0 \quad \text{for } v\text{-almost all } \omega \in \Omega.$$

Let N be the exceptional set of v-measure zero where the equation does not hold. Let

$$A := \{\omega \in \Omega: \varphi(g\omega) = \int \varphi(h\omega)\, \lambda_0(dh)\ \lambda_0\text{-a.e.}\}.$$

If we show that

(1) $A \in \mathscr{A}$,

(2) $\Omega \setminus N \subseteq A$ and hence $v(\Omega \setminus A) = 0$,

(3) $A \in \mathscr{A}_i$,

(4) $\int \varphi(h\omega)\, \lambda_0(dh) = \int \varphi(hg\omega)\, \lambda_0(dh)$ if $\omega \in A$, $g \in G$,

then the proof can be completed as follows.

Define

$$\psi(\omega) = \begin{cases} \int \varphi(h\omega)\, \lambda_0(dh) & \text{if} \quad \omega \in A, \\ 0 & \text{if} \quad \omega \notin A. \end{cases}$$

To show that ψ is G-invariant we note that $\omega \in A$ implies

$$\psi(g\omega) = \int \varphi(hg\omega)\, \lambda_0(dh) = \int \varphi(h\omega)\, \lambda_0(dh) = \psi(\omega),$$

whereas $\omega \notin A$ implies both $\psi(\omega) = 0$ and $\psi(g\omega) = 0$ since $g\omega \notin A$. The critical function ψ solves the problem since for $\omega \in A \setminus N$ we have $\varphi(\omega) = \varphi(h\omega)$ λ_0-a.e. which implies

$$\varphi(\omega) = \int \varphi(h\omega)\, \lambda_0(dh) = \psi(\omega).$$

It remains to prove assertions (1)–(4).

Assertion (1) follows from the fact that A is the set where the $\mathscr{A}$-measurable function

$$\omega \mapsto \int \left| \int \varphi(h\omega)\, \lambda_0(dh) - \varphi(g\omega) \right| \lambda_0(dg), \quad \omega \in \Omega,$$

vanishes. For the proof of (2) we note that $\omega \notin N$ implies $\varphi(h\omega) = \varphi(\omega)$ λ_0-a.e., hence $\omega \in A$. Next, let us prove (4). If $\omega \in A$ then we denote

$$N_\omega = \{k \in G: \varphi(k\omega) \neq \int \varphi(h\omega)\, \lambda_0(dh)\}$$

and observe that $\lambda_0(N_\omega) = 0$. Then $\lambda_0(N_\omega g^{-1}) = 0$, and since $N_\omega g^{-1}$ $= \{k \in G: kg \in N_\omega\} = \{k \in G: \varphi(kg\omega) \neq \int \varphi(h\omega)\, \lambda_0(dh)\}$

we obtain

$$\int \varphi(kg\omega)\,\lambda_0(dk) = \int\int \varphi(h\omega)\,\lambda_0(dh)\,\lambda_0(dk) = \int \varphi(h\omega)\,\lambda_0(dh).$$

Finally we show that (3) is true. If $\omega \in A$ and $g \in G$ then $\lambda_0(N_\omega g^{-1}) = 0$ implies that

$$\varphi(kg\omega) = \int \varphi(h\omega)\,\lambda_0(dh) \quad \text{for} \quad \lambda_0\text{-almost every } k \in G,$$

and from (4) it follows that

$$\int \varphi(h\omega)\,\lambda_0(dh) = \int \varphi(hg\omega)\,\lambda_0(dh).$$

Combining these equations we obtain

$$\varphi(kg\omega) = \int \varphi(hg\omega)\,\lambda_0(dh)$$

for λ_0-almost every $k \in G$. This implies $g\omega \in A$. □

It follows that for dominated experiments E the equivalence $F_i \underset{2}{\sim} E_i$ holds true. Under the additional conditions of Lemma 31.4 we obtain $F_i \underset{2}{\sim} S_*(E)$.

In the rest of this section we illustrate the method of reduction by invariance by a special case.

Let $(H, \langle .,. \rangle$ be a Euclidean space. The orthogonal group of H is denoted by $O(H)$.

31.8 Definition. A probability measure $P|\mathscr{B}(H)$ is *isotropic* if $P \circ g^{-1} = P$ for every $g \in O(H)$.

Suppose that $L \subseteq H$ is a linear subspace.

31.9 Definition. Let $P|\mathscr{B}(H)$ be a probability measure. For every $a \in L$ let $P_a := \varepsilon_a * P$. Then the experiment $E = (H, \mathscr{B}(H), \{P_a\colon a \in L\})$ is the *shift generated by* P and *spanned by* L.

In the following we consider a fixed isotropic probability measure $P|\mathscr{B}(H)$ and E denotes the shift generated by P and spanned by L.

Define $O_L(H) := \{A \in O(H)\colon AL \subseteq L\}$. It is easy to see that $AL = L$ and $AL^\perp = L^\perp$ for every $A \in O_L(H)$. For simplicity we identify a linear subspace with the group of translations generated by the subspace. In this sense $O_L(H) \times L$ denotes the group consisting of $g\colon x \mapsto Ax + b$, $x \in H$, where $A \in O_L(H)$ and $b \in L$.

31.10 Lemma. *The shift E is invariant under the group $G = O_L(H) \times L$.*

Proof. Let $g\colon x \mapsto Ax + b$, $x \in H$, where $A \in O_L(H)$ and $b \in L$. If $P_a = \varepsilon_a * P$, $a \in L$, then

$$\begin{aligned}\mathscr{L}(g|P_a)(t) &= e^{i\langle t,b\rangle}\hat{P}_a(A't) = e^{i\langle t,Aa+b\rangle}\hat{P}(A't)\\ &= e^{i\langle t,Aa+b\rangle}\hat{P}(t) = \hat{P}_{Aa+b}(t), \quad t\in H.\end{aligned}$$

Since $Aa+b\in L$ the assertion is proved. □

A *linear hypothesis* is a linear subspace $L_0\subseteq L$. Then $(L_0, L\setminus L_0)$ is called *linear testing problem.* Let

$$O_{L_0,L}(H)=\{A\in O(H)\colon AL\subseteq L, AL_0\subseteq L_0\}.$$

It follows that $AL_0=L_0$ and $A(L\setminus L_0)=L\setminus L_0$ if $A\in O_{L_0,L}(H)$.

31.11 Lemma. *The testing problem $(L_0, L\setminus L_0)$ for E is invariant under the group $G_0=O_{L_0,L}(H)\times L_0$.*

Proof. Similar to the proof of Lemma 31.10. □

We want to find a maximal invariant map S for the group G_0. To this end we need some technical prerequisites.

31.12 Remark. Let p_L and p_{L_0} denote the orthogonal projections of H onto L and L_0, respectively.

(1) If $A\in O_{L_0,L}(H)$ then $Ap_L=p_LA$ and $Ap_{L_0}=p_{L_0}A$.
To prove this let $x\in H$ and $y\in L$. Then

$$\langle p_LAx,y\rangle=\langle Ax,y\rangle=\langle x,A'y\rangle=\langle p_Lx,A'y\rangle=\langle Ap_Lx,y\rangle.$$

A similar argument works for L_0.

$$\text{(2)}\quad \begin{aligned}O_{L_0,L}(H)=\{&Ap_{L_0}+B(p_L-p_{L_0})+C(\mathrm{id}_H-p_L)\colon A\in O(L_0),\\ &B\in O(L_0^\perp\cap L), C\in O(L^\perp)\}.\end{aligned}$$

If $D\in O_{L_0,L}(H)$ then define $A=D|_{L_0}$, $B=D|_{L_0^\perp\cap L}$, $C=D|_{L^\perp}$. This yields the desired decomposition. Conversely, it is almost obvious, that any mapping which admits such a decomposition is in $O_{L_0,L}(H)$.

31.13 Theorem. *The mapping*

$$S\colon x\mapsto(\|x-p_L(x)\|, \|p_L(x)-p_{L_0}(x)\|),\quad x\in H,$$

is maximal G_0-invariant.

Proof. To prove invariance let $g\colon x\mapsto Ax+b$, $x\in H$, where $A\in O_{L_0,L}(H)$ and $b\in L_0$. Then we have

$$\begin{aligned}\|gx-p_Lgx\| &= \|Ax-p_LAx+b-p_Lb\| = \|Ax-Ap_Lx\|\\ &= \|x-p_Lx\|,\ x\in H,\quad\text{and}\end{aligned}$$

$$\|p_L gx - p_{L_0} gx\| = \|p_L Ax - p_{L_0} Ax + p_L b - p_{L_0} b\|$$
$$= \|Ap_L x - Ap_{L_0} x\| = \|p_L x - p_{L_0} x\|, \; x \in H.$$

To prove maximal invariance assume $Tx = Ty$. We have to construct an element $g: x \mapsto Ax + b$, $x \in H$, of G_0 such that $gx = y$. From $Tx = Ty$ it follows that $\|x - p_L x\| = \|y - p_L y\|$ and $\|p_L x - p_{L_0} x\| = \|p_L y - p_{L_0} y\|$. We may find $B \in O(L_0^\perp \cap L)$ and $C \in O(L^\perp)$ such that $B(p_L x - p_{L_0} x) = p_L y - p_{L_0} y$ and $C(x - p_L x) = y - p_L y$. Putting $A = p_{L_0} \oplus B(p_L - p_{L_0}) \oplus C(\mathrm{id}_H - p_L)$ and $b = p_{L_0} y - p_{L_0} x$ which satisfies $A \in O_{L_0, L}(H)$ and $b \in L_0$, we obtain

$$Ax + b = p_{L_0} x + B(p_L x - p_{L_0} x) + C(x - p_L x) + p_{L_0} y - p_{L_0} x$$
$$= p_{L_0} y + (p_L y - p_{L_0} y) + (y - p_L y) = y. \qquad \square$$

31.14 Examples. (1) Let $L = H$ and $L_0 = \{0\}$. Then $S: x \mapsto \|x\|$, $x \in H$, is maximal invariant under $G = O(H) \times H$.

(2) If $L = H$ but $L_0 \subseteq H$ is arbitrary, then $S: x \mapsto \|x - p_{L_0} x\|$, $x \in H$, is maximal invariant under $G = O_{L_0}(H) \times L_0$.

(3) If $L_0 = \{0\}$ but $L \subseteq H$ is arbitrary then $S: x \mapsto (\|x - p_L(x)\|, \|p_L(x)\|)$, $x \in H$, is maximal invariant under $G = O_L(H)$.
It is possible to compute the distribution of S if $P = N_H$, the standard Gaussian measure on H.

31.15 Theorem. *Let $S = (S_1, S_2)$ be the maximal invariant of 31.13. If $P = N_H$ then S_1 and S_2 are independent, $\mathscr{L}(S_1 | P_a) = \chi^2_{\dim H - \dim L}$ and $\mathscr{L}(S_2 | P_a) = \chi^2_{\dim L - \dim L_0}(\|a - p_{L_0} a\|^2)$, $a \in L$.*

Proof. We denote $h = \dim L_0$, $k = \dim L$ and $n = \dim H$. Moreover, we choose an orthonormal base $e_1, \ldots, e_n$ of H in such a way $e_1, \ldots, e_h$ is a base of L_0 and $e_1, \ldots, e_k$ is a base of L. Then

$$Sx = \Big(\sum_{i=k+1}^{n} \langle e_i, x \rangle^2, \sum_{i=h+1}^{k} \langle e_i, x \rangle^2 \Big), \quad x \in H.$$

It is clear that the random variables $X_i: x \mapsto \langle e_i, x \rangle$, $1 \leq i \leq n$, are independent and that

$$\mathscr{L}(X_i | P_a) = \nu_{\langle a, e_i \rangle, 1}, \quad 1 \leq i \leq n.$$

Hence

$$\mathscr{L}\Big(\sum_{i=k+1}^{n} X_i^2 | P_a \Big) = \chi^2_{n-k}$$

and

$$\mathscr{L}\Big(\Big(\sum_{i=h+1}^{k} X_i^2 | P_a \Big) = \chi^2_{k-h}\Big(\sum_{i=h+1}^{k} \langle a, e_i \rangle^2 \Big). \qquad \square$$

A different situation arises if not only the shift parameter but also a scale parameter is unknown. For $a \in L$ and $\sigma > 0$ let $P_{a,\sigma}: B \mapsto P\{x \in H: \sigma x + a \in B\}$, $B \in \mathscr{B}(H)$. In the following we consider the experiment $F = (H, \mathscr{B}(H), \{P_{a,\sigma}: a \in L, \sigma > 0\})$. For simplicity we identify $\mathbb{R}^+$ with the group of transformations $\sigma: x \mapsto \sigma x$, $x \in H$, $\sigma \in \mathbb{R}^+$.

31.16 Lemma. *The experiment F is invariant under the group $G = \mathbb{R}^+ \times O_L(H) \times L$.*

Proof. Let $g: x \mapsto \tau A x + b$, $ax \in H$, where $\tau > 0$, $A \in O_L(H)$ and $b \in L$. If $a \in L$ and $\sigma > 0$, then

$$\begin{aligned} \hat{\mathscr{L}}(g \mid P_{a,\sigma})(t) &= e^{i\langle t, b\rangle} \hat{P}_{a,\sigma}(\tau A' t) \\ &= e^{i\langle t, \tau A a + b\rangle} \hat{P}(\sigma \tau A' t) = e^{i\langle t, \tau A a + b\rangle} \hat{P}(\sigma \tau t) \\ &= \hat{P}_{\tau A a + b, \sigma\tau}(t), \quad t \in H. \qquad \square \end{aligned}$$

Let $L_0 \subseteq L$ be a subspace. Then $L_0 \times \mathbb{R}^+$ is called a linear hypothesis and $(L_0 \times \mathbb{R}^+, (L \setminus L_0) \times \mathbb{R}^+)$ is a linear testing problem.

31.17 Lemma. *The testing problem $(L_0 \times \mathbb{R}^+, (L \setminus L_0) \times \mathbb{R}^+)$ for F is invariant under the group $G_1 = \mathbb{R}^+ \times O_{L_0,L}(H) \times L_0$.*

Proof. Similar to the proof of Lemma 31.16. $\square$

31.18 Theorem. *Suppose that* $\dim L < \dim H$. *Then the mapping*

$$S: x \mapsto \begin{cases} \dfrac{\|p_L x - p_{L_0} x\|}{\|x - p_L x\|} & \text{if } x - p_L x \neq 0, \\ +\infty & \text{if } x - p_L x = 0,\ p_L x - p_{L_0} x \neq 0, \\ -1 & \text{if } x - p_L x = 0,\ p_L x - p_{L_0} x = 0, \end{cases}$$

is maximal G_1-invariant.

Proof. To prove invariance let $g: x \mapsto \sigma A x + b$, $x \in H$, where $\sigma > 0$, $A \in O_{L_0,L}(H)$ and $b \in L_0$. From Theorem 31.13 it follows that

$$\begin{aligned} &\|p_L g x - p_{L_0} g x\| = \sigma \|p_L x - p_{L_0} x\|, \\ &\|g x - p_L g x\| = \sigma \|x - p_L x\|. \end{aligned}$$

This implies that S is invariant.

Let us prove maximal invariance. If $Sx = Sy$ then there exists $\alpha > 0$ such that

$$\begin{aligned} &\alpha \|p_L x - p_{L_0} x\| = \|p_L y - p_{L_0} y\|, \\ &\alpha \|x - p_L x\| = \|y - p_L y\|. \end{aligned}$$

We may find $B \in O(L_0^{\perp} \cap L)$ and $C \in O(L^{\perp})$ such that $\alpha B(p_L x - p_{L_0} x) = p_L y - p_{L_0} y$ and $\alpha C(x - p_L x) = y - p_L y$.

Putting $A = p_{L_0} + \alpha B(p_L - p_{L_0}) + \alpha C(\mathrm{id}_H - p_L)$ and $b = p_{L_0} y - p_{L_0} x$ proves the assertion as before in Theorem 31.13. □

31.19 Corollary. *Suppose* $\dim L < \dim H$ *and* $P \ll \lambda_H$. *Then*

$$S\colon x \mapsto \frac{\|p_L x - p_{L_0} x\|}{\|x - p_L x\|}, \quad x \in H, \quad P_a\text{-a.e.}, \quad a \in L_0 .$$

Proof. Obvious. □

31.20 Corollary. *Let* $P = N_H$. *The distribution of* S *under* $P_{a,\sigma}$, $a \in L$, $\sigma > 0$, *is*

$$\mathscr{L}(S \mid P_{a,\sigma}) = F_{\dim L - \dim L_0, \dim H - \dim L}\left(\frac{\|a - p_{L_0}(a)\|^2}{\sigma^2}\right).$$

Proof. Apply Theorem 31.15. □

32. The theorem of Hunt and Stein

Suppose that G is a locally compact group with countable base for its topology. The Borel-σ-field of G is denoted by $\mathscr{B}(G)$. Let λ_r be a right Haar measure of G.

32.1 Definition. The group G is *amenable* if there is a sequence of compact subsets $K_n \uparrow G$ such that for every $g \in G$

$$\lim_{n \to \infty} \sup_{B \in \mathscr{B}} \left| \frac{\lambda_r(Bg \cap K_n)}{\lambda_r(K_n)} - \frac{\lambda_r(B \cap K_n)}{\lambda_r(K_n)} \right| = 0 .$$

The sequence (K_n) is called a *summing sequence* for G.

32.2 Remarks. (1) Every compact group is amenable since there exists an invariant probability measure.

(2) A sequence of compacts (K_n) is a summing sequence iff for every $g \in G$

$$\lim_{n \to \infty} \sup_{\varphi \in \mathscr{F}(G, \mathscr{B}(G))} \frac{1}{\lambda_r(K_n)} \int_{K_n} |\varphi(hg) - \varphi(h)| \lambda_r(dh) = 0 .$$

This follows from Lemma 2.3.

(3) A sequence of compacts (K_n) is a summing sequence iff for every $g \in G$

$$\lim_{n\to\infty} \frac{\lambda_r(K_n \triangle K_n g^{-1})}{\lambda_r(K_n)} = 0.$$

This follows from Lemma 2.4.

For further remarks see Discussion 48.12.

32.3 Example. A Euclidean space is amenable since it is an Abelian group. Let us give a direct proof of this fact. For $\alpha > 0$ let $K_\alpha = \{x \in H: \|x\| \leqq \alpha\}$. Then we have $K_{\sqrt{n}} + K_{n-\sqrt{n}} \subseteq K_n$ which implies that $K_{n-\sqrt{n}} \subseteq K_n - t$ for every $t \in K_{\sqrt{n}}$. We observe that

$$\lim_{n\to\infty} \frac{\lambda(K_n \backslash (K_n - t))}{\lambda(K_n)} \leqq \lim_{n\to\infty} \frac{\lambda(K_n \backslash K_{n-\sqrt{n}})}{\lambda(K_n)}$$
$$= \lim_{n\to\infty} \left(1 - \frac{\lambda(K_{n-\sqrt{n}})}{\lambda(K_n)}\right) = 0.$$

This proves the assertion.

Now we continue the general discussion of Section 31. In particular we suppose that the experiment $E = (\Omega, \mathscr{A}, \{P_\vartheta: \vartheta \in \Theta\})$ is G-invariant. Two points ϑ_1 and ϑ_2 of Θ are connected by G if there exists $g \in G$ such that $P_{\vartheta_2} = P_{\vartheta_1} \circ g^{-1}$. This is an equivalence relation on Θ and the equivalence classes are called the orbits of G on Θ. For simplicity we denote the set of orbits by Θ/G.

32.4 Lemma. *If a critical function $\varphi \in \mathscr{F}(\Omega, \mathscr{A})$ is $\mathscr{P}$-almost G-invariant then the power function of φ is constant on the orbits of Θ.*

If the power function $\vartheta \mapsto P_\vartheta \varphi$ of a critical function is constant on the orbits $\bar{\vartheta} \in \Theta/G$ then we denote

$$P_{\bar{\vartheta}}\varphi := P_\vartheta \varphi \quad \text{if} \quad \vartheta \in \bar{\vartheta} \in \Theta/G.$$

32.5 Theorem (Hunt and Stein). *Suppose that E is dominated and that G is amenable. Then for every critical function $\varphi \in \mathscr{F}(\Omega, \mathscr{A})$ there exists a $\mathscr{P}$-almost G-invariant critical function ψ such that for all $\bar{\vartheta} \in \Theta/G$*

$$\inf_{\vartheta\in\bar{\vartheta}} P_\vartheta \varphi \leqq P_{\bar{\vartheta}}\psi \leqq \sup_{\vartheta\in\bar{\vartheta}} P_\vartheta \varphi.$$

Proof. W.l.g. we assume that $\nu|\mathscr{A}$ is a probability measure being equivalent with $\mathscr{P}$. Let $\varphi \in \mathscr{F}(\Omega, \mathscr{A})$ be an arbitrary critical function. Let (K_n) be a summing sequence and denote $\mu_n := \lambda_r(.\cap K_n)/\lambda_r(K_n)$, $n \in \mathbb{N}$. We define a sequence of critical functions

$$\psi_n(\omega) := \int \varphi(g\omega)\, \mu_n(dg), \; \omega \in \Omega, \; n \in \mathbb{N},$$

and choose an $L_1(\nu)$-convergent subsequence $(\psi_{n_i})_{i\in\mathbb{N}} \subseteq (\psi_n)_{n\in\mathbb{N}}$. This implies the existence of a critical function $\psi \in \mathscr{F}(\Omega, \mathscr{A})$ such that

$$\lim_{k\to\infty} P_\vartheta \psi_{n_k} = P_\vartheta \psi \quad \text{if} \quad \vartheta \in \Theta .$$

We will prove that ψ has the desired properties. For every $\vartheta \in \Theta$ we have

$$P_\vartheta \psi_{n_k} = \iint \varphi(g\omega)\, \mu_{n_k}(dg)\, P_\vartheta(d\omega) = \int P_\vartheta(\varphi \circ g)\, \mu_{n_k}(dg)$$

which implies

$$\inf_{\sigma \in \vartheta} P_\sigma \varphi \leqq P_\vartheta \psi_{n_k} \leqq \sup_{\sigma \in \vartheta} P_\sigma \varphi \quad \text{if} \quad \vartheta \in \bar{\vartheta} \in \Theta / G .$$

This proves the asserted inequalities.

From Remark 32.2 (3) we obtain that

$$\lim_{k\to\infty} (\psi_{n_k}(g\omega) - \psi_{n_k}(\omega)) = 0 \quad \text{if} \quad \omega \in \Omega,\ g \in G .$$

This implies that for every $A \in \mathscr{A}$

$$\lim_{k\to\infty} \int_A (\psi_{n_k}(g\omega) - \psi_{n_k}(\omega))\, \nu(d\omega) = 0 .$$

We know from $L_1(\nu)$-convergence of $(\psi_{n_k})_{k\in\mathbb{N}}$ that

$$\lim_{k\to\infty} \int_A \psi_{n_k}(\omega)\, \nu(d\omega) = \int_A \psi(\omega)\, \nu(d\omega), \quad A \in \mathscr{A} .$$

Moreover, we note that $(\psi_{n_k})_{k\in\mathbb{N}}$ is also $L_1(\nu \circ g^{-1})$-convergent for every $g \in G$. Indeed, if $\nu(A) = 0$ then $P_\vartheta(A) = 0$ for every $\vartheta \in \Theta$, hence $P_\vartheta(g^{-1}A) = 0$ for every $\vartheta \in \Theta$. Since $\nu \sim \mathscr{P}$ we obtain $\nu(g^{-1}A) = 0$. Thus we have shown that $\nu \circ g^{-1} \ll \nu$ and therefore $\dfrac{d\nu \circ g^{-1}}{d\nu} \in L_1(\nu)$ which yields the asserted property. Hence we have

$$\lim_{k\to\infty} \int_A \psi_{n_k}(g\omega)\, \nu(d\omega) = \int_A \psi(g\omega)\, \nu(d\omega), \quad A \in \mathscr{A} .$$

Now

$$\int_A (\psi(g\omega) - \psi(\omega))\, \nu(d\omega) = 0 \quad \text{if} \quad A \in \mathscr{A} ,$$

proves that ψ is ν-almost G-invariant. □

32.6 Remark. If G is a compact group then the critical function ψ can be chosen as

$$\psi(\omega) := \int \varphi(g\omega)\, \lambda_r(dg), \quad \omega \in \Omega .$$

Let us mention some statistical implications of Theorem 32.5. For this, we assume that (H, K) is a G-invariant testing problem. For a G-invariant testing problem (H, K) the sets H and K are unions of certain orbits $\bar{\vartheta} \in \Theta/G$. Sometimes among all $\mathscr{P}$-almost G-invariant tests there is an optimal one. This optimal invariant test has interesting properties within the class of all critical functions.

For simplicity we assume in the following that there is a dominating measure $\nu|\mathscr{A}$ such that $(\Omega, \mathscr{A}, \nu)$ is perfect. If there is a maximal G-invariant mapping S then E_i and $S_*(E)$ are equivalent for testing problems (Theorems 31.4 and 31.7).

32.7 Theorem. *Suppose that E is dominated and G is amenable. Suppose further that S is maximal G-invariant. If $S_*(E)$ admits an optimal unbiased level-α-test $\psi^* \in \mathscr{F}_\alpha(H, K)$ then $\psi^* \circ S$ satisfies*

$$P_{\bar{\vartheta}}(\psi^* \circ S) \leqq \sup_{\vartheta \in \bar{\vartheta}} P_\vartheta \varphi \quad \textit{if} \quad \bar{\vartheta} \subseteq H, \quad \textit{and}$$

$$P_{\bar{\vartheta}}(\psi^* \circ S) \geqq \inf_{\vartheta \in \bar{\vartheta}} P_\vartheta \varphi \quad \textit{if} \quad \bar{\vartheta} \subseteq K,$$

for every critical function $\varphi \in \mathscr{F}_\alpha(H, K)$.

Proof. In view of Theorem 32.5 it is sufficient to show that

$$P_\vartheta(\psi^* \circ S) \leqq P_\vartheta(\varphi) \quad \text{if} \quad \bar{\vartheta} \subseteq H, \quad \text{and}$$
$$P_\vartheta(\psi^* \circ S) \geqq P_\vartheta(\varphi) \quad \text{if} \quad \bar{\vartheta} \subseteq K,$$

for every $\mathscr{P}$-almost G-invariant function $\varphi \in \mathscr{F}_\alpha(H, K)$. By Theorems 31.4 and 31.7 we need only consider critical functions of the form $\varphi = \psi \circ S$ where ψ is an unbiased level-α-test of $S_*(E_i)$. Now the assertion follows from the optimum property of ψ^*. □

A critical function with the properties of $\psi^* \circ S$ in the preceding theorem is sometimes called a *maximin-test*.

Finally, let us prove another property of optimal invariant tests. Recall, that for $\alpha \in [0, 1]$ the function

$$\chi_\alpha(H, K): \vartheta \mapsto \begin{cases} \inf \{P_\vartheta \varphi: \varphi \in \mathscr{F}_\alpha(H, K)\} & \text{if} \quad \vartheta \in H, \\ \sup \{P_\vartheta \varphi: \varphi \in \mathscr{F}_\alpha(H, K)\} & \text{if} \quad \vartheta \in K, \end{cases}$$

is called envelope power function for $\mathscr{F}_\alpha(H, K)$.

32.8 Theorem. *Assume that E is dominated and G is amenable. Suppose further that S is maximal G-invariant. If $S_*(E_i)$ admits an optimal unbiased level-α-test ψ^* then $\psi^* \circ S$ satisfies*

$$\sup_{\vartheta \in \bar{\vartheta}} |P_\vartheta(\psi^* \circ S) - \chi_\alpha(H, K)(\vartheta)| \leqq \sup_{\vartheta \in \bar{\vartheta}} |P_\vartheta \varphi - \chi_\alpha(H, K)(\vartheta)|$$

for all critical functions $\varphi \in \mathscr{F}_\alpha(H, K)$ and every orbit $\bar{\vartheta} \subseteq \Theta/G$.

Proof. First we note that $\chi_\alpha(H, K)$ is G-invariant. This follows immediately from that fact that $\varphi \in \mathscr{F}_\alpha(H, K)$ iff $\varphi \circ g \in \mathscr{F}_\alpha(H, K)$, $g \in G$. Now, if $\bar{\vartheta} \subseteq H$ then we obtain

$$0 \leqq P_{\bar{\vartheta}}(\psi^* \circ S) - \chi_\alpha(H, K)(\bar{\vartheta}) = \sup_{\vartheta \in \bar{\vartheta}} (P_\vartheta(\psi^* \circ S) - \chi_\alpha(H, K)(\vartheta))$$

$$\leqq \sup_{\vartheta \in \bar{\vartheta}} (P_\vartheta \varphi - \chi_\alpha(H, K)(\vartheta)) = \sup_{\vartheta \in \bar{\vartheta}} |P_\vartheta \varphi - \chi_\alpha(H, K)(\vartheta)|$$

whenever $\varphi \in \mathscr{F}_\alpha(H, K)$. A similar argument proves the assertion in case $\bar{\vartheta} \subseteq K$. □

To illustrate the preceding theory we show that the maximin tests obtained in Section 30 are exactly the best invariant tests under the group considered in 31.8ff. Hence, the maximin property can be understood as a consequence of the Theorem 32.7.

Let $(H, \langle .,. \rangle)$ be a Euclidean space, $\mathscr{B}(H)$ the Borel-σ-field of H and $N_H | \mathscr{B}(H)$ the standard Gaussian measure of H. We consider the Gaussian shift experiment $E = (H, \mathscr{B}(H), \{P_a: a \in L\})$ where $P_a = \varepsilon_a * N_H$ and $L \subseteq H$ is a linear subspace. Consider the linear testing problems $(L_0, L \setminus L_0)$ for E where $L_0 \subseteq L$ is a linear subspace. We keep the notation of Section 31. It is easy to see that the group $G_0 = O_{L, L_0} \times L_0$ is amenable.

32.9 Theorem. *For* $\alpha \in [0, 1]$ *let* k_α *be such that* $P_0\{x \in H: \|p_L(x) - p_{L_0}(x)\| > k_\alpha\} = \alpha$. *Then the test*

$$\varphi^*(x) = \begin{cases} 1 & \text{if} \quad \|p_L(x) - p_{L_0}(x)\| > k_\alpha, \\ 0 & \text{if} \quad \|p_L(x) - p_{L_0}(x)\| < k_\alpha, \end{cases} \qquad x \in H,$$

is optimal invariant in $\mathscr{F}_\alpha(H, K)$.

Proof. Consider the experiment $S_*(E) = (\mathbb{R}_+ \times \mathbb{R}_+, \mathscr{B}(\mathbb{R}_+ \times \mathbb{R}_+), \{\mathscr{L}(S_1, S_2 | P_a): a \in L\})$. From Theorem 31.15 it follows that $\varrho: \mathbb{R}_+ \times \mathbb{R}_+ \to \mathbb{R}_+: (x, y) \mapsto y$ is $S_*(E)$-sufficient. The testing problem $(L_0, L \setminus L_0)$ for the experiment

$$\varrho_*(S_*(E)) = (\mathbb{R}_+, \mathscr{B}(\mathbb{R}_+), \{\chi^2_{\dim L - \dim L_0}(\|a - p_{L_0}(a)\|^2): a \in L\})$$

may be rephrased as the testing problem $(\{0\}, (0, \infty))$ for the experiment

$$(\mathbb{R}_+, \mathscr{B}(\mathbb{R}_+), \{\chi^2_{\dim L - \dim L_0}(t): t \geqq 0\})$$

which is a m.l.r. experiment. It follows from Theorem 9.13 that the test

$$\psi^*(y) = \begin{cases} 1 & \text{if} \quad y > t_\alpha, \\ 0 & \text{if} \quad y < t_\alpha, \end{cases}$$

where t_α satisfies $\chi^2_{\dim L - \dim L_0}(\psi^*) = \alpha$, is an optimal unbiased level-α-test for the testing problem $(\{0\}, (0, \infty))$. Then $(x, y) \mapsto \psi^*(y)$ is an optimal unbiased level-α-test of $(L_0, L \backslash L_0)$ for $S_*(E)$. □

Now, we consider the experiment $F = (H, \mathscr{B}(H), \{P_{a,\sigma}: a \in L, \sigma > 0\})$. It is again easy to see that the group $G_1 = \mathbb{R}_+ \times O_{L, L_0} \times L_0$ is amenable.

32.10 Theorem. *Suppose that* $\dim L < \dim H$. *For every* $\alpha \in [0, 1]$ *let* k_α *be such that*

$$P_{0,1}\{x \in H: \frac{\|p_L(x) - p_{L_0}(x)\|}{\|x - p_L(x)\|} > k_\alpha\} = \alpha.$$

Then the test

$$\varphi^*(x) = \begin{cases} 1 & \text{if } \dfrac{\|p_L(x) - p_{L_0}(x)\|}{\|x - p_L(x)\|} > k_\alpha, \\ 0 & \text{if } \dfrac{\|p_L(x) - p_{L_0}(x)\|}{\|x - p_L(x)\|} < k_\alpha, \end{cases} \qquad x \in H,$$

is optimal invariant in $\mathscr{F}_\alpha(H, K)$.

Proof. The proof is similar to the proof of Theorem 32.9. □

Chapter 7: Theory of Estimation

Chapters 2–6 are concerned exclusively with the theory of testing hypotheses. Their topics are classical in the sense that there is a far reaching agreement concerning their theoretical and practical significance. A theory of estimation which is classical in the same sense does not exist. This is not due to a lack of theoretically interesting results in estimation theory. There are diverging opinions concerning the practical value of different approaches.

Historically, the original approach to parameter estimation was to restrict the estimates under consideration by a side condition in order to exclude strongly biased estimates. This approach is very similar to ideas of testing, since fixing a certain level is nothing else than imposing a side condition. Common side conditions in estimation theory are e.g. median unbiasedness and mean unbiasedness. But already at this point statisticians do not agree which of both is more useful from a statistical point of view. Moreover, sometimes side conditions are not compatible with admissibility being required by decision theory.

The less controversial situation in questions of testing may be due to the fact that with Neyman-Pearson tests a method of construction is at our disposal whose applicability reaches far beyond the case of binary experiments. In fact, in Chapters 2–6 all experiments are somehow reduced to experiments with monotone likelihood ratios whose analysis relies solely on the Neyman-Pearson lemma. According to the prevailing opinion for estimation the maximum likelihood method plays the role of a universal method of construction. However, adherents of this opinion are attacked violently by the so-called Bayesians and the discussion is complicated by ideological arguments on the "true character of probability". Without taking up this discussion let us look briefly at the problem of a universal method of constructing estimates.

Chapter 2 makes clear that Neyman-Pearson tests essentially are the solution of the problem of minimizing the sum of error probabilities for binary experiments. This problem can also be solved for finite experiments, and the solution is nothing else than the maximum likelihood method. However, for arbitrary experiments this is no longer true. There are two possibilities. Either one extends the minimization problem from finite experiments to arbitrary experiments. Then one obtains as solution those particular Bayes estimates which are in the terminology of Wolfowitz known as maximum probability estimates. Or one extends the solution of the minimization problem for finite experiments to arbitrary experiments. Then one obtains the maximum likelihood method. In general, the maximum likelihood method is not the solution of the generalized minimization problem. Till now there does not exist any general decision-theoretic optimization problem whose solution is the maximum likelihood method. Only within the framework of the asymptotic theory it will be possible to give some theoretical justification to the maximum likelihood method.

After these general remarks let us consider more thorougly the contents of Chapter 7. To begin with we fix the terminology in Section 33. Here the concepts of Section 6 are extended to those of Wald's decision theory.

Section 34 deals with median unbiased estimation of a linear function on a Gaussian shift experiment. This problem can be solved to a large extent solely by the Neyman-Pearson lemma. We do not conceal that the theory of median unbiased estimation can be put in much more general terms. For this, the reader is referred to Pfanzagl [1970b, 1971 and 1979]. The admissibility proof of Theorem 34.5 which only relies on the Neyman-Pearson lemma is due to Pfanzagl.

The theory of mean unbiased estimates which is presented in Section 35 does not rely on any order structure of the paramater space but makes use of a reduction by sufficiency. This is the best-known part of estimation theory, therefore we only discuss few examples. Moreover, we do not follow the tradition of presenting the Cramér-Rao inequality. But we discuss detailed the converse of the theorem of Blackwell-Rao and Lehmann-Scheffé which is due to Bahadur [1957]. More information on mean unbiased estimation can be found in Schmetterer [1974].

In analogy to the theory of testing hypotheses the next topic should be the role of invariance in estimation. However, as best invariant estimates usually have a Bayesian representation, we first have to establish the technical foundations of the Bayesian formalism in Sections 36 and 37.

Section 36 is concerned with the possibility and the consequences of integration over the parameter space from a general point of view. Desintegrating the mixtures of the underlying probability measures yields estimates which are well-known from Sections 34 and 35. In Section 37 we introduce general Bayes estimates which cover notions such as maximum probability estimates and Pitman estimates. We admit non-finite measures as prior distributions. Handling finite prior measures has been wellknown for many years. But the case of arbitrary prior measures often gave rise to difficulties. LeCam [1973] settled the problems by introducing the integrability condition 36.1.

In Section 38 we are after all prepared for discussing the role of invariance properties of the experiment in estimation theory. First, we restrict ourselves to full shift experiments on locally compact groups. The main result is the generalization of the convolution theorem (Theorem 38.10) which implies both the ordinary convolution theorem (Theorem 38.13) and the minimax property of the identity (Theorem 38.16). As an illustration we discuss shift experiments on Euclidean spaces where the estimation problem is solved for subconvex loss functions by means of Anderson's Lemma (Anderson [1955]). This example yields the complete solution of the problem of estimating arbitrary linear maps on Gaussian shift experiments by means of invariance theory. Lemma 38.3 is taken from Torgersen [1972]. Our proof of the convolution theorem follows Boll [1955], and thus relies on the theory of Bayes estimates.

Full shift experiments mainly occur as limit experiments in the asymptotic theory. For finite sample sizes the situation usually is somewhat more complicated. E.g. when considering independent replications of full Euclidean shifts, one does not obtain full shifts but shifts whose parameter spaces are linear subspaces of the sample space. The appropriate framework for handling such cases is the so-called structure model (in Fraser's terminology). We treat structure models as generally as possible, but always considering the application to Euclidean shifts with linear restrictions. The presentation is based on Section 38 since every structural model can be decomposed into a mixture of full shifts (Theorem 39.9). Thus, we obtain a convolution theorem (Theorem 39.25) and a representation of minimax estimates (Theorem 39.28). Application to Euclidean shifts yields the usual representations of best equivariant estimates as Pitman estimates.

The chapter is closed by Section 40 containing the most important facts on admissibility of estimators of a single parameter. The results and proofs are due to Blyth [1951], and Stein [1959].

33. Basic notions of estimation

Suppose that $\Theta \neq \emptyset$ is an arbitrary set and $E = (\Omega, \mathscr{A}, \{P_\vartheta : \vartheta \in \Theta\})$ is an experiment.

Let us introduce the terminology of Wald's decision theory.

33.1 Definition. Suppose that D is a topological space which is called *decision space*. Any Markov kernel $\varrho: \Omega \times \mathscr{B}_0(D) \to [0,1]$ is called a *decision function* and the set of all decision functions is denoted by $\mathscr{R}(E, D)$.

For every $\vartheta \in \Theta$ the linear function

$$f \mapsto f \varrho P_\vartheta := \int\int f(x)\, \varrho(\omega, dx)\, P_\vartheta(d\omega), \quad f \in \mathscr{C}_b(D),$$

is called *distribution* of ϱ under P_ϑ. A decision function $\varrho \in \mathscr{R}(E, D)$ is *nonrandomized* if $\varrho(.,B) \in \{0,1\}$ P_ϑ-a.e. for every $\vartheta \in \Theta$ and all $B \in \mathscr{B}_0(D)$.

33.2 Remark. If $\kappa: \Omega \to D$ is an $\mathscr{A}$-measurable mapping then $\varrho(.,B) := 1_B \circ \kappa$, $B \in \mathscr{B}_0(D)$, is a nonrandomized decision function. For this reason we shall often call the map κ itself a nonrandomized decision function. Conversely, if E is dominated and $\mathscr{B}_0(D)$ is separable then for every nonrandomized decision function $\varrho \in \mathscr{R}(E, D)$ there exists an $\mathscr{A}$-measurable mapping $\kappa\colon \Omega \to D$ such that $\varrho(., B) = 1_B \circ \kappa$ P_ϑ-a.e., $\vartheta \in \Theta$. To show this, let $M \in \mathscr{A}$ be such that $\varrho(\omega, B) \in \{0, 1\}$ for every $B \in \mathscr{B}_0(D)$, $\omega \in M$. Then for every $\omega \in M$ there exists exactly one atom $B(\omega)$ of $\mathscr{B}_0(D)$ such that $\varrho(\omega, B(\omega)) = 1$. Define $\kappa\colon \Omega \to D$ such that $\kappa(\omega) \in B(\omega)$ if $\omega \in M$ and arbitrary, but measurable elsewhere. Then κ is measurable since $\{\kappa \in B\} \cap M = \{\omega \in M\colon \varrho(\omega, B) = 1\}$ and obviously has the desired property.

33.3 Definition. Suppose that $(W_\vartheta)_{\vartheta \in \Theta}$ is a family of $\mathscr{B}_0(D)$-measurable functions $W_\vartheta\colon D \to \mathbb{R}$ each of which is bounded from below. The family $(W_\vartheta)_{\vartheta \in \Theta}$ is called *loss function* and for every $\varrho \in \mathscr{R}(E, D)$

$$W_\vartheta \varrho P_\vartheta := \iint W_\vartheta(x)\, \varrho(\omega, dx)\, P_\vartheta(d\omega), \quad \vartheta \in \Theta,$$

is called *risk* of ϱ with respect to $(W_\vartheta)_{\vartheta \in \Theta}$. A tripel consisting of Θ, of a decision space D and a loss function $(W_\vartheta)_{\vartheta \in \Theta}$ is called a *decision problem* (for Θ).

33.4 Example. The most simple case of decision problems are testing problems. In this case the decision space D is a partition $\{H, K\}$ of Θ and for every $\varrho \in \mathscr{R}(E, D)$ the function $\varrho(.. K)$ is in $\mathscr{F}(\Omega, \mathscr{A})$. It is clear that to each critical function in $\mathscr{F}(\Omega, \mathscr{A})$ there is a corresponding decision function $\varrho \in \mathscr{R}(E, D)$. The most common type of a loss function for testing problems is:

$$W_\vartheta(K) = 1_H(\vartheta), \quad \text{and} \quad W_\vartheta(H) = 1_K(\vartheta), \quad \vartheta \in \Theta.$$

Then for $\varphi \in \mathscr{F}$ the power function can be written as

$$\vartheta \mapsto P_\vartheta \varphi = \begin{cases} W_\vartheta \varrho P_\vartheta & \text{whenever} \quad \vartheta \in H, \\ 1 - W_\vartheta \varrho P_\vartheta & \text{whenever} \quad \vartheta \in K, \end{cases}$$

where $\varrho = (1 - \varphi)\, \varepsilon_H + \varphi\, \varepsilon_K$.

33.5 Definition. A decision problem $(\Theta, D, (W_\vartheta)_{\vartheta \in \Theta})$ is called an *estimation problem* if there is a function $f\colon \Theta \to D$ such that W_ϑ depends on ϑ only through f, $\vartheta \in \Theta$.

As the reader will notice a testing problem is an estimation problem iff the loss functions W_ϑ coincide for all $\vartheta \in H$ and for all $\vartheta \in K$. A decision problem with $\Theta = D$ is always an estimation problem since one may take $f = \mathrm{id}_\Theta$.

We say that a loss function $(W_\vartheta)_{\vartheta \in \Theta}$ satisfies a certain condition if every W_ϑ, $\vartheta \in \Theta$, satisfies this condition.

33.6 Remark. Let us collect some important conditions which are frequently used for loss functions.

(1) A function $W: D \to \mathbb{R}$ is *level compact* if $\{W \leqq \alpha\}$ is compact for every $\alpha < \sup W$. Note, that a level-compact function is either unbounded or continuous at infinity.

(2) Suppose that D is a linear space. A function $W: D \to [0, \infty)$ is *separating* if $W(0) = 0$ and 0 is an inner point of some level set $\{W \leqq \alpha\}$ with $\alpha < \sup W$.

(3) Suppose again that D is a linear space. A function $W: D \to [0, \infty)$ is *subconvex* if the level-sets $\{W \leqq \alpha\}$ are convex and centrally symmetric. If $D = \mathbb{R}$ then $W: \mathbb{R} \to [0, \infty)$ is subconvex iff $W = \ell \circ |.|$ where ℓ is increasing.

(4) Suppose that D is a normed space. Then $W: \mathbb{R} \to [0, \infty)$ is of *finite order* if $W \leqq C_1 |.|^p + C_2$ for some $p < \infty$, $C_1 < \infty$, $C_2 < \infty$.

33.7 Definition. Suppose that D is a decision space and $(W_\vartheta)_{\vartheta \in \Theta}$ a loss function. A decision function $\varrho_1 \in \mathscr{R}(E, D)$ is *better* than a decision function $\varrho_2 \in \mathscr{R}(E, D)$ if

$$W_\vartheta \varrho_1 P_\vartheta \leqq W_\vartheta \varrho_2 P_\vartheta \quad \text{for all} \quad \vartheta \in \Theta .$$

It is an aim of statistical decision theory to find decision functions whose risk is small for many $\vartheta \in \Theta$.

33.8 Definition. Suppose that D is a decision space and $(W_\vartheta)_{\vartheta \in \Theta}$ a loss function. If $\mathscr{C} \subseteq \mathscr{R}(R, D)$ then the *envelope risk function* of $\mathscr{C}$ is

$$\vartheta \mapsto \inf\{W_\vartheta \varrho P_\vartheta: \varrho \in \mathscr{R}(E, D)\}, \quad \vartheta \in \Theta .$$

A decision function $\varrho^* \in \mathscr{C}$ is *optimal* in $\mathscr{C}$ at ϑ if

$$W_\vartheta \varrho^* P_\vartheta = \inf\{W_\vartheta \varrho P_\vartheta: \varrho \in \mathscr{R}(E, D)\} .$$

It is *uniformly optimal* in $\mathscr{C}$ if it is optimal at every $\vartheta \in \Theta$.

Obviously, one cannot expect the existence of uniformly optimal decision functions in $\mathscr{C} = \mathscr{R}(E, D)$.

33.9 Examples. (1) Consider a binary experiment $E = (\Omega, \mathscr{A}, \{P_1, P_2\})$ and let $D = \Theta = \{1, 2\}$ and $W_\vartheta(x) = 1$ if $x \neq \vartheta$ and $= 0$ if $x = \vartheta$, $x \in D, \vartheta \in \Theta$. Then it follows from Theorem 14.2 that any decision function satisfying

$$\varrho^*(.,1) = 1 - \varrho^*(.,0) = \begin{cases} 1 & \text{if} \quad \dfrac{dP_2}{dP_1} > 1, \\[2ex] 0 & \text{if} \quad \dfrac{dP_2}{dP_1} < 1, \end{cases}$$

minimizes the sum $W_1 \varrho P_1 + W_2 \varrho P_2$, $\varrho \in \mathscr{R}(E, D)$.

(2) Consider a finite experiment $E = (\Omega, \mathscr{A}, \{P_1, \ldots, P_k\})$ and let $D = \Theta = \{1, 2, \ldots, k\}$ and $W_\vartheta(x) = 1$ if $x \neq \vartheta$ and $= 0$ if $x = \vartheta$, $x \in D$, $\vartheta \in \Theta$. It is easy to see, that for every $\varrho \in \mathscr{R}(E, D)$

$$\sum_{i=1}^{k} W_i \varrho P_i = 1 - \sum_{i=1}^{k} P_i \varrho(.,i).$$

Therefore, minimizing the sum of the risks is equivalent with maximizing $\sum_{i=1}^{k} P_i \varrho(.,i)$. Let $\nu|\mathscr{A}$ be a σ-finite measure dominating $\{P_1, \ldots, P_k\}$. Similarly as before, this optimization problem is solved by any decision function satisfying

$$\varrho^*(.,i) = 1 \quad \text{if} \quad \frac{dP_i}{d\nu} = \max_{1 \leqq j \leqq k} \frac{dP_j}{d\nu}.$$

Decision functions of this type are called *maximum likelihood estimates.*

Another possibility is to hope for uniformly optimal decision functions if $\mathscr{C} \subseteq \mathscr{R}(E, D)$ does not contain "strongly biased" elements. Therefore we have to generalize the notion of unbiasedness which has been introduced in Definition 7.8.

33.10 Lemma. *Suppose that (H, K) is a testing problem for Θ. If $\varphi \in \mathscr{F}$ let $\varrho = (1-\varphi)\,\varepsilon_H + \varphi\,\varepsilon_K$, and $W_\vartheta(H) = \alpha 1_K(\vartheta)$, $W_\vartheta(K) = (1-\alpha) 1_H(\vartheta)$, $\vartheta \in \Theta$. Then φ is an unbiased level-α-test for (H, K) iff*

$$W_\vartheta \varrho P_\vartheta = \inf\{W_\sigma \varrho P_\vartheta : \sigma \in \Theta\}, \quad \vartheta \in \Theta.$$

Proof. Since

$$W_\sigma \varrho P_\vartheta = \begin{cases} (1-\alpha) P_\vartheta \varphi & \text{if} \quad \sigma \in H, \\ \alpha(1 - P_\vartheta \varphi) & \text{if} \quad \sigma \in K, \end{cases}$$

we have $W_\vartheta \varrho P_\vartheta = \inf\{W_\sigma \varrho P_\vartheta : \sigma \in \Theta\}$, $\vartheta \in \Theta$, iff

$$(1-\alpha) P_\vartheta \varphi \leqq \alpha(1 - P_\vartheta \varphi) \quad \text{whenever} \quad \vartheta \in H, \quad \text{and}$$
$$\alpha(1 - P_\vartheta \varphi) \leqq (1-\alpha) P_\vartheta \varphi \quad \text{whenever} \quad \vartheta \in K.$$

This proves the assertion. □

This lemma is a formal motivation of the following definition.

33.11 Definition. Suppose that D is a decision space and $(W_\vartheta)_{\vartheta \in \Theta}$ is a loss function. A decision function $\varrho \in \mathscr{R}(E, D)$ is $(W_\vartheta)_{\vartheta \in \Theta}$-*unbiased* if

$$W_\vartheta \varrho P_\vartheta = \inf\{W_\sigma \varrho P_\vartheta : \sigma \in \Theta\}, \ \vartheta \in \Theta.$$

33.12 Example. Suppose that $f: \Theta \to \mathbb{R}$ is a function such that $f(\Theta)$ is open in $\mathbb{R}$. Let $D = \mathbb{R}$ and $W_\vartheta(x) = |x - f(\vartheta)|$, $(x, \vartheta) \in \mathbb{R} \times \Theta$. A nonrandomized and for every $\vartheta \in \Theta$ P_ϑ-integrable estimate $\kappa: \Omega \to \mathbb{R}$ is $(W_\vartheta)_{\vartheta \in \Theta}$-unbiased if

$$\int |\kappa - f(\vartheta)|\, dP_\vartheta = \inf\{\int |\kappa - f(\sigma)|\, dP_\vartheta : \sigma \in \Theta\}.$$

We show that this is the case iff

$$P_\vartheta\{\kappa \geqq f(\vartheta)\} \geqq \frac{1}{2}, \quad \vartheta \in \Theta, \quad \text{and}$$

$$P_\vartheta\{\kappa \leqq f(\vartheta)\} \geqq \frac{1}{2}, \quad \vartheta \in \Theta.$$

The second condition says nothing else than that $f(\vartheta)$ is a median of $\mathscr{L}(\kappa | P_\vartheta)$ for every $\vartheta \in \Theta$.

First, assume that $f(\vartheta)$ is a median of $\mathscr{L}(\kappa | P_\vartheta)$ for every $\vartheta \in \Theta$. If $f(\sigma) \geqq f(\vartheta)$ then

$$|x - f(\vartheta)| - |x - f(\sigma)| = \begin{cases} f(\sigma) - f(\vartheta) & \text{if} \quad x > f(\sigma), \\ 2x - (f(\vartheta) + f(\sigma)) & \text{if} \quad f(\vartheta) \leqq x \leqq f(\sigma), \\ -(f(\sigma) - f(\vartheta)) & \text{if} \quad x < f(\vartheta), \end{cases}$$

and thus

$$|x - f(\vartheta)| - |x - f(\sigma)| \leqq \begin{cases} f(\sigma) - f(\vartheta) & \text{if} \quad x > f(\vartheta), \\ 0 & \text{if} \quad x = f(\vartheta), \\ -(f(\sigma) - f(\sigma)) & \text{if} \quad x < f(\vartheta). \end{cases}$$

It follows that

$$\begin{aligned} &\int |\kappa - f(\vartheta)| \, dP_\vartheta - \int |\kappa - f(\sigma)| \, dP_\vartheta \\ &\quad \leqq (f(\sigma) - f(\vartheta)) \, P_\vartheta\{\kappa > f(\vartheta)\} - (f(\sigma) - f(\vartheta)) \, P_\vartheta\{\kappa \leqq f(\vartheta)\} \\ &\quad \leqq (f(\sigma) - f(\vartheta)) \cdot \frac{1}{2} - (f(\sigma) - f(\vartheta)) \cdot \frac{1}{2} = 0. \end{aligned}$$

A similar argument applies for $f(\sigma) \leqq f(\vartheta)$. Assume conversely that κ is $(W_\vartheta)_{\vartheta \in \Theta}$-unbiased. Let $f(\sigma) = f(\vartheta) + \varepsilon$, $\varepsilon > 0$. It follows that

$$\begin{aligned} 0 &\geqq \int |\kappa - f(\vartheta)| \, dP_\vartheta - \int |\kappa - f(\sigma)| \, dP_\vartheta \\ &\geqq \varepsilon P_\vartheta\{\kappa \geqq f(\sigma)\} - \varepsilon P_\vartheta\{\kappa < f(\vartheta)\} - \varepsilon P_\vartheta\{f(\vartheta) \leqq \kappa < f(\vartheta) + \varepsilon\}. \end{aligned}$$

For $\varepsilon \to 0$ we obtain

$$\begin{aligned} 0 &\geqq P_\vartheta\{\kappa > f(\vartheta)\} - P_\vartheta\{\kappa < f(\vartheta)\} - P_\vartheta\{\kappa = f(\vartheta)\} \\ &= 1 - 2 P_\vartheta\{\kappa \leqq f(\vartheta)\} \end{aligned}$$

which proves $P_\vartheta\{\kappa \leqq f(\vartheta)\} \geqq \frac{1}{2}$. The second inequality is proved in a similar way.

The preceding example shows that the following definition is a particular case of Definition 33.11.

33.13 Definition. A nonrandomized estimate $\kappa: \Omega \to \mathbb{R}$ is a *median-unbiased estimate* of a function $f: \Theta \to \mathbb{R}$ if

$$P_\vartheta\{\kappa \geqq f(\vartheta)\} \geqq \frac{1}{2}, \quad \vartheta \in \Theta, \quad \text{and}$$

$$P_\vartheta\{\kappa \leqq f(\vartheta)\} \geqq \frac{1}{2}, \quad \vartheta \in \Theta.$$

It is sometimes possible to obtain median-unbiased estimates which are uniformly optimal in the class of all median-unbiased estimates. We discuss results of this type in Section 34.

33.14 Example. Suppose that $f: \Theta \to \mathbb{R}$ is a function such that $f(\Theta)$ is open in $\mathbb{R}$. Let $D = \mathbb{R}$ and $W_\vartheta(x) = |x - f(\vartheta)|^2$, $(x, \vartheta) \in \mathbb{R} \times \Theta$. A nonrandomized and for every $\vartheta \in \Theta$ twice P_ϑ-integrable estimate $\kappa: \Omega \to \mathbb{R}$ is $(W_\vartheta)_{\vartheta \in \Theta}$-unbiased if

$$\int |\kappa - f(\vartheta)|^2 \, dP_\vartheta = \inf\{\int |\kappa - f(\vartheta)|^2 \, dP_\sigma : \sigma \in \Theta\}.$$

We show that this is the case iff

$$P_\vartheta \kappa = f(\vartheta) \quad \text{for all} \quad \vartheta \in \Theta.$$

It is clear that $P_\vartheta \kappa = f(\vartheta)$, $\vartheta \in \Theta$, implies that κ is $(W_\vartheta)_{\vartheta \in \Theta}$-unbiased. For the proof of the converse note that the minimum property implies for every $\sigma \in \Theta$

$$2 \int \kappa \, dP_\vartheta (f(\sigma) - f(\vartheta)) \leqq (f(\sigma) - f(\vartheta)) (f(\sigma) + f(\vartheta)).$$

It follows that

$$\int \kappa \, dP_\vartheta \leqq \frac{1}{2} (f(\sigma) + f(\vartheta)) \quad \text{if} \quad f(\sigma) > f(\vartheta), \quad \text{and}$$

$$\int \kappa \, dP_\vartheta \geqq \frac{1}{2} (f(\sigma) + f(\vartheta)) \quad \text{if} \quad f(\sigma) < f(\vartheta).$$

Since $f(\Theta)$ is open the assertion follows.

33.15 Definition. A nonrandomized estimate $\kappa: \Omega \to \mathbb{R}$ is a *mean-unbiased* estimate of a function $f: \Theta \to \mathbb{R}$ if it is P_ϑ-integrable for all $\vartheta \in \Theta$ and $P_\vartheta \kappa = f(\vartheta)$, $\vartheta \in \Theta$.

Sometimes it is possible to obtain mean-unbiased estimates which are uniformly optimal in the class of all mean unbiased estimates. Some theory of mean-unbiased estimation is presented in Section 35.

Which kind of unbiasedness of a decision function is appropriate depends on the problem. It is clear that median-unbiasedness is related to order structures whereas mean-unbiasedness is a natural condition if the problem has a linear structure.

33.16 Definition. Suppose that D is a decision space and $(W_\vartheta)_{\vartheta\in\Theta}$ is a loss function. A decision function $\varrho^* \in \mathscr{R}(E, D)$ is *minimax* if

$$\sup_{\vartheta\in\Theta} W_\vartheta \varrho^* P_\vartheta = \inf_{\varrho\in\mathscr{R}(E,D)} \sup_{\vartheta\in\Theta} W_\vartheta \varrho P_\vartheta .$$

Although it is trivial we note that any minimax decision function with constant risk is uniformly optimal in the class of all decision functions with constant risk. Minimaxity plays an important role for many estimation problems but sometimes it is useless for distinguishing a particular decision function as the following example shows.

33.17 Example. Suppose that E is an exponential experiment of rank 1 and (H, K) is a one-sided testing problem. Let $\alpha \in [0,1]$ and consider the loss function of Lemma 33.10. If $\varphi \in \mathscr{F}_\beta(H, K)$, $\beta \in [0,1]$, the maximal risk of φ is $\max\{(1-\alpha)\beta, \alpha(1-\beta)\}$ and since $\bigcup_{0\leq\beta\leq 1} \mathscr{F}_\beta(H, K)$ is a complete class of tests the minimax risk is

$$\inf_{0\leq\beta\leq 1} \max\{(1-\alpha)\beta, \alpha(1-\beta)\} = \alpha(1-\alpha).$$

It follows that every test in $\mathscr{F}_\alpha(H, K)$ is a minimax test for the loss function under consideration. Hence additional properties such as admissibility are needed for choosing a test.

Finally, we generalize the notions of Definitions 7.12 and 7.13 to the present situation.

33.18 Definition. Suppose that D is a decision space and $(W_\vartheta)_{\vartheta\in\Theta}$ is a loss function. Let $\mathscr{R}_0 \subseteq \mathscr{R}(E, D)$. A subset $\mathscr{C} \subseteq \mathscr{R}_0$ is called *$\mathscr{R}_0$-complete* for the decision problem $(\Theta, D, (W_\vartheta)_{\vartheta\in\Theta})$ if for every $\varrho \in \mathscr{R}_0$ there exists a better decision function $\sigma \in \mathscr{C}$.

An $\mathscr{R}$-complete class $\mathscr{C}$ is simply called complete.

33.19 Definition. Suppose that D is a decision space and $(W_\vartheta)_{\vartheta\in\Theta}$ is a loss function. Let $\mathscr{R}_0 \subseteq \mathscr{R}(E, D)$. A function $f\colon \Theta \to \bar{\mathbb{R}}$ is *$\mathscr{R}_0$-admissible* for the decision problem $(\Theta, D, (W_\vartheta)_{\vartheta\in\Theta})$ if in $\mathscr{R}_0$ there is no better risk function available than f. A decision function $\varrho \in \mathscr{R}(E, D)$ is *$\mathscr{R}_0$-admissible* if its risk function is $\mathscr{R}_0$-admissible.

$\mathscr{R}$-admissibility is simply called admissibility. An admissible decision function with constant risk is minimax.

34. Median unbiased estimation for Gaussian shifts

Suppose that $(H, \langle .,. \rangle)$ is a Euclidean space, $\mathscr{B}(H)$ the Borel-σ-field of H and $N_H|\mathscr{B}(H)$ the standard Gaussian measure of H. We consider a linear subspace $L \subseteq H$ and the experiment $E = (H, \mathscr{B}(H), \{P_t: t \in L\})$, where $P_t = \varepsilon_t * N_H$. The problem is to estimate a linear function $f: L \to \mathbb{R}$.

We choose as decision space the two-point compactification of $\mathbb{R}$, i.e. $D := \overline{\mathbb{R}}$. The elements $\varrho \in \mathscr{R}(E, \overline{\mathbb{R}})$ are called estimates. Let $W: [0, \infty) \to [0, \infty)$ be a nondecreasing function with $W(0) = 0$ and define the risk of an estimate $\varrho \in \mathscr{R}(E, \overline{\mathbb{R}})$ by

$$R(\varrho, t) := \iint W(|x - f(t)|)\, \varrho(\omega, dx)\, P_t(d\omega), \quad t \in L,$$

where $W(\infty) := \sup W$.

The following extends Definition 33.12. For convenience we denote $(\varrho P_t)(A) := 1_A \varrho P_t$, $A \in \mathscr{B}(\overline{\mathbb{R}})$, $t \in L$.

34.1 Definition. Let $\varrho \in \mathscr{R}(E, \overline{\mathbb{R}})$. Then ϱ is a *median unbiased estimate* of f for the experiment E if

$$(\varrho P_t)([f(t), \infty]) \geqq \frac{1}{2}, \quad \text{and}$$

$$(\varrho P_t)([-\infty, f(t)]) \geqq \frac{1}{2}$$

for every $t \in L$.

34.2 Lemma. *Every median unbiased estimate ϱ of f satisfies*

$$(\varrho P_t)([f(t) - c, f(t) + d]) \leqq \Phi\left(\frac{d}{\|f\|}\right) - \Phi\left(\frac{-c}{\|f\|}\right)$$

for all $c > 0$, $d > 0$, $t \in L$.

Proof. Let $e \in L$ be the unit vector with $e \perp \ker f$ and $f(e) > 0$. This implies $f(e) = \|f\|$. Define $t_1 = t - \dfrac{c}{\|f\|} e$ and $t_2 = t + \dfrac{d}{\|f\|} e$. Since ϱ is median unbiased for f it follows that

$$(\varrho P_{t_1})([-\infty, f(t) - c]) \geqq \frac{1}{2},$$

$$(\varrho P_{t_2})([f(t) - d, \infty]) \geqq \frac{1}{2}.$$

Lemma 28.1 implies that

$$(\varrho P_t)([-\infty, f(t)-c]) \geqq \Phi\left(-\left\|\frac{c}{\|f\|}e\right\|\right) = \Phi\left(-\frac{c}{\|f\|}\right)$$

and

$$(\varrho P_t)([f(t)+d, \infty]) \geqq \Phi\left(-\left\|\frac{d}{\|f\|}e\right\|\right) = \Phi\left(-\frac{d}{\|f\|}\right).$$

Hence we obtain that

$$\begin{aligned}
&(\varrho P_t)((f(t)-c, f(t)+d)) \\
&\quad = (\varrho P_t)([-\infty, f(t)+d)) - (\varrho P_t)([-\infty, f(t)-c]) \\
&\quad \leqq 1 - \Phi\left(-\frac{d}{\|f\|}\right) - \Phi\left(-\frac{c}{\|f\|}\right) = \Phi\left(\frac{d}{\|f\|}\right) - \Phi\left(-\frac{c}{\|f\|}\right).
\end{aligned}$$

A continuity argument completes the proof. □

We obtain a universal lower bound for the risk functions of median unbiased estimates.

34.3 Theorem. *Suppose that W is lower semicontinuous. Every median unbiased estimate $\varrho \in \mathscr{R}(E, \bar{\mathbb{R}})$ satisfies*

$$R(\varrho, t) \geqq \int W(\|f\| \cdot |s|)\, \nu_{0,1}(ds), \quad t \in L.$$

Proof. Let $0 = t_0 < t_1 < t_2 < \ldots < t_k$, $k \in \mathbb{N}$ and define

$$W_0 := \sum_{i=1}^{k} (W(t_i) - W(t_{i-1}))\, 1_{(t_i, \infty)}.$$

Let $\mathscr{W}$ be the class of all functions which can be obtained in this way. Every $W_0 \in \mathscr{W}$ is lower semicontinuous, nondecreasing, bounded and satisfies $W_0 \leqq W$. Moreover, we have $W = \sup \mathscr{W}$. This follows from lower semicontinuity of W. From Lemma 34.2 we obtain that

$$\iint W_0(|x - f(t)|)\, \varrho(\omega, dx)\, P_t(d\omega) \geqq \int W_0(\|f\| \cdot |s|)\, \nu_{0,1}(ds)$$

for every $W_0 \in \mathscr{W}$. This proves the assertion. □

34.4 Corollary. *The non-randomized estimate $\kappa^* = f \circ p_L$ is a median unbiased estimate of f and is uniformly optimal among all median unbiased estimates $\varrho \in \mathscr{R}(E, \bar{\mathbb{R}})$ of f.*

Proof. It is obvious that

$$R(\kappa^*, t) = \int W(|f \circ p_L|)\, dN_H = \int W(\|f\| \cdot |s|)\, \nu_{0,1}(ds), \quad t \in L.$$

Since $\mathscr{L}(f \circ p_L | P_t) = \nu_{f(t), \|f\|^2}$, $t \in L$, we see that κ^* is median unbiased for f. □

As a final result of this section will prove that the estimate $\kappa^* = f \circ p_L$ is even an admissible estimate of f. Due to the importance of this fact we shall give two proofs of it. The first proof is limited to particular loss functions. However, the basic idea is very simple.

34.5 Theorem. *Suppose that* $W = 1 - 1_{[0,c)}$, $c > 0$. *Then* $\kappa^* = f \circ p_L$ *is an admissible estimate in* $\varrho \in \mathscr{R}(E, \bar{\mathbb{R}})$.

Proof. (Pfanzagl). First we note that for every $\varrho \in \mathscr{R}(E, \bar{\mathbb{R}})$

$$R(\varrho, t) = (\varrho P_t)([f(t) + c, \infty)) + (\varrho P_t)([-\infty, f(t) - c]),$$

and

$$\int W(|f \circ p_L|)\, dN_H = 2\Phi\left(-\frac{c}{\|f\|}\right).$$

Let $\alpha := \inf_{t \in L} (\varrho P_t)([f(t) + c, \infty])$. Assuming that

$$\sup_{t \in L} (\varrho P_t)([f(t) + c, \infty] \cup [-\infty, f(t) - c]) \leqq 2\Phi\left(-\frac{c}{\|f\|}\right)$$

we show $\alpha = \Phi\left(-\frac{c}{\|f\|}\right)$. The relation

$$\inf_{t \in L} (\varrho P_t)([-\infty, f(t) - c]) = \Phi\left(-\frac{c}{\|f\|}\right)$$

is proved similarly.

For every $t \in L$ define $b(t) := t + \frac{2c}{\|f\|} e$ where $e \in L$ is as in the proof of 34.2. Then we obtain

$$\begin{aligned}
&(\varrho P_{b(t)})([f(b(t)) + c, \infty]) \\
&\qquad = (\varrho P_{b(t)})\{x \in \bar{\mathbb{R}}: |x - f(b(t))| \geqq c\} \\
&\qquad\quad - (\varrho P_{b(t)})\{x \in \bar{\mathbb{R}}: x - f(b(t)) \leqq -c\} \\
&\qquad = (\varrho P_{b(t)})([f(b(t)) + c, \infty] \cup [-\infty, f(b(t))] - c) - 1 \\
&\qquad\quad + (\varrho P_{b(t)})((f(b(t)) - c, \infty]) \\
&\qquad = (\varrho P_{b(t)})([f(b(t)) + c, \infty] \cup [-\infty, f(b(t)) - c]) - 1 \\
&\qquad\quad + (\varrho P_{b(t)})((f(t) + c, \infty]).
\end{aligned}$$

Since

$$\inf_{t \in L} (\varrho P_t)((f(t) + c, \infty]) \leqq \inf_{t \in L} (\varrho P_t)([f(t) + c, \infty]) = \alpha$$

it follows from Lemma 28.1 that

$$\inf_{t \in L} (\varrho P_{b(t)}) ((f(t) + c, \infty]) \leqq \Phi\left(N_\alpha + \frac{2c}{\|f\|}\right).$$

Hence we obtain that

$$\begin{aligned} &\alpha + 1 - \Phi\left(N_\alpha + \frac{2c}{\|f\|}\right) \\ &\leqq \sup_{t \in L} (\varrho P_t) ([f(t) + c, \infty] \cup [-\infty, f(t) - c]) \\ &\leqq 2\Phi\left(-\frac{c}{\|f\|}\right). \end{aligned}$$

This inequality can be written as

$$\Phi(N_\alpha) + \Phi\left(-N_\alpha - \frac{2c}{\|f\|}\right) \leqq 2\Phi\left(-\frac{c}{\|f\|}\right)$$

or

$$\begin{aligned} &\Phi\left(-\frac{c}{\|f\|} + \left[N_\alpha + \frac{c}{\|f\|}\right]\right) + \Phi\left(-\frac{c}{\|f\|} - \left[N_\alpha + \frac{c}{\|f\|}\right]\right) \\ &\leqq 2\Phi\left(-\frac{c}{\|f\|}\right). \end{aligned}$$

Elementary analysis shows that the function

$$h \mapsto \Phi(x + h) + \Phi(x - h) - 2\Phi(x), \quad h \in \mathbb{R},$$

for fixed $x < 0$ is non-negative and attains zero iff $h = 0$. This implies $N_\alpha = -\frac{c}{\|f\|}$ which yields $\alpha = \Phi\left(-\frac{c}{\|f\|}\right)$. Hence the assertion. □

It is not difficult to see that the preceding assertion is also valid if $W = 1 - 1_{[0,c]}$, $c > 0$. The charm of the argument lies in the fact that it rests only on the Neyman-Pearson lemma in the version of Lemma 28.1. The proof of the assertion in its full generality requires some elementary Bayesian techniques. Therefore we postpone it to Section 40.

Finally we extend the preceding results to a slightly more general situation. For $t \in L$ and $\sigma > 0$ let $P_{t,\sigma} = \mathscr{L}(\sigma \,\mathrm{id} + t \mid N_H)$. In the following we consider the experiment $F = (H, \mathscr{B}(H), \{P_{t,\sigma}: t \in L, \sigma > 0\})$.

For every $\sigma > 0$ the experiment $F_\sigma = (H, \mathscr{B}(H), \{P_{t,\sigma}: t \in L\})$ is of the same type as the experiment E if the vector space H is endowed with the inner product $\langle .,. \rangle_\sigma := \frac{1}{\sigma^2} \langle .,. \rangle$. It is natural to call an estimate $\varrho \in \mathscr{R}(F, \overline{\mathbb{R}})$ median-unbiased for F iff it is median-unbiased for every F_σ, $\sigma > 0$. We denote

$$R(\varrho, t, \sigma) = \iint W(|x - f(t)|) \, \varrho(\cdot, dx) \, dP_{t,\sigma}, \quad t \in L, \sigma > 0.$$

34.6 Theorem. *Every median unbiased estimate* ϱ *of* f *satisfies for every* $t \in L$, $\sigma > 0$,

$$P_{t,\sigma}\varrho(.,[f(t)-c, f(t)+d]) \leqq \Phi\left(\frac{d}{\|f\|}\right) - \Phi\left(\frac{-c}{\|f\|}\right), \quad c>0,\ d>0,$$

and

$$R(\varrho, t, \sigma) \geqq \int W(\|f\| \cdot |s|)\, \nu_{0,\sigma^2}(ds).$$

Proof. Apply Lemma 34.2 and Theorem 34.3 to F_σ, $\sigma > 0$. □

34.7 Corollary. *The estimate* $\kappa^* = f \circ p_L$ *is a median unbiased estimate of* f *and optimal among all median unbiased estimates of* f.

35. Mean unbiased estimation

Suppose that $\Theta \neq \emptyset$ is an arbitrary set and $E = (\Omega, \mathscr{A}, \{P_\vartheta: \vartheta \in \Theta\})$ an experiment in $\mathscr{E}(\Theta)$. Denote $\mathscr{P} = \{P_\vartheta: \vartheta \in \Theta)$. For the purpose of this section the elements of $\bigcap_{\vartheta \in \Theta} \mathscr{L}^2(\Omega, \mathscr{A}, P_\vartheta)$ are called estimates.

35.1 Definition. A function $f: \Theta \mapsto \mathbb{R}$ admits an *unbiased estimate* κ if κ satisfies $f(\vartheta) = P_\vartheta(\kappa)$, $\vartheta \in \Theta$. The set of all (mean)-unbiased estimates of f is denoted by $H(f)$.

35.2 Definition. Suppose that $f: \Theta \to \mathbb{R}$ admits unbiased estimates. An estimate $\kappa^* \in H(f)$ is called an *unbiased estimate of uniformly minimal variance* if

$$P_\vartheta((\kappa^* - f(\vartheta))^2) = \inf_{\kappa \in H(f)} P_\vartheta((\kappa - f(\vartheta))^2), \quad \vartheta \in \Theta.$$

From Steiner's formula it follows that for any two estimates $\kappa_1 \in H(f)$, $\kappa_2 \in H(f)$, and every $\vartheta \in \Theta$

$$P_\vartheta((\kappa_1 - f(\vartheta))^2) \leqq P_\vartheta((\kappa_2 - f(\vartheta))^2) \quad \text{iff} \quad P_\vartheta(\kappa_1^2) \leqq P_\vartheta(\kappa_2^2).$$

35.3 Lemma. *If* κ_1 *and* κ_2 *in* $H(f)$ *are of uniformly minimal variance then* $\kappa_1 = \kappa_2$ P_ϑ*-a.e.*, $\vartheta \in \Theta$.

Proof. Since $\frac{1}{2}(\kappa_1 + \kappa_2) \in H(f)$ and

$$\int \left(\frac{\kappa_1 + \kappa_2}{2}\right)^2 dP_\vartheta \leqq \frac{1}{2}\int \kappa_1^2\, dP_\vartheta + \frac{1}{2}\int \kappa_2^2\, dP_\vartheta, \quad \vartheta \in \Theta,$$

it follows that this inequality is even an equality and that

$$\int(\kappa_1-\kappa_2)^2\,dP_\vartheta=0,\quad \vartheta\in\Theta. \qquad \square$$

35.4 Lemma. *Suppose that $\mathscr{A}_1 \subseteq \mathscr{A}$ is E-sufficient. For any $\kappa\in H(f)$ let*

$$E(\kappa|\mathscr{A}_1)=P_\vartheta(\kappa|\mathscr{A}_1)\;P_\vartheta\text{-a.e.},\quad \vartheta\in\Theta.$$

Then $E(\kappa|\mathscr{A}_1)\in H(f)$ and

$$P_\vartheta(E(\kappa|\mathscr{A}_1)^2)\leqq P_\vartheta(\kappa^2),\quad \vartheta\in\Theta.$$

Proof. This is an immediate consequence of Jensen's inequality. $\square$

An experiment E is called *2-complete* if for every estimate κ

$$P_\vartheta\kappa=0,\ \vartheta\in\Theta \quad\text{implies}\quad \kappa=0,\ P_\vartheta\text{-a.e.},\ \vartheta\in\Theta.$$

This is a slightly weaker condition than completeness, defined in Theorem 16.4.

35.5 Theorem (Blackwell [1947], and Lehmann and Scheffé [1950]). *Suppose that $\mathscr{A}_1\subseteq\mathscr{A}$ is E-sufficient and that $E|\mathscr{A}_1$ is 2-complete. If $H(f)\neq\emptyset$ then there is an unbiased estimate of uniformly minimal variance κ^*, and κ^* satisfies*

$$\kappa^*=P_\vartheta(\kappa|\mathscr{A}_1)\quad P_\vartheta\text{-a.e.},\quad \vartheta\in\Theta,\ \kappa\in H(f).$$

Proof. Let κ_1 and κ_2 be elements of $H(f)$. Since

$$\int(E(\kappa_1|\mathscr{A}_1)-E(\kappa_2|\mathscr{A}_1))\,dP_\vartheta=0\quad\text{if}\quad \vartheta\in\Theta,$$

completeness of $\mathscr{A}_1$ implies that $E(\kappa_1|\mathscr{A}_1)=E(\kappa_2|\mathscr{A}_1)$ P_ϑ-a.e., $\vartheta\in\Theta$. Hence there is a function $\kappa^*\in H(f)$ satisfying

$$\kappa^*=E(\kappa|\mathscr{A}_1)\quad P_\vartheta\text{-a.e.},\ \vartheta\in\Theta,\quad\text{whenever}\quad \kappa\in H(f).$$

According to the preceding lemma, κ^* is of uniformly minimal variance. $\square$

In other words, every $\mathscr{A}_1$-measurable estimate κ is an unbiased estimate of uniformly minimal variance of its mean $f\colon \vartheta\mapsto P_\vartheta(\kappa)$, $\vartheta\in\Theta$.

35.6 Corollary. *Suppose that the conditions of Theorem 35.5 are satisfied. Then the unbiased estimate of minimal variance $\kappa^*\in H(f)$ satisfies*

$$\int W(\kappa^*)\,dP_\vartheta\leqq\int W(\kappa)\,dP_\vartheta,\quad \vartheta\in\Theta,\ \kappa\in H(f),$$

for every convex function $W\colon\mathbb{R}\to\mathbb{R}$ which is bounded from below.

Proof. The assertion follows from $\kappa^*=P_\vartheta(\kappa|\mathscr{A}_1)$ P_ϑ-a.e., and Jensen's inequality. $\square$

35.7 Example. Let $(H, \langle .,. \rangle)$ be a Euclidean space, $L \subseteq H$ a linear subspace. Then p_L is a sufficient mapping for the experiment $E = (H, \mathscr{B}(H), \{N_H * \varepsilon_a : a \in L\})$. Let us show that $\mathscr{P} = \{N_H * \varepsilon_a : a \in L\}$ is 2-complete for the σ-field $\mathscr{A}_1 = p_L^{-1}(\mathscr{B}(H))$. For this, let $g = h \circ p_L$ be such that $P_a g = 0$ for all $a \in L$. This implies that

$$0 = P_a g = (2\pi)^{-\dim H/2} \int_L \int_L h(x)\, e^{-\frac{\|x\|^2}{2}}\, e^{-\frac{\|y\|^2}{2}}\, e^{\langle x, a\rangle}\, e^{-\frac{\|a\|^2}{2}}\, dx\, dy$$

$$= C(a) \int_L h(x)\, e^{\langle x, a\rangle}\, e^{-\frac{\|x\|^2}{2}}\, dx$$

for every $a \in L$. From Theorem 5.7 we obtain that

$$h^+(x)\, e^{-\frac{\|x\|^2}{2}} = h^-(x)\, e^{-\frac{\|x\|^2}{2}} \quad \lambda_L\text{-a.e.}$$

which proves $g = 0$ P_a-a.e., $a \in L$. Hence every function $f \circ p_L$ is an unbiased estimate of uniformly minimal variance of its mean. If f is linear then $f \circ p_L \in H(f)$.

35.8 Example. Keeping the notation of the preceding example, consider the experiment $F = (H, \mathscr{B}(H), \{P_{a,\sigma} : a \in L, \sigma > 0\})$ where $P_{a,\sigma} = \mathscr{L}(\sigma\,\mathrm{id} + a \mid N_H)$. It is again easy to show that $S: x \mapsto (p_L(x), \|x - p_L(x)\|)$, $x \in H$, is sufficient for F, and that $\mathscr{P} = \{P_{a,\sigma} : a \in L, \sigma > 0\}$ is 2-complete for $S^{-1}(\mathscr{B}(H))$. Therefore, the unbiased estimates of uniformly minimal variance are exactly the estimates κ which depend on $x \in H$ through S.

For short, let us call any unbiased estimate of uniformly minimal variance simply *optimal*. Theorem 35.5 states that under the conditions imposed there the set of all optimal estimates is a linear space, which is generated by a σ-field.

It is our aim to show that the assumptions of Theorem 35.5 are necessary. Moreover, we want to obtain some information on the structure of the set of optimal estimates in such cases when the assumptions of Theorem 35.5 are not satisfied.

35.9 Lemma (Rao [1952]). *An estimate κ^* is optimal iff $P_\vartheta(\kappa^* v) = 0$ for every $\vartheta \in \Theta$ and every $v \in H(0)$.*

Proof. An estimate κ^* is optimal iff for every $\vartheta \in \Theta$ and every $v \in H(0)$ the function $\lambda \mapsto P_\vartheta((\kappa^* + \lambda v)^2)$, $\lambda \in \mathbb{R}$, attains its minimum at $\lambda = 0$. This is the case iff $P_\vartheta(\kappa^* v) = 0$. $\square$

Let D be the set of all estimates κ such that there exists an optimal unbiased estimate of $\vartheta \mapsto P_\vartheta(\kappa)$, $\vartheta \in \Theta$. If $\kappa \in D$ let $\pi(\kappa)$ be a version of the optimal estimate of $\vartheta \mapsto P_\vartheta(\kappa)$, $\vartheta \in \Theta$.

35.10 Lemma. *The set D is a linear space and π is a linear idempotent mapping. The set $\pi(D)$ of all optimal estimates is a linear space, too.*

Proof. Let κ_1, κ_2 be estimates in D and let $\lambda, \mu \in \mathbb{R}$. It follows from Lemma (35.9) that $\lambda\pi(\kappa_1) + \mu\pi(\kappa_2)$ is an optimal estimate. This proves the assertion. □

In the following we topologize the space of estimates $\bigcap_{\vartheta\in\Theta} \mathscr{L}^2(\Omega, \mathscr{A}, P_\vartheta)$ by the family of semi-norms $\kappa \mapsto P_\vartheta(\kappa^2)^{1/2}$, $\vartheta \in \Theta$.

35.11 Lemma. *The linear space $\pi(D)$ is closed and π: $D \to \pi(D)$ is uniformly continuous.*

Proof. From Lemma 35.9 it is clear that $\pi(D)$ is closed. Thus we need only prove that π is uniformly continuous. Let κ_1, κ_2 be arbitrary elements of D. Then

$$\begin{aligned} P_\vartheta((\pi(\kappa_1) - \pi(\kappa_2))^2) &= P_\vartheta((\pi(\kappa_1 - \kappa_2))^2) \\ &\leqq P_\vartheta((\kappa_1 - \kappa_2)^2), \quad \vartheta \in \Theta, \end{aligned}$$

which proves the assertion. □

Now we introduce the class $\mathscr{A}_0 := \{A \in \mathscr{A}: 1_A \in \pi(D)\}$. It follows from Lemma 35.9 that

$$A \in \mathscr{A}_0 \quad \text{iff} \quad \int_A v\, dP_\vartheta = 0 \quad \text{whenever} \quad v \in H(0), \quad \vartheta \in \Theta.$$

35.12 Lemma. (1) *$\mathscr{A}_0$ is a σ-field.*

(2) *Every $\mathscr{A}_0$-measurable estimate is in $\pi(D)$.*

(3) *$E|\mathscr{A}_0$ is 2-complete.*

(4) *If $\mathscr{A}_1$ is E-sufficient then $\mathscr{A}_0 \subseteq \mathscr{A}_1(P_\vartheta)$ for every $\vartheta \in \Theta$.*

Proof. (1) It is easy to see that $\mathscr{A}_0$ is a Dynkin system. Moreover, if $A \in \mathscr{A}_0$ then $1_A v \in H(0)$ if $v \in H(0)$. Therefore, $\mathscr{A}_0$ is $\cap$-stable and a σ-field.

(2) This is proved by induction, using Lemma 35.9.

(3) Let κ be an $\mathscr{A}_0$-measurable estimate. If $P_\vartheta(\kappa) = 0$ for every $\vartheta \in \Theta$ then $\kappa \in H(0)$ and hence

$$\int_A \kappa\, dP_\vartheta = 0 \quad \text{whenever} \quad A \in \mathscr{A}_0, \ \vartheta \in \Theta.$$

It follows that $\kappa = 0$ P_ϑ-a.e., $\vartheta \in \Theta$. This means that $E|\mathscr{A}_0$ is 2-complete.

(4) Assume that $\mathscr{A}_1$ is an E-sufficient σ-field. If $A \in \mathscr{A}_0$ then $1_A \in \pi(D)$ and from Lemma 35.4 we obtain that also $E(1_A|\mathscr{A}_1) \in \pi(D)$. Hence we have

$$1_A = E(1_A|\mathscr{A}_1)\ P_\vartheta\text{-a.e.}, \quad \vartheta \in \Theta.$$

If we denote $B = \{E(1_A|\mathscr{A}_1) = 1\}$, then $B \in \mathscr{A}_1$ and $A = B$ (P_ϑ), $\vartheta \in \Theta$. □

The following assertion shows that the mapping π is almost a conditional expectation.

35.13 Theorem (Bahadur [1957]). *The mapping π: $D \to \pi(D)$ has the following properties:*

(1) If $\kappa \in D$ and if h is $\mathscr{A}_0$-measurable and bounded, then $\kappa h \in D$ and $\pi(\kappa h) = \pi(\kappa) h$.

(2) If $\kappa \in D$ and if $\pi(\kappa)$ is $\mathscr{A}_0$-measurable, then $\pi(\kappa) = P_\vartheta(\kappa|\mathscr{A}_0)$ P_ϑ-a.e., $\vartheta \in \Theta$.

Proof. (1) Let $\kappa \in D$ and h be $\mathscr{A}_0$-measurable and bounded. First we note that

$$\int (\kappa h - \pi(\kappa) h) dP_\vartheta = \int (\kappa - \pi(\kappa)) h \, dP_\vartheta = 0, \quad \vartheta \in \Theta.$$

since $\kappa - \pi(\kappa) \in H(0)$. It follows that $\pi(\kappa) \cdot h$ is a mean-unbiased estimate of g: $\vartheta \mapsto P_\vartheta(\kappa h)$. If $v \in H(0)$ then $hv \in H(0)$ and therefore

$$\int \pi(\kappa) h v \, dP_\vartheta = 0, \quad \vartheta \in \Theta.$$

This implies that $\pi(\kappa) \cdot h$ is optimal.

(2) The property just proved implies that for $\kappa \in D$ and $A \in \mathscr{A}_0$ we have

$$\int_A \pi(\kappa) dP_\vartheta = \int \pi(\kappa) 1_A \, dP_\vartheta = \int \pi(\kappa 1_A) dP_\vartheta = \int_A \kappa \, dP_\vartheta, \quad \vartheta \in \Theta.$$

Hence, if $\pi(\kappa)$ is $\mathscr{A}_0$-measurable, it is a version of $P_\vartheta(\kappa|\mathscr{A}_0)$. □

The second assertion of Theorem 35.13 leads to the question, whether a given optimal estimate is $\mathscr{A}_0$-measurable.

35.14 Theorem (Bahadur [1957]). *If an optimal estimate is bounded, then it is $\mathscr{A}_0$-measurable.*

Proof. Let κ be a bounded optimal estimate. Then $\kappa v \in H(0)$ for every $v \in H(0)$. By induction we obtain that κ^n is optimal for all $n \in \mathbb{N}$. If p is a polynomial on $\mathbb{R}$ then $p \circ \kappa$ is optimal. Since $\overline{\kappa(\Omega)}$ is compact the Stone-Weierstrass theorem implies that $\varphi \circ \kappa$ is optimal whenever φ: $\mathbb{R} \to \mathbb{R}$ is continuous. If $U \subseteq \mathbb{R}$ is open then it follows that $1_U \circ \kappa$ is optimal and therefore $\{\kappa \in U\} \in \mathscr{A}_0$. Hence κ is $\mathscr{A}_0$-measurable. □

Now we arrive at the desired converse of Theorem 35.5.

35.15 Theorem (Bahadur [1957]). *Assume that E is dominated. If for every* *function which admits a bounded unbiased estimate there exists an optimal estimate then $\mathscr{A}_0$ is E-sufficient.*

Proof. We prove that $\mathscr{A}_0$ is pairwise sufficient for E. The rest follows from Theorem (20.4). Let P_1 and P_2 be arbitrary elements of $\mathscr{P}=\{P_\vartheta: \vartheta \in \Theta\}$. Complete the pair (P_1, P_2) to a sequence $(P_n)_{n\in\mathbb{N}} \subseteq \mathscr{P}$ such that $Q := \sum_{k\in\mathbb{N}} 2^{-k} P_k$ is equivalent with $\mathscr{P}$. Then the densities $\frac{dP_i}{dQ}$, $i=1,2$, can be assumed to be bounded.

We have to show that $\frac{dP_i}{dQ}$, $i=1,2$, are $\mathscr{A}_0$-measurable. Let $h_i = \pi\left(\frac{dP_i}{dQ}\right)$, $i=1,2$. Then $P_\vartheta(h_i v)=0$ if $\vartheta\in\Theta$, $v\in H(0)$, and therefore $Q(h_i v)=0$, $v\in H(0)$. On the other hand we have $P_i(v)=0$ and hence $Q\left(v\frac{dP_i}{dQ}\right)=0$, $v\in H(0)$. This implies

$$Q\left(\left(h_i - \frac{dP_i}{dQ}\right)v\right)=0, \quad v\in H(0).$$

But $h_i - \frac{dP_i}{dQ}$ is itself an element of $H(0)$ which implies

$$Q\left(\left(h_i - \frac{dP_i}{dQ}\right)^2\right)=0.$$

We obtain that $\frac{dP_i}{dQ}$ is optimal and in view of its boundedness $\mathscr{A}_0$-measurable. □

35.16 Corollary. *Assume that E is dominated. If for all $A\in\mathscr{A}$ the functions $\vartheta\mapsto P_\vartheta(A)$ admit optimal estimates then $\mathscr{A}_0$ is E-suffcient.*

Proof. Let $f: \Theta\to\mathbb{R}$ and such that there is a bounded unbiased estimate κ of f. By Theorem 35.15 we have to show that there exists an optimal unbiased estimate of f. Since κ is bounded we may find a sequence of step functions (κ_n) such that $\|\kappa_n-\kappa\|_u\to 0$ and (eventually by choosing a subsequence)

$$\sum_{n=1}^{\infty} \|\kappa_n-\kappa_{n+1}\|_u < \infty.$$

By assumption, for every κ_n there is an optimal estimate κ_n^* of $\vartheta\mapsto P_\vartheta(\kappa_n)$, $\vartheta\in\Theta$, $n\in\mathbb{N}$. It follows that for every $\vartheta\in\Theta$

$$\|\kappa_n^*-\kappa_{n+1}^*\|_{2,\vartheta} \leqq \|\kappa_n-\kappa_{n+1}\|_{2,\vartheta} \leqq \|\kappa_n-\kappa_{n+1}\|_u, \quad n\in\mathbb{N},$$

and thus

$$\sum_{n=1}^{\infty} \|\kappa_n^*-\kappa_{n+1}^*\|_{2,\vartheta} < \infty, \quad \vartheta\in\Theta.$$

Let $P_0 \in C(\mathscr{P})$ such that $\mathscr{P} \sim P_0$. Then, obviously,

$$\sum_{n=1}^{\infty} \|\kappa_n^* - \kappa_{n+1}^*\|_{2,P_0} < \infty$$

and it follows that (κ_n^*) has a P_0-a.e. limit κ^*. Now, it is not difficult to see that κ^* is an optimal unbiased estimate of f. □

36. Estimation by desintegration

Suppose that (T, d) is a metric space which is locally compact and separable. Let $\mathscr{B}(T)$ be its Borel σ-field. For the following, we choose a Borel measure $\mu|\mathscr{B}(T)$, that means $\mu(K) < \infty$ if $K \subseteq T$ is compact, and keep it fixed. Let us consider an experiment $E = (\Omega, \mathscr{A}, \{P_t: t \in T\})$ in $\mathscr{E}(T)$.

The experiment E is called *$\mathscr{B}(T)$-measurable* if $t \mapsto P_t(A)$ is $\mathscr{B}(T)$-measurable for every $A \in \mathscr{A}$. If E is $\mathscr{B}(T)$-measurable then we may define the measure $P(\mu)$: $A \mapsto \int P_t(A)\,\mu(dt)$, $A \in \mathscr{A}$. The experiment E is called *weakly continuous* if $t \mapsto P_t(A)$ is continuous for every $A \in \mathscr{A}$. Since in this case E is separable, the set $\mathscr{P} = \{P_t: t \in T\}$ is dominated and for every σ-finite measure $\nu|\mathscr{A}$ with $\mathscr{P} \ll \nu$ the function $(\omega, t) \mapsto \frac{dP_t}{d\nu}(\omega)$, $(\omega, t) \in \Omega \times T$, can be chosen $\mathscr{A} \times \mathscr{B}(T)$-measurable (Lemma 4.6).

36.1 Definition. Suppose that E is measurable. Then E is *μ-integrable* if for every $s \in T$ and every $\varepsilon > 0$ there is a critical function $\varphi \in \mathscr{F}(\Omega, \mathscr{A})$ such that

$$P_s\varphi < \varepsilon \quad \text{and} \quad \int_T P_t(1-\varphi)\,\mu(dt) < \infty.$$

In other words, E is μ-integrable if every testing problem $(\{s\}, T\backslash\{s\})$, $s \in T$, admits a test of arbitrary small level whose power function differs from one by a μ-integrable function. It is clear that E is μ-integrable for every bounded measure $\mu|\mathscr{B}(T)$.

36.2 Remark. The critical function of the preceding definition may be replaced by a critical region. Indeed, choose a critical function φ such that

$$P_s\varphi < \varepsilon^2 \quad \text{and} \quad \int_T P_t(1-\varphi)\,\mu(dt) < \infty.$$

Then $A = \{\varphi > \varepsilon\}$ satisfies

$$P_s(A) < \varepsilon \quad \text{and} \quad \int_T P_t(A')\,\mu(dt) < \infty.$$

The following assertion is the most convenient criterion to check μ-integrability of E.

36.3 Theorem. *A weakly continuous experiment E is μ-integrable iff $P(\mu)|\mathscr{A}$ is is σ-finite.*

Proof. Assume that E is μ-integrable and let $s \in T$. From 36.2 it follows that there is a sequence $(A_n)_{n \in \mathbb{N}} \subseteq \mathscr{A}$ such that $P_s(A_n) \uparrow 1$ and $P(\mu)(A_n) < \infty$ for every $n \in \mathbb{N}$. Hence there is a set $D_s \in \mathscr{A}$, $P_s(D_s) = 1$, such that $P(\mu)|\mathscr{A} \cap D_s$ is σ-finite. Let $S \subseteq T$ be a countable and dense subset. Then $D = \bigcup_{s \in S} D_s$ is such that $P_s(D) = 1$ if $s \in S$ and $P(\mu)|\mathscr{A} \cap D$ is σ-finite. Since E is weakly continuous it follows that $P_t(D) = 1$ for every $t \in T$. Hence $P(\mu)(D') = 0$ which proves the assertion.

Assume conversely that $P(\mu)|\mathscr{A}$ is σ-finite. Then there exists a sequence $(A_n)_{n \in \mathbb{N}} \subseteq \mathscr{A}$ such that $A_n \uparrow \Omega$ and $P(\mu)(A_n) < \infty$, $n \in \mathbb{N}$. This proves the assertion. □

36.4 Corollary. *A weakly continuous experiment E is μ-integrable iff any of the following conditions is fulfilled:*

(1) $\int \frac{dP_t}{dP_s} \mu(dt) < \infty$ *P_s-a.e. for every $s \in T$.*

(2) *There is a dominating measure $\nu|\mathscr{A}$ such that* $\int \frac{dP_t}{d\nu} \mu(dt) < \infty$ *ν-a.e.*

(3) $\int \frac{dP_t}{d\nu} \mu(dt) < \infty$ *ν-a.e. for every dominating measure $\nu|\mathscr{A}$.*

Proof. Assume that E is μ-integrable. Then assertions (3) and (2) follow immediately from

$$\int \frac{dP_t}{d\nu} \mu(dt) = \frac{dP(\mu)}{d\nu} \quad \nu\text{-a.e.}$$

since $P(\mu)$ is σ-finite. Similarly it is shown that (1) is valid. Now assume that (2) is satisfied. To prove that E is μ-integrable let $C_n := \{\int \frac{dP_t}{d\nu} \mu(dt) \leqq n\}$, $n \in \mathbb{N}$, and let $D_n \uparrow \Omega$, $D_n \in \mathscr{A}$, $n \in \mathbb{N}$, such that $\nu(D_n) < \infty$, $n \in \mathbb{N}$. Then $A_n := C_n \cap D_n$, $n \in \mathbb{N}$, satisfy $P(\mu)(A_n) < \infty$, $n \in \mathbb{N}$, and $\nu(\Omega \setminus \bigcup_{n \in \mathbb{N}} A_n) = 0$. Hence $P(\mu)$ is σ-finite.

Finally, assume that (1) holds. Let $\nu|\mathscr{A}$ be a probability measure which is equivalent to $\{P_t: t \in T\}$ and is of the form $\nu = \sum_{k \in \mathbb{N}} 2^{-k} P_{s_k}$ where $(s_k)_{k \in \mathbb{N}}$ is dense in T. Then we have

$$\int \frac{dP_t}{d\nu} \mu(dt) \leqq 2^k \int \frac{dP_t}{dP_{s_k}} \mu(dt) < \infty \quad P_{s_k}\text{-a.e.}, \ k \in \mathbb{N}.$$

It follows that $N = \{\int \frac{dP_t}{dv}\,\mu(dt) = \infty\}$ satisfies $P_{s_k}(N) = 0$ for every $k \in \mathbb{N}$ and hence $v(N) = 0$. $\square$

Although much more general cases will be discussed in subsequent sections let us illustrate these concepts by some typical simple examples.

36.5 Examples. Suppose that $(H, \langle .,. \rangle)$ is a Euclidean space, $L \subseteq H$ a linear subspace and $n = \dim H$, $k = \dim L$. The Lebesgue measure of H is denoted by λ_H.

(1) Let $P \ll \lambda_H$ be a probability measure and denote $h = \frac{dP}{d\lambda_H}$. Consider the shift $E = (H, \mathscr{B}(H), \{P_a: a \in L\})$, where $P_a = \varepsilon_a * P$. Choose $\mu = \lambda_L$. Then

$$\frac{dP(\lambda_L)}{d\lambda_H}(x) = \int_L h(x-a)\,\lambda_L(da)$$
$$= \int_L h(x - p_L(x) + a)\,\lambda_L(da), \quad x \in H.$$

Since

$$\int_{L^\perp}\int_L h(y+a)\,\lambda_L(da)\,\lambda_{L^\perp}(dy) = P(H) = 1$$

it follows that $dP(\lambda_L)/d\lambda_H < \infty \quad \lambda_H$-a.e.

This proves that E is λ_L-integrable. In the special case where $L = H$ we obtain even $P(\lambda_H) = \lambda_H$. For later purposes we note that $a \mapsto P_a$, $a \in L$, is continuous for the variational distance in any case. This is a consequence of Remark 3.1.

(2) Now, assume that $\dim L < \dim H$ and consider the shift with scale parameter $F = (H, \mathscr{B}(H), \{P_{a,\sigma}: a \in L, \sigma > 0\})$, where $P_{a,\sigma} = \mathscr{L}(\sigma\,\mathrm{id} + a | P)$, $a \in L$, $\sigma > 0$. Choose $\mu(da, d\sigma) = \lambda_L(da) \otimes \frac{1}{\sigma}\,d\sigma$. Then

$$\frac{dP(\mu)}{d\lambda_H}(x) = \int_{\mathbb{R}^+}\int_L \frac{1}{\sigma^{n+1}}\,h\left(\frac{x-a}{\sigma}\right)\lambda_L(da)\,d\sigma$$
$$= \int_{\mathbb{R}^+}\int_L \frac{1}{\sigma^{n+1}}\,h\left(\frac{x - p_L(x) + a}{\sigma}\right)\lambda_L(da)\,d\sigma, \quad x \in H.$$

Now, we put $y = \frac{a}{\sigma}$, $\alpha = \frac{1}{\sigma}\|x - p_L(x)\|$, which leads to

$$\frac{dP(\mu)}{d\lambda_H}(x) = \frac{1}{\|x - p_L(x)\|^{n-k}}$$
$$\cdot \int_{\mathbb{R}^+}\int_L \alpha^{n-k-1}\,h(\alpha\frac{x - p_L(x)}{\|x - p_L(x)\|} + y)\,\lambda_L(dy)\,d\alpha, x \in H.$$

Let $S=\{z\in L^{\perp}: \|z\|=1\}$ and let τ be the uniform distribution on S. We want to show that $dP(\mu)/d\lambda_H<\infty$ λ_H-a.e. and for this we show that

$$\int_S\int_{\mathbb{R}^+}\int_L \alpha^{n-k-1}h(\alpha z+y)\,\lambda_L(dy)\,d\alpha\,\tau(dz)=1\,.$$

But this is almost immediate since $(\alpha,z,y)\mapsto\alpha^{n-k-1}h(\alpha z+y)$ is a version of $dP/d(\lambda_{\mathbb{R}^+}\otimes\tau\otimes\lambda_L)$. Hence F is μ-integrable. It follows from Remark (3.1) that for shifts with scale parameter the mapping $(a,\sigma)\mapsto P_{a,\sigma}$, $(a,\sigma)\in L\times\mathbb{R}^+$, is continuous for the variational distance.

36.6 Definition. A measurable function $f\colon T\to\mathbb{R}$ is (E,μ)-*integrable* if E is $(|f|\mu)$-integrable.

If E is μ-integrable, then every bounded function f is (E,μ)-integrable.

36.7 Remark. Let $f\colon T\to\mathbb{R}$ be a measurable function. Theorem 36.3 and Corollary 36.4 imply that the following assertions are equivalent:

(1) The measurable function $f\colon T\to\mathbb{R}$ is (E,μ)-integrable.

(2) The measure $P(|f|\mu)\colon A\mapsto\int P_t(A)|f(t)|\,\mu(dt)$, $A\in\mathscr{A}$, is σ-finite.

(3) $\int|f(t)|\dfrac{dP_t}{dP_s}\mu(dt)<\infty$ P_s-a.e. for every $s\in T$.

(4) There is a dominating measure $\nu|\mathscr{A}$ such that $\int|f(t)|\dfrac{dP_t}{d\nu}\mu(dt)<\infty$ ν-a.e.

(5) $\int|f(t)|\dfrac{dP_t}{d\nu}\mu(dt)<\infty$ ν-a.e. for every dominating measure $\nu|\mathscr{A}$.

If E is μ-integrable and $f\colon T\to\mathbb{R}$ is (E,μ)-integrable then the RN-derivative

$$\frac{dP(f\mu)}{dP(\mu)}:=\frac{dP(f^+\mu)}{dP(\mu)}-\frac{dP(f^-\mu)}{dP(\mu)}$$

is well defined. The idea of using this RN-derivative as an estimate of f could be called *estimation by desintegration* with respect to the measure $\mu|\mathscr{B}$.

36.8 Examples. (1) Consider the shift of Example 36.5 (1). Let $p>0$ and suppose that $P(\|.\|^p)<\infty$. Then

$$\begin{aligned}\frac{dP(\|.\|^p\lambda_L)}{d\lambda_H}(x)&=\int_L\|a-p_L(x)\|^p h(x-p_L(x)+a)\,\lambda_L(da)\\&\le 2^p\int_L\|x-p_L(x)+a\|^p h(x-p_L(x)+a)\,\lambda_L(da)\\&\quad+2^p\|x\|^p\int h(x-p_L(x)+a)\,\lambda_L(da),\quad x\in H.\end{aligned}$$

The second term is finite λ_H-a.e. by Example 36.5 (1). The first term is also finite since

$$\int_{L^\perp}\int_L \|y+a\|^p h(y+a)\,\lambda_L(da)\,\lambda_{L^\perp}(dy) = P(\|.\|^p) < \infty .$$

Hence $\|.\|^p$ is (E, λ_L)-integrable.

(2) Assume that $\dim L < \dim H$. For the shift F with scale parameter the same assertion is valid. Let $p > 0$ and $\int \frac{\|x\|^p}{\|x - p_L(x)\|^p} P(dx) < \infty$. Then we obtain

$$\begin{aligned}
&\frac{dP(\|.\|^p \mu)}{d\lambda_H}(x) \\
&\leqq 2^p \int_{\mathbb{R}^+}\int_L \frac{1}{\sigma^{n+1}} \|x - p_L(x) + a\|^p\, h\left(\frac{x - p_L(x) + a}{\sigma}\right) \lambda_L(da)\, d\sigma \\
&\quad + 2^p \int_{\mathbb{R}^+}\int_L \frac{1}{\sigma^{n+1}} \|x\|^p\, h\left(\frac{x - p_L(x) + a}{\sigma}\right) \lambda_L(da)\, d\sigma \\
&= \frac{2^p}{\|x - p_L(x)\|^{n-k}} \int_{\mathbb{R}^+}\int_L \alpha^{n-k-1-p} \|\alpha \frac{x - p_L(x)}{\|x - p_L(x)\|} + y\|^p \cdot \\
&\quad h(\alpha \frac{x - p_L(x)}{\|x - p_L(x)\|} + y)\, \lambda_L(dy)\, d\alpha \\
&\quad + \frac{2^p \|x\|^p}{\|x - p_L(x)\|^{n-k}} \int_{\mathbb{R}^+}\int_L \alpha^{n-k-1} h(\alpha \frac{x - p_L(x)}{\|x - p_L(x)\|} + y)\, \lambda_L(dy)\, d\alpha, \\
&\quad x \in H.
\end{aligned}$$

We know from Example 36.5 (2) that the second term is finite λ_H-a.e. For the first term this is also valid since

$$\begin{aligned}
&\int_S \int_{\mathbb{R}^+}\int_L \alpha^{n-k-1-p} \|\alpha z + y\|^p h(\alpha z + y)\, \lambda_L(dy)\, d\alpha\, \tau(dz) \\
&= \int \frac{\|x\|^p}{\|x - p_L(x)\|^p} P(dx) < \infty .
\end{aligned}$$

Hence $\|.\|^p$ is (F, μ)-integrable. (If we only assume that $P(\|.\|^p) < \infty$ then it follows that $(a, \sigma) \mapsto \left(\frac{1}{\sigma}\|a\|\right)^p$, $(a, \sigma) \in L \times \mathbb{R}_+$ is (F, μ)-integrable.)

(3) If we specialize $P = N_H$ in (1) then every linear function $f\colon L \to \mathbb{R}$ is (E, λ_H)-integrable. We have

$$\frac{dP(f\lambda_L)}{dP(\lambda_L)} = \frac{dP(f\lambda_L)}{d\lambda_H} \Big/ \frac{dP(\lambda_L)}{d\lambda_H}$$

$$= \frac{\int_L f(a) \exp(-\frac{1}{2}\|x-a\|^2)\, \lambda_L(da)}{\int_L \exp(-\frac{1}{2}\|x-a\|^2)\, \lambda_L(da)}$$

and from $\|x-a\|^2 = \|x - p_L(x)\|^2 + \|p_L(x) - a\|^2$ it follows that

$$\frac{dP(f\lambda_L)}{dP(\lambda_L)} = f \circ p_L.$$

(4) If we specialize $P = N_H$ in (2) then it is not difficult to see that the condition is satisfied iff $n-k>p$. If $n-k>1$ then every linear function $f\colon L \to \mathbb{R}$ if (F,μ)-integrable and we obtain in a similar way as for (3)

$$\frac{dP(f\mu)}{dP(\mu)} = f \circ p_L.$$

Now, let us introduce posterior distributions. The basic idea is as follows. The mixture

$$A \times B \mapsto \int_B P_t(A)\, \mu(dt), \quad A \in \mathscr{A},\ B \in \mathscr{B}(T),$$

is decomposed along $(\Omega, \mathscr{A})$ by a kernel $F\colon \Omega \times \mathscr{B}(T) \to [0,1]$ such that

$$\int_B P_t(A)\, \mu(dt) = \int_A F(\omega, B)\, P(\mu)\,(d\omega), \quad A \in \mathscr{A},\ B \in \mathscr{B}(T).$$

Any kernel with this property will be called posterior distribution.

36.9 Definition. Suppose that E is weakly continuous and μ-integrable. A stochastic kernel $F\colon \Omega \times \mathscr{B}(T) \to [0,1]$ is called a *posterior distribution* (with respect to μ) if

$$F(B) := F(.,B) \in \frac{dP(1_B\mu)}{dP(\mu)}, \quad B \in \mathscr{B}(T).$$

36.10 Lemma. *Suppose that E is weakly continuous and μ-integrable. Then there exist posterior distributions.*

Proof. Let $\nu|\mathscr{A}$ be a dominating measure and let $Q|\mathscr{B}$ be an arbitrary probability measure. Let

$$N = \left\{ \int \frac{dP_t}{d\nu}\, \mu(dt) \notin (0,\infty) \right\}.$$

Then $P(\mu)(N) = 0$. For every $B \in \mathscr{B}$ define

$$F(B) = \begin{cases} \int_B \frac{dP_t}{d\nu}\,\mu(dt) \Big/ \int \frac{dP_t}{d\nu}\,\mu(dt) & \text{on} \quad \Omega \setminus N, \\ Q(B) & \text{on} \quad N. \end{cases}$$

Then we have for every $A \in \mathscr{A}$ with $P(\mu)(A) < \infty$ and every $B \in \mathscr{B}(T)$

$$\begin{aligned} \int_A F(B)\,dP(\mu) &= \int_{A\setminus N} \int_B \frac{dP_t}{d\nu}\,\mu(dt)\,d\nu \\ &= \int_B P_t(A\setminus N)\,\mu(dt) = P(1_B\mu)(A). \end{aligned}$$

This proves the assertion. □

The preceding lemma also gives us a method for computing posterior distributions.

36.11 Examples. (1) Consider the shift of Example 36.5 (1). It is easy to see that a posterior distribution is

$$F(x, B) = \frac{\int_B \frac{dP}{d\lambda_H}(x-a)\,\lambda_L(da)}{\int \frac{dP}{d\lambda_H}(x-a)\,\lambda_L(da)}, \qquad (x, B) \in H \times \mathscr{B}(L).$$

If we specialize $P = N_H$ then we obtain that $F(x, .) = \varepsilon_{p_L(x)} * N_L$, $x \in H$.

(2) Now, consider the shift with scale parameter of Example (36.5) (2). Then a posterior distribution is

$$F(x, B) = \frac{\iint_B \frac{1}{\sigma^{n+1}} \frac{dP}{d\lambda_H}\left(\frac{x-a}{\sigma}\right) d\sigma\,\lambda_L(da)}{\iint \frac{1}{\sigma^{n+1}} \frac{dP}{d\lambda_H}\left(\frac{x-a}{\sigma}\right) d\sigma\,\lambda_L(da)}, \qquad (x, B) \in H \times \mathscr{B}(L \times \mathbb{R}^+).$$

Specializing to $P = N_H$ does not lead to a considerable simplification.

We need a representation of posterior distributions which does not rely on a dominating measure. It is obtained in Theorem 36.14 after some preparations.

36.12 Lemma. *Suppose that E is weakly continuous. Then*

$$P_s\left\{\int_B \frac{dP_t}{dP_s}\,\mu(dt) < \frac{1}{2}\mu(B)\right\} \leqq 4 \sup_{t\in B} \|P_s - P_t\|, \quad B \in \mathscr{B}, s \in T.$$

Proof. The assertion is trivial if $\mu(B) = 0$. If $\mu(B) > 0$ then we have

$$P_s\left\{\int_B \frac{dP_t}{dP_s}\,\mu(dt) < \frac{1}{2}\,\mu(B)\right\}$$

$$= P_s\left\{\mu(B) - \int_B \frac{dP_t}{dP_s}\,\mu(dt) > \frac{1}{2}\,\mu(B)\right\}$$

$$\leqq P_s\left\{\int_B \left|1 - \frac{dP_t}{dP_s}\right| \mu(dt) > \frac{1}{2}\,\mu(B)\right\}$$

$$\leqq \frac{2}{\mu(B)} \int\int_B \left|1 - \frac{dP_t}{dP_s}\right| dP_s\,\mu(dt)$$

$$\leqq 4 \sup_{t \in B} \| P_s - P_t \|. \qquad \square$$

Recall, that by definition E is continuous if $t \mapsto P_t$ is continuous for the variational distance.

36.13 Corollary. *Suppose that E is continuous and $\mu(U) > 0$ for every open $U \subseteq T$, $U \neq \emptyset$. Then*

$$\int_U \frac{dP_t}{dP_s}\,\mu(dt) > 0 \quad P_s\text{-a.e.}$$

for every $s \in U$ and every open $U \subseteq T$, $U \neq \emptyset$.

Proof. Let $U \subseteq T$ be open, $s \in U$, and choose $\varepsilon > 0$ such that $B(s, \varepsilon) := \{t \in T\colon \| P_s - P_t \| < \varepsilon\} \subseteq U$. Then

$$P_s\left\{\int_U \frac{dP_t}{dP_s}\,\mu(dt) = 0\right\}$$

$$\leqq P_s\left\{\int_{B(s,\varepsilon)} \frac{dP_t}{dP_s}\,\mu(dt) < \frac{1}{2}\,\mu(B(s,\varepsilon))\right\} \leqq 4\varepsilon. \qquad \square$$

36.14 Theorem. *Suppose that E is continuous, μ-integrable and that $\mu(U) > 0$ for every open $U \subseteq T$, $U \neq \emptyset$. Then every posterior distribution F satisfies*

$$F(B) = \frac{\int_B \frac{dP_t}{dP_s}\,\mu(dt)}{\int \frac{dP_t}{dP_s}\,\mu(dt)} \quad P_s\text{-a.e.},\ B \in \mathscr{B}(T),\ s \in T.$$

Proof. Let $B \in \mathscr{B}(T)$. By definition of a posterior distribution we have for every $A \in \mathscr{A}$

$$\int_A F(B)\, dP(\mu) = P(1_B \mu)(A) = \int_B P_t(A)\, \mu(dt).$$

Let $N \in \mathscr{A}$ be such that $P_s(N) = 0$ and $P_t(A \setminus N) = \int_A \frac{dP_t}{dP_s}\, dP_s$, $t \in T$. The existence of such a set N follows from weak continuity of E. Let $t \in T$. From Corollary (36.13) it follows that $\int \frac{dP_t}{dP_s}\, \mu(dt) > 0$ P_s-a.e. Thus we obtain

$$\int_{A\setminus N} F(B)\, dP(\mu) = \int_B \int_{A\setminus N} \frac{dP_t}{dP_s}\, \mu(dt)\, dP_s$$

$$= \int_{A\setminus N} \frac{\int_B \frac{dP_t}{dP_s}\, \mu(dt)}{\int \frac{dP_t}{dP_s}\, \mu(dt)} \int \frac{dP_t}{dP_s}\, \mu(dt)\, dP_s .$$

The assertion follows since $\int \frac{dP_t}{dP_s}\, \mu(dt) = \frac{dP(\mu)}{dP_s}$ on $\Omega \setminus N$. □

36.15 Corollary. *Suppose that the conditions of Theorem 36.14 are satisfied. A measurable function $f\colon T \to \mathbb{R}$ is (E, μ)-integrable iff*

$$\int |f(t)|\, F(dt) < \infty \quad P_s\text{-a.e., } s \in T.$$

In this case

$$\frac{dP(f\mu)}{dP(\mu)} = \int f\, dF \quad P_s\text{-a.e., } s \in T.$$

Proof. For the first assertion combine 36.7 (3), 36.13 and 36.14. The second follows from Lemma 36.10. □

Finally, we prove a useful approximation lemma.

36.16 Lemma. *Suppose that E is continuous. Let $K \subseteq T$ be compact and $f\colon K \to \mathbb{R}$ $\mathscr{B}(T)$-measurable and bounded. Then for every $\varepsilon > 0$ there are a measurable partition $B_1, \ldots, B_M$ of K, points $t_i \in B_i$, $1 \leqq i \leqq M$, and $\alpha_i \in \mathbb{R}$, $1 \leqq i \leqq M$, such that*

$$P_s \left| \int_K f(t) \frac{dP_t}{dP_s}\, \mu(dt) - \sum_{i=1}^{M} \alpha_i \frac{dP_{t_i}}{dP_s}\, \mu(B_i) \right| < \varepsilon, \quad s \in T.$$

Proof. Let $\varepsilon > 0$ and $K \subseteq T$ compact. If $\mu(K) = 0$ or $\|f\|_u := \sup_K |f| = 0$ then the assertion is trivial. Therefore, we may assume that $\mu(K) > 0$ and $\|f\|_u > 0$. Since E is continuous there exists $\delta > 0$ such that

$$P_s\left|\frac{dP_{t_1}}{dP_s} - \frac{dP_{t_2}}{dP_s}\right| \leqq \|P_{t_1} - P_{t_2}\| < \frac{\varepsilon}{2\mu(K)\|f\|_u}$$

$$\text{whenever} \quad |t_1 - t_2| < \delta,\ t_1, t_2 \in K,\ s \in T.$$

Since f is bounded there is a step function $g = \sum_{i=1}^{M} \alpha_i 1_{B_i}$ such that $\|g\|_u \leqq \|f\|_u$ and $\|f-g\|_u < \frac{\varepsilon}{2\mu(K)}$. The sets B_i, $1 \leqq i \leqq M$, may be chosen such that $\operatorname{diam} B_i < \delta$, $1 \leqq i \leqq M$, and $\{B_i: 1 \leqq i \leqq M\}$ is a partition of K. We obtain

$$P_s\left|\int_K f(t)\frac{dP_t}{dP_s}\mu(dt) - \sum_{i=1}^{M}\alpha_i\frac{dP_{t_i}}{dP_s}\mu(B_i)\right|$$

$$= P_s\left|\int_K (f(t)-g(t))\frac{dP_t}{dP_s}\mu(dt) + \sum_{i=1}^{M}\int_{B_i} g(t)\left(\frac{dP_t}{dP_s} - \frac{dP_{t_i}}{dP_s}\right)\mu(dt)\right|$$

$$\leqq \int_K\int |f(t)-g(t)|\,dP_t\,\mu(dt) + \sum_{i=1}^{M}\int_{B_i}\int |g(t)|\left|\frac{dP_t}{dP_s} - \frac{dP_{t_i}}{dP_s}\right| dP_s\,\mu(dt)$$

$$\leqq \frac{\varepsilon}{2\mu(K)}\cdot\mu(K) + \frac{\varepsilon}{2\mu(K)}\cdot\sum_{i=1}^{M}\mu(B_i) < \varepsilon. \qquad \square$$

37. Generalized Bayes estimates

We keep the notations and assumptions of Section 36.

In the following we consider a loss function $W = (W_t)_{t\in T}$, given by $W_t: T \to [0,\infty)$, $t \in T$, such that $(s,t) \mapsto W_t(s)$, $(s,t) \in T \times T$, is $\mathscr{B}(T) \times \mathscr{B}(T)$-measurable and $W(0) = 0$. If $\varrho \in \mathscr{R}(E,T)$ is an estimate then the risk of ϱ with respect to W is given by

$$W_t\varrho P_t := \int\int W_t(s)\,\varrho(\omega, ds)\,P_t(d\omega),\ t \in T.$$

For convenience let us introduce the notations

$$W_t\varrho: \omega \mapsto \int W_t(s)\,\varrho(\omega, ds), \quad \omega \in \Omega,\ t \in T,$$

and

$$\varrho P_t: B \mapsto \int \varrho(\omega, B) P_t(d\omega), \quad B \in \mathscr{B}, \ t \in T.$$

We discuss first Bayes estimates assuming that $\mu|\mathscr{B}(T)$ is a finite measure. Generalized Bayes estimates are the extension of this concept to non-finite measures $\mu|\mathscr{B}(T)$. Recall that F denotes the posterior distribution w.r.t. μ.

37.1 Definition. Suppose that $\mu|\mathscr{B}(T)$ is finite and W is μ-integrable. An estimate $\varrho^* \in \mathscr{R}(E, T)$ is called a *Bayes estimate* (with respect to μ and W) if

$$\int W_t \varrho^* P_t \mu(dt) \leqq \int W_t \varrho P_t \mu(dt) \quad \text{for all} \quad \varrho \in \mathscr{R}(E, T).$$

37.2 Theorem. *Suppose that E is weakly continuous, $\mu|\mathscr{B}(T)$ is finite and W is μ-integrable. If an estimate $\varrho^* \in \mathscr{R}(E, T)$ is a Bayes estimate then for every $s \in T$*

$$\int (W_t \varrho^*)(\omega) F(\omega, dt) \leqq \int W_t(s) F(\omega, dt) \ P(\mu)\text{-a.e.}$$

Proof. Assume that there exists $s_0 \in T$ and $A \in \mathscr{A}$ with $P(\mu)(A) > 0$ such that

$$\int W_t(s_0) F(\omega, dt) < \int (W_t \varrho^*)(\omega) F(\omega, dt) \quad \text{if} \quad \omega \in A.$$

Define an estimate $\varrho \in \mathscr{R}(E, T)$ by

$$\varrho(\omega, .) = \begin{cases} \varrho^*(\omega, .) & \text{if} \quad \omega \notin A, \\ \varepsilon_{s_0} & \text{if} \quad \omega \in A. \end{cases}$$

Then it is easy to see that

$$\int W_t \varrho P_t \mu(dt) < \int W_t \varrho^* P_t \mu(dt). \qquad \square$$

If E is weakly continuous and $\mu(U) > 0$ if $U \subseteq T$ is open, then $P(\mu) \sim \{P_t: t \in T\}$. In this case in the preceding assertion the exceptional set is of P_t-measure zero for every $t \in T$.

The assertion of Theorem 37.2 is the starting point for the definition of generalized Bayes estimates.

37.3 Definition. A *loss function* $(W_t)_{t \in T}$ is (E, μ)-*integrable* if for every $s \in T$ the function $t \mapsto W_t(s)$, $t \in T$, is (E, μ)-integrable.

37.4 Definition. Suppose that E is μ-integrable and $(W_t)_{t \in T}$ is (E, μ)-integrable. An estimate $\varrho^* \in \mathscr{R}(E, T)$ is a *generalized Bayes estimate* (with respect to μ and W) if

$$\int (W_t \varrho^*)(\omega) F(\omega, dt) \leqq \int W_t(s) F(\omega, dt) \quad P_r\text{-a.e.}$$

for all $s \in T$ and $r \in T$.

37.5 Remark. Let us make some comments on the preceding definition. First we note that the inequality may be written as

$$\int \left(\int W_t(s')\, F(\omega, dt) \right) \varrho^*(\omega, ds') \leqq \int W_t(s)\, F(\omega, dt) \quad P_r\text{-a.e.}, \ r \in T, \ s \in T.$$

Assume for the moment that

$$\omega \mapsto \inf_{s \in T} \int W_t(s)\, F(\omega, dt), \quad \omega \in \Omega,$$

is $\mathscr{A}$-measurable. Letting

$$B(\omega) := \{ s' \in T \colon \int W_t(s')\, F(\omega, dt) = \inf_{s \in T} \int W_t(s)\, F(\omega, dt) \}, \quad \omega \in \Omega,$$

we see that ϱ^* is a generalized Bayes estimate iff

$$\varrho^*(\omega, B(\omega)) = 1 \quad P_t\text{-a.e.}, \quad t \in T.$$

The preceding remark shows that the existence of generalized Bayes estimates depends on regularity properties of the posterior risks $s \mapsto \int W_t(s)\, F(\omega, dt)$, $s \in T$, $\omega \in \Omega$. We do not intend to state the most general set of conditions which implies the existence of generalized Bayes estimates, since for most special cases existence follows just from a moment's reflection. However, we will work out a set of conditions which is useful in many cases.

First, let us consider examples.

37.6 Examples. (1) Let us consider again the shift on a Euclidean space $(H, \langle \cdot, \cdot \rangle)$ which has been introduced in Example 36.5 (1). Define the loss function by $W_a(b) = \|b - a\|^2$, $a, b \in L$, and assume that P possesses finite moments up to the order 2. Then

$$\kappa^*(x) = \int a F(x, da) = \frac{\int a \dfrac{dP}{d\lambda_H}(x - a)\, \lambda_L(da)}{\int \dfrac{dP}{d\lambda_H}(x - a)\, \lambda_L(da)}, \quad x \in H,$$

is a generalized Bayes estimate.

(2) Keep the situation of (1) but let

$$W_a(b) = \begin{cases} 1 & \text{if } \|b - a\| > c, \\ 0 & \text{if } \|b - a\| < c, \end{cases} \quad b \in L, \ a \in L.$$

The pertaining generalized Bayes estimates are called *Maximum Probability Estimates*.

(3) Now we specialize the case under (1) to $P = N_H$. Then it is easy to see that for both types of loss functions $\kappa^* = p_L$ is a generalized Bayes estimate. It

will turn out in Section 38 that this is even valid for a considerably larger class of loss functions.

(4) Finally let us consider a Gaussian shift with scale parameter and define μ as in Example 36.5 (2). Define the loss function by $W_{a,\sigma}(b, \tau) = \frac{1}{\sigma^2} \|b - a\|^2$, $a, b \in H$, $\sigma, \tau > 0$. Then it is not difficult to see that $\kappa^* = p_L$ is a generalized Bayes estimate.

Now we approach the announced existence theorem.

In the following let $(H, \langle \cdot, \cdot \rangle)$ be a Euclidean space and assume that $T = H$. Moreover let $\mu = \lambda_H$ and $W_t(s) = W(s - t)$ where $W: T \to [0, \infty)$ is a measurable function with $W(0) = 0$. An experiment $E \in \mathscr{E}(T)$ is μ-integrable of order $p \geqq 0$ if it is $f\mu$-integrable for $f: t \mapsto \|t\|^p$, $t \in T$. If W is of order p and E is λ_H-*integrable of order* p then $(W_t)_{t \in H}$ is (E, λ_H)-integrable.

37.7 Lemma. *Suppose that E is continuous and λ_H-integrable of order p. If W is of order p then the posterior risk functions*

$$s \mapsto \int W(s - t)\, F(dt), \quad s \in H,$$

are continuous P_r-a.e. for every $r \in H$.

Proof. Choose $s \in H$ and $r \in H$. Let $B(s, \delta_1) \subseteq H$ be such that $W(u - t) \leqq C_3 \|t\|^p + C_4$ if $u \in B(s, \delta_1)$ and $t \in H$. Since E is λ_H-integrable of order p it follows that

$$\int \|t\|^p F(dt) < \infty \quad P_r\text{-a.e.}, \quad r \in H.$$

The exceptional set $N \in \mathscr{A}$ can be chosen independently of $r \in H$. Now let $\varepsilon > 0$ arbitrary and fix some $\omega \notin N$. There exists $a_\varepsilon \geqq 0$ such that

$$\int_{\|t\|^p > a_\varepsilon} \|t\|^p F(\omega, dt) < \frac{\varepsilon}{3C_3}.$$

Define $W_{(\varepsilon)} := \min\{W, C_3 a_\varepsilon + C_4\}$. We may find $\delta \in (0, \delta_1)$ such that

$$\left| \int W_{(\varepsilon)}(u - t)\, F(\omega, dt) - \int W_{(\varepsilon)}(s - t)\, F(\omega, dt) \right| < \frac{\varepsilon}{3}$$

whenever $\|u - s\| < \delta$. This follows from continuity of convolutions. Hence we obtain for every $u \in B(s, \delta)$

$$\begin{aligned}
&\left| \int W(u - t)\, F(\omega, dt) - \int W(s - t)\, F(\omega, dt) \right| \\
&\leqq \left| \int W_{(\varepsilon)}(u - t)\, F(\omega, dt) - \int W_{(\varepsilon)}(s - t)\, F(\omega, dt) \right| \\
&+ \int (W - W_{(\varepsilon)})(u - t)\, F(\omega, dt) + \int (W - W_{(\varepsilon)})(s - t)\, F(\omega, dt) \\
&\leqq \frac{\varepsilon}{3} + 2C_3 \int_{\|t\|^p > a_\varepsilon} \|t\|^p F(\omega, dt) \leqq \varepsilon. \quad \square
\end{aligned}$$

37.8 Theorem. *Suppose that E is continuous and λ_H-integrable of order p. Assume further that W is separating, level-compact and of order p. Then there exist generalized Bayes estimates.*

Proof. The measurability question of Remark 37.5 is settled by Lemma 37.7. If we can prove that $B(\omega) \neq \emptyset$ on a set $A \in \mathscr{A}$ with $P_s(A) = 1$, $s \in H$, then the assertion follows from the existence theorem on measurable selections, Theorem 6.10.

1st step: Let $s \in H$ and $\varepsilon > 0$. First we note that there exists a $b < \sup W$ such that

$$P_s\{\int W(s-t)\, F(dt) > b\} < \varepsilon.$$

To prove this we first assume that W is not bounded. Since W is (E, λ_H)-integrable there exists a compact set $K \subseteq H$ and $\delta > 0$ such that

$$P_s\{\int_{H \setminus K} W(s-t)\, F(dt) > \delta\} < \varepsilon.$$

The assertion follows since $W(s-.)$ is bounded on K.

Now, assume that W is bounded and separating. Let $c < \sup W$ be such that $B = \{t \in T\colon\ W(s-t) \leqq c\}$ is a neighbourhood of s. From Lemma 36.12 we obtain that there is an $\eta > 0$ such that

$$P_s\{F(B) < \eta\} < \varepsilon.$$

The number η can be chosen such that $c < \sup W - \eta$. We obtain that

$$\begin{aligned}\int W(s-t)\, F(dt) &\leqq \sup W \cdot F(B') + (\sup W - \eta)\, F(B)\\ &= \sup W \cdot (1 - F(B)) + \sup W \cdot F(B) - \eta F(B)\\ &= \sup W - \eta F(B).\end{aligned}$$

Hence it follows that

$$P_s\{\int W(s-t)\, F(dt) > \sup W - \eta^2\} \leqq P_s\{F(B) < \eta\} < \varepsilon.$$

2nd step: Let $s \in H$ and $\varepsilon > 0$. We show that there exist a compact set $K \subseteq H$ and a number $0 < \delta < \varepsilon$, such that

$$P_s\{\inf_{x \in H \setminus K} \int W(x-t)\, F(dt) > \inf_{y \in H} \int W(y-t)\, F(dt) + \delta\} > 1 - \varepsilon.$$

Since $\varepsilon > 0$ is arbitrary this implies that $B(\omega) \neq \emptyset$ P_s-a.e. According to the first step there exists a $b < \sup W$ such that

$$P_s\{\int W(s-t)\, F(dt) \leqq b\} \geqq 1 - \frac{\varepsilon}{2}.$$

Let $0 < \delta < \varepsilon$ be such that $(b + \delta)/(1 - \delta) < \sup W$. Choose a compact set $C \subseteq H$ satisfying

$$P_s\{F(C) < 1 - \delta\} < \frac{\varepsilon}{2},$$

and let

$$A_\varepsilon := \{\int W(s-t)\,F(dt) \leqq b\} \cap \{F(C) \geqq 1 - \delta\}.$$

Then we have $P_s(A_\varepsilon) > 1 - \varepsilon$. Since W is level-compact there exists a compact set $K_\varepsilon \subseteq H$ such that $t \in C$ and $x \notin K_\varepsilon$ imply $W(x-t) > (b+\delta)/(1-\delta)$. Then we obtain for every $x \notin K_\varepsilon$ that on the set A_ε

$$\begin{aligned}\int W(x-t)\,F(dt) &\geqq \int_C W(x-t)\,F(dt) \\ &> \frac{b+\delta}{1-\delta} F(C) \geqq b + \delta \geqq \int W(s-t)\,F(dt) + \delta \\ &\geqq \inf_{y \in H} \int W(y-t)\,F(dt) + \delta. \quad \square\end{aligned}$$

As the proof of the preceding theorem shows there exist generalized Bayes estimates which are even non-randomized estimates.

38. Full shift experiments and the convolution theorem

Let G be a locally compact group with countably generated topology. Let λ_r and λ_ℓ be a pair of right and left invariant measures such that $\mathscr{L}(\sigma|\lambda_r) = \lambda_\ell$ if $\sigma: x \mapsto x^{-1}$, $x \in G$. The Borel-σ-field of G is denoted by $\mathscr{B}(G)$. The modulus function of G is denoted by Δ.

38.1 Definition. Let $P|\mathscr{B}(G)$ be a probability measure on G. Then the experiment $E = (G, \mathscr{B}(G), \{\varepsilon_t * P: t \in G\})$ is called the *full shift experiment* generated by P. For short we denote $P_t := \varepsilon_t * P$, $t \in G$.

38.2 Remark. The following formulas are immediate. A measurable function is P-integrable iff it is P_t-integrable and

$$\int f\,dP_t = \int f(tx)\,P(dx), \quad t \in G.$$

In particular, we have $P_t(A) = P(t^{-1}A)$, $t \in G$, $A \in \mathscr{B}$. If $P \ll \lambda_\ell$ then $P_t \ll \lambda_\ell$, $t \in G$, and

$$\frac{dP_t}{d\lambda_\ell}(x) = \frac{dP}{d\lambda_\ell}(t^{-1}x) \quad \lambda_\ell\text{-a.e.}, \quad t \in G.$$

38.3 Lemma. (Torgersen [1972]). *Suppose that E is the full shift experiment generated by P. Then the following assertions are equivalent:*

(1) $P \ll \lambda_\ell$,
(2) $\{P_t : t \in G\}$ *is dominated,*
(3) $\{P_t : t \in G\} \sim \lambda_\ell$,
(4) E *is weakly continuous,*
(5) E *is continuous.*

Proof: (1) $\Rightarrow$ (2): Let $A \in \mathscr{B}(G)$. Then

$$(\varepsilon_t * P)(A) = \int 1_A(tx)\, P(dx) = P(t^{-1}A), \quad t \in G.$$

If $\lambda_\ell(A) = 0$ then $\lambda_\ell(t^{-1}A) = 0$ and hence $(\varepsilon_t * P)(A) = 0$.

(2) $\Rightarrow$ (3): Let $Q|\mathscr{B}(G)$ be a probability measure such that $Q \sim \{P_t : t \in G\}$. If $A \in \mathscr{B}(G)$ and $t \in G$ then $Q(t^{-1}A) = 0$ implies $P_s(t^{-1}A) = 0$ for every $s \in G$. Hence we obtain $P_{ts}(A) = 0$ for all $s \in G$ and there $Q(A) = 0$. It follows that $Q(A) = 0$ iff

$$\begin{aligned} 0 &= \int Q(t^{-1}A)\, \lambda_\ell(dt) = \iint 1_A(tx)\, Q(dx)\, \lambda_\ell(dt) \\ &= \int \lambda_\ell(Ax^{-1})\, Q(dx) = \lambda_\ell(A) \int \Delta(x^{-1})\, Q(dx), \end{aligned}$$

where Δ is the modulus function of G. Since $\Delta > 0$ we obtain $Q \sim \lambda_\ell$.

(3) $\Rightarrow$ (1): Obvious.

(5) $\Rightarrow$ (4) $\Rightarrow$ (2): Obvious.

(3) $\Rightarrow$ (5): It is a well known fact that for every $f \in \mathscr{L}^1(G, \mathscr{B}(G), \lambda_\ell)$

$$\lim_{t \to e} \int |f(x) - f(t^{-1}x)|\, \lambda_\ell(dx) = 0.$$

Since

$$\frac{d(\varepsilon_t * P)}{d\lambda_\ell}(x) = \frac{dP}{d\lambda_\ell}(t^{-1}x), \quad x \in G,\ t \in G,$$

the assertion follows. □

Suppose that G is Abelian and let G be the *character group* of G, i.e. the group of all homomorphisms $\chi: G \to \{z \in \mathbb{C} : |z| = 1\}$. The Fourier transform of a probability measure $P|\mathscr{B}(G)$ is

$$\hat{P}: \chi \mapsto \int \chi\, dP, \quad \chi \in G^*.$$

It is well known (see e.g. Parthasarathy [1967]) that two probability measures on $\mathscr{B}(G)$ coincide iff their Fourier transforms coincide.

38.4 Lemma. *Suppose that G is Abelian. If $\hat{P}(\chi) \neq 0$, $\chi \in G^*$, then the full shift experiment E consists of pairwise different probability measures.*

Proof. Assume that $P_t = P_s$, $s, t \in G$. Then it follows that for every $\chi \in G^*$

$$\int \chi(x)\, P_t(dx) = \int \chi(x)\, P_s(dx)$$

and therefore $\chi(s) = \chi(t)$ for every $\chi \in G^*$. This proves $s = t$. □

Estimation for full shift experiments depends on the methods developed in Sections 36 and 37.

38.5 Lemma. *Every full shift experiment E is λ_r-integrable.*

Proof. Let us show that $\int P_t \lambda_r(dt) = \lambda_r$. If $A \in \mathscr{B}(G)$ then we have

$$\begin{aligned}\int P_t(A)\, \lambda_r(dt) &= \int\int 1_A(tx)\, P(dx)\, \lambda_r(dt) \\ &= \int\int 1_A(tx)\, \lambda_r(dt)\, P(dx) = \lambda_r(A).\end{aligned}$$ □

38.6 Example. The main example in the present section will be a full shift on a Euclidean space $(H, \langle\cdot,\cdot\rangle)$. For this case the preceding assertion can be improved to the following fact: If P has finite p-th moments then E is λ_H-integrable of order p. This is the particular case of Example 36.8 (1), where $H = L$.

Throughout the following we suppose that E is a dominated full shift experiment generated by the probability measure $P|\mathscr{B}(G)$.

Let us compute the posterior distribution given λ_r. A particular case of the following lemma is contained in Example 36.11 (1).

38.7 Lemma. *The posterior distribution with respect to λ_r is $F(x, .) = \varepsilon_x * \check{P}$, $x \in G$, where $\check{P} = \mathscr{L}(\sigma|P)$.*

Proof. Let $A \in \mathscr{B}(G)$. Then we have

$$\begin{aligned}\int_A \frac{dP}{d\lambda_\ell}(t^{-1}x)\, \lambda_r(dt) &= \int 1_A(t^{-1}) \frac{dP}{d\lambda_\ell}(tx)\, \lambda_\ell(dt) \\ &= \Delta(x) \int 1_A(xt^{-1}) \frac{dP}{d\lambda_\ell}(t)\, \lambda_\ell(dt) \\ &= \Delta(x) \int 1_A(xt^{-1})\, P(dt) = \Delta(x)\, \check{P}(x^{-1}A).\end{aligned}$$

Hence it follows from the proof of Lemma 36.10 that

$$F(x, A) = \frac{\Delta(x)\, \check{P}(x^{-1}A)}{\Delta(x)} = \check{P}(x^{-1}A).$$ □

At this point the reader should recall Definition 32.1 where amenable groups are introduced. Amenability is the reason of the optimum properties of certain estimates. We have been concerned with a similar situation before in Section 32.

First, we state some approximation lemmas for posterior distributions.

38.8 Lemma. *Suppose that G is amenable. Then for every probability measure $Q|\mathscr{B}(G)$ and every summing sequence (K_n)*

$$\lim_{n\to\infty} \frac{1}{\lambda_r(K_n)} \int_{K_n} (\varepsilon_x * Q)(K_n')\,\lambda_r(dx) = 0.$$

Proof. The assertion follows from

$$\begin{aligned}
&\frac{1}{\lambda_r(K_n)} \int_{K_n} (\varepsilon_x * Q)(K_n')\,\lambda_r(dx) \\
&= \frac{1}{\lambda_r(K_n)} \int 1_{K_n}(x) \int (1 - 1_{K_n}(xt))\,Q(dt)\,\lambda_r(dx) \\
&= \int Q(dt) \frac{1}{\lambda_r(K_n)} \int (1_{K_n}(x) - 1_{K_n}(x) 1_{K_n}(xt))\,\lambda_r(dx) \\
&\leqq \int Q(dt) \frac{1}{\lambda_r(K_n)} \int_{K_n} |1_{K_n}(x) - 1_{K_n}(xt)|\,\lambda_r(dx). \quad \square
\end{aligned}$$

38.9 Lemma. *Suppose that G is amenable. Let F be the posterior distribution of E given λ_r. Then for every summing sequence*

$$\lim_{n\to\infty} \frac{1}{\lambda_r(K_n)} \int\int_{K_n} \|F - F(.|K_n)\|\,dP_t\,\lambda_r(dt) = 0.$$

Proof. Since $\|F - F(.|K_n)\| = F(K_n')$, $n \in \mathbb{N}$, and since $F(x,.) = \varepsilon_x * \check{P}$ we need only show that

$$\lim_{n\to\infty} \frac{1}{\lambda_r(K_n)} \int_{K_n}\int (\varepsilon_x * \check{P})(K_n')\,P_t(dx)\,\lambda_r(dt) = 0.$$

We have

$$\int (\varepsilon_x * \check{P})(K_n')\,(\varepsilon_t * P)(dx) = (\varepsilon_t * P * \check{P})(K_n')$$

and therefore we may apply Lemma (38.8) with $Q = P * \check{P}$. $\square$

Every probability measure $Q|\mathscr{B}(G)$ defines an estimate $\varrho \in \mathscr{R}(E, G)$ by

$$\varrho(x,.) := \varepsilon_x * Q, \quad x \in G.$$

Such estimates satisfy $\varrho P_t = P_t * Q$, $t \in G$.

38.10 Definition. An estimate $\varrho \in \mathscr{R}(E, G)$ is a *convolution kernel* if $\varrho(x,.) = \varepsilon_x * Q$, $x \in G$, for some probability measure $Q \in \mathscr{B}(G)$.

38.11 Remarks. (1) An estimate $\varrho \in \mathscr{R}(E, G)$ is a convolution kernel iff

$\varrho(tx, tA) = \varrho(x, A)$, $x \in G$, $t \in G$, $A \in \mathscr{B}(G)$. Obviously, the condition is necessary. To show sufficiency, we define $Q := \varrho(e, .)$ which implies $\varrho(x, A) = Q(x^{-1}A) = (\varepsilon_x * Q)(A)$, $x \in G$, $A \in \mathscr{B}(G)$.

(2) Since $P_t = \varepsilon_t * P$, $t \in G$, the distributions of a convolution kernel satisfy an invariance condition, namely $\varrho P_t = \varepsilon_t * \varrho P$, $t \in G$. The latter property gives rise to the following definition.

38.12 Definition. An estimate $\varrho \in \mathscr{R}(E, G)$ is *equivariant* if $\varrho P_t = \varepsilon_t * \varrho P$, $t \in G$.

38.13 Remarks. (1) An estimate $\varrho \in \mathscr{R}(E, G)$ is equivariant iff $(\varrho P_t)(tA) = (\varrho P)(A)$, $t \in G$, $A \in \mathscr{B}(G)$.

(2) Consider the special case where $G = (H, \langle \cdot, \cdot \rangle)$ is a Euclidean space and $P = N_H$. In this case a non-randomized estimate $\kappa: H \to H$ is equivariant iff it is of the form $\kappa(x) = x + a$ P-a.e. for some $a \in H$. To see this note that equivariance implies

$$\int f(\kappa(x)) P_t(dx) = \int f(\kappa(s + x) - s) P_t(dx)$$

for all $s, t \in H$ and every $f \in \mathscr{C}_b(H)$. Since the Gaussian shift experiment is complete it follows that $\kappa(s + x) = \kappa(x) + s$ P-a.e., $s \in H$. An application of Fubini's theorem yields

$$P^2\{(s, x): \kappa(s + x) = s + \kappa(x)\} = 0.$$

Hence there exists $x_0 \in H$ such that $\kappa(s + x_0) = s + \kappa(x_0)$ for P-almost every $s \in H$. Now, taking $a = \kappa(x_0) - x_0$ proves the assertion.

The last remark shows that sometimes non-randomized equivariant estimates are almost convolution kernels. Can a similar assertion be proved for arbitrary equivariant estimates?

In the following theorem it is shown that even the distributions of non-equivariant estimates are "in the mean" convolutions.

38.14 Theorem. *Suppose that G is amenable and let (K_n) be a summing sequence. Then for every $\varrho \in \mathscr{R}(E, G)$ there exist probability measures $Q_n | \mathscr{B}(G)$, $n \in \mathbb{N}$, such that*

$$\lim_{n \to \infty} \left\| \frac{1}{\lambda_r(K_n)} \int_{K_n} \varepsilon_{t^{-1}} * \varrho P_t \lambda_r(dt) - P * Q_n \right\| = 0.$$

Proof. Recall that for every $\mathscr{B}(G) \otimes \mathscr{B}(G)$-measurable bounded function $h: G^2 \to \mathbb{R}$ we have

$$\int_{K_n} \int h(x, t) P_t(dx) \lambda_r(dt) = \int_{K_n} \iint h(x, t) F(dt | K_n)(x) P_s(dx) \lambda_r(ds),$$

$n \in \mathbb{N}$. We obtain for every $A \in \mathscr{B}(G)$

$$\frac{1}{\lambda_r(K_n)} \int_{K_n} (\varrho P_t)(tA)\, \lambda_r(dt)$$

$$= \frac{1}{\lambda_r(K_n)} \int_{K_n} \iint \varrho(x, tA)\, F(dt|K_n)(x)\, P_s(dx)\, \lambda_r(ds)$$

$$= \frac{1}{\lambda_r(K_n)} \int_{K_n} \iint \varrho(x, tA)\, (\varepsilon_x * \check{P})\, (dt)\, P_s(dx)\, \lambda_r(ds) + R_n(A)$$

where

$$|R_n(A)| \leqq \frac{1}{\lambda_r(K_n)} \int_{K_n} \int \|F - F(.|K_n)\|\, dP_t \lambda_r(dt).$$

By Lemma 38.9 it follows that

$$\lim_{n\to\infty} \sup_{A \in \mathscr{B}(G)} |R_n(A)| = 0.$$

If we denote

$$Q_n\colon A \mapsto \frac{1}{\lambda_r(K_n)} \int_{K_n} \int \varrho(x, xA)\, P_s(dx)\, \lambda_r(ds), \quad A \in \mathscr{B}(G),\ n \in \mathbb{N},$$

then we obtain

$$\frac{1}{\lambda_r(K_n)} \int_{K_n} (\varrho P_t)(tA)\, \lambda_r(dt)$$

$$= R_n(A) + \frac{1}{\lambda_r(K_n)} \int_{K_n} \iint \varrho(x, xtA)\, \check{P}(dt)\, P_s(dx)\, \lambda_r(ds)$$

$$= R_n(A) + \int Q_n(tA)\, \check{P}(dt) = R_n(A) + (P * Q_n)\, (A),$$

which proves the assertion. □

A first important consequence is the convolution theorem.

38.15 Theorem. (Boll [1955]). *Suppose that G is amenable. Then for every equivariant estimate $\varrho \in \mathscr{R}(E, G)$ there exists a probability measure $Q|\mathscr{B}(G)$ such that $\varrho P_t = P_t * Q$, $t \in G$.*

Proof. Since ϱ is equivariant we obtain from Theorem 38.14 a sequence of probability measures $Q_n|\mathscr{B}(G)$, $n \in \mathbb{N}$, such that

$$\lim_{n\to\infty} \|\varrho P - P * Q_n\| = 0.$$

Let $Q|\mathscr{B}(G)$ be a vague limit point of $(Q_n)_{n\in\mathbb{N}}$. Then for every $f \in \mathscr{C}_{00}(G)$ we have

$$f\varrho P = \int f d(P * Q).$$

Since ϱP is a probability measure the same is true for $P * Q$ and Q. □

38.16 Corollary. *Suppose that G is amenable. Then for every equivariant estimate there exists a convolution kernel with the same distribution.*

Let $W: G \to [0, \infty)$ be a lower semicontinuous function and define the loss function by $W_t(x) := W(t^{-1}x)$, $x \in G$, $t \in G$. Then the risk of an estimate $\varrho \in \mathscr{R}(E, G)$ is given by

$$W_t \varrho P_t = \int\int W(t^{-1}y)\, \varrho(x, dy)\, P_t(dx), \quad t \in G.$$

If ϱ is a convolution kernel defined by $Q|\mathscr{B}(G)$ then

$$W_t \varrho P_t = \int W d(P * Q), \quad t \in G.$$

By the convolution theorem for amenable groups the risk of any equivariant estimate is also of this form. The maximal risk of arbitrary estimates can be bounded from below by the risks of convolution kernels.

38.17 Theorem. *Suppose that G is amenable. Then for every estimate $\varrho \in \mathscr{R}(E, G)$ there is a probability measure $Q|\mathscr{B}(G)$ such that*

$$\sup_{t \in G} W_t \varrho P_t \geqq \int W d(P * Q)$$

for every level-compact function $W: G \to [0, \infty)$.

Proof. From Theorem 38.14 we obtain a sequence of probability measures $Q_n|\mathscr{B}(G)$, $n \in \mathbb{N}$, such that

$$\sup_{t \in G} f\varrho P_t \geqq \limsup_{n \to \infty} \int f d(P * Q_n), \quad f \in \mathscr{C}_b(G).$$

If the right hand side is zero for all $f \in \mathscr{C}_{00}(G)$ then it follows that

$$\sup_{t \in G} W_t \varrho P_t = W(\infty)$$

and the assertion is valid with arbitrary Q. Otherwise, let $Q_0|\mathscr{B}(G)$ be a vague limit point of $(Q_n)_{n \in \mathbb{N}}$, $Q_0 \neq 0$. Then $P * Q_0$ is a vague limit point of $(P * Q_n)_{n \in \mathbb{N}}$. Let $Q = \dfrac{1}{Q_0(G)} \cdot Q_0$. Then $Q|\mathscr{B}(G)$ is a probability measure. If $f \in \mathscr{C}_0^+(G)$ then we have

$$\liminf_{n \to \infty} \int f d(P * Q_n) \leqq \int f d(P * Q_0) \leqq \int f d(P * Q)$$

and therefore for every level compact function $f \in \mathscr{C}_b(G)$ we have (since

$\sup f - f \in \mathscr{C}_0^+(G)$)

$$\limsup_{n\to\infty} \int f d(P * Q_n) \geqq \int f d(P * Q)$$

We obtain that

$$\sup_{t\in G} f\varrho P_t \geqq \int f d(P * Q)$$

for every level compact function $f \in \mathscr{C}_b(G)$ and the proof is finished by Lemma 6.4. □

38.18 Corollary. *Let $W: G \to [0, \infty)$ be lower semicontinuous and suppose that there is a point $y_0 \in G$ such that*

$$\int W(x \cdot y_0)\, P(dx) \leqq \int W(x \cdot y)\, P(dx) \quad \text{if} \quad y \in G.$$

Then the non-randomized estimate κ: $x \mapsto x \cdot y_0$, $x \in G$, has the following properties:

(1) *κ is optimal (for W) among all convolution kernels.*

(2) *If G is amenable then κ is optimal (for W) among all equivariant estimates.*

(3) *If G is amenable and W is level-compact then κ is a minimax estimate (for W).*

Proof. (1) is obvious, (2) follows from Theorem 38.15 and (3) follows from Theorem 38.17. □

Now we turn to the case where G is a Euclidean space, denoted by $(H, \langle\cdot,\cdot\rangle)$.

38.19 Example. Let $W(x) = \|x\|^2$, $x \in H$. Then the assumption of the preceding corollary is fulfilled with $y_0 = \int x P(dx)$, provided the first moment exists. Hence, $\kappa: x \mapsto x + y_0$, $x \in H$, is a minimax estimate whatever $P|\mathscr{B}(H)$ looks like. If $P|\mathscr{B}(H)$ is centrally symmetric then the first moment is zero if it exists and hence, the identity is minimax for quadratic loss. This easy fact can be extended very far as we shall do below.

38.20 Lemma. *Let C, $D \subseteq H$ be convex sets which are centrally symmetric. Then*

$$\lambda((C + y) \cap D) \leqq \lambda(C \cap D), \quad y \in H.$$

Proof. In view of Theorem (6.1) we may assume that C and D are closed. It is clear that we may even assume that C and D are compact. For any convex, compact set $A \subseteq H$ let $S(A) := \frac{1}{2}A + \frac{1}{2}(-A)$. Then it is easy to see that $S((C + y) \cap D) \subseteq C \cap D$, using that C and D are convex and centrally symmetric. Hence, for the assertion it is sufficient to show that $\lambda(S(A)) \geqq \lambda(A)$ for any compact, convex set $A \subseteq H$. But this is an easy consequence of the Brunn-Minkowski Theorem 6.2. For this, put $k := \dim H$ and note that

$$\lambda^{\frac{1}{k}}(S(A)) = \lambda^{\frac{1}{k}}\left(\frac{1}{2}A + \frac{1}{2}(-A)\right) \geqq \frac{1}{2}\lambda^{\frac{1}{k}}(A) + \frac{1}{2}\lambda^{\frac{1}{k}}(-A) = \lambda^{\frac{1}{k}}(A). \qquad \square$$

38.21 Lemma. (Anderson [1955]). *Let $P \ll \lambda$. Suppose that $-\dfrac{dP}{d\lambda}$ and $W: H \to [0, \infty)$ are subconvex. Then*

$$\int W\,dP \leqq \int W(x+y)\,P(dx), \quad y \in H.$$

Proof. Let $C \subseteq H$ be convex and centrally symmetric. Then from Lemma 38.20 it follows that for every $\alpha \geqq 0$, $y \in H$

$$\begin{aligned} P(C+y) &= \int_0^\infty \lambda\left((C+y) \cap \left\{\frac{dP}{d\lambda} > \alpha\right\}\right) d\alpha \\ &\leqq \int_0^\infty \lambda\left(C \cap \left\{\frac{dP}{d\lambda} > \alpha\right\}\right) d\alpha = P(C), \quad y \in H. \end{aligned}$$

Putting $C = \{W \leqq \beta\}$, $\beta \geqq 0$, we obtain

$$P\{W > \beta\} \leqq P\{W(.+y) > \beta\}, \quad \beta \geqq 0,\ y \in H,$$

and therefore

$$\begin{aligned} \int W\,dP &= \int_0^\infty P\{W > \beta\}\,d\beta \leqq \int_0^\infty P\{W(.+y) > \beta\}\,d\beta \\ &= \int W(.+y)\,dP, \quad y \in H. \qquad \square \end{aligned}$$

At this point we could apply Corollary 38.18 to obtain that under the assumptions of Lemma 38.21 the identity is the optimal equivariant estimate. However, for the verification of the minimax property without assuming level-compactness of W we have to go back to Theorem 38.14.

38.22 Theorem. *Let $P \ll \lambda$. Suppose that $-\dfrac{dP}{d\lambda}$ and $W: H \to [0, \infty)$ are subconvex. Then $\kappa: x \mapsto x$, $x \in H$, is a minimax estimate (for W).*

Proof. W.l.g. we may assume that W is lower semicontinuous. Let $\varrho \in \mathscr{R}(E, H)$ be an arbitrary estimate. Then from Theorem (38.14) we obtain a sequence of probability measures $Q_n | \mathscr{B}(H)$, $n \in \mathbb{N}$, such that

$$\sup_{h \in H} W_h \varrho P_h \geqq \limsup_{n \to \infty} \int (W \cap a)\,d(P * Q_n)$$

for every $a>0$. Since with W also $W\cap a$, is lower semicontinuous and subconvex, it follows that

$$\sup_{h\in H} W_h \varrho P_h \geqq \int (W\cap a)\,dP, \quad a>0.$$

From

$$\int W\,dP = \sup_{a>0} \int (W\cap a)\,dP$$

the assertion follows. □

The question whether the identity is the only equivariant estimate with minimal risk is answered by the following corollary.

38.23 Corollary. *Let $P \ll \lambda$ and $\hat{P}(z) \neq 0$, $z\in H$. Suppose that $W: H \to [0,\infty)$ is level-compact and such that*

$$\int W\,dP < \int W(x+y)\,P(dx) \quad \textit{if} \quad y \neq 0.$$

Then an equivariant estimate $\varrho \in \mathscr{R}(E,H)$ has minimal risk (for W) iff $\varrho(x,A) = 1_A(x)$ P-a.e., $A\in\mathscr{B}(H)$.

Proof. Since $\varrho P = P * Q$ for some probability measure $Q|\mathscr{B}(H)$ it follows that

$$\int W\,dP = \int W\,d(P*Q).$$

First, we show that $Q=\varepsilon_0$. For $\alpha \geqq 0$ let $D_\alpha = \{x\in H: \|x\| \leqq \alpha\}$. Define

$$M_\alpha := \inf_{z\notin D_\alpha} \int W(y+z)\,P(dy).$$

These infima are attained since level-compactness implies

$$\lim_{z\to\infty} \int W(y+z)\,P(dy) = \sup W.$$

Hence $M_\alpha > \int W\,dP$ for every $\alpha>0$. We have

$$\begin{aligned}\int W\,d(P*Q) &= \iint W(y+z)\,P(dy)\,Q(dz)\\ &\geqq Q(D'_\alpha)\,M_\alpha + Q(D_\alpha)\,M_0\\ &= (1-Q(D_\alpha))\,M_\alpha + Q(D_\alpha)\,M_0.\end{aligned}$$

It follows that $Q(D_\alpha)=1$ for every $\alpha>0$ and therefore $Q=\varepsilon_0$.

Thus, we obtain $\varrho P = P$. Equivariance of ϱ implies that for every $t\in H$ and $A\in\mathscr{B}(H)$

$$\int \varrho(x+t, A)\,P(dx) = P(A-t).$$

Let $K\subseteq H$ be compact. Since shifts are λ-integrable

$$\int P(K-t)\,\lambda(dt) < \infty,$$

and hence

$$\int e^{-i\langle z,t-x\rangle} \int \varrho(t,K)\, P(dx)\, \lambda(dx)$$
$$= \int e^{-i\langle z,t\rangle} P(K-t)\, \lambda(dt), \quad z \in H.$$

By Fubini's theorem this yields

$$\hat{P}(z) \int e^{-i\langle z,t\rangle} \varrho(t,K)\, \lambda(dt)$$
$$= \hat{P}(z) \int e^{-i\langle z,t\rangle} 1_K(t)\, \lambda(dt)$$

which proves the assertion. □

The idea of the following proof has been used also by Ibragimov and Has'minskii [1981].

38.24 Discussion. (Equality in Anderson's Lemma). If $P = N_H$ then

$$\int W\,dP = \int W(.+y)\,dP \quad \text{implies} \quad y = 0,$$

for every subconvex function $W: H \to [0,\infty)$ which is level-compact, separating and of finite order. It should be noted that no of these latter conditions can be omitted without compensation.

To prove this, let $y \neq 0$ and recall the proof of Anderson's Lemma 38.21. In view of this proof it is sufficient to show that there is some $\beta_0 < \sup W$ such that

$$P\{W > \beta\} < P\{W(.+y) > \beta\}$$

for all $\beta \geqq \beta_0$. Choose β_0 in such a way that $\{W \leqq \beta_0\}$ contains 0 as inner point. This is possible since W is separating. Let $\beta_0 \leqq \beta < \sup W$ and denote $C = \{W \leqq \beta\}$. Then we have

$$P(H \setminus C) < P(H \setminus (C-y))$$

iff

$$\lambda\left((C-y) \cap \left\{\frac{dP}{d\lambda} > \alpha\right\}\right) < \lambda\left(C \cap \left\{\frac{dP}{d\lambda} > \alpha\right\}\right)$$

for some $\alpha > 0$. This is the inequality we shall prove below.

Let $\alpha := \sup\left\{\gamma\colon C \subseteq \left\{\frac{dP}{d\lambda} > \gamma\right\}\right\}$. Then it follows that $C \subseteq \left\{\frac{dP}{d\lambda} \geqq \alpha\right\}$.

Moreover, we show that

$$\partial C \cap \left\{\frac{dP}{d\lambda} = \alpha\right\} \neq \emptyset.$$

For this let $\delta_n \downarrow 0$ and choose $x_n \in C \cap \left\{\frac{dP}{d\lambda} < \alpha + \delta_n\right\}$, $n \in \mathbb{N}$. Then

$\alpha \leqq \frac{dP}{d\lambda}(x_n) < \alpha + \delta_n$, $n \in \mathbb{N}$, and there is an accumulation point x_0 of (x_n) satisfying $\frac{dP}{d\lambda}(x_0) = \alpha$. Since C is closed we have $x_0 \in C$, and since $\mathring{C} \subseteq \left\{\frac{dP}{d\lambda} > \alpha\right\}$, we have $x_0 \in \partial C$. Thus, we obtain

$$x_0 \in \partial C \cap \left\{\frac{dP}{d\lambda} = \alpha\right\}.$$

Next, let us show that

$$x_0 \notin S\left((C+y) \cap \left\{\frac{dP}{d\lambda} \geqq \alpha\right\}\right).$$

Assuming the contrary, namely

$$\begin{aligned} x_0 \in S\left((C+y) \cap \left\{\frac{dP}{d\lambda} \geqq \alpha\right\}\right) \\ = \frac{1}{2}(C+y) \cap \left\{\frac{dP}{d\lambda} \geqq \alpha\right\} \\ + \frac{1}{2}(C-y) \cap \left\{\frac{dP}{d\lambda} \geqq \alpha\right\}, \end{aligned}$$

it would follow that

$$x_0 = \frac{1}{2}(x_1+y) + \frac{1}{2}(x_2-y) = \frac{1}{2}(x_2+x_2),$$

where $x_1, x_2 \in C$, $x_1 + y \in \left\{\frac{dP}{d\lambda} \geqq \alpha\right\}$, $x_1 - y \in \left\{\frac{dP}{d\lambda} \geqq \alpha\right\}$. Since $C \subseteq \left\{\frac{dP}{d\lambda} \geqq \alpha\right\}$ and since x_0 is a boundary point of the strictly convex set $\left\{\frac{dP}{d\lambda} \geqq \alpha\right\}$ we obtain that necessarily $x_1 = x_2 = x_0$. But

$$x_0 + y \in \left\{\frac{dP}{d\lambda} \geqq \alpha\right\} \quad \text{and} \quad x_0 - y \in \left\{\frac{dP}{d\lambda} \geqq \alpha\right\},$$

is a contradiction to the fact that x_0 is a boundary point of the strictly convex set $\left\{\frac{dP}{d\lambda} \geqq \alpha\right\}$.

It follows that for some $\varepsilon > 0$

$$B(x_0, \varepsilon) \subseteq \left(S\left((C+y) \cap \left\{\frac{dP}{d\lambda} > \alpha\right\}\right)\right)'.$$

On the other hand $x_0 \in \partial C \cap \left\{\frac{dP}{d\lambda} = \alpha\right\}$. Therefore

$$\left(1 - \frac{\varepsilon}{2}\right) x_0 \in \mathring{C} \cap \left\{\frac{dP}{d\lambda} > \alpha\right\}.$$

This is due to the fact that $0 \in \mathring{C}$ and $0 \in \left\{\frac{dP}{d\lambda} > \alpha\right\}$. (Otherwise one could separate $\left(1 - \frac{\varepsilon}{2}\right) x_0$ from $\mathring{C}$ and produce a contradiction to $x_0 \in \bar{C}$). Now, it is clear that the open set $U := B\left(\left(1 - \frac{\varepsilon}{2}\right) x_0, \frac{\varepsilon}{4}\right)$ satisfies

$$U \cap S\left((C+y) \cap \left\{\frac{dP}{d\lambda} > \alpha\right\}\right) = \emptyset, \quad \text{but}$$

$$U \cup S\left((C+y) \cap \left\{\frac{dP}{d\lambda} > \alpha\right\}\right) \subseteq C \cap \left\{\frac{dP}{d\lambda} > \alpha\right\}.$$

This implies

$$\lambda\left(S\left((C+y) \cap \left\{\frac{dP}{d\lambda} > \alpha\right\}\right) < \lambda\left(C \cap \left\{\frac{dP}{d\lambda} > \alpha\right\}\right)\right).$$

Another application of the Brunn-Minowski theorem as in the proof of Lemma 38.20 proves the asserted inequality.

Now, we are in a position to present a complete solution of the estimation problem for Gaussian shift experiments with linear restrictions.

Let $L \subseteq H$ be a linear subspace and consider the experiment $E = (H, \mathscr{B}(H), \{N_H * \varepsilon_t : t \in L\})$. This is not a full shift experiment if $L \neq H$. We deal with the problem of estimating a linear function $f: L \to \mathbb{R}^k$ where we assume w.l.g. that f is surjective. This means, that the decision space is $D = \mathbb{R}^k$ and the loss function is of the form $W_t(y) := W(y - f(t))$, $y \in \mathbb{R}^k$, $t \in L$, where $W: \mathbb{R}^k \to [0, \infty)$. We shall prove that the non-randomized estimate $\kappa = f \circ p_L$ is the best possible choice.

38.25 Remark. In the proofs of the following assertions we shall frequently use a reduction of the problem. Let

$$F = (H, \mathscr{B}(H), \{N_H * \varepsilon_t : t \perp \ker f\})$$

and let $G := \kappa_* F$. To describe the experiment G we endow $\mathbb{R}^k$ with the inner product

$$\langle\langle y_1, y_2 \rangle\rangle := \langle x_1, x_2 \rangle \quad \text{if} \quad y_i = f(x_i),\ x_i \perp \ker f, \quad i = 1, 2.$$

With this inner product we have

$$\mathscr{L}(\kappa | N_H * \varepsilon_t) = N_{\mathbb{R}^k} * \varepsilon_{f(t)}, \quad t \perp \ker f,$$

and thus

$$G = (\mathbb{R}^k, \mathscr{B}^k, \{N_{\mathbb{R}^k} * \varepsilon_{f(t)} : t \perp \ker f\}).$$

The point is that G is a full shift experiment where the theory of the present section can be applied. Moreover, since $\kappa = f \circ p_L$ is a suffcient mapping, G and F are statistically isomorphic experiments. (The question whether E and G are statistically isomorphic makes no sense in our framework since E and G have different parameter spaces.)

Our first result is concerned with the convolution theorem. For convenience we denote $P_t = N_H * \varepsilon_t$, $t \in L$, $Q_t = N_{\mathbb{R}^k} * \varepsilon_{f(t)}$, $t \perp \ker f$.

38.26 Theorem. *Let $\varrho \in \mathscr{R}(E, \mathbb{R}^k)$ be an estimate which is "equivariant for the estimation of f" in the following sense:*

$$\varrho P_t = \varepsilon_{f(t)} * (\varrho P_0), \quad t \in L.$$

Then there exists a probability measure $R | \mathscr{B}^k$ such that

$$\varrho P_t = \mathscr{L}(f \circ p_L | P_t) * R, \quad t \in L.$$

Proof. Since $\varrho \in \mathscr{R}(E, \mathbb{R}^k)$ and $\mathscr{R}(F, \mathbb{R}^k) = \mathscr{R}(E, \mathbb{R}^k)$ we have $\varrho \in \mathscr{R}(F, \mathbb{R}^k)$. The experiments F and G are statistically isomorphic and therefore there exists $\tau \in \mathscr{R}(G, \mathbb{R}^k)$ such that $\tau Q_t = \varrho P_t$, $t \perp \ker f$. By Theorem 38.15 there exists $R | \mathscr{B}^k$ such that

$$\varrho P_t = \tau Q_t = Q_t * R, \quad t \perp \ker f,$$

or in other words

$$\varepsilon_{f(t)} * (\varrho P_0) = N_{\mathbb{R}^k} * \varepsilon_{f(t)} * R, \quad t \perp \ker f.$$

Since $t \in L$ occurs on both sides only through f the equation is valid even for every $t \in L$. □

Next, we show that $\kappa = f \circ p_L$ is a minimax estimate.

38.27 Theorem. *Assume that W is lower semicontinuous and subconvex. Then*

$$\inf_{\varrho \in \mathscr{R}(E, \mathbb{R}^k)} \sup_{t \in L} W_t \varrho P_t = \int W(f \circ p_L) \, dN_H.$$

Proof. Let $\varrho \in \mathscr{R}(E, \mathbb{R}^k)$ and choose $\tau \in \mathscr{R}(G, \mathbb{R}^k)$ as in the preceding proof. Then

$$\sup_{t\in L} W_t\varrho P_t \geqq \sup_{t\perp\ker f} W_t\varrho P_t = \sup_{t\perp\ker f} W_t\tau Q_t$$

$$= \int W\,dQ_0 = \int W(f\circ p_L)\,dN_H.$$

This proves the assertion. □

Finally, we consider the uniqueness problem.

38.28 Theorem. *Assume that the subconvex function* $W\colon \mathbb{R}^k \to [0,\infty)$ *is level-compact, separating and of finite order. Then every equivariant estimate* $\varrho \in \mathscr{R}(E, \mathbb{R}^k)$ *(in the sense of Theorem (28.26)) with*

$$W_t\varrho P_t = \int W(f\circ p_L)\,dN_H, \quad t\in L,$$

satisfies

$$\varrho(x, B) = 1_B(f\circ p_L(x)) \quad \lambda\text{-a.e.}, \quad B\in\mathscr{B}^k.$$

Proof. Choose $\tau \in \mathscr{R}(G, \mathbb{R}^k)$ as in the proof of Theorem 38.26. Then Corollary 38.23 and Discussion 38.24 imply that

$$\tau(.\,, B) = 1_B \quad Q_0\text{-a.e.}, \quad B\in\mathscr{B}^k,$$

or in other words

$$\int_A \varrho(.\,, B)\,dN_H = \int_A 1_B\circ\kappa\,dN_H$$

for all $B\in\mathscr{B}^k$, $A\in\kappa^{-1}(\mathscr{B}^k)$. If we put $A = \kappa^{-1}(B)$ then it follows that

$$\int_{\kappa^{-1}(B)} \varrho(.\,, B)\,dN_H = N_H(\kappa^{-1}(B)), \quad B\in\mathscr{B}^k,$$

and hence

$$\varrho(x, B) = 1 \quad \text{if} \quad f\circ p_L(x)\in B \quad \lambda_H\text{-a.e.} \qquad \square$$

It is clear that the preceding discussion carries over to the case with an additional scale parameter $\sigma > 0$.

If $P \neq N_H$ then the reduction used in Remark 38.25 is not possible since $\kappa = f\circ p_L$ need not be a sufficient mapping. This is one of the reasons for the development of the theory of the next section.

39. The structure model

In this paragraph we consider a situation which generalizes the case of full shift experiments considered in Section 38.

39.1 Example. Let $P \ll \lambda|\mathscr{B}^1$ and consider the n-fold product $E^n = (\mathbb{R}^n, \mathscr{B}^n, \{(P * \varepsilon_t)^n : t \in \mathbb{R}\})$, $n \in \mathbb{N}$, of the full shift generated by P. The translation group $G = \mathbb{R}$ operates on the sample space $\Omega = \mathbb{R}^n$ by

$$g\omega = (\omega_1 + g, \omega_2 + g, \ldots, \omega_n + g), \quad g \in G, \omega \in \Omega.$$

The orbits of the group action form a partition of Ω. Each orbit is isomorphic with the operating group. Therefore, we can identify the points $\omega \in \Omega$ by the following procedure: Let $M = \{\omega \in \Omega: \sum_{i=1}^{n} \omega_i = 0\}$. This is a cross section of orbits, i.e. it intersects each orbit in exactly one point. Each $\omega \in \Omega$ can be decomposed in the following way:

$$\omega = \frac{1}{n}\sum_{i=1}^{n} \omega_i + \left(\omega_1 - \frac{1}{n}\sum_{i=1}^{n} \omega_i, \ldots, \omega_n - \frac{1}{n}\sum_{i=1}^{n} \omega_i\right).$$

Denoting

$$T(\omega) = \frac{1}{n}\sum_{i=1}^{n} \omega_i, \quad \text{and}$$

$$S(\omega) = \left(\omega_1 - \frac{1}{n}\sum_{i=1}^{n} \omega_i, \ldots, \omega_n - \frac{1}{n}\sum_{i=1}^{n} \omega_i\right),$$

we obtain $\omega = T(\omega) + S(\omega)$, where

$$T(g + \omega) = g + T(\omega), \quad \omega \in \Omega, g \in G,$$

and

$$S(g + \omega) = S(\omega), \quad \omega \in \Omega, g \in G.$$

In other words T is equivariant and S is invariant.

Let $(\Omega, \mathscr{A})$ be a measurable space and let G be a group operating on Ω. We assume that G is a locally compact group with countably generated topology and the operation $(g, \omega) \mapsto g\omega$, $g \in G$, $\omega \in \Omega$, is $(\mathscr{B}(G) \otimes \mathscr{A})$-measurable. Let λ_r and λ_ℓ be a pair of right and left invariant measures such that $\mathscr{L}(\sigma|\lambda_r) = \lambda_\ell$ if $\sigma: g \mapsto g^{-1}$, $g \in G$.

The following analysis is based on one fundamental assumption.

39.2 Assumption. There is an $(\mathscr{A}, \mathscr{B}(G))$-measurable map $T: \Omega \to G$, which satisfies $T(g\omega) = gT(\omega)$ whenever $g \in G$ and $\omega \in \Omega$.

The following example generalizes Example 39.1.

39.3 Example. Suppose that $\Omega = H$ where $(H, \langle \cdot, \cdot \rangle)$ is a Euclidean space and let $L \subseteq H$ be a linear subspace. Then $G = L$ operates on H by the operation $x\omega := x + \omega$, $x \in G$, $\omega \in H$. It is clear that the orthogonal projection $T = p_L$ satisfies the condition of Assumption 39.2.

39.4 Example. As before let $\Omega = H$ and $L \subseteq H$ be a linear subspace satisfying $\dim L < \dim H$. But now let the semidirect product $G = \mathbb{R}^+ \times L$ operate on H by $(\sigma, s)\omega := \sigma\omega + s$, $(\sigma, s) \in \mathbb{R}^+ \times L$, $\omega \in H$. If we define $T_1 = \mathrm{id}_H - p_L$ and $T_2 = p_L$ then $T = (\|T_1(.)\|, T_2)$ satisfies the condition of Assumption 39.2 for $\omega \in H \setminus L$. To see this we have to show that

$$\begin{aligned} T(\sigma\omega + s) &= (\sigma, s)\, T(\omega) \\ &= (\sigma, s)\, (\|T_1(\omega)\|, T_2(\omega)) \\ &= (\sigma \|T_1(\omega)\|, \sigma T_2(\omega) + s). \end{aligned}$$

But this is immediate since

$$\|T_1(\sigma\omega + s)\| = \|\sigma T_1(\omega) + T_1(s)\| = \sigma \|T_1(\omega)\|$$

and

$$T_2(\sigma\omega + s) = \sigma T_2(\omega) + T_2(s) = \sigma T_2(\omega) + s.$$

For $\omega \in L$ the function T does not map into $\mathbb{R}^+ \times L$. However, for our purposes it does not matter to replace $\Omega = H$ by $\Omega = H \setminus L$ since L is a subset of Lebesgue measure zero. Denote $k = \dim L$. Easy computations show that $\lambda_\ell(d\sigma, ds) = \dfrac{1}{\sigma^{k+1}}\, d\sigma \otimes \lambda_L(ds)$ is a left-invariant measure on G and $\lambda_r(d\sigma, ds) = \dfrac{1}{\sigma}\, d\sigma \otimes \lambda_L(ds)$ is right-invariant.

39.5 Lemma. *The mapping* $S: \omega \mapsto (T\omega)^{-1}\omega$, $\omega \in \Omega$, *is maximal invariant under the operation of* G, *i.e. it satisfies*

(1) $S(\omega) = S(g\omega), \quad \omega \in \Omega,\ g \in G,$

(2) $S(\omega_1) = S(\omega_2)$ *implies* $\omega_1 = g\omega_2$ *for some* $g \in G$.

Proof. (1) This follows from

$$\begin{aligned} S(g\omega) &= (T(g\omega))^{-1}(g\omega) = (gT(\omega))^{-1}(g\omega) \\ &= (T\omega)^{-1} g^{-1} g\omega = (T\omega)^{-1}\omega = S(\omega). \end{aligned}$$

(2) If $S(\omega_1) = S(\omega_2)$ then $(T\omega_1)^{-1}\omega_1 = (T\omega_2)^{-1}\omega_2$ and therefore $\omega_1 = T\omega_1 \cdot (T\omega_2)^{-1}\omega_2$. □

39.6 Lemma. *The set* $\mathrm{im}\, S$ *intersects each orbit in exactly one point. Every* $\omega \in \Omega$ *admits a unique decomposition* $\omega = g \cdot s$ *where* $g \in G$ *and* $s \in \mathrm{im}\, S$, *namely* $g = T(\omega)$, $s = S(\omega)$.

Proof. The definition of S shows that $S(\omega)$ and ω are on the same orbit for every $\omega \in \Omega$. Property (1) implies that $\mathrm{im}\, S$ intersects each orbit at most at one point, i.e. $\operatorname{im} S$ is a cross section of orbits. The existence of the asserted decomposition follows from $\omega = T(\omega)\, S(\omega)$, $\omega \in \Omega$. To prove uniqueness let $\omega = gs$, $g \in G$, $s \in \operatorname{im} S$. This implies that $S(\omega) = S(gs) = S(s) = s$ and therefore $T(\omega)s = gs$. Applying T we obtain

$$T(\omega)\, T(s) = T((T\omega)s) = T(gs) = gT(s)$$

and therefore $T(\omega) = g$. □

39.7 Corollary. *The set* $\operatorname{im} S$ *is in* $\mathscr{A}$ *since* $\operatorname{im} S = T^{-1}\{e\}$.

Proof. If $s = S(\omega) = T^{-1}(\omega)\omega$ then $T(s) = T^{-1}(\omega) \cdot T(\omega) = e$. If conversely $s \in T^{-1}\{e\}$ then $T(s) = e$ and therefore $S(s) = T^{-1}(s) \cdot s = s$. □

39.8 Examples. In the case of Example 39.3 the maximal invariant is $S\colon x \mapsto x - p_L(x)$, $x \in H$. For Example 39.4 we have $S\colon x \mapsto \dfrac{x - p_L(x)}{\|x - p_L(x)\|}$, $x \in H$. In the second case $\operatorname{im} S = L^{\perp} \cap \{x \in H\colon \|x\| = 1\}$.

39.9 Remarks. At the first glance Assumption 39.2 might seem to be very restrictive. More familiar are the following two assumptions:

(1) There is a *cross section* M of the orbits of G on Ω. This means that for every $\omega \in \Omega$ the set $M \cap \{g\omega\colon g \in G\}$ contains exactly one element.

(2) The isotropic subgroups of all $\omega \in \Omega$ coincide. (The isotropic subgroup of $\omega \in \Omega$ is $\{g \in G\colon g\omega = \omega\}$).

Let $H \subseteq G$ be the common isotropic subgroup. Since H is a normal subgroup we may replace G by the factor group G/H. Then the common isotropic subgroup of every $\omega \in \Omega$ is $H = \{e\}$.

It is clear that our Assumption 39.2 implies conditions (1) and (2) with $M = \operatorname{im} S$ and $H = \{e\}$. However, apart from measurability questions also the converse is true since each $\omega \in \Omega$ admits a unique decomposition as $\omega = g \cdot s$ with $g \in G$ and $s \in M$. Defining $T(\omega) = g$ iff $\omega = g \cdot s$ yields a mapping $T\colon \Omega \to G$ which satisfies $T(g\omega) = gT(\omega)$, $g \in G$, $\omega \in \Omega$.

39.10 Definition. Let $P|\mathscr{A}$ be a probability measure. For every $g \in G$ let $P_g\colon A \mapsto P(g^{-1}A)$, $A \in \mathscr{A}$. Then the experiment $E = (\Omega, \mathscr{A}, \{P_g\colon g \in G\})$ is called *structure model* generated by P if the group operation satisfies condition 39.2.

The cases considered in Examples 39.1, 39.3 and 39.4 are structure models.

In the following we denote $P_S := \mathscr{L}(S|P)$. It is clear that $P_S = \mathscr{L}(S|P_g)$, $g \in G$, (by (39.5)).

39.11 Remark. We define the measures

$$\lambda_\ell * P_S\colon A \mapsto \iint 1_A(gs)\,\lambda_\ell(dg)\,P_S(ds), \quad A \in \mathscr{A}, \quad \text{and}$$
$$\lambda_r * P_S\colon A \mapsto \iint 1_A(gs)\,\lambda_r(dg)\,P_S(ds), \quad A \in \mathscr{A}.$$

It is clear that both measures are σ-finite since λ_ℓ and λ_r are σ-finite and P_S is finite. Moreover, we observe that

$$(\lambda_\ell * P_S)(A) = \int_A \Delta \circ T\, d(\lambda_r * P_S), \quad A \in \mathscr{A}.$$

where Δ is the modulus function of the group G. Since $\operatorname{im} \Delta \subseteq (0, \infty)$ it follows that $\lambda_\ell * P_S \sim \lambda_r * P_S$.

39.12 Lemma. *Every structure model is λ_r-integrable since $P(\lambda_r) = \lambda_r * P_S$.*

Proof. If $A \in \mathscr{A}$ and $g \in G$ then we have

$$\begin{aligned}\int P(g^{-1}A)\,\lambda_r(dg) &= \iint 1_A(g\omega)\,\lambda_r(dg)\,P(d\omega)\\ &= \iint 1_A(gT(\omega)s)\,\lambda_r(dg)\,P_S(ds)\\ &= \iint 1_A(gs)\,\lambda_r(dg)\,P_S(ds) = (\lambda_r * P_S)(A).\end{aligned}$$ □

39.13 Lemma. *The measure $\lambda_\ell * P_S$ is invariant, i.e.*

$$(\lambda_\ell * P_S)(gA) = (\lambda_\ell * P_S)(A), \quad g \in G,\ A \in \mathscr{A}.$$

Proof. For $g_1 \in G$ and $A \in \mathscr{A}$ we have

$$(\lambda_\ell * P_S)(g_1 A) = \iint 1_{g_1 A}(gs)\,\lambda_\ell(dg)\,P_S(ds).$$

Since $1_{g_1 A}(gs) = 1_A(g_1^{-1} gs)$ and since λ_ℓ is left invariant on G the assertion follows. □

39.14 Theorem. *For every structure model the following assertions are equivalent:*

(1) $P \ll \lambda_\ell * P_S$,
(2) $\mathscr{P}$ *is dominated,*
(3) $\mathscr{P} \ll \lambda_\ell * P_S$,
(4) E *is weakly continuous,*
(5) E *is continuous.*

Proof. (1) ⇔ (3): Let $A \in \mathscr{A}$. Then

$$P_g(A) = P(g^{-1}A) = \iint 1_{g^{-1}A}(hs) \frac{dP}{d(\lambda_\ell * P_S)}(hs)\, \lambda_\ell(dh)\, P_S(ds)$$

$$= \iint 1_A(ghs) \frac{dP}{d(\lambda_\ell * P_S)}(hs)\, \lambda_\ell(dh)\, P_S(ds)$$

$$= \iint 1_A(hs) \frac{dP}{d(\lambda_\ell * P_S)}(g^{-1}hs)\, \lambda_\ell(dh)\, P_S(ds).$$

This implies $P_g \ll \lambda_\ell * P_S$.

(2) $\Rightarrow$ (5): Let $Q|\mathscr{A}$ be a probability measure such that $Q \sim \{P_g: g \in G\}$. We claim that $Q \ll Q(\lambda_r)$. Indeed, if $Q(\lambda_r)(A) = 0$ then there exists a $g \in G$ such that $Q(g^{-1}A) = 0$. This implies $P_h(g^{-1}A) = 0$ for every $h \in G$ and therefore $P_h(A) = 0$ for every $h \in G$. Hence $Q(A) = 0$.

By Lemma 39.12 we have $Q(\lambda_r) = \lambda_r * Q_S$ and Remark 39.11 implies $\lambda_\ell * Q_S \sim \lambda_r * Q_S$. It follows that $Q \ll \lambda_\ell * Q_S$ and therefore $\mathscr{P} \ll \lambda_\ell * Q_S$. Lemma 39.13 implies that $\lambda_\ell * Q_S$ is an invariant measure and therefore

$$\frac{dP_g}{d(\lambda_\ell * Q)}(\omega) = \frac{dP}{d(\lambda_\ell * Q)}(g^{-1}\omega) \quad \lambda_\ell * Q\text{-a.e.}, \quad g \in G.$$

The Lemma of Riemann-Lebesgue shows that $g_n \to g$ implies

$$\lim_{n\to\infty} \int \left| \frac{dP}{d(\lambda_\ell * Q_S)}(g^{-1}hs) - \frac{dP}{d(\lambda_\ell * Q_S)}(g_n^{-1}hs) \right| \lambda_\ell(dh) = 0$$

for Q_S-almost every $s \in \operatorname{im} S$. Hence

$$\lim_{n\to\infty} \frac{dP_{g_n}}{d(\lambda_\ell * Q_S)} = \frac{dP_g}{d(\lambda_\ell * Q_S)} \quad (\lambda_\ell * Q_S)$$

and Scheffé's lemma (Remark (3.1)) proves (5).

(5) $\Rightarrow$ (4): Obvious.

(4) $\Rightarrow$ (3): Weak continuity implies $\mathscr{P} \ll P(\lambda_r)$. Since $P(\lambda_r) = \lambda_r * P_S \sim \lambda_\ell * P_S$ the assertion follows.

(3) $\Rightarrow$ (2): Obvious. □

As an easy consequence we see immediately that condition (3) may be strengthened to $\mathscr{P} \sim \lambda_\ell * P_S$ since $\lambda_r * P_S = P(\lambda_r) \ll \mathscr{P}$ and $\lambda_r * P_S \sim \lambda_\ell * P_S$.

39.15 Examples. (1) When we are dealing with a situation like Example 39.3 then we usually assume $P \ll \lambda_H$. Let $h = \dfrac{dP}{d\lambda_H}$. It follows that

$$P(A) = \int_A h(p_L(x) + x - p_L(x))\, \lambda_H(dx)$$

$$= \iint_A h(y+z)\, \lambda_L(dy)\, \lambda_{L^\perp}(dz) = \int_A h\, d(\lambda_L * \lambda_{L^\perp})$$

for all $A \in \mathscr{B}(G)$. Therefore we have

$$\frac{dP_S}{d\lambda_{L^\perp}}(y) = \int h(x+y)\,\lambda_L(dx), \quad y \in L^\perp.$$

(2) Things are more complicated with Example 39.4. Here we observe that

$$P(A) = \int_A h\left(\|x - p_L(x)\| \frac{x - p_L(x)}{\|x - p_L(x)\|} + p_L(x)\right) \lambda_H(dx)$$

$$= \iint_A h\left(\|z\| \cdot \frac{z}{\|z\|} + y\right) \lambda_L(dy)\,\lambda_{L^\perp}(dz), \quad A \in \mathscr{B}.$$

Let τ be the uniform distribution on $\{z \in L^\perp : \|z\| = 1\}$. Using transformation to polar coordinates one sees that $\mathscr{L}(\|.\| \,|\, \lambda_{L^\perp})$ is a measure with τ-density $\sigma \mapsto C\sigma^{n-k-1}$, $\sigma > 0$, where $n = \dim H$ and $k = \dim L$. Then it follows that

$$P(A) = \iiint_A C\alpha^n h(\alpha s + y) \frac{1}{\alpha^{k+1}}\, d\alpha\, \tau(ds)\, \lambda_L(dy), \quad A \in \mathscr{B},$$

and therefore

$$\frac{dP_S}{d\tau}(s) = \iint C\alpha^n h(\alpha s + y) \frac{1}{\alpha^{k+1}}\, d\alpha\, \lambda_L(dy), \quad s \in \operatorname{im} S.$$

39.16 Lemma. *Suppose that G is Abelian.* If $\hat{\mathscr{P}}(T|P)(\chi) \neq 0$, $\chi \in G^*$, *then the structure model consists of pairwise different probability measures.*

Proof. Assume that $P_{g_1} = P_{g_2}$ for some $g_1, g_2 \in G$. Then it follows that for every $\chi \in G^*$

$$\int \chi(T(\omega))\, P_{g_1}(d\omega) = \int \chi(T(\omega))\, P_{g_2}(d\omega)$$

and therefore $\chi(g_1) = \chi(g_2)$ for every $\chi \in G^*$. This proves $g_1 = g_2$. □

39.17 Examples. The assertion of the preceding lemma can be verified directly in particular cases. Let $f \in \mathscr{C}_0(H)$. If in Example 39.3 there exists an $a \in L$, $a \neq 0$, such that $P_a = P$ then $P_{na} = P$ for all $n \in \mathbb{N}$ which implies

$$\int f(x + na)\, P(dx) = \int f(x)\, P(dx), \quad n \in \mathbb{N}.$$

Since $f(x + na) \to 0$, $x \in H$, as $n \to \infty$, it follows that $P = 0$.

As for Example 39.4 similar considerations lead to

$$\int f\left(\sigma^n x + \frac{\sigma^n - 1}{\sigma - 1} a\right) P(dx) = \int f(x)\, P(dx), \quad n \in \mathbb{N},$$

which admits only $P = 0$, or $P = \varepsilon_{a/(1-\sigma)}$ if $\sigma \neq 1$.

39.18 Lemma. *The invariant σ-field*

$$\mathscr{A}_i = \{A \in \mathscr{A}: gA = A \quad \text{if} \quad g \in G\}$$

is generated by the mapping S, i.e. $A \in \mathscr{A}_i$ *iff* $A = S^{-1}(A)$.

Proof. Follows from Lemma 39.5. □

The decomposition which is proved in the following theorem is basic for the rest of the present section. It is shown that a structure model is a mixture of full shifts.

39.19 Theorem. *Suppose that* $E = (\Omega, \mathscr{A}, \{P_g: g \in G\})$ *is a dominated structure model. Then for every* $s \in \operatorname{im} S$ *there exists a full shift* $E^s = (G, \mathscr{B}(G), \{P_g^s: g \in G\})$ *such that:*

(1) $\omega \mapsto P_g^{S(\omega)}$ *is a version of the conditional distribution under* P_g *of T given* $\mathscr{A}_i$,

(2) $P_g(A) = \int P_g^s(A_s)\, P_S(ds), \quad g \in G, \quad A \in \mathscr{A}, \quad$ *where* $\quad A_s = \{h \in G: hs \in A\}$, $s \in \operatorname{im} S$.

Proof. First, we note that for every $C \in \mathscr{B}(\operatorname{im} S)$

$$\int_C \int \frac{dP}{d(\lambda_\ell * P_S)}(hs)\, \lambda_\ell(dh)\, P_S(ds) = P\{S \in C\} = P_S(C).$$

This implies that

$$\int \frac{dP}{d(\lambda_\ell * P_S)}(hs)\, \lambda_\ell(dh) = 1 \quad P_S\text{-a.e.}$$

For those $s \in \operatorname{im} S$ for which the equality holds define

$$P_g^s(B) = \int_B \frac{dP}{d(\lambda_\ell * P_S)}(g^{-1}hs)\, \lambda_\ell(dh), \quad B \in \mathscr{B}(G),\ g \in G.$$

For the rest define $\{P_g^s: g \in G\}$ to be any shift experiment. It is then clear that for every $s \in \operatorname{im} S$ the experiments

$$E^s := (G, \mathscr{B}(G), \{P_g^s: g \in G\})$$

are shift experiments.

(1) We have to show that for every $B \in \mathscr{B}(G)$ and $C \in \mathscr{B}(\operatorname{im} S)$

$$P_g\{T \in B, S \in C\} = \int_C P_g^s(B)\, P_S(ds), \quad g \in G.$$

This is easily seen from

$$\int_C P_g^s(B)\,P_S(ds) = \int_C\int_B \frac{dP}{d(\lambda_\ell * P_S)}(g^{-1}hs)\,\lambda_\ell(dh)$$

$$= P_g\{hs\colon h\in B, s\in C\} = P_g\{T\in B, S\in C\}.$$

(2) The second assertion need only be proved for sets $A\in\mathscr{A}$ of the form

$$A = \{hs\colon h\in B, s\in C\},\quad B\in\mathscr{B}(G),\ C\in\mathscr{B}(\operatorname{im} S).$$

But this has been done already under (1). □

39.20 Discussion (Fisher's fiducial distribution). (1) Let us first discuss the particular case of a full shift. Having observed $\omega\in\Omega$ one might be interested in the covering probability of the random set $\omega\cdot B$ where $B\in\mathscr{B}(G)$. It is obvious by a moment's reflection that

$$P_g\{\omega\in\Omega\colon g\in\omega\cdot B\} = \check{P}(B),\quad B\in\mathscr{B},\ g\in G.$$

The interesting feature of this equation is the fact that the right hand does not depend on $g\in G$. Therefore, $\check{P}(B)$ can be interpreted as the probability that $\omega\cdot B$ covers the unknown parameter $g\in G$.

(2) Now, we turn to structure models and attempt to establish a similar relation. The preceding Theorem 39.19 shows that

$$P_g^s\{h\in G\colon g\in h\cdot B\} = \check{P}^s(B),\quad B\in\mathscr{B},\ g\in G,\ s\in\operatorname{im} S.$$

Again, the right hand does not depend on $g\in G$ and therefore the number $\check{P}^{S(\omega)}(B)$ is the covering probability of the random set $T(\omega)\cdot B$, given $S(\omega)$. We may put the covering probability into

$$\check{P}^{S(\omega)}(B) = \check{P}^{S(\omega)}_{T(\omega)}(T(\omega)\cdot B).$$

The distribution $\check{P}^{S(\omega)}_{T(\omega)}$ has been called *fiducial distribution* by R.A. Fisher. It is the most important case in statistics where a posterior analysis of an experiment is possible without using a prior distribution.

(3) There is a strong relation of fiducial distributions and posterior distributions. Let us prove that, *independently of the choice of S and T* the fiducial distribution coincides with the posterior distribution for λ_r.

Choose $\omega = hs$ and $B\in\mathscr{B}(G)$. Then

$$\int_B \frac{dP}{d(\lambda_\ell * P_S)}(g^{-1}\omega)\,\lambda_r(dg) = \int_B \frac{dP}{d(\lambda_\ell * P_S)}(g^{-1}hs)\,\lambda_r(dg)$$

$$= \int 1_B(g^{-1})\,\frac{dP}{d(\lambda_\ell * P_S)}(ghs)\,\lambda_\ell(dg)$$

$$= \Delta(h)\int 1_B(hg^{-1})\,\frac{dP}{d(\lambda_\ell * P_S)}(gs)\,\lambda_\ell(dg)$$

$$= \Delta(T(\omega))\int 1_B(T(\omega)\cdot g^{-1})\,\frac{dP}{d(\lambda_\ell * P_S)}(g\cdot S(\omega))\,\lambda_\ell(dg).$$

Hence, the posterior distribution F for λ_r is

$$F(\omega, B) = \frac{\int_B \frac{dP}{d(\lambda_\ell * P_S)}(g^{-1}\omega)\,\lambda_r(dg)}{\int \frac{dP}{d(\lambda_\ell \circ P_S)}(g^{-1}\omega)\,\lambda_r(dg)}$$

$$= \frac{\int 1_B(T(\omega)g^{-1})\,\frac{dP}{d(\lambda_\ell * P_S)}(g\cdot S(\omega))\,\lambda_\ell(dg)}{\int \frac{dP}{d(\lambda_\ell * P_S)}(g\cdot S(\omega))\,\lambda_\ell(dg)}$$

$$= \int 1_B(T(\omega)g^{-1})\,P^{S(\omega)}(dg) = \check{P}^{S(\omega)}_{T(\omega)}(B),$$

where $\omega \in \Omega$, $B \in \mathscr{B}$. This leads to a simpler formula for the covering probabilities:

$$\check{P}^{S(\omega)}(B) = F(\omega, T(\omega)\cdot B), \quad \omega \in \Omega, \quad B \in \mathscr{B}.$$

(4) The posterior distributions for λ_r satisfy an invariance condition, namely

$$F(g\omega, gB) = \check{P}^{S(g\omega)}((T(g\omega))^{-1}\cdot gB) = \check{P}^{S(\omega)}(T\omega^{-1}B)$$
$$= F(\omega, B), \quad \omega \in \Omega, \quad B \in \mathscr{B}(G), \quad g \in G.$$

This leads to a further modification of the covering probabilities:

$$\check{P}^{S(\omega)}(B) = F(S(\omega), B), \quad \omega \in \Omega, \quad B \in \mathscr{B}.$$

(5) It must be stressed that the fiducial method is only a computational method and does not distinguish any particular estimator T satisfying Assumption 39.2. A suitable choice of T should be such that the covering probabilities are large in some sense. E.g. if for some $B \in \mathscr{B}(G)$ there exists an estimator T satisfying Assumption (39.2) and

$$F(\omega, T(\omega)\cdot B) = \sup_{g\in G} F(\omega, g\cdot B), \quad \omega \in \Omega,$$

then the confidence region $T(\omega)\cdot B$ has maximal covering probability.

(6) The preceding remarks can be extended literally to the computation of conditional risks given $S(\omega)$. Since (4) implies

$$\int 1_B(h^{-1}g)\,P^s_g(dh) = \int 1_B(h)\,F(s, dh), \quad s \in \operatorname{im} S, \quad B \in \mathscr{B}(G), \quad g \in G,$$

the conditional risk with respect to a loss function $W\colon G \to [0, \infty)$ is

$$\int W(g^{-1}h)\,P^s_g(dh) = \int W(h^{-1})\,F(s, dh), \quad s \in \operatorname{im} S, \quad g \in G.$$

In other words, given $S(\omega)$ the conditional risk of $T(\omega)$ is

$$\int W(h^{-1})\,F(S(\omega), dh) = \int W(h^{-1}.\,T(\omega))\,F(\omega, dh).$$

But the latter is nothing else than the posterior risk of T with respect to λ_r and the loss function $(W(g^{-1}.))_{g\in G}$. Thus, in case of structure models, we have obtained an interpretation of the posterior risk as a conditional risk without any need of a prior distribution. In this sense, generalized Bayes estimates with respect to λ_r can be viewed as estimates minimizing conditional risk functions.

In the following it is our aim to find estimators which are optimal with respect to the unconditional risk functions. It will turn out that this is the same class which minimizes the conditional risks.

(39.21) Remark (Decomposition of estimates). We keep the notation of Theorem 39.19. Then we have for every bounded $\mathscr{A}$-measurable function $f: \Omega \to \mathbb{R}$

$$P_g(f|\mathscr{A}_i) = \int f(hS)\, P_g^S(dh), \quad g \in G.$$

Consider an estimate $\varrho \in \mathscr{R}(E, G)$. For every $s \in \operatorname{im} S$ we may construct another estimate ϱ^s: $(h, B) \mapsto \varrho(hs, B)$, $(h, B) \in G \times \mathscr{B}$. It is clear that $\varrho^s \in \mathscr{R}(E^s, G)$, and we have

$$\varrho P_g = \int \varrho^s P_g^s P_S(ds), \quad g \in G.$$

This follows from

$$\begin{aligned}\int (\varrho^s P_g^s)(B) P_S(ds) &= \iint \varrho(hs, B)\, P_g^s(dh)\, P_S(ds)\\ &= \int \varrho(\omega, B) P_g(d\omega) = (\varrho P_g)(B), \quad B \in \mathscr{B}.\end{aligned}$$

39.22 Definition. An estimate $\varrho \in \mathscr{R}(E, G)$ is *equivariant* iff $\varrho P_g = \varepsilon_g * (\varrho P)$ for every $g \in G$.

39.23 Definition. An estimate $\varrho \in \mathscr{R}(E, G)$ is a *convolution kernel if* $\varrho(g\omega, gA) = \varrho(\omega, A)$ for all $\omega \in \Omega$, $g \in G$, $A \in \mathscr{B}(G)$.

It is clear that every convolution kernel is equivariant. A non-randomized estimate $\kappa: \Omega \to G$ is a convolution kernel iff $\kappa(g\omega) = g\kappa(\omega)$, $g \in G$, $\omega \in \Omega$.

39.24 Remark (Decomposition of convolution kernels). If $\varrho \in \mathscr{R}(E, G)$ is a convolution kernel then we may write $\varrho(\omega, B) = \varrho(T(\omega) S(\omega), B) = \varrho(S(\omega), T^{-1}(\omega) B)$, $\omega \in \Omega$, $B \in \mathscr{B}(G)$. If we denote $Q^s(B) := \varrho(s, B)$, $s \in \operatorname{im} S$, $B \in \mathscr{B}(G)$ then we have $\varrho(hs, B) = Q^s(h^{-1} B)$, $h \in G$, $s \in \operatorname{im} S$, $B \in \mathscr{B}(G)$. It follows that in this case (with the notation of Theorem 39.19).

$$\begin{aligned}(\varrho P_g)(B) &= \iint \varrho(hs, B)\, P_g^s(dh)\, P_S(ds)\\ &= \iint Q^s(h^{-1} B)\, P_g^s(dh)\, P_S(ds)\\ &= \int (P_g^s * Q^s)(B)\, P_S(ds).\end{aligned}$$

This explains the term "convolution kernel". Conversely, each stochastic kernel $s \mapsto Q^s|\mathscr{B}(G)$, $s \in \operatorname{im} S$, defines a convolution kernel according to $\varrho(\omega, B) = Q^{S(\omega)}\{T^{-1}(\omega) \cdot B\}$.

The following is an extension of the convolution theorem to structure models.

39.25 Theorem. *Suppose that G is amenable. Then for every equivariant estimate $\varrho \in \mathscr{R}(E, G)$ there exists a stochastic kernel $s \mapsto Q^s|\mathscr{B}(G)$, $s \in \operatorname{im} S$, such that*

$$\varrho P_g = \int (P_g^s * Q^s)\, P_S(ds), \quad g \in G.$$

Proof. For $\varrho \in \mathscr{R}(E, G)$, $s \in \operatorname{im} S$, define

$$Q_n^s \colon B \mapsto \frac{1}{\lambda_r(K_n)} \int\limits_{K_n}\!\!\int \varrho(hs, hB)\, P_g^s(dh)\, \lambda_r(dg), \quad B \in \mathscr{B}(G), \quad n \in \mathbb{N},$$

where (K_n) is a summing sequence. Then it follows from Theorem 38.14 that

$$\lim_{n \to \infty} \sup_{B \in \mathscr{B}(G)} \left| \frac{1}{\lambda_r(K_n)} \int\limits_{K_n} (\varrho^s P_g^s)(gB)\, \lambda_r(dg) - (P^s * Q_n^s)(B) \right| = 0,$$

$s \in \operatorname{im} S$. Let $f \in \mathscr{C}_{00}(G)$ and $\varphi \in L^1(\operatorname{im} S, P_S)$ be arbitrary. For convenience denote

$$A_n(f, \varphi) = \frac{1}{\lambda_r(K_n)} \int\limits_{K_n} \left[\iint f(g^{-1}h)\, (\varrho^s P_g^s)(dh)\, \varphi(s)\, P_S(ds)\right] \lambda_r(dg)$$

and

$$B_n(f, \varphi) = \iint f(h)\, (P^s * Q_n^s)(dh)\, \varphi(s)\, P_S(ds).$$

By weak compactness of bilinear functions and by Theorem 6.11 there is an accumulation point $Q \colon s \mapsto Q^s|\mathscr{B}(G)$ of the sequence $Q_n \colon s \mapsto Q_n^s|\mathscr{B}(G)$, $n \in \mathbb{N}$, for the topology of pointwise convergence on $\mathscr{C}_{00}(G) \times L^1(\operatorname{im} S, P_S)$ and a subsequence $\mathbb{N}_0 \subseteq \mathbb{N}$ such that

$$\begin{aligned} \lim_{n \in \mathbb{N}_0} A_n(f, \varphi) &= \lim_{n \in \mathbb{N}_0} B_n(f, \varphi) \\ &= \iint f(h)\, (P^s * Q^s)(dh)\, \varphi(s)\, P_S(ds) \end{aligned}$$

for all $f \in \mathscr{C}_{00}(G)$ and $\varphi \in L^1(\operatorname{im} S, P_S)$. Since ϱ is equivariant we have

$$A_n(f, 1) = f\varrho P, \quad f \in \mathscr{C}_{00}(G), \quad n \in \mathbb{N},$$

and therefore

$$f\varrho P = \iint f\, d(P^s * Q^s)\, P_S(ds), \quad f \in \mathscr{C}_{00}(G).$$

Since

$$1 = 1 \varrho P = \iint 1 \, d(P^s * Q^s) \, P_S(ds)$$

it follows that $Q: s \mapsto Q^s$ can be adjusted P_S-a.e. to be a non-degenerate stochastic kernel. This proves the assertion. □

39.26 Corollary. *Assume that G is amenable. Then for every equivariant estimate there exists a convolution kernel with the same distribution.*

Let $W: G \to [0, \infty)$ be a lower semicontinuous function, let the loss function be $(W(g^{-1} \cdot))_{g \in G}$, and define the risk of an estimate $\varrho \in \mathscr{R}(E, G)$ by

$$W_g \varrho P_g := \iint W(g^{-1} y) \, \varrho(\omega, dy) \, P_g(d\omega), \quad g \in G.$$

It is clear that the risk of an equivariant estimate is independent of $g \in G$. If ϱ is a convolution kernel defined by $Q: s \mapsto Q^s | \mathscr{B}(G)$ then

$$\begin{aligned} W_g \varrho P_g &= \iint W(g^{-1} y) \, (P_g^s * Q^s)(dy) \, P_S(ds) \\ &= \iiint W(g^{-1} xy) \, P_g^s(dx) \, Q^s(dy) \, P_S(ds) \\ &= \iiint W(xy) \, P^s(dx) \, Q^s(dy) \, P_S(ds) \\ &= \iint W(y) \, (P^s * Q^s)(dy) \, P_S(ds). \end{aligned}$$

39.27 Corollary. *Suppose that G is amenable. Then for every estimate $\varrho \in \mathscr{R}(E, G)$ there is a stochastic kernel $Q: s \mapsto Q^s | \mathscr{B}(G)$ such that*

$$\sup_{g \in G} W_g \varrho P_g \geqq \iint W(y) \, (P^s * Q^s)(dy) \, P_S(ds)$$

for every level-compact function W.

Proof. We may copy the first part of the proof of Theorem 39.24. Then we obtain a possibly degenerate kernel $s \mapsto Q_0^s$, $s \in \operatorname{im} S$, satisfying

$$\lim_{n \in \mathbb{N}_0} A_n(f, 1) = \iint f \, d(P^s * Q_0^s) \, P_S(ds), \quad f \in \mathscr{C}_{00}(G).$$

Let $Q^s := \dfrac{1}{Q_0^s(G)} Q_0^s$, where $Q_0^s(G) > 0$, and Q^s an arbitrary probability measure on $\mathscr{B}(G)$, elsewhere. Then it follows that

$$\inf_{g \in G} f \varrho P_g \leqq \lim_{n \in \mathbb{N}_0} A_n(f, 1) \leqq \int f \, d(P^s * Q^s) \, P_S(ds)$$

for every $f \in \mathscr{C}_0(G)^+$. Hence, we have for every level-compact function $f \in \mathscr{C}_b(G)$

$$\sup_{g \in G} f \varrho P_g \geqq \int f \, d(P^s * Q^s) \, P_S(ds).$$

The proof is finished by Lemma 6.4. □

Note that Q is independent of the loss function W.

Similarly as in Section 38 we conclude that in case of an amenable group an optimal equivariant estimate is a minimax estimate. We have to discuss the question how to find uniformly optimal equivariant estimates.

39.28 Lemma. *Suppose that there is a measurable function* ψ: $\operatorname{im} S \to G$ *such that for every* $y \in G$

$$\int W(x\psi(s))\, P^s(dx) \leqq \int W(xy)\, P^s(dx) \quad P_S\text{-a.e.}$$

Then for the convolution kernel $\kappa\colon \omega \mapsto T(\omega)\,\psi(S(\omega))$, $\omega \in \Omega$, *the following assertions hold true:*

(1) κ *is uniformly optimal among all convolution kernels.*

(2) *If* G *is amenable then* κ *is uniformly optimal among all equivariant estimates and is a minimax estimate.*

Proof. (1) The risk of κ is

$$\int W(\kappa(\omega))\, P(d\omega) = \iint W(x\psi(s))\, P^s(dx)\, P_S(ds).$$

From the assumption it follows that κ minimizes the risk over all convolution kernels.

(2) This is a consequence of (1) and of Corollaries 39.26 and 39.27. □

It is rather obvious that the estimates defined in Theorem 39.24 are $(W_g)_{g\in G}$-unbiased if $W_g := W(g^{-1}.)$, $g \in G$.

The final assertion of this section will be that uniformly optimal equivariant estimates can be obtained as generalized Bayes estimates for λ_r. In view of Discussion 39.20 (4) and (6), these are just the estimates minimizing the conditional risks.

39.29 Theorem. *If a non-randomized generalized Bayes estimate* κ *with respect to* λ_r *is a convolution kernel then it is uniformly optimal among all convolution kernels. Hence, if* G *is amenable then* κ *is uniformly optimal among all equivariant estimates and minimax.*

Proof. From Lemma 39.12 we obtain that a dominated structure model is λ_r-integrable. Discussion 39.20 shows that $F = \check{P}^S_T$.

Now, let κ be a non-randomized, generalized Bayes estimate. By assumption, κ is even a convolution kernel. We note that for all $\omega \in \Omega$ and $h \in G$

$$\begin{aligned} &\int W(g\,T^{-1}(\omega)\,h)\, P^{S(\omega)}(dg) \\ &= \int W(g^{-1}h)\, \check{P}^{S(\omega)}_{T(\omega)}(dg) = \int W(g^{-1}h)\, F(\omega, dg). \end{aligned}$$

The defining property of generalized Bayes estimates implies that for every $h \in G$

$$\int W(g\,T^{-1}(\omega)\,\kappa(\omega))\,P^{S(\omega)}(dg) \leq \int W(gh)\,P^{S(\omega)}(dg) \quad \mathscr{P}\text{-a.e.}$$

Since κ is a convolution kernel, we have $T^{-1}(\omega)\,\kappa(\omega) = \psi(S(\omega))$ where ψ satisfies the condition of Lemma 39.28. This proves the assertion. □

Let us consider some examples.

39.30 Example. Consider the case of Example 39.3. Denote $h = \dfrac{dP}{d\lambda_H}$.

(1) Suppose that $W = \|\,.\,\|^2$ and that F satisfies appropriate integrability conditions. Then it follows from Example 37.6 (1), that

$$\kappa(x) = \frac{\int a h(x-a)\,\lambda_L(da)}{\int h(x-a)\,\lambda_L(da)}, \quad x \in H,$$

is a generalized Bayes estimate and a convolution kernel. Therefore it is optimal in the sense of Theorem 39.29.

(2) Let $P = N_H$ and W subconvex. If W is not bounded then assume that F satisfies appropriate integrability conditions. In view of Example 36.11 (1), a generalized Bayes estimate is obtained by minimizing

$$z' \mapsto \int W(z'-a)\,e^{-\frac{1}{2}\|p_L(x)-a\|^2}\,\lambda_L(da), \quad z' \in L,$$

for every $x \in H$. From Anderson's Lemma (38.21) we see that $\kappa = p_L$ is a generalized Bayes estimate and a convolution kernel. Therefore it is optimal in the sense of Theorem 39.29.

39.31 Example. Now we consider the case of Example 39.4. Let $h = \dfrac{dP}{d\lambda_H}$.

(1) Suppose that $W = \|\,.\,\|^2$ and that F satisfies appropriate integrability conditions. Then it follows that

$$\kappa_2(x) = \frac{\iint a h\left(\dfrac{x-a}{\sigma}\right)\dfrac{1}{\sigma^{n+3}}\,d\sigma\,\lambda_L(da)}{\iint h\left(\dfrac{x-a}{\sigma}\right)\dfrac{1}{\sigma^{n+3}}\,d\sigma\,\lambda_L(da)}, \quad x \in H,$$

is a generalized Bayes estimate and a convolution kernel, therefore optimal in the sense of Theorem 39.29.

(2) Let $P = N_H$ and W be subconvex. If W is not bounded then assume that F satisfies appropriate integrability conditions. Then a generalized Bayes estimate is obtained by minimizing

$$z' \mapsto \iint W\left(\frac{z'-a}{\sigma}\right) e^{-\frac{1}{\sigma^2}\|p_L(x)-a\|^2} \frac{1}{\sigma^{n+1}} \lambda_L(da)\,d\sigma, \quad z' \in L,$$

for every $x \in H$.

From Lemma 38.21 we see that the integral over L is minimized by $z' = p_L(x)$, independently of $\sigma > 0$. Hence $\kappa_2 = p_L$ is a generalized Bayes estimate and therefore optimal in the sense of Theorem 39.29.

40. Admissibility of estimators

In this section we discuss briefly some well-known facts concerning admissibility of estimates.

Let $E = (\Omega, \mathscr{A}, \{P_t: t \in L\})$ be a dominated structure model where the operating group is a Euclidean space $(L, \langle .,. \rangle)$. For convenience we denote the operation of L on Ω by "+". Let $W: L \to [0, \infty)$ be a subconvex function.

40.1 Definition. A generalized Bayes estimate for $(W(t-.))_{t \in L}$ and λ_L is called a *Pitman estimate* for W.

40.2 Examples. The following is a particular case of Example 39.29. Let $\Omega = \mathbb{R}^n$ and $L = \mathbb{R}$. Define the operation by

$$t + \omega = (t + \omega_1, \ldots, t + \omega_n), \quad t \in \mathbb{R}, \quad \omega \in \mathbb{R}^n.$$

(1) If $W(t) = t^2$, $t \in \mathbb{R}$, then the Pitman estimate is

$$\kappa(\omega) = \frac{\int t \frac{dP}{d\lambda_H}(\omega - t)\,dt}{\int \frac{dP}{d\lambda_H}(\omega - t)\,dt}, \quad \omega \in \Omega, \quad t \in \mathbb{R}.$$

(2) If $W(t) = |t|$, $t \in \mathbb{R}$, then any Pitman estimate is a median of the posterior distribution, hence satisfying

$$\frac{\int_{-\infty}^{\kappa(\omega)} \frac{dP}{d\lambda_H}(\omega - t)\,dt}{\int_{-\infty}^{+\infty} \frac{dP}{d\lambda_H}(\omega - t)\,dt} = \frac{1}{2}, \quad \omega \in \Omega.$$

(3) If $W(t) = 1 - 1_{[0,c)}(t)$, $t \in \mathbb{R}$, then the Pitman estimates are called maximum probability estimates since they satisfy

$$\int_{\kappa(\omega)-c}^{\kappa(\omega)+c} \frac{dP}{d\lambda_H}(\omega - t)\,dt = \sup_{s\in\mathbb{R}} \int_{s-c}^{s+c} \frac{dP}{d\lambda_H}(\omega - t)\,dt, \quad \omega \in \Omega.$$

(4) If $P = N_{\mathbb{R}^n}$ then in any case $\kappa(\omega) = \frac{1}{n}\sum_{i=1}^{n} \omega_i$, $\omega \in \Omega$, is a Pitman estimate.

40.3 Remark. Extending the preceding example, suppose that $\Omega = H$, $(H, \langle .,. \rangle)$ a Euclidean space and $L \subseteq H$ is linear subspace. If $P = N_H$ then Theorem 38.28 proves admissibility of $\kappa = p_L$ within the class of *equivariant* estimates (take $f = \mathrm{id}_L$). This result could be extended to $P \neq N_H$ if $-\frac{dP}{d\lambda_H}$ and W satisfy the assumptions of Corollary 38.23, using the decomposition of Theorem 39.19. But even for the Gaussian case $P = N_H$ it is known that $\kappa = p_L$ is inadmissible within the class of *all* estimates as soon as $\dim L > 2$, (James and Stein [1960]).

We are interested in this section in admissibility within the class of all estimates. In view of the preceding remark we confine ourselves to the case $\dim L = 1$, i.e. $L = \mathbb{R}$.

40.4 Definition. An estimate $\varrho \in \mathscr{R}(E, \bar{\mathbb{R}})$ is *almost admissible* if for any further estimate $\sigma \in \mathscr{R}(E, \mathbb{R})$ the inequalities

$$W_t \sigma P_t \leqq W_t \varrho P_t, \quad t \in \mathbb{R},$$

imply

$$W_t \sigma P_t = W_t \varrho P_t \quad \text{for } \lambda\text{-almost all } t \in \mathbb{R}.$$

40.5 Lemma. *Let $W(t) = t^2$, $t \in \mathbb{R}$. Suppose that $\varrho \in \mathscr{R}(E, \bar{\mathbb{R}})$ is almost admissible and satisfies*

$$\iint (x - t)^2 \varrho(\omega, dx)\, P_t(d\omega) < \infty, \quad t \in \mathbb{R}.$$

Then it follows that $\varrho \in \mathscr{R}(E, \mathbb{R})$, ϱ is admissible, nonrandomized and uniquely determined by its risk function.

Proof. Since the second moments are finite it follows that $\varrho(., \{+\infty, -\infty\}) = 0$ P_t-a.e., $t \in \mathbb{R}$. Hence $\varrho \in \mathscr{R}(E, \mathbb{R})$. Then

$$\int \left(\int |x - t|\, \varrho(\omega, dx)\right)^2 P_t(d\omega) \leqq \iint (x - t)^2 \varrho(\omega, dx)\, P_t(\omega) < \infty, \quad t \in \mathbb{R},$$

implies that

$$\int |x|\, \varrho(\omega, dx) < \infty \quad P_t\text{-a.e.}, \quad t \in \mathbb{R}.$$

Hence, the non-randomized estimator

$$\kappa = \int x \varrho(.,dx)$$

is well-defined. Easy computations yield

$$\begin{aligned} & W_t \varrho P_t - W_t \kappa P_t \\ & \quad = \int [\int x^2 \varrho(\omega, dx) - (\int x \varrho(\omega, dx))^2] \, P_t(d\omega), \quad t \in \mathbb{R}, \end{aligned}$$

and, since ϱ is almost admissible we arrive at

$$\int x^2 \varrho(.,dx) - (\int x \varrho(.,dx))^2 = 0 \quad P_t\text{-a.e.}, \quad t \in \mathbb{R}.$$

This means, that ϱ is non-randomized since it coincides with κ.

Now, let $\sigma \in \mathscr{R}(E, \bar{\mathbb{R}})$ be an estimator satisfying

$$W_t \sigma P_t \leqq W_t \kappa P_t, \quad t \in \mathbb{R}.$$

Then σ is almost admissible, too, and can be replaced by a nonrandomized estimator $\kappa_1 \colon \Omega \to \mathbb{R}$. It follows that

$$\int (\kappa_1 - t)^2 \, dP_t = \int (\kappa - t)^2 \, dP_t, \quad \lambda\text{-a.e.}$$

Applying the parallelogramm identity we note that

$$\begin{aligned} & \int \left(\frac{\kappa_1 + \kappa}{2} - t \right)^2 dP_t + \int \left(\frac{\kappa_1 - \kappa}{2} - t \right)^2 dP_t \\ & \qquad = \frac{1}{2} \int (\kappa_1 - t)^2 \, dP_t + \frac{1}{2} \int (\kappa - t)^2 \, dP_t, \quad t \in \mathbb{R}. \end{aligned}$$

This implies by admissibility of κ and κ_1, that

$$\int (\kappa_1 - \kappa)^2 \, dP_t = 0, \quad \lambda\text{-a.e.},$$

whence $\kappa_1 = \kappa$ P_t-a.e., $t \in \mathbb{R}$. □

The following assertion contains the basic idea of Blyth's method for proving admissibility. Let $h(t) = s(|t|)$, $t \in \mathbb{R}$, be a positive and continuous probability density such that $s \colon [0, \infty) \to (0, \infty)$ is decreasing. Later, we shall put

$$h(t) = \frac{1}{\pi(1+t^2)}, \; t \in \mathbb{R}, \quad \text{and} \quad h(t) = \frac{1}{\sqrt{2\pi}} \exp\left(-\frac{t^2}{2} \right), \quad t \in \mathbb{R}.$$

40.6 Theorem. *Let ϱ be the Pitman estimate for W. If*

$$\lim_{\varepsilon \to 0} \left(\int W_t \varrho P_t \cdot h(\varepsilon t) \, dt - \inf_{\sigma \in \mathscr{R}(E, \bar{\mathbb{R}})} \int W_t \sigma P_t \cdot h(\varepsilon t) \, dt \right) = 0,$$

then ϱ is almost admissible.

Proof. Assume that $\sigma \in \mathscr{R}(E, \bar{\mathbb{R}})$ satisfies

$$W_t \sigma P_t \leqq W_t \varrho P_t, \quad t \in \mathbb{R}.$$

If ϱ_ε denotes the Bayes estimate for W and the prior distribution μ_ε, $\frac{d\mu_\varepsilon}{d\lambda}: t \mapsto \varepsilon h(\varepsilon t)$, $t \in \mathbb{R}$, then we have

$$\int W_t \varrho_\varepsilon P_t \mu_\varepsilon(dt) \leqq \int W_t \sigma P_t \mu_\varepsilon(dt) \leqq \int W_t \varrho P_t \mu_\varepsilon(dt).$$

Consider the sets

$$M_{a,b} = \{|t| < a, W_t \varrho P_t > W_t \sigma P_t + b\}, \quad a > 0, b > 0.$$

Then

$$\begin{aligned} &\int W_t \varrho P_t \mu_\varepsilon(dt) - \int W_t \varrho_\varepsilon P_t \mu_\varepsilon(dt) \\ &\quad \geqq \int (W_t \varrho P_t - W_t \sigma P_t)\, \mu_\varepsilon(dt) \\ &\quad \geqq b\lambda(M_{a,b})\, \varepsilon h(\varepsilon a). \end{aligned}$$

The assumption then implies that $\lambda(M_{a,b}) = 0$. Hence the assertion. □

40.7 Discussion (Stein [1959]). Let us consider the case of $W(t) = t^2$, $t \in \mathbb{R}$. If $P|\mathscr{B}^1$ is centered and has a finite second moment, then the Pitman estimate is

$$\kappa(x) = \int t \frac{dP}{d\lambda}(x - t)\, dt = x - \int z P(dz) = x, \quad x \in \mathbb{R}.$$

The Bayes estimates κ_ε for the priors μ_ε are given by

$$\kappa_\varepsilon(x) = \int t F_\varepsilon(x, dt), \quad x \in \mathbb{R},$$

where F_ε denotes the posterior distribution of E and μ_ε. This gives

$$\begin{aligned} &\int W_t \kappa P_t h(\varepsilon t)\, dt - \int W_t \kappa_\varepsilon P_t h(\varepsilon t)\, dt \\ &\quad = \frac{1}{\varepsilon} \iint (x - t)^2 P_t(dx)\, \mu_\varepsilon(dt) - \frac{1}{\varepsilon} \iint (\kappa_\varepsilon(x) - t)^2 P_t(dx)\, \mu_\varepsilon(dt) \\ &\quad = \frac{1}{\varepsilon} \iint (x^2 - \kappa_\varepsilon^2(x) - 2t(x - \kappa_\varepsilon(x)))\, P_t(dx)\, \mu_\varepsilon(dt) \\ &\quad = \frac{1}{\varepsilon} \iiint (x^2 - \kappa_\varepsilon^2(x) - 2t(x - \kappa_\varepsilon(x)))\, F_\varepsilon(x, dt)\, P_s(dx)\, \mu_\varepsilon(ds) \\ &\quad = \frac{1}{\varepsilon} \iint (x^2 - \kappa_\varepsilon^2(x) - 2\kappa_\varepsilon(x)\,(x - \kappa_\varepsilon(x))\, P_s(dx)\, \mu_\varepsilon(ds) \\ &\quad = \frac{1}{\varepsilon} \iint (x - \kappa_\varepsilon(x))^2 P_s(dx)\, \mu_\varepsilon(ds). \end{aligned}$$

Since

$$x-\kappa_\varepsilon(x)=\int(x-t)\,F_\varepsilon(x,dt)=\frac{\int(x-t)\frac{dP}{d\lambda}(x-t)\,h(\varepsilon t)\,dt}{\int\frac{dP}{d\lambda}(x-t)\,h(\varepsilon t)\,dt},$$

we obtain

$$\begin{aligned}&\int W_t\kappa P_t h(\varepsilon t)\,dt-\int W_t\kappa_\varepsilon P_t h(\varepsilon t)\,dt\\&=\iint\left(\frac{\int(x-t)\frac{dP}{d\lambda}(x-t)\,h(\varepsilon t)\,dt}{\int\frac{dP}{d\lambda}(x-t)\,h(\varepsilon t)\,dt}\right)^2\frac{dP}{d\lambda}(x-t)\,h(\varepsilon t)\,dt\,dx\\&=\int\frac{(\int z\,h(\varepsilon(z-x))\,P(dz))^2}{\int h(\varepsilon(z-x))\,P(dz)}\,dx.\end{aligned}$$

Thus, an admissibility proof consists in a suitable choice of h such that the last expression tends to zero for $\varepsilon\to 0$.

40.8 Theorem (Stein [1959]). *Let* $W(t)=t^2$, $t\in\mathbb{R}$, *and* $P|\mathscr{B}^1$ *such that* $\int z\,P(dz)=0$, $\int z^2\,P(dz)<\infty$. *Then the Pitman estimate* $\kappa=\mathrm{id}_{\mathbb{R}}$ *is admissible and uniquely determined by its risk function.*

Proof. We continue the preceding discussion and note that

$$\begin{aligned}(\int z\,h(\varepsilon(z-x))\,P(dz))^2&=(\int z(h(\varepsilon(z-x))-h(\varepsilon x))\,P(dz))^2\\&\leqq\int z^2\,P(dz)\cdot\int(h(\varepsilon(z-x))-h(\varepsilon x))^2\,P(dz).\end{aligned}$$

Moreover, for $\varepsilon\leqq 1$ we have

$$\int h(\varepsilon(z-x))\,P(dz)\geqq P(-1,+1)\cdot\inf_{-1\leqq y\leqq 1}h(\varepsilon x+y).$$

Now, we specify $h(x):=\frac{1}{\pi}\cdot\frac{1}{1+x^2}$, $x\in\mathbb{R}$. Since

$$\lim_{z\to\infty}\frac{1+(z+1)^2}{1+z^2}=1,$$

there is some $c>0$ such that

$$\inf_{-1\leqq y\leqq 1}h(z+y)\geqq c\cdot h(z),\quad z\in\mathbb{R}.$$

Hence, we may estimate

$$\int \frac{(\int z h(\varepsilon(z-x)) P(dz))^2}{\int h(\varepsilon(z-x)) P(dz)} dx$$
$$\leqq \text{Const.} \int z^2 P(dz) \cdot \iint (h(\varepsilon(z-x) - h(\varepsilon x))^2 / h(\varepsilon x) dx\, P(dz).$$

Moreover, we have

$$\int (h(\varepsilon(z-x) - h(\varepsilon x))^2 / h(\varepsilon x) dx$$
$$= \int h^2(\varepsilon(z-x))/h(\varepsilon x) dx - 2\int h(\varepsilon(z-x)) dx + \int h(\varepsilon x) dx$$
$$= \int \frac{h^2(\varepsilon x)}{h(\varepsilon(x+z))} dx - \int h(\varepsilon x) dx$$
$$= \frac{1}{\pi} \frac{1+\varepsilon^2(x+z)^2}{(1+\varepsilon^2 x^2)^2} dx - \frac{1}{\pi} \int \frac{1}{1+\varepsilon^2 x^2} dx$$
$$= \frac{1}{\pi} \frac{2\varepsilon^2 xz + \varepsilon^2 z^2}{(1+\varepsilon^2 x^2)^2} dx = \varepsilon^2 z^2 \frac{1}{\pi} \int \frac{1}{(1+\varepsilon^2 x^2)^2} dx = \frac{\varepsilon z^2}{2}.$$

Thus, we obtain

$$\int \frac{(\int z h(\varepsilon(z-x)) P(dz))^2}{h(\varepsilon(z-x)) P(dz)} dx = \varepsilon.\ \text{Const.} \left(\int z^2 P(dz)\right)^2.$$

This proves the assertion. □

As a consequence we obtain a general result for an arbitrary structure model.

40.9 Theorem (Stein [1959]). *Let $E = (\Omega, \mathscr{A}, \{P_t : t \in \mathbb{R}\})$ be a structure model and assume that there exists a non-randomized convolution kernel $T_0 : \Omega \to \mathbb{R}$, which has a finite fourth moment. Then the Pitman estimate for $W(t) = t^2$, $t \in \mathbb{R}$, is admissible and uniquely determined by its risk function.*

Proof. Let S_0 be the maximal invariant based on T_0 and F the posterior distribution for λ. Then the Pitman estimate is (by Discussion (39.20))

$$T(\omega) = \int z F(\omega, dz) = \int (z + T_0(\omega)) F(S_0(\omega), dz)$$
$$= \int z \check{P}_0^{S_0(\omega)}(dz) + T_0(\omega) = T_0(\omega) - P_0(T_0 | \mathscr{A}_i)(\omega).$$

It follows that T has a finite fourth moment, too.

Let S be the maximal invariant based on T and denote by P_t^s, $t \in \mathbb{R}$, $s \in \operatorname{im} S$, the conditional distribution of T given $S = s$. We have to show that

$$\lim_{\varepsilon \to 0} \left(\iint (T-t)^2 dP_t h(\varepsilon t) dt - \iint (\kappa_\varepsilon - t)^2 dP_t h(\varepsilon t) dt\right) = 0,$$

where κ_ε is the Bayes estimator for the prior μ_ε, $\dfrac{d\mu_\varepsilon}{d\lambda}(x) = \varepsilon h(\varepsilon x)$, $x \in \mathbb{R}$. We have

$$\iint (T-t)^2\, dP_t h(\varepsilon t)\, dt = \iiint (z-t)^2\, P_t^s(dz)\, h(\varepsilon t)\, dt\, P_S(ds),$$

and

$$\iint (\kappa_\varepsilon - t)^2\, dP_t h(\varepsilon t)\, dt = \iiint (\kappa_\varepsilon(z+s)-t)^2\, P_t^s(dz)\, h(\varepsilon t)\, dt\, P_S(ds).$$

It is clear that for every fixed $s \in \operatorname{im} S$ the estimator $z \mapsto \kappa_\varepsilon(z+s)$, $z \in \mathbb{R}$, is the Bayes estimator for the conditional experiment $E_s = (\mathbb{R}, \mathscr{B}, \{P_t^s : t \in \mathbb{R}\})$ and μ_ε. Thus, applying Discussion 40.7 to each of these experiments, it remains to show that

$$\lim_{\varepsilon \to 0} \iint \frac{(\int z h(\varepsilon(z-x))\, P^s(dz))^2}{\int h(\varepsilon(z-x))\, P^s(dz)}\, dx\, P_S(ds) = 0.$$

Specifying $h(x) = \frac{1}{\pi} \cdot \frac{1}{1+x^2}$, $x \in \mathbb{R}$, and considering the proof of Theorem (40.8) it suffices to prove that

$$\int (\int z^2\, P^s(dt))^2\, P_S(ds) < \infty.$$

But this is an immediate consequence of

$$\iint z^4\, P^s(dz)\, P_S(ds) = \int T^4\, dP < \infty. \qquad \square$$

Now, we turn to the special case where $\Omega = \mathbb{R}$ and $P = \nu_{0,1}$. In this case, the result of Theorem 40.8 can be extended to a considerably larger class of loss functions.

40.10 Theorem (Blyth [1951]). *Let $E = (\mathbb{R}, \mathscr{B}, \{\nu_{t,1} : t \in \mathbb{R}\})$, $f = \mathrm{id}_{\mathbb{R}}$ and assume that W is separating and of finite order. Then the identity is admissible and uniquely determined by its risk function.*

Proof. The proof is divided into three parts.

(1) In the first part we shall show that the assumption of Theorem 40.6 is satisfied for $h(x) = 1/\sqrt{2\pi} \cdot \exp(-x^2/2)$, $x \in \mathbb{R}$. Since in the present case the identity is the Pitman estimator we have to show that

$$\int W(|t|)\, \nu_{0,1}(dt) - \inf_{\varrho \in \mathscr{R}(E, \overline{\mathbb{R}})} \int W_t \varrho P_t \nu_{0,1/\varepsilon}(dt) = O(\varepsilon).$$

To compute

$$\inf_{\varrho \in \mathscr{R}(E, \overline{\mathbb{R}})} \int W_t \varrho P_t \nu_{0,1/\varepsilon}(dt)$$

we consider the mixtures

$$\mu_\varepsilon(A \times B) := \int_B \nu_{t,1}(A)\, \nu_{0,\frac{1}{\varepsilon}}(dt), \quad A \in \mathscr{B}(\mathbb{R}), \quad B \in \mathscr{B}(\mathbb{R}),$$

$\varepsilon > 0$. The marginal distribution for the first coordinate is

$$\mu_\varepsilon(A \times \mathbb{R}) = \nu_{0,1+1/\varepsilon}(A), \quad A \in \mathscr{B}(\mathbb{R}),$$

and desintegration of μ_ε with respect to the first coordinate yields

$$\mu_\varepsilon(A \times B) = \int_A F_\varepsilon(x, B)\, \mu_\varepsilon(dx, \mathbb{R}), \quad A \in \mathscr{B}(\mathbb{R}), \quad B \in \mathscr{B}(\mathbb{R}),$$

where the posterior distribution is given by

$$F_\varepsilon(x, B) = \frac{\int_B \frac{d\nu_{t,1}}{d\lambda}(x)\, \nu_{0,1/\varepsilon}(dt)}{\int_{\mathbb{R}} \frac{d\nu_{t,1}}{d\lambda}(x)\, \nu_{0,1/\varepsilon}(dt)} = \nu_{x/(1+\varepsilon),\, 1/(1+\varepsilon)}(B),$$

$x \in \mathbb{R}$, $B \in \mathscr{B}(\mathbb{R})$. The estimates $\kappa_\varepsilon \colon x \mapsto \frac{x}{1+\varepsilon}$, $x \in \mathbb{R}$, $\varepsilon > 0$, minimize

$$s \mapsto \int W(|s - t|)\, F_\varepsilon(x, dt), \quad s \in \mathbb{R},$$

for every $x \in \mathbb{R}$ and therefore

$$\begin{aligned}
&\inf_{\varrho \in \mathscr{R}(E, \overline{\mathbb{R}})} \int W_t \varrho P_t \nu_{0,1/\varepsilon}(dt) \\
&= \int W_t \kappa_\varepsilon P_t \nu_{0,1/\varepsilon}(dt) \\
&= \int\int W\left(\left|\frac{x}{1+\varepsilon} - t\right|\right) \nu_{0,1}(dx)\, \nu_{0,1/\varepsilon}(dt) \\
&= \int W\left(\left|\frac{x}{\sqrt{1+\varepsilon}}\right|\right) \nu_{0,1}(dx).
\end{aligned}$$

Integration by parts yields

$$\begin{aligned}
&\int W(|t|)\, \nu_{0,1}(dt) - \int W\left(\left|\frac{x}{\sqrt{1+\varepsilon}}\right|\right) \nu_{0,1}(dx) \\
&= 2 \int_{[0,\infty)} (\Phi(+\alpha) - \Phi(+\alpha\sqrt{1+\varepsilon}))\, W(d\alpha) \\
&\leqq 2(\sqrt{1+\varepsilon} - 1) \int_{[0,\infty)} \alpha \cdot \varphi(+\alpha)\, W(d\alpha) = O(\varepsilon)
\end{aligned}$$

since $x > y > 0$ implies $|\Phi(x) - \Phi(y)| \leqq |x - y|\, \varphi(y)$. This proves that the identity is almost admissible.

(2) Let $\varrho_0 \in \mathscr{R}(E, \bar{\mathbb{R}})$ be such that $\sup_{t \in \mathbb{R}} W_t \varrho_0 P_t \leqq \int W(|t|) \nu_{0,1}(dt)$. In the second part of the proof we shall show that $\varrho_0(x, \{\infty\}) = 0$ λ-a.e.

The case where W is unbounded is obvious. Suppose that W is bounded. Let $\delta > 0$ be arbitrary and define $A = \{\varrho_0(., \{\infty\}) > \delta\}$. We prove that $\lambda(A) = 0$.

For every $x \in A$ we obtain

$$\begin{aligned}
&\iint W(|y-t|)\, \nu_{x/(1+\varepsilon),\, 1/(1+\varepsilon)}(dt)\, \varrho_0(x, dy) \\
&\geqq \delta\, W(\infty) + (1-\delta) \int W\left(\left|\frac{x}{1+\varepsilon} - t\right|\right) \nu_{x/(1+\varepsilon),\, 1/(1+\varepsilon)}(dt) \\
&= \delta\, W(\infty) + (1-\delta) \int W\left(\frac{|t|}{\sqrt{1+\varepsilon}}\right) \nu_{0,1}(dt),
\end{aligned}$$

which implies, again for $x \in A$,

$$\begin{aligned}
&\iint W(|y-t|)\, \nu_{x/(1+\varepsilon),\, 1/(1+\varepsilon)}(dt)\, \varrho_0(x, dy) - \int W\left(\frac{|t|}{\sqrt{1+\varepsilon}}\right) \nu_{0,1}(dt) \\
&\geqq \delta\left(W(\infty) - \int W\left(\frac{|t|}{\sqrt{1+\varepsilon}}\right) \nu_{0,1}(dt)\right) \\
&\geqq \delta\left(W(\infty) - \int W(|t|)\, \nu_{0,1}(dt)\right) \\
&\geqq \delta\left(W(\infty) - 2 \int_{[0,\infty)} \Phi(-\alpha)\, W(d\alpha)\right) =: \delta\eta > 0,
\end{aligned}$$

since W is separating.

If we integrate these inequalities by $\nu_{0,1+1/\varepsilon}$ then we obtain

$$\begin{aligned}
&\int W_t \varrho_0 P_t \nu_{0,1/\varepsilon}(dt) - \inf_{\varrho \in \mathscr{R}(E, \bar{\mathbb{R}})} \int W_t \varrho P_t \nu_{0,1/\varepsilon}(dt) \\
&\geqq \delta\eta \cdot \nu_{0,1+1/\varepsilon}(A)
\end{aligned}$$

which implies by part (1) of the proof that $\nu_{0,1+1/\varepsilon}(A) = O(\varepsilon)$, $\varepsilon \to 0$. Hence $\lambda(A) = 0$.

(3) In the third part we may therefore assume that $\varrho_0 \in \mathscr{R}(E, \mathbb{R})$. For simplicity we denote

$$g(\sigma, z) := \int_{[0,\infty)} (\Phi(z - \sigma\alpha) + \Phi(-z - \sigma\alpha) - 2\Phi(-\sigma\alpha))\, W(d\alpha),$$

where $\sigma > 0$, $z \in \mathbb{R}$. It is easy to see that this is well-defined since the integrand is non-negative and for fixed $\sigma > 0$, $z \in \mathbb{R}$, dominated by a W-integrable function.

Easy calculation and integration by parts yield

$$\iint W(|y-t|)\,\nu_{x/(1+\varepsilon),\,1/(1+\varepsilon)}(dt)\,\varrho_0(x,dy)-\int W\left(\left|\frac{x}{1+\varepsilon}-t\right|\right)\nu_{x/(1+\varepsilon),\,1/(1+\varepsilon)}(dt)$$

$$=\iint W\left(\left|y-\frac{x}{1+\varepsilon}-\frac{t}{\sqrt{1+\varepsilon}}\right|\right)\nu_{0,1}(dt)\,\varrho_0(x,dy)-\int W\left(\frac{|t|}{\sqrt{1+\varepsilon}}\right)\nu_{0,1}(dt)$$

$$=\int \varrho_0(x,dy)\,g\left(\sqrt{1+\varepsilon},\sqrt{1+\varepsilon}\,y-\frac{x}{\sqrt{1+\varepsilon}}\right),\quad x\in\mathbb{R}.$$

If we integrate by $\nu_{0,1+1/\varepsilon}$ then we obtain

$$\int W_t\varrho_0 P_t\nu_{0,1/\varepsilon}(dt)-\inf_{\varrho\in\mathscr{R}(E,\overline{\mathbb{R}})}\int W_t\varrho P_t\nu_{0,1/\varepsilon}(dt)$$

$$=\iint g\left(\sqrt{1+\varepsilon},\sqrt{1+\varepsilon}\,y-\frac{x}{\sqrt{1+\varepsilon}}\right)\varrho_0(x,dy)\,\nu_{0,1+1/\varepsilon}(dx).$$

By part (1) of the proof and Fatou's lemma we arrive at

$$\iint \liminf_{\varepsilon\to 0} g\left(\sqrt{1+\varepsilon},\sqrt{1+\varepsilon}\,y-\frac{x}{\sqrt{1+\varepsilon}}\right)\varrho_0(x,dy)\,\lambda(dx)=0.$$

It is not difficult to see that

$$\liminf_{\varepsilon\to 0} g\left(\sqrt{1+\varepsilon},\sqrt{1+\varepsilon}\,y-\frac{x}{\sqrt{1+\varepsilon}}\right)=g(1,y-x)$$

and that $z\mapsto g(1,z)$, $z\in\mathbb{R}$, is a non-negative continuous function which vanishes exactly at $z=0$. This proves the assertion. □

Now we return to the general case. Let $E=(H,\mathscr{B}(H),\{P_t\colon t\in L\})$ where H is a Euclidean space, $P_t=\varepsilon_t * N_H$, $t\in L$, and $f\colon L\to\mathbb{R}$ is a linear function.

40.11 Theorem (Blyth [1951]). *Suppose that the loss function W is separating and of finite order. Then* $f\circ p_L$ *is admissible for* $E|(\ker f)^\perp$ *and uniquely determined by its risk function on* $(\ker f)^\perp$.

Proof. Choose a unit vector $e\perp\ker f$, $e\in L$, such that $f(e)>0$. Define the subexperiment $F=(H,\mathscr{B}(H),\{N_H*\varepsilon_{\lambda e}\colon\lambda\in\mathbb{R}\})$. It is easy to see that $\kappa:=f\circ p_L$ is sufficient for F. We have

$$G:=\kappa_*(F)=(\mathbb{R},\mathscr{B},\{\nu_{\lambda\|f\|,\|f\|^2}\colon\lambda\in\mathbb{R}\}).$$

Therefore there exists $\tau\in\mathscr{R}(G,\overline{\mathbb{R}})$ such that

$$Q_\lambda(\varrho_0(.,B)|\kappa)=\tau(\kappa,B),\quad B\in\overline{\mathscr{B}},$$

where $Q_\lambda := N_H * \varepsilon_{\lambda e}$, $\lambda \in \mathbb{R}$. The decision function τ satisfies

$$\begin{aligned}&\iint W(|y-\lambda\|f\||)\,\tau(.,dy)\,d\nu_{\lambda\|f\|,\|f\|^2}\\ &\quad \leqq \int W(|y|)\,\nu_{0,\|f\|^2}(dy), \quad \lambda \in \mathbb{R}.\end{aligned}$$

By Theorem (40.10) it follows that $\tau(.,B) = 1_B$ λ-a.e., $B \in \bar{\mathscr{B}}$, and we obtain

$$\int_A \varrho_0(.,B)\,dN_H = \int_A 1_B \circ \kappa\, dN_H$$

whenever $A \in \kappa^{-1}(\bar{\mathscr{B}})$, $B \in \bar{\mathscr{B}}$. Choosing particularly $A = \kappa^{-1}(B)$ it follows that

$$\int_{\kappa^{-1}(B)} \varrho_0(.,B)\,dN_H = N_H(\kappa^{-1}(B))$$

and hence

$$\varrho(x,B) = 1 \quad \text{if} \quad f \circ p_L(x) \in B \quad \lambda_H\text{-a.e.}, \quad B \in \bar{\mathscr{B}}. \qquad \square$$

It is obvious how to generalize Theorem 40.11 to the situation considered at the end of Section 34.

Chapter 8: General Decision Theory

Statistical decision theory has been founded by Wald [1950] in order to classify the vast variety of statistical methods by general principles. The basic idea is to consider statistical experiments as games in the sense of von Neumann's theory of games. In special cases we have introduced the ideas of decision theory already in Sections 7 and 33. Early important results of the theory were the minimax theorem and the complete class theorem. Decision theory became a general framework for statistical purposes after it was possible to formulate important ideas of classical statistics such as sufficiency and asymptotic optimality in decision-theoretic terms. Both problems have been solved by LeCam [1964 and 1972] following previous attempts by Blackwell [1951 and 1953], and Hajek [1972].

We consider the problem of sufficiency in Chapter 9, and the foundations of asymptotic optimality in Chapter 10. In the present chapter we only present those basic facts of classical decision theory which have already been known to Wald, but we do this as generally as required later on.

The objects of statistics are statistical experiments. To apply linear functional analysis the underlying families of probability measures have to be embedded into suitable linear spaces. In case of a dominated family this is done in Section 24 by taking the L^1-space of an equivalent σ-finite measure. The generalization of this procedure to an arbitrary experiment leads to the L-space of Definition 41.3. The basic facts on L-spaces are presented in Section 41.

In Wald's decision theory the strategies of the statistician are given by kernels. However, this set of decision functions is not topologically complete. Therefore, it is convenient to complete it by considering arbitrary bilinear functions as generalized decision functions. This is the subject of Section 42. However, only decision functions in the narrow sense admit a statistical interpretation. Theorems 42.5 and 42.7 deal with the role of kernels within the class of generalized decision functions.

Generalized decision functions are bilinear functions on the product of the space of bounded continuous functions on a topological decision space and the L-space of the experiment. In this context the bounded continuous functions play the role of loss functions. For statistical purposes, however, it is necessary to admit also the upper envelopes of bounded continuous functions as loss functions. Therefore, the class of loss functions has to be extended to the set of lower semicontinuous functions. In Section 43 we show that after this extension the class of decision function in the narrow sense remains sufficiently large (Theorem 43.5).

Section 45 contains a functional analytic version of the minimax theorem which is specialized in Section 46 to the framework of decision theory. In Section 47 we prove a version of the complete class theorem.

To a large extent we follow LeCam [1974]. For the theory of Banach lattices we refer to Schaefer [1970 and 1974]. In order to avoid the Mackey-topology used by LeCam in the original proof of Theorem 42.5 we employ Lemma 42.4. In Section 45 we follow Heyer [1969].

The final section of this chapter is devoted to the general theorem of Hunt and Stein. Instead of a transformation group operating on the sample space we start with a group of stochastic operators on the L-space of the experiment. This generalizes the first situation, but will turn out later to be almost equivalent to it. We distinguish equivariant from strictly equivariant decision functions. In case of shift experiments or structure models, the latter concept coincides with that of convolution kernels. We prove a version of the theorem of Hunt and Stein which covers the original version in testing theory (Section 32) and the convolution theorems of Sections 38 and 39. Practically the whole of this section is well-known. Further information on this subject is contained in Luschgy [1984].

41. Experiments and their L-Spaces

Let $T \neq \emptyset$ be an arbitrary set and $E = (\Omega, \mathscr{A}, \mathscr{P})$ with $\mathscr{P} = \{P_t: t \in T\}$ an experiment.

Measure theoretic assertions of decision theory often are valid P_t-a.e., $t \in T$, i.e. $\mathscr{P}$-a.e. If E is a dominated experiment then by Lemma (20.3) there exists a probability measure $P_0 | \mathscr{A}$ such that $P_0 \sim \mathscr{P}$. Thus, the expression $\mathscr{P}$-a.e. may be replaced by P_0-a.e. The suitable functional analytic framework is then the pair $L_1(\Omega, \mathscr{A}, P_0)$ and $L_\infty(\Omega, \mathscr{A}, P_0)$, i.e. the L-space and the M-space of section 24. However, if E is not dominated then the question for a suitable functional analytic framework has a more complicated answer. It is the aim of the present section to find the right generalization of the concept of L-space.

Let $ca(\Omega, \mathscr{A})$ be the set of all bounded signed measures on $(\Omega, \mathscr{A})$. We begin with a reinterpretation of our original concept of L-spaces for dominated experiments.

41.1 Lemma. *Let $E \in \mathscr{E}(T)$ be a dominated experiment and let $\nu | \mathscr{A}$ be a σ-finite measure such that $\mathscr{P} \sim \nu$. Then*

$$L(E) = \{\mu \in ca(\Omega, \mathscr{A}): \mu \ll \nu\}.$$

Proof. Obvious. □

For a suitable generalization we need a representation of L-spaces which does not rely on dominating measures. For this, we prove

41.2 Theorem. *Let $E \in \mathscr{E}(T)$ be a dominated experiment. Then $\mu \in L(E)$ iff for every $\sigma \in ca(\Omega, \mathscr{A})$*

$$\sigma \perp P_t,\ t \in T, \quad \textit{implies} \quad \sigma \perp \mu.$$

Proof. Let $P_0 \in C(\mathscr{P})$ be such that $P_0 \sim \mathscr{P}$. Then we have

$$\sigma \perp P_t,\ t \in T, \quad \text{iff} \quad \sigma \perp P_0.$$

Indeed, if $\sigma \perp P_0$ then there is $A \in \mathscr{A}$ such that $P_0(A) = 0$ and $\sigma(A') = 0$. This implies $P_t(A) = 0$ for every $t \in T$ and therefore $P_t \perp \sigma$ for every $t \in T$. If conversely $P_t \perp \sigma$ for every $t \in T$ then let $A_i \in \mathscr{A}$ be such that $P_{t_i}(A_i) = 0$ and $\sigma(A_i') = 0$, $i \in \mathbb{N}$, where $P_0 = \sum_{i=1}^{\infty} \alpha_i P_{t_i}$. Then $A = \bigcap_{i=1}^{\infty} A_i$ satisfies $P_0(A) = 0$ and $\sigma(A') = 0$. Hence $\sigma \perp P_0$.

Therefore, we need only prove that $\mu \in L(E)$ iff

$$\sigma \perp P_0 \quad \text{implies} \quad \sigma \perp \mu.$$

If $\mu \in L(E)$ then $\mu \ll P_0$, and $\sigma \perp P_0$ obviously implies $\sigma \perp \mu$. If conversely μ satisfies the condition then let $A \in \mathscr{A}$ be such that $P_0(A) = 0$. Since $\mu|_A \perp P_0$ it follows that $\mu|_A \perp \mu$ which is only possible if $\mu(A) = 0$. Hence $\mu \ll P_0$, i.e. $\mu \in L(E)$. □

We take the preceding assertion as starting point for our concept of L-spaces.

41.3 Definition (LeCam [1955]). Let $E \in \mathscr{E}(T)$ be an arbitrary experiment. Then the *L-space of E* is

$$L(E) = \{\mu \in ca(\Omega, \mathscr{A}) \colon \sigma \perp \mu \quad \text{if} \quad \sigma \perp P_t,\ t \in T\}.$$

41.4 Corollary. *The L-space $L(E)$ of an experiment E is a Banach lattice for the variational norm.*

Recall, that a Banach lattice is *order complete* if every subset which has an upper bound has a least upper bound. It is a well-known fact that $ba(\Omega, \mathscr{A})$ and $ca(\Omega, \mathscr{A})$ are order complete Banach lattices (see Dunford and Schwartz, [1969]).

41.5 Lemma. *The L-space of an experiment is order complete.*

Proof. Let $\{\mu_i \colon i \in I\} \subseteq L(E)$ and denote $\mu = \sup_{i \in I} \mu_i$. Then it is clear that $\mu \in ca(\Omega, \mathscr{A})$. If $\sigma \in ca(\Omega, \mathscr{A})$ is such that $\sigma \perp P_t$ for every $t \in T$ then we have to show that $\sigma \perp \mu$. Since $\mu_i \in L(E)$, $i \in I$, it follows that $\sigma \perp \mu_i$, $i \in I$, i.e. $|\sigma| \cap |\mu_i| = 0$, $i \in I$. Now, from $\mu^- \leqq \mu_i^- \leqq |\mu_i|$, $i \in I$, we obtain $\mu^- \cap |\sigma| = 0$. On the other hand

$$\mu^+ \cap |\sigma| = \sup_{i \in I} \mu_i^+ \cup |\sigma| = \sup_{i \in I} \mu_i^+ + |\sigma| = \mu^+ + |\sigma|$$

implies $\mu^+ \perp \sigma$. Hence $\sigma \perp \mu$. □

Our next aim is to obtain more information about the relation between $L(E)$ and $ba(\Omega, \mathscr{A})$.

41.6 Lemma. *Each $\sigma \in ba(\Omega, \mathscr{A})$ admits a unique decomposition $\sigma = \sigma_1 + \sigma_2$ such that*

(1) $\sigma_1 \in L(E)$, $\sigma_2 \in L(E)^\perp$,
(2) *if* $\sigma \geqq 0$ *then* $\sigma_1 \geqq 0$, $\sigma_2 \geqq 0$.

Proof. The uniqueness of any decomposition satisfying (1) is clear. To show the existence of the decomposition we need only consider $\sigma \geqq 0$. We define

$$\sigma_1 = \sup \{\tau \in L(E) \colon 0 \leqq \tau \leqq \sigma\},$$
$$\sigma_2 = \sigma - \sigma_1 .$$

It is immediate that $\sigma_1 \geqq 0$, $\sigma_2 \geqq 0$. We have to show that $\sigma_2 \perp L(E)$. Let $\mu \in L(E)$ and $\varrho = \sigma_2 \cap |\mu|$. It is clear that $\varrho \in L(E)$ and therefore $\varrho + \sigma_1 \in L(E)$. But $\varrho + \sigma_1 \leqq \sigma_2 + \sigma_1 = \sigma$ which implies by the maximality of σ_1 that $\varrho = 0$. Hence $\sigma_2 \perp \mu$. □

41.7 Theorem. *There exists a positive linear operator T: $ba(\Omega, \mathscr{A}) \to L(E)$ satisfying the following conditions:*

(1) $\|T\| = 1$.
(2) $(T\sigma)(1) = \sigma(1)$ if $\sigma \geqq 0$.
(3) $T | L(E) = \mathrm{id}_{L(E)}$.

Proof. Let $\pi \in L(E)$ be arbitrary such that $\pi \geqq 0$, $\pi(1) = 1$. For $\sigma \in ba(\Omega, \mathscr{A})$ define $T(\sigma) = \sigma_1 + \sigma_2(1)\pi$, using the notation of Lemma 41.6. Then T is a positive linear operator satisfying (3). Condition (2) is obvious. For (1) we note that

$$\begin{aligned} \|T\sigma\| &= |T\sigma|\,(1) = |\sigma_1 + \sigma_2(1)\,\pi|\,(1) \\ &\leqq |\sigma_1|\,(1) + |\sigma_2|\,(1)\,\pi(1) = |\sigma_1 + \sigma_2|\,(1) = |\sigma|\,(1) = \|\sigma\| \end{aligned}$$

which implies $\|T\| \leqq 1$. Together with (2) it follows (1). □

The topological dual of $L(E)$ is called *M-space* of E and is denoted by $M(E)$.

41.8 Lemma. *Suppose that $E \in \mathscr{E}(T)$ is a dominated experiment and let $\nu|\mathscr{A}$ be a σ-finite measure such that $\mathscr{P} \sim \nu$. Then $M(E) = L_\infty(\Omega, \mathscr{A}, \nu)$.*

In general, every $f \in \mathscr{L}_b(\Omega, \mathscr{A})$ defines an element $\varphi_f \in M(E)$ according to $\varphi_f(\sigma) = \sigma(f)$, $\sigma \in L(E)$. If the mapping $f \mapsto \varphi_f$ is surjective onto $M(E)$ then E is called *coherent*. Dominated experiments are coherent.

We finish this section with an assertion concerning the relation between $M(E)$ and $\mathscr{L}_b(\Omega, \mathscr{A})$ for arbitrary experiments.

41.9 Lemma. *Let E be an arbitrary experiment. Then*

$$\{\varphi_f \in M(E): 0 \leqq f \leqq 1, f \in \mathscr{L}_b(\Omega, \mathscr{A})\}$$

is dense in

$$\{\varphi \in M(E): 0 \leqq \varphi(\sigma) \leqq \sigma(\Omega) \quad \textit{whenever } \sigma \geqq 0, \sigma \in L(E)\}$$

for the $L(E)$-topology of $M(E)$.

Proof. If the assertion is not true then there exists some $\varphi \in M$, $0 \leqq \varphi(\sigma) \leqq \sigma(\Omega)$ if $\sigma \geqq 0$, $\sigma \in L(E)$, and $\sigma \in L(E)$ such that

$$\sigma(f) \leqq c - \varepsilon < c \leqq \varphi(\sigma) \quad \text{if} \quad 0 \leqq f \leqq 1, f \in \mathscr{L}_b(\Omega, \mathscr{A}),$$

for some $c \in \mathbb{R}$, $\varepsilon > 0$. This implies

$$\sigma^+(\Omega) \leqq c - \varepsilon < c \leqq \varphi(\sigma) \leqq \varphi(\sigma^+) \leqq \sigma^+(\Omega)$$

which is not possible. Hence the assertion. □

42. Decision functions

Let $E = (\Omega, \mathscr{A}, \mathscr{P})$ be an experiment and let D be a topological space. The Baire σ-field of D is denoted by $\mathscr{B}_0(D)$. We consider D as space of possible decisions. Recall that a Markov kernel $\varrho: \Omega \times \mathscr{B}_0(D) \to [0, 1]$ is called decision function for E and D. The set of all decision functions is denoted by $\mathscr{R}(E, D)$.

42.1 Remark. Let $\varrho \in \mathscr{R}(E, D)$. For convenience we denote

$$f\varrho\mu = \iint f(x)\,\varrho(\omega, dx)\,\mu(d\omega),$$

if $f \in \mathscr{C}_b(D)$, $\mu \in L(E)$. Every decision function $\varrho \in \mathscr{R}(E, D)$ defines a bilinear function β_ϱ: $\mathscr{C}_b D) \times L(E) \to \mathbb{R}$ according to

$$\beta_\varrho(f, \mu) = f\varrho\mu \quad \text{if} \quad f \in \mathscr{C}_b(D),\ \mu \in L(E).$$

42.2 Definition. A *generalized decision function* for E and D is a bilinear function $\beta: \mathscr{C}_b(D) \times L(E) \to \mathbb{R}$ satisfying the following conditions:

(1) $|\beta(f, \mu)| \leqq \|f\|_u \|\mu\|$ if $f \in \mathscr{C}_b(D)$, $\mu \in L(E)$.

(2) $\beta(f, \mu) \geqq 0$ if $f \geqq 0$, $\mu \geqq 0$.

(3) $\beta(1, \mu) = \mu(\Omega)$ if $\mu \in L(E)$.

The set of all generalized decision functions is denoted by $\mathscr{B}(E, D)$. It is clear that for every $\varrho \in \mathscr{R}(E, D)$ we have $\beta_\varrho \in \mathscr{B}(E, D)$. The *weak topology* of $\mathscr{B}(E, D)$ is the topology of pointwise convergence on $\mathscr{C}_b(D) \times L(E)$.

42.3 Theorem. *The set $\mathscr{B}(E, D)$ of all generalized decision functions is convex and compact for the weak topology.*

Proof. $\mathscr{B}(E, D)$ is a convex, closed subset of the unit ball in $\mathscr{C}_b(D)^* \otimes L(E)^*$, which is compact for the $\mathscr{C}_b(D) \otimes L(E)$-topology of $\mathscr{C}_b(D)^* \otimes L(E)^*$. □

The next theorem is basic for the whole theory. For the proof of this theorem we need the following extension of Lemma 41.9.

42.4 Lemma. *Let E be an arbitrary experiment. Then the set of all linear functions on $L(E)^k$ which are of the form*

$$(\sigma_i)_{1 \leqq i \leqq k} \mapsto \sum_{i=1}^{k} \sigma_i(f_i),$$

$0 \leqq f_i \leqq 1$, $\sum_{i=1}^{k} f_i \leqq 1$, $f_i \in \mathscr{L}_b(\Omega, \mathscr{A})$, $1 \leqq i \leqq k$, *is dense in the set of all linear functions*

$$(\sigma_i)_{1 \leqq i \leqq k} \mapsto \sum_{i=1}^{k} \varphi_i(\sigma_i), \quad (\varphi_i)_{1 \leqq i \leqq k} \in M(E)^k,$$

which satisfy $\sum_{i=1}^{k} \varphi_i(\sigma) \leqq \sigma(1)$ *if* $\sigma \geqq 0$, $\sigma \in L(E)$, *(for the k-fold product of the $L(E)$-topology of $M(E)$).*

Proof. First, we note that every continuous linear function on $L(E)^k$ is of the form

$$(\sigma_i)_{1 \leqq i \leqq k} \mapsto \sum_{i=1}^{k} \varphi_i(\sigma_i), \quad (\varphi_i)_{1 \leqq i \leqq k} \in M(E)^k.$$

Therefore, we may identify $M(E)^k = (L(E)^k)^*$. It is then clear that every linear function on $M(E)^k$ which is continuous for the k-fold product of the $L(E)$-topology of $M(E)$, is of the form

$$(\varphi_i)_{1\leqq i\leqq k} \mapsto \sum_{i=1}^{k} \varphi_i(\sigma_i), \quad (\sigma_i)_{1\leqq i\leqq k} \in L(E)^k.$$

Now, if the assertion is not true then there exist $(\varphi_i)_{1\leqq i\leqq k} \in M(E)^*$ satisfying $\sum_{i=1}^{k} \varphi_i(\sigma) \leqq \sigma(1)$ for all $\sigma \geqq 0$, $\sigma \in L(E)$, and $(\sigma_i)_{1\leqq i\leqq k} \in L(E)^k$, such that

$$\sum_{i=1}^{k} \sigma_i(f_i) \leqq c - \varepsilon < c \leqq \sum_{i=1}^{k} \varphi_i(\sigma_i)$$

whenever $0 \leqq f_i \leqq 1$, $\sum_{i=1}^{k} f_i \leqq 1$, $f_i \in \mathscr{L}_b\Omega, \mathscr{A})$, $1 \leqq i \leqq k$, and for some $c \in \mathbb{R}$, $\varepsilon > 0$. Denoting $\sigma_0 := \bigcup_{i=1}^{k} \sigma_i$ we obtain from Lemma (6.7) that

$$\sigma_0^+(1) \leqq c - \varepsilon < c \leqq \sum_{i=1}^{k} \varphi_i(\sigma_i) \leqq \sum_{i=1}^{k} \varphi_i(\sigma_0^+) \leqq \sigma_0^+(1)$$

which is not possible. Hence the assertion. □

42.5 Theorem (LeCam [1964]). *The set $\{\beta_\varrho \in \mathscr{B}(E, D): \varrho \in \mathscr{R}(E, D)\}$ is dense in $\mathscr{B}(E, D)$ for the weak topology.*

Proof. Let $\beta \in \mathscr{B}(E, D)$. Choose $\varepsilon > 0$ and finite sets $\{f_1, f_2, \ldots, f_m\} \subseteq \mathscr{C}_b(D)$ and $\{\mu_1, \mu_2, \ldots, \mu_n\} \subseteq L(E)$. We will construct some $\varrho \in \mathscr{R}(E, D)$ such that

$$|\beta(f_i, \mu_j) - f_i \varrho \mu_j| < \varepsilon \quad \text{if} \quad 1 \leqq i \leqq m, \quad 1 \leqq j \leqq n.$$

W.l.g. we may assume that $\mu_j(\Omega) = 1$ and $\mu_j \geqq 0$, $1 \leqq j \leqq n$. By Lemma 6.6 there exists a finite partition of the unity $(p_k)_{1\leqq k\leqq p}$ on D such that each f_i, $1 \leqq i \leqq n$, varies less than $\frac{\varepsilon}{3}$ on the support of the p_k, $1 \leqq k \leqq p$. By Lemma (42.4) choose for every $k \in \{1, 2, \ldots, p\}$ some $h_k \in \mathscr{L}_b(\Omega, \mathscr{A})$ such that

$$|\beta(p_k, \mu_j) - \mu_j(h_k)| < \frac{\varepsilon}{3p(\sum_{i=1}^{m} \|f_i\|_u)} \quad \text{if} \quad 1 \leqq j \leqq n.$$

This implies that

$$\mu_j(\Omega) - \mu_j(\sum_{k=1}^{p} h_k) = \mu_j(1 - \sum_{k=1}^{p} h_k) < \frac{\varepsilon}{3\sum_{i=1}^{m} \|f_i\|_u}.$$

According to Lemma 42.4 the functions h_k may be chosen such that $0 \leqq h_k \leqq 1$, $1 \leqq k \leqq p$, and $\sum_{k=1}^{p} h_k \leqq 1$. Let us denote $h_0 = 1 - \sum_{k=1}^{p} h_k$.

Let $x_k \in \operatorname{supp}(p_k)$, $1 \leqq k \leqq p$, and let x_0 be arbitrary. Then we define

$$\varrho(\omega, B) = \sum_{k=0}^{p} h_k(\omega)\, 1_B(x_k), \quad B \in \mathscr{B}_0(D),\ \omega \in \Omega.$$

Obviously, we have $\varrho \in \mathscr{R}(E, D)$. Moreover it follows that for every μ_j, $1 \leqq j \leqq n$,

$$|\beta(f_i, \mu_j) - f_i \varrho \mu_j| = |\sum_{k=1}^{p} \beta(f_i p_k, \mu_j) - \sum_{k=0}^{p} f_i(x_k)\, \mu_j(h_k)|$$
$$\leqq |\sum_{k=1}^{p} (\beta(f_i p_k, \mu_j) - \beta(f_i(x_k)\, p_k, \mu_j)|$$
$$+ \sum_{k=1}^{p} |f_i(x_k)\, \beta(p_k, \mu_j) - f_i(x_k)\, \mu_j(h_k)| + \max_{1 \leqq i \leqq m} \|f_i\|_u\, \mu_j(1 - \sum_{k=1}^{p} h_k)$$
$$< |\beta(\sum_{k=1}^{p} (f_i - f_i(x_k))\, p_k, \mu_j)| + \sum_{k=1}^{p} |f_i(x_k)|\, |\beta(p_k, \mu_j) - \mu_j(h_k)| + \frac{\varepsilon}{3}$$
$$\leqq \frac{\varepsilon}{3} \beta(\sum_{k=1}^{p} p_k, \mu_j) + \sum_{k=1}^{p} |f_i(x_k)| \frac{\varepsilon}{3 \sum_{k=1}^{p} \|f_i\|_u} + \frac{\varepsilon}{3} \leqq \varepsilon. \qquad \square$$

In general, the sets $\mathscr{B}(E, D)$ and $\{\beta_\varrho \in \mathscr{B}(E, D)\colon \varrho \in \mathscr{R}(E, D)\}$ are not identical. The following assertions describe the most important cases where they are.

42.6 Lemma (Farrell [1967]). *If E is dominated and D is a locally compact space with countable base then for every $\beta \in \mathscr{B}(E, D)$ there exists a kernel $\varrho\colon \Omega \times \mathscr{B}(D) \to [0, 1]$ such that*

$$\beta(f, \mu) = f \varrho \mu \quad \text{if} \quad f \in \mathscr{C}_{00}(D),\ \mu \in L(E).$$

Proof. Essentially, this is Theorem 6.11. □

42.7 Theorem. *Suppose that E is dominated and D is a locally compact space with countable base. If $\beta \in \mathscr{B}(E, D)$ is such that $f \mapsto \beta(f, P_t)$ is a Daniell integral on $\mathscr{C}_b(D)$ for every $t \in T$, then there exists $\varrho \in \mathscr{R}(E, D)$ satisfying*

$$\beta(f, \mu) = f \varrho \mu \quad \text{if} \quad f \in \mathscr{C}_b(D),\ \mu \in L(E).$$

Proof. Apply Lemma 42.6 and note that

$$1 \varrho P_t = \sup\{f \varrho P_t\colon 0 \leqq f \leqq 1, f \in \mathscr{C}_{00}(D)\}$$
$$= \sup\{\beta(f, P_t)\colon 0 \leqq f \leqq 1, f \in \mathscr{C}_{00}(D)\} = \beta(1, P_t) = 1$$

for every $t \in T$. This implies $\varrho(\omega, D) = 1$ $\mathscr{P}$-a.e. Eventually improving ϱ on a set of $\mathscr{P}$-measure zero yields $\varrho \in \mathscr{R}(E, D)$. □

42.8 Corollary. *If E is dominated and D is a compact metric space then* $\mathscr{B}(E, D) = \{\beta_\varrho : \varrho \in \mathscr{R}(E, D)\}$.

Proof. This follows from Theorem 42.7 since on a compact space every Radon measure is a Daniell integral on $\mathscr{C}_b(D)$. □

We finish this section with a characterization of non-randomized decision functions. Recall that a decision function $\varrho \in \mathscr{R}(E, D)$ is non-randomized if $\varrho(., B) \in \{0, 1\}$ P_t-a.e. for every $t \in T$ and all $B \in \mathscr{B}_0(D)$.

42.9 Theorem. *Let $\varrho \in \mathscr{R}(E, D)$. The following assertions are equivalent:*

(1) *ϱ is non-randomized.*
(2) *$f^2 \varrho \mu = (f\varrho)^2 \mu$ for every $f \in \mathscr{L}_b(\mathscr{B}_0(D))$ and $\mu \in L(E)$.*
(3) *$f^2 \varrho P_t = (f\varrho)^2 P_t$ for every $f \in \mathscr{C}_b(D)$ and $t \in T$.*

Proof. (1) ⇒ (2): First we note, that by assumption

$$f^2 \varrho P_t = (f\varrho)^2 P_t \quad \text{if} \quad f \in \mathscr{L}_b(\mathscr{B}_0(D)), \quad t \in T.$$

Fix $f \in \mathscr{L}_b(\mathscr{B}_0(D))$ and let $A = \{f^2 \varrho - (f\varrho)^2 > 0\}$. Since $f^2 \varrho - (f\varrho)^2 \geqq 0$ it follows that $P_t(A) = 0$, $t \in T$. Let $\mu \in L(E)$. Then $\mu|_A \perp P_t$ for every $t \in T$ and by definition of $L(E)$ this implies that $\mu|_A \perp \mu$. Hence $\mu(A) = 0$ and therefore

$$f^2 \varrho \mu = (f\varrho)^2 \mu.$$

(2) ⇒ (3): Obvious.

(3) ⇒ (1): It follows easily that

$$(1_B)^2 \varrho P_t = (1_B \varrho)^2 P_t, \quad t \in T,$$

whenever B is $\mathscr{C}_b(D)$-open. The system of all sets $B \in \mathscr{B}_0(D)$ with this property is a Dynkin system and therefore coincides with $\mathscr{B}_0(D)$. □

43. Lower semicontinuity

Let $f: D \to \mathbb{R}$ be a lower semicontinuous function which is bounded from below. If D is a separable metric space then there is a sequence $(\varphi_n) \subseteq \mathscr{C}_b(D)$, such that $\varphi_n \uparrow f$. In this case we have for every $\varrho \in \mathscr{R}(E, D)$

$$f\varrho\mu = \sup\{\varphi\varrho\mu : \varphi \leqq f, \varphi \in \mathscr{C}_b(D)\}, \quad \mu \in L^+(E).$$

This motivates the following definition.

43.1 Definition. If $f: D \to \mathbb{R}$ is lower semicontinuous and bounded from below then

$$\beta(f, \mu) := \sup \{\beta(\varphi, \mu) : \varphi \leqq f, \varphi \in \mathscr{C}_b(D)\}, \quad \mu \in L^+(E).$$

43.2 Theorem. *If E is dominated and D is a compact metric space then for every $\beta \in \mathscr{B}(E, D)$ there exists $\varrho \in \mathscr{R}(E, D)$ such that*

$$\beta(f, \mu) = f\varrho\mu$$

for every $\mu \in L^+(E)$ and every lower semicontinuous function $f: D \to \mathbb{R}$ which is bounded from below.

Proof. Since $\mathscr{C}(D)$ is separable if D is a compact metric space there exists a sequence $(\varphi_n) \subseteq \mathscr{C}(D)$, $\varphi_n \leqq f$, $\varphi_n \uparrow f$. If $\varrho \in \mathscr{R}(E, D)$ is chosen as in Theorem (42.7) and $\mu \in L(E)$ then it follows that

$$f\varrho\mu = \sup_{n \in \mathbb{N}} \varphi_n \varrho\mu = \sup_{n \in \mathbb{N}} \beta(\varphi_n, \mu) = \beta(f, \mu).$$

The last equality holds since $\beta(., \mu)$ is a Daniell integral on $\mathscr{C}(D)$. □

The following theorem is related to Theorem 42.7.

43.3 Theorem. *Suppose that E is dominated and D is a locally compact space with countable base. Let $\beta \in \mathscr{B}(E, D)$. If there exist unbounded level compact functions $f_t: D \to \mathbb{R}$ such that*

$$0 < \beta(f_t, P_t) < \infty \quad \textit{for every } t \in T$$

then $\beta = \beta_\varrho$ for some $\varrho \in \mathscr{R}(E, D)$.

Proof. In view of Theorem 42.7 we need only show that $\beta(., P_t)$ is a Daniell integral on $\mathscr{C}_b(D)$ for every $t \in T$. Let $t \in T$ and choose $\varepsilon > 0$. Then

$$K := \{f_t \leqq \frac{1}{\varepsilon} \beta(f_t, P_t)\}$$

is compact and

$$g := \frac{1}{\varepsilon} \beta(f_t, P_t) \cdot (1 - 1_K) \leqq f_t.$$

Since g is lower semicontinuous we obtain $\beta(g, P_t) \leqq \beta(f_t, P_t)$ which implies $\beta(1 - 1_K, P_t) \leqq \varepsilon$. This proves the assertion. □

In general, an element $\beta \in \mathscr{B}(E, D)$ need not be of the form $\beta = \beta_\varrho$ for some $\varrho \in \mathscr{R}(E, D)$. Nevertheless, one may prove an assertion related to Theorem 43.2. Recall, that if D is locally compact then $\mathscr{C}_0(D)$ is the space of all continuous functions on D which vanish at infinity. We have $\mathscr{C}_0(D) = \overline{\mathscr{C}_{00}(D)}$ for the uniform topology.

43.4 Lemma. *Suppose that E is dominated and D is a locally compact space with countable base. Then for every $\beta \in \mathscr{B}(E, D)$ there exists a decision function $\varrho \in \mathscr{R}(E, D)$ such that*

$$\beta(f, \mu) \leqq f\varrho\mu \quad \textit{if} \quad f \in \mathscr{C}_0(D)^+,\ \mu \in L(E)^+.$$

Proof. Let $\beta \in \mathscr{B}(E, D)$ and choose ϱ_0 according to Lemma 42.6. Let $A = \{\omega \in \Omega : \varrho_0(\omega, D) > 0\}$ and let $P|\mathscr{B}(D)$ be an arbitrary probability measure. Define

$$\varrho(\omega, B) = \begin{cases} \dfrac{\varrho_0(\omega, B)}{\varrho_0(\omega, D)} & \text{if} \quad \omega \in A, \\ P(B) & \text{if} \quad \omega \notin A, \end{cases}$$

$B \in \mathscr{B}(D)$. Then it follows for $f \in \mathscr{C}_0(D)^+$, $\mu \in L(E)^+$, that

$$\begin{aligned} \beta(f, \mu) = f\varrho_0\mu &= \int \int_D f(x)\, \varrho_0(\omega, dx)\, \mu(d\omega) \\ &= \int_A \int_D f(x)\, \varrho_0(\omega, dx)\, \mu(d\omega) \\ &\leqq \int_A \int_D f(x)\, \varrho(\omega, dx)\, \mu(d\omega) \\ &\leqq \int \int_D f(x)\, \varrho(\omega, dx)\, \mu(d\omega) = f\varrho\mu. \qquad \square \end{aligned}$$

43.5 Theorem. *Suppose that E is dominated and D is a locally compact space with countable base. Then for every $\beta \in \mathscr{B}(E, D)$ there exists a decision function $\varrho \in \mathscr{R}(E, D)$ such that*

$$f\varrho\mu \leqq \beta(f, \mu),\ \mu \in L(E)^+,$$

for every level-compact function $f: D \to \mathbb{R}$.

Proof. First, let $f: D \to \mathbb{R}$ be level-compact and in $\mathscr{C}_b(D)$. Then $\sup f - f$ is in $\mathscr{C}_0(D)^+$ and the assertion is an immediate consequence of Lemma 43.4. Now, let $f: D \to \mathbb{R}$ be arbitrary level-compact. Let $\mathscr{H} = \{g \in \mathscr{C}_b(D): g \leqq f,\ g$ level-compact$\}$. Then we know from Lemma 6.4 that $f = \sup \mathscr{H}$. For $\beta \in \mathscr{B}(E, D)$ choose ϱ according to Lemma 43.4.

We obtain for $\mu \in L(E)^+$

$$\begin{aligned} \beta(f, \mu) &\geqq \sup\{\beta(g, \mu): g \in \mathscr{H}\} \\ &\geqq \sup\{g\varrho\mu: g \in \mathscr{H}\} = f\varrho\mu \end{aligned}$$

since for $\varrho\mu$ the generalized Levi-theorem is valid. $\square$

44. Risk functions

Let $T \neq \emptyset$ be an arbitrary set. Assume that D is a topological space. The space D will play the role of the decision space.

44.1 Definition. A family $W = (W_t)_{t \in T}$ of functions $W_t\colon D \to \mathbb{R}$, $t \in T$, which are bounded from below and $\mathscr{B}_0(D)$-measurable, is called a *loss function*. A property is attributed to $W = (W_t)_{t \in T}$ if each W_t, $t \in T$, has the property.

44.2 Definition. Let $\beta \in \mathscr{B}(E, D)$ and let W be a lower semicontinuous loss function. The *risk* of β at $t \in T$ with respect to W is $\beta(W_t, P_t)$. The risk of $\varrho \in \mathscr{R}(E, D)$ is the risk of $\beta_\varrho \in \mathscr{B}(E, D)$ and is denoted by $W_t \varrho P_t$, $t \in T$. The functions $t \mapsto \beta(W_t, P_t)$, $t \in T$, and $t \mapsto W_t \varrho P_t$, $t \in T$, are called *risk functions*.

44.3 Definition. If W is a loss function then (T, D, W) is called a *decision problem*. The sets

$$R(E, D, W) = \{(\beta(W_t, P_t))_{t \in T}\colon \beta \in \mathscr{B}(E, D)\} \subseteq \mathbb{R}^T$$

and

$$R_0(E, D, W) = \{(W_t \varrho P_t)_{t \in T}\colon \varrho \in \mathscr{R}(E, D)\} \subseteq \mathbb{R}^T$$

are called the *risk sets* of the experiment E for the decision problem (T, D, W).

44.4 Lemma. *If W is a bounded continuous loss function then $R(E, D, W) \subseteq \mathbb{R}^T$ is convex and compact and $\overline{R_0(E, D, W)} = R(E, D, W)$.*

Proof. This follows from Theorems 42.3 and 42.5. □

Let us consider the behaviour of risk sets under restrictions of the parameter space. Let $T_0 \subseteq T$ and let $p_{T_0}\colon \mathbb{R}^T \to \mathbb{R}^{T_0}$ the projection.

44.5 Theorem. *Let W be a bounded continuous loss function. If $T_0 \subseteq T$ then*

$$p_{T_0}(R_0(E, D, W)) = R_0(E_{T_0}, D, W), \quad \textit{and}$$
$$p_{T_0}(R(E, D, W)) = R(E_{T_0}, D, W).$$

Proof. Since $\mathscr{R}(E, D) = \mathscr{R}(E_{T_0}, D)$ the first equation is obvious. It follows that

$$\begin{aligned} R(E_{T_0}, D, W) &= \overline{R_0(E_{T_0}, D, W)} = \overline{p_{T_0}(R_0(E, D, W))} \\ &\supseteq p_{T_0}(\overline{R_0(E, D, W)}) = p_{T_0}(R(E, D, W)) \end{aligned}$$

since p_{T_0} is continuous. On the other hand compactness of $R(E, D, W)$ implies that $p_{T_0}(R(E, D, W))$ is compact, too, and we obtain

$$R(E_{T_0}, D, W) = \overline{R_0(E_{T_0}, D, W)} = \overline{p_{T_0}(R_0(E, D, W))}$$
$$\subseteq \overline{p_{T_0}(R(E, D, W))} = p_{T_0}(R(E, D, W)).$$

This proves the assertion. □

45. A general minimax theorem

In this section we present a general version of the minimax theorem in a purely functional analytic framework. The application to decision theory, in particular the minimax theorem of decision theory is considered in the next paragraph.

Let T be a locally compact space and let $\mathscr{M}^1_{00}(T)$ be the space of all probability measures on $\mathscr{B}(T)$ with compact support. Each $m \in \mathscr{M}^1_{00}(T)$ defines a linear function on $\mathscr{C}(T)$. The space $\mathscr{C}(T)$ is topologized with the topology of uniform convergence on compacts.

45.1 Example. Let $T \neq \emptyset$ be an arbitrary set endowed with the discrete topology. Then $\mathscr{M}^1_{00}(T) = S_T$ and $\mathscr{C}(T) = \mathbb{R}^T$.

45.2 Definition. Let $M \subseteq \mathscr{C}(T)$ be an arbitrary set. The *lower envelope* of M is the function

$$m \mapsto \psi_M(m) := \inf\{\textstyle\int f\,dm \colon f \in M\}, \quad m \in \mathscr{M}^1_{00}(T).$$

45.3 Definition. Let $M \subseteq \mathscr{C}(T)$ be an arbitrary set. Then

$$\alpha(M) := \bigcup_{f \in M} \{g \in \mathscr{C}(T) \colon f \leqq g\}.$$

45.4 Remark. If $M \subseteq \mathscr{C}(T)$ is compact then $\alpha(M)$ is closed in $\mathscr{C}(T)$. To see this, let $g \in \overline{\alpha(M)}$. Then for every compact $K \subseteq T$ and every $\varepsilon > 0$

$$F_{K,\varepsilon} = \{h \in M \colon h(t) \leqq g(t) + \varepsilon \quad \text{if } t \in K\} \neq \emptyset.$$

The family of closed sets $F_{K,\varepsilon}$ is directed from below and therefore

$$\bigcap \{F_{K,\varepsilon} \colon K \text{ compact}, \varepsilon > 0\} \neq \emptyset.$$

This proves that $g \in \alpha(M)$.

Recall that a set $M \subseteq \mathscr{C}(T)$ is called *subconvex* if for $f_1 \in M$, $f_2 \in M$ and $\alpha \in (0,1)$ there is $f_3 \in M$ such that $f_3 \leqq \alpha f_1 + (1-\alpha) f_2$. Every convex set is subconvex. Moreover, if M is directed from below then it is subconvex, too. If M is subconvex then $\alpha(M)$ is convex.

45.5 Remark. For every $M \subseteq \mathscr{C}(T)$ and $m \in \mathscr{M}_{00}^1(T)$ we have

$$\psi_M(m) = \psi_{\overline{\alpha(M)}}(m).$$

The following assertion is the basic separation theorem.

45.6 Theorem (LeCam [1964]). *Let $M_1 \subseteq \mathscr{C}(T)$, $M_2 \subseteq \mathscr{C}(T)$. Assume that M_2 is subconvex. Then the following assertions are equivalent:*

(1) *For every $f \in M_1$ there is some $g \in \overline{\alpha(M_2)}$ such that $g \leqq f$.*

(2) *$\psi_{M_2}(m) \leqq \psi_{M_1}(m)$ for every $m \in \mathscr{M}_{00}^1(T)$.*

Proof. (1) $\Rightarrow$ (2): Assertion (1) implies that $\psi_{\overline{\alpha(M_2)}}(m) \leqq \psi_{M_1}(m)$ for every $m \in \mathscr{M}_{00}^1(T)$. Remark 45.5 proves (2).

(2) $\Rightarrow$ (1): Assuming the contrary there exists $f \in M_1$ such that $g \nleqq f$ for every $g \in \overline{\alpha(M_2)}$. Hence $f \notin \overline{\alpha(M_2)}$. Since $\overline{\alpha(M_2)}$ is convex and closed there is a continuous linear function L on $\mathscr{C}(T)$ such that

$$L(f) < \inf\{L(g): g \in \overline{\alpha(M_2)}\}.$$

Since $\alpha(M_2) = M_2 + \mathscr{C}_+(T)$ the linear function L must be positive and hence is a Radon measure on $\mathscr{C}_{00}(T)$. It can be normalized in such a way that

$$L(h) = \int h\,dm, \quad h \in \mathscr{C}(T),$$

for some $m \in \mathscr{M}_{00}^1(T)$. Thus we obtain

$$\psi_{M_1}(m) < \psi_{\overline{\alpha(M_2)}}(m) = \psi_{M_2}(m)$$

which contradicts (2). □

45.7 Corollary. *Let $M_1 \subseteq \mathscr{C}(T)$, $M_2 \subseteq \mathscr{C}(T)$. Assume that M_2 is subconvex and $\alpha(M_2)$ is closed. Then the following assertions are equivalent:*

(1) *For every $f \in M_1$ there is some $g \in M_2$ such that $g \leqq f$.*

(2) *$\psi_{M_2}(m) \leqq \psi_{M_1}(m)$ for every $m \in \mathscr{M}_{00}^1(T)$.*

We apply the preceding results to obtain a version of the well-known minimax theorem.

45.8 Theorem (Minimax Theorem). *Let T be a convex, compact subset of locally convex space and let Y be a convex subset of a vector space. Assume that $f: T \times Y \to \mathbb{R}$ satisfies the following conditions:*

(1) *$t \mapsto f(t, y)$ is continuous and concave on T for every $y \in Y$.*

(2) *$y \mapsto f(t, y)$ is convex on Y for every $t \in T$.*

Then

$$\inf_{y \in Y} \sup_{t \in T} f(t, y) = \sup_{t \in T} \inf_{y \in Y} f(t, y).$$

Proof. The inequality "$\geqq$" is obvious. To prove the reversed inequality let $\alpha \in (-\infty, \infty]$ such that

$$\sup_{t \in T} \inf_{y \in Y} f(t, y) \leqq \alpha.$$

We have to show that

$$\inf_{y \in Y} \sup_{t \in T} f(t, y) \leqq \alpha.$$

If $\alpha = \infty$ nothing is to be proved. If $\alpha < \infty$ let $M_1 = \{\alpha\} \subseteq \mathscr{C}(T)$ and

$$M_2 = \{f(.,y): y \in Y\} \subseteq \mathscr{C}(T).$$

The set M_2 is subconvex. For $m \in \mathscr{M}^1_{00}(T)$ let t_m be the barycenter of m on T. Then we obtain

$$\begin{aligned} \psi_{M_2}(m) &= \inf\{\textstyle\int g\,dm: g \in M_2\} \\ &\leqq \inf_{y \in Y} f(t_m, y) \leqq \alpha = \psi_{M_1}(m). \end{aligned}$$

Theorem (45.6) implies the existence of $g \in \overline{\alpha(M_2)}$ such that $g \leqq \alpha$. For every $\varepsilon > 0$ there is $y_\varepsilon \in Y$ such that $f(.,y_\varepsilon) \leqq \alpha + \varepsilon$ and therefore

$$\inf_{y \in Y} \sup_{t \in T} f(t, y) \leqq \alpha + \varepsilon. \qquad \square$$

45.9 Corollary. *Assume that the conditions of Theorem 45.8 are satisfied. Then there is $t_0 \in T$ such that*

$$\inf_{y \in Y} \sup_{t \in T} f(t, y) = \inf_{y \in Y} f(t_0, y).$$

Proof. The function $t \mapsto \inf_{y \in Y} f(t, y)$ is upper semicontinuous on T. If there is $t_0 \in T$ such that $\inf_{y \in Y} f(t_0, y) = \infty$ then the assertion is immediate. If $\inf_{y \in Y} f(t, y) < \infty$, $t \in T$, then the function is bounded on T and attains its supremum. Now, the assertion follows from Theorem 45.8. $\square$

46. The minimax theorem of decision theory

Now, we apply the results of the preceding section to the particular case which is described in Example 45.1. Let $E = (\Omega, \mathscr{A}, \{P_t: t \in T\})$ be an experiment and D a topological decision space. We consider an arbitrary subset $\mathscr{B} \subseteq \mathscr{B}(E, D)$ which is weakly compact and convex.

46.1 Lemma (LeCam [1964]). *Assume that W is a bounded, continuous loss function. Let $T_0 \subseteq T$ be an arbitrary subset. For every $f \in \mathbb{R}^{T_0}$ the following assertions are equivalent:*

(1) *There exists $\beta \in \mathscr{B}$ such that $f(t) \geqq \beta(W_t, P_t)$ for every $t \in T_0$.*

(2) *$\int f\,dm \geqq \inf\{\int \beta(W_t, P_t)\,dm\colon \beta \in \mathscr{B}\}$ for every $m \in S_{T_0}$.*

Proof. It is obvious that (1) $\Rightarrow$ (2). To prove (2) $\Rightarrow$ (1), we define $M_1 = \{f\}$ and $M_2 = \{(\beta(W_t, P_t))_{t \in T_0}\colon \beta \in \mathscr{B}\}$. Condition (2) implies that $\underline{\psi_{M_2}}(m) \leqq \psi_{M_1}(m)$ for every $m \in S_{T_0}$. From Theorem (45.6) we obtain some $g \in \alpha(M_2)$ such that $g \leqq f$. Since $\mathscr{B}$ is compact and $p_{T_0}\colon \mathbb{R}^T \to \mathbb{R}^{T_0}$ is continuous it follows that M_2 is compact and hence $\overline{\alpha(M_2)} = \alpha(M_2)$. This proves the assertion. □

46.2 Corollary. *The assertion of Lemma 46.1 is also valid if W is an arbitrary lower semicontinuous loss function.*

Proof. The implication (1) $\Rightarrow$ (2) is obvious. To prove (2) $\Rightarrow$ (1) let $\mathscr{V}$ be the set of all bounded, continuous loss functions $V \leqq W$. Condition (2) implies

$$\int f\,dm \geqq \inf\{\int \beta(V_t, P_t)\,dm\colon \beta \in \mathscr{B}\}$$

for every $m \in S_{T_0}$ and $V \in \mathscr{V}$. Hence Lemma (46.1) implies that for every $V \in \mathscr{V}$

$$\{\beta \in \mathscr{B}\colon \beta(V_t, P_t) \leqq f(t) \quad \text{if} \quad t \in T_0\} \neq \emptyset.$$

Since $\mathscr{B}$ is compact and $\mathscr{V}$ is directed from above we have

$$\bigcap_{V \in \mathscr{V}} \{\beta \in \mathscr{B}\colon \beta(V_t, P_t) \leqq f(t) \quad \text{if} \quad t \in T_0\} \neq \emptyset$$

and any element of this intersection satisfies (1). □

46.3 Theorem (Minimax Theorem). *For every lower semicontinuous loss function W*

$$\inf_{\beta \in \mathscr{B}} \sup_{t \in T} \beta(W_t, P_t) = \sup_{m \in S_T} \inf_{\beta \in \mathscr{B}} \int \beta(W_t, P_t)\, m(dt).$$

Proof. The inequality "$\geqq$" is obvious. For the proof of the reversed inequality we denote

$$\alpha = \sup_{m \in S_T} \inf_{\beta \in \mathscr{B}} \int \beta(W_t, P_t)\, m(dt).$$

If $\alpha = \infty$ then nothing has to be proved. If $\alpha < \infty$ then we put $f(t) = \alpha$, $t \in T$, and apply Corollary 46.2. □

46.4 Corollary. *For every lower semicontinuous loss function W there is some $\beta_W \in \mathscr{B}$ such that*

$$\sup_{t\in T} \beta_W(W_t, P_t) = \inf_{\beta\in\mathscr{B}} \sup_{t\in T} \beta(W_t, P_t).$$

Proof. The assertion has been actually proved in the proof of Theorem 46.3. □

46.5 Theorem. *Assume that E is dominated and D is a compact metric space. Then for every lower semicontinuous loss function W the following assertions hold:*

(1) $$\inf_{\varrho\in\mathscr{R}(E,D)} \sup_{t\in T} W_t\varrho P_t = \sup_{m\in S_T} \inf_{\varrho\in\mathscr{R}(E,D)} \int W_t\varrho P_t m(dt).$$

(2) *There is some* $\varrho_W \in \mathscr{R}(E, D)$ *such that*

$$\sup_{t\in T} W_t\varrho_W P_t = \inf_{\varrho\in\mathscr{R}(E,D)} \sup_{t\in T} W_t\varrho P_t.$$

Proof. This is an immediate consequence of Theorem 43.2 if it is applied to Theorem 46.3 and Corollary 46.4. □

46.6 Theorem. *Assume that E is dominated and D is a locally compact space with countable base. Then for every level-compact loss function W the following assertions hold:*

(1) $$\inf_{\varrho\in\mathscr{R}(E,D)} \sup_{t\in T} W_t\varrho P_t = \sup_{m\in S_T} \inf_{\varrho\in\mathscr{R}(E,D)} \int W_t\varrho P_t m(dt).$$

(2) *There is some* $\varrho_W \in \mathscr{R}(E, D)$ *such that*

$$\sup_{t\in T} W_t\varrho_W P_t = \inf_{\varrho\in\mathscr{R}(E,D)} \sup_{t\in T} W_t\varrho P_t.$$

Proof. The inequalities "$\geqq$" are obvious in both cases. The opposite inequalities follow from Theorem 43.5 if it is applied to Theorem 46.3 and Corollary 46.4. □

47. Bayes solutions and the complete class theorem

47.1 Definition. Let $m \in S_T$. A generalized decision function $\beta_0 \in \mathscr{B}(E, D)$ is called *Bayes solution* for $m \in S_T$ and W if

$$\int \beta_0(W_t, P_t) m(dt) = \inf_{\beta\in\mathscr{B}(E,D)} \int \beta(W_t, P_t) m(dt).$$

It is obvious that for every bounded continuous loss function W and for every

$m \in S_T$ there is a Bayes solution $\beta_0 \in \mathscr{B}(E, D)$. This is due to the fact that $\beta \mapsto \int \beta(W_t, P_t)m(dt)$ is continuous on the compact set $\mathscr{B}(E, D)$.

47.2 Lemma. *Assume that W is a lower semicontinuous loss function. Let $m \in S_T$. Then for every $\beta \in \mathscr{B}(E, D)$*

$$\int \beta(W_t, P_t)m(dt) = \sup_{V \in \mathscr{V}} \int \beta(V_t, P_t)m(dt)$$

where $\mathscr{V}$ is the set of all bounded, continuous loss functions $V \leqq W$.

Proof. The assertion is obvious since for every $\varepsilon > 0$ we may find $V \in \mathscr{V}$ such that $\beta(W_t, P_t) \leqq \beta(V_t, P_t) + \varepsilon$ for every $t \in \operatorname{supp}(m)$. □

We note the easy fact that for bounded loss functions W the function $m \mapsto \int \beta(W_t, P_t)m(dt)$ is continuous on S_α, $\alpha \in A(T)$, for every $\beta \in \mathscr{B}(E, D)$.

47.3 Theorem. *For every lower semicontinuous loss function W and every $m \in S_T$ there exist Bayes solutions.*

Proof. From the preceding lemma it follows that the mapping

$$\beta \mapsto \int \beta(W_t, P_t)m(dt), \quad \beta \in \mathscr{B}(E, D),$$

is lower semicontinuous. Hence it attains its infimum on the compact set $\mathscr{B}(E, D)$. □

47.4 Corollary. *For every lower semicontinuous loss function W and every $m \in S_T$*

$$\inf_{\beta \in \mathscr{B}(E, D)} \int \beta(W_t, P_t)m(t) = \sup_{V \in \mathscr{V}} \inf_{\beta \in \mathscr{B}(E, D)} \int \beta(V_t, P_t)m(dt),$$

where $\mathscr{V}$ denotes the set of all bounded continuous loss functions $V \leqq W$.

Proof. The inequality "$\geqq$" is obvious. To prove "$\leqq$" let

$$\alpha = \sup_{V \in \mathscr{V}} \inf_{\beta \in \mathscr{B}(E, D)} \int \beta(V_t, P_t)m(dt).$$

We observe that for every $V \in \mathscr{V}$ the sets

$$\{\beta \in \mathscr{B}(E, D): \int \beta(V_t, P_t)m(dt) \leqq \alpha\} \neq \emptyset.$$

Hence also the intersection of all these sets is non-empty and therefore contains some $\beta_0 \in \mathscr{B}(E, D)$ such that

$$\sup_{V \in \mathscr{V}} \int \beta_0(V_t, P_t)m(dt) \leqq \alpha.$$

Now the assertion follows from Lemma 47.2. □

If W is an arbitrary lower semicontinuous loss function then in general $\overline{R_0(E, D, W)} \neq R(E, D, W)$. The lower envelopes of $R_0(E, D, W)$ and $R(E, D, W)$ need not coincide. The preceding assertion, however, implies that at least the following is valid.

47.5 Corollary. *For every lower semicontinuous loss function and every $m \in S_T$*

$$\inf_{\beta \in \mathscr{B}(E, D)} \int \beta(W_t, P_t) m(dt) = \sup_{V \in \mathscr{V}} \inf_{\varrho \in \mathscr{R}(E, D)} \int V_t \varrho P_t m(dt),$$

where $\mathscr{V}$ denotes the set of all bounded continuous loss functions $V \leqq W$.

Our next aim is to prove the complete class theorem.

47.6 Definition. A generalized decision function $\beta_0 \in \mathscr{B}(E, D)$ is an *extended Bayes solution* for the loss function W if for every $\varepsilon > 0$ there is $m_\varepsilon \in S_T$ such that

$$\int \beta_0(W_t, P_t) m_\varepsilon(dt) \leqq \inf\{\int \beta(W_t, P_t) m_\varepsilon(dt) + \varepsilon \colon \beta \in \mathscr{B}(E, D)\}.$$

The following is a rather weak version of the complete class theorem. However, it is valid for unbounded loss functions.

47.7 Theorem. *Assume that W is a lower semicontinuous loss function. For every $\beta \in \mathscr{B}(E, D)$ there exists an extended Bayes solution $\beta_0 \in \mathscr{B}(E, D)$ such that*

$$\beta_0(W_t, P_t) \leqq \beta(W_t, P_t) \quad \textit{if} \quad t \in T.$$

Proof. Let

$$\psi(m) := \inf\{\int \sigma(W_t, P_t) m(dt) \colon \sigma \in \mathscr{B}(E, D)\}, \quad m \in S_T.$$

Note that $\psi(m) < \infty$ for every $m \in S_T$ since $W = (W_t)_{t \in T}$ is real-valued. If $\varepsilon := \inf_{m \in S_T} (\int \beta(W_t, P_t) m(dt) - \psi(m))$ then

$$\int (\beta(W_t, P_t) - \varepsilon) m(dt) \geqq \psi(m) \quad \text{for every } m \in S_T.$$

Now from Lemma (46.1) we obtain $\beta_0 \in \mathscr{B}(E, D)$ such that

$$\beta_0(W_t, P_t) \leqq \beta(W_t, P_t) - \varepsilon \quad \text{if} \quad t \in T.$$

From the definition of ε it follows that

$$\inf_{m \in S_T} (\int \beta_0(W_t, P_t) m(dt) - \psi(m)) = 0.$$

Hence β_0 is an extended Bayes solution. □

47.8 Corollary. *Assume that W is a bounded, lower semicontinuous loss function. Then for every $\beta \in \mathscr{B}(E, D)$ and every $\alpha \in A(T)$ there is a Bayes solution $\beta_\alpha \in \mathscr{B}(E, D)$ such that*

$$\beta_\alpha(W_t, P_t) \leqq \beta(W_t, P_t) \quad \text{if} \quad t \in \alpha.$$

Proof. The proof of Theorem 47.7 remains valid if S_T is replaced by S_α for a particular $\alpha \in A(T)$. We obtain $\beta_\alpha \in \mathscr{B}(E, D)$ such that

$$\beta_\alpha(W_t, P_t) \leqq \beta(W_t, P_t) \quad \text{if} \quad t \in \alpha, \quad \text{and}$$
$$\inf_{m \in S_\alpha} \left(\int \beta_\alpha(W_t, P_t) m(dt) - \psi(m)\right) = 0.$$

In view of the note preceding Theorem 47.3 it follows that for bounded loss functions W the function ψ is upper semicontinuous and therefore the infimum is attained on S_α. □

The following is the Complete Class Theorem.

47.9 Theorem (Complete Class Theorem). *Assume that W is a bounded, lower semicontinuous loss function. Then for every $\beta \in \mathscr{B}(E, D)$ there exists a weak limit of Bayes solutions $\beta_0 \in \mathscr{B}(E, D)$ such that*

$$\beta_0(W_t, P_t) \leqq \beta(W_t, P_t) \quad \textit{for every } t \in T.$$

Proof. For every $\alpha \in A(T)$ there is a Bayes solution β_α such that

$$\beta_\alpha(W_t, P_t) \leqq \beta(W_t, P_t) \quad \text{if} \quad t \in \alpha.$$

Let $\mathscr{B}_0$ be the set of all Bayes solutions in $\mathscr{B}(E, D)$. Hence for every $\alpha \in A(T)$

$$\bar{\mathscr{B}}_0 \cap \{\sigma \in \mathscr{B}(E, D): \sigma(W_t, P_t) \leqq \beta(W_t, P_t) \quad \text{if} \quad t \in \alpha\} \neq \emptyset.$$

For reasons of lower semicontinuity these sets are closed and therefore their intersection is non-empty. □

48. The generalized theorem of Hunt and Stein

Let $E = (\Omega, \mathscr{A}, \{P_t: t \in T\})$ be an experiment and G a locally compact group with countable base for its topology. The Borel-σ-field of G is denoted by $\mathscr{B}(G)$.

48.1 Definition. A positive linear mapping M: $L(E) \to L(E)$ is a *stochastic operator* if $\|M\sigma\| = \|\sigma\|$ if $\sigma \in L(E)$, $\sigma \geqq 0$. A family $(M_g)_{g \in G}$ of stochastic operators is a *group* if $M_{g_1 \circ g_2} = M_{g_1} \circ M_{g_2}$ for $g_1, g_2 \in G$ and $M_e = \mathrm{id}_{L(E)}$. It is a *measurable group* of stochastic operators if $g \mapsto (M_g \mu)(A)$ is $\mathscr{B}(G)$-measurable for all $\mu \in L(E)$ and $A \in \mathscr{A}$.

48.2 Definition. Let $(M_g)_{g \in G}$ be a group of stochastic operators on $L(E)$. The experiment is *invariant* under $(M_g)_{g \in G}$ if $M_g P_t \in \{P_s: s \in T\}$ for all $g \in G$ and $t \in T$.

48.3 Example. Let E be a dominated experiment and G a group of measurable transformations $g: \Omega \to \Omega$ where $(g, \omega) \mapsto g\omega$, $(g, \omega) \in G \times \Omega$, is $\mathscr{B}(G) \otimes \mathscr{A}$-measurable. This is the situation considered in Section 31. There we have called E a G-invariant experiment if $P_t \circ g^{-1} \in \{P_s: s \in T\}$ for all $t \in T$, $g \in G$. Particular cases of G-invariant experiments are the shift experiments of Section 38 and the structure models of Section 39.

Let us show that G-invariance of Section 31 is a special case of the situation described in Definition 48.2. For $\mu \in L(E)$ define $M_g \mu := \mu \circ g^{-1}$, $g \in G$. First we have to show that $M_g \mu \in L(E)$, $g \in G$. This is an easy consequence of G-invariance and Lemma 41.1. It is clear that $(M_g)_{g \in G}$ is a group of stochastic operators and that E is invariant under $(M_g)_{g \in G}$. Since the operation $(g, \omega) \mapsto g\omega$, $(g, \omega) \in G \times \Omega$, is $\mathscr{B}(G) \otimes \mathscr{A}$-measurable Fubini's theorem implies that $(M_g)_{g \in G}$ is a measurable group.

We introduce the notion of a G-invariant decision problem.

48.4 Definition. Assume that E is invariant under $(M_g)_{g \in G}$. Let (T, D, W) be a decision problem where G operates on D continuously from the left. The decision problem (T, D, W) is called *G-invariant* if

$$P_t = M_g P_s \quad \text{implies} \quad W_s(x) = W_t(gx), \quad x \in D,$$

whenever $s, t \in T$ and $g \in G$.

Let us illustrate this concept by the most important examples.

48.5 Examples. (1) Let (H, K) be a testing problem in the classical sense, i.e. a partition of $\{P_t: t \in T\}$ into two sets H and K. To put it into the terms of general decision theory let $D = \{0, 1\}$ and $W_t(1) = 1_H(P_t)$, $W_t(0) = 1_K(P_t)$, $t \in T$. If $M_g H \subseteq H$ and $M_g K \subseteq K$ for all $g \in G$ then obviously the decision problem (T, D, W) is G-invariant. Specifying to the case of Example 48.3 we see that G-invariant testing problems in the sense of Definition 31.1 are G-invariant decision problems.

(2) Let $T = D = G$ and assume that $P_t = M_g P_s$ iff $t = gs$, whenever $g \in G$, $t \in G$. This is the case with estimation problems for shift experiments or structure models. Let $W_g(h) := W(g^{-1}h)$ where $W: G \to \mathbb{R}$ is a $\mathscr{B}(G)$-measurable function which is bounded from below. Then $P_t = M_g P_s$ implies $t = gs$ and hence

$$W_s(x) = W(s^{-1}x) = W(t^{-1}gx) = W_t(gx), \quad x \in G.$$

Thus (G, G, W) is a G-invariant decision problem.

48.6 Definition. Assume that E is invariant under $(M_g)_{g \in G}$ and that G operates on D continuously from the left. A generalized decision function $\beta \in \mathscr{B}(E, D)$ is *equivariant* if

$$\beta(f \circ g, P_t) = \beta(f, M_g P_t), f \in \mathscr{C}_b(D), t \in T, g \in G.$$

It is *strictly equivariant* if

$$\beta(f \circ g, \mu) = \beta(f, M_g \mu), f \in \mathscr{C}_b(D), \mu \in L(E), g \in G.$$

The distinction between equivariance and strict equivariance becomes clear if we specialize to the case of Example 48.3.

48.7 Example. Consider the situation of Example (48.3). Let $\varrho \in \mathscr{R}(E, D)$. Then ϱ is equivariant in the sense of the preceding definition iff

$$\int\int f(gx)\, \varrho(\omega, dx)\, P_t(d\omega) = \int\int f(x)\, \varrho(g\omega, dx)\, P_t(d\omega)$$

for all $f \in \mathscr{C}_b(D)$, $g \in G$ and $t \in T$. For shift experiments and structure models this is exactly the concept of equivariance considered there. Now, let $\nu | \mathscr{A}$ be a σ-finite measure such that $\mathscr{P} \sim \nu$. A decision function $\varrho \in \mathscr{R}(E, D)$ is strictly equivariant in the sense of Definition 48.6 iff

$$\int\int f(gx)\, \varrho(\omega, dx)\, h(\omega)\, \nu(d\omega) = \int\int f(x)\, \varrho(g\omega, dx)\, h(\omega)\, \nu(d\omega)$$

for all $f \in \mathscr{C}_b(D)$, $g \in G$ and $h \in L^1(\nu)$. This implies

$$\int f(gx)\, \varrho(\omega, dx) = \int f(x)\, \varrho(g\omega, dx) \quad \nu\text{-a.e.}$$

for all $f \in \mathscr{C}_b(D)$ and $g \in G$. In Sections 38 and 39 a convolution kernel was defined by the condition

$$\varrho(\omega, B) = \varrho(g\omega, gB), \quad \omega \in \Omega, g \in G, B \in \mathscr{B}(D).$$

The following assertion gives conditions where strict equivariance can be improved to the latter property. Essentially, this is a lifting theorem but we present a complete proof, not relying on general lifting theorems. The situation is similar to that of Theorem 31.7.

First, we have to discuss briefly a question of measurability.

48.8 Lemma. *Consider the situation of Example 48.3 and assume that D is a locally compact space with countable base for its topology. Then*

$$(g, \omega) \mapsto \varrho(g\omega, gB), \quad (g, \omega) \in G \times \Omega,$$

is $\mathscr{B}(G) \otimes \mathscr{A}$-measurable for every $\varrho \in \mathscr{R}(E, G)$, $B \in \mathscr{B}(D)$.

Proof. For $\mathscr{C}_{00}(D)$ let $\mathscr{T}_p$ the topology of pointwise convergence on D and $\mathscr{T}_u$ the uniform topology of D. Then $\mathscr{T}_p \subseteq \mathscr{T}_u$, but since every ball $\{f \in \mathscr{C}_{00}(D): \|f\|_u < \alpha\} \subseteq \mathscr{B}(\mathscr{T}_p)$ and since there is a countable base of $\mathscr{T}_u$ consisting of balls it follows that $\mathscr{B}(\mathscr{T}_p) = \mathscr{B}(\mathscr{T}_u)$ on $\mathscr{C}_{00}(D)$. For every $f \in \mathscr{C}_{00}(D)$ the map

$$F_f\colon G \mapsto \mathscr{C}_{00}(D)\colon g \mapsto f(g^{-1}.)$$

is $\mathscr{T}_p$-continuous and hence $\mathscr{B}(\mathscr{T}_p)$-, and $\mathscr{B}(\mathscr{T}_u)$-measurable. Moreover, $(\omega, f) \mapsto \int f(x)\varrho(\omega, dx)$, $(\omega, f) \in \Omega \times \mathscr{C}_{00}(D)$, is $\mathscr{A} \otimes \mathscr{B}(\mathscr{T}_u)$-measurable. Now, the composition of measurable mappings implies that

$$(g, \omega) \mapsto \int f(g^{-1}x)\varrho(g\omega, dx), \quad (g, \omega) \in G \times \Omega,$$

is $\mathscr{B}(G) \otimes \mathscr{A}$-measurable for every $f \in \mathscr{C}_{00}(D)$.

Finally, a standard argument proves the assertion. □

48.9 Theorem. *Consider the situation of Example 48.3 and assume that D is a locally compact space with countable base for its topology. Then for every strictly equivariant $\varrho \in \mathscr{R}(E, D)$ there exists a strictly equivariant decision function $\varrho_0 \in \mathscr{R}(E, D)$ such that*

(1) $\varrho_0(\omega, B) = \varrho(\omega, B)$, $B \in \mathscr{B}(D)$, *and*

(2) $\varrho_0(g\omega, gB) = \varrho_0(\omega, B)$, $g \in G$, $B \in \mathscr{B}(D)$

on a set $A \in \mathscr{A}$ with $P_t(A) = 1$, $t \in T$.

Proof. Assume that $\nu|\mathscr{A}$ is a σ-finite measure being equivalent to $\mathscr{P} = \{P_t\colon t \in T\}$ and let λ be a right Haar measure of G. Since λ is σ-finite there exists a probability measure $\lambda_0|\mathscr{B}(G)$ which is equivalent to λ. This implies

$$\lambda_0(B) = 0 \quad \text{iff} \quad \lambda_0(Bg) = 0, \qquad B \in \mathscr{B}(G), \quad g \in G.$$

Let $\varrho \in \mathscr{R}(E, D)$ be strictly equivariant. Let $\mathscr{B}_0 \subseteq \mathscr{B}(D)$ be a countable field which generates $\mathscr{B}(D)$. In the following unions or intersections of families with indices $B \in \mathscr{B}(D)$ are equal with the corresponding countable unions or intersections with $B \in \mathscr{B}_0$, since two measures which coincide on $\mathscr{B}_0$ necessarily coincide on $\mathscr{B}(D)$.

We have

$$\nu \bigcup_{B \in \mathscr{B}(D)} \{\omega \in \Omega\colon \varrho(\omega, B) \neq \varrho(g\omega, gB)\} = 0$$

for every $g \in G$ which implies

$$(\nu \otimes \lambda_0) \bigcup_{B \in \mathscr{B}(D)} \{(\omega, g) \in \Omega \times G: \varrho(\omega, B) \neq \varrho(g\omega, gB)\} = 0.$$

Hence we obtain

$$\lambda_0 \bigcup_{B \in \mathscr{B}(D)} \{g \in G: \varrho(g\omega, gB) \neq \varrho(\omega, B)\} = 0 \quad \nu\text{-a.e.}$$

Let N be the exceptional set of ν-measure zero where the equation does not hold. Define

$$A := \bigcap_{B \in \mathscr{B}(D)} \{\omega \in \Omega: \varrho(g\omega, gB) = \int \varrho(h\omega, hB)\, \lambda_0(dh)\ \lambda_0\text{-a.e.}\}.$$

As soon we have shown that

(1) $A \in \mathscr{A}$,

(2) $\Omega \setminus N \subseteq A$ and hence $\nu(\Omega \setminus A) = 0$,

(3) $A \in \mathscr{A}_i$,

(4) $\int \varrho(h\omega, hB)\, \lambda_0(dh) = \int \varrho(hg\omega, hgB)\, \lambda_0(dh)$ if $\omega \in A$, $g \in G$, $B \in \mathscr{B}(D)$

the proof can be completed as follows.

Define

$$\varrho_0(\omega, B) = \begin{cases} \int \varrho(h\omega, hB)\, \lambda_0(dh) & \text{if } \omega \in A,\ B \in \mathscr{B}(D), \\ \varrho(\omega, B) & \text{if } \omega \notin A,\ B \in \mathscr{B}(D). \end{cases}$$

In order to show that ϱ_0 is strictly equivariant we note that $\omega \in A$ implies by (4) that

$$\begin{aligned} \varrho_0(g\omega, gB) &= \int \varrho(hg\omega, hgB)\, \lambda_0(dh) \\ &= \int \varrho(h\omega, hB)\, \lambda_0(dh) = \varrho_0(\omega, B) \end{aligned}$$

for all $B \in \mathscr{B}(D)$. The decision function ϱ_0 solves the problem since for $\omega \in A \setminus N$ we have

$$\varrho(\omega, B) = \varrho(g\omega, gB) \quad \lambda_0\text{-a.e.}, \quad B \in \mathscr{B}(D),$$

and therefore

$$\varrho(\omega, B) = \int \varrho(h\omega, hB)\, \lambda_0(dh) = \varrho_0(\omega, B), \quad B \in \mathscr{B}(D).$$

It remains to prove assertions (1)–(4).

Assertion (1) follows from the fact that A is the set where the $\mathscr{A}$-measurable functions

$$\omega \mapsto \int \left| \int \varrho(h\omega, hB)\, \lambda_0(dh) - \varrho(g\omega, gB) \right| \lambda_0(dg), \quad \omega \in \Omega,$$

$B \in \mathscr{B}_0$, vanish. For the proof of (2) we note that $\omega \notin N$ implies $g \mapsto \varrho(g\omega, gB)$ is constant λ_0-a.e. and therefore $\omega \in A$. Next let us prove (4).

If $\omega \in A$ then we denote

$$N_\omega = \bigcup_{B \in \mathscr{B}(D)} \{k \in G: \varrho(k\omega, kB) \neq \int \varrho(h\omega, hB)\, \lambda_0(dh)\}$$

and observe that $\lambda_0(N_\omega) = 0$. For arbitrary $g \in G$ it follows that $\lambda_0(N_\omega g^{-1}) = 0$. Since

$$N_\omega g^{-1} = \{k \in G: kg \in N_\omega\}$$

$$= \bigcup_{B \in \mathscr{B}(D)} \{k \in G: \varrho(kg\omega, kgB) \neq \int \varrho(h\omega, hB)\, \lambda_0(dh)\},$$

we obtain

$$\int \varrho(kg\omega, kgB)\, \lambda_0(dk) = \int \varrho(h\omega, hB)\, \lambda_0(dh)$$

for all $B \in \mathscr{B}(D)$. This proves (4).

Finally, we show that (3) is true. If $\omega \in A$ then $\lambda_0(N_\omega g^{-1}) = 0$ implies that for every $g \in G$

$$\varrho(kg\omega, kgB) = \int \varrho(h\omega, hB)\, \lambda_0(dh), \quad B \in \mathscr{B}(D), \quad \lambda_0\text{-a.e.}$$

Combining this with (4) we get for all $g \in G$

$$\varrho(kg\omega, kgB) = \int \varrho(hg\omega, hgB)\, \lambda_0(dh), \quad B \in \mathscr{B}(D), \quad \lambda_0\text{-a.e.},$$

and replacing B by $g^{-1}B$

$$\varrho(kg\omega, kB) = \int \varrho(hg\omega, hB)\, \lambda_0(dh) \quad B \in \mathscr{B}(D), \quad \lambda_0\text{-a.e.}$$

This implies $g\omega \in A$. □

48.10 Corollary. *Assume that E is a shift experiment or a structure model. Then for every strictly equivariant $\varrho \in \mathscr{R}(E, G)$ there exists a convolution kernel $\varrho_0 \in \mathscr{R}(E, G)$ such that $\varrho_0(\omega, B) = \varrho(\omega, B)$, $B \in \mathscr{B}(D)$, on a set $A \in \mathscr{A}$ with $P_t(A) = 1$, $t \in T$.*

Proof. From the proof of Theorem 48.9 it is clear that ϱ_0 can be chosen on $\Omega \setminus A$ to be a convolution kernel. □

Now we approach the proof of a general version of the Hunt-Stein theorem.

For convenience, call s and t *connected by G* if there exists $g \in G$ such that $P_t = M_g P_s$. This is an equivalence relation on T and the equivalence classes are called the *orbits* of G on T. Let us denote the set of orbits by T/G.

48.11 Lemma. *Assume that E is invariant under $(M_g)_{g \in G}$ and (T, D, W) is G-invariant where W is bounded and continuous. If $\beta \in \mathscr{B}(E, D)$ is equivariant then $t \mapsto \beta(W_t, P_t)$, $t \in T$, is constant on the orbits in T/G.*

Proof. Let $P_t = M_g P_s$. Then

$$\beta(W_t, P_t) = \beta(W_t, M_g P_s) = \beta(W_t \circ g, P_t) = \beta(W_s, P_s). \qquad \square$$

48.12 Discussion. The main technical tool for the following is a fixed point property.

(1) Let X be a topological vector space and $\mathcal{M}$ a family of continuous linear mappings $\varphi: X \to X$. The family has the *fixed point property* if every compact, convex set $K \subseteq X$ such that $\varphi(K) \subseteq K$, $\varphi \in \mathcal{M}$, contains a fixed point of $\mathcal{M}$, i.e. a point $x_0 \in K$ satisfying $\varphi(x_0) = x_0$ for every $\varphi \in \mathcal{M}$.

(2) A *representation* of a group G is a homomorphism $g \mapsto T_g$ of G into the space of all continuous linear mapping $T: X \to X$ of a topological vector space X.

(3) The group G has the *fixed point property* if every representation of G has the fixed point property.

(4) It is well known and will suffice for our purposes that every Abelian group has the fixed point property. This is the Markov-Kakutani fixed point theorem. For a proof see Dunford-Schwartz [1967, Theorem V. 10.6].

(5) The fixed point property is closely related to amenability. Amenability is a weaker condition than the fixed point property. If G is connected then both conditions are equivalent to each other. For a survey discussion of the interrelationships between various conditions related to these concepts, see Bondar and Milnes [1981].

48.13 Theorem (Generalized Theorem of Hunt and Stein). *Assume that E is invariant under a group $(M_g)_{g \in G}$ and G operates on D continuously from the left. If G has the fixed point property then for every $\beta \in \mathscr{B}(E, D)$ there exists a strictly equivariant decision function $\beta_0 \in \mathscr{B}(E, D)$ such that*

$$\sup_{g \in G} \beta(f \circ g^{-1}, M_g \mu) \geqq \beta_0(f, \mu)$$

for every $\mu \in L(E)^+$ and every lower semicontinuous function $f: D \to \mathbb{R}$.

Proof. For every $g \in G$ let $\beta_g: (f, \mu) \mapsto \beta(f \circ g^{-1}, M_g \mu), f \in \mathscr{C}_b(D), \mu \in L(E)$. Let K be the closed convex hull of $\{\beta_g: g \in G\}$ in $\mathscr{B}(E, D)$. If X denotes the topological vector space of continuous bilinear functions on $\mathscr{C}_b(D) \times L(E)$, then for every $g \in G$ the map $T_g: X \to X$ defined by

$$T_g(\gamma): (f, \mu) \mapsto \gamma(f \circ g^{-1}, M_g \mu), \ (f, \mu) \in \mathscr{C}_b(D) \times L(E), \ \gamma \in X,$$

is continuous and linear. Hence, (T_g) is a representation of G and satisfies $T_g(K) \subseteq K, g \in G$. By assumption, K contains a fixed point β_0 of (T_g). Since β_0 is a fixed point it is strictly equivariant and since $\beta_0 \in K$, it satisfies the asserted condition. $\square$

48.14 Remark. (1) The results of the previous chapters where we have used amenability admit a similar, much easier proof if the condition of amenability is replaced by the fixed point property. This is particularly valid of the classical Hunt-Stein theorem (Theorem 32.5) and of Boll's convolution theorem (Theorem 38.15).

(2) Conversely, the preceding assertion can be proved under the assumption of amenability by the technical means of previous chapters provided that $g \mapsto \beta(f \circ g^{-1}, M_g \mu)$, $g \in G$, is $\mathscr{B}(G)$-measurable, $f \in \mathscr{C}_b(D)$, $\mu \in L(E)$. Let us sketch the proof for this case.

Let (K_n) be a summing sequence of compacts $K_n \subseteq G$, $n \in \mathbb{N}$, and define $\lambda_n = \lambda_r(.|K_n)$, $n \in \mathbb{N}$. Denote

$$\beta_n: (f, \mu) \mapsto \int \beta(f \circ h^{-1}, M_h \mu)\, \lambda_n(dh), f \in \mathscr{C}_b(D),\ \mu \in L(E),\ n \in \mathbb{N}.$$

From Theorem 42.3 it follows that there exists a weak accumulation point $\beta_0 \in \mathscr{B}(E, D)$ of $(\beta_n)_{n \in \mathbb{N}}$. If β_0 is equivariant then the asserted inequality is obvious. Let us prove that β_0 is even strictly equivariant.

The choice of $(\lambda_n)_{n \in \mathbb{N}}$ implies that for every $g \in G$ and all $f \in \mathscr{C}_b(D)$, $\mu \in L(E)$,

$$\lim_{n \to \infty} \left| \int \beta(f \circ g^{-1} \circ h^{-1}, M_{hg} \mu)\, \lambda_n(dh) - \int \beta(f \circ h^{-1}, M_h \mu)\, \lambda_n(dh) \right| = 0.$$

It follows that

$$\lim_{n \to \infty} |\beta_n(f \circ g^{-1}, M_g \mu) - \beta_n(f, \mu)| = 0$$

for all $g \in G$, $f \in \mathscr{C}_b(D)$ and $\mu \in L(E)$. It is now clear that every weak accumulation point of $(\beta_n)_{n \in \mathbb{N}}$ is strictly equivariant.

(3) The preceding remark can be applied to $\varrho \in \mathscr{R}(E, D)$, since in this case $g \mapsto (f \circ g^{-1}) \varrho M_g$, $g \in G$, is $\mathscr{B}(G)$-measurable for all $f \in \mathscr{C}_b(D)$, $\mu \in L(E)$. For the proof consider the function F defined by

$$F(g, h) = f \circ g^{-1} \varrho M_h \mu, \quad (g, h) \in G^2,$$

for some $f \in \mathscr{C}_b(D)$, $\mu \in L(E)$, $\varrho \in \mathscr{R}(E, D)$. Then it is clear that $g \mapsto F(g, h)$, $g \in G$, is continuous for every $h \in G$, and $h \mapsto F(g, h)$, $h \in G$, is measurable for every $g \in G$. Let $(g_n) \subseteq G$ be countable and dense, and let d be a distance generating the topology of G. Then

$$\{(g, h) \in G^2: F(g, h) \leqq \alpha\} = \bigcap_{k=1}^{\infty} \bigcup_{n=1}^{\infty} \left\{(g, h) \in G^2: F(g_n, h) \leqq \alpha + \frac{1}{k},\ d(g_n, g) < \frac{1}{k}\right\},$$

$\alpha \in \mathbb{R}$, which implies that F is $\mathscr{B}(G) \otimes \mathscr{B}(G)$-measurable. Since for every $D \in \mathscr{B}(G) \otimes \mathscr{B}(G)$ the set $\{g \in G: (g, g) \in D\}$ is in $\mathscr{B}(G)$, the assertion follows.

48.15 Corollary. *Assume that E is invariant under $(M_g)_{g\in G}$ and G operates on D continuously from the left. If G has the fixed point property then for every $\beta \in \mathscr{B}(E, D)$ there exists a strictly equivariant decision function $\beta_0 \in \mathscr{B}(E, D)$ such that*

$$\sup_{t\in\bar{t}} \beta(W_t, P_t) \geqq \sup_{t\in\bar{t}} \beta_0(W_t, P_t)$$

for every $\bar{t} \in T/G$ and every lower semicontinuous loss function W of an invariant decision problem (T, D, W).

If E is dominated and D is a locally compact space with countable base then the preceding assertions can be improved.

48.16 Theorem. *Suppose that E is dominated and D is a locally compact space with countable base. Consider the case of Example 48.3 and assume that G operates on D continuously from the left. Assume further that there exist strictly equivariant elements in $\mathscr{R}(E, D)$. If G is amenable then for every $\beta \in \mathscr{B}(E, D)$ there exists a strictly equivariant decision function $\varrho \in \mathscr{R}(E, D)$ such that*

$$\sup_{g\in G} \beta(f \circ g^{-1}, M_g \mu) \geqq f\varrho\mu$$

for every $\mu \in L(E)^+$ and every level compact function $f\colon D \to \mathbb{R}$.

Proof. In view of Theorem 43.5 we may assume without loss of generality that $\beta \in \mathscr{R}(E, D)$. Then Remark 48.14 (2) and (3), implies the existence of a strictly equivariant $\beta_0 \in \mathscr{B}(E, D)$ such that

$$\sup_{g\in G} \beta(f \circ g^{-1}, M_g \mu) \geqq \beta_0(f, \mu), \quad \mu \in L(E)^+,$$

for every lower semicontinuous $f\colon D \to \mathbb{R}$.

We prove that there exists a strictly equivariant decision function $\varrho \in \mathscr{R}(E, D)$ such that

$$\beta_0(f, \mu) \geqq f\varrho\mu, \quad \mu \in L(E)^+,$$

for every level compact function $f\colon D \to \mathbb{R}$. For β_0 choose a kernel ϱ_0 according to Lemma 42.6. Let ϱ_1 be any strictly equivariant decision function in $\mathscr{R}(E, D)$. Define

$$\varrho(\omega, B) := \varrho_0(\omega, B) + (1 - \varrho_0)(\omega, D)\,\varrho_1(\omega, B), \quad \omega \in \Omega,\ B \in \mathscr{B}(D).$$

It is then clear that $\varrho \in \mathscr{R}(E, D)$. It is also clear that ϱ is strictly equivariant since $\varrho_0(\omega, D) = \varrho_0(g\omega, D)$ $\mathscr{P}$-a.e. If $f \in \mathscr{C}_b(D)$ is level compact then $\sup f - f \in \mathscr{C}_0^+(D)$ and for $\mu \in L(E)^+$ we obtain

$$\beta(\sup f - f, \mu) = (\sup f - f)\,\varrho_0\mu \leqq (\sup f - f)\,\varrho\mu.$$

This implies

$$\beta(f, \mu) \geqq f \varrho \mu .$$

Now Lemma 6.4 proves the assertion. □

It is obvious that a similar conclusion as in Corollary 48.15 is possible.

Chapter 9: Comparison of Experiments

The main difference between the usual decision theory and the theory of experiments can be explained as follows. It is the aim of decision theory to investigate a fixed statistical experiment, e.g. to find an optimal decision rule. In contrast to decision theory the theory of experiments considers the relations between different experiments. In this sense, most of the preceding theory in this book could be subsumed under the label of decision theory. However, problems concerning sufficiency and invariance point into the direction of the theory of experiments.

The starting point of the theory of experiments was the problem of comparison of experiments, initiated by Blackwell [1951]. Blackwell introduced a statistically natural concept for the comparison of general experiments which extends the ideas we have used previously in connection with binary experiments (Section 15) and with dominated experiments (Section 22). In Section 49 we discuss the relations between the various definitions.

The essential point of the theory of experiments is that the basic order relation between experiments, first defined in rather general terms, can be transformed in such a way that it becomes analytically tractable. In Chapter 3 this has already been done for binary experiments in an elementary way, using the Neyman-Pearson lemma, only. Now, in the general case, things are more complicated and we divide the procedure into several steps.

First of all, by means of the minimax theorem the order relation can be expressed in terms of the Bayesian risks for priors with finite support. It is even sufficient to consider only uniform priors. This reduction is carried through in Section 49. At this point the order relation is still based on all possible decision problems for a given parameter space. A suitable standardization of decision problems simplifies matters considerably without changing the order relation. It turns out that we need only consider decision spaces which are convex polyhedra, and loss functions which are projections (Sections 50 and 51). The next step is to express the Bayesian risks for uniform priors and standard decision problems in terms of integrals over concave functions, and to express the order relation between the experiments in terms of these integrals (Section 52). This procedure of transforming the order relation goes back to Blackwell [1951 and 1953], and has been generalized by LeCam [1964]. It is also discussed by Torgersen [1970].

In Section 53 we show that the Hellinger transforms characterize the equivalence classes of experiments. As a consequence we obtain that also the distributions of the likelihood processes have this property, thus extending previous results of Section 25.

We distinguish two different order relations between experiments. The coarser one considers testing problems only whereas the finer one admits arbitrary decision problems for the comparison of experiments. In Section 54 we present a few results essentially going back to Torgersen [1970]. Among others, it is shown that both order relations coincide for binary experiments. For arbitrary experiments only the corresponding equivalence relations are identical.

In Sections 24 and 25 we have proved that for dominated experiments the order relation based on testing problems can be expressed in terms of stochastic operators between the corresponding *L*-spaces. This characterization is extended in Section 55 to the randomization criterion which is the general formulation of the idea of sufficiency. Initiated by Blackwell [1951] the final version is due to LeCam [1964].

For every equivalence class of experiments with finite parameter space there is a standard measure on the unit simplex. There is even a one-to-one correspondence between equivalence classes and standard measures. This can be shown in an elementary way and is known since the papers of Blackwell [1951 and 1953]. In case of infinite parameter spaces the situation is more difficult. For every equivalence class of experiments there is a uniquely determined projective system of standard measures which corresponds to a conical measure, using the terminology of Choquet [1969]. It took some time until it was possible to give a correct proof of the converse. Our proof, given in Sections 56 and 57 follows Siebert [1979]. As a consequence we observe that every projective system of experiments possesses a projective limit.

In Section 58 we consider again the idea of invariant experiments. By means of the preceding theory it turns out that essentially one concept of invariance subsumes all definitions considered before.

The order structure on the space of experiments leads to a definition of a natural topology. This is done by means of a distance, called deficiency. With this distance the space of equivalence classes of experiments is a complete metric space. For infinite parameter spaces the metric topology differs from the weak topology which is the coarsest topology such that all projections to finite subexperiments are continuous. Endowed with the weak topology the space of experiments is a compact space. This is the content of Section 59, going back to LeCam [1972].

49. Basic concepts

Let $T \neq \emptyset$ be an arbitrary set. We consider experiments $E \in \mathscr{E}(T)$ and $F \in \mathscr{E}(T)$. These experiments are described by

$$E = (\Omega_1, \mathscr{A}_1, \{P_t: t \in T\})$$

and

$$F = (\Omega_2, \mathscr{A}_2, \{Q_t: t \in T\}).$$

Furthermore we consider decision problems (T, D, W) consisting of a topological space D and a loss function $W = (W_t)_{t \in T}$, where $W_t: D \to \mathbb{R}$, $t \in T$. For any loss function W we define

$$\| W_t \| = \sup \{ | W_t(x) | : x \in D \}, \quad t \in T.$$

49.1 Definition. Let (T, D, W) be a decision problem with a lower semicontinuous loss function W and let $\varepsilon \geqq 0$. Then the experiment E is *ε-deficient* with respect to the experiment F *for the decision problem* (T, D, W) if for every $\beta_2 \in \mathscr{B}(F, D)$ there is $\beta_1 \in \mathscr{B}(E, D)$ such that

$$\beta_1(W_t, P_t) \leqq \beta_2(W_t, Q_t) + \varepsilon \| W_t \|, \quad t \in T.$$

In this case we denote $E \underset{(D,W)}{\overset{\varepsilon}{\supseteq}} F$.

The reader observes immediately that the preceding definition makes only sense for $\varepsilon > 0$ if the loss function W is bounded.

If $E \underset{(D,W)}{\overset{0}{\supseteq}} F$ then we denote $E \underset{(D,W)}{\supseteq} F$. The relation "$\underset{(D,W)}{\supseteq}$" is an order relation. If $E \underset{(D,W)}{\supseteq} F$ then E is called *more informative* than F for (T, D, W). If $E \underset{(D,W)}{\supseteq} F$ and $F \underset{(D,W)}{\supseteq} E$ then E and F are called *equivalent* and we denote $E \underset{(D,W)}{\sim} F$.

49.2 Lemma. *Assume that W is a bounded, lower semicontinuous loss function. Then $E \underset{(D,W)}{\supseteq} F$ holds iff $E \underset{(D,W)}{\overset{\varepsilon}{\supseteq}} F$ for every $\varepsilon > 0$.*

Proof. This is an immediate consequence of the weak compactness of $\mathscr{B}(E, D)$. □

In Chapters 3 and 4 we have considered order relations between experiments which are closely related to the concept of the preceding definition. Let us recall what we have done and put it into slightly more general terms.

In Chapter 3, Section 15, we have considered the relation "$\underset{2}{\overset{\varepsilon}{\supseteq}}$" for binary experiments and in Chapter 4, Section 22, we have considered the order relation "$\underset{2}{\supseteq}$" for general dominated experiments. Recall the definitions:

Let $\varepsilon \geqq 0$ and let $E, F \in \mathscr{E}(T)$ be dominated experiments. Then the experiment E is ε-deficient with respect to the experiment F for testing problems if for every testing problem (H, K) and for every $\varphi_2 \in \mathscr{F}(\Omega_2, \mathscr{A}_2)$ there is $\varphi_1 \in \mathscr{F}_1(\Omega_1, \mathscr{A}_1)$ such that

$$P_t\varphi_1 \leqq Q_t\varphi_2 + \frac{\varepsilon}{2} \quad \text{if} \quad t \in H,$$

$$P_t\varphi_1 \geqq Q_t\varphi_2 - \frac{\varepsilon}{2} \quad \text{if} \quad t \in K.$$

In this case we denote $E \overset{\varepsilon}{\underset{2}{\supseteq}} F$. This relation is related to Definition 49.1 as follows.

49.3 Lemma. *Let $\varepsilon \geqq 0$ and let $E, F \in \mathscr{E}(T)$ be dominated experiments. Then $E \overset{\varepsilon}{\underset{2}{\supseteq}} F$ iff $E \overset{\varepsilon}{\underset{(D,W)}{\supseteq}} F$ for every decision problem where the decision space D contains exactly two elements.*

Proof. (1) Assume that $E \overset{\varepsilon}{\underset{2}{\supseteq}} F$. Let $D = \{0,1\}$ and W an arbitrary loss function. We define

$$H = \{t \in T\colon W_t(1) \geqq W_t(0)\}, \quad K = \{t \in T\colon W_t(1) < W_t(0)\}.$$

In view of Corollary 42.8 we choose some $\varrho_2 \in \mathscr{R}(F, D)$ and denote $\varphi_2 = \varrho_2(.,1)$. Obviously, $\varphi_2 \in \mathscr{F}(\Omega_2, \mathscr{A}_2)$ and according to $E \overset{\varepsilon}{\underset{2}{\supseteq}} F$ there is $\varphi_1 \in \mathscr{F}(\Omega_1, \mathscr{A}_1)$ such that

$$P_t\varphi_1 \leqq Q_t\varphi_2 + \frac{\varepsilon}{2} \quad \text{if} \quad t \in H,$$

$$P_t\varphi_1 \geqq Q_t\varphi_2 - \frac{\varepsilon}{2} \quad \text{if} \quad t \in K.$$

Let $\varrho_1 = \varphi_1\varepsilon_1 + (1-\varphi_1)\varepsilon_0$ where ε_1 and ε_0 denote the Dirac measures at 1 resp. 0. We note that

$$\begin{aligned} W_t\varrho_1 P_t &= W_t(1)P_t\varphi_1 + W_t(0)P_t(1-\varphi_1) \\ &= W_t(0) + P_t\varphi_1(W_t(1) - W_t(0)) \end{aligned}$$

and

$$\begin{aligned} W_t\varrho_2 Q_t &= W_t(1)Q_t\varphi_2 + W_t(0)Q_t(1-\varphi_2) \\ &= W_t(0) + Q_t\varphi_2(W_t(1) - W_t(0)). \end{aligned}$$

It follows that

$$\begin{aligned} W_t\varrho_1 P_t - W_t\varrho_2 Q_t &= (W_t(1) - W_t(0))\,(P_t\varphi_1 - Q_t\varphi_2) \\ &\leqq |W_t(1) - W_t(0)| \cdot \frac{\varepsilon}{2} \leqq \varepsilon \| W_t \|. \end{aligned}$$

Hence we have $E \underset{(D,W)}{\overset{\varepsilon}{\supseteq}} F$.

(2) Assume conversely that $E \underset{(D,W)}{\overset{\varepsilon}{\supseteq}} F$ for every decision problem where the decision space D contains exactly two elements. If (H, K) is an arbitrary testing problem then we define $D = \{0, 1\}$ and

$$W_t(0) = \begin{cases} -\frac{1}{2} & \text{if } t \in H, \\ +\frac{1}{2} & \text{if } t \in K, \end{cases} \qquad W_t(1) = \begin{cases} +\frac{1}{2} & \text{if } t \in H, \\ -\frac{1}{2} & \text{if } t \in K. \end{cases}$$

Let $\varphi_2 \in \mathscr{F}(\Omega_2, \mathscr{A}_2)$. Then for $\varrho_2 = \varphi_2 \varepsilon_1 + (1 - \varphi_2)\varepsilon_0$ there is $\varrho_1 \in \mathscr{R}(E, D)$ such that

$$W_t\varrho_1 P_t \leqq W_t\varrho_2 Q_t + \frac{\varepsilon}{2}, \quad t \in T.$$

Denoting $\varphi_1 = \varrho_1(.,1)$ we obtain

$$W_t\varrho_1 P_t = \begin{cases} -\frac{1}{2}(1 - P_t\varphi_1) + \frac{1}{2} P_t\varphi_1 & \text{if } t \in H, \\ -\frac{1}{2} P_t\varphi_1 + \frac{1}{2}(1 - P_t\varphi_1) & \text{if } t \in K, \end{cases}$$

and

$$W_t\varrho_2 Q_t = \begin{cases} -\frac{1}{2}(1 - Q_t\varphi_2) + \frac{1}{2} Q_t\varphi_2 & \text{if } t \in H, \\ -\frac{1}{2} Q_t\varphi_2 + \frac{1}{2}(1 - Q_t\varphi_2) & \text{if } t \in K. \end{cases}$$

It follows that

$$-\frac{1}{2}(1 - P_t\varphi_1) + \frac{1}{2} P_t\varphi_1 \leqq -\frac{1}{2}(1 - Q_t\varphi_2) + \frac{1}{2} Q_t\varphi_2 + \frac{\varepsilon}{2} \quad \text{if } t \in H,$$

and

$$-\frac{1}{2} P_t\varphi_1 + \frac{1}{2}(1 - P_t\varphi_1) \leqq -\frac{1}{2} Q_t\varphi_2 + \frac{1}{2}(1 - Q_t\varphi_2) + \frac{\varepsilon}{2} \quad \text{if } t \in K.$$

This proves $E \underset{2}{\overset{\varepsilon}{\supseteq}} F$. $\square$

We generalize the notion $E \overset{\varepsilon}{\underset{2}{\supseteq}} F$ to the case of not necessarily dominated experiments.

49.4 Definition. Let $\varepsilon \geqq 0$. Then the experiment E is *ε-deficient* with respect to the experiment F *for testing problems* ($E \overset{\varepsilon}{\underset{2}{\supseteq}} F$) if $E \overset{\varepsilon}{\underset{(D,W)}{\supseteq}} F$ for every decision problem where the decision space contains exactly two elements.

The following definition extends the spirit of the relation "$\overset{\varepsilon}{\underset{2}{\supseteq}}$" to general decision problems.

49.5 Definition. Let $\varepsilon \geqq 0$. The experiment E is *ε-deficient* with respect to the experiment F ($E \overset{\varepsilon}{\supseteq} F$) if $E \overset{\varepsilon}{\underset{(D,W)}{\supseteq}} F$ for every decision problem (T, D, W) with a bounded, continuous loss function W.

It is obvious that $E \overset{\varepsilon}{\supseteq} F$ implies $E \overset{\varepsilon}{\underset{2}{\supseteq}} F$. In general, the converse is not true. Later it will be shown that the converse is at least valid for binary experiments (see Section 54).

If $E \overset{0}{\supseteq} F$ then we denote $E \supseteq F$. The relation "$\supseteq$" is an order relation. If $E \supseteq F$ then E is called *more informative* than F. If $E \supseteq F$ and $F \supseteq E$ then E and F are called *equivalent* and we denote $E \sim F$.

It is obvious that $E \supseteq F$ iff $E \overset{\varepsilon}{\supseteq} F$ for for every $\varepsilon > 0$.

49.6 Corollary. *Let $\varepsilon \geqq 0$. If $E \overset{\varepsilon}{\supseteq} F$ then $E \overset{\varepsilon}{\underset{(D,W)}{\supseteq}} F$ for every decision problem (T, D, W) with a lower semicontinuous loss function W.*

Proof. Choose $\delta > 0$ arbitrary and let (T, D, W) be a decision problem with a lower semicontinuous loss function W. Let $\mathscr{V}_\delta$ be the set of all bounded, continuous loss functions $V \leqq W$ such that $\inf W_t - \delta \| W_t \| \leqq V_t \leqq W_t$, $t \in T$. It is clear that for every bounded, continuous loss function $V_t \leqq W$ there is $V \in \mathscr{V}_\delta$ such that $V_1 \leqq V \leqq W$. Moreover, each $V \in \mathscr{V}_\delta$ satisfies $\| V_t \| \leqq \| W_t \| \, (1 + \delta)$, $t \in T$. If $\beta_2 \in \mathscr{B}(F, D)$ then $E \overset{\varepsilon}{\supseteq} F$ implies

$$\bigcap_{t \in T} \{\beta \in \mathscr{B}(E, D) \colon \beta(V_t, P_t) \leqq \beta_2(W_t, Q_t) + \varepsilon(1 + \delta) \| W_t \|\} \neq \emptyset$$

for every $V \in \mathscr{V}_\delta$. Since $\mathscr{V}_\delta$ is directed from above it follows that

$$\bigcap_{V \in \mathscr{V}_\delta} \bigcap_{t \in T} \{\beta \in \mathscr{B}(E, D) \colon \beta(V_t, P_t) \leqq \beta_2(W_t, Q_t) + \varepsilon \| W_t \|\} \neq \emptyset.$$

This proves the assertion. □

By means of the Minimax Theorem a necessary and sufficient condition for

$E \overset{\varepsilon}{\underset{(D,W)}{\supseteq}} F$ can be established in terms of Bayesian risks which is the key of all following considerations.

49.7 Theorem (Blackwell [1951]). *Assume that* (T, D, W) *is a decision problem with a lower semicontinuous loss function. Let* $\varepsilon \geqq 0$. *Then* $E \overset{\varepsilon}{\underset{(D,W)}{\supseteq}} F$ *holds iff for every* $m \in S_T$

$$\inf_{\beta_1 \in \mathscr{B}(E,D)} \int \beta_1(W_t, P_t)\, m(dt)$$
$$\leqq \inf_{\beta_2 \in \mathscr{B}(F,D)} \int \beta_2(W_t, Q_t)\, m(dt) + \varepsilon \int \| W_t \| \, m(dt).$$

Proof. Apply Corollary (45.7) to

$$M_2 = \{(\beta_1(W_t, P_t))_{t \in T} \colon \beta_1 \in \mathscr{B}(E, D)\}, \quad \text{and}$$
$$M_1 = \{(\beta_2(W_t, Q_t) + \varepsilon \| W_t \|)_{t \in T} \colon \beta_2 \in \mathscr{B}(F, D)\}. \qquad \square$$

If (T, D, W) is a decision problem with a bounded, continuous loss function W, then the infima in the preceding theorem may be restricted to $\mathscr{R}(E, D)$ and $\mathscr{R}(F, D)$, respectively.

For $\alpha \in A(T)$ let E_α be the restriction of E to be parameter space α. It turns out that the comparison of experiments may be phrased in terms of the finite subexperiments, only.

49.8 Corollary. *Assume that* (T, D, W) *is a decision problem with a bounded continuous loss function. Let* $\varepsilon \geqq 0$. *Then the following assertions are equivalent:*

(1) $E \overset{\varepsilon}{\underset{(D,W)}{\supseteq}} F$.

(2) $E_\alpha \overset{\varepsilon}{\underset{(D,W)}{\supseteq}} F_\alpha$ *for every* $\alpha \in A(T)$.

Proof. It is clear that $\mathscr{R}(E, D) = \mathscr{R}(E_\alpha, D)$ and $\mathscr{R}(F, D) = \mathscr{R} F_\alpha, D)$ for every $\alpha \in A(T)$. Hence the assertion is an immediate consequence of Theorem 49.7. $\square$

Finally, we show that in Theorem (49.7) the prior measures m may be replaced by the uniform distribution.

49.9 Corollary (Blackwell [1951]). *Let* $\varepsilon \geqq 0$ *and let* D *be a decision space. Then the following assertions are equivalent:*

(1) $E \overset{\varepsilon}{\underset{(D,W)}{\supseteq}} F$ *for every bounded continuous loss function* W.

(2) *For every* $\alpha \in A(T)$ *and every bounded continuous loss function* W

$$\inf_{\varrho_1 \in \mathscr{R}(E,D)} \sum_{t\in\alpha} W_t \varrho_1 P_t \leqq \inf_{\varrho_2 \in \mathscr{R}(F,D)} \sum_{t\in\alpha} W_t \varrho_2 Q_t + \varepsilon \sum_{t\in\alpha} \| W_t \| .$$

Proof. It is clear that (1) $\Rightarrow$ (2). Let us prove (2) $\Rightarrow$ (1). Let $m \in S_T$ and let W be a bounded, continuous loss function. Let $\alpha \in A(T)$ be such that $m \in S_\alpha$. We define another loss function $\bar{W}$ by

$$\bar{W}(x,t) = |\alpha| \, m\{t\} \, W(x,t), \quad x \in D, \quad t \in T.$$

Then it follows that

$$\begin{aligned} \inf_{\varrho_1 \in \mathscr{R}(E,D)} \int W_t \varrho_1 P_t m(dt) &= \inf_{\varrho_1 \in \mathscr{R}(E,D)} \frac{1}{|\alpha|} \sum_{t\in\alpha} \bar{W}_t \varrho_1 P_t \\ &\leqq \inf_{\varrho_2 \in \mathscr{R}(F,D)} \frac{1}{|\alpha|} \sum_{t\in\alpha} \bar{W}_t \varrho_2 Q_t + \varepsilon \frac{1}{|\alpha|} \sum_{t\in\alpha} \| \bar{W}_t \| \\ &= \inf_{\varrho_2 \in \mathscr{R}(F,D)} \int W_t \varrho_2 Q_t m(dt) + \varepsilon \int \| W_t \| m(dt). \qquad \square \end{aligned}$$

50. Standard decision problems

50.1 Definition. A decision problem (T, D, L) is a *standard decision problem* for a parameter space T if $D \subseteq \mathbb{R}^T$ is a convex, compact subset and if $L_t\colon D \to \mathbb{R}$ is the projection onto the tth coordinate of $\mathbb{R}^T$, $t \in T$.

It will be shown in the next paragraph that comparison of experiments may be based on the consideration of standard decision problems only. In this section we discuss the reduction of arbitrary decision problems to standard decision problems. Let us consider an experiment $E \in \mathscr{E}(T)$ such that $E = (\Omega, \mathscr{A}, \{P_t\colon t \in T\})$.

50.2 Lemma. *Let* (T, D, L) *be a standard decision problem. Then for every* $\varrho \in \mathscr{R}(E, D)$ *there is a nonrandomized decision function* $\varrho_0 \in \mathscr{R}(E, D)$ *such that* $L_t \varrho_0 P_t = L_t \varrho P_t$, $t \in T$.

Proof. For every $\omega \in \Omega$ let $b(\omega)$ be the barycenter of $\varrho(\omega, .)$ in D. Since L_t is affine-linear on D for every $t \in T$ the non-randomized decision function $\varrho_0\colon \omega \mapsto b(\omega)$ satisfies

$$(L_t \varrho)(\omega) = \int L_t(x) \, \varrho(\omega, dx) = (b(\omega))_t = (L_t \varrho_0)(\omega).$$

It remains to show that ϱ_0 is $(\mathscr{A}, \mathscr{B}_0(D))$-measurable. Since $\omega \mapsto (L_t \varrho_0)(\omega)$ is $\mathscr{A}$-measurable for every $t \in T$ and since $\{L_t\colon t \in T\}$ separates points of the compact set D the Stone-Weierstraß theorem implies that $f \circ \varrho_0$ is $\mathscr{A}$-measurable for every $f \in \mathscr{C}(D)$. Hence ϱ_0 is $\mathscr{B}_0(D)$-measurable. □

50.3 Definition. A nonrandomized decision function $\varrho_0 \in \mathscr{R}(E, D)$ is called *simple* if it attains only finitely many values in D.

50.4 Lemma. *Let* (T, D, L) *be a standard decision problem. Then the set* $\{(L_t \varrho_0 P_t)_{t \in T}: \varrho_0 \in \mathscr{R}(E, D)$ *is simple nonrandomized*$\}$ *is dense in* $R(E, D, L)$.

Proof. It follows from Lemma 50.2 that the set $\{(L_t \varrho_0 P_t)_{t \in T}: \varrho_0 \in \mathscr{R}(E, D)$ is nonrandomized$\}$ coincides with $\{(L_t \varrho P_t)_{t \in T}: \varrho \in \mathscr{R}(E, D)\}$ which itself is dense in $R(E, D, L)$. Hence the assertion follows by a standard argument using the fact that D is totally bounded. □

The following assertion shows that, given an experiment $E \in \mathscr{E}(T)$, for every decision problem (T, D, W) there is a standard decision problem (T, D_0, L) such that the risk sets $R(E, D, W)$ and $R(E, D_0, L)$ coincide. Thus, the analysis of an experiment E may be based on the consideration of standard decision problems only.

50.5 Theorem (Blackwell [1951]). *Let* (D, W) *be a decision problem with a bounded, continuous loss function* W. *If* D_0 *denotes the closed, convex hull of* $\{(W_t(x))_{t \in T}: x \in D\}$ *then* $R(E, D, W) = R(E, D_0, L)$.

Proof. (1) Let us prove $R(E, D, W) \subseteq R(E, D_0, L)$. By Lemma 44.4 it is sufficient to prove $R_0(E, D, W) \subseteq R_0(E, D_0, L)$. If $\varrho \in \mathscr{R}(E, D)$ then for every $\omega \in \Omega$ we define $\varrho_0(\omega, .)$ to be the one-point measure which is concentrated at $(\int W_t(x)\, \varrho(\omega, dx))_{t \in T}$. Then we have

$$\int W_t(x)\, \varrho(\omega, dx) = \int L_t(x)\, \varrho_0(\omega, dx)$$

for every $\omega \in \Omega$ and $t \in T$ which proves that $(W_t \varrho P_t)_{t \in T} \in R_0(E, D_0, L)$.

(2) Let us show that $R(E, D_0, L) \subseteq R(E, D, W)$. To this end we show that $R_0(E, D, W)$ is dense in $R(E, D_0, L)$ and apply Lemma 44.4. Since the risks of the simple decision functions are dense in $R(E, D_0, L)$ it is sufficient to prove that every neighbourhood of the risk of a simple decision function contains elements of $R_0(E, D, W)$. Let $\varrho_0 \in \mathscr{R}(E, D_0)$ be a simple decision function and let

$$U = \{y \in \mathbb{R}^T: |y_t - L_t \varrho_0 P_t| < \varepsilon \quad \text{if} \quad t \in \alpha\}$$

for some $\varepsilon > 0$, $\alpha \in A(T)$. The decision function ϱ_0 is of the form

$$\varrho_0(\omega, B) = \sum_{i=1}^{k} 1_{A_i}(\omega)\, 1_B(x_i), \quad \omega \in \Omega, \quad B \in \mathscr{B}(D),$$

where $(A_1, A_2, \ldots, A_k)$ is an $\mathscr{A}$-measurable partition of Ω and $x_i \in D_0$, $1 \leqq i \leqq k$. From the definition of D_0 it follows that there are $m_i \in S_D$, $1 \leqq i \leqq k$, such that

$$|\int W_t dm_i - (x_i)_t| < \varepsilon \quad \text{if} \quad t \in \alpha, \quad 1 \leqq i \leqq k.$$

We define

$$\varrho(\omega, B) = \sum_{i=1}^{k} 1_{A_i}(\omega) m_i(B), \quad \omega \in \Omega, \quad B \in \mathscr{B}(D).$$

Obviously, $\varrho \in \mathscr{R}(E, D)$ and it remains to show that $(W_t \varrho P_t)_{t \in T} \in U$. This is the case since for every $t \in \alpha$

$$|W_t \varrho P_t - L_t \varrho_0 P_t| = |\sum_{i=1}^{k} \int W_t dm_i P_t(A_i) - \sum_{i=1}^{k} (x_i)_t P_t(A_i)|$$

$$\leqq \sum_{i=1}^{k} |\int W_t dm_i - (x_i)_t| P_t(A_i) < \varepsilon. \qquad \square$$

It is convenient to call decision problems (T, D_1, W_1) and (T, D_2, W_2) *equivalent* if $R(E, D_1, W_1) = R(E, D_2, W_2)$ for every experiment $E \in \mathscr{E}(T)$. Thus we have proved that for every decision problem (T, D, W) with a bounded continuous loss function there is an equivalent standard decision problem.

51. Comparison of experiments by standard decision problems

Let us consider experiments $E = (\Omega_1, \mathscr{A}_1, \{P_t : t \in T\})$ and $F = (\Omega_2, \mathscr{A}_2, \{Q_t : t \in T\})$. The reduction which has been achieved in the preceding paragraph yields immediately the following criterion.

51.1 Theorem. *Let $\varepsilon \geqq 0$. Then $E \overset{\varepsilon}{\supseteq} F$ holds iff $E \underset{(D_0, L)}{\overset{\varepsilon}{\supseteq}} F$ for every standard decision problem (T, D_0, L).*

Another consequence is concerned with testing problems.

51.2 Theorem. *Let $\varepsilon \geqq 0$. Then $E \underset{2}{\overset{\varepsilon}{\supseteq}} F$ iff $E \underset{(D_0, L)}{\overset{\varepsilon}{\supseteq}} F$ for every standard decision problem (T, D_0, L) with $D_0 = \text{co}\{x_1, x_2\}$, $x_1 \in \mathbb{R}^T$, $x_2 \in \mathbb{R}^T$.*

Proof. We know that $E \underset{2}{\overset{\varepsilon}{\supseteq}}$ F iff $E \underset{(D, W)}{\overset{\varepsilon}{\supseteq}} F$ for every decision problem (T, D, W) where D contains exactly two elements. By Theorem 50.5 for every such decision problem there is an equivalent standard decision problem (D_0, L) with $D_0 = \text{co}\{x_1, x_2\}$, $x_1 \in \mathbb{R}^T$, $x_2 \in \mathbb{R}^T$. Let conversely (D_0, L) be a standard decision problem where $D_0 = \operatorname{co}\{x_1, x_2\}$. This is by Theorem 50.5 equivalent with the ordinary problem $(\{x_1, x_2\}, L)$. □

In the following we apply Corollary 49.9 to standard decision problems. Let us recall some notations. For every $\alpha \in A(T)$ the set $\mathbb{R}^\alpha$ consists of all points $x \in \mathbb{R}^T$ with support contained in α. The projection from $\mathbb{R}^T$ to $\mathbb{R}^\alpha$ is denoted by p_α.

We begin with a simple fact concerning testing problems.

51.3 Theorem. *Let* $\varepsilon \geqq 0$. *Then* $E \overset{\varepsilon}{\underset{2}{\supseteq}} F$ *iff for every* $\alpha \in A(T)$ *and for every standard decision problem* (T, D_α, L) *where* $D_\alpha = \operatorname{co}\{x_1, x_2\}$, $x_1 \in \mathbb{R}^\alpha$, $x_2 \in \mathbb{R}^\alpha$,

$$\inf_{\varrho_1 \in \mathscr{R}(E, D_\alpha)} \sum_{t \in \alpha} L_t \varrho_1 P_t \leqq \inf_{\varrho_2 \in \mathscr{R}(F, D_\alpha)} \sum_{t \in \alpha} L_t \varrho_2 Q_t + \varepsilon \sum_{t \in \alpha} \|L_t\|.$$

Proof. We know from Corollary 49.8 that $E \overset{\varepsilon}{\underset{2}{\supseteq}} F$ iff $E_\alpha \overset{\varepsilon}{\underset{2}{\supseteq}} F_\alpha$ for every $\alpha \in A(T)$. By Corollary 49.9 the second assertion is equivalent to

$$\inf_{\varrho_1 \in \mathscr{R}(E, D^{(\alpha)})} \sum_{t \in \alpha} W_t \varrho_1 P_t \leqq \inf_{\varrho_2 \in \mathscr{R}(F, D^{(\alpha)})} \sum_{t \in \alpha} W_t \varrho_2 Q_t + \varepsilon \sum_{t \in \alpha} \|W_t\|$$

for every $\alpha \in A(T)$ and every decision problem $(D^{(\alpha)}, W)$ where $D^{(\alpha)}$ contains exactly two elements and W is a bounded, continuous loss function. In view of Theorem 50.5 for every such decision problem $(D^{(\alpha)}, W)$ there is an equivalent standard decision problem (D_α, L) where $D_\alpha = \operatorname{co}\{x_1, x_2\}$, $x_i \in \mathbb{R}^\alpha$, $i = 1, 2$, and $\|L_t\| = \|W_t\|$, $t \in \alpha$. □

The interesting feature of the following result is the fact that only convex polyhedra need to be taken into consideration to obtain a criterion for $E \overset{\varepsilon}{\supseteq} F$.

51.4 Theorem. *Let* $\varepsilon \geqq 0$. *Then* $E \overset{\varepsilon}{\supseteq} F$ *holds iff for every* $\alpha \in A(T)$ *and for every standard decision problem* (T, D_α, L) *where* D_α *is a convex polyhedron in* $\mathbb{R}^\alpha$

$$\inf_{\varrho_1 \in \mathscr{R}(E, D_\alpha)} \sum_{t \in \alpha} L_t \varrho_1 P_t \leqq \inf_{\varrho_2 \in \mathscr{R}(F, D_\alpha)} \sum_{t \in \alpha} L_t \varrho_2 Q_t + \varepsilon \sum_{t \in \alpha} \|L_t\|.$$

Proof. A similar argument as in the proof of Theorem 51.3 shows that $E \overset{\varepsilon}{\supseteq} F$ iff for every $\alpha \in A(T)$ and every standard decision problem (D_α, L) where $D_\alpha \subseteq \mathbb{R}^\alpha$ is convex and compact

$$\inf_{\varrho_1 \in \mathscr{R}(E, D_\alpha)} \sum_{t \in \alpha} L_t \varrho_1 P_t \leqq \inf_{\varrho_2 \in \mathscr{R}(F, D_\alpha)} \sum_{t \in \alpha} L_t \varrho_2 Q_t + \varepsilon \sum_{t \in \alpha} \|L_t\|.$$

Hence the condition of the present theorem is necessary for $E \overset{\varepsilon}{\supseteq} F$. To prove sufficiency let $\alpha \in A(T)$ and let $D_\alpha \subseteq \mathbb{R}^\alpha$ be convex and compact. For any $\varepsilon_1 > 0$

we choose a simple decision function $\bar{\varrho}_2 \in \mathscr{R}(F, D_\alpha)$ such that

$$\sum_{t \in \alpha} L_t \bar{\varrho}_2 Q_t \leqq \inf_{\varrho_2 \in \mathscr{R}(F, D_\alpha)} \sum_{t \in \alpha} L_t \varrho_2 Q_t + \varepsilon_1 \sum_{t \in \alpha} \|L_t\|.$$

Let $D_{\alpha,1}$ be the convex hull of the image of $\bar{\varrho}_2$. Since $D_{\alpha,1}$ is a convex polyhedron it follows from the condition of the present theorem that

$$\begin{aligned} \inf_{\varrho_1 \in \mathscr{R}(E, D_\alpha)} \sum_{t \in \alpha} L_t \varrho_1 P_t &\leqq \inf_{\varrho_1 \in \mathscr{R}(E, D_{\alpha,1})} \sum_{t \in \alpha} L_t \varrho_1 P_t \\ &\leqq \inf_{\varrho_2 \in \mathscr{R}(F, D_{\alpha,1})} \sum_{t \in \alpha} L_t \varrho_2 Q_t + \varepsilon \sum_{t \in \alpha} \|L_t\| \\ &\leqq \inf_{\varrho_2 \in \mathscr{R}(F, D_\alpha)} \sum_{t \in \alpha} L_t \varrho_2 Q_t + (\varepsilon + \varepsilon_1) \sum_{t \in \alpha} \|L_t\|. \qquad \square \end{aligned}$$

52. Concave function criteria

Let $T \neq \emptyset$. The dual $(\mathbb{R}_+^T)^*$ of $\mathbb{R}_+^T$ is the set of all $x \in \mathbb{R}_+^T$ with finite support. Recall the terminology of Section 45.

52.1 Definition. Let $D \subseteq (\mathbb{R}_+^T)^*$ be a bounded set. Then

$$\psi_D \colon \mathbb{R}_+^T \to \mathbb{R}_+ \colon y \mapsto \inf \{\langle x, y \rangle \colon x \in D\}$$

is called *lower envelope* of D.

Note that for any $D \subseteq (\mathbb{R}_+^T)^*$ we have $\psi_D = \psi_{\overline{\mathrm{co}}\, D}$. Hence any lower envelope is the lower envelope of a closed convex set. The lower envelope of a convex polyhedron $D = \mathrm{co}\{x_1, x_2, \ldots, x_n\}$ is given by $\psi_D(y) = \min\{\langle x_i, y \rangle \colon 1 \leqq i \leqq n\}$, $y \in \mathbb{R}_+^T$. It is easy to see that

$$\begin{aligned} &\psi_{D_1} \cap \psi_{D_2} = \psi_{\overline{\mathrm{co}}(D_1 \cup D_2)}, \\ &\lambda_1 \psi_{D_1} + \lambda_2 \psi_{D_2} = \psi_{\lambda_1 D_1 + \lambda_2 D_2}, \\ &\psi_D(-y) = \psi_{(-D)}(y), \quad y \in \mathbb{R}^T, \end{aligned}$$

for any sets $D_1, D_2, D \subseteq (\mathbb{R}_+^T)^*$ and $\lambda_1 \geqq 0$, $\lambda_2 \geqq 0$.

52.2 Lemma. *Any lower envelope is upper semicontinuous, concave and positively homogeneous.*

Proof. Obvious. $\square$

It is clear that the lower envelope of a convex polyhedron is even continuous.

52.3 Definition. If ψ_D is the lower envelope of a convex, compact subset $D \subseteq (\mathbb{R}_+^T)^*$ then the *norm* of ψ_D is defined by

$$\|\psi_D\| = \sum_{t \in T} \sup_{x \in D} |x_t|.$$

It is easy to see that $\|\psi_D\| = \sum_{t \in T} \max\{-\psi_D(e_t), -\psi_D(-e_t)\}$. If (T, D, L) is a standard decision problem then $\|\psi_D\| = \sum_{t \in T} \|L_t\|$.

52.4 Lemma. *The lower envelope ψ_D of a convex, compact subset $D = (\mathbb{R}_+^T)^*$ satisfies*

$$|\psi_D(y_1) - \psi_D(y_2)| \leqq \|\psi_D\| \, |y_1 - y_2|_\infty, \, y_i \in \mathbb{R}_+^T, \quad i = 1, 2.$$

Proof. Easy. □

52.5 Definition. Let $E = (\Omega, \mathscr{A}, \{P_t : t \in T\})$ be an experiment. For every $\alpha \in A(T)$ let $T_\alpha : \Omega \to \mathbb{R}_+^T$ be such that

$$(T_\alpha(\omega))_t = \begin{cases} \dfrac{dP_t}{d \sum\limits_{s \in \alpha} P_s}(\omega) & \text{if } t \in \alpha, \\[2ex] 0 & \text{if } t \notin \alpha. \end{cases}$$

Then $\sigma_\alpha = \mathscr{L}(T_\alpha | \sum_{s \in \alpha} P_s)$ is called *standard measure* of $E_\alpha = (\Omega, \mathscr{A}, \{P_t : t \in \alpha\})$ and $(\sigma_\alpha)_{\alpha \in A(T)}$ is the system of standard measures of E.

It is obvious that the mapping T_α is E_α-sufficient for every $\alpha \in A(T)$.

52.6 Lemma. *Let $E \in \mathscr{E}(T)$ be an experiment and let (T, D, L) be a standard decision problem. Then for every $\alpha \in A(T)$ and every nonrandomized $\varrho \in \mathscr{R}(E, D)$ there exists an $\mathscr{A}(T_\alpha)$-measurable decision function $\varrho_0 \in \mathscr{R}(E, D)$ such that $\varrho_0 \in P_t(\varrho | \mathscr{A}(T_\alpha))$, $t \in \alpha$.*

Proof. Let ϱ_1 be any version of the conditional expectation of ϱ given $\mathscr{A}(T_\alpha)$. We will prove that

$$P_t\{\varrho_1 \notin D\} = 0 \quad \text{if} \quad t \in \alpha.$$

Let M be the family of all affine-linear functionals $\ell : \mathbb{R}_+^\alpha \to \mathbb{R}_+$ satisfying $\ell(x) \leqq 0$ if $x \in D$. Then

$$\{\varrho_1 \notin D\} = \bigcup_{\ell \in M} \{\ell \circ \varrho_1 > 0\}.$$

If $M_0 \subseteq M$ is countable and dense in M then

$$\{\varrho_1 \notin D\} = \bigcup_{\ell \in M_0} \{\ell \circ \varrho_1 > 0\}.$$

We note that $\ell \circ \varrho_1 \in P_t(\ell \circ \varrho | \mathscr{A}(T_\alpha))$ if $t \in \alpha$ and therefore $\ell \circ \varrho_1 \leqq 0$ P_t-a.e. if $t \in \alpha$. Hence ϱ_1 can be adjusted to obtain ϱ_0. □

As has been shown in Theorem 51.4 the comparison of experiments may be based on the Bayesian risks for standard decision problems. These Bayesian risks may be expressed as integrals of the standard measures over concave functions.

52.7 Theorem (Blackwell [1951]). *Let $E \in \mathscr{E}(T)$ and let $(\sigma_\alpha)_{\alpha \in A(T)}$ be the associated system of standard measures. Then for every $\alpha \in A(T)$ and for every standard decision problem (T, D_α, L) where $D_\alpha \subseteq \mathbb{R}^\alpha_+$*

$$\inf_{\varrho \in \mathscr{R}(E, D_\alpha)} \sum_{t \in \alpha} L_t \varrho P_t = \int_{S_\alpha} \psi_{D_\alpha} d\sigma_\alpha .$$

Proof. It is sufficient to consider nonrandomized decision functions $\varrho \in \mathscr{R}(E, D_\alpha)$ which in the following are viewed as mappings $\varrho: \Omega \to D_\alpha$. According to Lemma 52.6 we may assume that $\varrho = \varrho_0 \circ T_\alpha$. It is then clear that

$$\sum_{t \in \alpha} L_t \varrho P_t = \int \langle \varrho_0(y), y \rangle \, \sigma_\alpha(dy).$$

Thus we obtain immediately that

$$\inf_{\varrho \in \mathscr{R}(E, D_\alpha)} \sum_{t \in \alpha} L_t \varrho P_t \geqq \int \psi_{D_\alpha}(y) \, \sigma_\alpha(dy).$$

To prove the reversed inequality choose $\varepsilon > 0$ and let $(x_n)_{n \in \mathbb{N}}$ be a sequence which is dense in D_α. For every $y \in S_\alpha$ define $\varrho_\varepsilon(y) \in D_\alpha$ in such a way that $\varrho_\varepsilon(y) = x_k$ if $k \in \mathbb{N}$ is the smallest integer satisfying

$$\langle x_k, y \rangle \leqq \psi_{D_\alpha}(y) + \varepsilon .$$

Then $\varrho_\varepsilon: S_\alpha \to D_\alpha$ is a measurable function as is easily seen from

$$\begin{aligned} &\{y_\alpha \in S_\alpha: \varrho_\varepsilon(y) = x_k\} \\ &= \bigcap_{i=1}^{k-1} \{y \in S_\alpha: \langle x_i, y \rangle > \psi_{D_\alpha}(y) + \varepsilon\} \cap \{y \in S_\alpha: \langle x_k, y \rangle \leqq \psi_{D_\alpha}(y) + \varepsilon\}. \end{aligned}$$

Moreover, we have

$$\begin{aligned} \inf_{\varrho \in \mathscr{R}(E, D_\alpha)} \sum_{t \in \alpha} L_t \varrho P_t &\leqq \sum_{t \in \alpha} L_t(\varrho_\varepsilon \circ T_\alpha) P_t \\ &= \int \langle \varrho_\varepsilon(y), y \rangle \, \sigma_\alpha(dy) \leqq \int \psi_{D_\alpha}(y) \, \sigma_\alpha(dy) + \varepsilon . \end{aligned}$$ □

52.8 Corollary. *Let $\varepsilon \geqq 0$ and let $(\sigma_\alpha)_{\alpha \in A(T)}$ and $(\tau_\alpha)_{\alpha \in A(T)}$ be the system of standard measures of experiments E and F. Then $E \overset{\varepsilon}{\supseteq} F$ holds iff for every $\alpha \in A(T)$ and for every convex polyhedron $D_\alpha \subseteq \mathbb{R}^\alpha$*

$$\int \psi_{D_\alpha} d\sigma_\alpha \leqq \int \psi_{D_\alpha} d\tau_\alpha + \varepsilon \| \psi_{D_\alpha} \| .$$

Proof. Combine Theorem 51.4 and Theorem 52.7. □

It is easy to formulate a similar criterion for the relation $E \underset{2}{\overset{\varepsilon}{\supseteq}} F$. Related questions will be considered in Section 54.

52.9 Lemma. *Assume that $M \subseteq S_T$ is compact and convex. Then for every upper semicontinuous, concave function $f: M \to \mathbb{R}$ there is a closed, convex set $D \subseteq (\mathbb{R}^T)^*$ such that*

$$f(y) = \inf\{\langle x, y \rangle : x \in D\}, \quad y \in M.$$

Proof. Since M is compact there exists $\alpha \in A(T)$ such that $M \subseteq S_\alpha$. We will show that the assertion is true for $D = \{x \in (\mathbb{R}^T)^* : \langle x, y \rangle \geqq f(y) \text{ if } y \in M\}$. Let $W = \{(y, \beta) \in M \times \mathbb{R} : f(y) \geqq \beta\}$. Then $W \subseteq \mathbb{R}^T \times \mathbb{R}$ is closed and convex. Choose $\varepsilon > 0$ and $y_0 \in M$. Then $(y_0, f(y_0) + \varepsilon) \notin W$ and hence there exist $x_0 \in (\mathbb{R}^T)^*$, $\gamma \in \mathbb{R}$, such that

$$\langle x_0, y_0 \rangle + \gamma(f(y_0) + \varepsilon) \leqq c < c + \delta \leqq \langle x_0, y \rangle + \gamma\beta$$

whenever $y \in M$, $\beta \leqq f(y)$. Putting $y = y_0$ and $\beta = f(y_0)$ it follows that $\gamma < 0$. We normalize x_0 in such a way that $\gamma = -1$ and obtain

$$\langle x_0, y_0 \rangle - f(y_0) - \varepsilon \leqq \langle x_0, y \rangle - f(y) \quad \text{if} \quad y \in M.$$

Since $y_0 \in S_\alpha$ and $M \subseteq S_\alpha$ there is a translation $x_1 \in (\mathbb{R}^T)^*$ of x_0 such that

$$\langle x_1, y_0 \rangle - f(y_0) - \varepsilon = 0 \leqq \langle x_1, y \rangle - f(y) \quad \text{if} \quad y \in M.$$

We obtain $x_1 \in D$ and $f(y_0) \leqq \langle x_1, y_0 \rangle = f(y_0) + \varepsilon$. This proves the assertion. □

52.10 Corollary (Blackwell [1951]). *Let $(\sigma_\alpha)_{\alpha \in A(T)}$ and $(\tau_\alpha)_{\alpha \in A(T)}$ be the systems of standard measures of experiments E and F. Then $E \supseteq F$ iff for every $\alpha \in A(T)$ and for every concave, upper semicontinuous function $f: S_\alpha \to \mathbb{R}$*

$$\int f \, d\sigma_\alpha \leqq \int f \, d\tau_\alpha .$$

Proof. From Corollary 52.8 it follows that the condition is sufficient for $E \supseteq F$ since every support function ψ_{D_α} with $D_\alpha \subseteq \mathbb{R}^\alpha$ is concave and upper semicontinuous on S_α. Conversely, the condition is necessary in view of Lemma 52.9. □

53. Hellinger transforms and standard measures

Recall that if $E \in \mathscr{E}(T)$ is an experiment then E_α, $\alpha \in A(T)$, denotes the restriction of E to the parameter set $\alpha \subseteq T$. In the following we define $0^0 = 1$.

53.1 Definition. Let $E = (\Omega, \mathscr{A}, \{P_t: t \in T\})$ be an experiment and let $\mathscr{B} \subseteq \mathscr{A}$ be a finite subfield of $\mathscr{A}$. If $B_1, B_2, \ldots, B_m$ are the atoms of $\mathscr{B}$ then the *conditional Hellinger transform* given $\mathscr{B}$ is

$$H(E_\alpha|\mathscr{B})(z) := \sum_{j=1}^{m} \prod_{t\in\alpha} P_t^{z_t}(B_j)$$

if $\alpha \in A(T)$, $z \in S_\alpha$.

53.2 Remark. Recall Hölder's inequality for nonnegative numbers a_{t_j}, $t \in T$, $1 \leqq j \leqq m$:

$$\sum_{j=1}^{m} \prod_{t\in\alpha} a_{t_j}^{z_t} \leqq \prod_{t\in\alpha} \left(\sum_{j=1}^{m} a_{t_j}\right)^{z_t} \quad \text{if} \quad z \in S_\alpha, \quad \alpha \in A(T).$$

53.3 Lemma. *Let $E \in \mathscr{E}(T)$ be an experiment and $\mathscr{B} \subseteq \mathscr{A}$ a finite subfield of $\mathscr{A}$. Then $0 \leqq H(E_\alpha|\mathscr{B}) \leqq 1$ on S_α for every $\alpha \in A(T)$.*

Proof. It is obvious that $H(E_\alpha|\mathscr{B}) \geqq 0$. Hölder's inequality implies for every $z \in S_\alpha$

$$H(E_\alpha|\mathscr{B})(z) = \sum_{j=1}^{m} \prod_{t\in\alpha} P_t^{z_t}(B_j) \leqq \prod_{t\in\alpha} \left(\sum_{j=1}^{m} P_t(B_j)\right)^{z_t} = 1. \qquad \square$$

53.4 Lemma. *Let $E \in \mathscr{E}(T)$ be an experiment and let $\mathscr{B}_1$ and $\mathscr{B}_2$* be finite subfields of $\mathscr{A}$. Then

$$\mathscr{B}_1 \subseteq \mathscr{B}_2 \quad \text{implies} \quad H(E_\alpha|\mathscr{B}_1) \geqq H(E_\alpha|\mathscr{B}_2) \quad \text{on} \quad S_\alpha$$

for every $\alpha \in A(T)$.

Proof. The relation $\mathscr{B}_1 \subseteq \mathscr{B}_2$ implies that the atoms of $\mathscr{B}_2$ are a finer partition of Ω than the atoms of $\mathscr{B}_1$. This means that every atom of $\mathscr{B}_1$ is the union of pairwise disjoint atoms of $\mathscr{B}_2$. Now the assertion follows from the fact that for any union $C_1 \cup C_2$ of disjoint sets $C_1 \in \mathscr{A}$, $C_2 \in \mathscr{A}$, Hölder's inequality implies

$$\begin{aligned}\prod_{t\in\alpha} P_t^{z_t}(C_1 \cup C_2) &= \prod_{t\in\alpha} (P_t(C_1) + P_t(C_2))^{z_t} \\ &\leqq \prod_{t\in\alpha} P_t^{z_t}(C_1) + \prod_{t\in\alpha} P_t^{z_t}(C_2). \qquad \square\end{aligned}$$

53.5 Definition. If $E \in \mathscr{E}(T)$ then for every $\alpha \in A(T)$ the *Hellinger transform*

$H(E_\alpha)\colon S_\alpha \to [0,1]$ is defined by

$$H(E_\alpha)(z) = \inf\{H(E_\alpha|\mathscr{B})(z)\colon \mathscr{B} \subseteq \mathscr{A} \text{ a finite subfield}\}.$$

53.6 Theorem. *Let $E = (\Omega, \mathscr{A}, \{P_t\colon t \in T\})$ be an experiment. If $\alpha \in A(T)$ and if $\nu|\mathscr{A}$ is a σ-finite measure dominating $\{P_t\colon t \in \alpha\}$ then*

$$H(E_\alpha)(z) = \int \prod_{t\in\alpha} \left(\frac{dP_t}{d\nu}\right)^{z_t} d\nu, \quad z \in S_\alpha.$$

Proof. It is sufficient to prove the assertion for probability measures $\nu|\mathscr{A}$.

(1) Let $\mathscr{B} \subseteq \mathscr{A}$ be a finite subfield with atoms $(B_1, B_2, \ldots, B_m)$. Then we have for every $j \in \{1, 2, \ldots, m\}$, $z \in S_\alpha$,

$$\int_{B_j} \prod_{t\in\alpha} \left(\frac{dP_t}{d\nu}\right)^{z_t} d\nu \leqq \prod_{t\in\alpha} \Big(\int_{B_j} \frac{dP_t}{d\nu}\, d\nu\Big)^{z_t} = \prod_{t\in\alpha} P_t^{z_t}(B_j)$$

and this implies

$$\int \prod_{t\in\alpha} \left(\frac{dP_t}{d\nu}\right)^{z_t} d\nu \leqq \sum_{j=1}^{m} \prod_{t\in\alpha} P_t^{z_t}(B_j).$$

Thus we obtain

$$\int \prod_{t\in\alpha} \left(\frac{dP_t}{d\nu}\right)^{z_t} d\nu \leqq H(E_\alpha)(z), \quad z \in S_\alpha.$$

(2) To prove the reversed inequality let $\varepsilon > 0$ and $z \in S_\alpha$ be arbitrary, and choose a finite subfield $\mathscr{B} \subseteq \mathscr{A}$ in such a way that the functions

$$f_t = \sum_{j=1}^{m} \frac{P_t(B_j)}{\nu(B_j)} 1_{B_j}, \quad t \in \alpha, \quad z_t > 0,$$

satisfy

$$\left\| \frac{dP_t}{d\nu} - f_t \right\|_1^{z_t} \leqq \frac{\varepsilon}{|\alpha|}, \quad t \in \alpha, \quad z_t > 0.$$

Since $\nu|\mathscr{A}$ is a probability measure the possibility of such a choice follows from martingale theorems. Let $\alpha = \{t_1, t_2, \ldots, t_n\}$. Then we obtain

$$\left| \int \prod_{t\in\alpha} \left(\frac{dP_t}{d\nu}\right)^{z_t} d\nu - \sum_{j=1}^{m} \prod_{t\in\alpha} P_t^{z_t} B_j) \right|$$

$$\leqq \int \left| \prod_{t\in\alpha,\, z_t>0} \left(\frac{dP_t}{d\nu}\right)^{z_t} - \prod_{t\in\alpha,\, z_t>0} f_t^{z_t} \right| d\nu$$

$$\leqq \sum_{t_i \in \alpha,\, z_{t_i} > 0} \int \left| \left(\frac{dP_{t_i}}{dv}\right)^{z_{t_i}} - f_{t_i}^{z_{t_i}} \right| \prod_{k<i} f_{t_k}^{z_{t_k}} \prod_{k>i} \left(\frac{dP_{t_k}}{dv}\right)^{z_{t_k}} dv$$

$$\leqq \sum_{t_i \in \alpha,\, z_{t_i} > 0} \left[\left(\int \left| \left(\frac{dP_{t_i}}{dv}\right)^{z_{t_i}} - f_{t_i}^{z_{t_i}} \right|^{\frac{1}{z_{t_i}}} dv \right)^{z_{t_i}} \prod_{k<i} \left(\int f_{t_k} dv \right)^{z_{t_k}} \prod_{k>i} \left(\int \frac{dP_{t_k}}{dv} dv \right)^{z_{t_k}} \right]$$

$$= \sum_{t \in \alpha,\, z_t > 0} \left(\int \left| \left(\frac{dP_t}{dv}\right)^{z_t} - f_t^{z_t} \right|^{\frac{1}{z_t}} dv \right)^{z_t}$$

$$\leqq \sum_{t \in \alpha,\, z_t > 0} \left(\int \left| \frac{dP_t}{dv} - f_t \right| dv \right)^{z_t} < \varepsilon.$$

(Use the fact that $|x^z - y^z| < |x - y|^z$ if $x \geqq 0$, $y \geqq 0$, $0 < z < 1$.) This proves the assertion. □

53.7 Remarks. (1) If $z \in S_\alpha$ then we denote

$$\psi_z\colon S_\alpha \to \mathbb{R}\colon x \mapsto \prod_{t \in \alpha} x_t^{z_t}.$$

The function ψ_z is continuous and concave on S_α. However, for $x \in \partial S_\alpha$ the functions $z \mapsto \psi_z(x)$, $z \in S_\alpha$, are not continuous. From the preceding theorem it follows that $H(E_\alpha)(z) = \int_{S_\alpha} \psi_z \, d\sigma_\alpha$, $z \in S_\alpha$, where σ_α is the standard measure of E_α, $\alpha \in A(T)$.

(2) From the formula of Theorem 53.6 it follows immediately that $H(E_\alpha)(z) = H(E_\beta)(z)$ if $z \in S_\beta$, $\beta \subseteq \alpha$.

Recalling the terminology of Section 5 it is clear that $H(E_\alpha)$ is the Hellinger transform of the standard measure σ_α, $\alpha \in A(T)$. This yields the following uniqueness assertion.

53.8 Corollary. *Let $E \in \mathscr{E}(T)$, $F \in \mathscr{E}(T)$. For $\alpha \in A(T)$ let σ_α be the standard measure of E_α and let τ_α be the standard measure of F_α. Then the following assertions are equivalent:*

(1) $E \sim F$,

(2) $E_\alpha \sim F_\alpha$ *for every* $\alpha \in A(T)$,

(3) $\sigma_\alpha = \tau_\alpha$ *for every* $\alpha \in A(T)$,

(4) $H(E_\alpha) = H(F_\alpha)$ *for every* $\alpha \in A(T)$.

Proof. It follows from Corollary 52.8 that (1) ⇔ (2). From Corollary 52.10 we obtain (2) ⇒ (4), Theorem 5.19 yields (4) ⇒ (3) and (3) ⇒ (2) is another consequence of Corollary 52.8. □

53.9 Corollary. *Assume that T is a finite set and let σ, τ be the standard* *measures of E and F. Then the following assertions are equivalent:*

(1) $E \sim F$

(2) $\sigma = \tau$,

(3) $H(E) = H(F)$.

Proof. It is clear that (1) $\Rightarrow$ (2) $\Leftrightarrow$ (3). The assertion follows from the fact that $H(E) = H(F)$ implies $H(E_\alpha) = H(F_\alpha)$ for every $\alpha \in A(T)$. □

The following is a useful lemma which allows to reduce equivalence of experiments to equality of likelihood ratio processes. It is an extension of Corollary 25.9.

53.10 Theorem. *Let E and F be experiments in $\mathscr{E}(T)$ and let $\mathscr{P} = \{P_t\colon t \in T\}$ and $\mathscr{Q} = \{Q_t\colon t \in T\}$ the corresponding sets of probability measures. Then $E \sim F$ iff*

$$\mathscr{L}\left(\left(\frac{dP_t}{dP_s}\right)_{t\in T}\middle|\, P_s\right) = \mathscr{L}\left(\left(\frac{dQ_t}{dQ_s}\right)_{t\in T}\middle|\, Q_s\right)$$

for every $s \in T$.

Proof. In view of the preceding results and because the distribution of a stochastic process is determined by its finite dimensional marginal distributions it is sufficient to prove the assertion for finite sets $T \neq \emptyset$. But this has been done already in Corollary 25.6. □

54. Comparison of experiments by testing problems

Let us explore the relation between comparison of experiments by general decision problems and by testing problems. As indicated previously both concepts coincide for binary experiments. To prove this we need a formula to transform integrals for σ_E into integrals for $\mu_E = \mathscr{L}\left(\frac{dP_2}{dP_1}\middle|\, P_1\right)$ where $E = (P_1, P_2)$ is a binary experiment. Then we are in a position to apply the results of Chapter 3.

54.1 Lemma. *Let E be a binary experiment and ψ_D the lower envelope of a convex, compact set $D \subseteq \mathbb{R}^2$. Then*

$$\int \psi_D \, d\sigma_E = \psi_D(0, 1) + \int [\psi_D(1, t) - \psi_D(0, t)]\, \mu_E(dt).$$

Proof. Let $E = (P_1, P_2)$. Elementary computations yield

$$\int \psi_D d\sigma_E = \int_{\eta_1=0} \psi_D(\eta_1,\eta_2)\,\sigma_E(d\eta_1,d\eta_2) + \int_{\eta_1>0} \psi_D(\eta_1,\eta_2)\,\sigma_E(d\eta_1,d\eta_2)$$
$$= \int_{\eta_1=0} \psi_D(0,1)\,\eta_2\,\sigma_E(d\eta_1,d\eta_2) + \int_{\eta_1>0} \psi_D\left(1,\frac{\eta_2}{\eta_1}\right)\eta_1\,\sigma_E(d\eta_1,d\eta_2)$$
$$= \psi_D(0,1)\,P_2\left\{\frac{dP_1}{d(P_1+P_2)}=0\right\} + \int \psi_D\left(1,\frac{dP_2}{dP_1}\right)dP_1$$
$$= \psi_D(0,1)\,(1-\int t\,\mu_E(dt)) + \int \psi_D(1,t)\,\mu_E(dt). \qquad \square$$

54.2 Theorem (Torgersen [1970]). *Let $E=(P_1,P_2)$ and $F=(Q_1,Q_2)$ be binary experiments. Then for every $\varepsilon \geqq 0$ the relation $E \underset{2}{\overset{\varepsilon}{\supseteq}} F$ is valid iff $E \overset{\varepsilon}{\supseteq} F$.*

Proof. Only one direction of the assertion is not trivial. Assume that $E \underset{2}{\overset{\varepsilon}{\supseteq}} F$.

Then we obtain from Theorem 17.1 that

$$\int f d\mu_E \leqq \int f d\mu_F + \frac{\varepsilon}{2}(f'(0)+f(\infty))$$

for every concave, increasing function $f\colon [0,\infty)\to[0,\infty)$, $f(0)=0$. Let $D\subseteq \mathbb{R}^2$ be an arbitrary convex polyedron. Then

$$\psi_D(y) = \min\{\langle x_i, y\rangle\colon 1\leqq i\leqq n\}, \quad y\in\mathbb{R},$$

if $D=\operatorname{co}\{x_1,x_2,\ldots,x_n\}$. We have to show that

$$\int \psi_D d\sigma_E \leqq \int \psi_D d\sigma_F + \varepsilon\|\psi_D\|.$$

Let us denote $x_i=(\xi_i,\eta_i)$, $1\leqq i\leqq n$. Then we have $\|\psi_D\| = \max\limits_{1\leqq i\leqq n}|\xi_i| + \max\limits_{1\leqq i\leqq n}|\eta_i|$. We denote $u=\min\limits_{1\leqq i\leqq n}\xi_i$ and $v=\min\limits_{1\leqq i\leqq n}\eta_i$. Since

$$\int \psi_D d\sigma_E = \int \psi_D d\sigma_E - \int u y_1\, d\sigma_E(y) + u = \int \psi_{D-(u,0)}\, d\sigma_E + u$$

and similarly

$$\int \psi_D d\sigma_F = \int \psi_{D-(u,0)}\, d\sigma_F + u$$

we obtain from Lemma 54.1 that

$$\int \psi_D d\sigma_E - \int \psi_D d\sigma_F = \int \psi_{D-(u,0)}\, d\sigma_E - \int \psi_{D-(u,0)}\, d\sigma_F$$
$$= \int [\psi_{D-(u,0)}(1,t) - vt]\,\mu_E(dt) - \int [\psi_{D-(u,0)}(1,t)-vt]\,\mu_F(dt)$$
$$= \int \min_{1\leqq i\leqq n}((\xi_i-u)+t(\eta_i-v))\,\mu_E(dt) - \int \min_{1\leqq i\leqq n}((\xi_i-u)+t(\eta_i-v))\,\mu_F(dt).$$

Considering the function

$$f(t) = \min_{1 \leqq i \leqq n} ((\xi_i - u) + t(\eta_i - v)), \quad t \geqq 0,$$

we observe that it is concave. It is increasing since $\eta_i - v \geqq 0$, $1 \leqq i \leqq n$. If $u = \xi_{i_1}$, $v = \eta_{i_2}$, then we have

$$f(0) = \min_{1 \leqq i \leqq n} (\xi_i - u) = \xi_{i_1} - u = 0,$$

$$f'(0) = \min_{\xi_i = u} (\eta_i - v) \leqq 2 \max_{1 \leqq i \leqq n} |\eta_i|,$$

$$f(\infty) = \min_{\eta_i = v} (\xi_i - u) \leqq 2 \max_{1 \leqq i \leqq n} |\xi_i|.$$

Thus, we obtain that

$$\begin{aligned} \int \psi_D d\sigma_E - \int \psi_D d\sigma_F &= \int f d\mu_E - \int f d\mu_F \\ &\leqq \frac{\varepsilon}{2} (f'(0) + f(\infty)) \\ &\leqq \varepsilon \left(\max_{1 \leqq i \leqq n} |\xi_i| + \max_{1 \leqq i \leqq n} |\eta_i| \right) \end{aligned}$$

which proves the assertion. □

We return to experiments with an arbitrary parameter space $T \neq \emptyset$. Let us prove that at least the equivalence relations "$\sim$" and "$\underset{2}{\sim}$" are identical. For dominated experiments this is a consequence of Theorem 25.8, Corollary 25.9 and Theorem 53.10.

Let us consider experiments $E = (\Omega_1, \mathscr{A}_1, \mathscr{P} = \{P_t : t \in T\})$ and $F = (\Omega_2, \mathscr{A}_2, \mathscr{Q} = \{Q_t : t \in T\})$. Let $(\sigma_\alpha)_{\alpha \in A(T)}$ and $(\tau_\alpha)_{\alpha \in A(T)}$ be the systems of standard measures of E and F. The following is an extension of Theorem 22.5.

54.3 Lemma (Torgersen [1970]). *Let* $\varepsilon \geqq 0$. *Then* $E \overset{\varepsilon}{\underset{2}{\supseteq}} F$ *iff*

$$\left\| \sum_{t \in T} a_t P_t \right\| \geqq \left\| \sum_{t \in T} a_t Q_t \right\| - \varepsilon \sum_{t \in T} |a_t|$$

for every $a \in (\mathbb{R}^T)^*$.

Proof. We obtain from Theorems 51.3 and 52.7 that $E \overset{\varepsilon}{\underset{2}{\supseteq}} F$ iff for every $\alpha \in A(T)$ and every pair $(x_1, x_2) \in \mathbb{R}^\alpha \times \mathbb{R}^\alpha$

$$\int \min_{i=1,2} \langle x_i, y \rangle \, \sigma_\alpha(dy) \leqq \int \min_{i=1,2} \langle x_i, y \rangle \, \tau_\alpha(dy) + \varepsilon \sum_{t \in \alpha} \max_{i=1,2} |(x_i)_t|.$$

It is sufficient for $E \overset{\varepsilon}{\underset{2}{\supseteq}} F$ to require the condition for all pairs $(x_1, x_2) \in \mathbb{R}^\alpha \times \mathbb{R}^\alpha$ which are centered at zero, i.e. $x_1 + x_2 = 0$. For such pairs we have

$$\min_{i=1,2} \langle x_i, y\rangle = -\frac{1}{2}|\langle x_1, y\rangle - \langle x_2, y\rangle|$$

and

$$\max_{i=1,2} |(x_i)_t| = \frac{1}{2}|x_{1,t} - x_{2,t}|.$$

It follows that $E \overset{\varepsilon}{\underset{2}{\supseteq}} F$ iff for every $\alpha \in A(T)$ and every pair $(x_1, x_2) \in \mathbb{R}^\alpha \times \mathbb{R}^\alpha$ such that $x_1 + x_2 = 0$

$$\int |\langle x_1, y\rangle - \langle x_2, y\rangle| \sigma_\alpha(dy)$$
$$\geqq \int |\langle x_1, y\rangle - \langle x_2, y\rangle| \tau_\alpha(dy) - \varepsilon \sum_{t\in\alpha} |x_{1,t} - x_{2,t}|.$$

This inequality is equivalent with

$$\int \left| \sum_{t\in\alpha} (x_{1,t} - x_{2,t}) \frac{dP_t}{d\sum_{s\in\alpha} P_s} \right| d\sum_{s\in\alpha} P_s$$
$$\geqq \int \left| \sum_{t\in\alpha} (x_{1,t} - x_{2,t}) \frac{dQ_t}{d\sum_{s\in\alpha} Q_s} \right| d\sum_{s\in\alpha} Q_s - \varepsilon \sum_{t\in\alpha} |x_{1,t} - x_{2,t}|.$$

Putting $a = x_1 - x_2$ we obtain the assertion. □

54.4 Corollary (Torgersen [1970]). *Let* $\varepsilon \geqq 0$. *Then* $E \overset{\varepsilon}{\underset{2}{\supseteq}} F$ *iff for every pair* $m_1 \in S_T$, $m_2 \in S_T$ *the binary experiments* $E_0 = (\int P_t m_1(dt), \int P_t m_2(dt))$ *and* $F_0 = (\int Q_t m_1(dt), \int Q_t m_2(dt))$ *satisfy* $E_0 \overset{\varepsilon}{\supseteq} F_0$.

Proof. Assume that $E \overset{\varepsilon}{\underset{2}{\supseteq}} F$. Let $m_1 \in S_T$, $m_2 \in S_T$. We have to show that

$$\|a \int P_t m_1(dt) + b \int P_t m_2(dt)\|$$
$$\geqq \|a \int Q_t m_1(dt) + b \int Q_t m_2(dt)\| - \varepsilon(|a| + |b|)$$

for all $a \in \mathbb{R}$, $b \in \mathbb{R}$. From the preceding theorem we know that

$$\|a \int P_t m_1(dt) + b \int P_t m_2(dt)\|$$
$$\geqq \|a \int Q_t m_1(dt) + b \int Q_t m_2(dt)\| - \varepsilon \sum_{t\in T} |a m_1\{t\} + b m_2\{t\}|.$$

The assertion follows from the fact that

$$\sum_{t\in T} |a m_1\{t\} + b m_2\{t\}| \leqq |a| + |b|.$$

Assume conversely that the condition is satisfied and let $a \in (\mathbb{R}^T)^*$. If $a_t \geqq 0$ for every $t \in T$ or if $a_t \leqq 0$ for every $t \in T$ then it is easy to obtain

$$\|\sum_{t\in T} a_t P_t\| \geqq \|\sum_{t\in T} a_t Q_t\| - \varepsilon \sum_{t\in T} |a_t|.$$

Otherwise let

$$m_1\{t\} = a_t^+ / \sum_{s\in T} a_s^+,\ m_2\{t\} = a_t^- / \sum_{s\in T} a_s^-, \quad t \in T.$$

It follows that

$$\begin{aligned}\|\sum_{t\in T} a_t P_t\| &\geqq \|\sum_{t\in T} a_t Q_t\| - \varepsilon(|\sum_{s\in T} a_s^+| + |\sum_{s\in T} a_s^-|)\\ &= \|\sum_{t\in T} a_t Q_t\| - \varepsilon \sum_{t\in T} |a_t|.\end{aligned}$$

This proves the assertion. □

54.5 Theorem (Torgersen [1970]). *$E \underset{2}{\sim} F$ iff $E \sim F$.*

Proof. It is obvious that $E \sim F$ implies $E \underset{2}{\sim} F$. Assume conversely that $E \underset{2}{\sim} F$. Then for $\alpha \in A(T)$ and $m \in S_\alpha$ we put

$$P_1 = \frac{1}{|\alpha|} \sum_{t\in\alpha} P_t \quad \text{and} \quad Q_1 = \sum_{t\in\alpha} m\{t\}\, P_t,$$

$$P_2 = \frac{1}{|\alpha|} \sum_{t\in\alpha} Q_t \quad \text{and} \quad Q_2 = \sum_{t\in\alpha} m\{t\}\, Q_t.$$

Then Corollary 54.4 implies $(P_1, Q_1) \sim (P_2, Q_2)$. Hence we obtain from Corollary 16.5

$$\mathscr{L}\left(\frac{dQ_1}{dP_1}\middle| P_1\right) = \mathscr{L}\left(\frac{dQ_2}{dP_2}\middle| Q_2\right)$$

which implies

$$\mathscr{L}\left(\sum_{t\in\alpha} m\{t\} \frac{dP_t}{d\sum_{s\in\alpha} P_s}\middle| \frac{1}{|\alpha|}\sum_{s\in\alpha} P_s\right) = \mathscr{L}\left(\sum_{t\in\alpha} m\{t\} \frac{dQ_t}{d\sum_{s\in\alpha} Q_s}\middle| \frac{1}{|\alpha|}\sum_{s\in\alpha} Q_s\right).$$

Now an easy argument using uniqueness of Fourier transform yields

$$\mathscr{L}\left(\left(\frac{dP_t}{d\sum_{s\in\alpha} P_s}\right)_{t\in\alpha}\middle| \frac{1}{|\alpha|}\sum_{s\in\alpha} P_s\right) = \mathscr{L}\left(\left(\frac{dQ_t}{d\sum_{s\in\alpha} Q_s}\right)_{t\in\alpha}\middle| \frac{1}{|\alpha|}\sum_{s\in\alpha} Q_s\right).$$

This means that the systems of standard measures of E and F coincide. □

54.6 Corollary (LeCam [1964] and Torgersen [1970]). *The following assertions are equivalent:*

(1) $E \underset{2}{\sim} F$.
(2) $E \sim F$.
(3) *There is a linear isometry* M: $\overline{\text{span}}\,\mathscr{P} \to \overline{\text{span}}\,\mathscr{Q}$ *such that* $M(P_t) = Q_t$ *if* $t \in T$.

Proof. Apply Theorems 54.3 and 54.5. □

55. The randomization criterion

Let E and F be experiments in $\mathscr{E}(T)$. The aim of this section is to prove a general version of Theorem 25.8.

55.1 Definition. A *randomization* from E to F is a bilinear function R: $\mathscr{L}^b(\Omega_2, \mathscr{A}_2) \times L(E) \to \mathbb{R}$ satisfying the following conditions:

(1) If $f \geqq 0$, $\sigma \geqq 0$, then $R(f, \sigma) \geqq 0$.
(2) $|R(f, \sigma)| \leqq \|f\|_u \|\sigma\|$.
(3) $R(1, \sigma) = \sigma(\Omega_1)$.

The set of all randomizations from E to F is denoted by $\mathscr{B}(E, F)$.

55.2 Definition. A *stochastic operator* or *transition* from $L(E)$ to $L(F)$ is a positive linear map M: $L(E) \to L(F)$ such that $\|M\sigma\| = \|\sigma\|$ if $\sigma \in L(E)$, $\sigma \geqq 0$.

Every stochastic operator M: $L(E) \to L(F)$ defines a randomization R_M from E to F according to $R_M(f, \sigma) = (M\sigma)(f)$, $f \in \mathscr{L}_b(\Omega_2, \mathscr{A}_2)$, $\sigma \in L(E)$. E.g. condition (3) follows from

$$\begin{aligned} R_M(1, \sigma) &= (M\sigma)(1) = (M\sigma)(\Omega_2) = M(\sigma^+)(\Omega_2) - M(\sigma^-)(\Omega_2) \\ &= \|M(\sigma^+)\| - \|M(\sigma^-)\| = \|\sigma^+\| - \|\sigma^-\| \\ &= \sigma^+(\Omega_1) - \sigma^-(\Omega_1) = \sigma(\Omega_1). \end{aligned}$$

The converse is not true in general. If R is a randomization then there is a mapping M_R: $L(E) \to ba(\Omega_2, \mathscr{A}_2)$ which is defined by $M_R(\sigma)(f) = R(f, \sigma)$, $f \in \mathscr{L}_b(\Omega_2, \mathscr{A}_2)$, $\sigma \in L(E)$. The map M_R is a positive linear map such that $\|M_R(\sigma)\| = \|\sigma\|$, $\sigma \in L(E)$, $\sigma \geqq 0$. This is an easy consequence of the properties of R.

55.3 Definition. An experiment $F \in \mathscr{E}(T)$ is a *randomization of* E if there is a randomization $R \in \mathscr{B}(E, F)$ such that $Q_t = M_R P_t$ for every $t \in T$.

In Section 24 we have defined randomizations of dominated experiments. The following two assertions imply that both definitions are compatible.

55.4 Lemma. *For every randomization R from E to F there is a stochastic operator M: $L(E) \to L(F)$ such that*

$$\|MP_t - Q_t\| \leqq \|M_R P_t - Q_t\|, \quad t \in T.$$

Proof. By Theorem 41.7 there exists a positive linear operator T: $ba(\Omega_2, \mathscr{A}_2) \to L(F)$ satisfying $\|T\| = 1$, $(T\sigma)(1) = (1)$ if $\sigma \geqq 0$ and $T|L(F) = \mathrm{id}_{L(F)}$. Define $M := T \circ M_R$. Then

$$\begin{aligned}\|MP_t - Q_t\| &= \|TM_R P_t - Q_t\| = \|TM_R P_t - TQ_t\| \\ &= \|T(M_R P_t - Q_t)\| \leqq \|M_R P_t - Q_t\|.\end{aligned}$$

$t \in T$, which proves the assertion. □

55.5 Theorem. *An experiment $F \in \mathscr{E}(T)$ is a randomization of $E \in \mathscr{E}(T)$ iff there is a stochastic operator M: $L(E) \to L(F)$ such that $Q_t = MP_t$ for every $t \in T$.*

55.6 Remarks. (1) The set $\mathscr{B}(E, F)$ can be topologized by the weak topology which is the coarsest topology such that $R \mapsto R(f, \mu)$ is continuous for every $f \in \mathscr{L}_b(\Omega_2, \mathscr{A}_2)$, $\mu \in L(E)$. A similar argument as in Theorem 42.3 for $\mathscr{B}(E, D)$ shows that $\mathscr{B}(E, F)$ is compact for the weak topology.

(2) A subset of $\mathscr{B}(E, F)$ is the set $\mathscr{R}(E, F)$ of all stochastic kernels K: $\Omega_1 \times \mathscr{A}_2 \to [0, 1]$. If $K \in \mathscr{R}(E, F)$ then

$$R_K: (f, \mu) \mapsto \iint f(\omega_2)\, K(\omega_1, d\omega_2)\, \mu(d\omega_1),$$

$f \in \mathscr{L}_b(\Omega_2, \mathscr{A}_2)$, $\mu \in L(E)$, is an element of $\mathscr{B}(E, F)$. A copy of the proof of Theorem 42.5 shows that $\{R_K \in \mathscr{B}(E, F): K \in \mathscr{R}(E, F)\}$ is dense in $\mathscr{B}(E, F)$ for the weak topology. The only difference in the argument is as follows: The functions $f_1, \ldots, f_m$ have to be chosen in $\mathscr{L}_b(\Omega_2, \mathscr{A}_2)$ and w.l.g. we may choose step function. If $C_1, \ldots, C_p$ is an $\mathscr{A}_2$-measurable partition of Ω_2 such that each f_i, $1 \leqq i \leqq m$, is constant on each C_k, $1 \leqq k \leqq p$, then we define $p_k := 1_{C_k}$, $1 \leqq k \leqq p$. Now the proof is literally the same as for Theorem 42.5.

(3) Suppose that E is a dominated experiment and $F = (\Omega_2, \mathscr{A}_2, \{Q_t: t \in T\})$ is such that Ω_2 is a locally compact space with countable base and $\mathscr{A}_2 = \mathscr{B}(\Omega_2)$. Then for every transition M: $L(E) \to L(F)$ there exists a kernel $K \in \mathscr{R}(E, F)$ such that $R_M = R_K$. The proof is easy. Indeed, $R_M \in \mathscr{B}(E, F)$ is such that $R_M(., P_t)$ is a Daniell integral on $\mathscr{C}_b(\Omega_2)$ for every $t \in T$. Then the existence of the kernel K follows similarly to Theorem 42.7.

Now, we approach the important randomization criterion. We follow LeCam [1964].

55.7 Lemma. *Let* $\varepsilon \geqq 0$ *and* $D = [-1, +1]^T$. *If* $E \overset{\varepsilon}{\supseteq} F$ *then for every* $\varrho_2 \in \mathscr{R}(F, D)$ *and every* $m \in S_T$ *there is an* $R \in \mathscr{B}(E, F)$ *such that*

$$\int L_t \varrho_2 (M_R P_t) m(dt) \leqq \int L_t \varrho_2 Q_t m(dt) + \varepsilon.$$

Proof. There is a nonrandomized decision function $\bar{\varrho}_2 \in \mathscr{R}(F, D)$ such that

$$\int L_t \bar{\varrho}_2 Q_t m(dt) = \int L_t \varrho_2 Q_t m(dt).$$

Let $\delta > 0$ be arbitrary. Since $E \overset{\varepsilon}{\supseteq} F$ there exists a nonrandomized simple decision function $\bar{\varrho}_1 \in \mathscr{R}(E, D)$ such that

$$\int L_t \bar{\varrho}_1 P_t m(dt) \leqq \int L_t \bar{\varrho}_2 Q_t m(dt) + \varepsilon + \delta.$$

It may be assumed that $\bar{\varrho}_1$ takes its values in the convex hull of the image of $\bar{\varrho}_2$. Let

$$\bar{\varrho}_1 = \sum_{i=1}^{m} x_i 1_{A_i}$$

where $x_i = \sum_{j=1}^{n} \alpha_{ij} y_j$, $\sum_{j=1}^{n} \alpha_{ij} = 1$, $y_j \in \operatorname{im} \bar{\varrho}_2$, $1 \leqq j \leqq n$, $1 \leqq i \leqq m$.

For every $j \in \{1, 2, \ldots, n\}$ let $\omega_j \in \Omega_2$ be such that $\bar{\varrho}_2(\omega_j) = y_j$. Then we define the randomization R by

$$R(f, \mu) = \sum_{i=1}^{m} \sum_{j=1}^{n} \alpha_{ij} f(\omega_j) \mu(A_i), \; f \in \mathscr{L}^b(\Omega_2, \mathscr{A}_2), \; \mu \in L(E).$$

It is obvious that $R \in \mathscr{B}(E, F)$. Moreover, for $t \in T$ we have

$$\begin{aligned} L_t \varrho_2 (M_R P_t) &= L_t \bar{\varrho}_2 (M_R P_t) = R(L_t \bar{\varrho}_2, P_t) \\ &= \sum_{i=1}^{m} \sum_{j=1}^{n} \alpha_{ij} \varrho_{2,t}(\omega_j) P_t(A_i) \\ &= \sum_{i=1}^{m} \sum_{j=1}^{n} \alpha_{ij} y_{j,t} P_t(A_i) \\ &= \sum_{i=1}^{m} x_{i,t} P_t(A_i) = L_t \bar{\varrho}_1 P_t, \end{aligned}$$

which proves that

$$\int L_t \varrho_2 (M_R P_t) m(dt) \leqq \int L_t \varrho_2 Q_t m(dt) + \varepsilon + \delta.$$

Since $\delta > 0$ was arbitrary we obtain

$$\inf_{R \in \mathscr{B}(E, F)} \left(\int L_t \varrho_2 (M_R P_t) m(dt) - \int L_t \varrho_2 Q_t m(dt) \right) \leqq \varepsilon.$$

Now the assertion follows since the infimum is attained on the compact set $\mathscr{B}(E, F)$. □

55.8 Lemma. *If $E \overset{\varepsilon}{\supseteq} F$ then for every $m \in S_T$ there exists a randomization $R \in \mathscr{B}(E, F)$ such that*

$$\int \|M_R P_t - Q_t\| m(dt) \leqq \varepsilon .$$

Proof. Let $D = [-1, +1]^T$. For convenience we denote

$$\Phi(M_R, \varrho, m) = \int L_t \varrho(M_R P_t) m(dt) - \int L_t \varrho\, Q_t m(dt)$$

if $R \in \mathscr{B}(E, F)$, $\varrho \in \mathscr{R}(F, D)$ and $m \in S_T$. Then the preceding assertion implies

$$\sup_{\varrho \in \mathscr{R}(F, D)} \inf_{R \in \mathscr{B}(E, F)} \Phi(M_R, \varrho, m) \leqq \varepsilon .$$

From the Minimax Theorem (Theorem 45.8) we obtain

$$\inf_{R \in \mathscr{B}(E, F)} \sup_{\varrho \in \mathscr{R}(F, D)} \Phi(M_R, \varrho, m) \leqq \varepsilon$$

for every $m \in S_T$. Since $R \mapsto \sup_{\varrho \in \mathscr{R}(F, D)} \Phi(M_R, \varrho, m)$ is lower semcontinuous on the compact set $\mathscr{B}(E, F)$ the infimum is attained. It remains to show that for every $R \in \mathscr{B}(E, F)$ and every $m \in S_T$

$$\sup_{\varrho \in \mathscr{R}(F, D)} \Phi(M_R, \varrho, m) = \int \|M_R P_t - Q_t\| m(dt).$$

First we note that obviously

$$\Phi(M_R, \varrho, m) \leqq \int \|M_R P_t - Q_t\| m(dt)$$

for every $\varrho \in \mathscr{R}(F, D)$. On the other hand, for $\varepsilon > 0$ and for every $t \in T$ there is a function $f_t \in \mathscr{L}_b(\Omega_2, \mathscr{A}_2)$, $\|f_t\|_u \leqq 1$, such that

$$\int f_t d(M_R P_t) - \int f_t dQ_t \geqq \|M_R P_t - Q_t\| - \varepsilon .$$

Let $\varrho_\varepsilon \in \mathscr{R}(F, D)$ be the nonrandomized decision function which is defined by $\varrho_\varepsilon = (f_t)_{t \in T}$ then we obtain

$$\Phi(M_R, \varrho_\varepsilon, m) \geqq \int \|M_R P_t - Q_t\| m(dt) - \varepsilon .$$

This proves the assertion. □

The following theorem is the randomization criterion. In the light of Sections 22–25 it solves the problem of „approximate sufficiency".

55.9 Theorem. (LeCam [1964]). *Let $\varepsilon \geqq 0$. Then $E \overset{\varepsilon}{\supseteq} F$ holds iff there exists $R \in \mathscr{B}(E, F)$ such that*

$$\|M_R P_t - Q_t\| \leqq \varepsilon \quad \textit{for every } t \in T .$$

Proof. (1) Assume that $E \overset{\varepsilon}{\supseteq} F$. Then we obtain from the preceding assertion that

$$\sup_{m \in S_T} \inf_{R \in \mathscr{B}(E,F)} \int \|M_R P_t - Q_t\| m(dt) \leqq \varepsilon .$$

We apply Corollary 45.7 with $\mathscr{M}^1_{00}(T) = S_T$. Let $M_1 = \{\varepsilon\}$ and

$$M_2 = \{(\|M_R P_t - Q_t\|)_{t \in T} \colon R \in \mathscr{B}(E, F)\} .$$

Clearly, M_2 is subconvex. The assumption implies $\psi_{M_2}(m) \leqq \psi_{M_1}(m)$ for every $m \in S_T$. The proof is finished if $\alpha(M_2)$ is closed in $\mathbb{R}^T$. But this is a consequence of Remark 45.4 if we put

$$f(t, R) = \|M_R P_t - Q_t\|, \quad t \in T, \quad R \in \mathscr{B}(E, F) .$$

(2) Assume that there is $R \in \mathscr{B}(E, F)$ such that $\|M_R P_t - Q_t\| \leqq \varepsilon$ for every $t \in T$. Let D be an arbitrary decision space. Then for every $\varrho_2 \in \mathscr{R}(F, D)$

$$\beta \colon \mathscr{C}_b(D) \times L(E) \to \mathbb{R} \colon (f, \mu) \mapsto f \varrho_2(M_2 \mu)$$

is an element of $\mathscr{B}(E, D)$ and it satisfies

$$\beta(W_t, P_t) \leqq W_t \varrho_2 Q_t + \varepsilon \|W_t\|$$

for every bounded continuous loss function $W \colon D \times T \to \mathbb{R}$. □

The range of M_R can be restricted to $L(F)$, thus obtaining the following extension of Theorem 25.6. For finite T, the second part is due to Blackwell [1953].

55.10 Corollary. (LeCam [1964]). (1) *Let $\varepsilon \geqq 0$. Then $E \overset{\varepsilon}{\supseteq} F$ iff there exists a stochastic operator M: $L(E) \to L(F)$ such that*

$$\|M P_t - Q_t\| \leqq \varepsilon \quad \text{if} \quad t \in T .$$

(2) *$E \supseteq F$ iff there exists a stochastic operator M: $L(E) \to L(F)$ such that $M P_t = Q_t$, $t \in T$.*

Proof. Theorem 55.9 and Lemma 55.4. □

The following version is in the spirit of Heyer [1982] and related to the concept of exhaustivity (see Section 23).

55.11 Corollary. *Suppose that E is a dominated experiment and $F = (\Omega_2, \mathscr{A}_2, \{Q_t \colon t \in T\})$ is such that Ω_2 is a locally compact space with countable base and $\mathscr{A}_2 = \mathscr{B}(\Omega_2)$.*

(1) *Let* $\varepsilon \geqq 0$. *Then* $E \overset{\varepsilon}{\supseteq} F$ *iff there exists a stochastic kernel* $K: \Omega_1 \times \mathscr{A}_2 \to [0,1]$ *such that*

$$\|KP_t - Q_t\| \leqq \varepsilon, \quad t \in T.$$

(2) $E \supseteq F$ *iff there exists a stochastic kernel* $K: \Omega_1 \times \mathscr{A}_2 \to [0,1]$ *such that*

$$KP_t = Q_t, \quad t \in T.$$

Proof. Corollary 55.10 and Remark 55.6 (3). □

As an application we prove a generalization of the convolution theorem.

55.12 Theorem. *Suppose that G is a locally compact group with countable base and* $P \ll \lambda_r$. *Let* $E = (G, \mathscr{B}(G), \{\varepsilon_g * P: g \in G\})$ *and* $F = (G, \mathscr{B}(G), \{\varepsilon_g * Q: g \in G\})$. *If G is amenable the the following assertions are valid:*

(1) (Torgersen [1972]) *Let* $\varepsilon \geqq 0$. *Then* $E \overset{\varepsilon}{\supseteq} F$ *iff there exists a probability measure* $K|\mathscr{B}(G)$ *such that* $\|P * K - Q\| \leqq \varepsilon$.

(2) (Boll [1955]) $E \supseteq F$ *iff there exists a probability measure* $K|\mathscr{B}(G)$ *such that* $P * K = Q$.

Proof. It is sufficient to prove (1). If there is a probability measure K such that $\|K * P - Q\| \leqq \varepsilon$ then it is clear that

$$\|\varepsilon_g * P * K - \varepsilon_g * Q\| = \|P * K - Q\| \leqq \varepsilon, \quad g \in G,$$

which implies $E \overset{\varepsilon}{\supseteq} F$ since $\mu \mapsto \mu * K$, $\mu \in L(E)$, defines a randomization from E to F. Assume conversely, that $E \overset{\varepsilon}{\supseteq} F$ and let R be a transition from E to F such that

$$\|M_R(\varepsilon_g * P) - (\varepsilon_g * Q)\| \leqq \varepsilon, \quad g \in G.$$

In view of Remark 55.6 (3), R can be supposed to be a kernel.

Let $(K_n)_{n \in \mathbb{N}}$ be a summing sequence of compact subsets of G. Define randomizations R_n from E to F, $n \in \mathbb{N}$, by

$$R_n(f, \mu) := \frac{1}{\lambda(K_n)} \int_{K_n} R(f \circ g^{-1}, \varepsilon_g * \mu)\, \lambda_r(dg),$$

$f \in \mathscr{L}_b(G, \mathscr{B}(G))$, $\mu \in L(E)$. Let $R_0 \in \mathscr{B}(E, F)$ be any weak accumulation point of $(R_n)_{n \in \mathbb{N}}$. Standard arguments yield $R_0(f \circ g^{-1}, \varepsilon_g * \mu) = R_0(f, \mu)$ if $f \in \mathscr{L}_b(G, \mathscr{B}(G))$ and $\mu \in L(E)$. Moreover, since the variational norm is lower semicontinuous for the $\mathscr{L}_b$-topology of $ba(G, \mathscr{B}(G))$, it follows that

$$\|M_{R_0} P - Q\| \leqq \limsup_{n \to \infty} \|M_{R_n} P - Q\|$$
$$\leqq \sup_{g \in G} \|M_R(\varepsilon_g * P) - (\varepsilon_g * Q)\| \leqq \varepsilon.$$

Next, we replace M_{R_0} by a stochastic kernel $\varrho \in \mathscr{R}(E, G)$. Let ϱ_0: $G \times \mathscr{B}(G) \to [0,1]$ be a kernel such that

$$R_0(f, \mu) = f\varrho_0\mu, \quad f \in \mathscr{C}_{00}(G), \ \mu \in L(E).$$

Define

$$\varrho(x, B) := \varrho_0(x, B) + (1 - \varrho_0(x, G))\, 1_B(x), \quad x \in G, \ B \in \mathscr{B}(G).$$

It is then clear that ϱ is strictly equivariant and hence there exists a probability measure $K|\mathscr{B}(G)$ such that $\varrho P = P * K$ (use Theorem 48.9 and cf. Remark 38.11 (1)). Moreover, we have

$$\begin{aligned} \|P * K - Q\| &= \|\varrho P - Q\| = |\varrho P - Q|(1) \\ &\leqq |\varrho_0 P - Q|(1) + (1 - \textstyle\int \varrho_0(., G)\, dP). \end{aligned}$$

Note that $\varrho_0 P \leqq M_{R_0} P$ and that $M_{R_0} P - \varrho_0 P$ is orthogonal to $\varrho_0 P - Q$. This implies that

$$1 - \textstyle\int \varrho_0(., G)\, dP = (M_{R_0} P)(1) - (\varrho_0 P)(1) = |M_{R_0} P - \varrho_0 P|(1)$$

and hence

$$\begin{aligned} \|P * K - Q\| &\leqq |\varrho_0 P - Q|(1) + |M_{R_0} P - \varrho_0 P|(1) \\ &= \|\varrho_0 P - Q\| + \|M_{R_0} P - \varrho_0 P\| = \|M_{R_0} P - Q\| \leqq \varepsilon. \end{aligned}$$

This proves the assertion. □

55.13 Remark. The assertion of Theorem 38.15 is a particular case of the preceding result. Let E be a full shift on an amenable group G then every equivariant estimate $\varrho \in \mathscr{R}(E, G)$ defines a full shift experiment $F = (G, \mathscr{B}, (G), \{\varepsilon_g * Q := g \in G\})$ with $Q = \varrho P$. Obviously, $E \supseteq F$ and hence the assertion by part (2) of Theorem 55.12.

Let $E = (\Omega_1, \mathscr{A}_1, \{P_t: t \in T\})$ and $F = (\Omega_2, \mathscr{A}_2, \{Q_t: t \in T\})$ be experiments in $\mathscr{E}(T)$ and assume that $E \supseteq F$. Then there is a transition M: $L(E) \to L(F)$ such that $MP_t = Q_t$, $t \in T$. It is clear that the transition M is uniquely determined on $\overline{\text{span}}\, \{P_t: t \in T\}$. The following improves this fact. We follow LeCam [1974].

Let $\mathscr{H}_0(T)$ be the set of all lower envelopes of finite subsets of $(\mathbb{R}^T)^*$ and let $\mathscr{H}(T)$ be the vector lattice which is generated by $\{p_t: t \in T\}$, where p_t: $\mathbb{R}^T \to \mathbb{R}$ denotes the projection onto the tth coordinate, $t \in T$.

55.14 Lemma. $\mathscr{H}(T) = \mathscr{H}_0(T) - \mathscr{H}_0(T)$.

Proof. It is clear that $\mathscr{H}_0(T) - \mathscr{H}_0(T) \subseteq \mathscr{H}(T)$. We have to show that $\mathscr{H}_0(T) - \mathscr{H}_0(T)$ is a vector lattice. Since $\mathscr{H}_0(T)$ is a convex cone the difference $\mathscr{H}_0(T) - \mathscr{H}_0(T)$ is a vector space. From

$$(\psi - \varphi)^+ = \psi - \psi \cap \varphi,$$
$$(\psi - \varphi)^- = \psi \cup \varphi - \varphi,$$

it follows that it is even a vector lattice. □

In the following we denote by $\mathrm{Lat}(E)$ the vector lattice which is generated by $\{P_t: t \in T\}$.

55.15 Lemma. *Let* $E = (\Omega, \mathscr{A}, \{P_t: t \in T\})$ *be an experiment. There exists exactly one vector lattice homomorphism* $\mathscr{H}(T) \to \mathrm{Lat}(E)$: $\varphi \mapsto P_\varphi$ *satisfying* $p_t \mapsto P_t$, $t \in T$.

Proof. Uniqueness is clear since $\{p_t: t \in T\}$ generates $\mathscr{H}(T)$. For proving existence define (see Definition 52.5)

$$P_\varphi := (\varphi \circ T_\alpha) \cdot \sum_{t \in \alpha} P_t$$

whenever $\varphi \in \mathscr{H}(T)$ depends only on the coordinates of $\alpha \in A(T)$, i.e. $\varphi \circ p_\alpha = \varphi$.

Since every $\varphi \in \mathscr{H}(T)$ is homogeneous it follows that P_φ is well defined. If $\varphi, \psi \in \mathscr{H}(T)$ and $\alpha \in A(T)$ is such that $\varphi \circ p_\alpha = \varphi$, $\psi \circ p_\alpha = \psi$, then the relations

$$P_{\xi\varphi + \eta\psi} = \xi P_\varphi + \eta P_\psi,$$
$$P_{\varphi \cap \psi} = P_\varphi \cap P_\psi,$$
$$P_{\varphi \cup \psi} = P_\varphi \cup P_\psi,$$

are obvious. This proves that $\varphi \mapsto P_\varphi$ is a lattice homomorphism. □

55.16 Theorem. (LeCam [1974]). *Let E and F be equivalent experiments in* $\mathscr{E}(T)$. *If* $M: L(E) \to L(F)$ *is a transition such that* $MP_t = Q_t$, $t \in T$, *then M is uniquely determined on* $\overline{\mathrm{Lat}(E)}$ *and it is an isometric Banach lattice isomorphism from* $\overline{\mathrm{Lat}(E)}$ *onto* $\overline{\mathrm{Lat}(F)}$.

Proof. If $\varphi \in \mathscr{H}_0(T)$ then there are $\{a_{t,i}: 1 \leqq i \leqq m, t \in \alpha\} \subseteq \mathbb{R}$ such that $P_\varphi = \min_{1 \leqq i \leqq m} \sum_{t \in \alpha} a_{t,i} P_t$. It follows that $MP_\varphi \leqq Q_\varphi$ for every $\varphi \in \mathscr{H}_0(T)$ since M is a positive operator. Moreover, we observe that for every $\varphi \in \mathscr{H}_0(T)$, $\varphi \circ p_\alpha = \varphi$,

$$P_\varphi(1) = \int \varphi \, d\sigma_\alpha = \int \varphi \, d\tau_\alpha = Q_\varphi(1).$$

This equation holds even for every $\varphi \in \mathscr{H}(T)$. Hence we obtain for $\varphi \in \mathscr{H}_0(T)$

$$\begin{aligned}\|Q_\varphi - MP_\varphi\| &= (Q_\varphi - MP_\varphi)(1) \\ &= Q_\varphi(1) - MP_\varphi(1) = Q_\varphi(1) - P_\varphi(1) = 0\end{aligned}$$

which implies $Q_\varphi = MP_\varphi$ if $\varphi \in \mathscr{H}_0(T)$ and therefore also if $\varphi \in \mathscr{H}(T)$.

It is obvious that Lat $(E) = \{P_\varphi : \varphi \in \mathscr{H}(T)\}$ and Lat $(F) = \{Q_\varphi : \varphi \in \mathscr{H}(T)\}$. Hence M is uniquely determined on Lat (E) and for reasons of continuity on $\overline{\text{Lat}}\,(E)$. It is clear that it is a Banach lattice homomorphism.

The proof is finished if we show that M is isometric on Lat (E). Since $Q_\varphi = MP_\varphi$ it is sufficient to show that $\|Q_\varphi\| = \|P_\varphi\|$ for every $\varphi \in \mathscr{H}(T)$. Since $\varphi \mapsto P_\varphi$ and $\varphi \mapsto Q_\varphi$ are lattice homomorphisms we have $P_{\varphi^+} = (P_\varphi)^+$, etc. ... It follows that

$$\begin{aligned}\|P_\varphi\| &= (P_\varphi)^+(1) + (P_\varphi)^-(1) = P_{\varphi^+}(1) + P_{\varphi^-}(1) \\ &= Q_{\varphi^+}(1) + Q_{\varphi^-}(1) = (Q_\varphi)^+(1) + (Q_\varphi)^-(1) = \|Q_\varphi\|\end{aligned}$$

for every $\varphi \in \mathscr{H}(T)$. □

If E is an arbitrary experiment then $L(E) \supseteq \overline{\text{Lat}\,(E)}$. It will be proved in the following sections that for every $E \in \mathscr{E}(T)$ there is an experiment $F \sim E$ such that $L(F) = \overline{\text{Lat}\,(F)}$.

A property of an experiment E is *hereditary* if also any experiment $F \subseteq E$ has this property.

55.17 Corollary. *Domination is an hereditary property, i.e. if E is dominated and $F \subseteq E$, then F is dominated, too.*

Proof. Let $E = (\Omega_1, \mathscr{A}_1, \mathscr{P} = \{P_t : t \in T\})$ be dominated. Then there exists $\nu \in L(E)$ such that $P_t \ll \nu$, $t \in T$. From Lemma 20.3 it follows, that we may assume $\nu \in \overline{\text{span}\,\mathscr{P}} \subseteq \overline{\text{Lat}\,E}$. Domination implies that for every $t \in T$

$$\begin{aligned}\lim_{k\to\infty} \|P_t - P_t \cap (k\nu)\| &= \lim_{k\to\infty} \int \left| \frac{dP_t}{d\nu} - \frac{dP_t}{d\nu} \cap k \right| d\nu \\ &= \lim_{k\to\infty} \int_{\frac{dP_t}{d\nu} \geq k} \left| \frac{dP_t}{d\nu} - k \right| d\nu = 0 .\end{aligned}$$

Let $F = (\Omega_2, \mathscr{A}_2, \{Q_t : t \in T\})$ and $M: L(E) \to L(F)$ be a transition such that $MP_t = Q_t$, $t \in T$. From Theorem 55.16 we obtain $M(P_t - P_t \cap (k\nu)) = MP_t - MP_t \cap kM\nu = Q_t - Q_t \cap kM\nu$, $t \in T$, and therefore

$$\lim_{k\to\infty} \|Q_t - Q_t \cap kM\nu\| = \lim_{k\to\infty} \|P_t - P_t \cap k\nu\| = 0, \quad t \in T.$$

This implies $Q_t \ll M\nu$, $t \in T$. □

56. Conical measures

The concept of conical measures is the technical key for a satisfactory representation theory of experiment types. In the present section we consider conical measures from a general point of view. They are discussed from the statistical point of view in Section 57.

Let $T \neq \emptyset$ be an arbitrary set. Recall that $\mathscr{H}_0(T)$ denotes the set of all lower envelopes of subsets of $(\mathbb{R}^T)^*$ and let $\mathscr{H}(T)$ be the vector lattice which is generated by the projections $\{p_t: t \in T\}$. From Lemma 55.14 we obtain that $\mathscr{H}(T) = \mathscr{H}_0(T) - \mathscr{H}_0(T)$.

56.1 Definition. A positive linear form M on $\mathscr{H}(T)$ is called a *conical measure*. The point $(Mp_t)_{t \in T} \subseteq \mathbb{R}^T$ is called the *resultant* of the conical measure.

We will prove the basic fact that every conical measure can be represented by some measure on the σ-field $\bigotimes_{t \in T} \mathscr{B}(\mathbb{R})$ which is generated by $\{p_t: t \in T\}$.

56.2 Lemma. *Let M be a conical measure. Then $\mathscr{N} = \{\varphi \in \mathscr{H}(T): M(|\varphi|) = 0\}$ is a vector lattice and $\tilde{C} = \{\tilde{\varphi} \in \mathscr{H}(T)/\mathscr{N}: \varphi \geqq 0\}$ is a proper cone, i.e. a convex cone with vertex $\tilde{0}$ satisfying $\tilde{C} \cap (-\tilde{C}) = \{\tilde{0}\}$.*

Proof. It is clear that $\mathscr{N}$ is a vector space. The relations

$$-(|\varphi_1| + |\varphi_2|) \leqq \varphi_1 \cap \varphi_2 \leqq \varphi_1 \cup \varphi_2 \leqq |\varphi_1| + |\varphi_2|$$

imply that $\mathscr{N}$ is even a vector lattice. The fact that $\tilde{C}$ is a convex cone of vertex $\tilde{0}$ follows because the mapping $\varphi \mapsto \tilde{\varphi}$ is linear. We have to show that $\tilde{C} \cap (-\tilde{C}) = \{\tilde{0}\}$. Let $\tilde{\varphi} \in \tilde{C} \cap (-\tilde{C})$. Then there are $\varphi_1 \in \tilde{\varphi}$, $\varphi_1 \geqq 0$, and $\varphi_2 \in \tilde{\varphi}$, $\varphi_2 \leqq 0$. Since $\varphi_1 - \varphi_2 \in \mathscr{N}$ we have $M(|\varphi_1 - \varphi_2|) = 0$. But $|\varphi_1 - \varphi_2| = |\varphi_1| + |\varphi_2|$ implies $\varphi_1 \in \mathscr{N}$, $\varphi_2 \in \mathscr{N}$, which proves the assertion. □

56.3 Lemma. *Let M be a conical measure. Then*

$$\tilde{\varphi}_1 \leqq \tilde{\varphi}_2 \quad \textit{iff} \quad \tilde{\varphi}_2 - \tilde{\varphi}_1 \in \tilde{C}$$

defines an order relation such that $\mathscr{H}(T)/\mathscr{N}$ is a vector lattice and $\varphi \mapsto \tilde{\varphi}$ is a vector lattice homomorphism.

Proof. It is clear that the relation "$\leqq$" on $\mathscr{H}(T)/\mathscr{N}$ is an order relation. For the second part we show that $(\varphi_1 \cup \varphi_2)^{\sim}$ is the least upper bound of $\tilde{\varphi}_1$ and $\tilde{\varphi}_2$. It is clear that $(\varphi_1 \cup \varphi_2)^{\sim} \geqq \tilde{\varphi}_1$ and $(\varphi_1 \cup \varphi_2)^{\sim} \geqq \tilde{\varphi}_2$. Let conversely $\tilde{\varphi}$ be any upper bound of $\{\tilde{\varphi}_1, \tilde{\varphi}_2\}$. Then $\tilde{\varphi} \geqq \tilde{\varphi}_1$ and $\tilde{\varphi} \geqq \tilde{\varphi}_2$ and therefore $\tilde{\varphi} - \tilde{\varphi}_1 \in \tilde{C}$ and $\tilde{\varphi} - \tilde{\varphi}_2 \in \tilde{C}$. In other words there are $\psi_1 \in \mathscr{N}$ and $\psi_2 \in \mathscr{N}$ such that

$$\varphi \geqq \varphi_1 + \psi_1, \quad \varphi \geqq \varphi_2 + \psi_2.$$

It follows that $(\varphi-\varphi_1)\cap(\varphi-\varphi_2)\geqq\psi_1\cap\psi_2$ and therefore $\varphi-(\varphi_1\cup\varphi_2)\geqq\psi_1\cap\psi_2\in\mathcal{N}$. Hence $\tilde{\varphi}\geqq(\varphi_1\cup\varphi_2)^\sim$. A similar argument shows that $(\varphi_1\cap\varphi_2)^\sim$ is the greatest lower bound of φ_1 and φ_2. □

56.4 Theorem (Choquet). *For every conical measure M there is a measure $\mu|\bigotimes_{t\in T}\mathscr{B}(\mathbb{R})$ such that $M\varphi=\int\varphi\,d\mu$ if $\varphi\in\mathscr{H}(T)$.*

Proof. The function $\varphi\mapsto M(|\varphi|)$ is a seminorm on $\mathscr{H}(T)$ which satisfies $M(\varphi_1+\varphi_2)=M\varphi_1+M\varphi_2$ if $\varphi_1\geqq 0$, $\varphi_2\geqq 0$. Let $H(T):=\mathscr{H}(T)/\mathcal{N}$ be the normed space with norm $\|\tilde{\varphi}\|_M:=M(|\varphi|)$. The completion $\hat{H}(T)$ of $H(T)$ with respect to $\|.\|_M$ is an Abstract L-space. Hence, by Theorem 6.9, there exists a measure space $(\Omega,\mathscr{A},\lambda)$ and a vector lattice isomorphism $\Phi\colon\hat{H}(T)\to L_1(\Omega,\mathscr{A},\lambda)$. Let us define

$$S\colon\mathscr{H}(T)\to L_1(\Omega,\mathscr{A},\lambda)\colon\varphi\mapsto\Phi(\tilde{\varphi}).$$

For every $\varphi\in\mathscr{H}_+(T)$ we have

$$M\varphi=\|\tilde{\varphi}\|_M=\int\Phi(\tilde{\varphi})\,d\lambda=\int S\varphi\,d\lambda.$$

We note the relation $S\varphi=\varphi\circ(Sp_t)_{t\in T}$ for every $\varphi\in\mathscr{H}(T)$. Indeed, the set of functions which satisfy the relation is a vector lattice which contains $\{p_t\colon t\in T\}$. If we define $\mu=\mathscr{L}((Sp_t)_{t\in T}|\lambda)$ then we obtain

$$M\varphi=\int S\varphi\,d\lambda=\int\varphi\circ(Sp_t)_{t\in T}\,d\lambda=\int\varphi\,d\mu$$

for every $\varphi\in\mathscr{H}(T)$. □

56.5 Corollary. *If $\mu|\bigotimes_{t\in T}\mathscr{B}(\mathbb{R})$ is constructed as in Theorem 56.4 then $\mathscr{H}(T)$ is dense in $L_1(\mu)$.*

Proof. Let $\varepsilon>0$. Since $H(T)$ is dense in $\hat{H}(T)$ and $\hat{H}(T)$ is lattice isomorphic to $L_1(\lambda)$, for every $g\in L_1(\lambda)$ there is $\varphi\in\mathscr{H}(T)$ such that $\|S\varphi-g\|_1<\varepsilon$. If $f\in L_1(\mu)$ then denote $g:=f\circ(Sp_t)_{t\in T}$ and let $\varphi\in\mathscr{H}(T)$ be such that $\|S\varphi-g\|_1<\varepsilon$. Then

$$\begin{aligned}\|\varphi-f\|_1&=\int|\varphi-f|\,d\mu=\int|\varphi\circ(Sp_t)_{t\in T}-f\circ(Sp_t)_{t\in T}|\,d\lambda\\&=\int|S\varphi-g|\,d\lambda<\varepsilon.\end{aligned}$$ □

57. Representation of experiments

Let us consider experiments $E\in\mathscr{E}(T)$ where $T\neq\emptyset$ is an arbitrary parameter set. The system of standard measures of an experiment satisfies a consistency relation. We note that a function $\varphi \in \mathscr{H}(T)$ depends on the coordinates $t \in \alpha$ only, $\alpha \subseteq A(T)$, if $\varphi \circ p_\alpha = \varphi$. Thereby $p_\alpha: \mathbb{R}^T \to \mathbb{R}^\alpha$ denotes the natural projection.

57.1 Lemma. *If $(\sigma_\alpha)_{\alpha \in A(T)}$ is the system of standard measures of an experiment $E \in \mathscr{E}(T)$ then it is consistent, i.e. it satisfies any of the following equivalent conditions:*

(1) $H(\sigma_\alpha)(z) = H(\sigma_\beta)(z)$ *if* $z \in S_\alpha \cap S_\beta$, $\alpha, \beta \in A(T)$.

(2) $\int \varphi \, d\sigma_\alpha = \int \varphi \, d\sigma_\beta$ *iff* $\alpha, \beta \in A(T)$, $\varphi \in \mathscr{H}(T)$ *and* $\varphi \circ p_\alpha = \varphi \circ p_\beta = \varphi$.

(3) $\sigma_\alpha = \mathscr{L}\left(\left(\frac{p_t}{\sum\limits_{s \in \alpha} p_s}\right)_{s \in \alpha} \Bigg| \left(\sum_{s \in \alpha} p_s\right) \sigma_\beta\right)$ *if* $\alpha \subseteq \beta$, $\alpha, \beta \in A(T)$.

Proof. First, we show that $(\sigma_\alpha)_{\alpha \in A(T)}$ necessarily satisfies condition (2). We may assume that $\alpha \subseteq \beta$. If we keep in mind that φ is positively homogeneous then it follows that

$$\int_{S_\alpha} \varphi \, d\sigma_\alpha = \int_\Omega \varphi\left(\left(\frac{dP_t}{d\sum\limits_{s \in \alpha} P_s}\right)_{t \in \alpha}\right) d\sum_{s \in \alpha} P_s$$

$$= \int_\Omega \varphi\left(\left(\frac{dP_t}{d\sum\limits_{s \in \alpha} P_s}\right)_{t \in \alpha}\right) \frac{d\sum\limits_{s \in \alpha} P_s}{d\sum\limits_{s \in \beta} P_s} \, d\sum_{s \in \beta} P_s$$

$$= \int_\Omega \varphi\left(\left(\frac{dP_t}{d\sum\limits_{s \in \alpha} P_s}\right)_{t \in \alpha} \frac{d\sum\limits_{s \in \alpha} P_s}{d\sum\limits_{s \in \beta} P_s}\right) d\sum_{s \in \beta} P_s$$

$$= \int_\Omega \varphi\left(\left(\frac{dP_t}{d\sum\limits_{s \in \beta} P_s}\right)_{t \in \alpha}\right) d\sum_{s \in \beta} P_s$$

$$= \int_\Omega \varphi\left(\left(\frac{dP_t}{d\sum\limits_{s \in \beta} P_s}\right)_{t \in \beta}\right) d\sum_{s \in \beta} P_s = \int_{S_\beta} \varphi \, d\sigma_\beta .$$

Next, let us prove the equivalence of (1) – (3).

(1) $\Rightarrow$ (3): Let $\alpha \subseteq \beta$, $\alpha, \beta \in A(T)$, $z \in S_\alpha$. Then

$$H(\sigma_\alpha)(z) = H(\sigma_\beta)(z) = \int_{S_\beta} \prod_{t\in\alpha} x_t^{z_t}\,\sigma_\beta(dx)$$

$$= \int_{S_\beta} \prod_{t\in\alpha} \left(\frac{x_t}{\sum_{s\in\alpha} x_s}\right)^{z_t} \left(\sum_{s\in\alpha} x_s\right) \sigma_\beta(dx)$$

$$= \int_{S_\alpha} \prod_{t\in\alpha} x_t^{z_t}\, \mathscr{L}\left(\left(\frac{p_t}{\sum_{s\in\alpha} p_s}\right)_{t\in\alpha} \middle| \left(\sum_{s\in\alpha} p_s\right)\sigma_\beta\right)(dx).$$

(3) ⇒ (2): This is similar to the proof of necessity of (2).
(2) ⇒ (1): Use Lemma 52.9. □

57.2 Corollary. *Let $(\sigma_\alpha)_{\alpha\in A(T)}$ be the system of standard measures of an experiment $E\in\mathscr{E}(T)$. Then*

$$M\varphi := \int \varphi\, d\sigma_\alpha \quad \textit{if} \quad \varphi\in\mathscr{H}(T) \quad \textit{and} \quad \varphi = \varphi\circ p_\alpha$$

is a conical measure of resultant $Mp_t = 1$, $t\in T$.

57.3 Definition. Let $E\in\mathscr{E}(T)$. Then the conical measure which is defined in Corollary 57.2 is the *conical measure of E* and is denoted by M_E.

57.4 Example. If $E = (\Omega, \mathscr{A}, \{P_t : t\in T\})$ is a dominated experiment then its conical measure can be given in a simpler form. Let $P_0|\mathscr{A}$ be a probability measure dominating $\mathscr{P}$. Let $\alpha\in A(T)$. For every $\varphi\in\mathscr{H}(T)$, $\varphi\circ p_\alpha = \varphi$, we have

$$M_E(\varphi) = \int \varphi\left(\left(\frac{dP_t}{d\sum_{s\in\alpha} P_s}\right)_{t\in\alpha}\right) d\sum_{s\in\alpha} P_s$$

$$= \int \varphi\left(\left(\frac{dP_t}{d\sum_{s\in\alpha} P_s}\right)_{t\in\alpha}\right) \frac{d\sum_{s\in\alpha} P_s}{dP_0}\, dP_0$$

$$= \int \varphi\left(\left(\frac{dP_t}{d\sum_{s\in\alpha} P_s}\,\frac{d\sum_{s\in\alpha} P_s}{dP_0}\right)_{t\in\alpha}\right) dP_0$$

$$= \int \varphi\left(\left(\frac{dP_t}{dP_0}\right)_{t\in\alpha}\right) dP_0.$$

We obtain a characterization of dominated experiments in terms of their conical measures.

57.5 Theorem. *An experiment $E \in \mathscr{E}(T)$ is dominated iff there exists a bounded measure $\mu | \bigotimes_{t \in T} \mathscr{B}(\mathbb{R}_+)$ such that*

$$M_E(\varphi) = \int \varphi \, d\mu, \quad \varphi \in \mathscr{H}(T).$$

Proof. (1) If E is dominated take a probability measure $P_0 | \mathscr{A}$ such that $\mathscr{P} \ll P_0$ and define $\mu = \mathscr{L}\left(\left(\frac{dP_t}{dP_0}\right)_{t \in T} \middle| P_0\right)$. Then Example (57.4) proves the assertion.

(2) Let $\mu | \bigotimes_{t \in T} \mathscr{B}(\mathbb{R}_+)$ be a bounded measure such that

$$M_E(\varphi) = \int \varphi \, d\mu, \quad \varphi \in \mathscr{H}(T).$$

Define $F = (\mathbb{R}_+^T, \bigotimes_{t \in T} \mathscr{B}(\mathbb{R}_+), \{Q_t: t \in T\})$ by $Q_t = p_t \mu$, $t \in T$. Then Q_t, $t \in T$, are probability measures since

$$\int p_t \, d\mu = M_E p_t = 1, \quad t \in T.$$

It is clear that μ dominates $\{Q_t: t \in T\}$. Moreover, we have $M_E = M_F$, since for $\varphi \circ p_\alpha = \varphi$, $\alpha \in A(T)$,

$$M_E \varphi = \int \varphi \, d\mu = \int \varphi \left(\left(\frac{p_t}{\sum_{s \in \alpha} p_s}\right)_{t \in \alpha}\right) \sum_{s \in \alpha} p_s \, d\mu = M_F \varphi.$$

This implies $E \sim F$ (Corollary 52.8) and by Corollary 55.17, E is dominated. □

57.6 Corollary. *If $E \in \mathscr{E}(T)$ is dominated then there exists a probability measure $Q_0 | \bigotimes_{t \in T} \mathscr{B}(\mathbb{R}_+)$ such that $F = (\mathbb{R}_+^T, \bigotimes_{t \in T} \mathscr{B}(\mathbb{R}_+), \{p_t Q_0: t \in T\})$ is equivalent to E.*

Is every conical measure the conical measure of an experiment? The following assertion settles this question.

57.7 Theorem (LeCam [1974]). *For every conical measure M on $\mathscr{H}(T)$ with resultant $Mp_t = 1$, $t \in T$, there is an experiment $E \in \mathscr{E}(T)$ such that $M = M_E$.*

Proof (Siebert [1979]). According to Theorem 56.4 there is a measure μ on $\bigotimes_{t \in T} \mathscr{B}(\mathbb{R})$ such that $M\varphi = \int \varphi \, d\mu$ if $\varphi \in \mathscr{H}(T)$. Let $E = (\Omega, \mathscr{A}, \{P_t: t \in T\})$ with $\Omega = \mathbb{R}^T$, $\mathscr{A} = \bigotimes_{t \in T} \mathscr{B}(\mathbb{R})$ and $P_t = p_t \mu$, $t \in T$. Obviously, P_t is a probability measure for every $t \in T$. Since every $\varphi \in \mathscr{H}(T)$ is positively homogeneous it follows that

$$M\varphi = \int \varphi \, d\mu = \int \varphi\left(\left(\frac{p_t}{\sum\limits_{s\in\alpha} p_s}\right)_{t\in\alpha}\right) \sum_{s\in\alpha} p_s \, d\mu$$

if $\varphi = \varphi \circ p_\alpha$. This proves $M = M_E$. □

The experiment E just constructed need not be dominated since μ need not be σ-finite.

57.8 Corollary. *Let $(\sigma_\alpha)_{\alpha \in A(T)}$ be a system of probability measures on $\bigotimes_{t\in T} \mathscr{B}(\mathbb{R})$ such that $\sigma_\alpha(S_\alpha) = 1$ if $\alpha \in A(T)$. Then $(\sigma_\alpha)_{\alpha\in A(T)}$ is the system of standard measures of an experiment $E \in \mathscr{E}(T)$ iff it is consistent in the sense of Lemma 57.1.*

Proof. It follows from Lemma 57.1 that the conditions are necessary. To prove sufficiency note that $M\colon \varphi \mapsto \int \varphi \, d\sigma_\alpha$, $\varphi \in \mathscr{H}(T)$, $\varphi = \varphi \circ p_\alpha$, defines a conical measure M of resultant $Mp_t = 1$, $t \in T$. There is an experiment $E \in \mathscr{E}(T)$ such that $M = M_E$. If $(\tau_\alpha)_{\alpha\in A(T)}$ denotes the system of standard measures of E then it follows by 52.8 that

$$\int \varphi \, d\sigma_\alpha = M\varphi = M_E\varphi = \int \varphi \, d\tau_\alpha$$

if $\varphi \in \mathscr{H}(T)$, $\varphi \circ p_\alpha = \varphi$. This implies $\sigma_\alpha = \tau_\alpha$ for every $\alpha \in A(T)$. □

57.9 Remark. The preceding theorem is of an elementary nature if T is a finite set. Let σ on $\mathscr{B}(S_T)$ be a probability measure such that $\int p_t \, d\sigma = 1$ if $t \in T$. Then $E_\sigma = (S_T, \mathscr{B}(S_T), \{p_t\sigma\colon t \in T\})$ is an experiment whose standard measure on S_T coincides with σ. The experiment E_σ is called the standard experiment of σ.

Comparison of experiments may be phrased in terms of conical measures.

57.10 Theorem. *Let $\varepsilon \geqq 0$ and let E and F be experiments in $\mathscr{E}(T)$ Then $E \overset{\varepsilon}{\supseteq} F$ iff*

$$M_E\varphi \leqq M_F\varphi + \varepsilon \quad \text{if} \quad \varphi \in \mathscr{H}_0(T), \quad \|\varphi\| = 1.$$

Proof. Apply Corollary 52.8. □

57.11 Corollary. *Let $E, F \in \mathscr{E}(T)$. Then $E \sim F$ iff $M_E = M_F$.*

Another consequence of the important Theorem 57.7 is the existence of projective limits of experiments.

57.12 Definition. A system of experiments $(E_{(\alpha)})_{\alpha\in A(T)}$ where $E_{(\alpha)} \in \mathscr{E}(\alpha)$, $\alpha \in A(T)$, is a *projective system* if $\alpha \subseteq \beta$ implies $(E_{(\beta)})_\alpha \sim E_\alpha$. An experiment

$E \in \mathscr{E}(T)$ is a *projective limit* of the projective system $(E_{(\alpha)})_{\alpha \in A(T)}$ if $E_\alpha \sim E_{(\alpha)}$ for every $\alpha \in A(T)$.

57.13 Corollary (LeCam [1972]). *For every projective system of experiments* $(E_{(\alpha)})_{\alpha \in A(T)}$ *there exists a projective limit* $E \in \mathscr{E}(T)$

Proof. If σ_α is the standard measure of $E_{(\alpha)}$, $\alpha \in A(T)$, then the system $(\sigma_\alpha)_{\alpha \in A(T)}$ satisfies conditions (1) and (2) of Corollary 57.8. Hence there is an experiment $E \in \mathscr{E}(T)$ such that σ_α is also the standard measure of E_α for every $\alpha \in A(T)$. This implies $E_\alpha \sim E_{(\alpha)}$ for every $\alpha \in A(T)$. □

Let us return to the problem considered below Theorem 55.16.

57.14 Corollary. *The experiment E constructed in Theorem 57.7 satisfies* $L(E) = \overline{\text{Lat}}\,(E) = L_1(\mu)$.

Proof. Clearly, $\overline{\text{Lat}\, E} \subseteq L(E)$. Let us identify $L_1(\mu)$ and $\{f\mu \colon f \in L_1(\mu)\}$. In order to show that $L(E) \subseteq L_1(\mu)$ consider $\sigma \in L(E)$, $\sigma \geqq 0$. Similarly as for Lemma 41.6 we may decompose $\sigma = \sigma_1 + \sigma_2$, $\sigma_1 \geqq 0$, $\sigma_2 \geqq 0$, where $\sigma_1 \in L_1(\mu)$ and $\sigma_2 \perp L_1(\mu)$. But $\sigma_2 \perp L_1(\mu)$ implies $\sigma_2 \perp P_t$, $t \in T$, and the defining property of $L(E)$ yields $\sigma_2 \perp \sigma$ which is only possible if $\sigma_2 = 0$. Hence, $\sigma = \sigma_1 \in L_1(\mu)$. Thus it remains to show that $\text{Lat}\,(E)$ is dense in $\{f\mu \colon f \in L_1(\mu)\}$. With the notations of Lemma 55.15 for every $\varphi \in \mathscr{H}(T)$ we have $P_\varphi = \varphi\mu$. According to Corollary 56.5 the set $\mathscr{H}(T)$ is dense in $L_1(\mu)$. This proves the assertion. □

57.15 Corollary. *For every experiment* $E \in \mathscr{E}(T)$ *there is an experiment* $F \sim E$ *such that* $L(F) = \overline{\text{Lat}}\,(F)$.

Proof. Applying to the conical measure M_E the construction of Theorem 57.7 there is an experiment F such that $M_E = M_F$ which satisfies $L(F) = \overline{\text{Lat}}\,(F)$ according to Corollary 57.14. □

58. Transformation groups and invariance

Let $E = (\Omega, \mathscr{A}, \{P_t \colon t \in T\})$ be an experiment and let G be a group.

58.1 Remark. Assume that there is a group $(M_g)_{g \in G}$ of stochastic operators on $L(E)$ such that E is invariant under $(M_g)_{g \in G}$. It follows from Corollary 55.10 that the experiments

$$M_g E := (\Omega, \mathscr{A}, \{M_g P_t: t \in T\}), \quad g \in G,$$

are equivalent with E.

If $P_s \neq P_t$ for $s \neq t$, then $(M_g)_{g \in G}$ defines an operation of G on T by

$$P_{gs} = M_g P_s, \quad g \in G, s \in T.$$

With this notation the experiments

$$(\Omega, \mathscr{A}, \{P_{gt}: t \in T\}), \quad g \in G,$$

are equivalent to E.

Now we start with a group G operating on T.

58.2 Definition. Assume that G operates on T. Then E is called *G-invariant* if E is equivalent to each of the experiments $(\Omega, \mathscr{A}, \{P_{gt}: t \in T\}), \quad g \in G$.

At first glance it seems that the notion of G-invariance is more general than the notion of invariance under the operation of a $(M_g)_{g \in G}$ of stochastic operators. However, this is not the case.

58.3 Theorem. *Assume that G operates on T and that E is G-invariant. Then there exists a group of stochastic operators $(M_g)_{g \in G}$ on $L(E)$ such that $P_{gt} = M_g P_t$ for all $g \in G$, $t \in T$.*

Proof. Let $E_0 \in \mathscr{E}(T)$ be such that $E_0 \sim E$ and $L(E_0) = \overline{\mathrm{Lat}(E_0)}$. Such an experiment exists by Corollary 57.15. First we show that E_0 is also G-invariant. Denote $E_0 = (\Omega_0, \mathscr{A}_0, \{Q_t: t \in T\})$. There are stochastic operators M_1: $L(E) \to L(E_0)$ and M_2: $L(E_0) \to L(E)$ such that $M_1 P_t = Q_t$ and $M_2 Q_t = P_t$, $t \in T$. This implies that $M_1 P_{gt} = Q_{gt}$ and $M_2 Q_{gt} = P_{gt}$ for all $t \in T$ and $g \in G$. It follows that

$$(\Omega, \mathscr{A}, \{P_{gt}: t \in T\}) \sim (\Omega_0, \mathscr{A}_0, \{Q_{gt}: t \in T\})$$

for every $g \in G$ which implies G-invariance of E_0. Now, since

$$E_0 \sim (\Omega_0, \mathscr{A}_0, \{Q_{gt}: t \in T\})$$

there is a stochastic operator $\bar{M}_g$: $L(E_0) \to L(E_0)$ such that $\bar{M}_g Q_t = Q_{gt}$, $t \in T$. It is clear that $\bar{M}_{g_1 \circ g_2} = \bar{M}_{g_1} \circ \bar{M}_{g_2}$ on the set $\{Q_t: t \in T\}$. But from Theorem 55.16 it follows that the group property is even valid on the whole of $L(E_0)$ and therefore $(\bar{M}_g)_{g \in G}$ is a group of stochastic operators. Now define

$$M_g := M_2 \circ \bar{M}_g \circ M_1, \quad g \in G.$$

It is clear that $(M_g)_{g \in G}$ is a family of stochastic operators satisfying $M_g P_t = P_{gt}$, $g \in G$, $t \in T$. It remains to show that $(M_g)_{g \in G}$ is a group of stochastic operators.

For this we note that $M_1 \circ M_2 = \mathrm{id}|_{L(E_0)}$. This follows from $(M_1 \circ M_2)(Q_t) = M_1(P_t) = Q_t$, $t \in T$, and from Theorem 55.16. Hence we obtain

$$M_{g_1 \circ g_2} = M_2 \circ \bar{M}_{g_1 \circ g_2} \circ M_1 = M_2 \circ \bar{M}_{g_1} \circ \bar{M}_{g_2} \circ M_1 = \\ = M_2 \circ \bar{M}_{g_1} \circ M_1 \circ M_2 \circ \bar{M}_{g_2} \circ M_1 = M_{g_1} \circ M_{g_2}.$$

This proves the assertion. □

58.4 Remark. Let $\mathscr{B}(G)$ be a σ-field on G and assume that the operation of G on T is measurable in the sense that $g \mapsto P_{gt}(A)$, $g \in G$, is $\mathscr{B}(G)$-measurable for every $A \in \mathscr{A}$. Then the preceding proof shows that $(M_g)_{g \in G}$ is a measurable group of stochastic operators. Hence the situation of G-invariant experiment is completely reduced the case considered in Section 48 and the Hunt-Stein theory can be applied.

For checking G-invariance it is convenient to have a criterion in terms of the likelihood processes.

58.5 Corollary. *Assume that G operates on T. Then E is G-invariant iff*

$$\mathscr{L}\left(\left(\frac{dP_t}{dP_s}\right)_{t \in T} \middle| P_s\right) = \mathscr{L}\left(\left(\frac{dP_{gt}}{dP_{gs}}\right)_{t \in T} \middle| P_{gs}\right)$$

for all $g \in G$ and $s \in T$.

Proof. Apply Theorem 53.10. □

We finish this section showing that every equivalence class of G-invariant experiments contains an experiment where the group of stochastic operators is induced by a group action on the sample space. However, we cannot show that the operation is measurable in the sense of Example 48.3.

58.6 Theorem. *Suppose that E is G-invariant. Then there exists an equivalent experiment $F = (\mathbb{R}_+^T, \bigotimes_{t \in T} \mathscr{B}(\mathbb{R}_+), \{Q_t : t \in T\})$ where G operates on $\mathbb{R}_+^T$ and $Q_{gt} = Q_t \circ g^{-1}$, $t \in T$, $g \in G$.*

Proof. Let $\mu | \bigotimes_{t \in T} \mathscr{B}(\mathbb{R}_+)$ be the measure which is constructed in the proof of Theorem 57.7. Let M be the conical measure of E and M_g the conical measure of $(\Omega, \mathscr{A}, \{P_{gt} : t \in T\})$, $g \in G$. Since E is G-invariant it follows that $M = M_g$, $g \in G$.

Let F be defined by $Q_t := p_t \mu$, $t \in T$. We define the operation of G on $\mathbb{R}_+^T$ by $gx := (x_{g^{-1}t})_{t \in T}$, $g \in G$, $x \in \mathbb{R}_+^T$. It is obvious that $g\colon \mathbb{R}_+^T \to \mathbb{R}_+^T$ is $\bigotimes_{t \in T} \mathscr{B}(\mathbb{R}_+)$-

measurable for every $g \in G$. For every $\varphi \in \mathscr{H}(T)$

$$\int \varphi \circ g \, d\mu = M_g(\varphi) = M(\varphi) = \int \varphi \, d\mu, \quad \varphi \in \mathscr{H}(T), \; g \in G,$$

and since $\mathscr{H}(T)$ is dense in $L_1(\mu)$ it follows that μ is invariant under the operation of G. We obtain

$$\begin{aligned} Q_{gt}(B) &= \int 1_B(x) \, p_{gt}(x) \, \mu(dx) = \int 1_B(x) \, p_t(g^{-1} x) \, \mu(dx) = \\ &= \int 1_B(gx) \, p_t(x) \, \mu(dx) = Q_t(g^{-1} B) \end{aligned}$$

if $g \in G$, $t \in T$, $B \in \bigotimes_{t \in T} \mathscr{B}(\mathbb{R}_+)$. This proves the assertion. □

59. Topological spaces of experiments

Let $T \neq \emptyset$ be an arbitrary set. Then $\mathscr{E}(T)$ denotes the collection of all experiments for the parameter space T. The elements of the quotient set $\mathscr{E}(T)/\sim$ are called *experiment types*. It should be recalled that $\mathscr{E}(T)/\sim$ $= \mathscr{E}(T)/\underset{2}{\sim}$. It is clear that $\mathscr{E}(T)/\sim$ is a set.

59.1 Definition. Let $E, F \in \mathscr{E}(T)$ and let

$$\delta(E, F) = \inf \{\varepsilon > 0 \colon E \overset{\varepsilon}{\supseteq} F\}.$$

Then $\Delta(E, F) = \max \{\delta(E, F), \delta(F, E)\}$ is called the *deficiency* between E and F.

59.2 Lemma. *The deficiency Δ is a pseudodistance on $\mathscr{E}(T)$.*

Proof. We have to prove that $\delta \colon \mathscr{E}(T) \times \mathscr{E}(T) \to \mathbb{R}$ satisfies the triangle inequality. But this inequality is the consequence of the fact that for $E, F, G \in \mathscr{E}(T)$

$$E \overset{\varepsilon_1}{\supseteq} F, \; F \overset{\varepsilon_2}{\supseteq} G \quad \text{implies} \quad E \overset{\varepsilon_1 + \varepsilon_2}{\supseteq} G. \qquad \square$$

Let $\dot{E} \in \mathscr{E}(T)/\sim$ be the equivalence class with $E \in \dot{E}$. We denote $\Delta(\dot{E}, \dot{F}) := \Delta(E, F)$, $E \in \mathscr{E}(T)$, $F \in \mathscr{E}(T)$. Then $(\mathscr{E}(T)/\sim, \Delta)$ is a metric space since $\Delta(E, F) = 0$ iff $E \sim F$.

There are several ways to express the deficiency between experiments.

59.3 Lemma. *If $E, F \in \mathscr{E}(T)$ then*

$$\Delta(E, F) = \sup \{|M_E \varphi - M_F \varphi| : \|\varphi\| \leqq 1, \; \varphi \in \mathscr{H}_0(T)\}.$$

Proof. This follows immediately from Theorem 57.10. □

59.4 Corollary. *If $E, F \in \mathscr{E}(T)$ then*

$$\Delta(E, F) = \sup\{\Delta(E_\alpha, F_\alpha): \alpha \in A(T)\}.$$

Proof. Note that $\mathscr{H}_0(T) = \bigcup_{\alpha \in A(T)} \mathscr{H}_0(\alpha)$ and apply the preceding lemma. □

59.5 Lemma. *Let* $E = (\Omega_1, \mathscr{A}_1, \{P_t: t \in T\})$ *and* $F = (\Omega_2, \mathscr{A}_2, \{Q_t: t \in T\})$. *Then*

$$\delta(E, F) = \inf\{\sup_{t \in T} \| M P_t - Q_t \|: M: L(E) \to L(F) \text{ is a stochastic operator}\}.$$

Proof. Apply Corollary 55.10. □

59.6 Corollary. *Let $E = (\Omega, \mathscr{A}, \{P_t: t \in T\})$ and $F = (\Omega, \mathscr{A}, \{Q_t: t \in T\})$ be experiments with the same sample space $(\Omega, \mathscr{A})$. Then*

$$\Delta(E, F) \leqq \sup_{t \in T} d_1(P_t, Q_t).$$

Proof. Since the identity defines a randomization from E to F it follows from Lemma 59.5 and Lemma 55.4 that

$$\delta(E, F) \leqq \sup_{t \in T} \| P_t - Q_t \|$$

which implies for reasons of symmetry

$$\Delta(E, F) \leqq \sup_{t \in T} \| P_t - Q_t \|. \quad □$$

To obtain the topological properties of experiment spaces we begin with considering the simplest case.

If T is a finite set then each $E \in \mathscr{E}(T)$ is characterized by its standard measure $\sigma_E \in \mathscr{S}_T$. From Remark 57.9 (1), we obtain that the mapping $E \mapsto \sigma_E$ is even surjective. Since $E \sim F$ implies $\sigma_E = \sigma_F$ the mapping $\dot{E} \mapsto \sigma_E$ is a bijection from $\mathscr{E}(T)/\sim$ onto $\mathscr{S}_T$. From Lemma 5.20 we know that $\mathscr{S}_T$ is compact for the weak topology.

59.7 Theorem. *If T is a finite set then $(\mathscr{E}(T)/\sim, \Delta)$ and $\mathscr{S}_T$ are topologically equivalent.*

Proof. The mapping $\sigma \mapsto \dot{E}_\sigma$ is a bijection from the compact space $\mathscr{S}_T$ onto the Hausdorff space $(\mathscr{E}(T)/\sim, \Delta)$. The assertion is proved if we show that the mapping is continuous.

Let $\sigma_n \to \sigma$ weakly where $(\sigma_n)_{n \in \mathbb{N}} \subseteq \mathscr{S}_T$. Then

$$\int \varphi \, d\sigma_n \to \int \varphi \, d\sigma \quad \text{if} \quad \varphi \in \mathscr{H}_0(T).$$

Since each function $\varphi \in \mathscr{H}_0(T)$ satisfies a Lipschitz condition with Lipschitz constant $\|\varphi\|$ it follows that $\{\varphi \in \mathscr{H}_0(T): \|\varphi\| \leqq 1\}$ is an equicontinuous and uniformly bounded set and therefore

$$\limsup_{n\to\infty} \{|\int \varphi\, d\sigma_n - \int \varphi\, d\sigma|: \varphi \in \mathscr{H}_0(T), \|\varphi\| \leqq 1\} = 0.$$

This implies $\Delta(E_{\sigma_n}, E_\sigma) \to 0$ in view of Corollary 52.8 or Lemma 59.3. □

59.8 Corollary. *If T is a finite set then $(\mathscr{E}(T)/\sim, \Delta)$ is a compact metric space.*

Let us return to the case when T is an arbitrary set.

59.9 Theorem (LeCam [1972]). *The metric space $(\mathscr{E}(T)/\sim, \Delta)$ is complete.*

Proof. Let $(E_n)_{n\in\mathbb{N}} \subseteq \mathscr{E}(T)$ be a Cauchy sequence for the pseudodistance Δ. Then for every $\alpha \in A(T)$ the sequence $(E_{n,\alpha})_{n\in\mathbb{N}} \subseteq \mathscr{E}(\alpha)$ is a Cauchy sequence and Corollary 59.8 implies that there is a limit $E_{(\alpha)}$. It is easy to see that $(E_{(\alpha)})_{\alpha\in A(T)}$ is a projective system and hence there is a projective limit $E \in \mathscr{E}(T)$. We have to show that E is a limit of $(E_n)_{n\in\mathbb{N}}$.

For every $\varepsilon > 0$ there is $N(\varepsilon) \in \mathbb{N}$ such that $\Delta(E_{n,\alpha}, E_{m,\alpha}) \leqq \varepsilon$, $\alpha \in A(T)$, if $n \geqq N(\varepsilon)$, $m \geqq N(\varepsilon)$. For fixed $n \in \mathbb{N}$ and $\alpha \in A(T)$ the function $F \mapsto \Delta(E_{n,\alpha}, F_\alpha)$ is continuous on $\mathscr{E}(\alpha)$ which implies $\Delta(E_{n,\alpha}, E_\alpha) \leqq \varepsilon$ if $n \geqq N(\varepsilon)$, $\alpha \in A(T)$. Now the assertion follows from Corollary 59.4. □

For arbitrary parameter spaces the Δ-topology of $\mathscr{E}(T)$ need not be compact. It will sometimes be called the *strong topology* of $\mathscr{E}(T)$ is contrast to the topology of the following definition.

59.10 Definition. The topology on $\mathscr{E}(T)/\sim$ which is generated by the family of pseudodistances $(E, F) \mapsto \Delta(E_\alpha, F_\alpha)$, $\alpha \in A(T)$, is called the *weak topology* of $\mathscr{E}(T)/\sim$.

If T is a finite set then obviously the strong and weak topology of $\mathscr{E}(T)$ coincide.

59.11 Theorem (LeCam [1972]). *The space of experiment types $\mathscr{E}(T)/\sim$ is compact for the weak topology.*

Proof. Let $\mathscr{F}$ be an ultrafilter in $\mathscr{E}(T)/\sim$. For every $\alpha \in A(T)$ let π_α: $\mathscr{E}(T)/\sim \to \mathscr{E}(\alpha)/\sim$ be the natural projection. As a first step we prove that $\pi_\alpha(\mathscr{F})$ is an ultrafilter for every $\alpha \in A(T)$. If $M \subseteq \mathscr{E}(\alpha)$ is an arbitrary set then $\pi_\alpha^{-1}(M) \in \mathscr{F}$ or $\pi_\alpha^{-1}(M') \in \mathscr{F}$. Hence $M = \pi_\alpha(\pi_\alpha^{-1}(M)) \in \pi_\alpha(\mathscr{F})$ or $M' = \pi_\alpha(\pi_\alpha^{-1}(M')) \in \pi_\alpha(\mathscr{F})$. This means that $\pi_\alpha(\mathscr{F})$ is an ultrafilter.

Since $\mathscr{E}(\alpha)/\sim$ is quasicompact the ultrafilter $\pi_\alpha(\mathscr{F})$ converges. Let

$\dot{E}_{(\alpha)} \in \mathscr{E}(\alpha)/\sim$ be a limit of $\pi_\alpha(\mathscr{F})$. As second step we prove that $(\dot{E}_{(\alpha)})_{\alpha \in A(T)}$ is a projective system.

Let $\alpha \subseteq \beta$. The filter $\pi_\beta(\mathscr{F})$ is finer than the filter of neighborhoods $\mathscr{U}_\beta(\dot{E}_\beta)$ of $\dot{E}_\beta$ in $\mathscr{E}(\beta)/\sim$, i.e. $\pi_\beta(\mathscr{F}) \supseteq \mathscr{U}_\beta(\dot{E}_\beta)$. The projection $\pi_{\beta\alpha}$: $\mathscr{E}(\beta)/\sim \to \mathscr{E}(\alpha)/\sim$ is continuous and therefore we have

$$\pi_{\beta\alpha}^{-1}(\mathscr{U}_\alpha(\pi_{\beta\alpha}(E_{(\beta)}))) \subseteq \mathscr{U}_\beta(\dot{E}_{(\beta)}) \subseteq \pi_\beta(\mathscr{F}).$$

This implies

$$\mathscr{U}_\alpha(\pi_{\beta\alpha}(\dot{E}_{(\beta)})) \subseteq \pi_{\beta\alpha}(\pi_\beta(\mathscr{F})) = \pi_\alpha(\mathscr{F})$$

whence we obtain $\pi_{\beta\alpha}(\dot{E}_{(\beta)}) \sim E_{(\alpha)}$.

According to Corollary 57.13 there is an experiment $E \in \mathscr{E}(T)$ such that $\dot{E}_{(\alpha)} \sim \pi_\alpha(E)$, $\alpha \in A(T)$. Since $\pi_\alpha(\mathscr{F}) \supseteq \mathscr{U}_\alpha(\pi_\alpha(\dot{E}))$, $\alpha \in A(T)$, we obtain

$$\mathscr{F} \supseteq \bigcup_{\alpha \in A(T)} \pi_\alpha^{-1} \mathscr{U}_\alpha(\pi_\alpha(E))$$

which proves that E is a limit of $\mathscr{F}$ for the weak topology. □

Chapter 10: Asymptotic Decision Theory

Practically, every result of asymptotic statistics relies either on weak convergence of experiments or on a stronger type of convergence. Besides the randomization criterion it was the second great success of the theory of experiments, when LeCam [1972 and 1979] was able to show that the main results of the local asymptotic theory (LeCam [1953] and Hajek [1972 and 1973]) can be proved exclusively under the assumption of weak convergence. This is the reason why we discuss in the present chapter weak convergence of experiments and its consequences from a general point of view. The results of this chapter are applied in Chapter 13 to obtain the classical assertions of asymptotic statistics.

The basic idea of asymptotic decision theory is simple and easily explained. Consider a weak convergent sequence of experiments. The object of the asymptotic investigation are sequences of decision functions. Every sequence of decision functions possesses accumulation points which are decision functions for the limit experiment. Now, it can be shown that the asymptotic properties of a sequence of decision functions are completely described by the properties of its accumulation points. In particular, a sequence of decision functions is asymptotically optimal in some sense iff the accumulation points are optimal in this sense for the limit experiment.

In Section 60 we discuss weak convergence of experiments. This type of convergence can be expressed in terms of convergence of the likelihood processes. Considering sequences instead of nets is justified under mild continuity conditions. In case of contiguity it is even sufficient to consider likelihood processes with a fixed base. This is proved in Section 61.

Convergence in distribution of decision functions is the subject of Section 62. We show that every sequence of decision function possesses accumulation points in distribution and that bounds for the risks of the sequence can be expressed in terms of the risks of the accumulation points. This leads to the important asymptotic minimax bound and renders assertions on asymptotic admissibility. Essentially, these are the main results of LeCam [1972]. However, we follow the improved presentation of LeCam [1979]. Moreover, the versions presented here are sufficiently general to cover also some classical local asymptotic results due to Bahadur [1964] and Pfanzagl [1970].

Concerning asymptotic admissibility, the assertions obtained in Section 62 are expressed in terms of convergence in distribution. In this respect they are much weaker than the corresponding classical assertions, which are contained in LeCam [1953] and Hajek [1972]. There it is proved that in the one-dimensional asymptotically normal case all sequences of decision function which attain the asymptotic minimax bound are stochastically equivalent. In LeCam [1979] this phenomenon is put into completely general terms. LeCam shows that stochastic equivalence is a consequence of the fact that the corresponding admissible decision function for the limit experiment is non-randomized and uniquely determined by its distribution. We present these results of LeCam in Section 63.

Some practically important decision functions are defined for each sample point by a minimum property depending on the corresponding path of a stochastic process, e.g. of the likelihood process. This is the case with maximum likelihood estimators and with generalized Bayes estimators. From the asymptotic point of view the question arises whether such a minimum property remains valid after passing to the limit. Let us put the problem more precisely. Consider a sequence of experiments converging weakly to a limit experiment. For each experiment of the sequence consider a decision function having a certain minimum property as described before. Then the question is whether the accumulation points of the sequence of decision functions share this minimum property. E.g. the question is whether the accumulation points of maximum likelihood estimates are maximum likelihood estimates for the limit experiment, or whether the accumulation points of generalized Bayes estimates are generalized Bayes estimates for the limit experiment.

In Section 64 this problem is considered in a rather general framework. It is shown that an invariance principle for the underlying sequence of stochastic processes is the technical key for a positive answer. For the case of maximum likelihood estimates such an approach is due to LeCam [1970]. It has been elaborated and extended to generalized Bayes estimates by Ibragimov and Has'minskii [1972 and 1973]. In both cases the authors require an invariance principle for the sequence likelihood processes themselves. However, there may be some doubt whether such an invariance principle for the likelihood processes is of any statistical meaning since it is not a necessary consequence of weak convergence of experiments.

In the case of generalized Bayes estimates the defining minimum property does not depend directly on the values of the likelihood processes but on stochastic processes which are integrals over the paths of the likelihood processes. In Sections 65–67 we show that weak convergence of experiments alone is sufficient for an invariance principle holding for these stochastic processes. Hence, in Section 67 we arrive at a positive answer to our propblem for the case of generalized Bayes estimates requiring only weak convergence of the underlying experiments. The results are taken from Strasser [1982].

60. Weakly convergent sequences of experiments

Let $T \neq \emptyset$ be an arbitrary set and (T_n) a sequence of subsets such that $T_n \uparrow T$. In the following we consider sequences of experiments $(E_n)_{n \in \mathbb{N}}$ where $E_n \in \mathscr{E}(T_n)$, $n \in \mathbb{N}$.

60.1 Definition. A sequence of experiments $E_n \in \mathscr{E}(T_n)$, $n \in \mathbb{N}$, *converges weakly* to $E \in \mathscr{E}(T)$ if $\Delta(E_{n,\alpha}, E_\alpha) \to 0$ for every $\alpha \in A(T)$.

It is clear that in case $T_n = T$, $n \in \mathbb{N}$, this definition is compatible with the notion of weak topology in the sense of Definition 59.10. The reason why we admit also $T_n \neq T$ will turn out when we are dealing with problems of asymptotic localization (see Section 82 and 83). Specifying the following to the case $T_n = T$, $n \in \mathbb{N}$, yields topological properties of $\mathscr{E}(T)/\sim$.

For convenience assertions which make sense for some $\alpha \in A(T)$ and for such $n \in \mathbb{N}$ that $\alpha \subseteq T_n$ are stated without the latter condition which is a matter of course.

60.2 Theorem. *A sequence $(E_n)_{n \in \mathbb{N}}$ converges weakly iff $(E_{n,\alpha})_{n \in \mathbb{N}}$ converges for every $\alpha \in A(T)$. In this case $(\lim_{n\to\infty} E_n)_\alpha \sim \lim_{n\to\infty} E_{n,\alpha}$ for every $\alpha \in A(T)$.*

Proof. It is clear that weak convergence of $(E_n)_{n \in \mathbb{N}}$ implies convergence of $(E_{n,\alpha})_{n \in \mathbb{N}}$ for every $\alpha \in A(T)$ and that in this case the asserted relation holds. Conversely, assume that $(E_{n,\alpha})_{n \in \mathbb{N}}$ converges for every $\alpha \in A(T)$. Then it is clear that the limits $\lim_{n\to\infty} E_{n,\alpha}$, $\alpha \in A(T)$, form a projective system. The projective limit is a weak limit of $(E_n)_{n \in \mathbb{N}}$. □

A simple consequence of the preceding assertion is that every weak Cauchy-sequence converges weakly. This follows from the completeness of $\mathscr{E}(\alpha)$ for every $\alpha \in A(T)$.

Another formulation of Theorem 60.2 is that $(E_n)_{n \in \mathbb{N}}$ converges weakly iff $(\dot{E}_{n,\alpha})_{n \in \mathbb{N}}$ has at most one accumulation point for every $\alpha \in A(T)$. This leads to the following criterion. Let $(\sigma_{n,\alpha})_{\alpha \in A(T)}$ and $(\sigma_\alpha)_{\alpha \in A(T)}$ be the system of standard measures of E_n, $n \in \mathbb{N}$, and of E.

60.3 Theorem. *A sequence of experiments $E_n \in \mathscr{E}(T_n)$, $n \in \mathbb{N}$, converges weakly to $E \in \mathscr{E}(T)$ iff any of the following conditions is satisfied:*

(1) *$(\sigma_{n,\alpha})_{n \in \mathbb{N}}$ converges weakly to σ_α for every $\alpha \in A(T)$.*
(2) *$(H(E_{n,\alpha}))_{n \in \mathbb{N}}$ converges pointwise on S_α to $H(E_\alpha)$ for every $\alpha \in A(T)$.*
(3) *$(M_{E_n}\varphi)_{n \in \mathbb{N}}$ converges to $M_E\varphi$ for every $\varphi \in \mathscr{H}_0(T)$, $\|\varphi\| \leq 1$.*
(4) $\left(\mathscr{L}\left(\left(\frac{dP_{n,t}}{dP_{n,s}}\right)_{t \in \alpha} \middle| P_{n,s}\right)\right)_{n \in \mathbb{N}}$ *converges weakly to* $\mathscr{L}\left(\left(\frac{dP_t}{dP_s}\right)_{t \in \alpha} \middle| P_s\right)$ *for every $\alpha \in A(T)$ and every $s \in \alpha$.*

Proof. It is clear that weak convergence is equivalent to condition (1). This is due to the fact that $(\mathscr{E}(\alpha)/\sim, \Delta)$ is topologically equivalent to the space $\mathscr{S}_\alpha$ of standard measures on S_α (confer Theorem 59.7).

(1) $\Rightarrow$ (2): The implication (1) $\Rightarrow$ (2) is obvious. The converse is valid since Hellinger transforms determine standard measures.

(1) $\Leftrightarrow$ (3): Use a similar argument as for the equivalence of (1) to (2).

(2) $\Rightarrow$ (4): As in the proof of Corollary 25.4 we see that convergence of the Hellinger transforms implies convergence of the Mellin transforms of $\mathscr{L}\left(\left(\frac{dP_{n,t}}{dP_{n,s}}\right)_{t\in\alpha} \middle| P_{n,s}\right)$, $n\in\mathbb{N}$, to the Mellin transform of $\mathscr{L}\left(\left(\frac{dP_t}{dP_s}\right)_{t\in\alpha} \middle| P_s\right)$, $s\in\alpha$, $\alpha\in A(T)$. An application of Theorem 5.16 proves (4).

(4) $\Rightarrow$ (1): The proof of Corollary 25.4 shows how the standard measures can be recovered from the finite dimensional marginal distributions of the likelihood processes. Hence, the assertion. □

60.4 Corollary. *A sequence of experiments $E_n\in\mathscr{E}(T_n)$, $n\in\mathbb{N}$, converges weakly iff any of the following conditions is satisfied:*

(1) $(\sigma_{n,\alpha})_{n\in\mathbb{N}}$ *converges weakly for every* $\alpha\in A(T)$.

(2) $(H(E_{n,\alpha}))_{n\in\mathbb{N}}$ *converges pointwise on* S_α *for every* $\alpha\in A(T)$.

(3) $(M_{E_n}\varphi)_{n\in\mathbb{N}}$ *converges for every* $\varphi\in\mathscr{H}_0(T)$, $\|\varphi\|\leqq 1$.

(4) $\left(\mathscr{L}\left(\left(\frac{dP_{n,t}}{dP_{n,s}}\right)_{t\in\alpha} \middle| P_{n,s}\right)\right)_{n\in\mathbb{N}}$ *converges weakly for every* $s\in\alpha$ *and every* $\alpha\in A(T)$.

Proof. Combine the compactness of $\mathscr{E}(\alpha)$, $\alpha\in A(T)$, with Theorem 60.2 and the uniqueness assertions of 53.8, 53.10 and 57.11. □

60.5 Corollary. *Assume that* $E_n\to E$ *weakly and* $F_n\to F$ *weakly where* $E_n\in\mathscr{E}(T_n)$, $F_n\in\mathscr{E}(T_n)$, $n\in\mathbb{N}$, $E, F\in\mathscr{E}(T)$. *Let* $\varepsilon\geqq 0$. *If* $E_n \overset{\varepsilon}{\supseteq} F_n$ *for every* $n\in\mathbb{N}$ *then* $E\overset{\varepsilon}{\supseteq} F$.

Although $\mathscr{E}(T)/\sim$ is a compact space for the weak topology it need not be sequentially compact. To obtain sequential compactness we need additional topological assumptions on the parameter set T.

Let us begin with a particular case.

60.6 Lemma. *If T is a countable set then every sequence of experiments $E_n\in\mathscr{E}(T_n)$, $n\in\mathbb{N}$, contains a weakly convergent subsequence.*

Proof. Apply that $\mathscr{E}(\alpha)$ is sequentially compact for every $\alpha\in A(T)$ and use a standard diagonal argument. □

60.7 Definition. Assume that (T, d) is a metric space. The experiment E is continuous if $t \mapsto P_t$ is *continuous*. The sequence of experiments $E_n \in \mathscr{E}(T_n)$, $n \in \mathbb{N}$, is *continuous in the limit* if for every $\varepsilon > 0$ and every $t \in T$ there is $\delta(\varepsilon, t) > 0$ such that

$$\limsup_{n \in \mathbb{N}} d_1(P_{n,s}, P_{n,t}) < \varepsilon \quad \text{if} \quad d(s,t) < \delta(\varepsilon, t).$$

Note that every equicontinuous sequence is continuous in the limit.

60.8 Lemma. *Let (T, d) be a metric space and assume that $E_n \to E$ weakly. Then E is continuous iff $(E_n)_{n \in \mathbb{N}}$ is continuous in the limit.*

Proof. This is due to the fact that

$$\lim_{n \to \infty} d_2(P_{n,s}, P_{n,t}) = d_2(P_s, P_t)$$

for every pair $(s, t) \in T \times T$. □

60.9 Theorem. *Let (T, d) be a separable metric space and assume that $(E_n)_{n \in \mathbb{N}}$ is continuous in the limit. Then $(E_n)_{n \in \mathbb{N}}$ contains a weakly convergent subsequence.*

Proof. Let $T_0 \subseteq T$ be countable and dense. Then there is a subsequence $\mathbb{N}_0 \subseteq \mathbb{N}$ such that $E_{n, T_0 \cap T_n} \to E_{T_0}$ weakly for $n \in \mathbb{N}_0$. We prove that $(E_n)_{n \in \mathbb{N}_0}$ is weakly convergent.

By Corollary 60.4 (3) it is sufficient to show that for $\alpha = \{s_1, \ldots, s_N\} \in A(T)$ and every $\varphi \in \mathscr{H}(T)$ with $\varphi \circ p_\alpha = \varphi$ the sequence $M_{E_n}(\varphi) = \int \varphi \, d\sigma_{n,\alpha}$, $n \in \mathbb{N}_0$, is a Cauchy sequence. Let $\varphi \in \mathscr{H}(T)$ and $\varphi \circ p_\alpha = \varphi$. Then φ can be represented in the form $\varphi = f \circ p_\alpha$ where $f\colon \mathbb{R}^{|\alpha|} \to \mathbb{R}$. Since φ is positively homogeneous and satisfies a Lipschitz condition the same is true of f. Let $\beta = \{t_1, \ldots, t_N\} \in A(T_0)$ and $\psi = f \circ p_\beta$. Then $\psi \in \mathscr{H}(T)$ and $\psi \circ p_\beta = \psi$. We have

$$\begin{aligned}
&\left| \int \varphi \, d\sigma_{n,\alpha} - \int \psi \, d\sigma_{n,\beta} \right| \\
&= \left| \int f\left(\left(\frac{dP_t}{d \sum_{s \in \alpha} P_s} \right)_{t \in \alpha} \right) d \sum_{s \in \alpha} P_s - \int f\left(\left(\frac{dP_t}{d \sum_{s \in \beta} P_s} \right)_{s \in \beta} \right) d \sum_{s \in \beta} P_s \right| \\
&= \left| \int f\left(\left(\frac{dP_t}{d \sum_{\alpha \cup \beta} P_s} \right)_{t \in \alpha} \right) d \sum_{\alpha \cup \beta} P_s - \int f\left(\left(\frac{dP_t}{d \sum_{\alpha \cup \beta} P_s} \right)_{t \in \beta} \right) d \sum_{\alpha \cup \beta} P_s \right| \\
&\leq \operatorname{Lip}(f) \sum_{i=1}^{N} \int \left| \frac{dP_{s_i}}{d \sum_{\alpha \cup \beta} P_s} - \frac{dP_{t_i}}{d \sum_{\alpha \cup \beta} P_s} \right| d \sum_{\alpha \cup \beta} P_s \\
&= 2 \operatorname{Lip}(f) \sum_{i=1}^{N} \| P_{s_i} - P_{t_i} \|.
\end{aligned}$$

The sequence $(\int \psi \, d\sigma_{n,\beta})_{n \in \mathbb{N}_0}$ is a Cauchy sequence. Since β can be chosen arbitrarily close to α we obtain that also $(\int \varphi \, d\sigma_{n,\alpha})_{n \in \mathbb{N}}$ is a Cauchy sequence. □

60.10 Corollary. *Let (T, d) be a separable metric space. Any equicontinuous subset of $\mathscr{E}(T)$ is weakly sequentially compact.*

61. Contiguous sequences of experiments

We keep the notations of the preceding paragraph.

61.1 Definition. A sequence of experiments $E_n \in \mathscr{E}(T_n)$, $n \in \mathbb{N}$, is *contiguous* if for every pair $(s, t) \in T \times T$ the sequences of probability measures $(P_{n,s})_{n \in \mathbb{N}}$ and $(P_{n,t})_{n \in \mathbb{N}}$ are mutually contiguous.

61.2 Definition. The experiment $E \in \mathscr{E}(T)$ is *homogeneous* if the probability measures P_t, $t \in T$, are mutually equivalent.

61.3 Theorem. *Assume that $E_n \to E$ weakly. Then E is homogeneous iff $(E_n)_{n \in \mathbb{N}}$ is contiguous.*

Proof. If $E_n \to E$ weakly then for each pair $(s, t) \in T \times T$ the binary experiments $(P_{n,s}, P_{n,t})$, $n \in \mathbb{N}$, converge to the binary experiment (P_s, P_t). This proves the assertion in view of Theorem 18.11. □

It should be noted that the weak limit of a sequence of homogeneous experiments need not be homogeneous.

For contiguous sequences of experiments weak convergence may be described in terms of one particular likelihood process. For the following we take an arbitrary element of T and keep it fixed. For convenience we denote it by 0.

61.4 Lemma. *If $E \in \mathscr{E}(T)$ then for every $\alpha \in A(T)$ there is a set $N \in \mathscr{A}$ such that $P_0(N) = 0$ and*

$$\left| H(E_\alpha)(z) - \int \prod_{t \in \alpha} \left(\frac{dP_t}{dP_0}\right)^{z_t} dP_0 \right| \leq \prod_{t \in \alpha} [P_t(N)]^{z_t}, \; z \in S_\alpha.$$

Proof. For $\alpha \in A(T)$ let $Q = \frac{1}{|\alpha|} \sum_{t \in \alpha} P_t$ and let $\left(\frac{dQ}{dP_0}, N\right)$ be a Lebesgue decomposition of Q with respect to P_0. Then, for $z \in S_\alpha$

$$H(E_\alpha)(z) = \int \prod_{t\in\alpha} \left(\frac{dP_t}{dQ}\right)^{z_t} dQ$$
$$= \int \prod_{t\in\alpha} \left(\frac{dP_t}{dP_0}\right)^{z_t} dP_0 + \int_N \prod_{t\in\alpha} \left(\frac{dP_t}{dQ}\right)^{z_t} dQ.$$

The assertion now follows from

$$\int_N \prod_{t\in\alpha} \left(\frac{dP_t}{dQ}\right)^{z_t} dQ \leqq \prod_{t\in\alpha} \left(\int_N \frac{dP_t}{dQ} dQ\right)^{z_t}. \qquad \square$$

61.5 Lemma. *If the sequence of experiments $E_n \in \mathscr{E}(T_n)$, $n \in \mathbb{N}$, is contiguous then for every $\alpha \in A(T)$ and every $z \in S_\alpha$*

$$\lim_{n\to\infty} \left| H(E_{n,\alpha})(z) - \int \prod_{t\in\alpha} \left(\frac{dP_{n,t}}{dP_{n,0}}\right)^{z_t} dP_{n,0} \right| = 0.$$

Proof. For $\alpha \in A(T)$ let $Q_n = \frac{1}{|\alpha|} \sum_{t\in\alpha} P_{n,t}$ and let $\left(\frac{dQ_n}{dP_{n,0}}, N_n\right)$ be a Lebesgue decomposition of Q_n with respect to $P_{n,0}$. Then $P_{n,0}(N_n) = 0$, $n \in \mathbb{N}$, implies

$$\lim_{n\to\infty} \prod_{t\in\alpha} P_{n,t}(N_n)^{z_t} = 0 \quad \text{if} \quad z \in S_\alpha.$$

Now, the assertion follows from Lemma 61.4. $\square$

61.6 Theorem. *If the sequence of experiments $E_n \in \mathscr{E}(T_n)$, $n \in \mathbb{N}$, is contiguous then $E_n \to E$ weakly iff for every $\alpha \in A(T)$*

$$\mathscr{L}\left(\left(\frac{dP_{n,t}}{dP_{n,0}}\right)_{t\in\alpha} \middle| P_{n,0}\right) \to \mathscr{L}\left(\left(\frac{dP_t}{dP_0}\right)_{t\in\alpha} \middle| P_0\right) \text{ weakly.}$$

Proof. If $E_n \to E$ weakly then the condition is satisfied in view of Theorem 60.3 (4). Conversely, assume that for every $\alpha \in A(T)$

$$\mathscr{L}\left(\left(\frac{dP_{n,t}}{dP_{n,0}}\right)_{t\in\alpha} \middle| P_{n,0}\right) \to \mathscr{L}\left(\left(\frac{dP_t}{dP_0}\right)_{t\in\alpha} \middle| P_0\right) \text{ weakly.}$$

Let $\alpha \in A(T)$. For simplicity denote

$$\mu_n := \mathscr{L}\left(\left(\frac{dP_{n,t}}{dP_{n,0}}\right)_{t\in\alpha} \middle| P_{n,0}\right), \quad n \in \mathbb{N}, \quad \text{and} \quad \mu := \mathscr{L}\left(\left(\frac{dP_t}{dP_0}\right)_{t\in\alpha} \middle| P_0\right).$$

Let us show that

$$\lim_{n\to\infty} \int \prod_{t\in\alpha} x_t^{z_t}\, d\mu_n = \int \prod_{t\in\alpha} x_t^{z_t}\, d\mu, \quad z \in \mathring{S}_\alpha.$$

First we note that for $a>0$ and $n\in\mathbb{N}$

$$\int_{\max_{t\in\alpha}|x_t|>a} \prod_{t\in\alpha} x_t^{z_t}\,d\mu_n \leqq \sum_{t\in\alpha} \int_{|x_t|>a} \prod_{s\in\alpha} x_s^{z_s}\,d\mu_n$$

$$\leqq \sum_{t\in\alpha}\prod_{s\in\alpha}\Big(\int_{|x_t|>a} x_s\,d\mu_n\Big)^{z_s} \leqq \sum_{t\in\alpha}\Big(\int_{|x_t|>a} x_t\,d\mu_n\Big)^{z_t}.$$

Now, Theorem 18.9 implies that

$$\lim_{a\to\infty}\sup_{n\in\mathbb{N}} \int_{\max_{t\in\alpha}|x_t|>a} \prod_{t\in\alpha} x_t^{z_t}\,d\mu_n = 0.$$

The same inequalities show that

$$\lim_{a\to\infty} \int_{\max_{t\in\alpha}|x_t|>a} \prod_{t\in\alpha} x_t^{z_t}\,d\mu = 0.$$

Thus, we obtain for every $z\in\mathring{S}_\alpha$ and every continuity point $a>0$ of

$$\mathscr{L}\Big(\max_{t\in\alpha}|x_t|\,\Big|\,\prod_{t\in\alpha} x_t^{z_t}\mu\Big)$$

$$\begin{aligned}
\int\prod_{t\in\alpha} x_t^{z_t}\,d\mu &\leqq \int_{\max_{t\in\alpha}|x_t|\leqq a} \prod_{t\in\alpha} x_t^{z_t}\,d\mu + R_1(a)\\
&= \lim_{n\to\infty}\int_{\max_{t\in\alpha}|x_t|\leqq a} \prod_{t\in\alpha} x_t^{z_t}\,d\mu_n + R_1(a)\\
&\leqq \liminf_{n\to\infty}\int\prod_{t\in\alpha} x_t^{z_t}\,d\mu_n + R_1(a)\\
&\leqq \limsup_{n\to\infty}\int\prod_{t\in\alpha} x_t^{z_t}\,d\mu_n + R_1(a)\\
&\leqq \lim_{n\to\infty}\int_{\max_{t\in\alpha}|x_t|\leqq a} \prod_{t\in\alpha} x_t^{z}\,d\mu_n + R_1(a) + R_2(a)\\
&= \int_{\max_{t\in\alpha}|x_t|\leqq a} \prod_{t\in\alpha} x_t^{z_t}\,d\mu + R_1(a) + R_2(a)\\
&\leqq \int\prod_{t\in\alpha} x_t^{z_t}\,d\mu + R_1(a) + R_2(a)
\end{aligned}$$

where

$$\lim_{a\to\infty}(|R_1(a)| + |R_2(a)|) = 0.$$

This proves the assertion. □

61.7 Corollary. *A contiguous sequence of experiments $E_n\in\mathscr{E}(T_n)$, $n\in\mathbb{N}$, converges weakly iff for every $\alpha\in A(T)$ the distributions*

$$\mathscr{L}\left(\left(\frac{dP_{n,t}}{dP_{n,0}}\right)_{t\in\alpha}\,\middle|\,P_{n,0}\right),\quad n\in\mathbb{N},\quad \textit{converge weakly.}$$

Proof. If $(E_n)_{n\in\mathbb{N}}$ converges weakly then the finite dimensional marginal distibutions of the likelihood processes converge weakly according to Theorem 60.3. On the other hand, if these distributions converge then Lemma 61.5 implies that the Hellinger transforms converge for every $\alpha \in A(T)$ which proves the converse. □

62. Convergence in distribution of decision functions

Let $T_n \uparrow T$ and assume that $(E_n)_{n\in\mathbb{N}}$ is a sequence of experiments $E_n \in \mathscr{E}(T_n)$, $n\in\mathbb{N}$, converging weakly to $E\in\mathscr{E}(T)$.

62.1 Definition. Let $\beta_n \in \mathscr{B}(E_n, D)$, $n\in\mathbb{N}$. The sequence $(\beta_n)_{n\in\mathbb{N}}$ *converges in distribution* to $\beta\in\mathscr{B}(E,D)$ if

$$\lim_{n\to\infty} \beta_n(f, P_{n,t}) = \beta(f, P_t), \quad f\in\mathscr{C}_b(D),\ t\in T.$$

It is easy to see that this definition is an extension of the corresponding elementary notions. If $(\kappa_n)_{n\in\mathbb{N}}$ is a sequence of $\mathscr{A}_n$-measurable estimates $\kappa_n\colon \Omega_n \to D$ then the corresponding decision functions are $\varrho_n(.,B) = 1_B\circ\kappa_n$, $n\in\mathbb{N}$, $B\in\mathscr{B}_0(D)$, and hence $(\mathscr{L}(\kappa_n|P_{n,t}))_{n\in\mathbb{N}}$ converges weakly to $\mathscr{L}(\kappa|P_t)$ for every $t\in T$ iff $(\varrho_n)_{n\in\mathbb{N}}$ converges in distribution to

$$\varrho\colon (\omega, B)\mapsto 1_B\circ\kappa(\omega),\ (\omega,B)\in\Omega\times\mathscr{B}_0(D).$$

Similarly, if $D=\{0,1\}$ and $\varrho_n(.,\{1\}) =: \varphi_n$, $n\in\mathbb{N}$, then $(\varrho_n)_{n\in\mathbb{N}}$ converges in distribution to ϱ iff the power functions $t\mapsto P_{n,t}\varphi_n$, $n\in\mathbb{N}$, converge pointwise to the power function of $\varphi := \varrho(.,\{1\})$.

62.2 Definition. An element $\beta\in\mathscr{B}(E,D)$ is an *accumulation point* (in distribution) of a sequence of generalized decision functions $\beta_n\in\mathscr{B}(E_n,D)$, $n\in\mathbb{N}$, if for every $\alpha\in A(T)$ and every finite set $G\subseteq\mathscr{C}_b(D)$ there is a subsequence $\mathbb{N}(\alpha,G)\subseteq\mathbb{N}$ such that

$$\lim_{n\in\mathbb{N}(\alpha,G)} \beta_n(f,P_{n,t}) = \beta(f,P_t), \quad f\in G,\ t\in\alpha.$$

62.3 Theorem. (LeCam [1979]). *Every sequence of generalized decision functions $\beta_n\in\mathscr{B}(E_n,D)$, $n\in\mathbb{N}$, has accumulation points $\beta\in\mathscr{B}(E,D)$.*

Proof. For every $\gamma\in A(T)$ and $n\in\mathbb{N}$ let $K_{n,\gamma}\colon \Omega\times\mathscr{A}_n\to[0,1]$ be a stochastic kernel such that

$$\|R_{K_{n,\gamma}}P_t - P_{n,t}\| < \Delta(E_{n,\gamma}, E_\gamma) + \frac{1}{n}, \quad t\in\gamma.$$

For this, confer Remark 55.6 (2), and Theorem 55.9. Then

$$\beta_{n,\gamma}: (f, \mu) \mapsto \beta_n(f, R_{K_{n,\gamma}}\mu), \quad f \in \mathscr{C}_b(D),\ \mu \in L(E),$$

are elements of $\mathscr{B}(E, D)$. Let β_γ be a weak accumulation point of $(\beta_{n,\gamma})_{n\in\mathbb{N}}$ and let β be a weak accumulation point of $(\beta_\gamma)_{\gamma\in A(T)}$ (cf. Theorem 42.3).

Fix $\alpha \in A(T)$ and a finite set $G \subseteq \mathscr{C}_b(D)$. We show that for every $\varepsilon > 0$ and every $n_0 \in \mathbb{N}$ there exists $n_\varepsilon \geqq n_0$ such that

$$|\beta_{n_\varepsilon}(f, P_{n_\varepsilon,t}) - \beta(f, P_t)| < \varepsilon, \quad f \in G,\ t \in \alpha.$$

First we note that there exists $\gamma \in A(T)$, $\gamma \supseteq \alpha$, such that

$$|\beta_\gamma(f, P_t) - \beta(f, P_t)| < \frac{\varepsilon}{3}, \quad f \in G,\ t \in \alpha.$$

Let $a := \max\{\|f\|_u : f \in G\}$ and $n_1 \in \mathbb{N}$ be such that

$$\Delta(E_{n,\gamma}, E_\gamma) + \frac{1}{n} < \frac{\varepsilon}{3a} \quad \text{if} \quad n \geqq n_1.$$

Then we choose $n_\varepsilon \geqq \max\{n_0, n_1\}$ in such a way that

$$|\beta_{n_\varepsilon,\gamma}(f, P_t) - \beta_\gamma(f, P_t)| < \frac{\varepsilon}{2}, \quad f \in G,\ t \in \alpha.$$

Since

$$\begin{aligned}
&|\beta_{n_\varepsilon}(f, P_{n_\varepsilon,t}) - \beta_{n_\varepsilon,\gamma}(f, P_t)| \\
&\quad = |\beta_{n_\varepsilon}(f, P_{n_\varepsilon,t}) - \beta_{n_\varepsilon}(f, R_{K_{n_\varepsilon,\gamma}} P_t)| \\
&\quad \leqq \|f\|\, \|P_{n_\varepsilon,t} - R_{K_{n_\varepsilon,\gamma}} P_t\| < \frac{\varepsilon}{3}, \quad f \in G,\ t \in \alpha,
\end{aligned}$$

the assertion is proved. □

It is now clear that a sequence $(\beta_n)_{n\in\mathbb{N}}$ which has exactly one accumulation point converges in distribution to this accumulation point.

62.4 Corollary. *Suppose that (T, D, W) is a decision problem with a lower semicontinuous loss function. Then every accumulation point $\beta \in \mathscr{B}(E, D)$ of a sequence $\beta_n \in \mathscr{B}(E_n, D)$, $n \in \mathbb{N}$, satisfies*

$$\beta(W_t, P_t) \leqq \limsup_{n\to\infty} \beta_n(W_t, P_{n,t}), \quad t \in T.$$

Proof. Let $V \leqq W$ be a bounded continuous loss function. Then for fixed $t \in T$ there exists a subsequence $\mathbb{N}_t \subseteq \mathbb{N}$ such that

$$\beta(V_t, P_t) = \lim_{n\in\mathbb{N}_t} \beta_n(V_t, P_{n,t}) \leqq \limsup_{n\to\infty} \beta_n(W_t, P_{n,t}).$$

Passing to the supremum over all $V \leqq W$ the assertion follows. □

Now, we arrive at the result which is the basis of asymptotic lower bounds of risk functions for a large variety of situations.

62.5 Theorem. *Suppose that (T, D, W) is a decision problem with a lower semicontinuous loss function. Let $\mathscr{B} \subseteq \mathscr{B}(E, D)$ be the set of all accumulation points of the sequence $\beta_n \in \mathscr{B}(E_n, D)$, $n \in \mathbb{N}$, and $\overline{\text{co}}\,\mathscr{B}$ its weakly closed convex hull. Then for every subset $T_0 \subseteq T$*

$$\liminf_{n\to\infty} \sup_{t\in T_0\cap T_n} \beta_n(W_t, P_{n,t}) \geqq \inf_{\beta\in\overline{\text{co}}\,\mathscr{B}} \sup_{t\in T_0} \beta(W_t, P_t).$$

Proof. Let $m \in S_{T_0}$ and $\alpha = \text{supp}(m)$. Choose a subsequence $\mathbb{N}_m \subseteq \mathbb{N}$ such that

$$\liminf_{n\to\infty} \int \beta_n(W_t, P_{n,t})m(dt) = \lim_{n\in\mathbb{N}_m} \int \beta_n(W_t, P_{n,t})m(dt).$$

Let $\beta \in \mathscr{B}(E, D)$ be an accumulation point of the sequence $(\beta_n)_{n\in\mathbb{N}_m}$. Obviously, this is also an accumulation point of the original sequence. It follows that for every bounded continuous loss function $V \leqq W$ there exists a subsequence $\mathbb{N}_V \subseteq \mathbb{N}_m$ satisfying

$$\lim_{n\in\mathbb{N}_V} \int \beta_n(V_t, P_{n,t})m(dt) = \int \beta(V_t, P_t)m(dt).$$

This implies that

$$\begin{aligned}\liminf_{n\to\infty} \int \beta_n(W_t, P_{n,t})m(dt) &= \lim_{n\in\mathbb{N}_m} \int \beta_n(W_t, P_{n,t})m(dt)\\ &\geqq \limsup_{n\in\mathbb{N}_m} \int \beta_n(V_t, P_{n,t})m(dt) \geqq \lim_{n\in\mathbb{N}_V} \int \beta_n(V_t, P_{n,t})m(dt)\\ &= \int \beta(V_t, P_t)m(dt).\end{aligned}$$

From Lemma 47.2 we obtain

$$\liminf_{n\to\infty} \int \beta_n(W_t, P_{n,t})m(dt) \geqq \int \beta(W_t, P_t)m(dt).$$

It follows that

$$\begin{aligned}&\liminf_{n\to\infty} \sup_{t\in T_0\cap T_n} \beta_n(W_t, P_{n,t})\\ &\quad= \liminf_{n\to\infty} \sup_{m\in S_{T_0\cap T_n}} \int \beta_n(W_t, P_{n,t})m(dt)\end{aligned}$$

$$\geqq \sup_{m \in S_{T_0}} \inf_{\beta \in \mathscr{B}} \int \beta(W_t, P_t) m(dt)$$

$$\geqq \sup_{m \in S_{T_0}} \inf_{\beta \in \overline{\text{co}}\, \mathscr{B}} \int \beta(W_t, P_t) m(dt).$$

An application of Theorem 46.3 completes the proof. □

A particular case is the famous asymptotic minimax bound for risk functions.

62.6 Corollary (LeCam [1972; 1979]). *Assume that the conditions of Theorem (62.5) are satisfied. Then for every sequence $\beta_n \in \mathscr{B}(E_n, D)$, $n \in \mathbb{N}$,*

$$\liminf_{n \to \infty} \sup_{t \in T_n} \beta_n(W_t, P_{n,t}) \geqq \inf_{\beta \in \mathscr{B}(E, D)} \sup_{t \in T} \beta(W_t, P_t).$$

Another application deals with admissibility. Recall, that a function $r\colon T \to (-\infty, +\infty]$ is an admissible risk function for E and (T, D, W) if for every $\beta \in \mathscr{B}(E, D)$

$$\beta(W_t, P_t) \leqq r(t), \quad t \in T, \quad \text{implies} \quad \beta(W_t, P_t) = r(t), \quad t \in T.$$

62.7 Theorem (LeCam [1972]). *Suppose that (T, D, W) is a decision problem with a lower semicontinuous loss function. Let $r\colon T \to (-\infty, +\infty]$ be an admissible risk function for E. If a sequence of $\beta_n \in \mathscr{B}(E_n, D)$, $n \in \mathbb{N}$, satisfies*

$$\limsup_{n \to \infty} \beta_n(W_t, P_{n,t}) \leqq r(t), \quad t \in T,$$

then

$$\lim_{n \to \infty} \beta_n(W_t, P_{n,t}) = r(t), \quad t \in T.$$

Proof. From Corollary 62.4 it follows that every accumulation point $\beta \in \mathscr{B}(E, D)$ of $(\beta_n)_{n \in \mathbb{N}}$ and even every $\beta \in \overline{\text{co}}\, \mathscr{B}$ satisfies

$$\beta(W_t, P_t) \leqq r(t), \quad t \in T,$$

which implies by admissibility that

$$\beta(W_t, P_t) = r(t), \quad t \in T,$$

for every $\beta \in \overline{\text{co}}\, \mathscr{B}$. Now Theorem 62.5 proves the assertion. □

Another version of this result is

62.8 Corollary. *Suppose that (T, D, W) is a decision problem with a lower semicontinuous loss function. Let $r\colon T \to (-\infty, +\infty]$ be an admissible risk function for E. If a sequence of $\beta_n \in \mathscr{B}(E_n, D)$, $n \in \mathbb{N}$, satisfies*

$$\liminf_{n\to\infty} \beta_n(W_{t_0}, P_{n,t_0}) < r(t_0)$$

for some $t_0 \in T$, *then there exists* $t_1 \in T$ *such that*

$$\limsup_{n\to\infty} \beta_n(W_{t_1}, P_{n,t_1}) > r(t_1).$$

63. Stochastic convergence of decision functions

Let $T_n \uparrow T$. Assume that $(E_n)_{n\in\mathbb{N}}$ is a sequence of experiments $E_n \in \mathscr{E}(T_n)$, $n \in \mathbb{N}$, converging weakly to $E \in \mathscr{E}(T)$. Let D be a topological decision space.

63.1 Definition. Let $\sigma_n \in \mathscr{R}(E_n, D)$ and $\tau_n \in \mathscr{R}(E_n, D)$, $n \in \mathbb{N}$, be two sequences of decision functions. The sequences $(\sigma_n)_{n\in\mathbb{N}}$ and $(\tau_n)_{n\in\mathbb{N}}$ are *stochastically equivalent* if

$$\lim_{n\to\infty} |f\sigma_n - f\tau_n| \, P_{n,t} = 0, \quad f \in \mathscr{C}_b(D), \quad t \in T.$$

It is immediate that stochastically equivalent sequences of decision functions have the same sets of accumulation points.

63.2 Remark. The concept of stochastic equivalence is closely related to convergence in measure of decision functions.

(1) Let (D, d) be a compact metric space. Let $A \subseteq \mathscr{C}_b(D)$ be the set of all functions satisfying

$$\|f\|_u \leqq 1 \quad \text{and} \quad |f(x) - f(y)| \leqq d(x, y), \quad x, y \in D.$$

Then by the Arzela-Ascoli-theorem it is easy to see that A is compact and

$$\sup\{|f(x) - f(y)| : f \in A\} = d(x, y), \quad x, y \in D.$$

Stochastic equivalence implies that

$$\lim_{n\to\infty} \int \sup_{f\in A} |f\sigma_n - f\tau_n| \, dP_{n,t} = 0, \quad t \in T,$$

which is equivalent to

$$\lim_{n\to\infty} \iiint d(x, y) \, \sigma_n(\omega, dx) \, \tau_n(\omega, dy) \, P_{n,t}(d\omega) = 0, \quad t \in T.$$

(2) Let (D, d) be a metric space which is separable and complete. From (1) it follows that

$$\lim_{n\to\infty} \int \int_K \int_K d(x, y) \, \sigma_n(\omega, dx) \, \tau_n(\omega, dy) \, P_{n,t}(d\omega) = 0, \quad t \in T,$$

for every compact $K \subseteq D$. Suppose that $(\sigma_n)_{n\in\mathbb{N}}$ and $(\tau_n)_{n\in\mathbb{N}}$ converge to some $\varrho \in \mathscr{R}(E, D)$ in distribution. Since ϱP_t is tight on $\mathscr{B}(D)$ we may find for every $\varepsilon > 0$ and $t \in T$ a compact set $K \subseteq D$ such that

$$\limsup_{n\to\infty} \int \sigma_n(., D\setminus K)\, dP_{n,t} < \varepsilon,$$

$$\limsup_{n\to\infty} \int \tau_n(., D\setminus K)\, dP_{n,t} < \varepsilon.$$

Then stochastic equivalence implies

$$\lim_{n\to\infty} (\sigma_n \otimes \tau_n) P_{n,t} \{(x, y) \in D^2: d(x, y) > \varepsilon\} = 0, \quad \varepsilon > 0.$$

(3) Let $D = \{0,1\}$ and denote $\varphi_n = \sigma_n(., \{1\})$, $\psi_n = \tau_n(., \{1\})$, $n \in \mathbb{N}$. Then it follows that

$$\lim_{n\to\infty} \int |\varphi_n - \psi_n|\, dP_{n,t} = 0, \quad n \in \mathbb{N}.$$

(4) Let (D, d) be a metric space which is separable and complete. Assume that there are sequences $\kappa_n: \Omega_n \to D$, $\pi_n: \Omega_n \to D$, $n \in \mathbb{N}$, satisfying

$$\varrho_n(., B) = 1_B \circ \kappa_n,\ \tau_n(., B) = 1_B \circ \pi_n, \quad n \in \mathbb{N},\ B \in \mathscr{B}(D).$$

Then, under the additional assuptions of (2)

$$\lim_{n\to\infty} P_{n,t}\{d(\kappa_n, \pi_n) > \varepsilon\} = 0, \quad \varepsilon > 0.$$

Suppose that two sequences of decision functions $\sigma_n \in \mathscr{R}(E_n, D)$ and $\tau_n \in \mathscr{R}(E_n, D)$, $n \in \mathbb{N}$, converge in distribution to the same limit $\varrho \in \mathscr{R}(E, D)$. When is it possible to conclude that the sequences $(\sigma_n)_{n\in\mathbb{N}}$ and $(\tau_n)_{n\in\mathbb{N}}$ are stochastically equivalent? The following is devoted to this question which is answered by Theorem 63.6.

Let $\beta \in \mathscr{B}(E, D)$. A *distributional neighborhood* of β is a set containing another set of the form

$$F = \{\gamma \in \mathscr{B}(E, D): |\gamma(f, P_s) - \beta(f, P_s)| < \varepsilon, f \in G, s \in \alpha\}$$

where $\alpha \in A(T)$ and $G \subseteq \mathscr{C}_b(D)$ is a finite subset and $\varepsilon > 0$. The system of distributional neighborhoods of β is a filter which is coarser than the filter of weak neighborhoods of β.

Let us call an element $\beta \in \mathscr{B}(E, D)$ *uniquely determined by its distribution* if $\gamma(f, P_s) = \beta(f, P_s)$ for all $f \in \mathscr{C}_b(D)$ and $s \in T$ implies $\gamma = \beta$.

63.3 Lemma. *Suppose that $\beta \in \mathscr{B}(E, D)$ is uniquely determined by its distribution. Then the filter of distributional neighborhoods of β coincides with the filter of weak neighborhoods of β.*

Proof. Let U be a weakly open neighborhood of β and denote by $\mathscr{F}$ the filter of distributional neighborhoods of β. Since β is uniquely determined by its distribution we have

$$\bigcap_{F\in\mathscr{F}} \bar{F} = \{\beta\},$$

where $\bar{F}$ denotes the weak closure of F, $F\in\mathscr{F}$. It follows that

$$\bigcap_{F\in\mathscr{F}} \bar{F}\setminus U = \emptyset,$$

and since $\mathscr{B}(E, D)$ is weakly compact, there exists $F\in\mathscr{F}$ such that $F\subseteq\bar{F}\subseteq U$. □

63.4 Remark. Let $E=(\Omega, \mathscr{A}, \{P_t: t\in T\})$ be a dominated experiment which is complete and let D be a locally compact decision space with countable base. Then every $\varrho\in\mathscr{R}(E, D)$ is uniquely determined by its distribution. To see this, let $\beta\in\mathscr{B}(E, D)$ be such that $\beta(f, P_t)=f\varrho P_t$ for all $f\in\mathscr{C}_b(D)$, $t\in T$. If ϱ_0 is a substochastic kernel such that $\beta(f, \mu)=f\varrho_0\mu$ if $f\in\mathscr{C}_{00}(D)$, $\mu\in L(E)$, then $f\varrho_0 P_t=f\varrho P_t$, $f\in\mathscr{C}_{00}(D)$, $t\in T$. It follows that ϱ_0 is a stochastic kernel and hence, $\beta\in\mathscr{R}(E, D)$. Now, completeness implies that $\beta=\varrho$.

63.5 Lemma (LeCam [1979]). *Suppose that* $E_n\to E$ *weakly and that* $\varrho_n\in\mathscr{R}(E_n, D)$, $n\in\mathbb{N}$, *converges to* $\varrho\in\mathscr{R}(E, D)$ *in distribution. If* ϱ *is non-randomized and uniquely determined by its distribution, then*

$$\lim_{n\to\infty} (f^2\varrho_n P_{n,t}-(f\varrho_n)^2 P_{n,t})=0, \quad f\in\mathscr{C}_b(D),\ t\in T.$$

Proof. Fix $f\in\mathscr{C}_b(D)$, $f\neq 0$, $t\in T$, and $\varepsilon>0$. We will construct a number $N(\varepsilon)$ such that

$$f^2\varrho_n P_{n,t}-(f\varrho_n)^2 P_{n,t}<\varepsilon \quad \text{if} \quad n\geqq N(\varepsilon).$$

Let $\mu=(f\varrho)\cdot P_t$ and define

$$U(\varrho, \varepsilon):=\{\beta\in\mathscr{B}(E, D): |\beta(f^2, P_t)-f^2\varrho P_t|<\frac{\varepsilon}{4}, |\beta(f, \mu)-f\varrho\mu|<\frac{\varepsilon}{8}\}.$$

Obviously, $U(\varrho, \varepsilon)$ is a weak neighborhood of ϱ, and in view of Lemma 63.3 there are $\alpha\in A(T)$, a finite subset $G\subseteq\mathscr{C}_b(D)$ and $\delta>0$ such that

$$\{\beta\in\mathscr{B}(E, D): |\beta(g, P_s)-g\varrho P_s|<\delta, g\in G, s\in\alpha\}\subseteq U(\varrho, \varepsilon).$$

Let $\gamma=\alpha\cup\{t\}$ and choose $N(\varepsilon)$ such that

$$\Delta(E_{n,\gamma}, E_\gamma)<\min\left\{\frac{\delta}{2\max\{\|g\|_u: g\in G\}}, \frac{\varepsilon}{4\|f\|_u^2}\right\}$$

and

$$|g\varrho_n P_{n,s} - g\varrho P_s| < \frac{\delta}{2} \quad \text{if} \quad s \in \alpha, g \in G,$$

whenever $n \geqq N(\varepsilon)$. For every $n \geqq N(\varepsilon)$ there is a kernel $K_n \in \mathscr{R}(E, E_n)$ such that

$$\|P_{n,s} - R_{K_n} P_s\| < \min\left\{\frac{\delta}{2\max\{\|g\|_u: g \in G\}}, \frac{\varepsilon}{4\|f\|_u}\right\}, \quad s \in \gamma,$$

(cf. Remark 55.6 (2)). Denoting $\sigma_n := \varrho_n R_{K_n} \in \mathscr{R}(E, D)$ we obtain

$$|g\sigma_n P_s - g\varrho P_s| < \delta, \quad s \in \alpha, n \geqq N(\varepsilon),$$

and therefore $\sigma_n \in U(\varrho, \varepsilon)$, $n \geqq N(\varepsilon)$. This implies by definition of $U(\varrho, \varepsilon)$

$$|f^2\sigma_n P_t - f^2\varrho P_t| < \frac{\varepsilon}{4},$$

$$|f\sigma_n(f\varrho \cdot P_t) - f\varrho((f\varrho) \cdot P_t)| < \frac{\varepsilon}{8}.$$

Since ϱ is non-randomized it follows from Theorem 42.9 that

$$\begin{aligned} 0 &\leqq f^2\sigma_n P_t - (f\sigma_n)^2 P_t \\ &\leqq f^2\sigma_n P_t - (f\sigma_n)^2 P_t + (f\sigma_n - f\varrho)^2 P_t \\ &= f^2\sigma_n P_t - f^2\varrho P_t - 2(f\sigma_n - f\varrho)(f\varrho \cdot P_t) \\ &\leqq \frac{\varepsilon}{4} + 2 \cdot \frac{\varepsilon}{8} = \frac{\varepsilon}{2}, \quad n \geqq N(\varepsilon). \end{aligned}$$

Now, the assertion follows from

$$\begin{aligned} &f^2\varrho_n P_{n,t} - (f\varrho_n)^2 P_{n,t} \\ &\qquad < f^2\varrho_n R_{K_n} P_t - (f\varrho_n)^2 R_{K_n} P_t + \frac{\varepsilon}{2} \\ &\qquad \leqq f^2\varrho_n R_{K_n} P_t - (f\varrho_n R_{K_n})^2 P_t + \frac{\varepsilon}{2} \\ &\qquad = f^2\sigma_n P_t - (f\sigma_n)^2 P_t + \frac{\varepsilon}{2} \leqq \varepsilon, \quad n \geqq N(\varepsilon). \qquad \square \end{aligned}$$

Now, we are in a position to give a complete solution of the question posed. Confer Theorem 23.10.

63.6 Theorem (LeCam [1979]). *Let $E \in \mathscr{E}(T)$ be an experiment and D a topological space. For any $\varrho \in \mathscr{R}(E, D)$ the following assertions are equivalent:*

(1) *Whenever a sequence of experiments $E_n \in \mathscr{E}(T_n)$, $n \in \mathbb{N}$, converges weakly to E and $\sigma_n \in \mathscr{R}(E_n, D)$, $n \in \mathbb{N}$, and $\tau_n \in \mathscr{R}(E_n, D)$, $n \in \mathbb{N}$, converge to ϱ in distribution, then $(\sigma_n)_{n\in\mathbb{N}}$ and $(\tau_n)_{n\in\mathbb{N}}$ are stochastically equivalent.*

(2) *ϱ is non-randomized and uniquely determined by its distribution.*

Proof. (1) $\Rightarrow$ (2): We define an experiment $F = (D \times \Omega, \mathscr{B}_0(D) \otimes \mathscr{A}, \{Q_t : t \in T\})$ by

$$Q_t : (f, g) \mapsto P_t(f\varrho \cdot g), \quad f \in \mathscr{L}_b(\mathscr{B}_0(D)), g \in \mathscr{L}_b(\mathscr{A}), t \in T.$$

Let us show that $E \sim F$. The relation $E \subseteq F$ is clear since for every $\tau \in \mathscr{R}(E, D)$ there is σ: $((x, \omega), B) \mapsto \tau(\omega, B)$, $(x, \omega) \in D \times \Omega$, $B \in \mathscr{B}_0(D)$, in $\mathscr{R}(F, D)$ satisfying

$$f\sigma Q_t = f\tau P_t, \quad t \in T, f \in \mathscr{C}_b(D).$$

Conversely, the mapping $T_1 : L(E) \to L(F)$ being defined by

$$T_1\mu : (f, g) \mapsto \mu(f\varrho \cdot g), \quad f \in \mathscr{L}_b(\mathscr{B}_0(D)), g \in \mathscr{L}_b(\mathscr{A}),$$

is a transition. This implies $E \supseteq F$.

Now we define a non-randomized decision function

$$\kappa : D \times \Omega \to D : (x, \omega) \mapsto x$$

for F. For every $f \in \mathscr{C}_b(D)$ we obtain

$$f\kappa Q_t = \int f \circ \kappa \, dQ_t = \iint f \circ \kappa(x, \omega)\, \varrho(\omega, dx)\, P_t(d\omega) = f\varrho P_t, \; t \in T.$$

On the other hand, σ: $((x, \omega), B) \mapsto \varrho(\omega, B)$, $(x, \omega) \in D \times \Omega$, $B \in \mathscr{B}_0(D)$, is in $\mathscr{R}(F, D)$ and satisfies

$$f\sigma Q_t = f\varrho P_t, \quad t \in T.$$

It follows that

$$f\sigma Q_t = f\kappa Q_t, \quad t \in T,$$

which implies by condition (1) that $|f\sigma - f\kappa| Q_t = 0$, $t \in T$, $f \in \mathscr{C}_b(D)$. A standard argument yields $|f\sigma - f\kappa|\mu = 0$ for all $\mu \in L(F)$ and therefore

$$f\sigma\mu = f\kappa\mu, \quad f \in \mathscr{C}_b(D), \mu \in L(F).$$

Putting $\mu = f \cdot Q_t$, $t \in T$, it follows that

$$(f\varrho)^2 P_t = f^2 \varrho P_t, \quad t \in T, f \in \mathscr{C}_b(D),$$

which implies that ϱ is non-randomized by Theorem 42.9.

It remains to show that ϱ is uniquely determined by its distribution. If $\varrho_1 \in \mathscr{R}(E, D)$ is such that $f\varrho_1 P_t = f\varrho P_t$, $f \in \mathscr{C}_b(D)$, $t \in T$, then a direct application of condition (1) implies that $|f\varrho - f\varrho_1| P_t = 0$, $f \in \mathscr{C}_b(D)$, $t \in T$, which proves the assertion.

(2) $\Rightarrow$ (1): Let $\varrho_n = \frac{1}{2}(\sigma_n + \tau_n)$, $n \in \mathbb{N}$. Since $(\varrho_n)_{n \in \mathbb{N}}$ converges to ϱ in distribution it follows from Lemma (63.5) that

$$\lim_{n \to \infty} (f^2 \varrho_n P_{n,t} - (f\varrho_n)^2 P_{n,t}) = 0, \quad f \in \mathscr{C}_b(D),\ t \in T.$$

Denoting $\varphi_n = \frac{1}{2}(\sigma_n - \tau_n)$, $n \in \mathbb{N}$, we have

$$\begin{aligned}(f\varphi_n)^2 + (f\varrho_n)^2 &= \tfrac{1}{2}[(f\sigma_n)^2 + (f\tau_n)^2] \\ &\leqq \tfrac{1}{2}[f^2\sigma_n + f^2\tau_n] = f^2\varrho_n,\end{aligned}$$

and therefore

$$(f\varphi_n)^2 \leqq f^2\varrho_n - (f\varrho_n)^2, \quad n \in \mathbb{N}.$$

This proves the assertion. □

There is an interesting consequence of the preceding assertions concerning the determination of decision functions by their distribution. It should be recalled that completeness is not a property of equivalence classes of experiments as can be seen from the case of exponential experiments. Therefore, in general, it may happen that a distribution determines the underlying decision function for one experiment whereas it does not for another equivalent experiment. However, if the underlying decision function is non-randomized then uniqueness carries over to the whole equivalence class. Confer also Theorem 23.9.

63.7 Corollary. *Let $\varrho \in \mathscr{R}(E, D)$. If there exists an experiment $F = (\Omega_1, \mathscr{A}_1, \{Q_t : t \in T\}) \sim E$ and $\sigma \in \mathscr{R}(F, D)$ such that*

$$f\varrho P_t = f\sigma Q_t, \quad f \in \mathscr{C}_b(D),\ t \in T,$$

where σ is non-randomized and uniquely determined by its distribution, then also ϱ is non-randomized and uniquely determined by its distribution.

64. Convergence of minimum estimates

Let (T, d) be a metric space and let $T_n \subseteq T$ be open subsets satisfying $T_n \uparrow T$. Let $(\Omega_n, \mathscr{A}_n, P_n)$, $n \in \mathbb{N}$, be a sequence of probability spaces and consider stochastic processes $(Z_n(t))_{t \in T_n}$, $n \in \mathbb{N}$, where $Z_n(t): \Omega_n \to (-\infty, +\infty]$ are $\mathscr{A}_n$-measurable functions, $n \in \mathbb{N}$. Assume that the stochastic processes $(Z_n(t))_{t \in T_n}$, $n \in \mathbb{N}$, are separable. Moreover, let $(\Omega, \mathscr{A}, P)$ be a probability space and let $(Z(t))_{t \in T}$ be a separable stochastic process where $Z(t): \Omega \to (-\infty, +\infty]$ is $\mathscr{A}$-measurable.

64.1 Examples. (1) The results of the present section may be applied to the following situation. Let $E_n = (\Omega_n, \mathscr{A}_n, \{P_{n,t}: t \in T_n\})$, $n \in \mathbb{N}$, and $E = (\Omega, \mathscr{A}, \{P_t: t \in T\})$ be experiments. Then we fix some $s \in T$, put $P_n := P_{n,s}$, $n \in \mathbb{N}$, $P := P_s$, and define

$$Z_n(t) = -\log \frac{dP_{n,t}}{dP_{n,s}}, \; t \in T_n, \; n \in \mathbb{N}, \quad \text{and}$$

$$Z(t) = -\log \frac{dP_t}{dP_s}, \; t \in T.$$

(2) In sections 65–67 we shall assume that T is a Euclidean space and apply the results of the present section to the same situation as under (1), but defining

$$Z_n(t) = \int W(t-s)\, F_n ds), \quad t \in T_n, \; n \in \mathbb{N}, \quad \text{and}$$
$$Z(t) = \int W(t-s)\, F(ds), \quad t \in T,$$

where $(W(.-s))_{s \in T}$ is a loss function and F_n are posterior distributions for E_n with respect to some prior measures μ_n, $n \in \mathbb{N}$.

For notational convenience we introduce

$$B_n^\varepsilon(\omega_n) := \{t \in T_n: Z_n(t)(\omega_n) \leqq \inf_{s \in T_n} Z_n(s)(\omega_n) + \varepsilon\}$$

and

$$B^\varepsilon(\omega) := \{t \in T: Z(t)(\omega) \leqq \inf_{s \in T} Z(s)(\omega) + \varepsilon\},$$

$n \in \mathbb{N}$, $\varepsilon \geqq 0$. The terminology which is introduced in the following definitions is motivated by its applications to decision theory.

64.2 Definition. A stochastic kernel $\varrho: \Omega \times \mathscr{B}(T) \to [0,1]$ is a *minimum estimate* for $(Z(t))_{t \in T}$ if $\varrho(., B^0) = 1$ P-a.e.

64.3 Definition. A sequence of stochastic kernels $\varrho_n: \Omega_n \times \mathscr{B}(T_n) \to [0,1]$, $n \in \mathbb{N}$, is a sequence of *asymptotic minimum estimates* if for every $\varepsilon > 0$

$$\lim_{n \to \infty} \int \varrho_n(., T_n \setminus B_n^\varepsilon)\, dP_n = 0.$$

64.4 Examples. (1) Consider the case of Example 64.1 (1). An estimate $\varrho \in \mathscr{R}(E, T)$ which is a minimum estimate for every P_s, $s \in T$, is a *maximum likelihood estimate*. A sequence of estimates $\varrho_n \in \mathscr{R}(E_n, T_n)$, $n \in \mathbb{N}$, which is a sequence of asymptotic minimum estimates for every sequence $(P_{n,s})_{n \in \mathbb{N}}$, $s \in T$, is a sequence of *asymptotic maximum likelihood estimates.*

(2) Consider the case of Example 64.1 (2). Then the respective estimates are called *Bayes estimates* and sequences of *asymptotic Bayes estimates.*

Now we state those conditions which are usually needed for a satisfactory theory of minimum estimates.

64.5 Conditions for $(Z(t))_{t \in T}$.

(1) For every $\varepsilon > 0$ there is a compact set $K \subseteq T$ such that

$$P\{\inf_{x \in T \setminus K} Z(x) \leqq \inf_{y \in T} Z(y) + \varepsilon\} < \varepsilon .$$

(2) The process $(Z(t))_{t \in T}$ has continuous paths P-a.e.

64.6 Conditions for $(Z_n(t))_{t \in T_n}$, $n \in \mathbb{N}$.

(1) For every $\varepsilon > 0$ there is a compact set $K \subseteq T$ such that

$$\limsup_{n \to \infty} P_n\{\inf_{x \in T_n \setminus K} Z_n(x) \leqq \inf_{y \in T_n} Z_n(y) + \varepsilon\} < \varepsilon .$$

(2) The processes $(Z_n(t))_{t \in T_n}$, $n \in \mathbb{N}$, have continuous paths P_n-a.e. and are equicontinuous and bounded on compacts in (P_n)-probability.

First, we consider the question of existence of minimum estimates.

64.7 Theorem. *Suppose, that conditions 64.5 (1) and (2), are satisfied. Then there exist minimum estimates for* $(Z(t))_{t \in T}$.

Proof. If we can prove that $P\{B^0(\omega) \neq \emptyset\} = 1$ then the assertion follows from the existence theorem for measurable selections, Theorem 6.10. For every $n \in \mathbb{N}$ let $K_n \subseteq T$ be a compact set such that

$$P\left\{\inf_{x \in T \setminus K_n} Z(x) \leqq \inf_{y \in T} Z(y) + \frac{1}{n}\right\} < \frac{1}{n} .$$

Since

$$\left\{\inf_{x \in T \setminus K_n} Z(x) > \inf_{y \in T} Z(y) + \frac{1}{n}\right\} \subseteq \{B^0 \neq \emptyset\} \quad P_n\text{-a.e.}$$

it follows that $P\{B^0 \neq \emptyset\} \geqq 1 - \frac{1}{n}$, $n \in \mathbb{N}$, which proves the assertion. □

64.8 Theorem. *Suppose that conditions 64.6 (1) and (2) are satisfied. Then there exist sequences of asymptotic minimum estimates which even satisfy*

$$\lim_{n \to \infty} \int \varrho_n(\,.\,, B_n^0)\, dP_n = 1 .$$

Proof. For every $k \in \mathbb{N}$ let $K_k \subseteq T$ be a compact set such that

$$\limsup_{n \to \infty} P_n\left\{\inf_{x \in T_n \setminus K_k} Z_n(x) \leqq \inf_{y \in T_n} Z_n(y) + \frac{1}{k}\right\} < \frac{1}{k} .$$

Let N_k be such that $n \geqq N_k$ implies $T_n \subseteq K_k$ and

$$P_n\left\{\inf_{x \in T_n \setminus K_k} Z_n(x) \leqq \inf_{y \in T_n} Z_n(y) + \frac{1}{k}\right\} < \frac{1}{k}.$$

Since

$$\left\{\inf_{x \in T_n \setminus K_k} Z_n(x) > \inf_{y \in T_n} Z_n(y) + \frac{1}{k}\right\} \subseteq \{B_n^0 \neq \emptyset\} \quad P_n\text{-a.e.},$$

it follows that $P_n\{B_n^0 \neq \emptyset\} \geqq 1 - \frac{1}{k}$ if $n \geqq N_k$, which implies that $\lim_{n\to\infty} P_n\{B_n^0 \neq \emptyset\} = 1$. From Theorem 6.10 follows the existence of measurable maps κ_n: $\{B_n^0 \neq \emptyset\} \to T_n$ such that $\kappa_n(\omega_n) \in B_n^0(\omega_n)$. Define κ_n arbitrary on $\{B_n^0 = \emptyset\}$ and $\varrho_n(\omega_n, B) := 1_B(\kappa_n(\omega_n))$, $\omega_n \in \Omega_n$, $B \in \mathscr{B}(T_n)$. □

64.9 Remark. The reader will note that the proof of Theorem 64.7 is a literal copy of the second part of the proof of Theorem 37.8, which proves the existence of generalized Bayes estimates. In a similar way we shall prove the existence of asymptotic Bayes estimates. For proving the existence of maximum likelihood estimates our Theorems 64.7 and 64.8 are less useful since in this case the stochastic processes $(Z_n(t))_{t \in T_n}$, $n \in \mathbb{N}$, depend on $s \in T$ whereas the maximum likelihood estimates must be constructed independently of $s \in T$.

64.10 Lemma. *Suppose that condition 64.6 (1), is satisfied. Then for every $\varepsilon > 0$ there exists a compact set $K \subseteq T$ such that*

$$\lim_{n\to\infty} P_n\{B_n^\varepsilon \subseteq K\} > 1 - \varepsilon, \quad n \in \mathbb{N}.$$

Proof. Let $\varepsilon > 0$. Choose $K \subseteq T$ such that

$$\limsup_{n\to\infty} P_n\{\inf_{x \in T_n \setminus K} Z_n(x) \leqq \inf_{y \in T_n} Z_n(y) + \varepsilon\} < \varepsilon.$$

Since

$$\{\inf_{x \in T_n \setminus K} Z_n(x) > \inf_{y \in T_n} Z_n(y) + \varepsilon\} \subseteq \{B_n^\varepsilon \subseteq K\}$$

the assertion is proved. □

64.11 Definition. A sequence of stochastic kernels $\varrho_n: \Omega_n \times \mathscr{B}(T_n) \to [0,1]$, $n \in \mathbb{N}$, is *uniformly tight* if for every $\varepsilon > 0$ there is a compact set $K \subseteq T$ such that

$$\limsup_{n\to\infty} P_n\{\varrho_n(.,K) < 1 - \varepsilon\} < \varepsilon.$$

64.12 Theorem. *Suppose that condition 64.6 (1), is satisfied. Then every* *sequence of asymptotic minimum estimates for* $(Z_n(t))_{t\in T_n}$, $n\in\mathbb{N}$, *is uniformly tight.*

Proof. Let $\varepsilon>0$. Choose $K\subseteq T$ according to Lemma 64.10. Then

$$\varrho_n(.,T_n\setminus K)\leqq\varrho_n(.,T_n\setminus B_n^\varepsilon)+\varrho_n(.,B_n^\varepsilon\setminus K),$$

$n\in\mathbb{N}$. This implies by definition that

$$\limsup_{n\to\infty}\int\varrho_n(.,T_n\setminus K)\,dP_n\leqq\limsup_{n\to\infty}\int\varrho_n(.,B_n^\varepsilon\setminus K)\,dP_n<\varepsilon$$

since

$$P_n\{\varrho_n(.,B_n^\varepsilon\setminus K)>0\}\leqq P_n\{B_n^\varepsilon\setminus K\neq\emptyset\}<\varepsilon$$

for sufficiently large $n\in\mathbb{N}$. □

This tightness assertion has important consequences.

64.13 Corollary. *Assume that* T *is a locally compact space. Suppose that conditions 64.6 (1) and (2), are satisfied. If a sequence of stochastic kernels* $\sigma_n\colon\Omega_n\times\mathscr{B}(T_n)\to[0,1]$, $n\in\mathbb{N}$, *is stochastically equivalent to a sequence of asymptotic minimum estimates for* $(Z_n(t))_{t\in T_n}$, $n\in\mathbb{N}$, *then* (σ_n) *is also a sequence of asymptotic minimum estimates for* $(Z_n(t))_{t\in T_n}$, $n\in\mathbb{N}$.

Proof. Let (ϱ_n) be a sequence of asymptotic minimum estimates for $(Z_n(t))_{t\in T_n}$, $n\in\mathbb{N}$, which is stochastically equivalent to (σ_n). Let $\varepsilon>0$ and choose a compact set $K\subseteq T$ such that for $n\geqq N(\varepsilon)$

$$\int\varrho_n(.,T_n\setminus K)\,dP_n<\frac{\varepsilon}{4},$$

$$\int\sigma_n(.,T_n\setminus K)\,dP_n<\frac{\varepsilon}{4}.$$

By condition 64.6 (2), there exists $\delta>0$ such that the sets

$$A_n:=\left\{\sup_{d(x,y)<\delta,\;x,y\in K}|Z_n(x)-Z_n(y)|\leqq\frac{\varepsilon}{2}\right\}$$

satisfy $P_n(A_n')<\frac{\varepsilon}{2}$ as soon as $K\subseteq T_n$. Hence, $P_n(A_n)\geqq1-\frac{\varepsilon}{2}$, and for all $x,y\in K$, $\omega\in\Omega_n$,

$$x\in B_n^{\varepsilon/2}(\omega),\ d(x,y)<\delta\quad\text{imply}\quad y\in B_n^\varepsilon(\omega),\quad n\in\mathbb{N}.$$

It follows that for $n\geqq N(\varepsilon)$

$$\int \varrho_n(., B_n^{\varepsilon/2})\, \sigma_n(., T_n \setminus B_n^{\varepsilon})\, dP_n$$
$$\leqq \frac{\varepsilon}{2} + \int \varrho_n(., K \cap B_n^{\varepsilon/2})\, \sigma_n(., K \setminus B_n^{\varepsilon})\, dP_n$$
$$\leqq \varepsilon + \int_{A_n} \varrho_n(., K \cap B_n^{\varepsilon/2})\, \sigma_n(., K \setminus B_n^{\varepsilon})\, dP_n$$
$$\leqq \varepsilon \int \Big(\iint_{d(x,y) \geqq \delta,\, x, y \in K} \varrho_n(., dx)\, \sigma_n(., dy)\Big)\, dP_n.$$

Stochastic equivalence implies

$$\limsup_{n\to\infty} \int \varrho_n(., B_n^{\varepsilon/2})\, \sigma_n(., T_n \setminus B_n^{\varepsilon})\, dP_n \leqq \varepsilon.$$

Since (ϱ_n) is a sequence of asymptotic minimum estimates it follows that

$$\limsup_{n\to\infty} \int \sigma_n(., T_n \setminus B_n^{\varepsilon})\, dP_n \leqq \varepsilon.$$

This proves that (σ_n) is also a sequence of asymptotic minimum estimates for $(Z_n(t))_{t \in T_n}$, $n \in \mathbb{N}$. □

64.14 Corollary. *Suppose that condition 64.5 and 64.6 are satisfied. Assume that for every $\alpha \in A(T)$*

$$\lim_{n\to\infty} \mathscr{L}((Z_n(t))_{t\in\alpha} | P_n) = \mathscr{L}((Z(t))_{t\in\alpha} | P), \quad \textit{weakly.}$$

Then for every compact $K \subseteq T$

$$\limsup_{n\to\infty} P_n\{B_n^0 \cap K \neq \emptyset\} \leqq \lim_{\varepsilon\downarrow 0} \limsup_{n\to\infty} P_n\{B_n^{\varepsilon} \cap K \neq \emptyset\}$$
$$\leqq P\{B^0 \cap K \neq \emptyset\}.$$

Proof. Let $K \subseteq T$ be compact. The first inequality is trivial. Moreover, we observe that

$$\lim_{\varepsilon\downarrow 0} P\{B^{\varepsilon} \cap K \neq \emptyset\} = P\{B^0 \cap K \neq \emptyset\}$$

since compactness of K implies

$$\bigcap_{\varepsilon > 0} \{B^{\varepsilon} \cap K \neq \emptyset\} = \{B^0 \cap K \neq \emptyset\} \quad P\text{-a.e.}$$

Hence, it suffices to show that

$$\limsup_{n\to\infty} P_n\{B_n^{\varepsilon} \cap K \neq \emptyset\} \leqq P\{B^{\varepsilon} \cap K \neq \emptyset\} + 2\varepsilon$$

for sufficiently small $\varepsilon > 0$. For every sufficiently small $\varepsilon > 0$ and $n \geqq N(\varepsilon)$ we have a compact set $K_\varepsilon \subseteq T$, $K_\varepsilon \supseteq K$, such that

$$P_n\{B_n^\varepsilon \subseteq K_\varepsilon\} > 1-\varepsilon \quad \text{and} \quad P\{B^\varepsilon \subseteq K_\varepsilon\} > 1-\varepsilon\,.$$

This follows from Lemma 64.10. Since

$$B_n^\varepsilon \cap K \neq \emptyset \quad \text{iff} \quad \inf_K Z_n \leqq \inf_{K_\varepsilon} Z_n + \varepsilon$$

whenever $B_n^\varepsilon \subseteq K_\varepsilon$ and $K_\varepsilon \subseteq T_n$, and since

$$B^\varepsilon \cap K \neq \emptyset \quad \text{iff} \quad \inf_K Z \leqq \inf_{K_\varepsilon} Z + \varepsilon$$

if $B^\varepsilon \subseteq K_\varepsilon$, and since from condition 64.6 (2) it follows that

$$\mathscr{L}((Z_n(t))_{t\in K_\varepsilon}|P_n) \to \mathscr{L}((Z(t))_{t\in K_\varepsilon}|P) \text{ weakly on } \mathscr{C}(K_\varepsilon)$$

we obtain

$$\begin{aligned}
&\limsup_{n\to\infty} P_n\{B_n^\varepsilon \cap K \neq \emptyset\}\\
&\quad \leqq \varepsilon + \limsup_{n\to\infty} P_n\{\inf_K Z_n \leqq \inf_{K_\varepsilon} Z_n + \varepsilon\}\\
&\quad \leqq \varepsilon + P\{\inf_K Z \leqq \inf_{K_\varepsilon} Z + \varepsilon\} \leqq 2\varepsilon + P\{B^\varepsilon \cap K \neq \emptyset\}\,.
\end{aligned}$$

Hence the assertion. □

Now, we arrive at the desired result concerning convergence in distribution of minimum estimates.

64.15 Theorem. *Suppose that conditions 64.5 and 64.6 are satisfied. Assume that for every $\alpha \in A(T)$*

$$\lim_{n\to\infty} \mathscr{L}((Z_n(t))_{t\in\alpha}|P_n) = \mathscr{L}((Z(t))_{t\in\alpha}|P) \quad \textit{weakly}.$$

If the stochastic process $(Z(t))_{t\in T}$ attains its infimum in exactly one point P-a.e., then every sequence of asymptotic minimum estimates for $(Z_n(t))_{t\in T_n}$, $n\in\mathbb{N}$, converges in distribution to the minimum estimate for $(Z(t))_{t\in T}$.

Proof. Assume that (ϱ_n) is a sequence of asymptotic minimum estimates for $(Z_n(t))_{t\in T_n}$, $n \in \mathbb{N}$. Let $K \subseteq T$ be compact. If $\varepsilon > 0$ and $K \subseteq T_n$, then we have

$$\int \varrho_n(.\,, K)\,dP_n \leqq \int \varrho_n(.\,, K\cap B_n^\varepsilon)\,dP_n + \int \varrho_n(.\,, T_n\setminus B_n^\varepsilon)\,dP_n\,.$$

This implies that

$$\begin{aligned}
\limsup_{n\to\infty} \int \varrho_n(.\,, K)\,dP_n &\leqq \limsup_{n\to\infty} P_n\{\varrho(.\,, K\cap B_n^\varepsilon) > 0\}\\
&\leqq \limsup_{n\to\infty} P_n\{K \cap B_n^\varepsilon \neq \emptyset\}\,.
\end{aligned}$$

Corollary 64.14 yields

$$\limsup_{n\to\infty} \int \varrho_n(.,K)\,dP_n \leqq P\{B^0 \cap K \neq \emptyset\}.$$

Let ϱ be the minimum estimate for $(Z(t))_{t\in T}$. Since card $B^0(\omega)=1$ P-a.e. it follows that ϱ is non-randomized and

$$P\{B^0 \cap K \neq \emptyset\} = P\{\varrho(.,K)=1\} = \int \varrho(.,K)\,dP.$$

This implies

$$\limsup_{n\to\infty} \int \varrho_n(.,K)\,dP_n \leqq \int \varrho(.,K)\,dP.$$

Now, uniform tightness completes the proof of the assertion. □

In the subsequent sections the previous results are applied to asymptotic Bayes estimation since thereby it is possible to guarantee conditions 64.5 and 64.6 in a statistically plausible way. The problem of maximum likelihood estimation is discussed below.

64.16 Remark. If conditions 64.5 and 64.6 are satisfied with the notations of Example 64.1 (1) for every $s\in T$, then the application of the previous results to maximum likelihood theory is a matter of routine. The problem consists in establishing the validity of those conditions. Weak convergence of experiments does not imply the second condition and thus, for an invariance principle for the likelihood processes usually additional assumptions have to be made. We shall return to this in Section 84.

65. Uniformly integrable experiments

Let (T,d) be a metric space which is locally compact and separable. A Borel measure is a measure $\mu\in\mathscr{B}(T)$ such that $\mu(K)<\infty$ for every compact $K\subseteq T$.

Let $T_n\subseteq T$, $n\in\mathbb{N}$, be a sequence of open subsets such that $T_n\uparrow T$. Consider a sequence of experiments $E_n=(\Omega_n,\mathscr{A}_n,\{P_{n,t}\colon t\in T_n\})$, $n\in\mathbb{N}$. Moreover, let (μ_n) be a fixed sequence of Borel measures on $\mathscr{B}(T)$.

The main assumption of this section is concerned with the separation of points from complements of their neighborhoods by tests. Recall Definition 36.1.

65.1 Definition. Suppose that the experiments E_n, $n\in\mathbb{N}$, are measurable. Then the sequence (E_n) is *uniformly* (μ_n)*-integrable* if for every $s\in T$ and every $\varepsilon>0$ there are a compact set $K\subseteq T$ and a sequence of critical functions

$\varphi_n \in \mathscr{F}(\Omega_n, \mathscr{A}_n)$, $n \in \mathbb{N}$, such that

$$P_{n,s}\varphi_n > 1 - \varepsilon \quad \text{and} \quad \int_{T_n \setminus K} P_{n,t}\varphi_n \mu_n(dt) < \varepsilon$$

as soon as $s \in T_n$ and $K \subseteq T_n$.

For an example where this condition is satisfied see Discussion 84.10. The terminology is justified by the following theorem.

65.2 Theorem. *Suppose that the experiments E_n, $n \in \mathbb{N}$, are separable and measurable. Then the sequence (E_n) is uniformly (μ_n)-integrable iff for every $s \in T$ and $\varepsilon > 0$ there is a compact set $K \subseteq T$ such that*

$$P_{n,s}\left\{ \int_{T_n \setminus K} \frac{dP_{n,t}}{dP_{n,s}} \mu_n(dt) > \varepsilon \right\} < \varepsilon$$

as soon as $s \in T_n$ and $K \subseteq T_n$.

Proof. (1) Assume that (E_n) is uniformly (μ_n)-integrable. Let $s \in T$ and $0 < \varepsilon < 1$. Choose a compact set $K \subseteq T$ and a sequence of tests $\varphi_n \in \mathscr{F}(\Omega_n, \mathscr{A}_n)$, $n \in \mathbb{N}$, in such a way that

$$P_{n,s}\varphi_n > 1 - \frac{\varepsilon^2}{2} \quad \text{and} \quad \int_{T_n \setminus K} P_{n,t}(\varphi_n)\, \mu_n(dt) < \frac{\varepsilon^2}{2}$$

as soon as $s \in T_n$ and $K \subseteq T_n$. Denote

$$B_n := \left\{ \int_{T_n \setminus K} \frac{dP_{n,t}}{dP_{n,s}} \mu_n(dt) > \varepsilon \right\}, \quad n \in \mathbb{N}.$$

Then it follows as soon as $s \in T_n$ and $K \subseteq T_n$ that

$$\begin{aligned} P_{n,s}(B_n) &= \int_{B_n} (1 - \varphi_n)\, dP_{n,s} + \int_{B_n} \varphi_n\, dP_{n,s} \\ &\leq P_{n,s}(1 - \varphi_n) + \frac{1}{\varepsilon} \iint_{T_n \setminus K} \varphi_n \frac{dP_{n,t}}{dP_{n,s}} \mu_n(dt)\, dP_{n,s} \\ &\leq \frac{\varepsilon^2}{2} + \frac{\varepsilon}{2} < \varepsilon. \end{aligned}$$

(2) Assume conversely that there is a compact set $K \subseteq T$ such that

$$P_{n,s}\left\{ \int_{T_n \setminus K} \frac{dP_{n,t}}{dP_{n,s}} \mu_n(dt) > \varepsilon \right\} < \varepsilon$$

for a given $\varepsilon > 0$, as soon as $s \in T_n$ and $K \subseteq T_n$.

Note, that there are sets $M_n \in \mathscr{A}_n$ such that $P_{n,s}(M_n) = 1$ and

$P_{n,t}|\mathscr{A}_n \cap M_n \ll P_{n,s}|\mathscr{A}_n \cap M_n$, $t \in T_n$, $n \in \mathbb{N}$. (The point is that M_n is independent of $t \in T_n$ which is possible in view of separability.) Let

$$C_n := M_n \cap \{ \int_{T_n \setminus K} \frac{dP_{n,t}}{dP_{n,s}} \mu_n(dt) < \varepsilon \}, \quad n \in \mathbb{N}.$$

Then we obtain that $P_{n,s}(C_n) > 1 - \varepsilon$ and

$$\int_{T_n \setminus K} P_{n,t}(C_n)\, \mu_n(dt) = \int_{T_n \setminus K} \int_{C_n} \frac{dP_{n,t}}{dP_{n,s}} dP_{n,s} \mu_n(dt)$$

$$= \int_{C_n} \int_{T_n \setminus K} \frac{dP_{n,t}}{dP_{n,s}} \mu_n(dt)\, dP_{n,s} < \varepsilon$$

as soon as $s \in T_n$ and $K \subseteq T_n$. □

Next, we consider the consequences of uniform integrability for posterior distributions. First, we need a lemma.

65.3 Lemma. *Suppose that (E_n) is equicontinuous and that $\mu_n(U) > 0$ if $U \subseteq T$ is open, $n \in \mathbb{N}$. Then for every $s \in T$ and every $\varepsilon > 0$ there is $\delta_0 > 0$ such that*

$$P_{n,s}\{ \int_{B(s,\delta)} \frac{dP_{n,t}}{dP_{n,s}} \mu_n(dt) < \frac{1}{2} \mu_n(B(s,\delta))\} < \varepsilon$$

as soon as $s \in T_n$ and if $0 < \delta < \delta_0$.

Proof. Let us apply Lemma 36.12. Choose $s \in T$ and let $N(s) = \min\{n \in \mathbb{N}: s \in T_n\}$. From equicontinuity it follows that for every $\varepsilon > 0$ there exists $\delta_0 > 0$ such that

$$\| P_{n,s} - P_{n,t} \| < \frac{\varepsilon}{2} \quad \text{if} \quad t \in T_n \quad \text{and} \quad d(s,t) < \delta_0 .$$

We may choose $\delta_0 > 0$ sufficiently small to guarantee that $B(s, \delta_0) \subseteq T_{N(s)}$. This proves the assertion. □

65.4 Definition. A sequence of estimates $\varrho_n \in \mathscr{R}(E_n, T)$, $n \in \mathbb{N}$, is *uniformly tight* if for every $s \in T$ and every $\varepsilon > 0$ there is a compact set $K \subseteq T$ such that

$$P_{n,s}\{\varrho_n(.,K) < 1 - \varepsilon\} < \varepsilon$$

as soon as $s \in T_n$ and $K \subseteq T_n$.

Throughout the following we assume that the sequence of Borel measures (μ_n) converges strongly to a Borel measure $\mu|\mathscr{B}(T)$ on every compact $K \subseteq T$.

65.5 Theorem. *Suppose that (E_n) is equicontinuous and that $\mu(U)>0$ if $U\subseteq T$ is open. Then (E_n) is uniformly (μ_n)-integrable iff the sequence of posterior distributions F_n with respect to μ_n, $n\in\mathbb{N}$, is uniformly tight.*

Proof. (1) Assume that (E_n) is uniformly integrable. Let $s\in T$ and $\varepsilon>0$. By Lemma (64.3) we may find $\eta>0$ such that

$$P_{n,s}\{\int\frac{dP_{n,t}}{dP_{n,s}}\,\mu_n(dt)<\eta\}<\frac{\varepsilon}{2}$$

for sufficiently large $n\in\mathbb{N}$. By Theorem (65.2) choose a compact set $K\subseteq T$ such that

$$P_{n,s}\{\int_{T_n\setminus K}\frac{dP_{n,t}}{dP_{n,s}}\,\mu_n(dt)>\varepsilon\eta\}<\frac{\varepsilon}{2}$$

as soon as $s\in T_n$ and $K\subseteq T_n$. Then it follows with Theorem 36.14 that

$$\begin{aligned}&P_{n,s}\{F_n(T_n\setminus K)>\varepsilon\}\\&\quad=P_{n,s}\{\int_{T_n\setminus K}\frac{dP_{n,t}}{dP_{n,s}}\,\mu_n(dt)>\varepsilon\int\frac{dP_{n,t}}{dP_{n,s}}\,\mu_n(dt)\}\\&\quad\leqq P_{n,s}\{\int_{T_n\setminus K}\frac{dP_{n,t}}{dP_{n,s}}\,\mu_n(dt)>\varepsilon\eta\}+\frac{\varepsilon}{2}<\varepsilon\end{aligned}$$

for sufficiently large $n\in\mathbb{N}$. This proves one part of the assertion since uniform tightness for a finite subset of $\mathbb{N}$ is trivial.

(2) Assume that the posterior distributions are uniformly tight. It is sufficient to prove the condition of Theorem 65.2 for sufficiently large $n\in\mathbb{N}$. Let $K_0\subseteq T$ be a compact subset satisfying

$$P_{n,s}\{F_n(K_0)<1-\varepsilon\}<\frac{\varepsilon}{3}$$

and

$$\mu_n(K_0)\geqq a>0,$$

for sufficiently large $n\in\mathbb{N}$. Čebysev's inequality yields

$$P_{n,s}\left\{\int_{K_0}\frac{dP_{n,t}}{dP_{n,s}}\,\mu_n(dt)>\frac{3\mu_n(K_0)}{\varepsilon}\right\}<\frac{\varepsilon}{3}.$$

Choose a compact set $K\subseteq T$, $K_0\subseteq K$, such that

$$P_{n,s}\left\{F_n(T_n\setminus K)>\frac{\varepsilon^2(1-\varepsilon)}{3a}\right\}<\frac{\varepsilon}{3}$$

as soon as $s \in T_n$, $K \subseteq T_n$. Then it follows that

$$P_{n,s}\left\{\int_{T_n\setminus K} \frac{dP_{n,t}}{dP_{n,s}}\,\mu_n(dt) > \varepsilon\right\}$$

$$\leqq \frac{\varepsilon}{3} + P_{n,s}\left\{\frac{\int_{T_n\setminus K} \frac{dP_{n,t}}{dP_{n,s}}\,\mu_n(dt)}{\int_{K_0} \frac{dP_{n,t}}{dP_{n,s}}\,\mu_n(dt)} > \frac{\varepsilon^2}{3\,\mu_n(K_0)}\right\}$$

$$= \frac{\varepsilon}{3} + P_{n,s}\left\{\frac{F_n(T_n\setminus K)}{F_n K_0)} > \frac{\varepsilon^2}{3\,\mu_n(K_0)}\right\}$$

$$\leqq 2\frac{\varepsilon}{3} + P_{n,s}\left\{F_n(T_n\setminus K) > \frac{\varepsilon^2}{3\,\mu_n(K_0)}\,(1-\varepsilon)\right\}$$

$$\leqq 2\frac{\varepsilon}{3} + P_{n,s}\left\{F_n(T_n\setminus K) > \frac{\varepsilon^2}{3a}\,(1-\varepsilon)\right\} < \varepsilon. \qquad \square$$

65.6 Corollary. *Suppose that (E_n) is equicontinuous and that $\mu(U) > 0$ if $U \subseteq T$ is open. If (E_n) is uniformly $(|f|\mu_n)$-integrable where $f\colon T \to \mathbb{R}^m$ is a $\mathscr{B}(T)$-measurable function, then for every $s \in T$ and $\varepsilon > 0$ there is a compact set $K \subseteq T$ such that*

$$P_{n,s}\{\int_{T_n\setminus K} |f(t)|\,F_n(dt) > \varepsilon\} < \varepsilon$$

as soon as $s \in T_n$, $K \subseteq T_n$.

Proof. Copy part (1) of the proof of Theorem 65.5. $\square$

The following two lemmas are of technical importance in the sequel.

65.7 Lemma. *Suppose that (E_n) is equicontinuous and uniformly (μ_n)-integrable. Assume further that $\mu(U) > 0$ if $U \subseteq T$ is open. Then for every $s \in T$, $\varepsilon > 0$, and every neighborhood U of s there exists $\eta > 0$ such that*

$$\lim_{n\to\infty} P_{n,s}\{F_n(U) > \eta\} > 1 - \varepsilon.$$

Proof. Let $s \in T$ and $\varepsilon > 0$. Choose $\delta > 0$ in such a way that $B(s,\delta) \subseteq U$ and that for sufficiently large $n \in \mathbb{N}$

$$P_{n,s}\left\{\int_{B(s,\delta)} \frac{dP_{n,t}}{dP_{n,s}}\,\mu_n(dt) < \frac{\mu_n(B(s,\delta))}{2}\right\} < \frac{\varepsilon}{3}.$$

This is possible by Lemma 65.3. In view of Theorem 65.2 we may find a compact set $K \subseteq T$ such that

$$P_{n,s}\left\{ \int\limits_{T_n \setminus K} \frac{dP_{n,t}}{dP_{n,s}} \mu_n(dt) > \frac{\varepsilon}{3} \right\} < \frac{\varepsilon}{3} \quad \text{if} \quad s \in T_n,\ K \subseteq T_n.$$

Moreover, Čebysev's inequality implies

$$P_{n,s}\left\{ \int\limits_{K} \frac{dP_{n,t}}{dP_{n,s}} \mu_n(dt) > \frac{3\mu_n(K)}{\varepsilon} \right\} < \frac{\varepsilon}{3},\ s \in T_n,\ K \subseteq T_n.$$

We obtain for sufficiently large $n \in \mathbb{N}$

$$P_{n,s}\left\{ F_n(U) < \frac{\mu_n(B(s,\delta))}{2} \Big/ \left(\frac{\varepsilon}{3} + \frac{3\mu_n(K)}{\varepsilon} \right) \right\}$$

$$\leqq P_{n,s}\left\{ \int\limits_{U} \frac{dP_{n,t}}{dP_{n,s}} \mu_n(dt) < \frac{\mu_n(B(s,\delta))}{2} \right\} + \frac{2\varepsilon}{3} < \varepsilon.$$

Choosing

$$0 < \eta \leqq \liminf_{n \to \infty} \frac{\mu_n(B(s,\delta))}{2} \Big/ \left(\frac{\varepsilon}{3} + \frac{3\mu_n(K)}{\varepsilon} \right)$$

proves the seertion. □

65.8 Lemma. *Suppose that (E_n) is equicontinuous and uniformly (μ_n)-integrable. Assume further that $\mu(U) > 0$ if $U \subseteq T$ is open. Then for every $s \in T$ and every $\varepsilon > 0$ there is $C(\varepsilon) < \infty$ such that*

$$P_{n,s}\left\{ F_n\left\{ \frac{dF_n}{d\mu} > C(\varepsilon) \right\} > \varepsilon \right\} < \varepsilon$$

as soon as $s \in T_n$.

Proof. Let $s \in T$ and $\varepsilon > 0$. Since the sequence of posterior distributions is uniformly tight it is sufficient to show that for every compact $K \subseteq T$ there exists $C(\varepsilon) < \infty$ such that

$$P_{n,s}\left\{ F_n\left(K \cap \left\{ \frac{dF_n}{d\mu_n} > C(\varepsilon) \right\} \right) > \varepsilon \right\} < \varepsilon$$

as soon as $s \in T_n$ and $K \subseteq T_n$. Moreover, we need only prove the assertion for sufficiently large $n \in \mathbb{N}$. W.l.g. let $\mu(K) > 0$. According to Lemma 65.3 there exists $\delta > 0$ such that

$$P_{n,s}\left\{ \int \frac{dP_{n,t}}{dP_{n,s}} \mu_n(dt) < \delta \right\} < \frac{\varepsilon}{3}$$

for sufficiently large $n \in \mathbb{N}$. Let $B_1, \ldots, B_k$ be a partition of K and $t_i \in B$, $1 \leqq i \leqq k$, such that

$$\sup\{\|P_{n,t} - P_{n,t_i}\| : t \in B_i\} < \frac{\delta\varepsilon^2}{6\mu_n(K)}, \quad 1 \leqq i \leqq k.$$

The existence of such a partition follows from equicontinuity, from compactness of K and from $\mu_n(K) \to \mu(K) > 0$. Let $C < \infty$ be an arbitrary constant. Since

$$\mu_n\left\{\frac{dF_n}{d\mu_n} > C\right\} \leqq \frac{1}{C}, \quad n \in \mathbb{N},$$

it follows that for sufficiently large $n \in \mathbb{N}$

$$P_{n,s}\left\{\int_{K \cap \{\frac{dF_n}{d\mu_n} > C\}} \frac{dP_{n,t}}{dP_{n,s}}\, \mu_n(dt) > \frac{1}{C}\sum_{i=1}^{k} \frac{dP_{n,t_i}}{dP_{n,s}} + \frac{\varepsilon\delta}{2}\right\}$$

$$\leqq P_{n,s}\left\{\int_{K \cap \{\frac{dF_n}{d\mu_n} > C\}} \frac{dP_{n,t}}{dP_{n,s}}\, \mu_n(dt) > \sum_{i=1}^{k} \frac{dP_{n,t_i}}{dP_{n,s}}\, \mu\left(B_i \cap \left\{\frac{dF_n}{d\mu_n} > C\right\}\right) + \frac{\varepsilon\delta}{2}\right\}$$

$$\leqq P_{n,s}\left\{\left|\int_{K \cap \{\frac{dF_n}{d\mu_n} > C\}} \frac{dP_{n,t}}{dP_{n,s}}\, \mu_n(dt) - \sum_{i=1}^{k} \int_{B_i \cap \{\frac{dF_n}{d\mu_n} > C\}} \frac{dP_{n,t}}{dP_{n,s}}\, \mu_n(dt)\right| > \frac{\varepsilon\delta}{2}\right\}$$

$$\leqq P_{n,s}\left\{\sum_{i=1}^{k} \int_{B_i \cap \{\frac{dF_n}{d\mu_n} > C\}} \left|\frac{dP_{n,t}}{dP_{n,s}} - \frac{dP_{n,t_i}}{dP_{n,s}}\right| \mu_n(dt) > \frac{\varepsilon\delta}{2}\right\}$$

$$\leqq \frac{2}{\varepsilon\delta} \sum_{i=1}^{k} \int_{B_i} \|P_{n,t} - P_{n,t_i}\|\, \mu_n(dt) \leqq \frac{2}{\varepsilon\delta} \cdot \frac{\delta\varepsilon^2}{6} = \frac{\varepsilon}{3}.$$

This implies

$$P_{n,s}\left\{F_n\left(K \cap \left\{\frac{dF_n}{d\mu_n} > C\right\}\right) > \varepsilon\right\}$$

$$\leqq \frac{\varepsilon}{3} + P_{n,s}\left\{\int_{K \cap \{\frac{dF_n}{d\mu_n} > C\}} \frac{dP_{n,t}}{dP_{n,s}}\, \mu_n(dt) > \varepsilon\delta\right\}$$

$$\leqq \frac{2\varepsilon}{3} + P_{n,s}\left\{\frac{1}{C}\sum_{i=1}^{k} \frac{dP_{n,t_i}}{dP_{n,s}} > \frac{\varepsilon\delta}{2}\right\}$$

$$\leqq \frac{2\varepsilon}{3} + \sum_{i=1}^{k} \frac{2}{C\varepsilon\delta} \cdot \int \frac{dP_{n,t_i}}{dP_{n,s}}\, dP_{n,s} \leqq \frac{2\varepsilon}{3} + \frac{2k}{C\varepsilon\delta}.$$

The assertion is proved if we choose $C(\varepsilon) > \dfrac{6k}{\varepsilon^2\delta}$. □

66. Uniform tightness of generalized Bayes estimates

In the following we consider the case where $(T, |\,.\,|)$ is a finite dimensional linear space and $\mu = \lambda_T$, the Lebesgue measure on T. In addition, the situation is the same as in the preceding section. Call the sequence (E_n) uniformly (μ_n)-integrable of order p if it is uniformly $(g\mu_n)$-integrable for $g: t \mapsto |t|^p$. Let $W: T \to [0, \infty)$, $W(0) = 0$, be a loss function.

66.1 Remark. In the following we denote

$$Z_n(t) := \int W(t-x) F_n(dx), \quad t \in T_n,\ n \in \mathbb{N}.$$

We shall permanently refer to Sections 64 and 65.

66.2 Definition. A sequence of estimates $\varrho_n \in \mathscr{R}(E_n, T_n)$, $n \in \mathbb{N}$, is a sequence of *asymptotic Bayes estimates* (for W and (μ_n)) if it is a sequence of asymptotic minimum estimates for $(Z_n(t))_{t \in T_n}$, $n \in \mathbb{N}$, for every sequence $(P_{n,s})$, $s \in T$.

66.3 Lemma. *Assume that (E_n) is equicontinuous and uniformly (μ_n)-integrable of order $p \geqq 1$. If W is of order p, level compact and separating then for every $\varepsilon > 0$ and every $s \in T$ there exists $b < \sup W$ such that*

$$P_{n,s}\{Z_n(s) > b\} < \varepsilon \quad \textit{as soon as} \quad s \in T_n.$$

Proof. Let $s \in T$ and $\varepsilon > 0$. First, we assume that W is not bounded. From Corollary 65.6 it follows that there is a compact set $K \subseteq T$ and $\delta > 0$ such that

$$P_{n,s}\{\int_{T_n \setminus K} W(s-t) F_n(dt) > \delta\} < \varepsilon$$

as soon as $s \in T_n$, $K \subseteq T_n$. Now the assertion follows since $W(s-.)$ is bounded on K.

Next assume that W is bounded and separating. Let $c < \sup W$ be such that $U = \{s \in T: W(s-t) \leqq c\}$ is a neighborhood of s. From Lemma 65.7 we obtain $\eta > 0$ such that

$$P_{n,s}\{F_n(U) < \sqrt{\eta}\} < \varepsilon$$

as soon as $U \subseteq T_n$. W.l.g. $\eta > 0$ can be chosen in such a way that $c < \sup W - \sqrt{\eta}$. From

$$\begin{aligned}\int W(s-t) F_n(dt) &\leqq \sup W \cdot F_n(T_n \setminus U) + (\sup W - \sqrt{\eta}) F_n(U)\\ &= \sup W(1 - F_n(U)) + \sup W \cdot F_n(U) - \sqrt{\eta}\, F_n(U)\\ &= \sup W - \sqrt{\eta} \cdot F_n(U)\end{aligned}$$

it follows that

$$P_{n,s}\{\int W(s-t)\,F_n(dt) > \sup W - \eta\} \leqq P_{n,s}\{F_n(U) < \sqrt{\eta}\} < \varepsilon. \qquad \square$$

66.4 Theorem. *Assume that (E_n) is equicontinuous and uniformly (μ_n)-integrable of order $p \geqq 1$. Assume further that W is of order p, level compact and separating. Then for every $s \in T$ and every $\varepsilon > 0$ there exists a compact set $K_\varepsilon \subseteq T$ such that*

$$P_{n,s}\{\inf_{x \in T_n \setminus K_\varepsilon} Z_n(x) \leqq \inf_{y \in T_n} Z_n(y) + \varepsilon\} < \varepsilon$$

as soon as $s \in T_n$, $K_\varepsilon \subseteq T_n$.

Proof. Let $s \in T$, $\varepsilon > 0$. By Lemma 66.3 there exists $b_0 \in (0, \sup W)$ such that

$$P_{n,s}\{\int W(s-t)\,F_n(dt) \leqq b_0\} \geqq 1 - \frac{\varepsilon}{2}$$

as soon as $s \in T_n$. Reducing $\varepsilon > 0$, if necessary, we achieve $(b_0 + \varepsilon)/(1-\varepsilon) < \sup W$. Let $C \subseteq T$ be compact and such that

$$P_{n,s}\{F_n(C) < 1 - \varepsilon\} < \frac{\varepsilon}{2}$$

as soon as $s \in T_n$, $C \subseteq T_n$. This is possible by Theorem 65.5.

Let

$$A_{n,\varepsilon} := \{\int W(s-t)\,F_n(dt) \leqq b_0\} \cap \{F_n(C) > 1 - \varepsilon\}.$$

Then $P_{n,s}(A_{n,\varepsilon}) > 1 - \varepsilon$. Now we choose a compact set $K_\varepsilon \subseteq T$ in such a way that

$$W(x-t) > \frac{b_0 + \varepsilon}{1-\varepsilon} \quad \text{whenever } t \in C \quad \text{and} \quad x \notin K_\varepsilon.$$

This is possible since W is level compact. If $x \notin K_\varepsilon$ then we obtain on $A_{n,\varepsilon}$

$$\begin{aligned}\int W(x-t)\,F_n(dt) &\geqq \int_C W(x-t)\,F_n(dt) > \frac{b_0+\varepsilon}{1-\varepsilon} F_n(C) \geqq b_0 + \varepsilon \\ &\geqq \int W(s-t)\,F_n(dt) + \varepsilon \geqq \inf_{y \in T_n} \int W(y-t)\,F_n(dt) + \varepsilon. \qquad \square\end{aligned}$$

As a consequence we obtain existence and tightness of asymptotic Bayes estimates.

66.5 Corollary. *Assume that the conditions of Theorem 66.4 are satisfied.*

(1) *There exist sequences of asymptotic Bayes estimates for W and (μ_n).*

(2) *Every sequence of asymptotic Bayes estimates for W and (μ_n) is uniformly tight.*

Proof. (1) Apply Theorem 64.8.
(2) Apply Theorem 64.12. □

67. Convergence of generalized Bayes estimates

First, we consider the general case where (T,d) is a metric space. Let us consider the situation of Section 65 but assume additionally that the sequence of experiments (E_n) converges weakly to an experiment $E \in \mathscr{E}(T)$.

Our first assertion is a basic approximation lemma.

67.1 Lemma. *Suppose that (E_n) is equicontinuous. Let $K \subseteq T$ be compact and $f\colon K \to \mathbb{R}^m$ $\mathscr{B}(T)$-measurable and bounded. Then for every $\varepsilon > 0$ there are a measurable partition $B_1, B_2, \ldots, B_M$ of K, points $t_i \in B_i$, $1 \leqq i \leqq M$, and $\alpha_i \in \mathbb{R}$, $1 \leqq i \leqq M$, such that*

$$P_{n,s}\left|\int_K f(t)\,\frac{dP_{n,t}}{dP_{n,s}}\,\mu_n(dt) - \sum_{i=1}^{M} \alpha_i\,\frac{dP_{n,t}}{dP_{n,s}}\,\mu_n(B_i)\right| < \varepsilon$$

whenever $s \in T_n$ and $K \subseteq T_n$.

Proof. The proof is almost the same as for Lemma 36.16. Let $\varepsilon > 0$ and $K \subseteq T$ compact. It is clear that $\sup\{\mu_n(K)\colon n \in \mathbb{N}\} =: C < \infty$. If $C = 0$ or $\|f\|_u = 0$ then the assertion is trivial. Assume that $C > 0$ and $\|f\|_u > 0$. From equicontinuity of (E_n) it follows that there exists $\delta > 0$ such that

$$P_{n,s}\left|\frac{dP_{n,t_1}}{dP_{n,s}} - \frac{dP_{n,t_2}}{dP_{n,s}}\right| < \frac{\varepsilon}{2C\|f\|_u} \quad \text{if} \quad d(t_1, t_2) < \delta,\ t_1, t_2 \in K,$$

whenever $s \in T_n$ and $K \subseteq T_n$. Since f is bounded there is a step function $g = \sum_{i=1}^{M} \alpha_i 1_{B_i}$ such that $\|g\|_u \leqq \|f\|_u$ and

$$\sup_{t \in K}\left|f(t) - \sum_{i=1}^{M} \alpha_i 1_{B_i}(t)\right| < \frac{\varepsilon}{2C}.$$

The sets B_i, $1 \leqq i \leqq M$, may be chosen in such a way that $\operatorname{diam} B_i < \delta$, $1 \leqq i \leqq M$, and that $\{B_i\colon 1 \leqq i \leqq M\}$ is a partition of K. Now the assertion follows by the chain of inequalities already considered in the proof of 36.16. □

67.2 Lemma. *Suppose that (E_n) is equicontinuous. Let $K \subseteq T$ be compact and $f\colon K \to \mathbb{R}^m$ $\mathscr{B}(T)$-measurable and bounded. If $E_n \to E$ then*

$$\mathscr{L}\Big(\int_K f(t)\,\frac{dP_{n,t}}{dP_{n,s}}\,\mu_n(dt)\,|\,P_{n,s}\Big) \to \mathscr{L}\Big(\int_K f(t)\,\frac{dP_t}{dP_s}\,\mu(dt)\,|\,P_s\Big) \quad \textit{weakly},$$

for every $s \in T$.

Proof. By Lemma 60.7 the limit experiment E is continuous. Let

$$\varphi_n = \int_K f(t)\,\frac{dP_{n,t}}{dP_{n,s}}\,\mu_n(dt), \quad n \in \mathbb{N}, \quad \text{and}$$

$$\varphi_0 = \int_K f(t)\,\frac{dP_t}{dP_s}\,\mu(dt).$$

Moreover, for a given $\varepsilon > 0$ choose a partition $B_1, B_2, \ldots, B_M$ of K, points $t_i \in B$ and $\alpha_i \in \mathbb{R}$, $1 \leqq i \leqq M$, according to Lemmas 67.1 and 36.16. Denote

$$\psi_n = \sum_{i=1}^{M} \alpha_i\,\frac{dP_{n,t_i}}{dP_{n,s}}\,\mu_n(B_i), \quad n \in \mathbb{N}, \quad \text{and}$$

$$\psi_0 = \sum_{i=1}^{M} \alpha_i\,\frac{dP_{t_i}}{dP_s}\,\mu(B_i).$$

Then we have

$$\mathscr{L}(\psi_n\,|\,P_{n,s}) \to \mathscr{L}(\psi_0\,|\,P_s) \quad \text{weakly},$$

$$P_{n,s}|\psi_n - \varphi_n| < \varepsilon \quad \text{as soon as} \quad s \in T_n,\ K \subseteq T_n,$$

and

$$P_s|\psi_0 - \varphi_0| < \varepsilon.$$

Since $\varepsilon > 0$ is arbitrary it follows by easy arguments that

$$\mathscr{L}(\varphi_n\,|\,P_{n,s}) \to \mathscr{L}(\varphi_0\,|\,P_s) \quad \text{weakly.} \qquad \square$$

The following two assertions are the basic facts for limit theorems on Bayes estimates.

67.3 Lemma. *Suppose that* (E_n) *is equicontinuous and uniformly* (μ_n)*-integrable. Then* E *is* μ*-integrable.*

Proof. By Corollary 36.4 it is sufficient to show that

$$P_s\left\{\int \frac{dP_t}{dP_s}\,\mu(dt) = \infty\right\} = 0, \quad s \in T.$$

Let $s \in T$, $\varepsilon > 0$. Choose a compact set $K_\varepsilon \subseteq T$ satisfying

$$P_{n,s}\left\{\int_{T_n\setminus K} \frac{dP_{n,t}}{dP_{n,s}}\,\mu_n(dt) > \varepsilon\right\} < \frac{\varepsilon}{2}$$

as soon as $s \in T_n$, $K_\varepsilon \subseteq T_n$. This is possible by Theorem 65.2. From Lemma 67.2 it follows that for every compact $K \supseteq K_\varepsilon$

$$P_s\left\{\int_{K\setminus K_\varepsilon} \frac{dP_t}{dP_s}\,\mu(dt) > \varepsilon\right\} < \frac{\varepsilon}{2}$$

which implies that

$$P_s\left\{\int_{T\setminus K_\varepsilon} \frac{dP_t}{dP_s}\,\mu(dt) > \varepsilon\right\} \leqq \frac{\varepsilon}{2}\cdot$$

Hence we obtain

$$\begin{aligned} &P_s\left\{\int \frac{dP_t}{dP_s}\,\mu(dt) > \varepsilon + 2\frac{\mu(K_\varepsilon)}{\varepsilon}\right\} \\ &\leqq P_s\left\{\int_{T\setminus K_\varepsilon} \frac{dP_t}{dP_s}\,\mu(dt) > \varepsilon\right\} + P_s\left\{\int_{K_\varepsilon} \frac{dP_t}{dP_s}\,\mu(dt) > 2\frac{\mu(K_\varepsilon)}{\varepsilon}\right\} \\ &< \frac{\varepsilon}{2} + \frac{\varepsilon}{2} < \varepsilon. \qquad \square \end{aligned}$$

67.4 Lemma. *Suppose that (E_n) is equicontinuous and uniformly (μ_n)-integrable of order $p \geqq 1$. Assume further that $\mu(U) > 0$ if $U \subseteq T$ is open. If $f\colon T \to \mathbb{R}^m$ is of order p then*

$$\mathscr{L}\left(\int f(t)\,F_n(dt)\,|\,P_{n,s}\right) \to \mathscr{L}\left(\int f(t)\,F(dt)\,|\,P_s\right) \quad \textit{weakly}$$

for every $s \in T$.

Proof. Let $s \in T$. It follows from Lemma 67.2 that for every compact $K \subseteq T$ with $s \in \mathring{K}$

$$\mathscr{L}\left(\int f(t)\,F_n(dt|K)\,|\,P_{n,s}\right) \to \mathscr{L}\left(\int f(t)\,F(dt|K)\,|\,P_s\right) \quad \text{weakly.}$$

Since

$$\begin{aligned} &\left|\int f(t)\,F_n(dt|K) - \int f(t)\,F_n(dt)\right| \\ &\quad \leqq F_n(T_n\setminus K)\int f(t)\,F_n(dt|K) + \int_{T_n\setminus K} f(t)\,F_n(dt) \end{aligned}$$

and

$$\begin{aligned} &\left|\int f(t)\,F(dt|K) - \int f(t)\,F(dt)\right| \\ &\quad \leqq F(T\setminus K)\int f(t)\,F(dt|K) + \int_{T\setminus K} f(t)\,F(dt) \end{aligned}$$

it follows from Theorem 65.5 and Corollary 65.6 that for every $\varepsilon > 0$ there is a compact set $K_\varepsilon \subseteq T$ such that

$$P_{n,s} | \int f(t)\, F_n(dt | K_\varepsilon) - \int f(t)\, F_n(dt) | < \varepsilon$$

as soon as $s \in T_n$, $K_\varepsilon \subseteq T_n$, and

$$P_s | \int f(t)\, F(dt | K_\varepsilon) - \int f(t)\, F(dt) | < \varepsilon .$$

Now, a similar argument as in the proof of Corollary 67.2 proves the assertion. □

From now, we assume that $(T, |\,.\,|)$ is a finite dimensional linear space and $\mu = \lambda_T$. Let $W: T \to [0, \infty)$ be a loss function.

67.5 Theorem. *Suppose that* (E_n) *is equicontinuous and uniformly* (μ_n)-*integrable of order* $p \geqq 1$. *Let* W *be of order* p. *Then the stochastic processes*

$$Z_n(t) := \int W(t - x)\, F_n(dx), \quad t \in T_n,\ n \in \mathbb{N},$$

are equicontinuous in $(P_{n,s})$-*probability for every* $s \in T$.

Proof. We have to show that for every $s \in T$, $x \in T$, and every $\varepsilon > 0$ there exists $\delta > 0$ such that

$$P_{n,s}\{ \sup_{y \in B(x,\delta)} |Z_n(y) - Z_n(x)| > \varepsilon\} < \varepsilon$$

as soon as $s \in T_n$, $B(x, \delta) \subseteq T_n$.

Choose $s \in T$, $x \in T$ and $\varepsilon > 0$ arbitrarily. Let $\delta_1 > 0$ be such that $W(y - t) \leqq C_3 |t|^p + C_4$ if $y \in B(x, \delta_1)$ and $t \in T$. Then we may find a compact set $K \subseteq T$ such that

$$P_{n,s}\left\{ \sup_{y \in B(x,\delta_1)} \int_{T_n \setminus K} W(y - t)\, F_n(dt) > \frac{\varepsilon}{4}\right\} < \frac{\varepsilon}{3}$$

as soon as $s \in T_n$ and $K \subseteq T_n$. This is clear by Corollary 65.6. Let $M_2 := \sup\{W(y - t): y \in B(x, \delta_1),\ t \in K\}$. By Lemma 65.8 there is $M_1 < \infty$ satisfying

$$P_{n,s}\left\{ F_n\left\{\frac{dF_n}{d\mu_n} > M_1\right\} > \frac{\varepsilon}{4 M_2}\right\} < \frac{\varepsilon}{3}$$

as soon as $s \in T_n$. Let $\delta_2 > 0$ be such that

$$\sup_{y \in B(x,\delta_2)} \int_K | W(y - t) - W(x - t) |\, \lambda_T(dt) < \frac{\varepsilon}{8 M_1}$$

which implies

$$\sup_{y \in B(x,\delta_2)} \int_K |W(y-t) - W(x-t)| \mu_n(dt) < \frac{\varepsilon}{4M_1}$$

for sufficiently large $n \in \mathbb{N}$. If we choose $\delta = \min\{\delta_1, \delta_2\}$ then it follows that

$$P_{n,s}\left\{\sup_{y \in B(x,\delta)} |Z_n(y) - Z_n(x)| > \varepsilon\right\}$$

$$\leqq P_{n,s}\left\{\sup_{y \in B(x,\delta)} \int_K |W(y-t) - W(x-t)| F_n(dt) > \frac{\varepsilon}{2}\right\}$$

$$+ 2P_{n,s}\left\{\sup_{y \in B(x,\delta)} \int_{T_n \setminus K} W(y-t) F_n(dt) > \frac{\varepsilon}{4}\right\}$$

$$\leqq P_{n,s}\left\{M_2 \cdot F_n\left\{\frac{dF_n}{d\mu_n} > M_1\right\}\right.$$

$$\left. + M_1 \cdot \sup_{y \in B(x,\delta)} \int_K |W(y-t) - W(x-t)| \mu_n(dt) > \frac{\varepsilon}{2}\right\} + \frac{2\varepsilon}{2}$$

$$\leqq P_{n,s}\left\{M_2 \cdot F_n\left\{\frac{dF_n}{d\mu_n} > M_1\right\} > \frac{\varepsilon}{4}\right\} + \frac{2\varepsilon}{4} < \varepsilon$$

for sufficiently large $n \in \mathbb{N}$. Since $(Z_n(x))_{x \in T_n}$ is continuous $P_{n,s}$-a.e. for every fixed $n \in \mathbb{N}$ by Lemma 37.7, the assertion follows. □

67.6 Corollary. *Suppose that (E_n) is equicontinuous and uniformly (μ_n)-integrable of order $p \geqq 1$. Assume further that W is separating, level-compact and of order p.*

(1) *If a sequence of estimates $\sigma_n \in \mathscr{R}(E_n, T_n)$, $n \in \mathbb{N}$, is stochastically equivalent with a sequence of asymptotic Bayes estimates then (σ_n) is also a sequence of asymptotic Bayes estimates.*

(2) *If the stochastic process $Z(t) := \int W(t-x) F(dx)$, $t \in T$, attains its infimum in at most a single point P_s-a.e., $s \in T$, then every sequence of asymptotic Bayes estimates converges in distribution to the generalized Bayes estimate of E.*

Proof. (1) Apply Corollary 64.13.

(2) Apply Theorem 64.15. □

67.7 Corollary. *Assume that the conditions of Corollary 67.6 (2), are satisfied. Then every sequence of estimates which converges in distribution to the generalized Bayes estimate of E is a sequence of asymptotic Bayes estimates. All sequences of asymptotic Bayes estimates are stochastically equivalent.*

Proof. The generalized Bayes estimate ϱ of E is non-randomized. Moreover, it is uniquely determined by its distribution since the distribution determines

$$M: A \mapsto \int_A \iint W(x-t)\,\varrho(\omega, dx)\,P_t(d\omega)\,\mu(dt), \quad A \in \mathscr{A},$$

and

$$\frac{dM}{dP(\mu)} = \iint W(x-t)\,\varrho(.\,, dx)\,F(dt).$$

Hence, Theorem 63.6 implies that all estimates which converge to ϱ in distribution are stochastically equivalent. In particular, they are stochastically equivalent to a given sequence of asymptotic Bayes estimates which exists by Corollary 66.5. By Corollary 67.6 the assertion follows. □

Chapter 11: Gaussian Shifts on Hilbert Spaces

In the preceding chapters we have met Gaussian shifts several times. The distinguished role which these experiments play in the classical theory is due to the fact that they admit a particularly simple statistical analysis. Roughly speaking, their theory can be presented in terms of linear algebra. However, in the last decades more and more statisticians came to the conclusion that practical statistical data almost never originate from Gaussian shift experiments. Nevertheless, experiments of this type are still of central theoretical significance. The reason are the results of asymptotic statistics.

The asymptotic theory of statistics deals with local approximations of experiments for large sample sizes by simpler experiments. Thereby it turns out that under mild smoothness conditions limit experiments are usually Gaussian shifts.

For the application of the asymptotic decision theory of Chapter 10 to cases where the limit is a Gaussian shift we need a complete statistical theory of Gaussian shift experiments. In case of finite dimensional parameter spaces the pertaining results are scattered over the preceding parts of this book (cf. sections 28, 30, 34, 38). The asymptotic theory of non-parametric methods leads, however, to limit experiments which are Gaussian shifts with infinite dimensional parameter spaces. This is the reason why we take up the theory of Gaussian shifts again and present it general enough to cover also the infinite dimensional case.

The case of infinite dimensional parameter spaces requires some technical tools which are collected in Section 68. It is concerned with linear processes and cylinder set measures. Section 69 deals with the general concept of a Gaussian shift experiment on a Hilbert space. We characterize the likelihood process of a Gaussian shift and show that linear processes define generalized decision functions in a canonical way.

Gaussian shift experiments are invariant under the translation group of the underlying Hilbert space. In case the Hilbert space is of finite dimension the Gaussian shift can be represented as full shift on this finite dimensional Hilbert space, generated by the standard normal distribution. But if the Hilbert space is not of finite dimension then such a representation is impossible since there is no standard normal distribution on such a Hilbert space. If the Hilbert space can be completed in a suitable way (Abstract Wiener spaces), it becomes possible to generate the Gaussian shift experiment through an operation of the Hilbert space on the sample space. These questions, together with some important examples, are discussed in Section 70.

In Sections 71 and 72 we present the theory of testing and estimation for general Gaussian shifts. Section 73 deals with the particular case of Abstract Wiener space representation which admits some simplification.

The content of this chapter is well-known. The first presentation in the literature from our viewpoint can be found in the thesis of Moussatat [1976] which was written under the guidance of LeCam. From there we take the proof of Theorem 71.14. The thesis of Moussatat also contains a particular case of the minimax bound given in Theorem 73.6. This theorem is formulated for the first time by Millar [1979] referring to unpublished results of LeCam. The general minimax bound of Theorem 72.7, although unpublished, should be well-known, too.

A presentation of the subject with a similar intention as ours is Millar [1983].

68. Linear stochastic processes and cylinder set measures

Let $(H, \langle .,. \rangle)$ be a separable Hilbert space. Any linear function Z: $H \to \mathscr{L}(\Omega, \mathscr{A})$, where $(\Omega, \mathscr{A})$ is a sample space, is called *linear process*.

68.1 Example. Let κ: $\Omega \to H$ be a measurable mapping. Then $Z(h) := \langle h, \kappa(.)\rangle$, $h \in H$, defines a linear process.

To exhibit another important example we need some basic facts on Gaussian processes.

68.2 Discussion. Let $T \neq \emptyset$ be an arbitrary set. A stochastic process $X = (\Omega, \mathscr{A}, P, (X_t)_{t \in T})$ is a *Gaussian process* if all finite dimensional marginal distributions of X are Gaussian distributions. The function

$$K\colon (s, t) \mapsto \int (X_s - P(X_s))(X_t - P(X_t))\, dP, \quad s, t \in T,$$

is the covariance of X. Obviously, the covariance K is positive semidefinite, i.e.

$$\sum_{i=1}^{k} \sum_{j=1}^{k} \alpha_i \alpha_j K(t_i, t_j) \geq 0$$

for every choice $(t_1, \ldots, t_k) \in T^k$, $(\alpha_1, \ldots, \alpha_k) \in \mathbb{R}^k$.

As a matter of fact, every positive semidefinite symmetric function K on T^2 is the covariance of a Gaussian process. To see this, let $\Omega = \mathbb{R}^T$, $\mathscr{A} = \mathscr{B}(\mathbb{R})^T$ and define for every $\alpha \in A(T)$ a probability measure $P_\alpha | \mathscr{B}(\mathbb{R})^\alpha$ by

$$\int \exp\left(i \sum_{t \in \alpha} x_t y_t\right) P_\alpha(dy) = \exp\left(-\frac{1}{2} \sum_{s \in \alpha} \sum_{t \in \alpha} x_s x_t K(s, t)\right),$$

$(x_t)_{t \in \alpha} \in \mathbb{R}^\alpha$. Then it is easy to see that $(P_\alpha)_{\alpha \in A(T)}$ is a projective system of Gaussian probability measures. Define $P|\mathscr{B}(\mathbb{R})^T$ to be the projective limit and take $X_t = p_t$, $t \in T$.

The case we are interested in arises when T itself is a Hilbert space $(H, \langle .,. \rangle)$. In this case $\langle .,. \rangle$ is positive definite and therefore the covariance function of a Gaussian process.

68.3 Definition. A Gaussian process $X = (\Omega, \mathscr{A}, P, (X(h))_{h \in H})$ is a *standard Gaussian process* (for H) if

(1) $\int X(h)\,dP = 0, \quad h \in H,$

(2) $\int X(h_1)X(h_2)\,dP = \langle h_1, h_2 \rangle, \quad h_1, h_2 \in H.$

The following is a useful characterization of standard Gaussian processes.

68.4 Theorem. *Let $X: H \to L^2(\Omega, \mathscr{A}, P)$. Then X is a standard Gaussian process iff X is linear and satisfies $\mathscr{L}(X(h)|P) = \nu_{0,||h||^2}$, $h \in H$.*

Proof. (1) Suppose that X is a standard Gaussian process. Let $(\alpha_1 \dots \alpha_n) \in \mathbb{R}^n$ and $(h_1 \dots h_n) \in H^n$, $n \in \mathbb{N}$. Then

$$\begin{aligned}\int\left(\sum_{i=1}^n \alpha_i X(h_i)\right)^2 dP &= \sum_{i=1}^n \sum_{j=1}^n \alpha_i \alpha_j \int X(h_i)X(h_j)\,dP \\ &= \sum_{i=1}^n \sum_{j=1}^n \alpha_i \alpha_j \langle h_i, h_j \rangle \\ &= \left\|\sum_{i=1}^n \alpha_i h_i\right\|^2.\end{aligned}$$

Hence, $\sum_{i=1}^n \alpha_i h_i = 0$ implies $\sum_{i=1}^n \alpha_i X(h_i) = 0$ P-a.e.

(2) Assume conversely, that X is linear and $\mathscr{L}(X(h)|P) = \nu_{0,||h||^2}$, $h \in H$. Let $(\alpha_1 \dots \alpha_n) \in \mathbb{R}^n$ and $(h_1 \dots h_n) \in H^n$, $n \in \mathbb{N}$. Then we have

$$\int \exp\left(i \sum_{k=1}^n \alpha_k X(h_k)\right) dP = \int \exp\left(iX\left(\sum_{k=1}^n \alpha_k h_k\right)\right) dP$$

$$= \exp\left(-\frac{1}{2}\left\|\sum_{k=1}^n \alpha_k h_k\right\|^2\right) = \exp\left(-\frac{1}{2}\sum_{k=1}^n \sum_{l=1}^n \alpha_k \alpha_l \langle h_k, h_l \rangle\right).$$

This implies that the vector $(X(h_1) \dots X(h_n))$ is jointly Gaussian with mean zero and covariance matrix $(\langle h_k, h_l \rangle)_{1 \le k, l \le n}$. □

68.5 Example. If H is of finite dimension then any standard Gaussian process $X: H \to L^2(\Omega, \mathscr{A}, P)$ can be written as $X(h) = \langle h, \kappa \rangle$, $h \in H$, where $\kappa: \Omega \to H$ is a random variable. E.g. take an orthonormal base $(e_1 \dots e_n)$ of H and define $\kappa := \sum_{i=1}^{n} X(e_i)e_i$.

It will turn out below that in case of an infinite dimensional Hilbert space H a standard Gaussian process can never be derived from a mapping $\kappa: \Omega \to H$.

68.6 Definition. Let $\mathscr{L}$ be the system of finite dimensional linear subspaces $L \subseteq H$. A family of Borel measures $\mu_L | \mathscr{B}(L)$, $L \in \mathscr{L}$, is a *cylinder set measure* if it is *projective*, i.e. if $L_1 \subseteq L_2$ implies $\mu_{L_1} = \mathscr{L}(p_{L_1} | \mu_{L_2})$.

68.7 Examples. (1) The system of standard Gaussian measures N_L, $L \in \mathscr{L}$, defines a cylinder set measure $N_H : (N_L)_{L \in \mathscr{L}}$. It is called the *standard Gaussian distribution* on H.

(2) Every linear process $Z: H \to \mathscr{L}(\Omega, \mathscr{A})$ defines a cylinder set measure according to the following construction: For every $L \in \mathscr{L}$ let $Z_L: \Omega \to L$ be such that $Z(h) = \langle h, Z_L \rangle$ if $h \in L$. Let $\mu_L = \mathscr{L}(Z_L | P)$ where $P | \mathscr{A}$ is a probability measure. Then $(\mu_L)_{L \in \mathscr{L}}$ is a cylinder set measure and is called the *distribution* of Z under $P (=: \mathscr{L}(Z | P))$.

(3) It is easy to see that the distribution of a standard Gaussian process is the standard Gaussian distribution.

68.8 Discussion. In a separable Hilbert space the Borel-σ-fields of the weak and the strong topology coincide since the closed balls are also weakly closed. Therefore, it is not ambiguous to speak of *the* Borel-σ-field of H $(=: \mathscr{B}(H))$. A Borel set $B \subseteq H$ is a *cylinder set* if there exists $L \in \mathscr{L}$ such that $B = (B \cap L) \oplus L^{\perp}$. The cylinder sets form a field which is denoted by $\mathscr{R}(H)$. It is clear that $\mathscr{R}(H)$ is a generating class for $\mathscr{B}(H)$. If μ is a cylinder set measure then it gives rise to a finitely additive set function on $\mathscr{R}(H)$, also denoted by μ, which is defined according to $\mu(B) := \mu_L(B \cap L)$, $B = (B \cap L) \oplus L^{\perp}$, $L \in \mathscr{L}$. This is well-defined by projectivity of $(\mu_L)_{L \in \mathscr{L}}$.

The question arises whether a cylinder set measure can be extended to a Borel measure.

68.9 Theorem. *If H is of infinite dimension then N_H cannot be extended to a Borel measure on $\mathscr{B}(H)$.*

Proof. We shall show that the outer measure of every ball is zero. If N_H could be extended to a Borel measure then the measure of the balls should increase to one as their radii tend to infinity.

Let $r > 0$ and $(e_j)_{j \in \mathbb{N}}$ an orthonormal base of H. Define $B_n = \{h \in H: \sum_{j=1}^{n} \langle h, e_j \rangle^2 \leq r^2\}$, $n \in \mathbb{N}$. Then $B_n \downarrow B(0, r)$ as $n \to \infty$. It will turn out that $N_H(B_n) \downarrow 0$ as $n \to \infty$.

The set B_n is a cylinder set whose base is the ball of radius r in the finite dimensional subspace $L_n = \text{span}\{e_1 \dots e_n\}$. Therefore,

$$\begin{aligned} N_H(B_n) &= N_{L_n}(B_n \cap L_n) \\ &= \frac{1}{(2\pi)^{\frac{n}{2}}} \int_{\sum_{i=1}^n x_i^2 \leqq r^2} \dots \int \exp\left(-\frac{1}{2}\sum_{i=1}^n x_i^2\right) dx_1 \dots dx_n \\ &\leqq \frac{1}{(2\pi)^{\frac{n}{2}}} \lambda_n(B(0,r)) = \frac{r^n}{2^{n/2}\Gamma\left(1+\frac{n}{2}\right)} \end{aligned}$$

which tends to zero as $n \to \infty$. The assertion follows. □

68.10 Corollary. *If H is of infinite dimension then a standard Gaussian process $(X(h))_{h \in H}$ cannot be represented as $X(h) = \langle h, \kappa(.)\rangle$, $h \in H$, where $\kappa: \Omega \to H$ is a Borel measurable function.*

Proof. If there existed a mapping κ generating a standard Gaussian process, then its distribution would be a Borel measure coinciding on $\mathcal{R}(H)$ with the standard Gaussian distribution. By Theorem 68.9, such a Borel measure does not exist. □

69. Gaussian shift experiments

Suppose that $(H, \langle .,. \rangle)$ is a Euclidean space. The *standard Gaussian shift* on $(H, \langle .,. \rangle)$ is the experiment $G = (H, \mathcal{B}(H), \{N_H * \varepsilon_h : h \in H\})$.

69.1 Definition. A *Gaussian shift* on a Euclidean space $(H, \langle .,. \rangle)$ is an experiment in $\mathscr{E}(H)$ which is equivalent to the standard Gaussian shift on $(H, \langle .,. \rangle)$.

In the following $(H, \langle .,. \rangle)$ denotes a separable Hilbert space. We extend the preceding definition.

69.2 Definition. A *Gaussian shift* on $(H, \langle .,. \rangle)$ is an experiment $E \in \mathscr{E}(H)$ such that for every finite dimensional subspace $L \subseteq H$ the experiment E_L is a Gaussian shift.

69.3 Lemma. (1) *Any two Gaussian shifts on the same Hilbert space are equivalent.*

(2) *Every experiment which is equivalent to a Gaussian shift is itself a Gaussian shift.*

Proof. It is obvious by definition that the assertions are true for Euclidean spaces. Hence, the general assertion follows by considering the restrictions to finite dimensional subspaces. □

In other words, the property of being a Gaussian shift is a property of equivalence classes of experiments and there is exactly one equivalence class for each Hilbert space which contains Gaussian shifts.

There is a strong relation between Gaussian shift experiments and standard processes.

69.4 Theorem. *An experiment $E = (\Omega, \mathscr{A}, \{P_h: h \in H\})$ is a Gaussian shift iff the stochastic process $(X(h))_{h\in H}$ which is defined by*

$$\frac{dP_h}{dP_0} = \exp(X(h) - \frac{1}{2}\|h\|^2), \quad h \in H,$$

is a standard Gaussian process under P_0.

Proof. In any case E is homogeneous and therefore its equivalence class is determined by the distribution of $(X(h))_{h\in H}$. Easy computations show that for a finite dimensional subspace $L \subseteq H$

$$\frac{d(N_L * \varepsilon_h)}{dN_L} = \exp(\langle h, \mathrm{id}_L\rangle - \frac{1}{2}\|h\|^2), \quad h \in L.$$

We observe that the distributions of $(\langle h, \mathrm{id}_L\rangle)_{h\in L}$ under N_L and $(X(h))_{h\in L}$ under P_0 coincide iff $(X(h))_{h\in H}$ is a standard Gaussian process. □

It should be noted that on a given probability space $(\Omega, \mathscr{A}, P)$ there exist several standard Gaussian processes which are different from each other. On the other hand the standard process which is associated with a particular Gaussian shift is uniquely determined P-a.e.

69.5 Definition. Let E be a Gaussian shift. The standard Gaussian process associated with E is called the *central process* of E.

69.6 Corollary. *For every standard process $(X(h))_{h\in H}$ there exists a Gaussian shift E for which $(X(h))_{h\in H}$ is central.*

Proof. If $(X(h))_{h\in H}$ is a standard process of $(\Omega, \mathscr{A}, P)$ then we define $P_0 := P$ and $P_h|\mathscr{A}$, $h \in H$, by

$$\frac{dP_h}{dP_0} = \exp(X(h) - \frac{1}{2}\|h\|^2), \quad h \in H.$$

It is easy to see that $(\Omega, \mathscr{A}, \{P_h: h \in H\})$ is an experiment. □

If $(H, \langle .,. \rangle)$ is a Euclidean space then a linear process $(X(h))_{h \in H}$ can be written as $X(h) = \langle h, X \rangle$, $h \in H$, where $X: \Omega \to H$ is a random variable. If $(X(h))_{h \in H}$ is central for a Gaussian shift E then let us call the random variable X central for E, too.

69.7 Examples. (1) Let $(H, \langle .,. \rangle)$ be a Euclidean space and $E = (H, \mathscr{B}(H), \{P_h: h \in H\})$ the standard Gaussian shift on H. Then $X = \mathrm{id}_H$ is central for E.

(2) Let $H = \mathbb{R}^k$ and $\langle x, y \rangle := x^t \Gamma y$ where Γ is a positive definite $(k \times k)$-matrix. Then $N_H = \nu_{0,\Gamma^{-1}}$. Since

$$\frac{d\nu_{h,\Gamma^{-1}}}{d\nu_{0,\Gamma^{-1}}}(x) = \exp(h^t \Gamma x - \frac{1}{2} h^t \Gamma h), \quad h \in H,\ x \in H,$$

the experiment $E = (\mathbb{R}^k, \mathscr{B}^k, \{\nu_{h,\Gamma^{-1}}: h \in \mathbb{R}^k\})$ is a standard Gaussian shift and $X = \mathrm{id}_H$ is central.

(3) Let $H = \mathbb{R}^k$ and $\langle .,. \rangle$ as before but let $E = (\mathbb{R}^k, \mathscr{B}^k, \{\nu_{\Gamma h,\Gamma}: h \in \mathbb{R}^k\})$. Then we have

$$\frac{d\nu_{\Gamma h,\Gamma}}{d\nu_{0,\Gamma}}(x) = \exp(h^t x - \frac{1}{2} h^t \Gamma h), \quad h \in H,\ x \in H,$$

which implies that E is a Gaussian shift and $X = \Gamma^{-1}\, \mathrm{id}_H$ is central. Note, that E is not a standard Gaussian shift on $(H, \langle .,. \rangle)$.

(4) Let $(H, \langle .,. \rangle)$ be an arbitrary Hilbert space and $L \subseteq H$ a finite dimensional space. Let $E = (\Omega, \mathscr{A}, \{P_h: h \in H\})$ be a Gaussian shift on H and E_L its restriction to L. If $(X(h))_{h \in H}$ is the central process of E and if $\{e_1, \ldots, e_n\}$ is an orthonormal basis of L then

$$X_L = \sum_{i=1}^{n} X(e_i) e_i$$

is the central random variable of E_L. This is due to the fact that for each $h \in L$

$$\begin{aligned} X(h) &= X(\sum_{i=1}^{n} \langle h, e_i \rangle e_i) \\ &= \sum_{i=1}^{n} X(e_i) \langle h, e_i \rangle = \langle h, \sum_{i=1}^{n} X(e_i) e_i \rangle . \end{aligned}$$

If L_1, L_2 are finite dimensional subspaces and $L_1 \subseteq L_2$ then it is clear from above that $X_{L_1} = p_{L_1} \circ X_{L_2}$.

(5) If $(H, \langle .,. \rangle)$ is a Euclidean space and $L \subseteq H$ is a linear subspace, then

$E = (H, \mathscr{B}(H), \{N_H * \varepsilon_h : h \in L\})$ is a Gaussian shift and p_L is its central random variable. This is the case considered in Section 30.

69.8 Remarks. (1) Let us compute the Hellinger transforms of a Gaussian shift. For $(z_1, \ldots, z_n) \in S_n$ and $h_i \in H$, $1 \leqq i \leqq n$, we have

$$\int \prod_{i=1}^{n} \left(\frac{dP_{h_i}}{dP_0}\right)^{z_i} dP_0 = \int \exp\left(\sum_{i=1}^{n} z_i \left(L(h_i) - \frac{1}{2}\|h_i\|^2\right)\right) dP_0$$

$$= \exp\left(-\frac{1}{2}\sum_{i=1}^{n} z_i \|h_i\|^2 + \frac{1}{2}\left\|\sum_{i=1}^{n} z_i h_i\right\|^2\right)$$

$$\cdot \int \exp\left(L\left(\sum_{i=1}^{n} z_i h_i\right) - \frac{1}{2}\left\|\sum_{i=1}^{n} z_i h_i\right\|^2\right) dP_0$$

$$= \exp\left(-\frac{1}{2}\sum_{i=1}^{n} z_i \|h_i\|^2 + \frac{1}{2}\left\|\sum_{i=1}^{n} z_i h_i\right\|^2\right).$$

Confer the result of Example 5.11.

(2) The Hellinger distance between two measures of a Gaussian shift is

$$d_2^2(P_{h_1}, P_{h_2}) = 1 - \exp\left(-\frac{1}{4}(\|h_1\|^2 + \|h_2\|^2) + \frac{1}{8}\|h_1 + h_2\|^2\right)$$

$$= 1 - \exp\left(-\frac{1}{8}\|h_1 - h_2\|^2\right), \quad h_1, h_2 \in H.$$

It follows that any Gaussian shift is uniformly continuous.

(3) Every Gaussian shift is translation invariant. This follows by easy computations from the Hellinger transforms given in (1).

69.9 Lemma. *Suppose that $(X(h))_{h \in H}$ is a stochastic process and $E = (\Omega, \mathscr{A}, \{P_h : h \in H\})$ an experiment. Then E is a Gaussian shift and $(X(h))_{h \in H}$ its central process iff*

(1) *the distribution* $\mathscr{L}\left(\log \frac{dP_{h_1}}{dP_0}, X(h_2) \,\middle|\, P_0\right)$ *is Gaussian with expectation* $\left(-\frac{1}{2}\|h_1\|^2, 0\right)$ *and covariance $\langle h_1, h_2 \rangle$, $h_i \in H$, $i = 1, 2$, and either*

(2) *E is a Gaussian shift or*

(3) *$(X(h))_{h \in H}$ is a standard process under P_0.*

Proof. It is clear that conditions (1) and (2) are necessary. Assume conversely, that (1) is satisfied. Then it follows that the variance of

$$\log \frac{dP_h}{dP_0} - X(h) + \frac{1}{2}\|h\|^2$$

under P_0 is zero for every $h \in H$. Hence, (2) and (3) imply each other. $\square$

69.10 Theorem. *A stochastic process $(X(h))_{h\in H}$ is central for the Gaussian shift $E = (\Omega, \mathscr{A}, \{P_h\colon h \in H\})$ iff*

$$\mathscr{L}(X(h_1)|P_{h_2}) = \nu_{\langle h_1, h_2\rangle, \|h_1\|^2} \quad \textit{for all} \quad h_1 \in H, h_2 \in H.$$

Proof. (1) Suppose that $(X(h))_{h\in H}$ is central. Let $h_1 \in H$, $h_2 \in H$. Then we obtain from translation invariance that

$$\begin{aligned}
\mathscr{L}(X(h_1)|P_0) &= \mathscr{L}\left(\log \frac{dP_{h_1}}{dP_0} + \frac{1}{2}\|h_1\|^2 \,\middle|\, P_0\right) \\
&= \mathscr{L}\left(\log \frac{dP_{h_1+h_2}}{dP_{h_2}} + \frac{1}{2}\|h_1\|^2 \,\middle|\, P_{h_2}\right) \\
&= \mathscr{L}\left(X(h_1) - \frac{1}{2}\|h_1+h_2\|^2 + \frac{1}{2}\|h_2\|^2 + \frac{1}{2}\|h_1\|^2 \,\middle|\, P_{h_2}\right) \\
&= \mathscr{L}(X(h_1) - \langle h_1, h_2\rangle | P_{h_2}).
\end{aligned}$$

(2) Conversely assume that $\mathscr{L}(X(h_1)|P_{h_2}) = \nu_{\langle h_1, h_2\rangle, \|h_1\|^2}$ for all $h_1 \in H$, $h_2 \in H$. A standard argument shows that for every $h \in H$ and $c \in \mathbb{R}$

$$\left(1_{\left\{\frac{dP_h}{dP_0} > \exp\left(c - \frac{1}{2}\|h\|^2\right)\right\}} - 1_{\{X(h) > c\}}\right)\left(\frac{dP_h}{dP_0} - \exp\left(c - \frac{1}{2}\|h\|^2\right)\right) \geqq 0 \quad P_0\text{-a.e.}$$

Moreover, the P_0-expectations of these expressions vanish. It follows that

$$P_0 | 1_{\left\{\log \frac{dP_h}{dP_0} + \frac{1}{2}\|h\|^2 > c\right\}} - 1_{\{X(h) > c\}} | = 0$$

for every $h \in H$ and $c \in \mathbb{R}$. This implies that

$$\log \frac{dP_h}{dP_0} = X(h) - \frac{1}{2}\|h\|^2 \quad P_0\text{-a.e.}, \quad h \in H. \qquad \square$$

69.11 Corollary. *Suppose that $(H, \langle .,. \rangle)$ is a Euclidean space. A random variable $X\colon \Omega \to H$ is central for the Gaussian shift $E = (\Omega, \mathscr{A}, \{P_h\colon h \in H\})$ iff $\mathscr{L}(X|P_h) = \varepsilon_h * N_H$, $h \in H$.*

If H is a finite dimensional Hilbert space then the central random variable $X\colon \Omega \to H$ is a non-randomized decision function in $\mathscr{R}(E, H)$. In general, however, the central process does not define a decision function in $\mathscr{R}(E, H)$.

A function $f: H \to \mathbb{R}$ is called a *cylinder function* if there is $L \in \mathscr{L}$ such that $f \circ p_L = f$. Let $Z = (Z(h))_{h \in H}$ be an arbitrary linear process. Such a process defines a system of random variables $(Z_L)_{L \in \mathscr{L}}$ which are connected by

$$Z_{L_1} = p_{L_1} \circ Z_{L_2} \quad \text{if} \quad L_1 \subseteq L_2 .$$

69.12 Remark. Suppose that the linear process Z is of the form $Z(h) = \langle h, \kappa \rangle$, $h \in H$, where $\kappa: \Omega \to H$ is a Borel measurable function. Then for every $L \in \mathscr{L}$ we have $Z_L = p_L \circ \kappa$. If $\beta \in \mathscr{B}(E, H)$ is the decision function which is defined by κ then

$$\begin{aligned} \beta(f, \mu) &= \int f \circ \kappa \, d\mu = \int f \circ p_L \circ \kappa \, d\mu \\ &= \int f \circ Z_L \, d\mu \end{aligned}$$

if $f \in \mathscr{C}_b(H)$ is a cylinder function satisfying $f \circ p_L = f$ for some $L \in \mathscr{L}$ and if $\mu \in L(E)$. For every $L \in \mathscr{L}$ the random variable $p_L \circ \kappa =: Z_L$ is also a decision function and since

$$\lim_{L \to H} \|x - p_L(x)\| = 0, \quad x \in H,$$

it follows that

$$\beta(f, \mu) = \lim_{L \to H} \int f \circ Z_L \, d\mu, \quad f \in \mathscr{C}_b(H), \, \mu \in L(E) .$$

In other words, β is the weak limit of $(Z_L)_{L \in \mathscr{L}}$ in $\mathscr{B}(E, H)$.

We shall show that for every linear process Z the limit of $(Z_L)_{L \in \mathscr{L}}$ exists in $\mathscr{B}(E, H)$. It should be noted that the following is not restricted to Gaussian shift experiments.

69.13 Theorem. *Suppose that* $Z = (Z(h))_{h \in H}$ *is a linear process. Then the net of random variables* $(Z_L)_{L \in \mathscr{L}}$ *converges in* $\mathscr{B}(E, H)$ *to a decision function* $\beta \in \mathscr{B}(E, H)$ *satisfying*

$$\beta(f, \mu) = \int f \circ Z_L \, d\mu \quad \textit{if} \quad f \circ p_L = f,$$

for cylinder functions $f \in \mathscr{C}_b(H)$ *and* $L \in \mathscr{L}$, *and* $\mu \in L(E)$.

Proof. For every $L \in \mathscr{L}$ let $\beta_L \in \mathscr{B}(E, H)$ be defined by

$$\beta_L(f, \mu) = \int f(Z_L) \, d\mu, \quad f \in \mathscr{C}_b(H), \, \mu \in L(E) .$$

Let $\beta \in \mathscr{B}(E, H)$ be any weak accumulation point of $(\beta_L)_{L \in \mathscr{L}}$. Then β has the asserted property. To show this let $L_1 \in \mathscr{L}$ and $f \in \mathscr{C}_b(H)$ such that $f \circ p_{L_1} = f$. Then for every $L \in \mathscr{L}$, $L \supseteq L_1$, it is clear that

$$\beta_L(f, \mu) = \int f(Z_L)\,d\mu = \int f(Z_{L_1})\,d\mu$$
$$= \beta_{L_1}(f, \mu), \quad \mu \in L(E),$$

which implies that

$$\beta(f, \mu) = \beta_{L_1}(f, \mu), \quad \mu \in L(E).$$

As a consequence we obtain that all weak accumulation points of $(\beta_L)_{L \in \mathscr{L}}$ coincide on the cylinder functions. To prove convergence we have to show that every weak accumulation point is uniquely determined by its value on the cylinder functions.

Let $f \in \mathscr{C}_b(H)$, $\mu \in L(E)$ and $\varepsilon > 0$. If β is a weak accumulation point of $(\beta_L)_{L \in \mathscr{L}}$ then there exists an $L \in \mathscr{L}$ such that

$$|\beta(f, \mu) - \beta_L(f, \mu)| < \varepsilon.$$

Since

$$\beta_L(f, \mu) = \int f(Z_L)\,d\mu$$
$$= \int (f \circ p_L)(Z_L)\,d\mu = \beta(f \circ p_L, \mu),$$

this implies

$$|\beta(f, \mu) - \beta(f \circ p_L, \mu)| < \varepsilon.$$

Since $f \circ p_L$ is a cylinder function, the assertion follows. $\square$

69.14 Definition. If $Z = (Z(h))_{h \in H}$ is a linear process then the limit $\beta_Z \in \mathscr{B}(E, H)$ of $(Z_L)_{L \in \mathscr{L}}$ is called the *decision function defined by Z.*

If $Z = (Z(h))_{h \in H}$ is a linear process of the form $Z(h) = \langle h, \kappa \rangle$, $h \in H$, where $\kappa: \Omega \to H$ is a Borel measurable mapping then every linear function $f: H \to \mathbb{R}^k$ defines an image $f \circ Z: \Omega \to \mathbb{R}^k$ by $f \circ Z: \omega \mapsto f(\kappa(\omega))$, $\omega \in \Omega$. The random variable $f \circ Z$ is characterized by the property $x^*(f \circ Z) = Z(f^*(x^*))$ if $x^* \in (\mathbb{R}^k)^*$. Such a construction can even be carried through if Z is an arbitrary linear process.

69.15 Lemma. *Let $Z = (Z(h))_{h \in H}$ be an arbitrary linear process and $f: H \to \mathbb{R}^k$ a continuous linear function. Then there exists a random variable $f \circ Z: \Omega \to \mathbb{R}^k$ which is uniquely determined by the property $x^*(f \circ Z) = Z(f^*(x^*))$, $x^* \in (\mathbb{R}^k)^*$.*

Proof. Uniqueness is clear. To prove existence let $H = L \oplus \ker f$ and $\{e_1 \ldots e_m\}$ an orthonormal base of L. Define $f \circ Z := \sum_{i=1}^{m} Z(e_i) f(e_i)$ and note that

$$\begin{aligned}
x^*(f\circ Z) &= \sum_{i=1}^{m} Z(e_i)\, x^*(f(e_i)) \\
&= \sum_{i=1}^{m} Z(e_i)\, \langle f^*(x^*), e_i\rangle \\
&= Z\Big(\sum_{i=1}^{m} \langle f^*(x^*), e_i\rangle\, e_i\Big) \\
&= Z(f^*(x^*)). \quad \square
\end{aligned}$$

An interesting particular case arises when $f\colon H \to \mathbb{R}$. Then $f \in H$ and $f\circ Z = Z(f)$.

With the notation of the preceding lemma the random variables Z_L, $L \in \mathscr{L}$, of Example 68.7 (2), defined by a linear process are nothing else than $Z_L = p_L \circ Z$, $L \in \mathscr{L}$. Moreover, it is almost obvious that $(f\circ g)\circ Z = f\circ(g\circ Z)$ if both sides are well defined.

69.16 Remark. (1) Let $L \in \mathscr{L}$ and let $E_L|_L$ be the restriction of the Gaussian shift E to the subspace L. If $X = (X(h))_{h\in H}$ is central for E then $X_L = p_L \circ X$ is central for $E|_L$.

(2) A particular case arises if $f\colon H \to \mathbb{R}^k$ is linear continuous and of rank k. If $L = (\ker f)^{\perp}$ then $p_L = f^* \circ (f\circ f^*)^{-1} \circ f$ and hence the central random variable of $E|_L$ is $f^* \circ (f\circ f^*)^{-1} \circ (f\circ X)$.

(3) Continuing the second case we reparametrize L by $f|_L\colon L \to \mathbb{R}^k$ which is a linear isomorphism. In order to get an isometry we endow $\mathbb{R}^k$ with the inner product defined by the matrix Γ of $(f\circ f^*)^{-1}$ and obtain that $f\circ X$ is the central variable of this experiment. To see this fact, note that

$$\|h\|^2 = f(h)^t\, \Gamma f(h) \quad \text{if} \quad h \in L,$$

and

$$X(h) = f(h)^t\, \Gamma f\circ X \quad \text{if} \quad h \in L.$$

The underlying experiment has representations given in Examples 69.7 (2) and (3).

70. Banach sample spaces

If $(H, \langle .,. \rangle)$ is a finite dimensional Hilbert space then there exists a Gaussian shift experiment on H whose sample space is H and whose central process is of the form $X(h) = \langle \mathrm{id}, h\rangle$, $h \in H$. If H is not of finite dimension then such a representation is not possible. The reason is that the standard Gaussian distribution N_H cannot be extended to a Borel measure on $\mathscr{B}(H)$.

Intuitively, the reason why cylinder set measures like the standard Gaussian distribution cannot be extended to Borel measures on H, is that H is too "small" in some sense. The extension works if H is completed in a suitable way. In many cases completion is done by embedding H into a Banach space B by means of a continuous, injective map $\tau: H \to B$.

70.1 Remark. Let $(B, \|\,.\,\|_B)$ be a separable Banach space and $\tau: H \to B$ a linear continuous mapping. Then it is possible to define the image $\mathscr{L}(\tau | N_H)$ of N_H under τ in the following way: A cylinder function on B is a function of the form $f \circ (x_1^*, \ldots, x_k^*)$ where $f | \mathbb{R}^k$ and $x_i^* \in B^*$, $1 \leqq i \leqq k$, $k \in \mathbb{N}$. If $g \in \mathscr{C}_b(B)$ is a cylinder function on B then

$$\mathscr{L}(\tau | N_H)(g) := \int g \circ \tau \, dN_H,$$

which is well defined since $g \circ \tau \in \mathscr{C}_b(H)$ is a cylinder function on H. It is clear that $\mathscr{L}(\tau | N_H)$ need not be a Borel measure on $\mathscr{B}(B)$. Analytically, we have $Q = \mathscr{L}(\tau | N_H)$ iff

$$\int \exp(i x^* \circ \tau) \, dN_H = \int \exp(i x^*) \, dQ$$

for all $x^* \in B^*$.

70.2 Definition. Let $(B, \|.\|_B)$ be a separable Banach space and $\tau: H \to B$ a linear continuous mapping which is injective and such that $f(H)$ is dense in B. If $\mathscr{L}(\tau | N_H)$ can be extended to a Borel measure $P | \mathscr{B}(B)$ then (H, B, τ) is called an *Abstract Wiener space.*

In the following we exhibit some important examples of Abstract Wiener spaces. In any of the cases considered in Theorems 70.3–70.5, it follows from the Stone-Weierstrass theorem that $\tau(H)$ is dense in B.

70.3 Theorem. *Let $H = L^2([0,1], \mathscr{B}([0,1]), \lambda)$ and $B = \{x \in \mathscr{C}([0,1]): x(0) = 0\}$. Consider the mapping $\tau: H \to B$ defined by $\tau(h): t \mapsto \int_0^t h \, d\lambda$, $0 \leqq t \leqq 1$. Then $\mathscr{L}(\tau | N_H)$ is a Borel measure on $\mathscr{B}(B)$ and coincides with the Wiener measure W. Thus, (H, B, τ) is an Abstract Wiener space.*

Proof. We need only show that $W = \mathscr{L}(\tau | N_H)$. To verify this we have to show that

$$\int \exp(i x^* \circ \tau) \, dN_H = \int \exp(i x^*) \, dW$$

for all $x^* \in B^*$. The dual space B consists of all signed Borel measures on $\mathscr{B}([0,1])$. It is sufficient to prove the equation only for linear combinations of one-point measure since these are weakly dense in B^*. Let

$$x^* = \sum_{k=1}^{n} \alpha_k \varepsilon_{t_k}, \ (\alpha_k) \in \mathbb{R}^n, \ (t_k) \in [0,1]^n.$$

We obtain

$$\int \exp(ix^*)\,dW = \int \exp\Big(i \sum_{k=1}^{n} \alpha_k x_{t_k}\Big)\, W(dx)$$

$$= \exp\left(-\frac{1}{2} \sum_{k=1}^{n} \sum_{l=1}^{n} \alpha_k \alpha_l \min\{t_k, t_l\}\right).$$

On the other hand we have

$$\int \exp(ix^* \circ \tau)\,dN_H = \int \exp\Big(i \sum_{k=1}^{n} \alpha_k \int_0^{t_k} h\,d\lambda\Big)\, N_H(dh)$$

$$= \int \exp\Big(i \int \Big(\sum_{k=1}^{n} \alpha_k 1_{[0,t_k)}\Big) h\,d\lambda\Big)\, N_H(dh)$$

$$= \int \exp\Big(i \Big\langle \sum_{k=1}^{n} \alpha_k \cdot 1_{[0,t_k)}, h \Big\rangle\Big)\, N_H(dh)$$

$$= \exp\left(-\frac{1}{2} \left\| \sum_{k=1}^{n} \alpha_k \cdot 1_{[0,t_k)} \right\|^2\right). \qquad \square$$

70.4 Theorem. *Let $H = \{h \in L^2([0,1], \mathscr{B}([0,1]), \lambda): \int h\,d\lambda = 0\}$ and $B = \{x \in \mathscr{C}([0,1]): x(0) = x(1) = 0\}$. Consider again the mapping $\tau\colon H \to B$ defined by $\tau(h)\colon t \mapsto \int_0^t h\,d\lambda$, $0 \leqq t \leqq 1$. Then $\mathscr{L}(\tau \mid N_H)$ is a Borel measure on $\mathscr{B}(B)$ and coincides with the distribution W_0 of the Brownian bridge on B. Thus, (H, B, τ) is an Abstract Wiener space.*

Proof. The proof is similar to the proof of Theorem 70.3. Again taking

$$x^* = \sum_{k=1}^{n} \alpha_k \varepsilon_{t_k}, \quad (\alpha_k) \in \mathbb{R}^n,\ (t_k) \in [0,1]^n,$$

we have

$$\int \exp(ix^*)\,dW_0 = \exp\left(-\frac{1}{2} \sum_{k=1}^{n} \sum_{l=1}^{n} \alpha_k \alpha_l (\min\{t_k, t_l\} - t_k \cdot t_l)\right)$$

and

$$\int \exp(ix^* \circ \tau)\,dN_H = \int \exp\Big(i \sum_{k=1}^{n} \alpha_k \int_0^{t_k} h\,d\lambda\Big)\, N_H(dh)$$

$$= \int \exp\Big(i \int \Big(\sum_{k=1}^{n} \alpha_k (1_{[0,t_k)} - t_k)\Big) h\,d\lambda\Big)\, N_H(dh)$$

$$= \exp\left(-\frac{1}{2} \left\| \sum_{k=1}^{n} \alpha_k (1_{[0,t_k)} - t_k) \right\|^2\right). \qquad \square$$

70.5 Theorem. *Suppose that F is a continuous distribution function on $\mathbb{R}$ and let $H = \{h \in L^2(\mathbb{R}, \mathscr{B}, F): \int h\,dF = 0\}$. Let $B = \mathscr{C}_0(\mathbb{R})$ and consider the mapping*

τ: $H \to B$ defined by $\tau(h)$: $t \mapsto \int_{-\infty}^{t} h\,dF$, $t \in \mathbb{R}$. Then $W_F := \mathscr{L}(\tau | N_H)$ is a Borel measure on $\mathscr{B}(B)$. Thus, (H, B, τ) is an Abstract Wiener space.

Proof. Let F^*: $\{x \in \mathscr{C}([0,1]): x(0) = x(1) = 0\} \to \mathscr{C}_0(\mathbb{R})$ be such that $F^*(x) = x \circ F$, $x \in \mathscr{C}([0,1])$. Define $W_F := \mathscr{L}(F^* | W_0)$. In other words, if $(\Omega, \mathscr{A}, P, (X_t)_{t \in [0,1]})$ is a Brownian bridge, then W_F is the distribution of the stochastic process $(\Omega, \mathscr{A}, P, (X_{F(t)})_{t \in \mathbb{R}})$. To show, that $W_F = \mathscr{L}(\tau | N_H)$, we take

$$x^* = \sum_{k=1}^{n} \alpha_k \varepsilon_{t_k}, \quad (\alpha_k) \in \mathbb{R}^n, \, (t_k) \in \mathbb{R}^n,$$

and observe that

$$\int \exp(ix^*)\,dW_F$$
$$= \exp\left(-\frac{1}{2} \sum_{k=1}^{n} \sum_{l=1}^{n} \alpha_k \alpha_l (\min\{F(t_k), F(t_l)\} - F(t_k), F(t_l))\right)$$

and

$$\int \exp(ix^* \circ \tau)\,dN_H = \int \exp(i \sum_{k=1}^{n} \alpha_k \int_0^{t_k} h\,dF) N_H(dh)$$
$$= \int \exp(i \int (\sum_{k=1}^{n} \alpha_k (1_{(-\infty, t_k)} - F(t_k)) h\,dF) N_H(dh)$$
$$= \exp\left(-\frac{1}{2} \left\| \sum_{k=1}^{n} \alpha_k (1_{(-\infty, t_k)} - F(t_k)) \right\|^2\right). \qquad \square$$

Next, we establish the existence of particular standard Gaussian processes for Abstract Wiener spaces.

70.6 Theorem. *Suppose that (H, B, τ) is an Abstract Wiener space. Then there exists a uniquely determined standard Gaussian process $(X(h))_{h \in H}$ on $(B, \mathscr{B}(B), P)$ with $X(h) \circ \tau = \langle h, . \rangle$, $h \in H$.*

Proof. Since τ is injective, $\operatorname{im} \tau^*$ is dense in H. Otherwise, there exists $h_0 \perp \operatorname{im} \tau^*$, $h_0 \in H \setminus \{0\}$, which implies $0 = \langle \tau^*(x^*), h_0 \rangle = x^*(\tau(h_0))$ for all $x^* \in B^*$. Hence $\tau(h_0) = 0$ which is a contradiction. Similarly, since $\operatorname{im} \tau$ is dense in B, τ^* is injective.

For every $h \in \operatorname{im} \tau^*$ let $X(h) = x^*$ if $\tau^*(x^*) = h$. Then $X(h)$ is well-defined since τ^* is injective. Moreover, if $\tau^*(x^*) = h$ we have

$$\mathscr{L}(X(h) | P) = \mathscr{L}(x^* | P) = \mathscr{L}(x^* \circ \tau | N_H)$$
$$= \mathscr{L}(\langle h, . \rangle | N_H) = \nu_{0, \|h\|^2}.$$

This implies that X: $\operatorname{im} \tau^* \to L^2(B, \mathscr{B}(B), P)$ is a linear isometric mapping, and therefore can be extended to the whole of H. By Theorem 68.4, X is a standard Gaussian process, and by construction it satisfies

$$X(h)\circ\tau = x^*\circ\tau = \langle \tau^*(x^*), .\rangle = \langle h, .\rangle$$

if $h = \tau^*(x^*)$. Since $\operatorname{im}\tau^*$ is dense in H, this is even true for every $h \in H$. □

70.7 Examples. (1) Consider the case of Theorem 70.3. Let $(X(h))_{h\in H}$ be the standard Gaussian process on B which satisfies $X(h)\circ\tau = \langle h, .\rangle$, $h \in H$. This process is usually called the *Wiener integral*. Let us compute the Wiener integral for particular functions. First, let $x \in \operatorname{im}\tau$, i.e. there exists a derivative $x' \in L^2([0,1])$. In this case, we have

$$X(h)(x) = \langle h, x'\rangle = \int_0^1 h(t)x'(t)\,dt = \int_0^1 h(t)\,dx(t),$$

where the latter integral is a Stieltjes integral. If $x \in B\setminus\operatorname{im}\tau$ then such an interpretation of $X(h)$ is no more possible for every $h \in H$. But, if $h \in \operatorname{im}\tau^*$ then we have by construction $X(h) = x^*$ if $h = \tau^*(x^*)$. E.g. if $h = \sum_{i=1}^k \alpha_i 1_{[0,t_i)}$ then, obviously, $h = (\sum_{i=1}^k \alpha_i\varepsilon_{t_i})\circ\tau = \tau^*(\sum_{i=1}^k \alpha_i\varepsilon_{t_i})$ and hence

$$\begin{aligned} X(h)(x) &= \sum_{i=1}^k \alpha_i\varepsilon_{t_i}(x) = \sum_{i=1}^k \alpha_i x(t_i) \\ &= \int_0^1 h(t)\,dx(t), \quad x \in B. \end{aligned}$$

These properties motivate the notation $X(h)(x) =: \int_0^1 h(t)\,dx(t)$ for arbitrary $h \in H$, $x \in B$. It should be kept in mind that in spite of this notation the Wiener integral is not a Stieltjes integral if $x \in B$ is not of bounded variation.

(2) Consider the case of Theorem 70.4. Let $(X(h))_{h\in H}$ be the standard Gaussian process on B, which satisfies $X(h)\circ\tau = \langle h, .\rangle$, $h \in H$. This is nothing else than the Wiener integral restricted to H and to the sample space B. Indeed, let $X(h)$, $h \in L^2[0,1]$, denote the Wiener-Integral and

$$I(f)(t) := f(0) + t(f(1) - f(0)), \quad f \in \mathscr{C}[0,1],\ t \in [0,1].$$

Noting that $W_0 = \mathscr{L}(\mathrm{id} - I|W)$ and $X(h)\circ I = 0$, $h \in H$, it can easily be checked that $(B, \mathscr{B}(B), W_0, (X(h)|_B)_{h\in H})$ satisfies the characteristic properties in Theorem 70.6.

(3) Finally, consider the case of Theorem 70.5. Also in this case the standard process $(X(h))_{h\in H}$ on $\mathscr{C}_0(\mathbb{R})$ which satisfies $X(h)\circ\tau = \langle h, .\rangle$, $h \in H$, can be expressed in terms of the Wiener integral. For this, recall that every continuous distribution function F has a right inverse F^{-1} being defined by

$$F^{-1}(s) = \inf\{x \in \mathbb{R}: F(x) \geqq s\}, \quad s \in (0,1).$$

The right inverse need not be continuous, but satisfies

$$s_1 \leqq s_2 \quad \text{iff} \quad F^{-1}(s_1) \leqq F^{-1}(s_2), \quad s_1, s_2 \in (0,1).$$

It can therefore be used for a transformation of Stieltjes integrals into Lebesgue integrals, namely

$$\int_{-\infty}^{+\infty} h\,dF = \int_0^1 h \circ F^{-1}\,d\lambda_1$$

for every $h \in L^2(F)$.

Now, we note that the Borel measure W_F on $\mathscr{C}_0(\mathbb{R})$ which is constructed in the proof of Theorem 70.5, gives probability 1 to the subset

$$\{x \circ F: x \in \mathscr{C}([0,1])\}.$$

If $y \in \mathscr{C}_0(\mathbb{R})$ is of this type, then $y \circ F^{-1}$ is in $\mathscr{C}([0,1])$ and we define

$$X(h)(y) := \int_0^1 h \circ F^{-1}(t)\,d(y \circ F^{-1})(t), \quad h \in L^2(F).$$

We shall prove that this is the standard Gaussian process of the desired nature. Let $y \in \mathscr{C}_0(\mathbb{R})$ be such that

$$y(t) = \int_{-\infty}^{t} g\,dF, \quad t \in \mathbb{R},$$

for some $g \in L^2(F)$. Then

$$(y \circ F^{-1})(s) = \int_{-\infty}^{F^{-1}(s)} g\,dF = \int_0^s g \circ F^{-1}\,d\lambda_1.$$

Hence, by definition of the Wiener integral we obtain

$$X(h)(y) = \int_0^1 (h \circ F^{-1})(g \circ F^{-1})\,d\lambda_1 = \int hg\,dF.$$

This proves the assertion since $y = \tau(g)$.

Abstract Wiener spaces admit a representation of Gaussian shift experiments as shift experiments in the usual sense.

70.8 Theorem. *Suppose that (H, B, τ) is an Abstract Wiener space and let $P_0 := \mathscr{L}(\tau \mid N_H)$. Let $(X(h))_{h \in H}$ be the standard Gaussian process on $(B, \mathscr{B}(B), P_0)$ satisfying $X(h) \circ \tau = \langle h, .\rangle$, $h \in H$. Then*

$$E = (B, \mathscr{B}(B), \{P_0 * \varepsilon_{\tau(h)}: h \in H\})$$

is a Gaussian shift on H and $(X(h))_{h \in H}$ its central process.

Proof. Denote $P_h := P * \varepsilon_{\tau(h)}$, $h \in H$. For every $h \in H$ let $Q_h | \mathscr{B}(B)$ be the Borel measure which is defined by

$$\frac{dQ_h}{dP_0}(x) = \exp(X(h)(x) - \frac{1}{2}\|h\|^2), \quad x \in B.$$

Then, by Theorem 69.4 $\{Q_h: h \in H\}$ is a Gaussian shift whose standard Gaussian process is X. It follows from Theorem 69.10 that

$$\mathscr{L}(X(h_1)|Q_{h_2}) = \nu_{\langle h_1, h_2 \rangle, \|h_1\|^2}, \quad h_i \in H, \ i = 1, 2.$$

The same is true with Q replaced by P since we shall show that the distribution $\mathscr{L}(X(h_1)|P_{h_2})$ is by definition the distribution of

$$x \mapsto X(h_1)(x + \tau(h_2)), \quad x \in B,$$

under the probability measure P_0. Indeed, if $h_1 = \tau^*(x^*)$ for some $x^* \in B^*$ then

$$\begin{aligned} X(h_1)(x + \tau(h_2)) &= x^*(x + \tau(h_2)) \\ &= x^*(x) + x^*(\tau(h_2)) \\ &= X(h_1)(x) + \langle h_1, h_2 \rangle. \end{aligned}$$

Thus, we obtain

$$\mathscr{L}(X(h_1)|P_{h_2}) = \nu_{\langle h_1, h_2 \rangle, \|h_1\|^2}$$

if $h_1 \in \operatorname{im} \tau^*$, and by continuity even for every $h_1 \in H$. It follows that

$$\mathscr{L}((X(h_1))_{h_1 \in H}|P_{h_2}) = \mathscr{L}((X(h_1))_{h_1 \in H}|Q_{h_2}), \quad h_2 \in H.$$

Since $X(\tau^*(x^*)) = x^*$, $x^* \in B^*$, we obtain

$$\mathscr{L}(x^*|P_h) = \mathscr{L}(x^*|Q_h), \quad h \in H, \ x^* \in B^*,$$

which yields $P_h = Q_h$, $h \in H$. □

70.9 Example. Consider the case of Theorem 70.3. The Gaussian shift experiment associated with this example is familiar in the signal detection theory and usually written as stochastic differential equation

$$dy(t) = dx(t) + h(t)\,dt, \quad 0 \leqq t \leqq 1,$$

where $h \in L^2([0, 1])$ is an unknown signal. The observation $dy(t)$ consists of the signal $h(t)\,dt$ and white noise $dx(t)$. In our terminology the equation should be written as

$$y(t) = x(t) + \int_0^t h(s)\,ds, \quad 0 \leqq t \leqq 1,$$

where $x, y \in \mathscr{C}([0,1])$ and x is a random element being governed by the Wiener measure. The central process of this experiment is the Wiener integral.

The cases of Theorems 70.4 and 70.5 are obtained as limit experiment in non-parametric statistical problems (see Sections 80, 82 and 83).

71. Testing for Gaussian shifts

Let $(H, \langle .,. \rangle)$ be an Hilbert space and $E = (\Omega, \mathscr{A}, \{P_h: h \in H\})$ a Gaussian shift experiment. For the case of a finite dimensional Hilbert space the problem of testing has been treated in Sections 28 and 30.

We begin with the analysis of testing problems concerning a continuous, linear function $f: H \to \mathbb{R}$. First, we consider one-sided testing problems. Let $H_1 = \{h \in H: f(h) \leqq 0\}$, $K_1 = \{h \in H: f(h) > 0\}$. Recall, that a critical function $\varphi \in \mathscr{F}(\Omega, \mathscr{A})$ is unbiased of level $\alpha \in [0,1]$ for the testing problem (H_1, K_1) if

$$P_h\varphi \leqq \alpha \quad \text{if} \quad f(h) \leqq 0 \quad \text{and}$$
$$P_h\varphi \geqq \alpha \quad \text{if} \quad f(h) > 0.$$

It is similar of level α for the testing problem (H_1, K_1) if $P_h\varphi = 0$ whenever $f(h) = 0$. Every critical function which is unbiased of level α is also similar of level α.

Let $e \in H$ be a unit vector such that $e \perp \ker f$ and $f(e) > 0$. Then $f(h) = \langle e, h \rangle \|f\|$, $h \in H$. Moreover, for every linear subspace $L \subseteq H$ such that $e \in L$ the norms $\|f|_L\|$ and $\|f\|$ are equal.

71.1 Lemma. *If $\varphi \in \mathscr{F}(\Omega, \mathscr{A})$ is similar of level α for the testing problem (H_1, K_1) then*

$$P_h\varphi \leqq \Phi\left(N_\alpha + \frac{f(h)}{\|f\|}\right) \quad \textit{if} \quad f(h) > 0,$$

$$P_h\varphi \geqq \Phi\left(N_\alpha + \frac{f(h)}{\|f\|}\right) \quad \textit{if} \quad f(h) \leqq 0.$$

Proof. Let $h \in H$ and let $L \subseteq H$ be a finite dimensional linear subspace containing h and e. Then $E|_L$ is a finite dimensional Gaussian shift and the assertion follows from Corollary 28.2 or Theorem 28.6. □

71.2 Definition. Suppose that $\varphi \in \mathscr{F}(\Omega, \mathscr{A})$ is similar of level α for (H_1, K_1). Then φ is *optimal of level* α for (H_1, K_1) at $h \in H$ if

$$P_h \varphi = \Phi\left(N_\alpha + \frac{f(h)}{\|f\|}\right).$$

It is *uniformly optimal of level* α for (H_1, K_1) if this is true for every $h \in H$.

71.3 Theorem. *Let $X = (X(h))_{h \in H}$ be the central process of E. A critical function $\varphi^* \in \mathscr{F}(\Omega, \mathscr{A})$ is uniformly optimal of level α for (H_1, K_1) iff*

$$\varphi^* = \begin{cases} 1 & \text{if } \dfrac{f \circ X}{\|f\|} > N_{1-\alpha} \\ 0 & \text{if } \dfrac{f \circ X}{\|f\|} < N_{1-\alpha} \end{cases}, \quad P_0\text{-a.e.}$$

Proof. From the proof of Lemma 69.15 we obtain that $f \circ X = X(e) \cdot \|f\|$. Since

$$\mathscr{L}(X(e) \mid P_h) = \nu_{\langle e, h\rangle, 1} = \nu_{f(h)/\|f\|, 1}, \quad h \in H,$$

it follows that φ^* is uniformly optimal. To prove uniqueness we note that optimality for E implies optimality for $E|_{(\ker f)^\perp}$. Thus, uniqueness follows from Corollary 26.5. □

It is clear that φ^* is admissible for (H_1, K_1).

71.4 Corollary. *If a critical function $\varphi^* \in \mathscr{F}(\Omega, \mathscr{A})$ is optimal of level α for (H_1, K_1) at any $h \in H$ with $f(h) \neq 0$, then φ^* is uniformly optimal.*

Proof. Let $L \subseteq H$ be a finite dimensional linear subspace containing h and e. Then Corollary 28.7 implies that φ^* is uniformly optimal on L, in particular on $\ker f^\perp$. This proves the assertion. □

Now, we turn to two-sided testing problems. From now on let $H_2 = \{h \in H: f(h) = 0\}$, $K_2 = \{h \in H: f(h) \neq 0\}$. Recall, that a critical function $\varphi \in \mathscr{F}(\Omega, \mathscr{A})$ is unbiased of level $\alpha \in [0, 1]$ for (H_2, K_2) if

$$P_h \varphi \leqq \alpha \quad \text{if} \quad f(h) = 0, \quad \text{and}$$
$$P_h \varphi \geqq \alpha \quad \text{if} \quad f(h) \neq 0.$$

71.5 Lemma. *If $\varphi \in \mathscr{F}(\Omega, \mathscr{A})$ is unbiased of level α for (H_2, K_2) then*

$$P_h \varphi \leqq \Phi\left(N_{\alpha/2} + \frac{f(h)}{\|f\|}\right) + \Phi\left(N_{\alpha/2} - \frac{f(h)}{\|f\|}\right), \quad h \in H.$$

Proof. Let $h \in H$. By Theorem 28.8 the assertion is valid for any finite dimensional subspace $L \subseteq H$ containing h and e. □

71.6 Definition. Suppose that $\varphi \in \mathscr{F}(\Omega, \mathscr{A})$ is unbiased of level α for (H_2, K_2). Then φ is *optimal of level* α for (H_2, K_2) at $h \in H$ if

$$P_h \varphi = \Phi\left(N_{\alpha/2} + \frac{f(h)}{\|f\|}\right) + \Phi\left(N_{\alpha/2} - \frac{f(h)}{\|f\|}\right).$$

It is *uniformly optimal of level* α for (H_2, K_2) if this is true for every $h \in H$.

71.7 Theorem. *Let $X = (X(h))_{h \in H}$ be the central process of E. A critical function $\varphi^* \in \mathscr{F}(\Omega, \mathscr{A})$ is uniformly optimal of level α for (H_2, K_2) iff*

$$\varphi^* = \begin{cases} 1 & \text{if } \dfrac{|f \circ X|}{\|f\|} > N_{1-\alpha/2} \\ 0 & \text{if } \dfrac{|f \circ X|}{\|f\|} < N_{1-\alpha/2} \end{cases}, \quad P_0\text{-a.e.}$$

Proof. The proof is similar to that of Theorem 71.3. □

It is clear that φ^* is admissible for (H_2, K_2).

71.8 Corollary. *If a critical function $\varphi^* \in \mathscr{F}(\Omega, \mathscr{A})$ is optimal of level α for (H_2, K_2) at any $h \in H$ with $f(h) \neq 0$, then φ^* is uniformly optimal.*

Proof. The proof is similar to the proof of Corollary 71.4, replacing 28.7 by 28.9. □

Next, we consider linear testing problems. Let $L_0 \subseteq H$ be a linear subspace of finite codimension. This means, that $L_0^\perp$ is a finite dimensional subspace. Examples of such cases arise if $L_0 = \ker f$ for some linear function $f: H \to \mathbb{R}^k$, $k \in \mathbb{N}$, or in a trivial way if H is of finite dimension. We consider the testing problem $H_3 = L_0$, $K_3 = H \setminus L_0$.

71.9 Definition. A critical function $\varphi \in \mathscr{F}(\Omega, \mathscr{A})$ is *unbiased of level* $\alpha \in [0,1]$ for (H_3, K_3) if

$$\begin{aligned} P_h \varphi &\leqq \alpha \quad \text{if} \quad h \in L_0, \\ P_h \varphi &\geqq \alpha \quad \text{if} \quad h \in H \setminus L_0. \end{aligned}$$

Define $B_c = \{h \in H: \|h - p_{L_0}(h)\| = c\}$, $c > 0$.

71.10 Theorem. *Let $X = (X(h))_{h \in H}$ be the central process of E. Let $\alpha \in [0,1]$ and choose $k_\alpha \in [0, \infty]$ such that $P_0\{\|(\mathrm{id}\text{-}p_{L_0}) \circ X\| > k_\alpha\} = \alpha$. Then the test*

$$\varphi^* = \begin{cases} 1 & \text{if} \quad \|(\text{id-}p_{L_0})\circ X\| > k_\alpha, \\ 0 & \text{if} \quad \|(\text{id-}p_{L_0})\circ X\| < k_\alpha, \end{cases}$$

is unbiased of level α *for* (H_3, K_3). *Moreover, if* $\varphi \in \mathscr{F}_\alpha(H_3, K_3)$ *then for every* $c > 0$

$$\inf_{h\in B_c} P_h\varphi \leqq \inf_{h\in B_c} P_h\varphi^*.$$

Proof. Let $c > 0$. Consider the experiment $(\Omega, \mathscr{A}, \{P_h: h \in L_0^\perp\})$ and the testing problem $\tilde{H}_3 = \{0\}$, $\tilde{K}_3 = L_0^\perp \backslash \{0\}$. Since φ is unbiased of level α for this restricted experiment and for the testing problem (H_3, K_3) it follows from Theorem 30.2 that

$$\inf_{h\in B_c} P_h\varphi \leqq \inf_{h\in B_c\cap L_0^\perp} P_h\varphi \leqq C_{k,c^2}(C_{k,0}^{-1}(\alpha))$$

where C_{k,c^2} is the distribution function of the non-central χ^2-distribution with $k := \dim(L_0^\perp)$ degrees of freedom and non-centrality parameter $c^2 \geqq 0$. It is clear that $\mathscr{L}(\|(\text{id-}p_{L_0})\circ X\|^2 | P_h)$ has the distribution function C_{k,c^2} with $c^2 = \|h - p_{L_0}(h)\|^2$, $h \in H$. This proves the assertion. □

71.11 Corollary. *Keep the notation of the preceding theorem. If a critical function* $\varphi \in \mathscr{F}(\Omega, \mathscr{A})$ *satisfies for at least one* $c > 0$

$$P_0\varphi \leqq \alpha,$$
$$P_h\varphi \geqq P_h\varphi^* \quad \text{if} \quad h \in B_c, \quad h \perp L_0,$$

then $\varphi = \varphi^*$ P_0*-a.e. Hence,* φ^* *is admissible for every testing problem* $(\{0\}, B_c \cap L_0^\perp)$ *and is uniquely determined by its power function on* $\{0\} \cup (B_c \cap L_0^\perp)$, $c > 0$.

Proof. Consider the experiment $(\Omega, \mathscr{A}, \{P_h: h \perp L_0\})$ and apply Corollary 30.3. □

71.12 Corollary. *Let* $C \subseteq L_0$ *be a closed convex subset. Then*

$$\varphi^* = \begin{cases} 1 & \text{if} \quad (\text{id-}p_{L_0})\circ X \notin C, \\ 0 & \text{if} \quad (\text{id-}p_{L_0})\circ X \in C, \end{cases}$$

is an admissible test for the testing problem $(L_0, H\backslash L_0)$ *and is uniquely determined by its power function.*

Proof. Apply Theorem 30.4 to the subexperiment $E|_{L_0^\perp}$ and to the testing problem $(\{0\}, L_0^\perp\backslash\{0\})$. □

71.13 Remark. Consider the problem of testing a linear function $f: H \to \mathbb{R}^k$. W.l.g., assume that $\text{im}(f) = \mathbb{R}^k$. Consider the testing problem $(\{f = 0\},$

$\{f \neq 0\}$). Then the Discussion (30.8) is literally valid if we replace the projection p_L by the central process $X = (X(h))_{h \in H}$ of E.

It remains to discuss the testing problem $(\{0\}, H \setminus \{0\})$. Since $L_0 = \{0\}$ is not of finite codimension the discussion 71.9–71.13 does not apply to this case. But we may extend the assertion of Corollary 71.12 obtaining at least a considerably large class of admissible tests for $(\{0\}, H \setminus \{0\})$. The proof follows that of Theorem 30.4.

71.14 Theorem (Moussatat [1976]). *Let $(h_n)_{n \in \mathbb{N}} \subseteq H$ and $(r_n)_{n \in \mathbb{N}} \subseteq \mathbb{R}$ be arbitrary sequences. Then*

$$\varphi^* = \begin{cases} 1 & \text{if } X(h_n) > r_n \text{ for some } n \in \mathbb{N}, \\ 0 & \text{if } X(h_n) \leqq r_n \text{ for every } n \in \mathbb{N}, \end{cases}$$

is an admissible test for the testing problem $(\{0\}, \{h \in H: h \neq 0\})$ and is uniquely determined by its power function.

Proof. If any $h_n = 0$ then either φ^* is a trivial test or it can be omitted in the definition of φ^*. Therefore we assume that $h_n \neq 0$, $n \in \mathbb{N}$. Suppose that there exists a critical function $\varphi \in \mathscr{F}(H, \mathscr{B}(H))$ such that $P_0 \varphi \leqq P_0 \varphi^*$ and $P_h \varphi \geqq P_h \varphi^*$ if $h \neq 0$. We shall prove that in this case $\varphi = \varphi^*$ P_0-a.e.

Assuming the contrary, i.e. $P_0\{\varphi \neq \varphi^*\} > 0$, it follows by $P_0 \varphi \leqq P_0 \varphi^*$ that $P_0\{\varphi^* > \varphi\} > 0$. It is clear that

$$\{\varphi^* > \varphi\} = \bigcup_{n \in \mathbb{N}} \{X(h_n) > r_n\} \cap \{\varphi < 1\}.$$

Hence, there exists some $n \in \mathbb{N}$ such that

$$P_0(\{X(h_n) > r_n\} \cap \{\varphi < 1\}) > 0.$$

Fix this particular $n \in \mathbb{N}$ and let $\lambda > 0$ be arbitrary. Since

$$P_{\lambda h_n} \varphi^* \leqq P_{\lambda h_n} \varphi,$$

we obtain

$$\begin{aligned} 0 &\geqq \int (\varphi^* - \varphi)\, dP_{\lambda h_n} = \int (\varphi^* - \varphi) \exp\left(\lambda X(h_n) - \frac{1}{2} \|\lambda h_n\|^2\right) dP_0 \\ &= \exp\left(-\frac{1}{2}\|\lambda h_n\|^2 + \lambda r_n\right) \int (\varphi^* - \varphi) \exp(\lambda (X(h_n) - r_n))\, dP_0 \\ &= \exp\left(-\frac{1}{2}\|\lambda h_n\|^2 + \lambda r_n\right) \Bigg(\int_{X(h_n) > r_n} (\varphi^* - \varphi) \exp(\lambda(X(h_n) - r_n))\, dP_0 \\ &\quad + \int_{X(h_n) \leqq r_n} (\varphi^* - \varphi) \exp(\lambda(X(h_n) - r_n))\, dP_0 \Bigg). \end{aligned}$$

As $\lambda \to \infty$ the second integral remains bounded. The first integral, however, tends to infinity since

$$\{X(h_n) > r_n\} \subseteq \{\varphi^* = 1\}.$$

Therefore we arrive at a contradiction for sufficiently large $\lambda > 0$. □

71.15 Remark. The assertion of Theorem 71.14 is an extension of 71.12 in the following sense: If the sequence $(h_n)_{n \in \mathbb{N}}$ is contained in a finite dimensional subspace $L \subseteq H$ then the critical function φ^* is of the form

$$\varphi^* = \begin{cases} 1 & \text{if} \quad p_L \circ X \notin C, \\ 0 & \text{if} \quad p_L \circ X \in C, \end{cases}$$

where $C = \bigcap_{n \in \mathbb{N}} \{h \in H: \langle h, h_n \rangle \leqq r_n\}$ is a closed, convex subset of H.

72. Estimation for Gaussian shifts

Again, let $(H, \langle .,. \rangle)$ be a separable Hilbert space and $E = (\Omega, \mathscr{A}, \{P_h: h \in H\})$ a Gaussian shift experiment.

Let $f: H \to \mathbb{R}$ be a continuous, linear function. Recall, that an estimate $\varrho \in \mathscr{R}(E, \bar{\mathbb{R}})$ is median unbiased for f if

$$P_h(\varrho(., (-\infty, f(h)])) \geqq \frac{1}{2},$$

$$P_h(\varrho(., [f(h), \infty)) \geqq \frac{1}{2},$$

for every $h \in H$. Let $e \in H$ be a unit vector such that $e \perp \ker f$ and $f(e) > 0$. Define the loss function by $W_h(x) = \ell(|x - f(h)|)$, $x \in \bar{\mathbb{R}}$, $h \in H$, where $\ell: [0, \infty] \to [0, \infty]$ is non-decreasing, $\ell(0) = 0$.

72.1 Lemma. *Suppose that ℓ is lower semicontinuous. Then every median unbiased estimate $\varrho \in \mathscr{R}(E, \bar{\mathbb{R}})$ satisfies*

$$W_h \varrho P_h \geqq \int \ell(|\,.\,|)\, d\nu_{0, \|f\|^2}, \quad h \in H.$$

Proof. Let $h \in H$ and let $L \subseteq H$ be a finite dimensional linear subspace containing h and e. Then $E|_L$ is a finite dimensional Gaussian shift and the assertion follows from Theorem 34.3 since $\|f\| = \|f|_L\|$. □

72.2 Definition. Suppose that W is lower semicontinuous and $\varrho \in \mathscr{R}(E, \bar{\mathbb{R}})$ is median unbiased. Then ϱ is *optimal median unbiased* (for W) at $h \in H$ if

$$W_h \varrho P_h = \int \ell(|\,.\,|)\, d\nu_{0, \|f\|^2},$$

and *uniformly optimal median unbiased* if this holds for every $h \in H$.

72.3 Theorem. *Let $X = (X(h))_{h \in H}$ be the central process of E. Then $\kappa = f \circ X$ is a uniformly optimal median unbiased estimate of f for every lower semicontinuous $\ell\colon [0, \infty] \to [0, \infty]$.*

Proof. The assertion follows from the obvious fact that $\mathscr{L}(\kappa | P_h) = \nu_{f(h), \|f\|^2}$, $h \in H$. □

72.4 Theorem. *Let $X = (X(h))_{h \in H}$ be the central process of E. Suppose that ℓ is lower semicontinuous, of finite order and separating. If $\varrho_0 \in \mathscr{R}(E, \overline{\mathbb{R}})$ satisfies*

$$W_h \varrho_0 P_h \leqq \int \ell(|\,.\,|)\, d\nu_{0, \|f\|^2} \quad \text{if} \quad h \perp \ker f,$$

then $\varrho_0(., \overline{\mathbb{R}} \setminus \{f \circ X\}) = 0$ P_0-a.e.

Proof. Copy the proof of Theorem 40.11 replacing p_L by X_L where $L = (\ker f)^\perp$. □

The preceding assertions offer a complete solution for the estimation problem of a linear function $f\colon H \to \mathbb{R}$. Before we enter the problem of estimating an arbitrary linear mapping f on H, we shall consider the estimation of the identity.

We begin with the case where H is a finite dimensional Hilbert space. This case has been treated already in Section 38, but only considering estimates in $\mathscr{R}(E, H)$. In view of the general decision theory we have also to take into consideration the estimates in $\mathscr{B}(E, H) \setminus \mathscr{R}(E, H)$.

Define the loss function by $W_h(x) = \ell(x - h)$, $x \in H$, $h \in H$, where $\ell\colon H \to [0, \infty)$ is a measurable function. The following assertion is an immediate consequence of Theorems 38.22 and 43.5 in case ℓ is level-compact.

72.5 Theorem. *Assume that* $\dim H < \infty$. *Let $\ell\colon H \to [0, \infty)$ be lower semicontinuous and subconvex. Then*

$$\inf_{\beta \in \mathscr{B}(E, H)} \sup_{h \in H} \beta(W_h, P_h) = \int \ell \circ X\, dP_0 = \int \ell\, dN_H.$$

Proof. W.l.g. we assume that E is a standard Gaussian shift. The inequality "$\leqq$" is obvious. The other is proved within several steps.

(1) Assume that $\ell = 1 - 1_C$ where

$$C = \bigcap_{i=1}^{k} \{x \in H: |\langle x, y_i \rangle| \leqq \beta_i\}, \quad y_i \in H, \beta_i \geqq 0.$$

Let $L = \text{span}\{y_1, \ldots, y_k\}$. The sets C and $C \cap L$ are closed, convex and centrally symmetric.

Moreover, $C \cap L$ is compact. To see this, let $\{y_{i_1} \ldots y_{i_m}\} \subseteq \{y_1 \ldots y_k\}$ be a base of L and $\{a_1 \ldots a_m\}$ its orthonormalization. Then for every $x \in C \cap L$ and $s = 1, \ldots, m$

$$|\langle x, a_s \rangle| \leqq \sum_{i=1}^{k} \beta_i \|y_i\|$$

which implies

$$\|x\|^2 = \sum_{s=1}^{m} |\langle x, a_s \rangle|^2 \leqq m\Big(\sum_{i=1}^{k} \beta_i \|y_i\|\Big)^2.$$

Moreover, we have $\ell \circ p_L = \ell$.

To prove the assertion for this particular choice of ℓ we note first that

$$\inf_{\beta \in \mathscr{B}(E, H)} \sup_{h \in H} \beta(W_h, P_h) \geqq \inf_{\beta \in \mathscr{B}(E, H)} \sup_{h \in L} \beta(W_h, P_h).$$

For every $\beta \in \mathscr{B}(E, H)$ we define $\bar{\beta} \in \mathscr{B}(E_L, L)$ by

$$\bar{\beta}: (g, \mu) \mapsto \beta(g \circ p_L, \mu), \quad g \in \mathscr{C}_b(L), \mu \in L(E).$$

Comparing the risks of β and $\bar{\beta}$ for $h \in L$, we obtain

$$\begin{aligned} \beta(W_h, P_h) &= \sup\{\beta(f, P_h): f \in \mathscr{C}_b(H), f \leqq W_h\} \\ &\geqq \sup\{\beta(g \circ p_L, P_h): g \in \mathscr{C}_b(L), g \circ p_L \leqq W_h\} \\ &= \sup\{\bar{\beta}(g, P_h): g \in \mathscr{C}_b(L), g \leqq W_h|_L\} \\ &= \bar{\beta}(W_h|_L, P_h), \quad h \in L, \end{aligned}$$

since $W_h \circ p_L = W_h$. This implies that

$$\inf_{\beta \in \mathscr{B}(E, H)} \sup_{h \in L} \beta(W_h, P_h) \geqq \inf_{\beta \in \mathscr{B}(E_L, L)} \sup_{h \in L} \beta(W_h|_L, P_h).$$

Now, $W_h|_L$ is level-compact and we arrive at

$$\begin{aligned} &\inf_{\beta \in \mathscr{B}(E_L, L)} \sup_{h \in L} \beta(W_h|_L, P_h) \\ &= \inf_{\varrho \in \mathscr{R}(E_L, L)} \sup_{h \in L} (W_h|_L)\varrho P_h = \int \ell(X_L)\, dP_0 = \int \ell\, dP_0, \end{aligned}$$

by Theorems 43.5 and 38.22.

(2) Let $C \subseteq H$ be an arbitrary closed, convex and centrally symmetric set. Consider the loss function $\ell = 1 - 1_C$. Let $\mathscr{V}_1$ be the class of loss functions considered in part (1) of the proof. Then $\mathscr{V}_1$ is directed from above and

$$\ell = \sup\{V \in \mathscr{V}_1 : V \leqq \ell\}.$$

To see the latter, consider any $x \notin C$. Then, by basic separation theorems, there are $y \in H$, $\beta \geqq 0$, such that

$$\langle y, x\rangle > \beta, \quad \text{but} \quad |\langle y, z\rangle| \leqq \beta \quad \text{if} \quad z \in C.$$

Let $D = \{z \in H : |\langle y, z\rangle| \leqq \beta\}$ and define $V = 1 - 1_D$. Then $C \subseteq D$ implies $V \leqq \ell$, and $x \notin D$ implies $V(x) = \ell(x)$.

If $V \in \mathscr{V}_1$ let $V_h := V(.-h)$. Now, the assertion follows for ℓ by

$$\begin{aligned}
&\inf_{\beta \in \mathscr{B}(E,H)} \sup_{h \in H} \beta(W_h, P_h) \\
&\geqq \sup_{V \in \mathscr{V}_1 : V \leqq \ell} \inf_{\beta \in \mathscr{B}(E,H)} \sup_{h \in H} \beta(V_h, P_h) \\
&= \sup_{V \in \mathscr{V}_1 : V \leqq \ell} \int V\,dP_0 = \int \ell\,dP_0 .
\end{aligned}$$

(3) Next, let ℓ be a simple function. If $\operatorname{im} \ell = \{\alpha_1, \ldots, \alpha_n\}$, $\alpha_1 < \alpha_2 < \ldots < \alpha_n$, then

$$\ell = \sum_{j=1}^{n} (\alpha_j - \alpha_{j-1}) V_j$$

where $\alpha_0 = 0$, $V_0 = 1$, $V_j = 1_{\{\ell > \alpha_{j-1}\}}$, $1 \leqq j \leqq n-1$.

We note, that for every $j = 1, \ldots, n-1$ the function V_j is of the type considered in part (2) of the proof.

Let $\mathscr{B}_i \subseteq \mathscr{B}(E, H)$ be the set of all strictly equivariant decision functions. Now, we apply the general Hunt-Stein-Theorem 48.13. Thus, we get

$$\begin{aligned}
&\inf_{\beta \in \mathscr{B}(E,H)} \sup_{h \in H} \beta(W_h, P_h) = \inf_{\beta \in \mathscr{B}_i} \beta(\ell, P_0) \\
&= \inf_{\beta \in \mathscr{B}_i} \sum_{j=1}^{n} (\alpha_j - \alpha_{j-1}) \beta(V_j, P_0) \\
&\geqq \sum_{j=1}^{n} (\alpha_j - \alpha_{j-1}) \inf_{\beta \in \mathscr{B}_i} \beta(V_j, P_0) \\
&= \sum_{j=1}^{n} (\alpha_j - \alpha_{j-1}) \inf_{\beta \in \mathscr{B}(E,H)} \sup_{h \in H} \beta(V_{j,h}, P_0) \\
&= \sum_{j=1}^{n} (\alpha_j - \alpha_{j-1}) \int V_j\,dP_0 = \int \ell\,dP_0 .
\end{aligned}$$

(4) Finally, let ℓ be arbitrary. Let $\mathscr{V}_3$ be the class of loss functions considered in part (3) of the proof. Then $\mathscr{V}_3$ is directed from above and

$$\ell = \sup\{V \in \mathscr{V}_3 : V \leqq \ell\}.$$

To see the latter,, we have to show that for every $x \in H$ and $\varepsilon > 0$ there exists $V \leqq \ell$, $V \in \mathscr{V}_3$, such that $\ell(x) \leqq V(x) + \varepsilon$. For this, let $\alpha < \ell(x) \leqq \alpha + \varepsilon$. Since $x \notin \{\ell \leqq \alpha\}$ there are $y \in H$, $\beta \geqq 0$, such that

$$\langle y, x\rangle > \beta, \quad \text{but } |\langle y, z\rangle| \leqq \beta \quad \text{if} \quad \ell(z) \leqq \alpha.$$

Let $C = \{z \in H: |\langle y, z\rangle| \leqq \beta\}$ and define $V = \alpha(1 - 1_C) \in \mathscr{V}_3$. Then $\{\ell \leqq \alpha\} \subseteq C$ which implies

$$V = \alpha(1 - 1_C) \leqq \alpha 1_{\{\ell > \alpha\}} \leqq \ell,$$

and $V(x) = \alpha \geqq \ell(x) - \varepsilon$, since $x \notin C$. □

72.6 Corollary. *Assume that the conditions of Theorem 72.5 are satisfied. Then the central random variable $X: \Omega \to H$ is a minimax estimate.*

Proof. Use Corollary 69.11. □

Next, we extend the preceding result to the general case where the dimension of H is not necessarily finite.

72.7 Theorem. *Suppose that $\ell: H \to [0, \infty)$ is lower semicontinuous and subconvex. Then*

$$\inf_{\beta \in \mathscr{B}(E, H)} \sup_{h \in H} \beta(W_h, P_h) = \sup_{L \in \mathscr{L}} \int_L \ell \, dN_L.$$

Proof. (1) In the first part we prove that the inequality "$\leqq$" is valid. For this we apply several times the Minimax Theorem 46.3:

$$\begin{aligned}
&\inf_{\beta \in \mathscr{B}(E, H)} \sup_{h \in H} \beta(W_h, P_h) \\
&= \sup_{m \in S_H} \inf_{\beta \in \mathscr{B}(E, H)} \int \beta(W_h, P_h) m(dh) \\
&= \sup_{L \in \mathscr{L}} \sup_{m \in S_L} \inf_{\beta \in \mathscr{B}(E, H)} \int \beta(W_h, P_h) m(dh) \\
&= \sup_{L \in \mathscr{L}} \inf_{\beta \in \mathscr{B}(E, H)} \sup_{h \in L} \beta(W_h, P_h) \\
&\leqq \sup_{L \in \mathscr{L}} \int \ell \circ X_L \, dP_0
\end{aligned}$$

since $X_L \in \mathscr{B}(E, H)$, $L \in \mathscr{L}$.

(2) For the proof of the reversed inequality we introduce the class $\mathscr{V}$ of functions $V: H \to [0, \infty)$, which are lower semicontinuous and subconvex, and in addition satisfy $V \circ p_L = V$ for some finite dimensional subspace $L \subseteq H$. This class satisfies

$$\ell = \sup \{V \in \mathscr{V} : V \leqq \ell\}$$

which follows from parts (2) and (4) of the proof of Theorem 72.5. Moreover, $\mathscr{V}$ is directed from above. To see this, let $V_1 \circ p_{L_1} = V_1$ and $V_2 \circ p_{L_2} = V_2$. If $L = \operatorname{span}\{L_1, L_2\}$ then $V_i \circ p_L = V_i$, $i = 1, 2$, and hence $(V_1 \cup V_2) \circ p_L = (V_1 \cup V_2)$.

(3) Let us prove that for every $V \in \mathscr{V}$ such that $V \circ p_L = V$

$$\inf_{\beta \in \mathscr{B}(E,H)} \sup_{h \in H} \beta(V_h, P_h) \geqq \int_L V dN_L .$$

First, it is clear that

$$\inf_{\beta \in \mathscr{B}(E,H)} \sup_{h \in H} \beta(V_h, P_h) \geqq \inf_{\beta \in \mathscr{B}(E,H)} \sup_{h \in L} \beta(V_h, P_h) .$$

Secondly, similarly to the argument in part (1) of the proof of Theorem 72.5 it is shown that

$$\inf_{\beta \in \mathscr{B}(E,H)} \sup_{h \in L} \beta(V_h, P_h) \geqq \inf_{\beta \in \mathscr{B}(E_L, L)} \sup_{h \in L} \beta(V_h|_L, P_h) .$$

Now, the assertion follows from Theorem 72.5.

(4) With part (3) of this proof we arrive at

$$\inf_{\beta \in \mathscr{B}(E,H)} \sup_{h \in H} \beta(W_h, P_h) \geqq \sup_{V \in \mathscr{V}: V \leqq \ell} \int_{L(V)} V dN_{L(V)}$$

where $L(V) \subseteq H$ is a finite dimensional subspace such that $V \circ p_{L(V)} = V$. It remains to show that

$$\sup_{V \in \mathscr{V}: V \leqq \ell} \int_{L(V)} V dN_{L(V)} = \sup_{L \in \mathscr{L}} \int_L \ell \, dN_L .$$

This is proved, showing that for each $V \in \mathscr{V}$

$$\int_{L(V)} V dN_{L(V)} = \sup_{L \in \mathscr{L}} \int_L V dN_L .$$

It is clear that $L(V) \subseteq L$ implies

$$\int_{L(V)} V dN_{L(V)} = \int_L V dN_L$$

since $V \circ p_L = V$, in this case. Thus, we need only show that $L_1 \subseteq L_2$ implies

$$\int_{L_1} V dN_{L_1} \leqq \int_{L_2} V dN_{L_2},$$

or equivalently,

$$\int_0^\infty N_{L_1}\{V > \alpha\} \, d\alpha \leqq \int_0^\infty N_{L_2}\{V > \alpha\} \, d\alpha .$$

In other words, we have to prove that for every centrally symmetric, closed convex set $C \subseteq H$

$$N_{L_1}(C \cap L_1) \geqq N_{L_2}(C \cap L_2).$$

If we put $D := C \cap L_2$ then this means

$$N_{L_2}((D \cap L_1) \oplus L_1^\perp) \geqq N_{L_2}(D)$$

where $L_1^\perp$ denotes the orthogonal complement of L_1 in L_2. But the last inequality follows from

$$\begin{aligned}\int_D dN_{L_2} &= \int_{L_1^\perp} \int_{L_1} 1_{D-x_2}(x_1) N_{L_1}(dx_1) N_{L_1^\perp}(dx_2)\\ &\leqq \int_{L_1^\perp} \int_{L_1} 1_D(x_1) N_{L_1}(dx_1) N_{L_1^\perp}(dx_2)\\ &= N_{L_2}((D \cap L_1) \oplus L_1^\perp),\end{aligned}$$

where we have used Lemma 38.20. □

72.8 Remark. Suppose that $\ell: H \to [0, \infty)$ is lower semicontinuous and subconvex. If $L_1 \subseteq L_2$ are finite dimensional subspaces of H then

$$\int_{L_1} \ell \, dN_{L_1} \leqq \int_{L_2} \ell \, dN_{L_2}.$$

This has been proved in part (4) of the preceding proof.

Now, it is easy to find minimax estimates of the identity.

72.9 Theorem. *Let $X = (X(h))_{h \in H}$ be the central process of E and $\beta_X \in \mathscr{B}(E, H)$ the decision function defined by X (according to Definition (69.14)). Suppose that $\ell: H \to [0, \infty)$ is lower semicontinuous and subconvex. Then β_X is a minimax estimate of the identity.*

Proof. Noting, that the assertion of Theorem 62.5 is valid also for the net $(X_L)_{L \in \mathscr{L}}$ in $\mathscr{B}(E, H)$, we obtain for every $L_0 \in \mathscr{L}$

$$\sup_{h \in L_0} \beta_X(W_h, P_h) \leqq \liminf_{L \to H} \sup_{h \in L_0} \int \ell(X_L - h) \, dP_h = \liminf_{L \to H} \int_L \ell \, dN_L$$

which implies that

$$\sup_{h \in H} \beta_X(W_h, P_h) \leqq \sup_{L \in \mathscr{L}} \int_L \ell \, dN_L.$$

Equality follows from Theorem 72.7. □

In many important applications the decision problem is of finite dimension in the sense that the loss function is a cylinder function.

72.10 Corollary. *Let $X = (X(h))_{h \in H}$ be the central process of E. Suppose that ℓ: $H \to [0, \infty)$ is lower semicontinuous and subconvex. If $L_0 \in \mathscr{L}$ is a subspace satisfying $\ell \circ p_{L_0} = \ell$, then*

$$\sup_{L \in \mathscr{L}} \int_L \ell \, dN_L = \int_{L_0} \ell \, dN_{L_0}$$

and the random variable X_{L_0} is a minimax estimate.

Proof. Since "$\geqq$" is trivial we need only prove "$\leqq$". Let $L \subseteq H$ be any finite dimensional subspace and let $L_1 = \operatorname{span}(L \cup L_0)$. Then by Corollary 72.8

$$\int_L \ell \, dN_L \leqq \int_{L_1} \ell \, dN_{L_1}$$

and

$$\int_{L_1} \ell \, dN_{L_1} = \int_{L_1} \ell \circ p_{L_0} dN_{L_1} = \int_{L_0} \ell \, d\mathscr{L}(p_{L_0} | N_{L_1})$$
$$= \int_{L_0} \ell \, dN_{L_0}. \qquad \square$$

An important application is the estimation of linear functions f: $H \to B$ with finite dimensional range B. The problem has two aspects leading essentially to the same solution. The first consists in defining $D = H$ and $\ell = \ell_1 \circ f$ where ℓ_1: $B \to [0, \infty)$. Denoting $L(f) := (\ker f)^{\perp}$ Theorem 72.7 and Corollary 72.10 lead to the minimax risk

$$\inf_{\beta \in \mathscr{B}(E, H)} \sup_{h \in H} \beta(W_h, P_h) = \int_{L(f)} \ell_1 \circ f dN_{L(f)}$$

and to the minimax estimate β_X. The second possibility is more natural.

72.11 Theorem. *Let B be a finite dimensional space and f: $H \to B$ a continuous, linear function such that* $\operatorname{im} f = B$. *Suppose that ℓ_1: $B \to [0, \infty)$ is lower semicontinuous and subconvex. Denote $L(f) := (\ker f)^{\perp}$.*

If $D = B$ and $W_h := \ell_1(. - f(h))$, $h \in H$, then

$$\inf_{\beta \in \mathscr{B}(E, H)} \sup_{h \in H} \beta(W_h, P_h) = \int_{L(f)} \ell_1 \circ f \, dN_{L(f)}.$$

The estimate $f \circ X$ is a minimax estimate.

Proof. The inequality "$\leqq$" is obvious since $f \circ X_{L(f)} \in \mathscr{B}(E, B)$. To prove the other inequality we show first that

$$\inf_{\beta \in \mathscr{B}(E, B)} \sup_{h \in H} \beta(W_h, P_h) \geqq \inf_{\beta \in \mathscr{B}(E_{L(f)}, L(f))} \sup_{h \in L(f)} \beta((\ell_1 \circ f)_h, P_h).$$

For this, let $\beta \in \mathscr{B}(E, B)$ and define $\bar{\beta} \in \mathscr{B}(E_{L(f)}, L(f))$ by

$$\bar{\beta}\colon (g, \mu) \mapsto \beta(g \circ f^{-1}, \mu), \quad g \in \mathscr{C}_b(L(f)),\ \mu \in L(E),$$

where $f^{-1}\colon B \to L(f)$ is the inverse of $f|_{L(f)}$. Then

$$\begin{aligned}\bar{\beta}((\ell_1 \circ f)_h, P_h) &= \sup\{\bar{\beta}(V, P_h)\colon V \leqq (\ell_1 \circ f)_h \text{ on } L(f),\ V \in \mathscr{C}_b(L(f))\}\\ &= \sup\{\beta(V \circ f^{-1}, P_h)\colon V \circ f^{-1} \leqq \ell_1(.-f(h)) \text{ on } B,\ V \in \mathscr{C}_b(L(f))\}\\ &\leqq \sup\{\beta(V_1, P_h)\colon V_1 \leqq \ell_1(.-f(h)) \text{ on } B,\ V_1 \in \mathscr{C}_b(B)\}\\ &= \beta(W_h, P_h), \quad h \in L(f).\end{aligned}$$

Now, the assertion follows since

$$\inf_{\beta \in \mathscr{B}(E_{L(f)}, L(f))} \sup_{h \in L(f)} \beta((\ell_1 \circ f)_h, P_h) = \int_{L(f)} \ell_1 \circ f \, dN_{L(f)}$$

is an immediate consequence of Theorem 72.5. It is clear that $f \circ X$ is a minimax estimate of f. □

72.12 Remark. Keep the assumptions of the preceding theorem. As to the computation of the minimax bound let $B = \mathbb{R}^k$. Then for $t \in \mathbb{R}^k$

$$\int \exp(it'f(x))\, dN_{L_0}(x) = \hat{N}_{L_0}(f^*(t)) = \exp\left(-\frac{1}{2} < f^*(t), f^*(t) >\right)$$

If $(a_1 \ldots a_k)$ is an orthonormal base of L_0 and if Γ is the matrix of $(f \circ f^*)^{-1}$ with respect to $(a_1 \ldots a_k)$ then

$$\mathscr{L}(f \mid N_{L_0}) = \nu_{0,\Gamma}$$

and hence

$$\int_{L_0} \ell_1 \circ f \, dN_{L_0} = \int_{\mathbb{R}^k} \ell_1 \, d\nu_{0,\Gamma}.$$

A uniqueness assertion is possible if we only consider equivariant estimates.

72.13 Corollary. *Suppose that the assumptions of Theorem 72.11 are satisfied. Assume further that ℓ_1 is level-compact and separating.*

Let $D = B$ and $W_h := \ell_1(.-f(h))$, $h \in H$. If $\beta \in \mathscr{B}(E, B)$ is equivariant and satisfies

$$\beta(W_0, P_0) = \int_{L(f)} \ell_1 \circ f \, dN_{L(f)}$$

then β coincides with the non-randomized estimate $f \circ X$.

Proof. Since $L(E) = L(E|_{L(f)})$ we may restrict our attention to the finite dimensional case where $H = L(f)$. Then the only difference to the assertion of Theorem 38.28 is that now we do not assume that $\beta \in \mathscr{R}(E, B)$.

First, we show that there exists an equivariant estimate $\varrho \in \mathscr{R}(E, B)$ such that

$$W_h \varrho P_h \leqq \beta(W_h, P_h), \quad h \in H.$$

For this, we copy the construction of Lemma 43.4. The kernel ϱ_0 obtained there satisfies

$$g(.-h)\varrho_0 P_h = \beta(g(.-h), P_h) = \beta(g, P_0) = g\varrho_0 P_0, \quad h \in H,$$

for all $g \in \mathscr{C}_{00}(B)$. It follows that

$$P_h(\varrho_0(.,B)) = P_0(\varrho_0(.,B)), \quad h \in H.$$

Let X be the central random variable of E. Since X is E-sufficient we may assume that ϱ_0 depends on $\omega \in \Omega$ through X. Hence, by completeness of $\{\mathscr{L}(X|P_h): h \in H\}$ we obtain that $\varrho_0(.,B) = \text{const}\ N_H$-a.e. The case $\varrho_0(.,B) = 0$ cannot happen since otherwise

$$\beta(W_h, P_h) = \ell_1(\infty) > \int \ell_1 \, dP_0, \quad h \in H,$$

which contradicts the assumption. Thus, having established $\varrho_0(.,B) > 0$ we copy the construction of Lemma 43.4 and observe that the decision function ϱ obtained there is equivariant. Now, we apply Theorem 38.28 and conclude that ϱ coincides with $f \circ X$. This implies

$$\beta(W_0 - \ell_1(\infty), P_0) = (W_0 - \ell_1(\infty))\varrho P_0.$$

On the other hand it is clear that

$$\beta(W_0 - \ell_1(\infty), P_0) = (W_0 - \ell_1(\infty))\varrho_0 P_0$$

by definition of ϱ_0. Since

$$(W_0 - \ell_1(\infty))\varrho P_0 = \frac{1}{\varrho_0(.,B)}(W_0 - \ell_1(\infty))\varrho_0 P_0$$

it follows that $\varrho_0(.,B) = 1$. Hence $\beta = \varrho_0 = \varrho = f \circ X$. □

As a consequence we obtain that the non-randomized estimate $f \circ X$ is uniquely determined by its distribution.

We finish this section with a general version of Boll's convolution theorem.

72.14 Remark. Let us call a linear process $Z = (Z(h))_{h \in H}$ equivariant if the decision function β_Z is equivariant, i.e. if

$$\beta_Z(f, P_0) = \beta_Z(f(.-h), P_h), \quad h \in H, f \in \mathscr{C}_b(H).$$

In terms of the linear process Z this means that

$$\mathscr{L}(Z(h_1) - \langle h_1, h_2 \rangle | P_{h_2}) = \mathscr{L}(Z(h_1)|P_0), \; h_i \in H, \; i = 1, 2.$$

E.g. every standard process is equivariant in this sense.

72.15 Theorem. *Suppose that $Z = (Z(h))_{h \in H}$ is an equivariant process. Then there exists a cylinder set probability measure $(Q_L)_{L \in \mathscr{L}}$ such that*

$$\mathscr{L}(Z_L|P_0) = N_L * Q_L, \quad L \in \mathscr{L}.$$

Proof. Since Z is equivariant, the random variables Z_L are equivariant estimates for the restricted Gaussian shifts $E|_L$, $L \in \mathscr{L}$. The existence of probability measures $Q_L|\mathscr{B}(L)$ such that

$$\mathscr{L}(Z_L|P_0) = N_L * Q_L, \quad L \in \mathscr{L},$$

follows immediately from Theorem 38.15. It remains to show that $(Q_L)_{L \in \mathscr{L}}$ is projective. Projectivity of $(Z_L)_{L \in \mathscr{L}}$ implies that for $L_1 \subseteq L_2$

$$\mathscr{L}(p_{L_1}|N_{L_2} * Q_{L_2}) = N_{L_1} * Q_{L_1}.$$

However, it is clear that

$$\mathscr{L}(p_{L_1}|N_{L_2} * Q_{L_2}) = N_{L_1} * \mathscr{L}(p_{L_1}|Q_{L_2})$$

which proves

$$Q_{L_1} = \mathscr{L}(p_{L_1}|Q_{L_2}). \qquad \square$$

73. Testing and estimation for Banach sample spaces

The results of Sections 71 and 72 can be given in a particular simple form if the underlying Gaussian shift is represented by an Abstract Wiener space.

Let (H, B, τ) be an Abstract Wiener space and $E = (B, \mathscr{B}(B), \{P_h: h \in H\})$ the Gaussian shift where $P_h = P_0 * \varepsilon_{\tau(h)}$, $h \in H$. The central process of E is denoted by $(X(h))_{h \in H}$. Recall, that the central process satisfies $X(h_1)(\tau(h_2)) = \langle h_1, h_2 \rangle$, $h_1, h_2 \in H$.

The tests of Theorems 71.3, 71.7 and 71.10 do not simplify very much when considered in the Abstract Wiener space representation. Therefore we confine ourselves to an example.

73.1 Example. Consider the case of Theorem 70.3 and Example 70.9. Then any linear continuous function f on H is of the form $f = \langle ., h_0 \rangle$, $h_0 \in H$. W.l.g. assume that $\|h_0\| = 1$. Since $f \circ X = X(h_0)$ is the Wiener integral the optimal test of Theorem 71.3 is

$$\varphi^*(x) = \begin{cases} 1 & \text{if } \int h_0 \, dx > N_{1-\alpha} \\ 0 & \text{if } \int h_0 \, dx < N_{1-\alpha} \end{cases}, \quad x \in \mathscr{C}([0,1]),$$

and a similar formula holds for the optimal test of Theorems 71.7 and 71.10.

A considerable simplification, however, is possible considering the testing problem $(\{0\}, H \setminus \{0\})$.

73.2 Theorem (Moussatat [1976]). *Let $C \subseteq B$ be a convex, closed subset. Then*

$$\varphi^*(x) = \begin{cases} 1 & \text{if } x \notin C, \\ 0 & \text{if } x \in C, \end{cases} \quad x \in B,$$

is an admissible test for the testing problem $(\{0\}, H \setminus \{0\})$ and is uniquely determined by its distribution.

Proof. We show that φ^* is of the form considered in Theorem 71.14. From basic separation theorems it follows that there exists a sequence $(x_n^*)_{n \in \mathbb{N}} \subseteq B^*$ such that

$$C = \{x \in B \colon x_n^*(x) \leqq r_n, \, n \in \mathbb{N}\}.$$

Let us define $h_n := \tau^*(x_n)$, $n \in \mathbb{N}$. The assertion is proved since from the proof of Theorem 70.6 we know that $X(h_n) = x_n^*$, $n \in \mathbb{N}$. □

73.3 Corollary. *Any test of the form*

$$\varphi^*(x) = \begin{cases} 1 & \text{if } \|x\|_B > c, \\ 0 & \text{if } \|x\|_B < c, \end{cases} \quad x \in B,$$

is an admissible test for the testing problem $(\{0\}, H \setminus \{0\})$ and is uniquely determined by its distribution.

Next, we attempt to compute the minimax bound in the case of estimating the linear mapping τ.

73.4 Discussion. Similar to the remarks preceding Theorem 72.11 we may distinguish two versions of this estimation problem. Let $\ell \colon B \to [0, \infty)$ be lower semicontinuous and subconvex.

(1) Define $D = H$ and $W_h \colon x \mapsto (\ell \circ \tau)\,(x - h)$, $x \in H$, $h \in H$. Then the minimax risk of this estimation problem is

$$\inf_{\beta \in \mathscr{B}(E,H)} \sup_{h \in H} \beta(W_h, P_h) = \sup_{L \in \mathscr{L}} \int_L \ell \circ \tau \, dN_L,$$

according to Theorem 72.7.

(2) Sometimes, however, one is dealing with estimation problems where $D = B$ and $W_h \colon x \mapsto \ell(x - \tau(h))$, $x \in B$, $h \in H$. Since the experiment E has

sample space B, the identity of B is in $\mathscr{B}(E, B)$ and therefore

$$\inf_{\beta \in \mathscr{B}(E,B)} \sup_{h \in H} \beta(W_h, P_h) \leqq \int \ell \, dP_0 .$$

We shall prove that even equality holds.

Our first assertion deals with part (1) of the preceding discussion. It will be shown that the minimax risk can be simplified in this case.

73.5 Theorem. *Suppose that ℓ: $B \to [0, \infty)$ is lower semicontinuous and subconvex. Then*

$$\sup_{L \in \mathscr{L}} \int_L \ell \circ \tau \, dN_L = \int \ell \, dP_0 .$$

Proof. Let $\mathscr{V}$ be the class of all lower semicontinuous subconvex functions $\tilde{\ell}$: $B \to [0, \infty)$ which depend on $x \in B$ through a finite subset $\{x_1^*, \ldots, x_k^*\} \subseteq B^*$ only. It should be clear from the preceding proofs of this section that $\mathscr{V}$ is directed from above and $\ell = \sup \{\tilde{\ell} \in \mathscr{V} : \tilde{\ell} \leqq \ell\}$. It is therefore sufficient to prove the assertion for $\tilde{\ell} \in \mathscr{V}$.

If $\tilde{\ell} \in \mathscr{V}$, then there exists a finite dimensional subspace $L_0 \subseteq H$ and a continuous, linear mapping π: $B \to L_0$ such that $\pi \circ \tau = p_{L_0}$ and $\tilde{\ell} = \tilde{\ell} \circ \tau \circ \pi$. For the proof of this assertion, let $x_1^*, \ldots, x_k^* \in B^*$ be such that $x - y \in \bigcap_{i=1}^{k} \ker x_i^*$ implies $\tilde{\ell}(x) = \tilde{\ell}(y)$. W.l.g. we assume that $x_1^*, \ldots, x_k^*$ are linearly independent and $f^*(x_1^*), \ldots, f^*(x_k^*)$ are an orthonormal system. Denote $e_i := f^*(x_i^*)$, $1 \leqq i \leqq k$, and define $L_0 = \operatorname{span}\{e_1, \ldots, e_k\}$. Then

$$\pi: B \to L_0: z \mapsto \sum_{i=1}^{k} x_i^*(z) e_i$$

is of the desired nature.

For the determination of the left side of the asserted equation we need only note that

$$(\tilde{\ell} \circ \tau) \circ p_{L_0} = (\tilde{\ell} \circ \tau) \circ (\pi \circ \tau) = \tilde{\ell} \circ \tau$$

and apply Lemma (72.10) to obtain

$$\sup_{\dim L < \infty} \int_L \tilde{\ell} \circ \tau \, dN_L = \int_{L_0} \tilde{\ell} \circ \tau \, dN_{L_0} .$$

For the determination of the right side we remember that $P_0 = \mathscr{L}(\tau | N_H)$ and hence

$$\begin{aligned} \int \tilde{\ell} \, dP &= \int \tilde{\ell} \circ \tau \circ \pi \, dP = \int \tilde{\ell} \circ \tau \circ \pi \circ \tau \, dN_H \\ &= \int \tilde{\ell} \circ \tau \circ p_{L_0} dN_H = \int_{L_0} \tilde{\ell} \circ \tau \, N_{L_0} . \end{aligned}$$

This completes the proof. □

Now, we prove that in part (2) of Discussion 73.4 even equality holds.

73.6 Theorem. *Let $D = B$ and W_h: $x \mapsto \ell(x - \tau(h))$, $x \in B$, $h \in H$, for a lower semicontinuous subconvex function ℓ: $B \to [0, \infty)$. Then*

$$\inf_{\beta \in \mathscr{B}(E, B)} \sup_{h \in H} \beta(W_h, P_h) = \int \ell \, dP_0 .$$

Proof. Let $\mathscr{V}$ be defined as in the proof of Theorem 73.5. It is sufficient to show that for every $\tilde{\ell} \in \mathscr{V}$

$$\inf_{\beta \in \mathscr{B}(E, B)} \sup_{h \in H} \beta(\tilde{W}_h, P_h) \geqq \int \tilde{\ell} \, dP_0$$

where $\tilde{W}_h$: $x \mapsto \tilde{\ell}(x - \tau(h))$, $x \in B$, $h \in H$.

Let $\tilde{\ell} \in \mathscr{V}$. Then, in view of the proof of Theorem 73.5, there is a finite dimensional subspace $L_0 \subseteq H$, and a continuous, linear mapping π: $B \to L_0$, such that $\pi \circ \tau = p_{L_0}$ and $\tilde{\ell} = \tilde{\ell} \circ \tau \circ \pi$.

We shall prove that for every $\beta \in \mathscr{B}(E, B)$ there exists a $\beta_0 \in \mathscr{B}(E, L_0)$ such that

$$\beta(W_h, P_h) \geqq \beta_0((\tilde{\ell} \circ \tau)_h, P_h), \quad h \in L_0 .$$

For this, let $\beta \in \mathscr{B}(E, B)$ and define $\beta_0 \in \mathscr{B}(E, L_0)$ by

$$\beta_0(g, \mu) = \beta(g \circ \pi, \mu), \quad g \in \mathscr{C}_b(L_0), \mu \in L(E) .$$

If $h \in L_0$, we have

$$\begin{aligned} &\beta_0((\tilde{\ell} \circ \tau)_h, P_h) \\ &\quad = \sup\{\beta_0(V, P_h): V \in \mathscr{C}_b(L_0), V \leqq \tilde{\ell} \circ \tau(. - h) \text{ on } L_0\} \\ &\quad = \sup\{\beta(V \circ \pi, P_h): V \in \mathscr{C}_b(L_0), V \circ \pi \leqq \tilde{\ell} \circ \tau(\pi(.) - h) \text{ on } B\} \\ &\quad \leqq \sup\{\beta(V, P_h): V \in \mathscr{C}_b(B), V \leqq \tilde{\ell}(. - \tau(h)) \text{ on } B\} \\ &\quad = \beta(W_h, P_h) . \end{aligned}$$

Hence, β_0 has the required property.

We obtain that

$$\begin{aligned} &\inf_{\beta \in \mathscr{B}(E, B)} \sup_{h \in H} \beta(\tilde{W}_h, P_h) \\ &\quad \geqq \inf_{\beta \in \mathscr{B}(E, L_0)} \sup_{h \in L_0} \beta((\tilde{\ell} \circ \tau)_h, P_h) = \int_{L_0} \tilde{\ell} \circ \tau \, dN_{L_0} . \end{aligned}$$

From the end of the proof of Theorem 73.5 we see that

$$\int_{L_0} \tilde{\ell} \circ f \, dN_{L_0} = \int \tilde{\ell} \, dP,$$

which proves the assertion. □

73.7 Corollary. *Suppose that the assumptions of Theorem 73.6 are satisfied. Then the identity on B is a minimax estimate.*

Chapter 12: Differentiability and Asymptotic Expansions

In the present chapter it is our aim to provide the technical foundation for a large class of applications of the asymptotic theory. The actual application of asymptotic decision theory to these examples is considered in Chapter 13.

The idea of independent replications of a statistical experiment is formalized by multiplication of experiments. Consider a triangular array of experiments and form the products of every row. The resulting sequence of experiments has accumulation points for the weak topology. The question arises how to describe all possible accumulation points and to give criteria for the convergence against certain types of accumulation points. For this problem a complete, general solution is known. The particular case of binary experiments is treated in LeCam [1969]. The case of arbitrary parameter spaces is considered in LeCam [1974], and in Janssen, Milbrodt and Strasser [1985].

In this book we do not consider the problem in full generality. We are only interested in the weak convergence of product experiments to Gaussian shifts. Weak convergence of product experiments to Gaussian shifts is proved most conveniently by means of a stochastic expansion of the likelihood process, as it has been done before already in the early papers of Wald. The present chapter is exclusively devoted to the proof of this expansion.

To be more precise, we have to establish a stochastic expansion of the logarithm of the likelihood process. The classical Taylor argument for this expansion is presented in Section 74. We use assumptions which are almost necessary. Related conditions which are necessary and sufficient can be found in LeCam [1969], in Oosterhoff and van Zwet [1979] and in Janssen, Milbrodt and Strasser, [1985].

Of basic importance for the following are the concepts of a differentiable curve in a family of probability measures and of a tangent vector of a family of probability measures. They have a considerably broader range of applications than we can present in this book. The reader is referred to Pfanzagl and Wefelmeyer [1982]. We confine ourselves to exhibit the relation between the tangent vector of a differentiable curve and the stochastic expansion of the likelihood process. This is done in Section 75.

In Section 76 we consider differentiable experiments with finite dimensional parameter space. This is the main subject of the classical asymptotic theory. The essential point is the construction of an inner product on the tangent space of the parameter set such that it becomes isomorphic to the tangent space of the experiment.

For some time there was considerable effort to find conditions as weak as possible which imply differentiability of an experiment. Our proposal in Section 77 is taken from LeCam [1970] and Hajek [1972]. The examples of Section 78 shall illustrate the usefullness of our conditions.

The preceding sections can be applied immediately to obtain the stochastic expansion for differentiable experiments in case of identical and independent replications. In this case the stochastic expansion is parametrized by the tangent space. However, in case of non-identical replications we have to parametrize by triangular arrays of tangent vectors. Such expansions are considered in Section 79. They occur in the literature for the first time in Hajek and Sidak [1967], in connection with rank tests. In view of the importance of this special case it is elaborated in full detail. Further information concerning the case of non-identical replications is contained in Moussatat [1976] and in Becker [1983].

74. Stochastic expansion of likelihood ratios

Consider a triangular array $E_{ni} = (\Omega_{ni}, \mathscr{A}_{ni}, (P_{ni}, Q_{ni}))$, $1 \leqq i \leqq k(n)$, $n \in \mathbb{N}$, of binary experiments. Assume that $k(n) \uparrow \infty$. Denote

$$E_n = (\Omega_n, \mathscr{A}_n, (P_n, Q_n)) := \prod_{i=1}^{k(n)} E_{ni}, \quad n \in \mathbb{N}.$$

For $1 \leqq i \leqq k(n)$, $n \in \mathbb{N}$, let $\left(\frac{dQ_{ni}}{dP_{ni}}, N_{ni}\right)$ be a Lebesgue decomposition of Q_{ni} with respect to P_{ni}. We are going to investigate the asymptotic behaviour of the likelihood ratios

$$\frac{dQ_n}{dP_n} = \prod_{i=1}^{k(n)} \frac{dQ_{ni}}{dP_{ni}}, \quad n \in \mathbb{N}.$$

74.1 Definition. A triangular array of functions $g_{ni} \in L^2(\Omega_{ni}, \mathscr{A}_{ni}, P_{ni})$, $1 \leqq i \leqq k(n)$, $n \in \mathbb{N}$, is a *Lindeberg array* if

$$(1) \quad \limsup_{n\to\infty} \sum_{i=1}^{k(n)} P_{ni}(g_{ni}^2) < \infty, \quad \text{and}$$

$$(2) \quad \lim_{n\to\infty} \sum_{i=1}^{k(n)} \int_{|g_{ni}|>\varepsilon} g_{ni}^2 \, dP_{ni} = 0, \quad \varepsilon > 0.$$

Our first assertion is basic. For simplicity we use the following notation: A sequence of random variables $r_n\colon \Omega_n \to \mathbb{R}$ is $o_{P_n}(1)$ if

$$\lim_{n\to\infty} P_n\{|r_n|>\varepsilon\}=0, \quad \varepsilon>0.$$

74.2 Theorem. *Suppose that* $g_{ni}:=2\left(\sqrt{\dfrac{dQ_{ni}}{dP_{ni}}}-1\right)$, $1\leqq i\leqq k(n)$, $n\in\mathbb{N}$, *is a Lindeberg array. Then for every* $n\in\mathbb{N}$

$$\frac{dQ_n}{dP_n}=\exp\left(\sum_{i=1}^{k(n)}(g_{ni}-P_{ni}(g_{ni}))-\frac{1}{2}\sum_{i=1}^{k(n)}P_{ni}(g_{ni}^2)-\sum_{i=1}^{k(n)}Q_{ni}(N_{ni})+o_{P_n}(1)\right)$$

Proof. First we note that

$$\log\frac{dQ_{ni}}{dP_{ni}}=2\log\left(\frac{1}{2}g_{ni}+1\right), \quad 1\leqq i\leqq k(n), \quad n\in\mathbb{N}.$$

A simple Taylor expansion yields

$$x-2\log\left(\frac{x}{2}+1\right)=\frac{x^2}{4}r(x) \quad \text{if} \quad x>-2,$$

where

$$r(x):=\int_0^1\frac{2(1-s)}{\left(1+\dfrac{sx}{2}\right)^2}\,ds, \quad x>-2,$$

satisfies $r(0)=1$ and

$$|r(x_1)-r(x_2)|\leqq C|x_1-x_2| \quad \text{if} \quad |x_1|<1, |x_2|<1.$$

We obtain that

$$\begin{aligned}\log\frac{dQ_n}{dP_n}&=\sum_{i=1}^{k(n)}g_{ni}-\frac{1}{4}\sum_{i=1}^{k(n)}g_{ni}^2\cdot r(g_{ni})\\&=\sum_{i=1}^{k(n)}g_{ni}-\frac{1}{4}\sum_{i=1}^{k(n)}g_{ni}^2+\frac{1}{4}\sum_{i=1}^{k(n)}g_{ni}^2(1-r(g_{ni})).\end{aligned}$$

For every $\varepsilon>0$ we have

$$\begin{aligned}&\limsup_{n\to\infty}P_n\{\max_{1\leqq i\leqq k(n)}|g_{ni}|>\varepsilon\}\\&\leqq\limsup_{n\to\infty}\sum_{i=1}^{k(n)}P_{ni}\{|g_{ni}|>\varepsilon\}\\&\leqq\limsup_{n\to\infty}\sum_{i=1}^{k(n)}\frac{1}{\varepsilon^2}\int_{|g_{ni}|>\varepsilon}g_{ni}^2\,dP_{ni}=0\end{aligned}$$

by assumption (2). We will prove that

$$\lim_{n\to\infty} P_n\left\{\left|\sum_{i=1}^{k(n)} g_{ni}^2 - \sum_{i=1}^{k(n)} P_{ni}(g_{ni}^2)\right| > \varepsilon\right\} = 0, \quad \varepsilon > 0.$$

Then the assertion follows from (1) as we shall see below. Choose $\varepsilon > 0$, $\delta > 0$, arbitrarily. For any random variable X let $\bar{X} = X \cdot 1_{\{|X| < \delta\}}$. Then either

$$P_n\left\{\left|\sum_{i=1}^{k(n)} g_{ni}^2 - \sum_{i=1}^{k(n)} P_{ni}(g_{ni}^2)\right| > \varepsilon\right\}$$
$$\leqq P_n\left\{\left|\sum_{i=1}^{k(n)} g_{ni}^2 - \sum_{i=1}^{k(n)} \overline{g_{ni}}^2\right| > \frac{\varepsilon}{3}\right\}$$
$$+ P_n\left\{\left|\sum_{i=1}^{k(n)} \overline{g_{ni}}^2 - \sum_{i=1}^{k(n)} P_{ni}(\overline{g_{ni}}^2)\right| > \frac{\varepsilon}{3}\right\}$$

or

$$\sum_{i=1}^{k(n)} \left| P_{ni}(g_{ni}^2) - P_{ni}(\overline{g_{ni}}^2)\right| > \frac{\varepsilon}{3}.$$

Since

$$P_n\left\{\left|\sum_{i=1}^{k(n)} g_{ni}^2 - \sum_{i=1}^{k(n)} \overline{g_{ni}}^2\right| > \frac{\varepsilon}{3}\right\} \leqq P_n\left\{\max_{1\leqq i\leqq k(n)} |g_{ni}| > \delta\right\},$$

$$P_n\left\{\left|\sum_{i=1}^{k(n)} \overline{g_{ni}}^2 - \sum_{i=1}^{k(n)} P_{ni}(\overline{g_{ni}}^2)\right| > \frac{\varepsilon}{3}\right\}$$
$$\leqq \frac{9}{\varepsilon^2}\sum_{i=1}^{k(n)} P_{ni}(\overline{g_{ni}}^4) \leqq \frac{9\delta^2}{\varepsilon^2}\sum_{i=1}^{k(n)} P_{ni}(g_{ni}^2),$$

and

$$\sum_{i=1}^{k(n)} |P_{ni}(g_{ni}^2) - P_{ni}(\overline{g_{ni}}^2)| \leqq \sum_{i=1}^{k(n)} \int_{|g_{ni}|>\delta} g_{ni}^2\, dP_{ni},$$

it follows that

$$\limsup_{n\to\infty} P_n\left\{\left|\sum_{i=1}^{k(n)} g_{ni}^2 - \sum_{i=1}^{k(n)} P_{ni}(g_{ni}^2)\right| > \varepsilon\right\}$$
$$\leqq \frac{9\delta^2}{\varepsilon^2} \limsup_{n\to\infty} \sum_{i=1}^{k(n)} P_{ni}(g_{ni}^2).$$

This proves the assertion since $\delta > 0$ can be chosen arbitrarily small and we arrive at the expansion

$$\frac{dQ_n}{dP_n} = \exp\left(\sum_{i=1}^{k(n)} g_{ni} - \frac{1}{4}\sum_{i=1}^{k(n)} P_{ni}(g_{ni}^2) + r_n\right), \quad n \in \mathbb{N},$$

where

$$\lim_{n\to\infty} P_n\{|r_n| > \varepsilon\} = 0, \quad \varepsilon > 0.$$

Now, we use Remark 2.13 and Lemma 2.10 noting that

$$P_{ni}(g_{ni}) = -2d_2^2(P_{ni}, Q_{ni}),$$
$$P_{ni}(g_{ni}^2) = 8d_2^2(P_{ni}, Q_{ni}) - 4Q_{ni}(N_{ni}),$$

$1 \leqq i \leqq k(n)$, $n \in \mathbb{N}$. This leads to the asserted expansion. □

We want to replace the Lindeberg array of Theorem 74.2 by an equivalent one.

74.3 Lemma. *Suppose that* $(g_{ni})_{1\leqq i\leqq k(n)}$, $n \in \mathbb{N}$, *and* $(h_{ni})_{1\leqq i\leqq k(n)}$, $n \in \mathbb{N}$, *are triangular arrays satisfying*

$$\lim_{n\to\infty} \sum_{i=1}^{k(n)} \int (g_{ni} - h_{ni})^2 \, dP_{ni} = 0.$$

(1) *If* $(g_{ni})_{1\leqq i\leqq k(n)}$, $n \in \mathbb{N}$, *is a Lindeberg array then* $(h_{ni})_{1\leqq i\leqq k(n)}$, $n \in \mathbb{N}$, *is a Lindeberg array, too.*

(2) $$\lim_{n\to\infty} \int \left(\sum_{i=1}^{k(n)} (g_{ni} - P_{ni}(g_{ni})) - \sum_{i=1}^{k(n)} (h_{ni} - P_{ni}(h_{ni})) \right)^2 dP_n = 0.$$

(3) $$\lim_{n\to\infty} \sum_{i=1}^{k(n)} (P_{ni}(g_{ni}^2) - P_{ni}(h_{ni}^2)) = 0.$$

Proof. (1) We have

$$\int h_{ni}^2 \, dP_{ni} \leqq \left(\sqrt{\int g_{ni}^2 \, dP_{ni}} + \sqrt{\int (h_{ni} - g_{ni})^2 \, dP_{ni}}\right)^2$$
$$\leqq 2\left(\int g_{ni}^2 \, dP_{ni} + \int (h_{ni} - g_{ni})^2 \, dP_{ni}\right).$$

This proves property 74.1 (1). For the second property we obtain similarly that

$$\limsup_{n\to\infty} \sum_{i=1}^{k(n)} \int_{|h_{ni}|>\varepsilon} h_{ni}^2 \, dP_{ni} \leqq \limsup_{n\to\infty} \sum_{i=1}^{k(n)} \int_{|h_{ni}|>\varepsilon} g_{ni}^2 \, dP_{ni}, \quad \varepsilon > 0.$$

Moreover, we have for $\varepsilon > 0$ and $n \in \mathbb{N}$

$$\sum_{i=1}^{k(n)} \int_{|h_{ni}|>\varepsilon} g_{ni}^2 \, dP_{ni} \leqq \sum_{i=1}^{k(n)} \int_{|g_{ni}|>\frac{\varepsilon}{2}} g_{ni}^2 \, dP_{ni} + \sum_{i=1}^{k(n)} \int_{|h_{ni}-g_{ni}|>\frac{\varepsilon}{2}} g_{ni}^2 \, dP_{ni}$$

and

$$\sum_{i=1}^{k(n)} \int_{|h_{ni}-g_{ni}|>\frac{\varepsilon}{2}} g_{ni}^2 \, dP_{ni} \leqq \sum_{i=1}^{k(n)} \int_{|g_{ni}|\geqq 1} g_{ni}^2 \, dP_{ni} + \frac{4}{\varepsilon^2} \sum_{i=1}^{k(n)} \int (h_{ni} - g_{ni})^2 \, dP_{ni}.$$

Putting terms together we arrive at property (2) of Definition 74.1.

(2) We have

$$\int \left(\sum_{i=1}^{k(n)} (g_{ni} - P_{ni}(g_{ni})) - \sum_{i=1}^{k(n)} (h_{ni} - P_{ni}(h_{ni})) \right)^2 dP_n$$
$$= \sum_{i=1}^{k(n)} \int (g_{ni} - h_{ni} - P_{ni}(g_{ni} - h_{ni}))^2 \, dP_{ni}$$
$$\leqq \sum_{i=1}^{k(n)} \int (g_{ni} - h_{ni})^2 \, dP_{ni}, \quad n \in \mathbb{N}.$$

(3) We have

$$\sum_{i=1}^{k(n)} (P_{ni}(g_{ni}^2) - P_{ni}(h_{ni}^2)) = \sum_{i=1}^{k(n)} P_{ni}((g_{ni} - h_{ni}) \cdot (g_{ni} + h_{ni}))$$
$$\leqq \sum_{i=1}^{k(n)} (\int (g_{ni} - h_{ni})^2 \, dP_{ni})^{1/2} (\int (g_{ni} + h_{ni})^2 \, dP_{ni})^{1/2}$$
$$\leqq (\sum_{i=1}^{k(n)} \int (g_{ni} - h_{ni})^2 \, dP_{ni})^{1/2} (\sum_{i=1}^{k(n)} \int (g_{ni} + h_{ni})^2 \, dP_{ni})^{1/2}.$$

Since

$$\int (g_{ni} + h_{ni})^2 \, dP_{ni} \leqq 2(\int g_{ni}^2 \, dP_{ni} + \int h_{ni}^2 \, dP_{ni})$$

it follows that

$$\limsup_{n \to \infty} \sum_{i=1}^{k(n)} \int (g_{ni} + h_{ni})^2 \, dP_{ni} < \infty$$

which proves the assertion. □

74.4 Corollary. *Suppose that $(h_{ni})_{1 \leqq i \leqq k(n)}$, $n \in \mathbb{N}$, is a Lindeberg array satisfying*

$$\lim_{n \to \infty} \sum_{i=1}^{k(n)} \int \left(\sqrt{\frac{dQ_{ni}}{dP_{ni}}} - 1 - \frac{1}{2} h_{ni} \right)^2 dP_{ni} = 0.$$

Then the expansion of Theorem 74.2 is valid (replacing (g_{ni}) by (h_{ni})).

Proof. Combine Theorem 74.2 and Lemma 74.3. □

75. Differentiable curves

Suppose that $(\Omega, \mathscr{A}, \nu)$ is a σ-finite measure space. Let $\mathscr{P}$ be the set of all probability measures on $(\Omega, \mathscr{A})$ which satisfy $P \ll \nu$. We identify $\mathscr{P}$ with a subset of $L^2(\Omega, \mathscr{A}, \nu)$ by $P \mapsto \left(\frac{dP}{d\nu}\right)^{1/2}$, $P \in \mathscr{P}$.

75.1 Definition. Let $\varepsilon > 0$. A curve $t \mapsto P_t$ from $(-\varepsilon, \varepsilon)$ to $\mathscr{P}$ is *differentiable* at $t = 0$ (or at P_0) if the map $t \mapsto \left(\frac{dP_t}{d\nu}\right)^{1/2}$, $t \in (-\varepsilon, \varepsilon)$, is differentiable at $t = 0$.

If $t \mapsto P_t$ is differentiable at $t = 0$ then the derivative is of the form $t \mapsto \frac{t}{2} h$, $t \in \mathbb{R}$, where $h \in L^2(\Omega, \mathscr{A}, \nu)$.

75.2 Theorem. *Let $h \in L^2(\Omega, \mathscr{A}, \nu)$. Then $t \mapsto \frac{t}{2} h$, $t \in \mathbb{R}$, is the derivative at $P_0 \in \mathscr{P}$ of a differentiable curve $t \mapsto P_t$ in $\mathscr{P}$, iff*

(1) *$h = g \cdot \sqrt{\frac{dP_0}{d\nu}}$ for some $g \in L^2(\Omega, \mathscr{A}, P_0)$, and*

(2) *$\int g\, dP_0 = 0$.*

Proof. (1) Let us show that $h = 0$ where $\frac{dP_0}{d\nu} = 0$ ν-a.e. Let $B_1 = \left\{\frac{dP_0}{d\nu} = 0, h < 0\right\}$. Then for every $\delta > 0$

$$\frac{1}{\delta^2} \int_{B_1} \left(\sqrt{\frac{dP_\delta}{d\nu}} - \sqrt{\frac{dP_0}{d\nu}} - \frac{\delta}{2} h\right)^2 d\nu$$

$$= \frac{1}{\delta^2} \int_{B_1} \left(\frac{dP_\delta}{d\nu} - \delta \sqrt{\frac{dP_\delta}{d\nu}} \cdot h + \frac{\delta^2}{4} h^2\right) d\nu \geqq \frac{1}{4} \int_{B_1} h^2\, d\nu .$$

For $\delta \to 0$ we obtain $\int_{B_1} h^2\, d\nu = 0$. Defining $B_2 = \left\{\frac{dP_0}{d\nu} = 0, h > 0\right\}$ we obtain in a similar way $\int_{B_2} h^2\, d\nu = 0$. Define $g = h\left(\frac{dP_0}{d\nu}\right)^{-1/2}$ where $dP_0/d\nu > 0$ and $g = 0$ elsewhere.

Next, we show that g satisfies condition (2). It is clear that

$$\lim_{t \to 0} \frac{1}{t^2} \int \left(\sqrt{\frac{dP_t}{dP_0}} - 1 - \frac{t}{2} g\right)^2 dP_0 = 0 .$$

Since L^2-convergence implies L^1-convergence we obtain from Remark 2.13

$$\frac{1}{2} \int g\, dP_0 = \lim_{t \to 0} \frac{1}{t} \int \left(\sqrt{\frac{dP_t}{dP_0}} - 1\right) dP_0 = - \lim_{t \to 0} \frac{2}{t} d_2^2(P_0, P_t) .$$

But differentiability implies

$$\lim_{t\to 0} \frac{1}{t^2} d_2^2(P_0, P_t) < \infty,$$

which proves that $\int g\, dP_0 = 0$.

(2) Let $g \in L^2(\Omega, \mathscr{A}, P_0)$ be such that condition (2) is satisfied. We have to define a curve $t \mapsto P_t$ which is differentiable at $t = 0$ and has derivative $t \mapsto \frac{t}{2} h$ with $h = g \cdot \sqrt{\frac{dP_0}{dv}}$. For this, let $f_0 := \frac{dP_0}{dv}$ and define

$$g_t := \left(1 - \frac{t^2}{4} \|h\|_{2,v}^2\right)^{1/2} \cdot f_0^{1/2} + \frac{t}{2} h, \ t \in \mathbb{R}.$$

Then for every $t \in \mathbb{R}$, $f_t := g_t^2$ is a probability density since

$$\int f_t\, dv = \left(1 - \frac{t^2}{4} \|h\|_{2,v}^2\right) \int f_0\, dv + \frac{t^2}{4} \int h^2\, dv = 1.$$

We have $f_t^{1/2} = |g_t|$, $t \in \mathbb{R}$. Let us prove that $t \mapsto |g_t|$ is differentiable at $t = 0$ in $L^2(\Omega, \mathscr{A}, v)$ with derivative $t \mapsto \frac{t}{2} h$. For this, we have to show that

$$\lim_{t\to 0} \frac{1}{t} \int \left(|g_t| - |g_0| - \frac{t}{2} h\right)^2 dv = 0.$$

First, we observe that

$$\lim_{t\to 0} \frac{1}{t} \left(|g_t(\omega)| - |g_0(\omega)| - \frac{t}{2} h(\omega)\right) = 0 \quad v\text{-a.e.}$$

This is trivial where $f_0(\omega) = 0$, and where $f_0(\omega) > 0$ there exists an $\varepsilon(\omega) > 0$ such that $|g_t(\omega)| = g_t(\omega)$ if $|t| < \varepsilon(\omega)$. Moreover, for sufficiently small t

$$\begin{aligned} \left|\frac{1}{t}(|g_t(\omega)| - |g_0(\omega)|)\right| &\leqq \frac{1}{|t|} |g_t(\omega) - g_0(\omega)| \\ &= \frac{1}{|t|} \left| \left(\sqrt{1 - \frac{t^2}{4} \|h\|_{2,v}^2} - 1\right) f_0^{1/2} + \frac{t}{2} h \right| \\ &\leqq f_0^{1/2} \left| \frac{\sqrt{1 - \frac{t^2}{4} \|h\|_{2,v}^2} - 1}{t} \right| + \frac{1}{2} |h| \leqq f_0^{1/2} + \frac{1}{2} |h|. \end{aligned}$$

Hence, the assertion follows from the theorem on dominated convergence. □

75.3 Definition. Let $\mathscr{P}_0 \subseteq \mathscr{P}$. An element $g \in L^2(\Omega, \mathscr{A}, P_0)$ is a *tangent vector* of $\mathscr{P}_0$ at $P_0 \in \mathscr{P}_0$ if there exists a differentiable curve $t \mapsto P_t$ in $\mathscr{P}_0$ whose derivative at P_0 is $t \mapsto \frac{t}{2} g \cdot \sqrt{\frac{dP_0}{dv}}$, $t \in \mathbb{R}$. The set of all tangent vectors of $\mathscr{P}_0$ at $P_0 \in \mathscr{P}_0$ is the tangent space $T_{P_0}(\mathscr{P}_0)$.

75.4 Corollary. $T_{P_0}(\mathscr{P}) = \{g \in L^2(\Omega, \mathscr{A}, P_0)\colon \int g\, dP_0 = 0\}$, *for every* $P_0 \in \mathscr{P}$.

If $E = (\Omega, \mathscr{A}, \{P_\vartheta\colon \vartheta \in \Theta\})$ is an experiment then we write $T_{P_{\vartheta_0}}(E) := T_{P_{\vartheta_0}}(\{P_\vartheta\colon \vartheta \in \Theta\})$.

It is sometimes useful to work with a subspace of $T_{P_0}(\mathscr{P})$ which is easier to handle. Define $D_{P_0}(\mathscr{P}) := \{g \in T_{P_0}(\mathscr{P})\colon g \text{ is bounded}\}$.

75.5 Lemma. *The linear subspace* $D_{P_0}(\mathscr{P})$ *is* $L_2(P_0)$*-dense in* $T_{P_0}(\mathscr{P})$.

Proof. Let $g_n = g \cdot 1_{\{|g|<n\}}$, $n \in \mathbb{N}$. Then $(g_n - P_0(g_n))$, $n \in \mathbb{N}$, is a sequence in $D_{P_0}(\mathscr{P})$ and approximates g since

$$\int (g_n - P_n(g_n) - g)^2\, dP_0 \leqq \int (g_n - g)^2\, dP_0 = \int_{|g|>n} g^2\, dP_0, \quad n \in \mathbb{N}. \qquad \square$$

75.6 Remark. There exists particularly simple curves $t \mapsto P_t$ which have tangent vectors in $D_{P_0}(\mathscr{P})$. Let g be bounded and such that $P_0(g) = 0$. Then define

$$\frac{dP_t}{dv} = (1 + tg)\frac{dP_0}{dv}, \quad |t| < \frac{1}{\|g\|_\infty}.$$

It is easy to see that $t \mapsto P_t$ is differentiable at $t = 0$ with tangent vector g. Indeed, we have

$$\frac{1}{t}\left(\sqrt{\frac{dP_t}{dv}} - \sqrt{\frac{dP_0}{dv}}\right) = \frac{1}{t}(\sqrt{1+tg} - 1) \cdot \sqrt{\frac{dP_0}{dv}}$$

which converges pointwise to $\frac{1}{2} g \left(\frac{dP_0}{dv}\right)^{1/2}$. L^2-convergence follows since $|\sqrt{1+tg} - 1| \leqq C \cdot t$ for sufficiently small t.

Before we are in a position to apply the results of Section 74 we need some information concerning the singular parts of P_t with respect to P_0. If $t \mapsto P_t$ is a curve let $\left(\frac{dP_t}{dP_0}, N_t\right)$ be a Lebesgue decomposition of P_t with respect to P_0.

75.7 Lemma. *If* $t \mapsto P_t$ *is differentiable then*

$$\lim_{t \to 0} \frac{1}{t^2} P_t(N_t) = 0.$$

Proof. Let g be the tangent vector of $t \mapsto P_t$ and $h = g \cdot \sqrt{\frac{dP_0}{d\nu}}$. We have

$$P_t(N_t) = \int_{N_t} \left(\sqrt{\frac{dP_t}{d\nu}} - \sqrt{\frac{dP_0}{d\nu}}\right)^2 d\nu$$

$$\leqq 2 \int_{N_t} \left(\sqrt{\frac{dP_t}{d\nu}} - \sqrt{\frac{dP_0}{d\nu}} - \frac{t}{2} h\right)^2 d\nu + 2 \int_{N_t} \left(\frac{t}{2} h\right)^2 d\nu .$$

Now, the assertion follows from differentiability and from condition (1) of Theorem 75.2. □

Thus, we arrive at the fundamental expansion for differentiable curves.

75.8 Theorem. *Suppose that* $t \mapsto P_t$ *is differentiable with tangent vector* $g \in T_{P_0}(\mathscr{P})$. *Then*

$$\frac{dP^n_{t/\sqrt{n}}}{dP^n_0}(\underline{\omega}) = \exp\left(\frac{t}{\sqrt{n}} \sum_{i=1}^n g(\omega_i) - \frac{t^2}{2} \|g\|^2_{P_0} + o_{P_0}(1)\right), \quad \underline{\omega} \in \Omega^n, \ n \in \mathbb{N}.$$

Proof. We have

$$\lim_{n \to \infty} n \int \left[\left(\frac{dP^n_{t/\sqrt{n}}}{dP_0}\right)^{1/2} - 1 - \frac{t}{2\sqrt{n}} g\right]^2 dP_0 = 0 .$$

It is clear that $h_{ni} := \frac{t}{\sqrt{n}} g$, $1 \leqq i \leqq n$, $n \in \mathbb{N}$, is a Lindeberg array. Hence, Corollary 74.4 implies

$$\frac{dP^n_{t/\sqrt{n}}}{dP^n_0}(\underline{\omega}) =$$

$$\exp\left(\frac{t}{\sqrt{n}} \sum_{i=1}^n (g(\omega_i) - P_0(g)) - \frac{t^2}{2} P_0(g^2) - \frac{n}{2} P_{t/\sqrt{n}}(N_{t/\sqrt{n}}) + o_{P_n}(1)\right).$$

From Theorem 75.2 and Lemma 75.7 we obtain the desired expansion. □

The final assertion makes clear that expansions may also be obtained without differentiability conditions.

75.9 Corollary. *Let* $g \in T_{P_0}(\mathscr{P})$. *A sequence* $(Q_n) \subseteq \mathscr{P}$ *satisfies*

$$\frac{dQ^n_n}{dP^n_0}(\underline{\omega}) = \exp\left(\frac{1}{\sqrt{n}} \sum_{i=1}^n g(\omega_i) - \frac{1}{2} \|g\|^2_{P_0} + o_{P_0}(1)\right),$$

$\underline{\omega} \in \Omega^n$, $n \in \mathbb{N}$, *iff*

$$\lim_{n\to\infty} \int \left[\sqrt{n}\left(\sqrt{\frac{dQ_n}{d\nu}} - \sqrt{\frac{dP_0}{d\nu}}\right) - \frac{1}{2} g \cdot \sqrt{\frac{dP_0}{d\nu}}\right]^2 d\nu = 0.$$

Proof. (1) Assume that the expansion of the likelihood ratios is valid. Moreover, let $t \mapsto P_t$ be a differentiable curve with tangent vector g. Then

$$\frac{dP^n_{1/\sqrt{n}}}{dP^n_0} - \frac{dQ^n_n}{dP^n_0} \to 0 \quad (P^n_0) \quad \text{as} \quad n \to \infty.$$

From the expansion it follows by Lemma 6.12 that the sequences of likelihood ratios are uniformly (P^n_0)-integrable which implies by contiguity that

$$\lim_{n\to\infty} d_1(P^n_{1/\sqrt{n}}, Q^n_n) = 0.$$

Hence,

$$\lim_{n\to\infty} \sqrt{n}\, d_2(P_{1/\sqrt{n}}, Q_n) = 0$$

which proves one part of the assertion.

(2) The converse follows from Corollary 74.4 provided that we show that

$$\lim_{n\to\infty} n\, Q_n(N_n) = 0$$

where $\left(\frac{dQ_n}{dP_0}, N_n\right)$ are Lebesgue decompositions of Q_n with respect to P_0, $n \in \mathbb{N}$. But this follows in quite the same way as in the proof of Lemma 75.7. □

It is obvious by a literal repetition of the proof that the preceding assertion remains valid if $g \in T_{P_0}(\mathscr{P})$ is replaced by a convergent sequence $(g_n) \subseteq T_{P_0}(\mathscr{P})$.

76. Differentiable experiments

Suppose that M is an open subset of a finite dimensional linear manifold. The underlying linear space is denoted by T and $|.|$ is any norm of T. We consider an experiment $E = (\Omega, \mathscr{A}, \{P_x : x \in M\})$. Subsequently, we always assume that E is separable and that densities are $\mathscr{A} \otimes \mathscr{B}(M)$-measurable.

76.1 Example. Let $M = \{x \in \mathbb{R}^k : \sum_{i=1}^k x_i = 1, 0 < x_i < 1, 1 \leq i \leq k\}$ and consider the experiment $E = (\Omega, \mathscr{A}, \{P_x : x \in M\})$ where $\Omega = \{1, 2, \ldots, k\}$, $\mathscr{A} = 2^\Omega$ and $P_x = \sum_{i=1}^k x_i \varepsilon_i$, $x \in M$. It is clear that M is an open subset of a linear manifold and the underlying linear space is $T = \{t \in \mathbb{R}^k : \sum_{i=1}^k t_i = 0\}$.

Suppose that E is dominated and let $\nu|\mathscr{A}$ be a σ-finite dominating measure. Then $x \mapsto \left(\frac{dP_x}{d\nu}\right)^{1/2}$, $x \in M$, maps into $L^2(\Omega, \mathscr{A}, \nu)$. In the following we assume that this map is differentiable. First, we note that this property does not depend on the dominating measure $\nu|\mathscr{A}$.

76.2 Lemma. *Suppose that E is dominated. Let $x_0 \in M$. Then the following assertions are equivalent:*

(1) *There exists a dominating σ-finite measure $\nu|\mathscr{A}$ such that $x \mapsto \left(\frac{dP_x}{d\nu}\right)^{1/2}$, $x \in M$, is differentiable at x_0.*

(2) *For every dominating σ-finite measure $\nu|\mathscr{A}$ the map $x \mapsto \left(\frac{dP_x}{d\nu}\right)^{1/2}$, $x \in M$, is differentiable at x_0.*

Proof. We leave the easy proof to the reader. □

From now on, we fix a dominating σ-finite measure $\nu|\mathscr{A}$. Let $F: x \mapsto 2\left(\frac{dP_x}{d\nu}\right)^{1/2}$, $x \in M$. (The factor 2 is to avoid confusing factors in subsequent formulas.) If F is differentiable at $x_0 \in M$, then the derivative $DF(x_0)$ is a linear map from T to $L^2(\Omega, \mathscr{A}, \nu)$ which satisfies

$$\int (F(x_0 + t) - F(x_0) - DF(x_0) \cdot t)^2 \, d\nu = o(|t|^2) \quad \text{as} \quad t \to 0 .$$

76.3 Definition. The experiment E is *differentiable* at $x_0 \in M$ if the map F is differentiable at x_0.

76.4 Theorem. *If E is differentiable at $x_0 \in M$ and $DF(x_0)$ is injective, then*

$$T_{P_{x_0}}(E) = \{g \in L^2(\Omega, \mathscr{A}, P_{x_0}) : g \cdot \sqrt{\frac{dP_{x_0}}{d\nu}} \in \operatorname{im} DF(x_0)\} .$$

Proof. Denote

$$D = \{g \in L^2(\Omega, \mathscr{A}, P_{x_0}) : g \sqrt{\frac{dP_{x_0}}{d\nu}} \in \operatorname{im} DF(x_0)\} .$$

(1) If $g \in D$ then g is the tangent vector of the differentiable curve $\xi \mapsto P_{x+\xi t}$, $\xi \in (-\varepsilon, \varepsilon)$, where $t \in T$ is such that $g \cdot \sqrt{\frac{dP_{x_0}}{d\nu}} = DF(x_0)(t)$. Hence $D \subseteq T_{P_{x_0}}(E)$.

(2) Let conversely $\xi \mapsto Q_\xi$, $\xi \in (-\varepsilon, \varepsilon)$, be a differentiable curve in $\{P_x : x \in M\}$ such that $Q_0 = P_{x_0}$. Since $DF(x_0)$ is injective there is an open

neighbourhood U of $x_0 \in M$ such that $F: U \to \{P_x: x \in M\}$ is a diffeomorphism. Then for some $\delta > 0$ the mapping $\psi: \xi \mapsto F^{-1}(Q_\xi)$, $\xi \in (-\delta, \delta)$, is a differentiable curve in M. Let $t := D\psi(0) \in T$ and g be the tangent vector of $\xi \mapsto Q_\xi$ at 0. It is then clear that

$$t = D\psi(0) = DF(x_0)^{-1} \cdot \left(g \cdot \sqrt{\frac{dP_{x_0}}{dv}}\right)$$

which implies that $DF(x_0)(t) = g\sqrt{\frac{dP_{x_0}}{dv}}$. Hence $g \in D$. Thus, we have proved $T_{P_{x_0}}(E) \subseteq D$. □

As a consequence we obtain that $\dim T_{P_{x_0}}(E) = \dim T$ if $DF(x_0)$ is one-to-one. Since on $T_{P_{x_0}}(E)$ there is a natural inner product, let us introduce an inner product on T such that $T_{P_{x_0}}(E) \cong T$ as inner product spaces.

76.5 Definition. Suppose that E is differentiable at $x \in M$. Then the bilinear function

$$B_x: (s, t) \mapsto \int (DF(x) \cdot s)(DF(x) \cdot t)\, dv, \quad s, t \in T,$$

is called *canonical covariance* of E at x.

The canonical covariance at $x \in M$ is positive definite iff $DF(x)$ is injective.

76.6 Corollary. *Suppose that E is differentiable at $x \in M$ and $DF(x)$ is injective. Then $T_{P_x}(E) \cong (T, B_x)$.*

76.7 Remark. If E is differentiable at $x \in M$ then

$$\frac{1}{8} B_x(s - t, s - t) = \lim_{\varepsilon \to 0} \frac{1}{\varepsilon^2} d_2^2(P_{x+\varepsilon s}, P_{x+\varepsilon t}).$$

This follows immediately from

$$d_2^2(P_{x+\varepsilon s}, P_{x+\varepsilon t}) = \frac{1}{8} \int (F(x+\varepsilon s) - F(x+\varepsilon t))^2\, dv.$$

76.8 Definition. Suppose that E is differentiable at $x \in M$ and $DF(x)$ is injective. The $\mathscr{A}$-measurable function $g_x: \Omega \to T$ which is defined by

$$DF(x) \cdot t = B_x(t, g_x) \cdot \sqrt{\frac{dP_x}{dv}}, \quad t \in T,$$

is called the *canonical derivative* of E at $x \in M$.

From this definition it is clear that the tangent vector of the differentiable curve $\xi \mapsto P_{x+\xi t}$, $\xi \in (-\varepsilon, \varepsilon)$, is $B_x(t, g_x)$, $x \in M$, $t \in T$.

76.9 Corollary. *Under the assumptions of 76.8 the canonical derivative g_x at $x \in M$ satisfies*

(1) $P_x(g_x) = 0$,
(2) $P_x(B_x(s, g_x) \cdot B_x(t, g_x)) = B_x(s, t)$, $s, t \in T$, *or briefly* $P_x(g_x \otimes g_x) = B_x$.

Proof. Apply Theorem 75.2 (2), and Definition 76.5. □

77. Conditions for differentiability

We keep the notation of the preceding section. In particular, recall that $F\colon x \mapsto 2\left(\frac{dP_x}{dv}\right)^{1/2}$, $x \in M$.

77.1 Definition. A linear function $DF(x)\colon T \to L^2(\Omega, \mathscr{A}, v)$ is a *derivative* of F at $x \in M$ *in P_x-measure* if

$$\lim_{t \to 0} \frac{1}{|t|}(F(x+t) - F(x) - DF(x) \cdot t) = 0 \text{ in } P_x\text{-measure.}$$

In many cases it is easy to find a derivative in P_x-measure. The problem is then to show that it is also a derivative in $L^2(\Omega, \mathscr{A}, v)$. Nevertheless, in any case we may define the positive semidefinite bilinear function

$$B_x(s, t) := \int (DF(x) \cdot s)(DF(x) \cdot t)\, dv, \quad s, t \in T.$$

77.2 Lemma. *Assume that for every $x \in M$ there exists a derivative of F at x in P_x-measure. If*

$$F(x+t) - F(x) = \int_0^1 DF(x + \xi t) \cdot t\, d\xi, \quad t \in T,$$

then

$$d_2^2(P_x, P_{x+t}) \leqq \frac{1}{8} \int_0^1 B_{x+\xi t}(t, t)\, d\xi, \quad t \in T.$$

Proof. We have

$$d_2^2 P_x, P_{x+t}) = \frac{1}{8} \int (F(x+t) - F(x))^2\, dv$$

$$= \frac{1}{8} \int \left(\int_0^1 DF(x + \xi t) \cdot t\, d\xi \right) \left(\int_0^1 DF(x + \eta t) \cdot t\, d\eta \right) dv$$

$$= \frac{1}{8} \int_0^1 \int_0^1 \left(\int DF(x+\xi t) \cdot t DF(x+\eta t) \cdot t \, dv \right) d\xi \, d\eta$$

$$\leqq \frac{1}{8} \int_0^1 \int_0^1 (B_{x+\xi t}(t, t))^{1/2} (B_{x+\eta t}(t, t))^{1/2} \, d\xi \, d\eta$$

$$\leqq \frac{1}{8} \int_0^1 B_{x+\xi t}(t, t) \, d\xi . \qquad \square$$

The following theorem reveals sufficient conditions for differentiability. It is in the spirit of Hajek [1972].

77.3 Theorem. *Assume that $DF(x)$ is a derivative of F at x in P_x-measure for every $x \in M$ and satisfies $DF(x) = 0$ where $\frac{dP_x}{dv} = 0$, v-a.e. If*

(1) *$F(x+t) - F(x) = \int_0^1 DF(x+\xi t) \cdot t \, d\xi$, v-a.e. $t \in T$, $x \in M$, and*

(2) *$(x, t) \mapsto B_x(t, t)$, $t \in T$, $x \in M$, is continuous,*

then E is differentiable on M.

Proof. Let $\varepsilon_n \to 0$ and $t_n \to t \in T$. We have to show that

$$(3) \quad \lim_{n\to\infty} \int \left(\frac{F(x+\varepsilon_n \cdot t_n) - F(x)}{\varepsilon_n} - DF(x) \cdot t \right)^2 dv = 0 .$$

In view of Lemma 77.2 and by assumption (2) we have

$$(4) \quad \limsup_{n\to\infty} \frac{1}{\varepsilon_n^2} \int (F(x+\varepsilon_n t_n) - F(x))^2 \, dv \leqq \int (DF(x)t)^2 \, dv .$$

Put $D = \left\{ \frac{dP_x}{dv} > 0 \right\}$. Then it follows that

$$\limsup_{n\to\infty} \frac{1}{\varepsilon_n^2} \int_D (F(x+\varepsilon_n t_n) - F(x))^2 \, dv \leqq \int_D (DF(x)t)^2 \, dv .$$

Since $DF(x)$ is a derivative of F at x in P_x-measure it follows by the Lemma of Scheffé that

$$(5) \quad \lim_{\varepsilon_n \to 0} \int_D \left(\frac{F(x+\varepsilon_n t_n) - F(x)}{\varepsilon_n} - DF(x) \cdot t \right)^2 dv = 0 ,$$

which implies that

$$\lim_{n\to\infty} \frac{1}{\varepsilon_n^2} \int_D (F(x+\varepsilon_n t_n) - F(x))^2 \, dv$$

$$= \int_D (DF(x) \cdot t)^2 \, dv = \int (DF(x) \cdot t)^2 \, dv .$$

Together with (4) this entails

$$\lim_{n\to\infty} \int_{D'} \left(\frac{F(x+\varepsilon_n t_n) - F(x)}{\varepsilon_n} - DF(x)\cdot t\right)^2 dv = 0$$

and by (5) we obtain (3). □

It follows from the proof of the preceding theorem that $DF(x)$ is the derivative in $L^2(\Omega, \mathscr{A}, v)$ and B_x the canonical covariance.

77.4 Example. Denote $\ell(\omega, x) := \log \frac{dP_x}{dv}(\omega)$, $\omega \in M$. Assume that the following conditions are satisfied:

(1) For every $\omega \in \Omega$ the function $x \mapsto \ell(\omega, x)$ is real valued and twice differentiable on M.

(2) The function $\omega \mapsto \ell'(\omega, x)$ is P_x-integrable and $P_x(\ell'(.,x)) = 0$, $x \in M$.

(3) The functions $\omega \mapsto \ell'(\omega, x) \otimes \ell'(\omega, x)$ and $\omega \mapsto \ell''(\omega, x)$ are P_x-integrable and

$$P_x(\ell'(.,x) \otimes \ell'(.,x)) = -P_x(\ell''(.,x)), \quad x \in M.$$

(4) The function $x \mapsto P_x(\ell''(.,x))$ is continuous on M.

This set of conditions is usually called the *Conditions of Cramer and Wald.* Some comments might be illuminating.

Condition (1) implies that the densities are strictly positive and finite on Ω for each $x \in M$. Conditions (2) and (3) are satisfied if differentiation can be interchanged with P_x-integration in a suitable way. In fact, the well-known property of the log-likelihood function

$$P_x(\ell(.,x)) = \sup_{y\in M} P_x(\ell(.,y))$$

implies that if $y \mapsto P_x(\ell(.,y))$ is differentiable at x then the derivative is zero. This is the background of regularity condition (2). If condition (2) is satisfied and if difficulties with interchanging derivation and integration are neglected, then we obtain

$$0 = D(P_x(\ell'(.,x))) = P_x(\ell''(.,x)) + P_x(\ell'(.,x) \otimes \ell'(.,x)).$$

This serves as a motivation of condition (3).

Let us show that conditions (1)–(4) imply differentiability of E. This is done by means of Theorem 77.3. Obviously,

$$DF(x) := \frac{1}{2} F(x) \cdot \ell'(.,x)$$

is a derivative of F at x in P_x-measure, $x \in M$. Moreover, it is clear that condition 77.3 (1), is satisfied. For the proof of 77.3 (2), we note that

$$B_x(t, t) = \int (\ell'(., x) \cdot t)^2 \, dP_x$$
$$= -\int \ell''(., x) \cdot (t, t) \, dP_x, \quad x \in M, \, t \in T.$$

Now, continuity follows from (4).

In the preceding example it was easy to derive condition 77.3 (1), since the densities are everywhere positive. If the densities are zero with positive ν-measure then things are more complicated.

77.5 Discussion (Hájek [1972]). Let $\nu | \mathscr{A}$ be a dominating measure and define $h(., x) := \frac{dP_x}{d\nu}$, $x \in M$. We consider the case where $M \subseteq \mathbb{R}$ is an open interval. The mapping F is given by $x \mapsto 2h^{1/2}(., x)$, $x \in M$. Let us establish the assumptions of Theorem 77.3 under the following conditions:

(1) The mapping $x \mapsto h(., x)$, $x \in M$, has a derivative $h'(., x) \in L^1(\Omega, \mathscr{A}, \nu)$, $x \in M$, in ν-measure, which is $\mathscr{A} \otimes \mathscr{B}(M)$-measurable.

(2) $h(\omega, x_2) - h(\omega, x_1) = \int_{x_1}^{x_2} h'(\omega, y) \, dy$ if $\omega \in \Omega$, $x_1 < x_2$.

(3) For every $x \in M$

$$0 < I(x) := \int \left(\frac{h'(., x)}{h(., x)} \right)^2 h(., x) \, d\nu < \infty$$

and $x \mapsto I(x)$, $x \in M$, is continuous.

Let us denote

$$s(., x) := \begin{cases} \dfrac{1}{2} \dfrac{h'(., x)}{h(., x)^{1/2}} & \text{where} \quad h(., x) > 0, \\ 0 & \text{otherwise}. \end{cases}$$

First, we have to show that $\frac{1}{2} DF(x) = s(., x)$, $x \in M$, is a derivative of $\frac{1}{2} F$ in P_x-measure. For this, we note that

$$\frac{h(., x + \varepsilon) - h(., x)}{\varepsilon} =$$
$$= \frac{h^{1/2}(., x + \varepsilon) - h^{1/2}(., x)}{\varepsilon} \cdot (h^{1/2}(., x + \varepsilon) + h^{1/2}(., x)),$$

$\varepsilon > 0$, $x \in M$. Then it is clear that on $D = \{h((., x) > 0\}$

$$\lim_{\varepsilon \to 0} \frac{1}{\varepsilon} (h^{1/2}(.,x+\varepsilon) - h^{1/2}(.,x)) = s(.,x) \text{ in } \nu\text{-measure.}$$

Moreover, we observe that $DF(x) = 0$ where $h(.,x) = 0$ by definition, and condition 77.3 (2), is satisfied by assumption (3). Thus, it remains to verify condition 77.3 (1).

Before we do so, we show that there are a set $N \in \mathscr{A}$, $\nu(N) = 0$, and for every $x \in M$ a number $\eta(x) > 0$ satisfying

$$\int_{x-\eta(x)}^{x+\eta(x)} |s(.,y)|\, dy < \infty \quad \text{on} \quad \Omega \setminus N.$$

For every $x \in M$ let $\delta(x) > 0$ be such that

$$\int_{x-\delta(x)}^{x+\delta(x)} I(y)\, dy < \infty.$$

Since

$$\int_{x-\delta(x)}^{x+\delta(x)} |s(.,y)|\, dy \leqq (2\delta(x))^{1/2} \left(\int_{x-\delta(x)}^{x+\delta(x)} s(.,y)^2\, dy \right)^{1/2}$$

it follows that

$$\int_{x-\delta(x)}^{x+\delta(x)} |s(.,y)|\, dy < \infty \quad \nu\text{-a.e.}$$

Let N_x be the pertaining exceptional set of ν-measure zero. Since $\{(x-\delta(x), x+\delta(x)) \colon x \in M\}$ covers M there exists a countable subcover. Let $(x_i)_{i \in \mathbb{N}}$ be such that $\{(x_i - \delta(x_i), x_i + \delta(x_i)) \colon i \in \mathbb{N}\}$ covers M. If we put $N = \bigcup_{i=1}^{\infty} N_{x_i}$ then the auxiliary assertion is proved.

Now, we begin with the proof of condition 77.3 (1). Let $\omega \in \Omega \setminus N$. We shall prove that for every pair $x_1 < x_2$, $x_i \in M$, $i = 1, 2$,

$$h(\omega, x_2)^{1/2} - h(\omega, x_1)^{1/2} = \int_{x_1}^{x_2} s(\omega, y)\, dy.$$

We have to distinguish two cases.

Case 1: Assume that $y \mapsto h(\omega, y)$ is positive on (x_1, x_2). Then it is clear that for every $\varepsilon > 0$

$$h(\omega, x_2 - \varepsilon)^{1/2} - h(\omega, x_1 + \varepsilon)^{1/2} = \int_{x_1+\varepsilon}^{x_2-\varepsilon} s(\omega, y)\, dy$$

since $y \mapsto h(\omega, y)$ is bounded away from zero on $[x_1 + \varepsilon, x_2 - \varepsilon]$. Now, the assertion follows from the choice of N.

Case 2: If x_1, x_2 are arbitrary the intervall (x_1, x_2) can be represented in the form

$$(x_1, x_2) = \bigcup_{i=1}^{\infty} (\alpha_i, \beta_i) \cup \{y \in (x_1, x_2): h(\omega, y) = 0\},$$

where (α_i, β_i), $i \in \mathbb{N}$, are disjoint intervals on which $y \mapsto h(\omega, y)$ is positive and $h(\omega, \alpha_i) = 0$ if $\alpha_i \neq x_1$, $h(\omega, \beta_i) = 0$ if $\beta_i \neq x_2$. It is then clear that

$$\begin{aligned} h(\omega, x_2)^{1/2} - h(\omega, x_1)^{1/2} &= \sum_{i=1}^{\infty} (h(\omega, \beta_i)^{1/2} - h(\omega, \alpha_i)^{1/2}) \\ &= \sum_{i=1}^{\infty} \int_{\alpha_i}^{\beta_i} s(\omega, y)\, dy = \int_{x_1}^{x_2} s(\omega, y)\, dy \end{aligned}$$

since $y \mapsto s(\omega, y)$ vanishes outside of $\bigcup_{i=1}^{\infty} (\alpha_i, \beta_i)$.

78. Examples of differentiable experiments

First, let us continue Example 76.1.

78.1 Example. Recall the notation of Example 76.1. If $\nu|\mathscr{A}$ denotes the counting measure then $F(x): j \mapsto 2\sqrt{x_j}$, $1 \leqq j \leqq k$, $x \in M$, and

$$DF(x): t \mapsto (t_j/\sqrt{x_j})_{1 \leqq j \leqq k}, \quad t \in T,\ x \in M,$$

is the derivative in ν-measure. It is clear that condition 77.3 (1), is satisfied. Moreover, we have

$$B_x(s, t) = \sum_{j=1}^{k} s_j t_j / x_j, \quad s, t \in T,\ x \in M,$$

which is continuous and therefore Theorem 77.3 implies that E is differentiable on M. Since the canonical covariance is even positive definite there exists a canonical derivative g_x at every $x \in M$; it is of the form

$$g_x: j \mapsto (-x_1, \ldots, -x_{j-1}, 1 - x_j, -x_{j+1}, \ldots, -x_k), \quad 1 \leqq j \leqq k.$$

Next, we turn to exponential experiments. For this, we assume that $M \subseteq \mathbb{R}^k$ is open, hence $T = \mathbb{R}^k$.

78.2 Theorem. *Suppose that $E \in \mathscr{E}(M)$ is an exponential experiment of rank k with densities*

$$\frac{dP_x}{d\nu} = C(x) \exp\left(\sum_{i=1}^{k} x_i T_i\right), \quad x \in M.$$

for some dominating σ-finite measure $\nu|\mathscr{A}$. *Then E is differentiable on M. The canonical covariance at* $x \in M$ *is*

$$B_x(s, t) := s' \Gamma_x t, \quad s, t \in T,$$

where $\Gamma_x(i, j) = P_x((T_i - P_x(T_i))(T_j - P_x(T_j)))$, $1 \leqq i, j \leqq k$.

Proof. For the following recall Theorem 77.3. We observe that there is a derivative in ν-measure at $x \in M$

$$DF(x) \cdot t = \frac{1}{2} F(x) \left(\frac{1}{C(x)} C'(x) \cdot t + \sum_{i=1}^{k} t_i T_i \right)$$
$$= \frac{1}{2} F(x) \sum_{i=1}^{k} t_i (T_i - P_x(T_i)),$$

by Lemma 5.6. The formula for B_x and 77.3 (1) are immediate.

Another application of Lemma 5.6 shows that Condition 77.3 (2) is satisfied which proves the assertion. □

The functions $T_1, \ldots, T_k$ are called *linearly independent* if $\sum_{i=1}^{k} \alpha_i T_i = \text{const}$ ν-a.e. implies $\alpha_1 = \ldots = \alpha_k = 0$.

78.3 Corollary. *Assume that the conditions of Theorem 78.2 are satisfied. If* $T_1, \ldots, T_k$ *are linearly independent then the canonical covariance at* $x \in M$ *is positive definite and the canonical derivative at* $x \in M$ *is*

$$g_x = \Gamma_x^{-1} (T_i - P_x(T_i))_{1 \leqq i \leqq k}.$$

Let us return to the general case considered in Section 76.

If $E = (\Omega, \mathscr{A}, \{P_x : x \in M\})$ and $\psi: U \to M$, $U \subseteq \mathbb{R}^\ell$, then we may define the experiment $\tilde{E} = (\Omega, \mathscr{A}, \{P_{\psi(y)} : y \in U\})$. In the following we assume that U is open.

78.4 Theorem. *Suppose that* $E = (\Omega, \mathscr{A}, \{P_x : x \in M\})$ *is differentiable on M with canonical covariances* B_x, $x \in M$. *If* $\psi: U \to M$ *is differentiable then* $\tilde{E} = (\Omega, \mathscr{A}, \{P_{\psi(y)} : y \in U\})$ *is differentiable on U and the canonical covariance at* $y \in U$ *is*

$$\tilde{B}_y(s, t) = B_{\psi(y)}(\psi'(y) \cdot s, \quad \psi'(y) \cdot t), \quad s, t \in \mathbb{R}^\ell.$$

Proof. Let $\nu|\mathscr{A}$ be any dominating σ-finite measure and denote $F: x \mapsto 2\left(\frac{dP_x}{d\nu}\right)^{1/2}$, $x \in M$, and $\tilde{F}: y \mapsto 2\left(\frac{dP_{\psi(y)}}{d\nu}\right)^{1/2}$, $y \in U$. Since F is differentiable on M and $\tilde{F} = F \circ \psi$ it is clear that $\tilde{F}$ is differentiable on U and $D\tilde{F}(y)$

$= DF(\psi(y)) \cdot \psi'(y)$, $y \in U$. The formula for the canonical covariance is immediate. $\square$

78.5 Corollary. *Assume that the conditions of Theorem 78.4 are satisfied.*

(1) *If B_x is positive definite, $x \in M$, and ψ is an immersion then $\tilde{B}_y$ is positive definite, $y \in U$.*

(2) *If g_x is the canonical derivative of E at $x \in M$, then the canonical derivative $\tilde{g}_y$ of $\tilde{E}$ at $y \in U$ satisfies*

$$B_{\psi(y)}(\psi'(y) \cdot s, \psi'(y) \cdot \tilde{g}_y) = B_{\psi(y)}(\psi'(y) \cdot s, g_{\psi(y)}), \quad s \in \mathbb{R}^{\ell}.$$

Proof. Assertion (1) is obvious. For (2), we note that

$$\begin{aligned} \tilde{B}_y(s, \tilde{g}_y) &= D\tilde{F}(y) \cdot s \left(\frac{dP_{\psi(y)}}{dv}\right)^{-1/2} \\ &= DF(\psi(y)) \cdot (\psi'(y) \cdot s) \left(\frac{dP_{\psi(y)}}{dv}\right)^{-1/2} \\ &= B_{\psi(y)}(\psi'(y) \cdot s, g_{\psi(y)}), \quad s \in \mathbb{R}^{\ell}. \quad \square \end{aligned}$$

78.6 Remark. Under the assumption (1) of Corollary 78.5 the canonical derivative of $\tilde{E}$ at $y \in U$ is uniquely determined by 78.5 (2). It can be given explicitely in the following way. Fix $y \in \mathbb{R}^{\ell}$ and let $A\colon \mathbb{R}^{\ell} \to T$ be a linear map. Define the adjoint A^* for $B_{\psi(y)}$ by

$$B_{\psi(y)}(As, t) = \tilde{B}_y(s, A^* t) \quad \text{if} \quad s \in \mathbb{R}^{\ell}, t \in T.$$

Since $\psi'(y)$ is of full rank the map $\psi'(y)^* \circ \psi'(y)$ is invertible. Then

$$\tilde{g}_y = (\psi'(y)^* \circ \psi'(y))^{-1} \circ \psi'(y)^* g_{\psi(y)}.$$

Let us apply the formulas obtained so far to a simple particular case.

78.7 Example. Suppose that $U \subseteq \mathbb{R}$ is an open interval and $\mathscr{P} = \{(p_1(y)), \ldots, p_k(y)\colon y \in U\}$ is a family of probability measures on $\{1, \ldots, k\}$. If $0 < p_i(y) < 1$, $y \in U$, $1 \leq i \leq k$, then $\psi\colon y \mapsto (p_1(y), \ldots, p_k(y))$, $y \in U$, maps U into the linear manifold M of Examples 76.1 and 78.1. Using the notations introduced there we have $(\Omega, \mathscr{A}, \mathscr{P}) = (\Omega, \mathscr{A}, \{P_{\psi(y)}\colon y \in U\}) =: \tilde{E}$. If ψ is differentiable then $\tilde{E}$ is differentiable on U. Let us compute the canonical covariance at $y \in U$. From Theorem 78.4 and Example 78.1 we obtain that

$$\tilde{B}_y(s, t) = stI(y), \quad s, t \in \mathbb{R},$$

where

$$I(y) = \sum_{i=1}^{k} \frac{(\psi_i'(y))^2}{\psi_i(y)} = P_{\psi(y)}((D_y \log \psi)^2).$$

In case $I(y) > 0$, the canonical derivative $\tilde{g}_y$ satisfies

$$sI(y)\tilde{g}_y = s \sum_{i=1}^{k} \frac{\psi_i'(y)}{\psi_i(y)} (g_{\psi(y)})_i, \quad s \in \mathbb{R},$$

hence we obtain

$$\tilde{g}_y \colon j \mapsto \frac{1}{I(y)} \cdot \frac{\psi_j'(y)}{\psi_j(y)}, \quad 1 \leqq j \leqq k.$$

In other words, $\tilde{g}_y = I(y)^{-1} D_y \log \psi$.

Some important examples are given as "smooth" subexperiments of exponential experiments. These are sometimes called *curved exponential experiments.*

78.8 Corollary. *Assume that the conditions of Theorem 78.2 are satisfied. If* $\psi \colon U \to M$ *is differentiable then* $\tilde{E} = (\Omega, \mathscr{A}, \{P_{\psi(y)} \colon y \in U\})$ *is differentiable on* U *and the canonical covariance at* $y \in U$ *is*

$$\tilde{B}_y(s, t) = s^t \tilde{\Gamma}_y t, \quad s, t \in \mathbb{R}^\ell,$$

where $\tilde{\Gamma}_y = \psi'(y)^t \Gamma_{\psi(y)} \psi'(y)$. *In case* $\Gamma_{\psi(y)}$ *is positive definite and* ψ *is an immersion then* $\tilde{\Gamma}_y$ *is positive definite, too, and the canonical derivative at* $y \in U$ *is*

$$\tilde{g}_y = \tilde{\Gamma}_y^{-1} \psi'(y)^t (T_i - P_{\psi(y)} T_i)_{1 \leqq i \leqq k}.$$

Proof. Differentiability and the form of the canonical covariance are consequences of Theorem 78.4. For the canonical derivative apply Corollaries 78.3 and 78.5. □

78.9 Example. Consider the experiment $\tilde{E} = (\mathbb{R}, \mathscr{B}, \{\nu_{a,\sigma^2} \colon a \in \mathbb{R}, \sigma^2 > 0\})$. Let $U = \{(a, \sigma^2) \colon a \in \mathbb{R}, \sigma^2 > 0\}$ and $M = \{(x_1, x_2) \colon x_1 \in \mathbb{R}, x_2 < 0\}$. If we define $P_x | \mathscr{B}^1$ by

$$\frac{dP_x}{d\lambda}(\omega) = C(x) \exp(x_1 \omega + x_2 \omega^2), \quad \omega \in \mathbb{R}, x \in M,$$

then we have $\nu_{a,\sigma^2} = P_{\psi(a,\sigma^2)}$ where $\psi(a, \sigma^2) = \left(\frac{a}{\sigma^2}, -\frac{1}{2\sigma^2}\right)$, $(a, \sigma^2) \in U$. The experiment $E = (\mathbb{R}, \mathscr{B}, \{P_x \colon x \in M\})$ is exponential of rank 2 and we may apply Corollary 78.8. Let $T_1(\omega) = \omega$, $T_2(\omega) = \omega^2$, $\omega \in \mathbb{R}$. We have

$$\operatorname{Var}_{a,\sigma^2}(T_1) = \sigma^2, \operatorname{Var}_{a,\sigma^2}(T_2) = 4a^2\sigma^2 + 2\sigma^4, \operatorname{Cov}_{a,\sigma^2}(T_1, T_2) = 2a\sigma^2$$

which yields

$$\Gamma_{\psi(a,\sigma^2)} = \begin{pmatrix} \sigma^2 & 2a\sigma^2 \\ 2a\sigma^2 & 4a^2\sigma^2 + 2\sigma^4 \end{pmatrix}.$$

Since

$$\psi'(a, \sigma^2) = \begin{pmatrix} \frac{1}{\sigma^2} & -\frac{a}{\sigma^4} \\ 0 & \frac{1}{2\sigma^4} \end{pmatrix}$$

is of full rank it follows that

$$\tilde{\Gamma}_{a,\sigma^2} = \begin{pmatrix} \frac{1}{\sigma^2} & 0 \\ 0 & \frac{1}{2\sigma^4} \end{pmatrix}.$$

The canonical derivative is given by

$$\begin{aligned} \tilde{g}_{a,\sigma^2}(\omega) &= \tilde{\Gamma}_y^{-1} \psi'(y)^t \begin{pmatrix} \omega - a \\ \omega^2 - a^2 - \sigma^2 \end{pmatrix} \\ &= (\Gamma_{\psi(y)} \cdot \psi'(y))^{-1} \begin{pmatrix} \omega - a \\ \omega^2 - a^2 - \sigma^2 \end{pmatrix} \\ &= \begin{pmatrix} 1 & 0 \\ -2a & 1 \end{pmatrix} \begin{pmatrix} \omega - a \\ \omega^2 - a^2 - \sigma^2 \end{pmatrix} = \begin{pmatrix} \omega - a \\ (\omega - a)^2 - \sigma^2 \end{pmatrix}, \quad \omega \in \mathbb{R}. \end{aligned}$$

78.10 Example. Consider the experiment

$$\tilde{E} = (\mathbb{R}^2, \mathscr{B}^2, \{\nu_{\binom{a}{b}, \begin{pmatrix} \sigma^2 & \kappa \\ \kappa & \tau^2 \end{pmatrix}}: (a, b, \sigma^2, \tau^2, \kappa) \in U\})$$

where $U = \{(a, b, \sigma^2, \tau^2, \kappa) \in \mathbb{R}^2 \times (0, \infty) \times (0, \infty) \times \mathbb{R}: \sigma^2\tau^2 - \kappa^2 > 0\}$. Then the Lebesgue densities of this experiment are

$$C \cdot \exp\left(\sum_{j=1}^{5} \psi_j(a, b, \sigma^2, \tau^2, \kappa) \cdot T_j \right)$$

where $T_1: (\omega_1, \omega_2) \mapsto \omega_1$, $T_2: (\omega_1, \omega_2) \mapsto \omega_2$, $T_3: (\omega_1, \omega_2) \mapsto \omega_1^2$, $T_4: (\omega_1, \omega_2) \mapsto \omega_2^2$, $T_5: (\omega_1, \omega_2) \mapsto \omega_1 \omega_2$,

and

$$\psi_1 = \frac{a\tau^2 - b\kappa}{\sigma^2\tau^2 - \kappa^2}, \quad \psi_2 = \frac{b\sigma^2 - a\kappa}{\sigma^2\tau^2 - \kappa^2}, \quad \psi_3 = \frac{-\tau^2}{2(\sigma^2\tau^2 - \kappa^2)},$$

$$\psi_4 = \frac{-\sigma^2}{2(\sigma^2\tau^2 - \kappa^2)}, \quad \psi_5 = \frac{\kappa}{\sigma^2\tau^2 - \kappa^2}.$$

If we define $P_x | \mathscr{B}^2$, $x \in M = \psi(U)$, by

$$\frac{dP_x}{d\lambda^2} = C(x) \exp\left(\sum_{j=1}^{5} x_j T_j \right)$$

then we have $\nu_{\binom{a}{b}, \begin{pmatrix} \sigma^2 & \kappa \\ \kappa & \tau^2 \end{pmatrix}} = P_{\psi(a, b, \sigma^2, \tau^2, \kappa)}$ where $\psi = (\psi_1, \psi_2, \ldots, \psi_5)$. The experiment $E = (\mathbb{R}^2, \mathscr{B}^2, \{P_x: x \in M\})$ is exponential and we may apply Corollary 78.8. Elementary computations yield the covariance matrix $\Gamma_{\psi(a, b, \sigma^2, \tau^2, \kappa)}$, given by

$$\begin{aligned}
&\operatorname{Var}(T_1) = \sigma^2 && \operatorname{Var}(T_2) = \tau^2 \\
&\operatorname{Cov}(T_1, T_2) = \kappa && \operatorname{Cov}(T_2, T_3) = = 2a\kappa \\
&\operatorname{Cov}(T_1, T_3) = 2a\sigma^2 && \operatorname{Cov}(T_2, T_4) = 2b\tau^2 \\
&\operatorname{Cov}(T_1, T_4) = 2b\kappa && \operatorname{Cov}(T_2, T_5) = b\kappa + a\tau^2 \\
&\operatorname{Cov}(T_1, T_5) = a\kappa + b\sigma^2
\end{aligned}$$

$$\begin{aligned}
&\operatorname{Var}(T_3) = 4a^2\sigma^2 + 2\sigma^4 \\
&\operatorname{Cov}(T_3, T_4) = 4ab\kappa + 2\kappa^2 \\
&\operatorname{Cov}(T_3, T_5) = 2\sigma^2\kappa + 2a^2\kappa + 2ab\sigma^2
\end{aligned}$$

$$\begin{aligned}
&\operatorname{Var}(T_4) = 4b^2\tau^2 + 2\tau^4 \\
&\operatorname{Cov}(T_4, T_5) = 2\tau^2\kappa + 2b^2\kappa + 2ab\tau^2
\end{aligned}$$

$$\operatorname{Var}(T_5) = \sigma^2\tau^2 + \kappa^2 + 2ab\kappa + a^2\tau^2 + b^2\sigma^2.$$

The Jacobian $\psi'(a, b, \sigma^2, \tau^2, \kappa)$ is (with $\Delta := \sigma^2\tau^2 - \kappa^2$)

$$\begin{pmatrix}
\frac{\tau^2}{\Delta} & \frac{-\kappa}{\Delta} & \frac{b\kappa\tau^2 - a\tau^4}{\Delta^2} & \frac{b\kappa\sigma^2 - a\kappa^2}{\Delta^2} & \frac{2\kappa a\tau^2 - b(\kappa^2 + \sigma^2\tau^2)}{\Delta^2} \\
\frac{-\kappa}{\Delta} & \frac{\sigma^2}{\Delta} & \frac{a\kappa\tau^2 - b\kappa^2}{\Delta^2} & \frac{a\kappa\sigma^2 - b\sigma^4}{\Delta^2} & \frac{2\kappa b\sigma^2 - a(\kappa^2 + \sigma^2\tau^2)}{\Delta^2} \\
0 & 0 & \frac{\tau^4}{2\Delta^2} & \frac{\kappa^2}{2\Delta^2} & \frac{-\kappa\tau^2}{\Delta^2} \\
0 & 0 & \frac{\kappa^2}{2\Delta^2} & \frac{\sigma^4}{2\Delta^2} & \frac{-\kappa\sigma^2}{\Delta^2} \\
0 & 0 & \frac{-\kappa\tau^2}{\Delta^2} & \frac{-\kappa\sigma^2}{\Delta^2} & \frac{\sigma^2\tau^2 + \kappa^2}{\Delta^2}
\end{pmatrix}$$

This gives at $(a, b, \sigma^2, \tau^2, \kappa)$

$$\Gamma_\psi \cdot \psi' = \begin{pmatrix} 1 & 0 & 0 & 0 & 0 \\ 0 & 1 & 0 & 0 & 0 \\ 2a & 0 & 1 & 0 & 0 \\ 0 & 2b & 0 & 1 & 0 \\ b & a & 0 & 0 & 1 \end{pmatrix}$$

and as canonical covariance

$$\tilde{\Gamma} = (\psi')^t \cdot \Gamma_\psi \cdot \psi' = \begin{pmatrix} \frac{\tau^2}{\Delta} & \frac{-\kappa}{\Delta} & 0 & 0 & 0 \\ \frac{-\kappa}{\Delta} & \frac{\sigma^2}{\Delta} & 0 & 0 & 0 \\ 0 & 0 & \frac{\tau^4}{2\Delta^2} & \frac{\kappa^2}{2\Delta^2} & \frac{-\kappa\tau^2}{\Delta^2} \\ 0 & 0 & \frac{\kappa^2}{2\Delta^2} & \frac{\sigma^4}{2\Delta^2} & \frac{-\kappa\sigma^2}{\Delta^2} \\ 0 & 0 & \frac{-\kappa\tau^2}{\Delta^2} & \frac{-\kappa\sigma^2}{\Delta^2} & \frac{\sigma^2\tau^2+\kappa^2}{\Delta^2} \end{pmatrix}.$$

The canonical derivative is given by

$$\tilde{g}_{a,b,\sigma^2,\tau^2,\kappa}(\omega_1, \omega_2) = (\Gamma_\psi \cdot \psi')^{-1} \begin{pmatrix} \omega_1 - a \\ \omega_2 - b \\ \omega_1^2 - a^2 - \sigma^2 \\ \omega_2^2 - b^2 - \tau^2 \\ \omega_1\omega_2 - \kappa - ab \end{pmatrix} =$$

$$= \begin{pmatrix} 1 & 0 & 0 & 0 & 0 \\ 0 & 1 & 0 & 0 & 0 \\ -2a & 0 & 1 & 0 & 0 \\ 0 & -2b & 0 & 1 & 0 \\ -b & -a & 0 & 0 & 1 \end{pmatrix} \cdot \begin{pmatrix} \omega_1 - a \\ \omega_2 - b \\ \omega_1^2 - a^2 - \sigma^2 \\ \omega_2^2 - b^2 - \tau^2 \\ \omega_1\omega_2 - \kappa - ab \end{pmatrix} = \begin{pmatrix} \omega_1 - a \\ \omega_2 - b \\ (\omega_1 - a)^2 - \sigma^2 \\ (\omega_2 - b)^2 - \tau^2 \\ (\omega_1 - a)(\omega_2 - b) - \kappa \end{pmatrix}.$$

79. The stochastic expansion of a differentiable experiment

Consider the case of Section 76 and keep the notation introduced there. We are interested in the stochastic expansion of the likelihood ratios

$$\prod_{i=1}^{k(n)} \left(\frac{dP_{x+t_{ni}}}{dP_x}(\omega_i)\right), \quad \underset{\sim}{\omega} \in \Omega^{k(n)}, \, n \in \mathbb{N},$$

where $(t_{ni})_{1 \leqq i \leqq k(n)}$, $n \in \mathbb{N}$, is a triangular array in T satisfying the following

79.1 Conditions.

(1) $\lim\limits_{n\to\infty} \max\limits_{1 \leqq i \leqq k(n)} |t_{ni}| = 0,$

(2) $\limsup\limits_{n\to\infty} \sum\limits_{i=1}^{k(n)} |t_{ni}|^2 < \infty,$

where $|.|$ is any norm on T. Since T is of finite dimension the validity of the conditions does not depend on the particular norm.

The main result of this section is

79.2 Theorem. *Suppose that E is differentiable at $x \in M$ and $DF(x)$ is injective. Let $(t_{ni})_{1 \leqq i \leqq k(n)}$, $n \in \mathbb{N}$, be a triangular array satisfying 79.1 (1) and (2). Then*

$$\prod_{i=1}^{k(n)} \frac{dP_{x+t_{ni}}}{dP_x}(\underset{\sim}{\omega}) = \exp\Big(\sum_{i=1}^{k(n)} B_x(t_{ni}, g_x(\omega_i)) - \frac{1}{2}\sum_{i=1}^{k(n)} B_x(t_{ni}, t_{ni}) + o_{P_x^n}(1)\Big),$$

$\underset{\sim}{\omega} \in \Omega^n, \quad n \in \mathbb{N}.$

Proof. Define $h_{ni}(\omega_i) := B_x(t_{ni}, g_x(\omega_i))$, $\omega_i \in \Omega$, $1 \leqq i \leqq k(n)$, $n \in \mathbb{N}$. We shall apply Corollary 74.4. For this, we have to show that $(h_{ni})_{1 \leqq i \leqq k(n)}$, $n \in \mathbb{N}$, is a Lindeberg array. Since $P_x(h_{ni}^2) = B_x(t_{ni}, t_{ni})$ by 76.9 (2), Condition 74.1 (1) follows from Assumption 79.1 (2).

For the proof of Condition 74.1 (2) we note that

$$\sum_{i=1}^{k(n)} \int\limits_{B_x(t_{ni}, g_x) > \varepsilon} B_x(t_{ni}, g_x)^2 \, dP_x$$
$$\leqq \sum_{i=1}^{k(n)} B_x(t_{ni}, t_{ni})) \int\limits_{B_x(g_x, g_x) > \frac{\varepsilon^2}{\max\limits_{1 \leqq i \leqq k(n)} B_x(t_{ni}, t_{ni})}} B_x(g_x, g_x) \, dP_x$$

which together with 79.1 (1) and (2) implies 74.1 (2) in view of $|g_x| \in L^2(\Omega, \mathscr{A}, P_x)$ and

$$\lim_{n\to\infty} P_x\left\{B_x(g_x, g_x) > \frac{\varepsilon^2}{\max\limits_{1 \leqq i \leqq k(n)} B_x(t_{ni}, t_{ni})}\right\} = 0.$$

Hence, $(h_{ni})_{1 \leqq i \leqq k(n)}$, $n \in \mathbb{N}$, is a Lindeberg array. To complete the assumptions of Corollary 74.4 we have to show that

$$\lim_{n \to \infty} \sum_{i=1}^{k(n)} \int \left(\sqrt{\frac{dP_{x+t_{ni}}}{dP_x}} - 1 - \frac{1}{2} B_x(t_{ni}, g_x) \right)^2 dP_x = 0 .$$

But this is an obvious consequence of differentiability of E at $x \in M$ and assumption 79.1 (2). Thus, we conclude by Corollary 74.4 that the asserted expansion is valid, since $P_x(g_x) = 0$ and $P_x(g_x \otimes g_x) = B_x$ by Corollary 76.9, and since a similar proof as for Lemma 75.7 implies by differentiability that

$$\lim_{n \to \infty} \sum_{i=1}^{k(n)} P_{x+t_{ni}}(N_{x+t_{ni}}) = 0 . \qquad \square$$

79.3 Corollary. *Suppose that F is differentiable at $x \in M$ and $DF(x)$ is injective. Then for every bounded sequence $(t_n) \subseteq T$*

$$\frac{dP^n_{x+\frac{1}{\sqrt{n}}t_n}}{dP^n_x}(\underline{\omega}) = \exp\left(B_x\left(t_n, \frac{1}{\sqrt{n}} \sum_{i=1}^{n} g_x(\omega_i) \right) - \frac{1}{2} B_x(t_n, t_n) + o_{P^n_x}(1) \right)$$

$\underline{\omega} \in \Omega^n$, $n \in \mathbb{N}$.

There is an important special case of Theorem 79.2 which we discuss a little more thoroughly.

79.4 Examples. (Hajek and Sidak [1967]). Let $M = \mathbb{R}$, $\dfrac{dP_x}{d\lambda} = f(. - x)$, $x \in \mathbb{R}$, and assume that the conditions of Discussion 77.5 are satisfied. It is clear that $I(x) =: I$, $x \in \mathbb{R}$, is independent of $x \in \mathbb{R}$. Then we have

$$B_x(s, t) = stI, \quad s, t, x \in \mathbb{R},$$

and

$$\tilde{g}_x = \frac{1}{I} \cdot \frac{\dot{f}(. - x)}{f(. - x)} \cdot 1_{\{f(. - x) > 0\}}, \quad x \in \mathbb{R}.$$

Recall, that the distribution function F of f has a right inverse

$$F^{-1}\colon s \mapsto \inf\{x \in \mathbb{R}\colon F(x) \geqq s\}, \quad s \in [0, 1].$$

Although $F^{-1} \circ F \neq \mathrm{id}_{\mathbb{R}}$ in general, it is nevertheless true that [loc. cit. p. 21, 34]

$$\frac{\dot{f} \circ F^{-1}}{f \circ F^{-1}}(F(x)) = \frac{\dot{f}(x)}{f(x)} \ \lambda\text{-a.e. on } \{f > 0\}.$$

Hence, defining $\varphi := -(\dot{f} \circ F^{-1} / f \circ F^{-1}) 1_{\{f \circ F^{-1} > 0\}}$ we may write

$$\tilde{g}_x = \frac{1}{I} \cdot \varphi(F(.-x))\ P_x\text{-a.e.}.$$

We note that $\varphi \in L^2([0,1])$ and [loc. cit. p. 19, 20]

$$\int_0^1 \varphi^2 \, d\lambda = I, \quad \int_0^1 \varphi \, d\lambda = 0.$$

If $(t_{ni})_{1 \leqq i \leqq k(n)}$, $n \in \mathbb{N}$, is a triangular array satisfying 79.1 (1) and (2), then we arrive at

$$\prod_{i=1}^{k(n)} \frac{dP_{x+t_{ni}}}{dP_x}(\underline{\omega}) = \exp\left(\sum_{i=1}^{k(n)} t_{ni} \cdot \varphi(F(\omega_i - x)) - \frac{I}{2} \sum_{i=1}^{k(n)} t_{ni}^2 + o_{P_x{}^n}(1)\right),$$

$\underline{\omega} \in \Omega^n$, $n \in \mathbb{N}$.

This form of the expansion is related to rank statistics. If $\underline{\omega} = (\omega_1, \ldots, \omega_n)$ is a random sample, let $R_{ni}(\underline{\omega})$ be the rank of ω_i in $\underline{\omega}$, $1 \leqq i \leqq n$. The idea of rank statistics is to replace $\varphi(F(\omega_i - x))$ by $\varphi\left(\frac{R_{ni}(\underline{\omega})}{n+1}\right)$ if φ is increasing, but for general φ it is technically more appropriate to replace $\varphi(F(\omega_i - x))$ by

$$n \int_{(R_{ni}(\omega)-1)/n}^{R_{ni}(\omega)/n} \varphi \, d\lambda, \quad 1 \leqq i \leqq n.$$

It has been shown by Hajek and Sidak [1967] that

$$\lim_{n\to\infty} \int \left[\sum_{i=1}^{k(n)} t_{ni} \left(n \int_{(R_{ni}(\omega)-1)/n}^{R_{ni}(\omega)/n} \varphi \, d\lambda - \varphi(F(\omega_i - x))\right)\right]^2 P_x^n(d\underline{\omega}) = 0.$$

(For the sake of completeness we prove this fact at the end of this section.) Thus, we arrive at the expansion

$$\prod_{i=1}^{k(n)} \frac{dP_{x+t_{ni}}}{dP_x} = \exp\left(\sum_{i=1}^{k(n)} t_{ni} \left(n \int_{(R_{ni}-1)/n}^{R_{ni}/n} \varphi \, d\lambda\right) - \frac{I}{2} \sum_{i=1}^{k(n)} t_{ni}^2 + o_{P_x^n}(1)\right).$$

This expansion is the starting point of the theory of rank tests.

79.5 Theorem. (Hajek and Sidak [1967]). *Suppose that the conditions of Example 79.4 are satisfied. Let $(t_{ni})_{1 \leqq i \leqq k(n)}$, $n \in \mathbb{N}$, be a triangular array satisfying 79.1 (1) and (2), and in addition $\sum_{i=1}^{k(n)} t_{ni} = 0$, $n \in \mathbb{N}$. Then*

$$\lim_{n\to\infty} \int \left[\sum_{i=1}^{k(n)} t_{ni} \left(n \int_{(R_{ni}(\omega)-1)/n}^{R_{ni}(\omega)/n} \varphi \, d\lambda - \varphi(F(\omega_i - x))\right)\right]^2 P_x^n(d\underline{\omega}) = 0, \quad x \in \mathbb{R}.$$

Proof. The proof is divided into several steps.

(1) Let

$$\varphi_n = \sum_{i=1}^{n} n \int_{\frac{i-1}{n}}^{\frac{i}{n}} \varphi\, d\lambda \cdot 1_{\left[\frac{i-1}{n}, \frac{i}{n}\right)}, \quad n \in \mathbb{N}.$$

Then $\varphi_n \in L^2([0,1])$, $\int_0^1 \varphi_n d\lambda = 0$, $n \in \mathbb{N}$, and $\int_0^1 (\varphi_n - \varphi)^2 d\lambda \to 0$ by well-known martingale theorems.

(2) Fix $x \in \mathbb{R}$ and let $U_{n,i}(\underline{\omega}) = F(\omega_i - x)$, $1 \leqq i \leqq n$, $\underline{\omega} \in \Omega^n$. Then it is clear that $U_{n,1}, \ldots, U_{n,n}$ are independent and uniformly distributed over $[0,1]$ under P_x^n. Let $(U_{n,[1]}, \ldots, U_{n,[n]})$ be the ordered sample $(U_{n,1}, \ldots, U_{n,n})$. Recall, that $(U_{n,[1]}, \ldots, U_{n,[n]})$ and $(R_{n,1}, \ldots, R_{n,n})$ are independent from each other for each $n \in \mathbb{N}$. Define

$$\psi_n = \sum_{i=1}^{n} P_x^n(\varphi(U_{n,[i]})) \cdot 1_{\left[\frac{i-1}{n}, \frac{i}{n}\right)}, \quad n \in \mathbb{N}.$$

Then $\psi_n \in L^2([0,1])$, $\int_0^1 \psi_n d\lambda = 0$, $n \in \mathbb{N}$, and $\int_0^1 (\psi_n - \varphi)^2 d\lambda \to 0$.

Again, the first two assertions are easy to see. The third is proved by Scheffés lemma. Jensen's inequality yields

$$\int_0^1 \psi_n^2 d\lambda \leqq \int_0^1 \varphi^2 d\lambda, \quad n \in \mathbb{N}.$$

A little more laborious is it to show that $\psi_n \to \varphi$ λ-a.e. To this end note that

$$\begin{aligned}\psi_n(s) &= P_x^n(\varphi(U_{n,[ns]+1})) \\ &= n! \cdot \int_0^1 \varphi(t) \frac{t^{[ns]}(1-t)^{n-[ns]-1}}{[ns]!\,(n-[ns]-1)!}\, dt \\ &=: \int_0^1 \varphi(t) f_n(t)\, dt, \quad s \in [0,1].\end{aligned}$$

Since $f_n(t) \to 0$ if $t \neq s$ and $\int_0^1 f_n(t)\, dt = 1$, $n \in \mathbb{N}$, it follows that $\psi_n(s) \to \varphi(s)$ for all Lebesgue points s of φ.

(3) Let us show that

$$\lim_{n\to\infty} \int \left(\psi_n\left(\frac{R_{n1}}{n+1}\right) - \varphi(U_{n,1}) \right)^2 dP_x^n = 0.$$

Evaluating the quadratic expression under the integral we get three terms. The first is

$$\int \psi_n^2\left(\frac{R_{n1}}{n+1}\right) dP_x^n = \sum_{i=1}^{n} \int_{R_{n1}=i} \psi_n^2\left(\frac{i}{n+1}\right) dP_x^n$$
$$= \frac{1}{n}\sum_{i=1}^{n} \psi_n^2\left(\frac{i}{n+1}\right) = \int_0^1 \psi_n^2\, d\lambda,$$

the second is

$$\int \varphi^2(U_{n,1})\, dP_x^n = \int_0^1 \varphi^2\, d\lambda,$$

and the third is

$$-2\int \psi_n\left(\frac{R_{n1}}{n+1}\right)\varphi(U_{n1})\, dP_x^n$$
$$= -2\sum_{i=1}^{n} \int_{R_{n1}=i} \psi_n\left(\frac{i}{n+1}\right)\varphi(U_{n,[i]})\, dP_x^n$$
$$= -\frac{2}{n}\sum_{i=1}^{n} \psi_n^2\left(\frac{i}{n+1}\right) = -2\int_0^1 \psi_n^2\, d\lambda.$$

Thus, we obtain

$$\int\left(\psi_n\left(\frac{R_{n1}}{n+1}\right) - \varphi(U_{n,1})\right)^2 dP_x^n$$
$$= \int_0^1 \psi_n^2\, d\lambda + \int_0^1 \varphi^2\, d\lambda - 2\int_0^1 \psi_n^2\, d\lambda$$
$$= \int_0^1 \varphi^2\, d\lambda - \int_0^1 \psi_n^2\, d\lambda$$

which tends to zero by part (2) of the proof.

(4) We show that

$$\lim_{n\to\infty} \int\left(\varphi_n\left(\frac{R_{n1}}{n+1}\right) - \varphi(U_{n,1})\right)^2 dP_x^n = 0.$$

Indeed, we have

$$\int\left(\psi_n\left(\frac{R_{n1}}{n+1}\right) - \varphi_n\left(\frac{R_{n1}}{n+1}\right)\right)^2 dP_x^n$$
$$= \frac{1}{n}\sum_{i=1}^{n}\left(\psi_n\left(\frac{i}{n+1}\right) - \varphi_n\left(\frac{i}{n+1}\right)\right)^2 = \int_0^1 (\psi_n - \varphi_n)^2\, d\lambda$$

which tends to zero by (1) and (2). Thus, (4) follows from (3).

(5) Now, we are in the position to prove the assertion of the theorem. Since

$$\varphi_n\left(\frac{R_{ni}}{n+1}\right) = n \int\limits_{(R_{ni}-1)/n}^{R_{ni}/n} \varphi\, d\lambda, \quad 1 \leqq i \leqq n,\ n \in \mathbb{N},$$

we need only show

$$\lim_{n\to\infty} P_x^n\left(\left[\sum_{i=1}^{k(n)} t_{ni}\left(\varphi_n\left(\frac{R_{ni}}{n+1}\right) - \varphi(U_{n,i})\right)\right]^2\right) = 0 .$$

Evaluating the quadratic expression under the integral we have

$$\sum_{i=1}^{k(n)} t_{ni}^2 \int \left(\varphi_n\left(\frac{R_{ni}}{n+1}\right) - \varphi(U_{ni})\right)^2 dP_x^n$$

$$+ \sum_{i\neq j} t_{ni} t_{nj} \int \left(\varphi_n\left(\frac{R_{ni}}{n+1}\right) - \varphi(U_{ni})\right)\left(\varphi_n\left(\frac{R_{nj}}{n+1}\right) - \varphi(U_{nj})\right) dP_x^n$$

$$= \left(\sum_{i=1}^{k(n)} t_{ni}^2\right) \int \left(\varphi_n\left(\frac{R_{n1}}{n+1}\right) - \varphi(U_{n1})\right)^2 dP_x^n$$

$$+ \left(\left(\sum_{i=1}^{k(n)} t_{ni}\right)^2 - \sum_{i=1}^{k(n)} t_{ni}^2\right) \int \left(\varphi_n\left(\frac{R_{n1}}{n+1}\right) - \varphi(U_{n1})\right)\left(\varphi_n\left(\frac{R_{n2}}{n+1}\right) - \varphi(U_{n2})\right) dP_x^n$$

$$\leqq 2\left(\sum_{i=1}^{k(n)} t_{ni}^2\right) \int \left(\varphi_n\left(\frac{R_{n1}}{n+1}\right) - \varphi(U_{n1})\right)^2 dP_n^n$$

which tends to zero by 79.1 (2) and part (4) of this proof. □

Chapter 13: Asymptotic Normality

This chapter combines the results of Chapters 10, 11 und 12. The general framework for the examples considered in Chapter 12 is the concept of asymptotic normality. It means that a sequence of experiments converges weakly against a Gaussian shift experiment the type of which is well-known to us from Chapter 11. From the results of Chapter 10 we obtain statistical assertions concerning the sequence of experiments.

In Section 80 we explain what is meant by an asymptotically normal sequence of experiments. For such a sequence the logarithms of the likelihood processes are approximately linear. This observation leads to the fundamental concept of a central sequence of stochastic processes or random variables. We illustrate asymptotic normality of some well-known examples considering both finite dimensional as well as infinite dimensional cases.

Before asymptotic decision theory was available in the form of Chapter 10 the most important instrument for proving asymptotic optimality of decision functions was the so-called exponential approximation. Essentially, exponential approximation can be found already in the early papers of Wald [1943] and LeCam [1953]. The hidden argument was isolated by LeCam [1960]. Let us mention the papers of Hajek [1972 and 1973], and Hajek and Sidak [1967] where the exponential approximation is applied in an explicit way. We present this method and its relation to an early idea of asymptotic sufficiency in Section 81. By way of example we obtain the famous result of Hajek and Sidak [1967] concerning asymptotic sufficiency of the vector of ranks. Finally, it is convenient to prove at this point the old theorem of Bernstein and v. Mises which became important again in the paper of LeCam [1953].

At this point we have to mention the concept of global asymptotic normality which is related to asymptotic sufficiency and is the intrinsic argument of Wald's paper [1943]. This path pointed out by Wald was continued by LeCam [1956], Hajek [1971], Michel and Pfanzagl [1970], and Pfanzagl [1972a] and [1972b]. Recently, the relation between local and global asymptotic normality has been investigated by Milbrodt, [1983], and by Droste, [1985].

Refinements of local asymptotic normality, rates of convergence and asymptotic optimality properties of higher order are considered by Pfanzagl [1985].

Sections 82 and 83 are concerned with testing and estimation for asymptically normal sequences of experiments. At this point we have to introduce the idea of local parametrization. We explain it by examples with independent, identically distributed observations. It turns out that decision problems of nonlinear, but smooth nature can be replaced after rescaling by linear decision problems. Thus, the theory of Chapter 11 becomes applicable for the limiting Gaussian shifts. We obtain a complete description of asymptotically optimal testing and estimation procedures, both for finite dimensional as well as for infinite dimensional situations. The results are illustrated by means of classical examples.

In Section 84 the reader can find some concluding remarks on how to obtain central sequences, which are known from the preceding to be the basis of optimal sequences of decision functions. We show that central sequences are characterized by the maximum likelihood property or by Bayesian optimality.

80. Asymptotic normality

Let $(H, \langle .,. \rangle)$ be a Hilbert space. Consider a sequence of experiments $E_n = (\Omega_n, \mathscr{A}_n, \{P_{n,h}: h \in H_n\})$, $n \in \mathbb{N}$, where $H_n \uparrow H$ as $n \to \infty$, $0 \in H_n$, $n \in \mathbb{N}$. Recall Definition 60.1.

80.1 Definition. The sequence $(E_n)_{n \in \mathbb{N}}$ is *asymptotically normal* if it converges weakly to a Gaussian shift on H.

80.2 Theorem. *The sequence of experiments E_n, $n \in \mathbb{N}$, is asymptotically normal iff the stochastic processes $(L_n(h))_{h \in H_n}$, $n \in \mathbb{N}$, defined by*

$$\frac{dP_{n,h}}{dP_{n,0}} = \exp\left(L_n(h) - \frac{1}{2}\,\|h\|^2\right), \quad h \in H_n,\ n \in \mathbb{N},$$

satisfy the following conditions:

(1) $\mathscr{L}(L_n(h) \mid P_{n,0}) \to \nu_{0,\|h\|^2}$ *weakly*, $h \in H$,

(2) $\alpha L_n(h_1) + \beta L_n(h_2) - L_n(\alpha h_1 + \beta h_2) \to 0 \quad (P_{n,0})$, *whenever* $\alpha, \beta \in \mathbb{R}$, $h_1 \in H$, $h_2 \in H$.

Proof. It is clear by Theorem 69.4 that $(E_n)_{n \in \mathbb{N}}$ is asymptotically normal iff the finite dimensional marginal distributions of $(L_n(h))_{h \in H_n}$ under $P_{n,0}$, $n \in \mathbb{N}$, converge weakly to the finite dimensional marginal distributions of a standard Gaussian process on $(H, \langle .,. \rangle)$. Therefore we have to show that conditions (1) and (2) are equivalent to such a property. But this is an immediate consequence of Theorem 68.4. □

80.3 Remark. Sometimes it is possible to split the sequence (L_n) into a sequence of linear processes (X_n) and a remainder term such that

$$L_n(h) = X_n(h) + o_{P_{n,0}}(1), \quad h \in H, n \in \mathbb{N}.$$

The following example illustrates this case.

80.4 Example. Let $(\Omega, \mathscr{A}, P_0)$ be a probability space. Let $H = \{g \in L^2(\Omega, \mathscr{A}, P_0): P_0(g) = 0\}$ and $M = \{g \in H: P_0(g^2) \leqq 4\}$. For every $g \in M$

$$\frac{dP_g}{dP_0} := \left(\frac{1}{2}g + \sqrt{1 - \frac{1}{4}P_0(g^2)}\right)^2$$

defines a probability measure $P_g \ll P_0$. Conversely, each $P \ll P_0$ admits a representation of the form $P = P_g$, with

$$g = 2\left(\sqrt{\frac{dP}{dP_0}} - a(P, P_0)\right).$$

Hence, the sets $\{P|\mathscr{A}: P \ll P_0\}$ and $\{P_g: g \in M\}$ coincide. Consider the experiment

$$E = (\Omega, \mathscr{A}, \{P_g: g \in M\}).$$

We are interested in the asymptotic behaviour of the product experiments $E^n = (\Omega^n, \mathscr{A}^n, \{P_g^n: g \in M\})$. To obtain a nondegenerate limit experiment we stabilize the sequence (E^n) by scale-transformations.

Let $H_n = \left\{g \in H: \frac{1}{\sqrt{n}} g \in M\right\}$ and define

$$E_n = (\Omega^n, \mathscr{A}^n, \{P^n_{1/\sqrt{n}\cdot g}: g \in H_n\}), \quad n \in \mathbb{N}.$$

Now it is clear that $H_n \uparrow H$ as $n \to \infty$. Moreover, from the second part of the proof of Theorem 75.2 it follows that $t \mapsto P_{tg}$, $t \in (-\varepsilon, \varepsilon)$, is a curve differentiable at $t = 0$ with tangent vector g. Therefore, from Theorem 75.8 we obtain the expansion

$$\frac{dP^n_{1/\sqrt{n}\cdot g}}{dP_0^n}(\underline{\omega}) = \exp\left(\frac{1}{\sqrt{n}} \sum_{i=1}^n g(\omega_i) - \frac{1}{2}P_0(g^2) + o_{P_0^n}(1)\right),$$

$\underline{\omega} \in \Omega^n$, $n \in \mathbb{N}$. With the notation

$$X_n(g): \underline{\omega} \mapsto \frac{1}{\sqrt{n}} \sum_{i=1}^n g(\omega_i), \quad \underline{\omega} \in \Omega^n,$$

the assumptions of Theorem 80.2 are satisfied which implies that (E_n) converges weakly to the Gaussian shift on H. By Theorems 70.5 and 70.8 this Gaussian shift sometimes can be represented by an Abstract Wiener space.

80.5 Definition. Suppose that (E_n) is asymptotically normal. A sequence of linear processes (X_n) satisfying

(1) $\mathscr{L}(X_n(h)|P_{n,0}) \to \nu_{0,\|h\|^2}$ weakly, $h \in H$,

(2) $$\frac{dP_{n,h}}{dP_{n,0}} = \exp\left(X_n(h) - \frac{1}{2}\|h\|^2 + o_{P_{n,0}}(1)\right), \quad n \in \mathbb{N}, h \in H,$$

is called a *central* sequence for (E_n).

If H is a Euclidean space then central sequences are always available.

80.6 Corollary. *Suppose that $(H, \langle .,. \rangle)$ is a Euclidean space. Then the sequence of experiments E_n, $n \in \mathbb{N}$, is asymptotically normal iff there exists a sequence of random variables X_n: $\Omega_n \to H$, $n \in \mathbb{N}$, such that*

(1) $\mathscr{L}(X_n|P_{n,0}) \to N_H$ *weakly, and*

(2) $$\frac{dP_{n,h}}{dP_{n,0}} - \exp\left(\langle h, X_n\rangle - \frac{1}{2}\|h\|^2\right) \to 0 \ (P_{n,0}), \textit{ whenever } h \in H.$$

Proof. It follows from the preceding theorem that the condition is sufficient. To prove necessity let $\{e_1, \ldots, e_k\}$ be an orthonormal base of H. Then we define (for sufficiently large $n \in \mathbb{N}$)

$$X_n := \sum_{i=1}^{k} \left(\log \frac{dP_{n,e_i}}{dP_{n,0}} + \frac{1}{2}\right) e_i$$

where the likelihood ratios are positive. Then condition (1) is satisfied. Condition (2) is also valid since the distributions

$$\mathscr{L}\left(\log \frac{dP_{n,h}}{dP_{n,0}} - \langle h, X_n\rangle + \frac{1}{2}\|h\|^2 \,\middle|\, P_{n,0}\right), \quad n \in \mathbb{N},$$

converge weakly to

$$\mathscr{L}\left(\log \frac{dP_h}{dP_0} - \langle h, X\rangle + \frac{1}{2}\|h\|^2 \,\middle|\, P_0\right) = \varepsilon_0$$

where $E = (\Omega, \mathscr{A}, \{P_h: h \in H\})$ denotes a Gaussian shift and

$$X := \sum_{i=1}^{k} \left(\log \frac{dP_{e_i}}{dP_0} + \frac{1}{2}\right) e_i$$

is a central map (cf. Example 69.7 (4)). □

80.7 Definition. Suppose that E_n, $n \in \mathbb{N}$, is asymptotically normal. Then every sequence of random variables X_n: $\Omega_n \to H$, $n \in \mathbb{N}$, satisfying conditions (1) and (2) of Corollary 80.6 is called a *central sequence* for $(E_n)_{n \in \mathbb{N}}$.

80.8 Example. Suppose that M is an open subset of a finite dimensional linear manifold with underlying linear space H. Let $E = (\Omega, \mathscr{A}, \{P_x: x \in M\})$ be an experiment which is differentiable with injective derivatives.

(1) (One-sample problem). Consider the product experiments $E^n = (\Omega^n, \mathscr{A}^n, \{P_y^n: y \in M\})$, $n \in \mathbb{N}$. We stabilize by a scale transformation around some fixed point $x \in M$ and obtain

$$E_n = (\Omega^n, \mathscr{A}^n, \{P^n_{x+h\cdot n^{-1/2}}: h \in H_n\}),$$

where $H_n = \{h \in H: \; x + \frac{1}{\sqrt{n}} h \in M\}$, $n \in \mathbb{N}$. Since the triangular array $t_{ni} := \frac{1}{\sqrt{n}} h$, $1 \leqq i \leqq n$, $n \in \mathbb{N}$, satisfies conditions 79.1 (1) and (2), we obtain from Theorem 79.2 that

$$\frac{dP^n_{x+hn^{-1/2}}}{dP^n_x}(\underline{\omega}) = \exp\left(B_x\left(h, \frac{1}{\sqrt{n}} \sum_{i=1}^{n} g_x(\omega_i)\right) - \frac{1}{2} B_x(h, h) + o_{P^n_x}(1)\right),$$

$\underline{\omega} \in \Omega^n$, $n \in \mathbb{N}$, $h \in H$. Since

$$\mathscr{L}\left(\underline{\omega} \mapsto \frac{1}{\sqrt{n}} \sum_{i=1}^{n} g_x(\omega_i) \,\middle|\, P^n_x\right) \to \nu_{0, P_x(g_x \otimes g_x)}$$

weakly, and since $P_x(g_x \otimes g_x) = B_x$, it follows that $\nu_{0, P_x(g_x \otimes g_x)} = N_{(H, B_x)}$ and the assumptions of Corollary 80.6 are satisfied. Hence, (E_n) converges weakly to the Gaussian shift on (H, B_x). A central sequence is given by

$$X_n: \underline{\omega} \mapsto \frac{1}{\sqrt{n}} \sum_{i=1}^{n} g_x(\omega_i), \quad \underline{\omega} \in \Omega^n, \; n \in \mathbb{N}.$$

(2) (Two-sample problem). Consider the product experiments

$$E^n = (\Omega^n, \mathscr{A}^n, \{P_{y_1}^{k_1(n)} \otimes P_{y_2}^{k_2(n)}: (y_1, y_2) \in M^2\}),$$

where $k_1(n) + k_2(n) = n$, $n \in \mathbb{N}$, and

$$\lim_{n\to\infty} \frac{k_1(n)}{n} = \alpha \in (0,1), \quad \lim_{n\to\infty} \frac{k_2(n)}{n} = \beta \in (0,1).$$

If we stabilize by a scale transformation around some fixed point $(x, x) \in M^2$ then we obtain

$$E_n = (\Omega^n, \mathscr{A}^n, \{P^{k_1(n)}_{x+h_1 n^{-1/2}} \otimes P^{k_2(n)}_{x+h_2 n^{-1/2}}: (h_1, h_2) \in H_n^2\}, \quad n \in \mathbb{N}.$$

Since the triangular array

$$t_{ni} = \begin{cases} \dfrac{1}{\sqrt{n}} h_1 & \text{if} \quad 1 \leqq i \leqq k_1(n), \\ \dfrac{1}{\sqrt{n}} h_2 & \text{if} \quad k_1(n)+1 \leqq i \leqq n, \end{cases} \qquad n \in \mathbb{N},$$

satisfies conditions 79.1 (1) and (2), we obtain from Theorem 79.2 that

$$\frac{d(P^{k_1(n)}_{x+h_1/\sqrt{n}} \otimes P^{k_2(n)}_{x+h_2/\sqrt{n}})}{dP^n_x}(\underline{\omega})$$
$$= \exp\Bigg(B_x(h_1, \frac{1}{\sqrt{n}} \sum_{i=1}^{k_1(n)} g_x(\omega_i)) + B_x(h_2, \frac{1}{\sqrt{n}} \sum_{i=k_1(n)+1}^{n} g_x(\omega_i))$$
$$- \frac{1}{2}\left(\frac{k_1(n)}{n} B_x(h_1, h_1) + \frac{k_2(n)}{n} B_x(h_2, h_2) \right) + o_{P^n_x}(1) \Bigg)$$
$$= \exp\Bigg(\alpha B_x(h_1, \sqrt{n} \frac{1}{k_1(n)} \sum_{i=1}^{k_1(n)} g_x(\omega_i))$$
$$+ \beta B_x(h_2, \sqrt{n} \frac{1}{k_2(n)} \sum_{i=k_1(n)+1}^{n} g_x(\omega_i))$$
$$- \frac{1}{2}(\alpha B_x(h_1, h_1) + \beta B_x(h_2, h_2)) + o_{P^n_x}(1) \Bigg),$$

$\underline{\omega} \in \Omega^n$, $n \in \mathbb{N}$, $(h_1, h_2) \in H^2$. On H^2 we define an inner product by

$$\left\langle\!\left\langle \begin{pmatrix} h_1 \\ h_2 \end{pmatrix}, \begin{pmatrix} \overline{h_1} \\ \overline{h_2} \end{pmatrix} \right\rangle\!\right\rangle := \alpha B_x(h_1, \overline{h_1}) + \beta B_x(h_2, \overline{h_2}).$$

Then it follows similarly as under part (1) that (E_n) converges weakly to the Gaussian shift on $(H^2, \langle\!\langle .,. \rangle\!\rangle)$. A central sequence is given by

$$X_n\colon \underline{\omega} \mapsto \begin{pmatrix} \sqrt{n} \dfrac{1}{k_1(n)} \displaystyle\sum_{i=1}^{k_1(n)} g_x(\omega_i) \\ \sqrt{n} \dfrac{1}{k_2(n)} \displaystyle\sum_{i=k_1(n)+1}^{n} g_x(\omega_i) \end{pmatrix}, \qquad \underline{\omega} \in \Omega^n, \ n \in \mathbb{N}.$$

80.9 Lemma. *Suppose that $(E_n)_{n \in \mathbb{N}}$ is asymptotically normal. Then any central sequences $(X_n)_{n \in \mathbb{N}}$ and $(Y_n)_{n \in \mathbb{N}}$ satisfy*

$$X_n(h) - Y_n(h) \to 0 \ (P_{n,0}), \quad h \in H.$$

Proof. Obvious by definition. □

The criterion for centrality in Theorem 80.12 is prepared by two lemmas.

80.10 Lemma. *Suppose that $(E_n)_{n\in\mathbb{N}}$ is asymptotically normal. A sequence of linear processes (X_n) is central iff for all $h_1, h_2 \in H$*

$$\mathcal{L}\left(\log\frac{dP_{n,h_1}}{dP_{n,0}}, X_n(h_2)\middle| P_{n,0}\right) \to \nu_{a,M} \quad \textit{weakly},$$

where

$$a = \begin{pmatrix} -\frac{1}{2}\|h_1\|^2 \\ 0 \end{pmatrix}, \qquad M = \begin{pmatrix} \|h_1\|^2 & \langle h_1, h_2\rangle \\ \langle h_1, h_2\rangle & \|h_2\|^2 \end{pmatrix}.$$

Proof. It is obvious that

$$\mathcal{L}(L_n(h_1), L_n(h_2)| P_{n,0}) \to \nu_{0,M} \quad \text{weakly}.$$

If (X_n) is central then this implies that

$$\mathcal{L}(L_n(h_1), X_n(h_2)| P_{n,0}) \to \nu_{0,M} \quad \text{weakly}.$$

Conversely, if the latter is true, then

$$\mathcal{L}(L_n(h) - X_n(h)| P_{n,0}) \to \varepsilon_0 \quad \text{weakly},$$

which implies $L_n(h) - X_n(h) = o_{P_{n,0}}(1)$, $h \in H$. □

80.11 Lemma. *Suppose that $(E_n)_{n\in\mathbb{N}}$ is asymptotically normal. If a sequence of linear processes (X_n) is central, then*

$$\mathcal{L}\left(\log\frac{dP_{n,h_1}}{dP_{n,0}}, X_n(h_2)\middle| P_{n,h_1}\right) \to \nu_{b,M} \quad \textit{weakly}$$

where

$$b = \begin{pmatrix} -\frac{1}{2}\|h_1\|^2 \\ \langle h_1, h_2\rangle \end{pmatrix}.$$

Proof. Let $f \in \mathscr{C}_{00}(\mathbb{R}^2)$ and $h_1, h_2 \in H$. Then with the notation of the preceding lemma we have

$$\begin{aligned}\lim_{n\to\infty} \int f\left(\log\frac{dP_{n,h_1}}{dP_{n,0}}, X_n(h_2)\right) dP_{n,h_1} &= \int_{\mathbb{R}^2} f(x,y)\, e^x\, \nu_{a,M}(dx,dy) \\ &= \int_{\mathbb{R}^2} f(x,y)\, \nu_{b,M}(dx,dy). \qquad \square\end{aligned}$$

For the following assertion recall Example 68.7 (2), according to which the distribution of a linear process is a cylinder set measure. Weak convergence or convolution of cylinder set measures $\mu = (\mu_L)_{L \in \mathscr{L}}$ has to be interpreted in terms of their components μ_L, $L \in \mathscr{L}$.

80.12 Theorem. *Suppose that (E_n) is asymptotically normal. A sequence of linear processes (X_n) is central iff*

$$\mathscr{L}(X_n | P_{n,h}) \to N_H * \varepsilon_h \quad \textit{weakly}, \quad h \in H.$$

Proof. In view of the preceding lemma it is clear that every central sequence has the asserted property. Conversely, the condition implies

$$\mathscr{L}(X_n(h_1) | P_{n,h_2}) \to \nu_{\langle h_1, h_2 \rangle, \|h_1\|^2} \quad \text{weakly}$$

for all $h_1, h_2 \in H$. A standard argument shows that for every $h \in H$, $c \in \mathbb{R}$ and $n \in \mathbb{N}$

$$\left(1_{\left\{\frac{dP_{n,h}}{dP_{n,0}} > e^{c - \frac{1}{2}\|h\|^2}\right\}} - 1_{\{X_n(h) > c\}}\right)\left(\frac{dP_{n,h}}{dP_{n,0}} - e^{c - \frac{1}{2}\|h\|^2}\right) \geqq 0 \quad P_{n,0} - \text{a.e.}$$

Moreover, by contiguity the $P_{n,0}$-expectations of these expressions converge to zero as $n \to \infty$. This implies that

$$P_{n,0}\left| 1_{\left\{\log \frac{dP_{n,h}}{dP_{n,0}} > c - \frac{1}{2}\|h\|^2\right\}} - 1_{\{X_n(h) > c\}} \right| \to 0,$$

for every $h \in H$, $c \in \mathbb{R}$. Now it is easy to see that

$$\log \frac{dP_{n,h}}{dP_{n,0}} = X_n(h) - \frac{1}{2}\|h\|^2 + o_{P_{n,0}}(1), \quad h \in H, \, n \in \mathbb{N}.$$

To show this fact, put $Y_n = \log \frac{dP_{n,h}}{dP_{n,0}} + \frac{1}{2}\|h\|^2$ and $Z_n = X_n(h)$, $n \in \mathbb{N}$. Since the distributions of (Y_n) and (Z_n) are uniformly tight, we may assume that they are concentrated on some compact $K \subseteq \mathbb{R}$. We know that for every $c \in \mathbb{R}$

$$\lim_{n \to \infty} P_{n,0}\{Y_n \leqq c < Z_n\} = 0, \quad \text{and} \quad \lim_{n \to \infty} P_{n,0}\{Z_n \leqq c < Y_n\} = 0.$$

Let $\varepsilon > 0$ and let $\{c_1, \ldots, c_N\}$ be an ε-net of K. Then

$$P_{n,0}\{|Y_n - Z_n| > \varepsilon\} \leqq \sum_{i=1}^{N} P_{n,0}\{Y_n \leqq c_i < Z_n\} + \sum_{i=1}^{N} P_{n,0}\{Z_n \leqq c_i < Y_n\},$$

which proves the assertion. □

Since a Gaussian shift is continuous any sequence $(E_n)_{n \in \mathbb{N}}$ which is asymptotically normal is continuous in the limit. However, such a sequence need not be equicontinuous. Recall that a sequence of continuous experiments is equicontinuous if for every $h \in H$ and every $\varepsilon > 0$ there exists a $\delta(\varepsilon, h) > 0$ such that

$$h_1 \in H_n,\ \|h_1 - h\| < \delta(\varepsilon, h) \quad \text{imply} \quad d_1(P_{n,h}, P_{n,h_1}) < \varepsilon .$$

80.13 Theorem. *Suppose that $(E_n)_{n\in\mathbb{N}}$ is an asymptotically normal sequence of continuous experiments and denote*

$$\frac{dP_{n,h}}{dP_{n,0}} = \exp\left(X_n(h) - \frac{1}{2}\|h\|^2 + r_n(h)\right), \quad h \in H_n,\ n \in \mathbb{N},$$

where $(X_n)_{n\in\mathbb{N}}$ is a central sequence. Then $(E_n)_{n\in\mathbb{N}}$ is equicontinuous on compact subsets $K \subseteq H$ iff any of the following conditions is satisfied:

(1) *For every convergent sequence $h_n \in H_n$, $n \in \mathbb{N}$, and every $\varepsilon > 0$*

$$\lim_{n\to\infty} P_{n,0}\{|r_n(h_n)| > \varepsilon\} = 0 .$$

(2) *For every compact $K \subseteq H$ and every $\varepsilon > 0$*

$$\lim_{n\to\infty} \sup_{h\in K} P_{n,0}\{|r_n(h)| > \varepsilon\} = 0 .$$

Proof. It is clear that conditions (1) and (2) are equivalent. Assume first, that $(E_n)_{n\in\mathbb{N}}$ is equicontinuous on compacts. Let $\lim\limits_{n\to\infty} h_n = h$. Then we have $\lim\limits_{n\to\infty} d_1(P_{n,h_n}, P_{n,h}) = 0$ and therefore

$$\lim_{n\to\infty} \int \left| \frac{dP_{n,h_n}}{dP_{n,0}} - \frac{dP_{n,h}}{dP_{n,0}} \right| dP_{n,0} = 0 .$$

This implies

$$\log \frac{dP_{n,h_n}}{dP_{n,0}} - \log \frac{dP_{n,h}}{dP_{n,0}} \to 0 \quad (P_{n,0})$$

which proves (1).

Assume conversely that (1) is satisfied. Choose $\delta(\varepsilon, h) > 0$ such that

$$d_2(\varepsilon_{h_1} * N_H, \varepsilon_h * N_H) < \frac{\varepsilon}{2\sqrt{2}} \quad \text{if} \quad |h_1 - h| \leqq \delta(\varepsilon, h).$$

If $(E_n)_{n\in\mathbb{N}}$ were not equicontinuous on compacts then there is a compact subset $K \subseteq H$ and $h \in K$ such that we may find a sequence of points $h_n \in K$, $|h_n - h| < \delta(\varepsilon, h)$, $n \in \mathbb{N}$, with

$$d_1(P_{n,h_n}, P_{n,h}) \geqq \varepsilon \quad \text{for some} \quad \varepsilon > 0 .$$

W.l.g. we assume that $(h_n)_{n\in\mathbb{N}}$ converges to $h_0 \in K$. Then it follows by Definition 80.1 and by Theorem 60.3 (4), that

$$\mathscr{L}\left(\log \frac{dP_{n,h}}{dP_{n,h}} \,\middle|\, P_{n,h}\right) \to \mathscr{L}\left(\log \frac{d(\varepsilon_{h_0} * N_H)}{d(\varepsilon_h * N_H)} \,\middle|\, \varepsilon_h * N_H\right), \quad \text{weakly.}$$

This implies

$$\begin{aligned}\limsup_{n\to\infty} d_1(P_{n,h_n}, P_{n,h}) &\leqq \sqrt{2} \lim_{n\to\infty} d_2(P_{n,h_n}, P_{n,h}) \\ &= \sqrt{2}\, d_2(\varepsilon_{h_0} * N_H, \varepsilon_h * N_H) < \frac{\varepsilon}{2}\end{aligned}$$

which contradicts the construction of $(h_n)_{n\in\mathbb{N}}$. □

If H is a Euclidean space then equicontinuity on compacts is equivalent to equicontinuity. In this case the convergent sequence (h_n) of condition (1) may be replaced by a bounded one, which is not necessarily convergent.

80.14 Example. The sequences (E_n) considered in Example 80.8 (1) and (2), are equicontinuous. This is clear since Theorem 79.2 remains applicable if the triangular arrays are defined to be

$$t_{ni} := \frac{1}{\sqrt{n}}\, h_n, \quad 1 \leqq i \leqq n,\ n \in \mathbb{N},$$

and

$$t_{ni} := \begin{cases} \dfrac{1}{\sqrt{n}}\, h_{n,1} & \text{if } \ 1 \leqq i \leqq k_1(n), \\ \dfrac{1}{\sqrt{n}}\, h_{n,2} & \text{if } \ k_1(n)+1 \leqq i \leqq n, \end{cases} \qquad n \in \mathbb{N},$$

respectively, where (h_n), $(h_{n,1})$ and $(h_{n,2})$ are convergent sequences in H.

80.15 Example. Consider the case of Example 80.4. The sequence (E_n) considered there is equicontinuous on compacts. To show this let $(g_n) \subseteq H$ be a convergent sequence. Then $P_{1/\sqrt{n}\cdot g_n}$ is given by

$$\sqrt{\frac{dP_{1/\sqrt{n}\cdot g_n}}{dv}} = \sqrt{\frac{dP_0}{dv}} \cdot \left|\left(\frac{1}{2\sqrt{n}}\, g_n + \sqrt{1 - \frac{1}{4n} P_0(g_n^2)}\right)\right|, \quad n \in \mathbb{N}.$$

Then arguments of part (2) of the proof of Theorem 75.2 imply that

$$\lim_{n\to\infty} \int \left[n\left(\sqrt{\frac{dP_{1/\sqrt{n}\cdot g_n}}{dv}} - \sqrt{\frac{dP_0}{dv}}\right) - \frac{1}{2} g_n \cdot \sqrt{\frac{dP_0}{dv}}\right]^2 dv = 0.$$

It follows by Corollary 75.9 (and the remark below Corollary 75.9) that the expansion

$$\frac{dP^n_{1/\sqrt{n}\cdot g_n}}{dP^n_0}(\omega) = \exp\left(\frac{1}{\sqrt{n}}\sum_{i=1}^n g_n(\omega_i) - \frac{1}{2}\|g_n\|^2_{P_0} + o_{P^n_0}(1)\right),$$

$\underline{\omega} \in \Omega^n$, $n \in \mathbb{N}$, is valid. Hence the assertion.

We finish this section with the discussion of an important example.

80.16 Example (Hajek and Sidak [1967] and Moussatat [1976]). Consider the case discussed in Theorem 79.2. For simplicity let $M = \mathbb{R}$. Define $H = \{h \in L^2([0,1]): \int_0^1 h\,d\lambda = 0\}$ and let

$$c_{ni}(h) := n \int_{\frac{i-1}{n}}^{\frac{i}{n}} h\,d\lambda, \quad 1 \leqq i \leqq n,\ h \in H.$$

It is then clear that $\sum_{i=1}^n c_{ni}(h) = 0$, $n \in \mathbb{N}$, $h \in H$. Fix $x \in \mathbb{R}$ and define

$$P_{n,h} := \prod_{i=1}^n P_{x+\frac{1}{\sqrt{n}}c_{ni}(h)}, \quad h \in H,\ n \in \mathbb{N}.$$

The triangular arrays $\left(\frac{1}{\sqrt{n}}c_{ni}(h)\right)_{1\leqq i \leqq n}$, $n \in \mathbb{N}$, satisfy 79.1 (1) and (2) for every $h \in H$. Therefore Theorem 79.2 yields the expansion

$$\begin{aligned}\frac{dP_{n,h}}{dP_{n,0}}(\underline{\omega}) &= \exp\left(\frac{1}{\sqrt{n}}\sum_{i=1}^n B_x(c_{ni}(h), g_x(\omega_i))\right.\\ &\qquad \left.- \frac{1}{2n}\sum_{i=1}^n B_x(c_{ni}(h), c_{ni}(h)) + o_{P_{n,0}}(1)\right)\\ &= \exp\left(B_x(1,1)\cdot\frac{1}{\sqrt{n}}\sum_{i=1}^n c_{ni}(h)\,g_x(\omega_i)\right.\\ &\qquad \left.- \frac{1}{2}B_x(1,1)\frac{1}{n}\sum_{i=1}^n c^2_{ni}(h) + o_{P_{n,0}}(1)\right),\end{aligned}$$

$\underline{\omega} \in \Omega^n$, $n \in \mathbb{N}$. Let $X_n\colon \Omega^n \to H$ be defined as

$$X_n\colon \underline{\omega} \mapsto \sqrt{n}\sum_{i=1}^n g_x(\omega_i)\cdot 1_{\left[\frac{i-1}{n},\frac{i}{n}\right)}, \quad \underline{\omega} \in \Omega^n,$$

and note that part (1) of the proof of Theorem 79.5 implies

$$\lim_{n\to\infty} \frac{1}{n} \sum_{i=1}^{n} c_{ni}^2(h) = \|h\|^2, \quad h \in H.$$

This gives the expansion

$$\frac{dP_{n,h}}{dP_{n,0}} = \exp\left(B_x(1,1)\langle X_n, h\rangle - \frac{1}{2} B_x(1,1)\|h\|^2 + o_{P_{n,0}}(1)\right), \quad n \in \mathbb{N}.$$

The central limit theorem implies

$$\mathscr{L}(\langle X_n, h\rangle \mid P_{n,0}) \to \nu_{0,\|h\|^2} \quad \text{weakly}.$$

Hence, by Theorem 80.3 the sequence of experiments

$$E_n = (\Omega^n, \mathscr{A}^n, \{P_{n,h}: h \in H\}), \quad n \in \mathbb{N},$$

is asymptotically normal for $(H, B_x(1,1)\langle .,.\rangle)$.

From the expansion it is clear that the sequence (X_n) is central in the sense of Definition (80.7). In case $\Omega = \mathbb{R}$ and $\frac{dP_x}{d\lambda} = f(.-x)$, $x \in \mathbb{R}$, the discussion of Example (79.4) tells us that also

$$X_n: \underset{\sim}{\omega} \mapsto \frac{1}{I}\sqrt{n} \sum_{i=1}^{n} \int_{(R_{ni}(\omega)-1)/n}^{R_{ni}(\omega)/n} \varphi\, d\lambda \cdot 1_{\left[\frac{i-1}{n}, \frac{i}{n}\right)}, \quad \underset{\sim}{\omega} \in \Omega^n,$$

is a central sequence for (E_n).

If $(h_n) \subseteq H$ is a convergent sequence then the triangular array $\left(\frac{1}{\sqrt{n}} c_{ni}(h_n)\right)_{1 \le i \le n}$, $n \in \mathbb{N}$, satisfies 79.1 (1) and (2), too. It follows that (E_n) is equicontinuous on compact subsets of H.

81. Exponential approximation and asymptotic sufficiency

The first assertion we prove states that a sequence $(E_n)_{n\in\mathbb{N}}$ which is asymptotically normal may be approximated in a stronger sense by a sequence of exponential experiments.

81.1 Theorem (LeCam [1960]). *Let $(H, \langle .,.\rangle)$ be a Euclidean space. Suppose that $(E_n)_{n\in\mathbb{N}}$ is asymptotically normal. Then there exists a sequence of exponential experiments $F_n = (\Omega_n, \mathscr{A}_n, \{Q_{n,h}: h \in H_n\})$, $n \in \mathbb{N}$, satisfying*

$$\lim_{n\to\infty} d_1(P_{n,h}, Q_{n,h}) = 0, \quad h \in H.$$

Let $(X_n)_{n\in\mathbb{N}}$ be a central sequence of random variables. The exponential experi-

ments F_n can be chosen such that

(1) $Q_{n,h} \ll P_{n,0}, \quad h \in H_n, n \in \mathbb{N}$,

$$(2) \quad \frac{dQ_{n,h}}{dP_{n,0}} = C_n(h) \exp(\langle h, X_n^* \rangle - \frac{1}{2}\|h\|^2), \quad h \in H_n, n \in \mathbb{N},$$

where

$$(3) \quad X_n^* = X_n \cdot 1_{\{\|X_n\| \leqq k_n\}}, n \in \mathbb{N}, k_n \uparrow \infty,$$

$$(4) \quad \lim_{n\to\infty} \sup_{\|h\| \leqq a} |C_n(h) - 1| = 0, \quad a > 0.$$

Proof. For convenience we introduce the notations

$$f_{n,h}(\omega_n) = \frac{dP_{n,h}}{dP_{n,0}}(\omega_n), \quad \omega_n \in \Omega_n,$$

$$g_{n,h}(\omega_n) = \frac{dQ_{n,h}}{dP_{n,0}}(\omega_n), \quad \omega_n \in \Omega_n,$$

$$\mu_h = \mathscr{L}(\exp|\nu_{-\frac{1}{2}\|h\|^2, \|h\|^2}), \quad h \in H.$$

First step: We show that the truncation $(k_n)_{n \in \mathbb{N}}$ can be chosen such that for every $a > 0$

$$\lim_{n\to\infty} \sup_{\|h\| \leqq a} |C_n(h) - 1| = 0.$$

Note that the family of functions

$$x \mapsto f_i(x, h) := \begin{cases} \exp(\langle x, h \rangle - \frac{1}{2}\|h\|^2) & \text{if } \|x\| \leqq i, \\ \exp(-\frac{1}{2}\|h\|^2) & \text{if } \|x\| > i, \end{cases}$$

$\|h\| \leqq i$, is uniformly bounded and equicontinuous on $\{\|x\| \leqq i\}$ for every $i \in \mathbb{N}$. This implies (applying e.g. Bhattacharya and Rao [1976: Theorem 2.4]) that

$$\lim_{n\to\infty} \sup_{\|h\| \leqq i} |\int f_i(x, h) \mathscr{L}(X_n | P_{n,0})(dx) - \int f_i(x, h) N_H(dx)| = 0$$

for every $i \in \mathbb{N}$. A standard argument yields a sequence $k_n \uparrow \infty$ such that

$$\lim_{n\to\infty} \sup_{\|h\| \leqq k_n} |\int f_{k_n}(x, h) \mathscr{L}(X_n | P_{n,0})(dx) - \int f_{k_n}(x, h) N_H(dx)| = 0.$$

Defining $X_n^* := X_n 1_{\{\|X_n\| \leqq k_n\}}$ we obtain

$$\lim_{n\to\infty} \sup_{\|h\| \leqq a} |\int \exp(\langle h, X_n^* \rangle - \frac{1}{2}\|h\|^2) \, dP_{n,0} - (N_H * \varepsilon_h)\{\|x\| \leqq k_n\}| = 0$$

for every $a>0$. Obviously, this implies

$$\lim_{n\to\infty} \sup_{\|h\|\leqq a} \left| \int \exp\left(\langle h, X_n^*\rangle - \frac{1}{2}\|h\|^2\right) dP_{n,0} - 1 \right| = 0, \quad a>0.$$

Since

$$C_n(h) = 1 \Big/ \int \exp\left(\langle h, X_n^*\rangle - \frac{1}{2}\|h\|^2\right) dP_{n,0}$$

the assertion is proved.

Second step: We note that

$$\limsup_{n\to\infty} d_1(P_{n,h}, Q_{n,h}) = \frac{1}{2} \limsup_{n\to\infty} \int |f_{n,h} - g_{n,h}| \, dP_{n,0}, \quad h\in H.$$

This is an immediate consequence of contiguity.

Let us prove that $\lim_{n\to\infty} |f_{n,h} - g_{n,h}| = 0 \ (P_{n,0})$ for every $h\in H$. Note that for every $\varepsilon>0$ there exists $c_\varepsilon<\infty$ such that

$$\lim_{n\to\infty} P_{n,0}\{\|X_n\| \geqq c_\varepsilon\} \leqq \varepsilon.$$

Let $d(\varepsilon) := \exp\left(c_\varepsilon\|h\| - \frac{1}{2}\|h\|^2\right)$. If we denote

$$r_n(h) := \log \frac{dP_{n,h}}{dP_{n,0}} - \langle h, X_n\rangle + \frac{1}{2}\|h\|^2, \quad h\in H,$$

then

$$\begin{aligned}
|f_{n,h} - g_{n,h}| &\leqq \left|f_{n,h} - \exp\left(\langle h, X_n^*\rangle - \frac{1}{2}\|h\|^2\right)\right| \\
&\quad + \left|\exp\left(\langle h, X_n^*\rangle - \frac{1}{2}\|h\|^2\right) - g_{n,h}\right| \\
&= \exp\left(\langle h, X_n\rangle - \frac{1}{2}\|h\|^2\right) \cdot \left|\exp r_n(h) - \exp(\langle h, X_n^*\rangle - \langle h, X_n\rangle)\right| \\
&\quad + \exp\left(\langle h, X_n^*\rangle - \frac{1}{2}\|h\|^2\right) |C_n(h) - 1|
\end{aligned}$$

implies

$$\begin{aligned}
&P_{n,0}\{|f_{n,h} - g_{n,h}| > \varepsilon\} \\
&\quad \leqq P_{n,0}\left\{\exp\left(\|h\|\cdot\|X_n\| - \frac{1}{2}\|h\|^2\right) > d(\varepsilon)\right\} \\
&\quad + P_{n,0}\left\{\left|\exp r_n(h) - \exp(\langle h, X_n^* > - \langle h, X_n\rangle)\right| > \frac{\varepsilon}{2d(\varepsilon)}\right\} \\
&\quad + P_{n,0}\left\{|C_n(h) - 1| > \frac{\varepsilon}{2d(\varepsilon)}\right\}.
\end{aligned}$$

This proves the assertion.

Third step: We prove that $(f_{n,h})_{n\in\mathbb{N}}$ is uniformly $(P_{n,0})$-integrable for every $h\in H$. By Lemma 6.12 we have to show that

$$\lim_{n\to\infty} \mathscr{L}(f_{n,h}|P_{n,0}) = \mu_h \quad \text{vaguely, and}$$

$$\lim_{n\to\infty} \int s\mathscr{L}(f_{n,h}|P_{n,0})(ds) = \int s\mu_h(ds).$$

The first equation is obvious. Moreover, we know that $\int s\mu_h(ds) = 1$. The second assertion follows from

$$\lim_{n\to\infty} \int s\mathscr{L}(f_{n,h}|P_{n,0})(ds) = \lim_{n\to\infty} \int \frac{dP_{n,h}}{dP_{n,0}}\, dP_{n,0}$$

and from contiguity.

Forth step: We note that $(g_{n,h})_{n\in\mathbb{N}}$ is uniformly $(P_{n,0})$-integrable for every $h\in H$. This is proved in the same way as in the 3rd step. In the present case this is almost immediate. □

81.2 Corollary. *Assume that the conditions of Theorem 81.1 are satisfied. If the sequence $(E_n)_{n\in\mathbb{N}}$ is even equicontinuous then the assertion of the preceding theorem can be improved to*

$$\lim_{n\to\infty} \sup_{\|h\|\leqq a} d_1(P_{n,h}, Q_{n,h}) = 0, \quad a>0.$$

The exponential approximation is closely related to the concept of asymptotic sufficiency.

81.3 Definition. Let $\mathscr{B}_n \subseteq \mathscr{A}_n$ be sub-σ-fields, $n\in\mathbb{N}$. The sequence $(\mathscr{B}_n)$ is *asymptotically sufficient* for (E_n) if

$$\lim_{n\to\infty} \left|\int \varphi_n dP_{n,h} - \int P_{n,0}(\varphi_n|\mathscr{B}_n)\, dP_{n,h}\right| = 0$$

for every sequence of critical functions $\varphi_n \in \mathscr{F}(\Omega_n, \mathscr{A}_n)$, $n\in\mathbb{N}$, and every $h\in H$.

81.4 Theorem. *Let H be a Hilbert space. If (E_n) is asymptotically normal and (X_n) is a central sequence in the sense of Definition 80.7 then $(\mathscr{A}(X_n))$ is asymptotically sufficient for (E_n).*

Proof. (1) Assume that H is of finite dimension. Then we may apply the exponential approximation of Theorem 81.1. Since $\mathscr{A}(X_n)$ is sufficient for F_n we have

$$\int_{A_n} \varphi_n dQ_{n,h} = \int_{A_n} Q_{n,0}(\varphi_n|\mathscr{A}(X_n))\, dQ_{n,h},$$

$A_n \in \mathscr{B}_n$, $\varphi_n \in \mathscr{F}(\Omega_n, \mathscr{A}_n)$, $n\in\mathbb{N}$, $h\in H_n$. This proves the assertion.

(2) If H is not of finite dimension let $h \in H$ and define $L = \{th: t \in \mathbb{R}\}$. Then $(\mathscr{A}(\langle h, X_n\rangle))$ is asymptotically sufficient for $(E_n|_{L \cap H_n})$. This implies that for every sequence $(\varphi_n)_{n \in \mathbb{N}}$

$$\lim_{n\to\infty} |\int \varphi_n dP_{n,h} - \int P_{n,0}(\varphi_n | \mathscr{A}(\langle h, X_n\rangle))\, dP_{n,h}| = 0.$$

Applying the exponential approximation to the subspace L we obtain

$$\begin{aligned}&\int P_{n,0}(\varphi_n|\mathscr{A}(\langle h, X_n\rangle))\, dP_{n,h}\\ &\quad = \int P_{n,0}(\varphi_n|\mathscr{A}(\langle h, X_n\rangle)) \frac{dQ_{n,h}}{dP_{n,0}}\, dP_{n,0} + o(1)\end{aligned}$$

and since $\mathscr{A}(\langle h, X_n\rangle) \subseteq \mathscr{A}(X_n)$ and $\dfrac{dQ_{n,h}}{dP_{n,0}}$ is $\mathscr{A}(\langle h, X_n\rangle)$-measurable, $n \in \mathbb{N}$, it follows that

$$\begin{aligned}&\int P_{n,0}(\varphi_n|\mathscr{A}(\langle h, X_n\rangle))\, dP_{n,h}\\ &\quad = \int P_{n,0}(\varphi_n|\mathscr{A}(X_n))\, dQ_{n,h} + o(1)\\ &\quad = \int P_{n,0}(\varphi_n|\mathscr{A}(X_n))\, dP_{n,h} + o(1).\end{aligned}$$

This proves that

$$\lim_{n\to\infty} |\int \varphi_n dP_{n,h} - \int P_{n,0}(\varphi_n|\mathscr{A}(X_n))\, dP_{n,h}| = 0. \qquad \square$$

A similar argument as in the preceding proof shows that every sequence of σ-fields $\mathscr{A}_n \supseteq \mathscr{A}(X_n)$, $n \in \mathbb{N}$, is asymptotically sufficient for (E_n).

81.5 Corollary. *If (E_n) is asymptotically normal and equicontinuous, and if (X_n) is a central sequence in the sense of Definition 80.7 then $\mathscr{A}(X_n)$ is asymptotically sufficient for (E_n) uniformly on compact subsets of H, i.e.*

$$\lim_{n\to\infty} \sup_{h\in K} |\int_{A_n} \varphi_n dP_{n,h} - \int_{A_n} P_{n,0}(\varphi_n|\mathscr{A}(X_n))\, dP_{n,h}| = 0$$

for every compact $K \subseteq H$, every sequence $A_n \in \mathscr{A}(X_n)$, $n \in \mathbb{N}$, and every sequence $\varphi_n \in \mathscr{F}(\Omega_n, \mathscr{A}_n)$, $n \in \mathbb{N}$.

81.6 Example (Hájek and Sidák [1967]). Consider Example 80.16 and especially the case $\Omega = \mathbb{R}$, $\dfrac{dP_x}{d\lambda} = f(.-x)$, $x \in \mathbb{R}$. For every $n \in \mathbb{N}$ let $\mathscr{B}_n = \mathscr{A}(R_{n1}, \ldots, R_{nn})$, i.e. the σ-field generated by the vector of ranks. Then $(\mathscr{B}_n)$ is asymptotically sufficient for (E_n) uniformly on compacts.

Another application of the exponential approximation is concerned with posterior distributions. For this, we have to restrict ourselves to Euclidean spaces $(H, \langle .,. \rangle)$. Let F_n be the posterior distribution with respect to the Lebesgue measure $\lambda_H|\mathscr{B}(H_n)$. In the following we assume that $\mathring{H}_n \uparrow H$.

81.7 Theorem. *Assume that* $(H, \langle .,. \rangle)$ *is a Euclidean space. Suppose that* $(E_n)_{n\in\mathbb{N}}$ *is an asymptotically normal sequence of continuous,* λ_H*-integrable experiments and* $(X_n)_{n\in\mathbb{N}}$ *is a central sequence for* (E_n). *Then*

$$\lim_{n\to\infty} \int d_1(F_n(.\,|K), (N_H * \varepsilon_{X_n})(.\,|K))\, dP_{n,0} = 0$$

for every compact $K \subseteq H$.

Proof. We keep the notation of the proof of Theorem 81.1. Then we have by Theorem 36.14

$$F_n(B) = \frac{\int_{B\cap H_n} f_{n,h}\,\lambda_H(dh)}{\int_{H_n} f_{n,h}\,\lambda_H(dh)}, \quad B \in \mathscr{B}(H),\ n \in \mathbb{N}.$$

Let us denote

$$G_n(B) := \frac{\int_{B\cap H_n} g_{n,h}\lambda_H(dh)}{\int_{H_n} g_{n,h}\lambda_H(dh)}, \quad B \in \mathscr{B}(H),\ n \in \mathbb{N}.$$

If $K \subseteq H$ is compact then for $n \geqq n_K$

$$\int_K \left| \frac{f_{n,h}}{\int_K f_{n,h}\lambda_H(dh)} - \frac{g_{n,h}}{\int_K g_{n,h}\lambda_H(dh)} \right| \lambda_H(dh)$$

$$= \int_K \left| \frac{f_{n,h}}{\int_K f_{n,h}\lambda_H(dh)} - \frac{f_{n,h}}{\int_K g_{n,h}\lambda_H(dh)} + \frac{f_{n,h}}{\int_K g_{n,h}\lambda_H(dh)} \right.$$

$$\left. - \frac{g_{n,h}}{\int_K g_{n,h}\lambda_H(dh)} \right| \lambda_H(dh)$$

$$\leqq \int_K f_{n,h}\lambda_H(dh) \frac{\left|\int_K f_{n,h}\lambda_H(dh) - \int_K g_{n,h}\lambda_H(dh)\right|}{\int_K f_{n,h}\lambda_H(dh)\cdot \int_K g_{n,h}\lambda_H(dh)}$$

$$+ \frac{1}{\int_K g_{n,h}\lambda(dh)} \int |f_{n,h} - g_{n,h}|\,\lambda_H(dh)$$

$$\leqq 2\,\frac{\int_K |f_{n,h} - g_{n,h}|\,\lambda_H(dh)}{\int_K g_{n,h}\lambda_H(dh)}.$$

This implies that

$$d_1(F_n(.|K), G_n(.|K))$$
$$\leqq 2 \frac{1}{\int_K C_n(h) \exp(\langle h, X_n^* \rangle - \frac{1}{2}\|h\|^2) \lambda_H(dh)}$$
$$\cdot \int_K |f_{n,h} - C_n(h) \exp(\langle h, X_n^* \rangle - \frac{1}{2}\|h\|^2)| \lambda_H(dh).$$

Choosing $a > 0$ arbitrarily and denoting

$$M_n := \left\{ \int_K C_n(h) \exp(\langle h, X_n^* \rangle - \frac{1}{2}\|h\|^2) \lambda_H(dh) \geqq \int_K C_n(h) \exp(-\|h\| a - \frac{1}{2}\|h\|^2) \lambda_H(dh) \right\}$$

we obtain

$$\int d_1(F_n(.|K), G_n(.|K)) \, dP_{n,0}$$
$$\leqq P_{n,0}(M_n') + \int_{M_n} d_1(F_n(.|K), G_n(.|K)) \, dP_{n,0}$$
$$\leqq P_{n,0}\{|X_n| > a\} + \frac{2 \int_K d_1(P_{n,h}, Q_{n,h}) \lambda_H(dh)}{\int_K C_n(h) \exp(-\|h\| a - \frac{1}{2}\|h\|^2) \lambda_H(dh)}.$$

This implies

$$\lim_{n \to \infty} \int d_1(F_n(.|K), G_n(.|K)) \, dP_{n,0} = 0$$

since $a > 0$ is arbitrary. Thus it remains to prove the assertion for G_n, $n \in \mathbb{N}$, instead of F_n, $n \in \mathbb{N}$.

For this we note that

$$\frac{\int_B \exp(\langle h, X_n^* \rangle - \frac{1}{2}\|h\|^2) \lambda_H(dh)}{\int \exp(\langle h, X_n^* \rangle - \frac{1}{2}\|h\|^2) \lambda_H(dh)} = (N_H * \varepsilon_{X_n^*})(B),$$

$B \in \mathscr{B}(H)$, $n \in \mathbb{N}$.

Similar reasoning as at the beginning yields

$$d_1(G_n(.|K), (N_H * \varepsilon_{X_n^*})(.|K)) \leq \frac{2 \int_K |C_n(h) - 1| \exp(\langle h, X_n^* \rangle - \frac{1}{2}\|h\|^2)\, \lambda_H(dh)}{\int_K \exp(\langle h, X_n^* \rangle - \frac{1}{2}\|h\|^2)\, \lambda_H(dh)}$$

$$\leq 2 \sup_{h \in K} |C_n(h) - 1|$$

for every compact $K \subseteq H$ and therefore

$$\lim_{n \to \infty} \int d_1(F(.|K), (N_H * \varepsilon_{X_n^*})(.|K))\, dP_{n,0} = 0.$$

Since

$$N_H * \varepsilon_{X_n} \neq N_H * \varepsilon_{X_n^*} \quad \text{iff} \quad \|X_n\| > k_n, \quad n \in \mathbb{N},$$

it follows that

$$\limsup_{n \to \infty} \int d_1(N_H * \varepsilon_{X_n^*}, N_H * \varepsilon_{X_n})\, dP_{n,0} = \lim_{n \to \infty} P_{n,0}\{\|X_n\| > k_n\} = 0$$

which proves the assertion. □

As a consequence we obtain a result which goes back to Bernstein and von Mises.

81.8 Corollary (LeCam, Wolfowitz [1953]). *If under the assumptions of Theorem 81.7 the sequence of posterior distribution is uniformly tight then*

$$\lim_{n \to \infty} \int d_1(F_n, N_H * \varepsilon_{X_n})\, dP_{n,0} = 0.$$

82. Application to testing hypotheses

Let $(H, \langle .,. \rangle)$ be a Hilbert space. Suppose that the sequence of experiments $E_n = (\Omega_n, \mathscr{A}_n, \{P_{n,h}: h \in H_n\})$, $n \in \mathbb{N}$, is asymptotically normal. Let $E = (\Omega, \mathscr{A}, \{P_h: h \in H\})$ be a Gaussian shift on H.

The basic idea is to handle testing problems for (E_n) by a transition to the limit experiment. For limit experiments which are Gaussian shifts linear testing problems admit a complete solution. However, the original testing problems for (E_n) need not be of a linear type. Nevertheless, transition to the limit transfers "smooth" testing problems into linear ones provided that the sequence (E_n) is obtained by a localization of the original parameter space.

We begin with some remarks on how a suitable localization of the parameter space transfers smooth testing problems into linear ones.

82.1 Discussion (The idea of localization). Suppose that M is an open subset of a linear manifold with underlying linear space T. Let $E_n = (\Omega_n, \mathscr{A}_n, \{P_{n,x}: x \in M\})$, $n \in \mathbb{N}$, be a sequence of experiments. Usually, testing hypotheses takes place around a fixed parameter point $x_0 \in M$ which is either known by prior experience or the result of an initial estimate. Statistical inference aims at the detection and the measurement of a deviation of the true value $x \in M$ from the starting point $x_0 \in M$.

Typically, $d_1(P_{n,x}, P_{n,y}) \to 1$ as $n \to \infty$ if $x \neq y$. Hence, the situation of the statistician is very different for different sample sizes $n \in \mathbb{N}$ and one cannot expect that the situation with small sample size can be approximated well by situations with large sample size. For an acceptable approximation it is necessary that at least the magnitude of $d_1(P_{n,x}, P_{n,y})$ behaves qualitatively stable as $n \to \infty$.

In many cases the key for the solution of this problem is a reparametrization of the sequence (E_n). Let us call the sequence (E_n) *localizable* at $x_0 \in M$ with $\delta_n \downarrow 0$, if

$$0 < \liminf_{n\to\infty} d_1(P_{n,x_0}, P_{n,x_0+\delta_n t}) \leqq \limsup_{n\to\infty} d_1(P_{n,x_0}, P_{n,x_0+\delta_n t}) < \infty$$

for $t \in T$, $t \neq 0$.

In such a case define $Q_{n,t} := P_{n,x_0+\delta_n t}$, $t \in T$, $n \in \mathbb{N}$, whenever $x_0 + \delta_n t \in M$. Consider the sequence of experiments

$$F_n = (\Omega_n, \mathscr{A}_n, \{Q_{n,t}: t \in \frac{1}{\delta_n}(M - x_0)\}), \quad n \in \mathbb{N}.$$

The sequence (F_n) satisfies for every $t \in T$

$$0 < \liminf_{n\to\infty} d_1(Q_{n,0}, Q_{n,t}) \leqq \limsup_{n\to\infty} d_1(Q_{n,0}, Q_{n,t}) < 1$$

iff $t \neq 0$. Thus, any weak limit experiment F of (F_n) is a non-degenerate one.

82.2 Example. Let M be an open subset of a finite dimensional linear manifold with underlying linear space T. Suppose that $E = (\Omega, \mathscr{A}, \{P_x: x \in M\})$ is a differentiable experiment with injective derivative at each $x \in M$. Assume further that $x \mapsto P_x$ is a homeomorphism. Then $x \mapsto P_x$ is even a diffeomorphism (considered as mapping from M into $L^2(\Omega, \mathscr{A}, \nu)$ for some dominating measure $\nu|\mathscr{A}$). We shall prove that (E^n) is localizable at every $x \in M$ with $\delta_n = n^{-1/2}$, $n \in \mathbb{N}$. We shall even prove the considerably stronger result that

(1) $$0 < \liminf_{n\to\infty} n\, d_2^2(P_x^n, P_{x+t_n/\sqrt{n}}^n) \leqq \limsup_{n\to\infty} n\, d_2^2(P_x^n, P_{x+t_n/\sqrt{n}}^n) < \infty$$

iff

(2) $$0 < \liminf_{n\to\infty} |t_n| \leqq \limsup_{n\to\infty} |t_n| < \infty .$$

Differentiability and regularity of the derivative together with Remark 76.7 imply that

$$(3)\quad 0<\liminf_{n\to\infty}\frac{d_2(P_x^n, P_{x+s_n}^n)}{|s_n|}\leqq\limsup_{n\to\infty}\frac{d_2(P_x^n, P_{x+s_n}^n)}{|s_n|}<\infty$$

whenever $s_n \to 0$. Thus, if (t_n) satisfies (2) it is immediate that (t_n) satisfies (1). Conversely, if (t_n) satisfies (1) then $t_n/\sqrt{n} \to 0$ since $x \mapsto P_x$ is a homeomorphism. Hence, (3) may be applied to $s_n = t_n/\sqrt{n}$ which yields that (t_n) satisfies (2).

82.3 Example. Consider the case of Example (80.4). Then the sequence (E^n) is localizable at $g = 0$ with $\delta_n = n^{-1/2}$, $n \in \mathbb{N}$. To see this recall from the proof of Theorem 75.2 that

$$\lim_{n\to\infty} n\,d_2^2(P_0, P_{g\cdot n^{-1/2}}) = \frac{1}{8}P_0(g^2).$$

This implies that

$$0<\liminf_{n\to\infty} n\,d_2^2(P_0, P_{g\cdot n^{-1/2}}) \leqq \limsup_{n\to\infty} n\,d_2^2(P_0, P_{g\cdot n^{-1/2}})<\infty$$

iff $g \neq 0$.

82.4 Discussion (Localization of testing problems). Keep the notation of Discussion 82.1. Let $f: M \to \mathbb{R}$ be differentiable at $x_0 \in M$, $f(x_0) = 0$, and $Df(x_0) \neq 0$. Consider the problem of testing $H_0 = \{f \leqq 0\}$, $K_0 = \{f > 0\}$ near x_0. A sequence of critical function (φ_n) is asymptotically unbiased of level $\alpha \in [0,1]$ for (H_0, K_0) if

$$\limsup_{n\to\infty} P_{n,x_n}\varphi_n \leqq \alpha \quad \text{if} \quad (x_n) \subseteq H_0,$$

$$\liminf_{n\to\infty} P_{n,x_n}\varphi_n \geqq \alpha \quad \text{if} \quad (x_n) \subseteq K_0,$$

for a sufficiently large class of sequences (x_n) such that (P_{n,x_n}) cannot be separated completely from (P_{n,x_0}), i.e.

$$\limsup_{n\to\infty} d_1(P_{n,x_0}, P_{n,x_n}) < 1.$$

This implies that

$$\limsup_{n\to\infty} P_{n,x_0+\delta_n t}\varphi_n \leqq \alpha \quad \text{if} \quad f(x_0+\delta_n t) \leqq 0,\ n \in \mathbb{N},$$

$$\liminf_{n\to\infty} P_{n,x_0+\delta_n t}\varphi_n \geqq \alpha \quad \text{if} \quad f(x_0+\delta_n t) > 0,\ n \in \mathbb{N},$$

for every $t \in H$.

Now, let (E_n) be equicontinuous. Then it is not difficult to show that a sequence of critical functions (φ_n) is asymptotically unbiased of level α for (H, K) iff

$$\limsup_{n\to\infty} P_{n,x_0+\delta_n t}\varphi_n \leqq \alpha \quad \text{if} \quad Df(x_0)(t) \leqq 0,$$

$$\liminf_{n\to\infty} P_{n,x_0+\delta_n t}\varphi_n \geqq \alpha \quad \text{if} \quad Df(x_0)(t) > 0.$$

Thus, in terms of the localized sequence (F_n) the critical functions (φ_n) are asymptotically unbiased of level α for the linear testing problem $H_1 = \{Df(x) \leqq 0\}$, $K_1 = \{Df(x) > 0\}$.

The preceding remarks indicate how the analysis of "smooth" testing problems in asymptotically normal situations can be reduced to the analysis of linear testing problems. In the following we restrict our interest to linear testing problems.

We begin with the analysis of testing problems concerning a continuous linear function $f\colon H \to \mathbb{R}$. The corresponding non-asymptotic theory has been discussed in Sections 28 and 71. First, we consider one-sided testing problems. Let $H_1 = \{h \in H\colon f(h) \leqq 0\}$, $K_1 = \{h \in H\colon f(h) > 0\}$.

82.5 Definition. (1) A sequence of critical functions $\varphi_n \in \mathscr{F}(\Omega_n, \mathscr{A}_n)$, $n \in \mathbb{N}$, is *asymptotically unbiased* of level $\alpha \in [0,1]$ for the testing problem (H_1, K_1) if

$$\limsup_{n\to\infty} P_{n,h}\varphi_n \leqq \alpha \quad \text{if} \quad f(h) \leqq 0, \quad \text{and}$$

$$\liminf_{n\to\infty} P_{n,h}\varphi_n \geqq \alpha \quad \text{if} \quad f(h) > 0.$$

(2) A sequence of critical functions $\varphi_n \in \mathscr{F}(\Omega_n, \mathscr{A}_n)$, $n \in \mathbb{N}$, is *asymptotically similar* of level $\alpha \in [0,1]$ for the testing problem (H_1, K_1) if

$$\lim_{n\to\infty} P_{n,h}\varphi_n = \alpha \quad \text{if} \quad f(h) = 0.$$

A sequence which is asymptotically unbiased of level α is asymptotically similar of level α. This is true since the sequence $(E_n)_{n\in\mathbb{N}}$ is continuous in the limit.

82.6 Lemma. *If a sequence of tests $\varphi_n \in \mathscr{F}(\Omega_n, \mathscr{A}_n)$, $n \in \mathbb{N}$, is asymptotically similar of level α for the testing problem (H_1, K_1) then*

$$\limsup_{n\to\infty} P_{n,h}\varphi_n \leqq \Phi\left(N_\alpha + \frac{f(h)}{\|f\|}\right) \quad \textit{if} \quad f(h) > 0,$$

$$\liminf_{n\to\infty} P_{n,h}\varphi_n \geqq \Phi\left(N_\alpha + \frac{f(h)}{\|f\|}\right) \quad \textit{if} \quad f(h) \leqq 0.$$

Proof. Apply Theorem 62.5 with $T_1 = \{h\}$. Note that the set $\mathscr{B}$ of accumulation points of (φ_n) is contained in $\mathscr{F}_\alpha^s(H_1, K_1)$ and so does $\overline{\text{co}}\,\mathscr{B}$. Thus, it follows that

$$\limsup_{n\to\infty} P_{n,h}\varphi_n \leqq \sup_{\varphi\in\mathscr{F}_\alpha^s(H_1,K_1)} P_h\varphi \quad \text{if} \quad f(h) > 0,$$

$$\liminf_{n\to\infty} P_{n,h}\varphi_n \geqq \inf_{\varphi\in\mathscr{F}_\alpha^s(H_1,K_1)} P_h\varphi \quad \text{if} \quad f(h) \leqq 0.$$

Now the assertion follows from Lemma 71.1. □

82.7 Definition. Suppose that $(\varphi_n)_{n\in\mathbb{N}}$ is asymptotically similar of level α for (H_1, K_1). Then $(\varphi_n)_{n\in\mathbb{N}}$ is *asymptotically optimal* of level α for (H_1, K_1) at $h \in H$ if

$$\lim_{n\to\infty} P_{n,h}\varphi_n = \Phi\left(N_\alpha + \frac{f(h)}{\|f\|}\right), \quad h\in H.$$

In the following we identify f with a point of H, i.e. "$f = \langle .,f\rangle$".

82.8 Theorem. *Let $(L_n)_{n\in\mathbb{N}}$ be defined as in Theorem (80.2). A sequence of critical functions $\varphi_n \in \mathscr{F}(\Omega_n, \mathscr{A}_n)$, $n\in\mathbb{N}$, is asymptotically optimal of level α for (H_1, K_1) iff it is stochastically equivalent to the sequence*

$$\psi_n = \begin{cases} 1 & \text{if} \quad L_n(f) > \|f\| N_{1-\alpha}, \\ 0 & \text{if} \quad L_n(f) < \|f\| N_{1-\alpha}, \end{cases} \qquad n\in\mathbb{N}.$$

Proof. It is clear from Theorem 80.12 that the sequence (ψ_n) is asymptotically optimal of level α for (H_1, K_1). Hence every sequence (φ_n) which is stochastically equivalent to (ψ_n) shares the optimality. Let us prove the converse by Theorem 63.6. Let X be central for the limit experiment E. Then (ψ_n) converges in distribution to

$$\psi = \begin{cases} 1 & \text{if} \quad f\circ X > \|f\| N_{1-\alpha}, \\ 0 & \text{if} \quad f\circ X \leqq \|f\| N_{1-\alpha}. \end{cases}$$

Now, ψ is non-randomized and by Theorem (71.3) ψ is uniquely determined by its distribution. Hence the assertion. □

82.9 Corollary. *If a sequence of critical functions $\varphi_n \in \mathscr{F}(\Omega_n, \mathscr{A}_n)$, $n\in\mathbb{N}$, which is asymptotically similar of level α for (H_1, K_1), is asymptotically optimal at some $h\in H$ with $f(h) \neq 0$, then it is asymptotically optimal.*

Proof. Every accumulation point $\varphi \in \mathscr{F}(H, \mathscr{B}(H))$ of $(\varphi_n)_{n\in\mathbb{N}}$ is similar of level α and optimal at $f(h) \neq 0$. From Corollary 71.4 it follows that φ is uniformly optimal. By Theorem 71.3, φ is the only accumulation point of $(\varphi_n)_{n\in\mathbb{N}}$ and $(\varphi_n)_{n\in\mathbb{N}}$ converges to φ in distribution. This proves the assertion. □

82.10 Remark. If there exists a central sequence (X_n) of processes for (E_n) then

$$\psi_n = \begin{cases} 1 & \text{if } f \circ X_n > \|f\| N_{1-\alpha}, \\ 0 & \text{if } f \circ X_n < \|f\| N_{1-\alpha}, \end{cases} \qquad n \in \mathbb{N},$$

is asymptotically optimal of level α for (H_1, K_1).

Now we turn to two-sided testing problems. From now on let $H_2 = \{h \in H: f(h) = 0\}$, $K_2 = \{h \in H: f(h) \neq 0\}$.

82.11 Definition. A sequence of critical functions $\varphi_n \in \mathscr{F}(\Omega_n, \mathscr{A}_n)$, $n \in \mathbb{N}$, is *asymptotically unbiased* of level $\alpha \in [0,1]$ for the testing problem (H_2, K_2) if

$$\limsup_{n \to \infty} P_{n,h} \varphi_n \leqq \alpha \quad \text{if} \quad f(h) = 0, \quad \text{and}$$

$$\liminf_{n \to \infty} P_{n,h} \varphi_n \geqq \alpha \quad \text{if} \quad f(h) \neq 0.$$

82.12 Lemma. *If a sequence of critical functions $\varphi_n \in \mathscr{F}(\Omega_n, \mathscr{A}_n)$, $n \in \mathbb{N}$, is asymptotically unbiased of level α for (H_2, K_2) then*

$$\limsup_{n \to \infty} P_{n,h} \varphi_n \leqq \Phi\left(N_{\alpha/2} + \frac{f(h)}{\|f\|}\right) + \Phi\left(N_{\alpha/2} - \frac{f(h)}{\|f\|}\right), \quad h \in H.$$

Proof. From Theorem 62.5 it follows similarly to the proof of Lemma 82.6 that

$$\limsup_{n \to \infty} P_{n,h} \varphi_n \leqq \sup_{\varphi \in \mathscr{F}_\alpha(H_2, K_2)} P_h \varphi, \quad h \in H.$$

Now the assertion follows from Lemma 71.5. □

82.13 Definition. Suppose that $(\varphi_n)_{n \in \mathbb{N}}$ is asymptotically unbiased of level α for (H_2, K_2). Then $(\varphi_n)_{n \in \mathbb{N}}$ is *asymptotically optimal* of level α for (H_2, K_2) at $h \in H$ if

$$\lim_{n \to \infty} P_{n,h} \varphi_n = \Phi\left(N_{\alpha/2} + \frac{f(h)}{\|f\|}\right) + \Phi\left(N_{\alpha/2} - \frac{f(h)}{\|f\|}\right).$$

82.14 Theorem. *Let $(L_n)_{n \in \mathbb{N}}$ be defined as in Theorem 80.2. A sequence of critical functions $\varphi_n \in \mathscr{F}(\Omega_n, \mathscr{A}_n)$, $n \in \mathbb{N}$, is asymptotically optimal of level α for (H_2, K_2) iff it is stochastically equivalent to the sequence*

$$\psi_n = \begin{cases} 1 & \text{if } |L_n(f)| > \|f\| N_{1-\frac{\alpha}{2}}, \\ 0 & \text{if } |L_n(f)| < \|f\| N_{1-\frac{\alpha}{2}}, \end{cases} \qquad n \in \mathbb{N}.$$

Proof. The proof is similar to the proof of Theorem 82.8 employing Theorem 71.7 instead of 71.3. □

82.15 Corollary. *If a sequence of critical functions $\varphi_n \in \mathscr{F}(\Omega_n, \mathscr{A}_n)$, $n \in \mathbb{N}$, which is asymptotically unbiased of level α for (H_2, K_2), is asymptotically optimal at some $h \in H$ with $f(h) \neq 0$, then it is asymptotically optimal.*

Proof. The proof is similar to the proof of Corollary 82.9. □

82.16 Remark. If there exists a central sequence (X_n) of processes for (E_n) then

$$\psi_n = \begin{cases} 1 & \text{if} \quad |f \circ X_n| > \|f\| \, N_{1-\alpha}, \\ 0 & \text{if} \quad |f \circ X_n| < \|f\| \, N_{1-\alpha}, \end{cases} \qquad n \in \mathbb{N},$$

is asymptotically optimal of level α for (H_2, K_2).

82.17 Example. Let us consider the two-sample problem for the location-scale family of the Gaussian distribution. We have to combine Examples 80.8 (2), and 78.9. The parameter space $U = \mathbb{R} \times (0, \infty)$ has the tangent space $H = \mathbb{R}^2$. Therefore, the sequence (E_n) converges weakly to the Gaussian shift on $(\mathbb{R}^4, \ll .,\, \gg)$, where

$$\ll \begin{pmatrix} s_1 \\ s_2 \\ s_3 \\ s_4 \end{pmatrix}, \begin{pmatrix} t_1 \\ t_2 \\ t_3 \\ t_4 \end{pmatrix} \gg = (s_1, s_2) \begin{pmatrix} \dfrac{1}{\sigma^2} & 0 \\ 0 & \dfrac{1}{2\sigma^4} \end{pmatrix} \begin{pmatrix} t_1 \\ t_2 \end{pmatrix}$$

$$+ (s_3, s_4) \begin{pmatrix} \dfrac{1}{\sigma^2} & 0 \\ 0 & \dfrac{1}{2\sigma^4} \end{pmatrix} \begin{pmatrix} t_3 \\ t_4 \end{pmatrix}$$

and $x = (a, \sigma^2)$. A central sequence is given by

$$X_n \colon \underline{\omega} \mapsto \begin{pmatrix} \sqrt{n} \dfrac{1}{k_1(n)} \sum\limits_{i=1}^{k_1(n)} \begin{pmatrix} \omega_i - a \\ (\omega_i - a)^2 - \sigma^2 \end{pmatrix} \\ \sqrt{n} \dfrac{1}{k_2(n)} \sum\limits_{i=k_1(n)+1}^{n} \begin{pmatrix} \omega_i - a \\ (\omega_i - a)^2 - \sigma^2 \end{pmatrix} \end{pmatrix}, \quad \underline{\omega} \in \Omega^n,\ n \in \mathbb{N}.$$

Let $f(a_1, \sigma_1^2, a_2, \sigma_2^2) = a_1 - a_2$, which yields $Df(a, \sigma^2)\,(s_1, s_2, s_3, s_4) = s_1 - s_3$. We have

$$Df(a, \sigma^2) = \ll \begin{pmatrix} \sigma^2 \\ 0 \\ -\sigma^2 \\ 0 \end{pmatrix}, . \gg$$

and thus obtain that $\| Df(a, \sigma^2) \| = \sqrt{2\sigma^2}$. Therefore an optimal sequence of critical functions for (H_1, K_1) is given by

$$\varphi_n = \begin{cases} 1 \\ & \text{if } \dfrac{\sqrt{n}\left(\dfrac{1}{k_1(n)}\sum\limits_{i=1}^{k_1(n)}\omega_i - \dfrac{1}{k_2(n)}\sum\limits_{i=k_1(n)+1}^{n}\omega_i\right)}{\sqrt{2\sigma^2}} \begin{matrix} > \\ \\ < \end{matrix} N_{1-\alpha}, \\ 0 \end{cases}$$

$n \in \mathbb{N}$. To eliminate the dependence on σ^2 one may replace $2\sigma^2$ by

$$\frac{1}{k_1(n)}\sum_{i=1}^{k_1(n)}\omega_i^2 + \frac{1}{k_2(n)}\sum_{i=k_1(n)+1}^{n}\omega_i^2 - \left(\frac{1}{k_1(n)}\sum_{i=1}^{k_1(n)}\omega_i\right)^2 - \left(\frac{1}{k_2(n)}\sum_{i=k_1(n)+1}^{n}\omega_i\right)^2$$

which gives a stochastically equivalent sequence of critical functions not depending on $x = (a, \sigma^2)$.

82.18 Example. Consider Example 80.4 and let $\varphi: \Omega \to \mathbb{R}$ be $\mathscr{A}$-measurable and bounded. Let $f: P \mapsto \int \varphi\, dP - \int \varphi\, dP_0$, $P \ll P_0$, and consider the non-parametric testing problem $H_1 = \{f \leqq 0\}$, $K_1 = \{f > 0\}$.

Since, as is easily seen,

$$f(P_g) = \frac{1}{4}\int \varphi g^2\, dP_0 + \sqrt{1 - \frac{1}{4}P_0(g^2)}\int g\varphi\, dP_0 = \int g\varphi\, dP_0 + o(\sqrt{P_0(g^2)})$$

we have $Df(P_0): g \mapsto \int \varphi g\, dP_0$, $g \in H$, which means that $(\varphi - P_0(\varphi)) \in H$ is the derivative of f at P_0. Thus, we obtain an asymptotically optimal sequence of critical functions

$$\psi_n(\underline{\omega}) = \begin{cases} 1 \text{ if } \dfrac{1}{\sqrt{n}}\sum\limits_{i=1}^{n}(\varphi(\omega_i) - P_0(\varphi)) > \|\varphi - P_0(\varphi)\|_{P_0}\cdot N_{1-\alpha}, \\ 0 \text{ if } \dfrac{1}{\sqrt{n}}\sum\limits_{i=1}^{n}(\varphi(\omega_i) - P_0(\varphi)) < \|\varphi - P_0(\varphi)\|_{P_0}\cdot N_{1-\alpha}, \end{cases}$$

$\underline{\omega} \in \Omega^n$, $n \in \mathbb{N}$.

82.19 Remark. The preceding example is a little more subtle if $\varphi \in L^2(\Omega, \mathscr{A}, P_0)$ is not bounded. The point is that in this case f is only defined on a dense subset of H, but has a derivative in H. Thus, the localized testing problem $(\{Df(P_0) \leqq 0\}, \{Df(P_0) > 0\})$ may be treated as above, but its relation to the original testing problem $(\{f \leqq 0\}, \{f > 0\})$ must be treated more carefully than it has been done in Discussion 82.4. This topic is treated in the literature under the label "von Mises-functionals". The reader will easily note that Discussion 82.4 can be carried through when f is only defined on a dense subset of M, but has a derivative in the tangent space of M.

Now, we turn to linear testing problems. Let $L_0 \subseteq H$ be a linear subspace of finite codimension and consider the testing problem $H_3 = L_0$, $K_3 = H \setminus L_0$. The corresponding non-asymptotic theory has been discussed in Sections 30 and 71.

82.20 Definition. A sequence of critical functions $\varphi_n \in \mathscr{F}(\Omega_n, \mathscr{A}_n)$, $n \in \mathbb{N}$, is *asymptotically unbiased* of level $\alpha \in [0, 1]$ for the testing problem (H_3, K_3) if

$$\limsup_{n\to\infty} P_{n,h}\varphi_n \leqq \alpha \quad \text{if} \quad h \in L_0,$$

$$\liminf_{n\to\infty} P_{n,h}\varphi_n \geqq \alpha \quad \text{if} \quad h \in H \setminus L_0.$$

For the following, we denote $B_c = \{h \in H: \|h - p_{L_0}(h)\| = c\}$, $c > 0$.

82.21 Theorem. *Assume that $(E_n)_{n\in\mathbb{N}}$ is equicontinuous and suppose that (X_n) is a central sequence of processes for (E_n). For $\alpha \in [0, 1]$ let k_α be as in Theorem 71.10. Then the following assertions are true:*

(1) The sequence of critical functions

$$\varphi_n^* = \begin{cases} 1 & \text{if} \quad \|(\mathrm{id} - p_{L_0}) \circ X_n\| > k_\alpha, \\ 0 & \text{if} \quad \|(\mathrm{id} - p_{L_0}) \circ X_n\| < k_\alpha, \end{cases}$$

is asymptotically unbiased of level α for (H_3, K_3).

(2) If (φ_n) is another sequence which is asymptotically unbiased of level α for (H_3, K_3) then

$$\limsup_{n\to\infty} \inf_{h\in B_c} P_{n,h}\varphi_n \leqq \lim_{n\to\infty} \inf_{h\in B_c} P_{n,h}\varphi_n^*.$$

(3) If (φ_n) is any sequence of critical functions satisfying for at least one $c > 0$

$$\limsup_{n\to\infty} P_{n,0}\varphi_n \leqq \alpha, \quad \textit{and}$$

$$\liminf_{n\to\infty} P_{n,h}\varphi_n \geqq \lim_{n\to\infty} P_{n,h}\varphi_n^* \quad \textit{whenever} \quad h \in B_c,\ h \perp L_0,$$

then (φ_n) is stochastically equivalent to (φ_n^*).

Proof. It is clear that (φ_n^*) converges in distribution to the test φ^* of Theorem 71.10. Hence, the assertion follows from Theorem 71.10 and Corollary 71.11, applying Theorems 62.5 and 63.6. □

82.22 Example (Goodness of fit in the discrete case). Consider Example 76.1 and let $p: \Theta \to M$ be a differentiable mapping from an open subset $\Theta \subseteq \mathbb{R}^l$,

$l < k$, into M. We want to consider the testing problem $(\Theta, M \setminus \Theta)$. For this we localize the problem around some point $p(\vartheta) \in M$, $\vartheta \in \Theta$. Then a similar reasoning as that of Discussion (82.4) changes our problem into the testing problem $(L_0, H \setminus L_0)$ where $H = \{t \in \mathbb{R}^k: \sum_{i=1}^{k} t_i = 0\}$ is the tangent space of M and $L_0 = T_{p(\vartheta)}(p(\Theta))$.

The results of Examples 78.1 and 80.8 show that the sequence $E_n = (\Omega^n, \mathscr{A}^n, \{P^n_{p(\vartheta)+t/\sqrt{n}}: t \in H\})$, $n \in \mathbb{N}$, converges to the Gaussian shift on $(H, B_{p(\vartheta)})$ where

$$B_{p(\vartheta)}(s, t) = s' \cdot \begin{pmatrix} \frac{1}{p_1(\vartheta)} & & 0 \\ & \ddots & \\ 0 & & \frac{1}{p_k(\vartheta)} \end{pmatrix} \cdot t, \quad s, t \in H.$$

A central sequence is given by

$$X_n = \frac{1}{\sqrt{n}} \cdot \begin{pmatrix} S_1 - n \cdot p_1(\vartheta) \\ \vdots \\ S_k - n \cdot p_k(\vartheta) \end{pmatrix}, \quad n \in \mathbb{N},$$

where S_j is the frequency of the event j in a sample, $1 \leqq j \leqq k$.

For the construction of the asymptotically optimal sequence of tests according to Theorem 82.21 we have to find a sequence of random variables $Y_n: \Omega^n \to L_0$, which is stochastically equivalent to $(p_{L_0} \circ X_n)$. For this, the usual procedure is as follows: Let $(\hat{\vartheta}_n)$ be a sequence of estimates $\hat{\vartheta}_n: \Omega^n \to \Theta$ such that $(\sqrt{n}(\hat{\vartheta}_n - \vartheta))_{n \in \mathbb{N}}$ is central for $F_{n,\vartheta} = (\Omega^n, \mathscr{A}^n, \{P^n_{p(\vartheta+s/\sqrt{n})}: s \in \mathbb{R}^l\})$, $n \in \mathbb{N}$, for every $\vartheta \in \Theta$. The existence of such estimates is discussed in Section 84. It follows that

$$\sqrt{n}(p(\hat{\vartheta}_n) - p(\vartheta)) = p'(\vartheta)(\sqrt{n}(\hat{\vartheta}_n - \vartheta)) + o_{P^n_{p(\vartheta)}}(1).$$

From Theorem 78.4 we see that $(p'(\vartheta)(\sqrt{n}(\hat{\vartheta}_n - \vartheta)))_{n \in \mathbb{N}}$ is a central sequence for $(E_n | L_0)_{n \in \mathbb{N}}$ and hence stochastically equivalent to $(p_{L_0} \circ X_n)_{n \in \mathbb{N}}$. The same is then true of $(\sqrt{n}(p(\hat{\vartheta}_n) - p(\vartheta)))_{n \in \mathbb{N}}$.

Putting terms together we arrive at an asymptotically optimal sequence of tests of the form

$$\varphi_n^* = \begin{cases} 1 & \text{if } \sum_{j=1}^{k} \frac{(S_j - n p_j(\hat{\vartheta}_n))^2}{n p_j(\vartheta)} > k_\alpha, \\ 0 & \text{if } \sum_{j=1}^{k} \frac{(S_j - n p_j(\hat{\vartheta}_n))^2}{n p_j(\vartheta)} < k_\alpha, \end{cases} \quad n \in \mathbb{N}.$$

The parameter ϑ in the denominator can also be replaced by $(\hat{\vartheta}_n)$, thus obtaining a stochastically equivalent sequence of critical functions. This is the usual χ^2-test for goodness of fit problems in the discrete case.

Our last example deals with the application of Theorem 73.2 to tests of the Kolmogoroff-Smirnoff type.

82.23 Example. (Goodness of fit in the continuous case). Let $P_0|\mathscr{B}_1$ be a non-atomic probability measure with distribution function F_0. We parametrize the set of probability measures $P \ll P_0$ as we have done in Example 80.4, thus obtaining an experiment $E = (\mathbb{R}, \mathscr{B}^1, \{P_g: g \in M\})$ where

$$M = \{g \in H: P_0(g^2) \leqq 4\} \quad \text{and} \quad H = \{g \in L^2(P_0): P_0(g) = 0\}.$$

We want to consider the testing problem $(\{0\}, M \setminus \{0\})$. Localization around P_0 according to 82.3 yields the sequence of experiments

$$E_n = (\mathbb{R}^n, \mathscr{B}^n, \{P^n_{1/\sqrt{n}\cdot g}: g \in H_n\}),$$

where $H_n = \{g \in H: P_0(g^2) \leqq 4n\}$, $n \in \mathbb{N}$. We shall show that the sequence of critical functions (called Kolmogoroff-Smirnoff-tests)

$$\varphi_n^* = \begin{cases} 1 & \text{if } \sup\limits_{\mathbb{R}} \sqrt{n}\,|F_n - F_0| > c, \\[2ex] 0 & \text{if } \sup\limits_{\mathbb{R}} \sqrt{n}\,|F_n - F_0| \leqq c, \end{cases}$$

(where F_n denotes the empirical distribution function for the sample size n), is asymptotically admissible. To be precise, if (φ_n) is any other sequence satisfying

$$\limsup_{n\to\infty} P_0^n \varphi_n \leqq \liminf_{n\to\infty} P_0^n \varphi_n^*, \quad \text{and}$$

$$\liminf_{n\to\infty} P^n_{1/\sqrt{n}\cdot g}\, \varphi_n \geqq \limsup_{n\to\infty} P^n_{1/\sqrt{n}\cdot g}\, \varphi_n^*, \quad g \in H,$$

then it is stochastically equivalent to (φ_n^*). According to Theorems 62.7 and 63.6 we need only show that (φ_n^*) converges in distribution to a critical function φ^* for the limit experiment, which is admissible, non-randomized and uniquely determined by its distribution.

The limit experiment of (E_n) is a Gaussian shift on $H = \{g \in L^2(\mathbb{R}, \mathscr{B}, P_0): \int g\,dP_0 = 0\}$ and by Theorems 70.5 and 70.8 has the representation

$$E = (\mathscr{C}_0(\mathbb{R}), \mathscr{B}(\mathscr{C}_0(\mathbb{R})), \{W_{F_0} * \varepsilon_{\tau(g)}: g \in H\})$$

where $\tau(g): t \mapsto \int\limits_{-\infty}^{t} g\,dP_0$, $t \in \mathbb{R}$. Consider the critical function

$$\varphi^*: x \mapsto \begin{cases} 1 & \text{if } \sup\limits_{\mathbb{R}} |x(t)| > c, \\[2ex] 0 & \text{if } \sup\limits_{t\in\mathbb{R}} |x(t)| \leqq c, \end{cases} \qquad x \in \mathscr{C}_0(\mathbb{R}).$$

By Theorem 73.2, the non-randomized critical function φ^* is admissible and uniquely determined by its distribution. It remains to show that (φ_n^*) converges in distribution to φ^*. But this is an immediate consequence of the wellknown invariance principles for the empirical distribution function. (See e.g. Parthasarathy [1967: Ch. 7, Theorem 9.1]).

82.24 Remark. Replacing in the preceding example the tests φ_n^* by

$$\psi_n^* = \begin{cases} 1 & \text{if} \quad n\int (F_n - F_0)^2 \, dF_0 > c, \\ 0 & \text{if} \quad n\int (F_n - F_0)^2 \, dF_0 \leqq c, \end{cases}$$

(called Cramer-von Mises tests), would lead to a similar conclusion. The reason is that under suitable conditions (ψ_n^*) converges in distribution to

$$\psi^*\colon x \mapsto \begin{cases} 1 & \textit{if} \quad \int x^2 \, dF_0 > c, \\ 0 & \text{if} \quad \int x^2 \, dF_0 \leqq c, \end{cases}$$

and $x \mapsto \int x^2 \, dF_0$, $x \in \mathscr{C}_0(\mathbb{R})$, is a continuous and convex function on $\mathscr{C}_0(\mathbb{R})$.

83. Application to estimation

Consider the same situation as in the preceding section.

83.1 Remark. The application of the results of this section is again mainly concerned with suitable localizations of experiments around some fixed points of the original parameter space (cf. Discussion 82.1). But in contrast to testing, for estimation problems it is usually not possible to treat the problem only locally around some fixed point. It is rather desirable to obtain estimates which have optimum properties for every localization around any point of the original parameter space.

83.2 Discussion (Localization of estimation problems). Keep the notation of Discussions 82.1 and 82.4. Let $f\colon M \to \mathbb{R}$ be differentiable at $x_0 \in M$ and $Df(x_0) \neq 0$. Consider the problem of estimating f which is to be localized around some point $x_0 \in M$.

A sequence of estimates $\kappa_n\colon \Omega^n \to \mathbb{R}$ is asymptotically median unbiased for the estimation of f if

$$\liminf_{n\to\infty} P_{n,x_n}\{\kappa_n \geqq f(x_n)\} \geqq \frac{1}{2},$$

$$\liminf_{n\to\infty} P_{n,x_n}\{\kappa_n \leqq f(x_n)\} \geqq \frac{1}{2},$$

for a sufficiently large class of sequences $(x_n) \subseteq M$ such that (P_{n,x_n}) cannot be separated completely from (P_{n,x_0}). This implies that

$$\liminf_{n\to\infty} P_{n,x_0+\delta_n t}\{\kappa_n \geqq f(x_0+\delta_n t)\} \geqq \frac{1}{2},$$

$$\liminf_{n\to\infty} P_{n,x_0+\delta_n t}\{\kappa_n \leqq f(x_0+\delta_n t)\} \geqq \frac{1}{2},$$

for every $t \in H$. If (E_n) is equicontinuous then it is not difficult to show that (κ_n) is asymptotically median unbiased for f iff

$$\liminf_{n\to\infty} P_{n,x_0+\delta_n t}\left\{\frac{1}{\delta_n}(\kappa_n - f(x_0)) \geqq Df(x_0)(t)\right\} \geqq \frac{1}{2},$$

$$\liminf_{n\to\infty} P_{n,x_0+\delta_n t}\left\{\frac{1}{\delta_n}(\kappa_n - f(x_0)) \leqq Df(x_0)(t)\right\} \geqq \frac{1}{2},$$

for every $t \in H$. Thus, in terms of the localized problem the sequence $\left(\frac{1}{\delta_n}(\kappa_n - f(x_0))\right)_{n\in\mathbb{N}}$ must be asymptotically median unbiased for the estimation of the linear function $Df(x_0)$ on H.

Similarly, we shall call the sequence (κ_n) locally asymptotically optimal in some sense around $x_0 \in M$ if $\left(\frac{1}{\delta_n}(\kappa_n - f(x_0))\right)_{n\in\mathbb{N}}$ is asymptotically optimal for the estimation of $Df(x_0)$ in the respective sense for the localized sequence (E_n). To see the justification for this, note that

$$\int \ell\left(\left|\frac{1}{\delta_n}(\kappa_n - f(x_0+\delta_n t))\right|\right) dP_{n,x_0+\delta_n t}$$
$$= \int \ell\left(\left|\frac{1}{\delta_n}(\kappa_n - f(x_0)) - Df(x_0)(t)\right|\right) dP_{n,x_0+\delta_n t} + o(1)$$

provided that ℓ is sufficiently smooth.

Finally, two sequences of estimates $(\kappa_n^{(1)})$ and $(\kappa_n^{(2)})$ are locally asymptotically equivalent around $x_0 \in M$ if

$$\frac{1}{\delta_n}(\kappa_n^{(1)} - \kappa_n^{(2)}) \to 0\ (P_{n,x_0+\delta_n t}), \quad t \in H.$$

We begin with the problem of estimating a linear function $f\colon H \to \mathbb{R}$. The corresponding non-asymptotic theory has been discussed in Sections 34 and 72.

83.3 Definition. A sequence of estimates $\varrho_n \in \mathscr{R}(E_n, \overline{\mathbb{R}})$, $n \in \mathbb{N}$, is *asymptotically median unbiased* for f if

$$\liminf_{n\to\infty} (\varrho_n P_{n,h})([f(h),\infty]) \geqq \frac{1}{2}, \quad \text{and}$$

$$\liminf_{n\to\infty} (\varrho_n P_{n,h})([-\infty, f(h)]) \geqq \frac{1}{2}$$

for every $h \in H$.

Let $\ell: [0,\infty] \to [0,\infty]$ be a non-decreasing function with $\ell(0) = 0$. Define the loss function by $W_h(x) := \ell(|x - f(h)|)$, $x \in \bar{\mathbb{R}}$, $h \in H$.

83.4 Theorem (Pfanzagl [1970]). *Suppose that ℓ is lower semicontinuous. If $\varrho_n \in \mathscr{R}(E_n, \bar{\mathbb{R}})$, $n \in \mathbb{N}$, is asymptotically median unbiased for f then*

$$\liminf_{n\to\infty} W_h \varrho_n P_{n,h} \geqq \int \ell(|.|)\, d\nu_{0,\|f\|^2}, \quad h \in H.$$

Proof. From Corollary 42.8 we obtain that $\mathscr{B}(E, \bar{\mathbb{R}})$ may be identified with $\mathscr{R}(E, \bar{\mathbb{R}})$. Let $\mathscr{F} \subseteq \mathscr{R}(E, \bar{\mathbb{R}})$ be the set of all median unbiased estimates for f. It is easy to see that $\mathscr{F}$ is weakly closed and convex, and that every accumulation point of (ϱ_n) is in $\mathscr{F}$. Hence, combining Lemma 72.1 and Theorem 62.5 the assertion follows. □

83.5 Theorem (LeCam [1953] and Hájek [1972]). *Suppose that ℓ is lower semicontinuous, of finite order and separating. If a sequence of estimates $\varrho_n \in \mathscr{R}(E_n, \bar{\mathbb{R}})$, $n \in \mathbb{N}$, satisfies*

$$\limsup_{n\to\infty} W_h \varrho_n P_{n,h} \leqq \int \ell(|.|)\, d\nu_{0,\|f\|^2}, \quad h \in H,$$

then (ϱ_n) is stochastically equivalent to $(L_n(f))_{n\in\mathbb{N}}$, ($(L_n)$ is defined as in Theorem 80.2.)

Proof. Every weak accumulation point $\beta \in \mathscr{B}(E, \bar{\mathbb{R}})$ of (ϱ_n) satisfies by Corollary 62.4

$$\beta(W_h, P_h) \leqq \int \ell(|.|)\, d\nu_{0,\|f\|^2}, \quad h \in H.$$

From Theorem 72.4 we obtain that $f \circ X$, where X is central for E, is the only accumulation point of (ϱ_n). Hence, (ϱ_n) and $L_n(f)$ converge to $f \circ X$ in distribution. Now, an application of Theorem 63.6 proves the assertion. □

83.6 Remarks. (1) The preceding assertion also implies that the bound given there is the asymptotic minimax bound. However, it will be seen later, that this is also valid without ℓ being of finite order and separating.

(2) If there exists a central sequence (X_n) for (E_n) then $(L_n(f))$ may be replaced by $(f \circ X_n)$.

83.7 Discussion. (1) At this point we have to discuss the question whether there exist sequences of estimates $(\varrho_n) \in \mathscr{R}(E_n, \bar{\mathbb{R}})$, $n \in \mathbb{N}$, which attain the lower bound in the sense that

$$\lim_{n\to\infty} W_h \varrho_n P_{n,h} = \int \ell(|.|)\,d\nu_{0,\|f\|^2}, \quad h \in H.$$

From Theorem 83.5 we see that such a sequence must be stochastically equivalent to $(L_n(f))_{n\in\mathbb{N}}$. If ℓ is bounded then $(L_n(f))$ in fact attains the asymptotic bound since

$$\mathscr{L}(L_n(f)|P_{n,h}) \to \nu_{f(h),\|f\|^2} \quad \text{weakly}, \quad h \in H,$$

and discontinuities of ℓ do not matter since they are of Lebesgue measure zero. But, if ℓ is unbounded then we have to impose additional conditions to achieve the desired convergence. E.g. if ℓ is of order $p > 0$ then it is sufficient to require that $(L_n(f))$ is uniformly p-times integrable, i.e.

$$\lim_{a\to 0} \sup_{n\in\mathbb{N}} \int_{|L_n(f)|>a} |L_n(f)|^p\,dP_{n,h} = 0, \quad h \in H.$$

(2) Another possibility of dealing with this problem is as follows. For practical purposes it is realistic to suppose that the loss function is bounded and continuous, but it is not realistic to assume that the loss function is known. One has to take into consideration a set $\mathscr{V}$ of bounded continuous loss functions. Let W be the upper envelope of $\mathscr{V}$. With this interpreation the asymptotically interesting risks are rather

(a) $\sup_{V\in\mathscr{V}} \limsup_{n\to\infty} V_h \varrho_n P_{n,h}, \quad h \in H,$

than

(b) $\limsup_{n\to\infty} W_h \varrho_n P_{n,h}, \quad h \in H.$

It is easy to see that the assertions of Theorems 83.4 and 83.5 remain valid replacing (b) by (a). But, doing so it follows that the sequence $(L_n(f))$ attains the bound in any case.

83.8 Example. The famous classical formulations of the preceding results are mainly concerned with the case considered in Discussion 77.5. The local asymptotic estimation problem is concerned with the experiments

$$E_n = (\Omega^n, \mathscr{A}^n, \{P^n_{x+tn^{-1/2}} : t \in H_n\}), \quad n \in \mathbb{N},$$

and estimating the function $x \mapsto x$, $x \in M$, is equivalent to estimating $t \mapsto t$, $t \in H$, for the localized problems. Then a sequence of estimates $\kappa_n: \Omega^n \to M$, $n \in \mathbb{N}$, is locally asymptotically optimal in the sense of Theorems 83.4 and 83.5

(cf. also Discussion 83.2) iff

$$\sqrt{n}\,(\kappa_n(\underline{\omega}) - x) = \frac{1}{I(x)} \cdot \frac{1}{\sqrt{n}} \sum_{i=1}^{n} \frac{h'(\omega_i, x)}{h(\omega_i, x)} 1_{\{h(.,x)>0\}}(\omega_i) + o_{P_x^n}(1),$$

$\underline{\omega} \in \Omega^n$, $n \in \mathbb{N}$. (Centrality follows from 79.4 or 80.8).

83.9 Example. Consider the case of Example 82.18 with $P_0(\varphi) = 0$. Then

$$\kappa_n\colon \underline{\omega} \mapsto \frac{1}{n} \sum_{i=1}^{n} \varphi(\omega_i), \quad \underline{\omega} \in \Omega^n,\ n \in \mathbb{N}$$

is a locally asymptotically optimal sequence of estimates in the sense of Theorems 83.4 and 83.5.

83.10 Example. Let us discuss a generalization of the preceding example. In the literature it is treated under the label of "minimum contrast estimation". Let $\psi(x, t) = (\varphi(x) - t)^2$, $x \in \mathbb{R}$, $t \in \mathbb{R}$. Then f satisfies

$$\int \psi(x, f(P))\, P(dx) = \inf_{t \in \mathbb{R}} \int \psi(x, t)\, P(dx),$$

and the optimal sequence of estimates $\kappa_n\colon \underline{x} \mapsto \frac{1}{n} \sum_{i=1}^{n} \varphi(x_i)$ satisfies

$$(1) \qquad \sum_{i=1}^{n} \psi(x_i, \kappa_n(\underline{x})) = \inf_{t \in \mathbb{R}} \sum_{i=1}^{n} \psi(x_i, t), \quad \underline{x} \in \mathbb{R}^n.$$

This relation between the functional f and the optimal estimator sequence is also valid for more general functions $\psi\colon \mathbb{R}^2 \to \mathbb{R}$.

For simplicity we omit any discussion of regularity conditions. Let $\psi\colon \mathbb{R}^2 \to \mathbb{R}$ be sufficiently smooth and such that

$$t \mapsto \int \psi(x, t)\, P(dx), \quad t \in \mathbb{R},$$

has a unique minimum for every $P \ll P_0$, say $f(P)$. Let

$$\dot{\psi}(x, t) = \frac{\partial}{\partial t} \psi(x, t), \quad \ddot{\psi}(x, t) = \frac{\partial^2}{\partial t^2} \psi(x, t).$$

Then, by the implicit function theorem, the function $g \mapsto f(P_g)$, $g \in H$, has the derivative at P_0

$$g \mapsto -\frac{\int \dot{\psi}(x, f(P_0))\, g\, P_0(dx)}{\int \ddot{\psi}(x, f(P_0))\, P_0(dx)}, \quad g \in H,$$

or in other words

$$\hat{\kappa}_n: \underset{\sim}{x} \mapsto \frac{1}{\int \ddot{\psi}(x, f(P_0))\, P_0(dx)} \left(-\frac{1}{n} \sum_{i=1}^{n} \dot{\psi}(x_i, f(P_0)) \right), \quad \underset{\sim}{x} \in \mathbb{R}^n,$$

is a sequence of estimates which is locally asymptotically optimal in the sense of Theorems 83.4 and 83.5. Suppose that (κ_n) is defined by equation (1) and neglect questions of existence and measurability. Let us show that (κ_n) and $(\hat{\kappa}_n)$ are locally asymptotically equivalent, i.e.

$$\sqrt{n}(\kappa_n - \hat{\kappa}_n) \to 0 \quad (P_0^n).$$

For this, we have to assume that the distributions of $(\sqrt{n}(\kappa_n - f(P_0))_{n \in \mathbb{N}}$ are uniformly tight. This is a consistency property depending on ψ, the proof of which is not discussed in this book. But if tightness is fulfilled, then the expansion

$$\begin{aligned} 0 &= \sum_{i=1}^{n} \dot{\psi}(x_i, \kappa_n(\underset{\sim}{x})) \\ &= \sum_{i=1}^{n} \dot{\psi}(x_i, f(P_0)) + (\kappa_n(\underset{\sim}{x}) - f(P_0)) \sum_{i=1}^{n} \ddot{\psi}(x_i, f(P_0)) + \ldots \end{aligned}$$

yields

$$\begin{aligned} 0 &= \frac{1}{\sqrt{n}} \sum_{i=1}^{n} \dot{\psi}(x_i, f(P_0)) + \\ &\quad + \sqrt{n}(\kappa_n(\underset{\sim}{x}) - f(P_0)) \cdot \frac{1}{n} \sum_{i=1}^{n} \ddot{\psi}(x_i, f(P_0)) + \ldots \end{aligned}$$

which obviously indicates stochastic equivalence of (κ_n) and $(\hat{\kappa}_n)$, (cf. Levit [1975] and Pfanzagl [1982]).

Now, we turn to the problem of estimating a linear mapping $f: H \to \mathbb{R}^k$. The corresponding non-asymptotic theory has been discussed in sections 38 and 72. Let $\ell: \mathbb{R}^k \to [0, \infty)$ be a function and define $W_h(x) := \ell(x - f(h))$, $x \in \mathbb{R}^k$, $h \in H$. Denote by $\mathscr{K}$ the system of all compact subsets of H. Let $L(f) = (\ker f)^\perp$. For convenience we denote (in view of Corollary 72.10)

$$\int \ell \circ f \, dN_H := \int_{L(f)} \ell \circ f \, dN_{L(f)}.$$

83.11 Theorem. *Suppose that $\ell: \mathbb{R}^k \to [0, \infty)$ is lower semicontinuous and subconvex. Then every sequence of estimates $(\varrho_n) \in \mathscr{R}(E_n, \mathbb{R}^k)$ satisfies*

$$\sup_{K \in \mathscr{K}} \liminf_{n \to \infty} \sup_{h \in K} W_h \varrho_n P_{n,h} \geqq \int \ell \circ f \, dN_H.$$

Proof. For fixed $K \in \mathscr{K}$ it follows from Theorem 62.5 that

$$\liminf_{n\to\infty} \sup_{h\in K} W_h \varrho_n P_{n,h} \geqq \inf_{\beta\in\mathscr{B}(E,\mathbb{R}^k)} \sup_{h\in K} \beta(W_h, P_h).$$

An application of the Minimax theorem 46.3 and of Theorem 72.11 yields

$$\sup_{K\in\mathscr{K}} \inf_{\beta\in\mathscr{B}(E,\mathbb{R}^k)} \sup_{h\in K} \beta(W_h, P_h)$$

$$= \inf_{\beta\in\mathscr{B}(E,\mathbb{R}^k)} \sup_{h\in H} \beta(W_h, P_h) = \int \ell \circ f \, dN_H. \qquad \square$$

83.12 Remarks. (1) Perhaps the reader did expect instead of Theorem 83.11 the weaker assertion

$$\liminf_{n\to\infty} \sup_{h\in H_n} W_h \varrho_n P_{n,h} \geqq \int \ell \circ f \, dN_H.$$

But, under general assumptions there is no hope of obtaining estimates (ϱ_n) such that

$$\limsup_{n\to\infty} \sup_{h\in H_n} W_h \varrho_n P_{n,h} = \int \ell \circ f \, dN_H.$$

(2) Suppose that (X_n) is central for (E_n) and X is central for E. Then we have

$$\mathscr{L}(f\circ X_n | P_{n,h}) \to \mathscr{L}(f\circ X | P_h) \quad \text{weakly}, \quad h \in H.$$

If (E_n) is equicontinuous on compacts and if ℓ is bounded and continuous then this implies

$$\lim_{n\to\infty} \sup_{h\in K} \int W_h(f\circ X_n)\, dP_{n,h} = \int \ell \circ f \, dN_H, \quad \text{for all} \quad K \in \mathscr{K}.$$

If ℓ is not bounded and continuous then the remarks of Discussion 83.7 apply.

(3) A particular case arises when $\dim H < \infty$ and $f = \mathrm{id}_H$. Then any central sequence is asymptotically minimax in the sense discussed above.

According to James and Stein [1960] the identity is not an admissible estimate for a finite dimensional Gaussian shift and quadratic loss if $\dim H > 2$. Therefore, an extension of the uniqueness assertion 83.5 cannot be expected, in general. However, a reduction of the class of estimates under consideration leads to an admissibility assertion.

83.13 Definition. A sequence of estimates $\varrho_n \in \mathscr{R}(E_n, \mathbb{R}^k)$, $n \in \mathbb{N}$, is *asymptotically equivariant* (for the estimation of f) if

$$\lim_{n\to\infty} |g \varrho_n P_{n,h} - g(.+f(h)) \varrho_n P_{n,h}| = 0$$

for all $g \in \mathscr{C}_b(\mathbb{R}^k)$ and $h \in H$.

83.14 Remark. Suppose that ℓ is lower semicontinuous and subconvex. If (ϱ_n) is asymptotically equivariant then it is clear from Theorems 62.5 and 72.11 that

$$\liminf_{n\to\infty} W_h \varrho_n P_{n,h} \geqq \int \ell \circ f \, dN_H, \quad h \in H,$$

since every accumulation point of (ϱ_n) has constant risk. If in addition the sequence (ϱ_n) has a limit probability distribution, i.e. if there exists a probability measure $R|\mathscr{B}^k$ such that

$$\lim_{n\to\infty} g \varrho_n P_{n,0} = \int g \, dR, \quad g \in \mathscr{C}_b(\mathbb{R}^k),$$

then

$$R = \mathscr{L}(f \circ X | N_H) * Q$$

where $Q|\mathscr{B}^k$ is another probability measure. This is the famous *asymptotic convolution theorem*, due to Hajek [1970]. The reason is that all accumulation points of (ϱ_n) are equivariant in the sense of 38.26 and have the same distribution which can be represented as a convolution in view of the convolution theorem 38.26.

Now, we arrive at the announced admissibility assertion. Although it is not really necessary we assume that (E_n) possesses a central sequence (X_n).

83.15 Theorem. *Suppose that ℓ is subconvex, level compact, separating and of finite order. If a sequence of estimates $\varrho_n \in \mathscr{R}(E_n, \mathbb{R}^k)$, $n \in \mathbb{N}$, is asymptotically equivariant and satisfies*

$$\limsup_{n\to\infty} W_h \varrho_n P_{n,h} \leqq \int \ell \circ f \, dN_H, \quad h \in H,$$

then $(\varrho_n)_{n\in\mathbb{N}}$ is stochastically equivalent to $(f \circ X_n)_{n\in\mathbb{N}}$ where $(X_n)_{n\in\mathbb{N}}$ is any central sequence of $(E_n)_{n\in\mathbb{N}}$.

Proof. Every weak accumulation point $\beta \in \mathscr{B}(E, \mathbb{R}^k)$ of $(\varrho_n)_{n\in\mathbb{N}}$ is equivariant and satisfies by 62.4 and 72.11

$$\beta(W_h, P_h) = \int \ell \circ f \, dN_H, \quad h \in H.$$

From Corollary 72.13 we obtain that β coincides with the non-randomized estimate $f \circ X$. Therefore $f \circ X$ is the only accumulation point of $(\varrho_n)_{n\in\mathbb{N}}$. Hence $(\varrho_n)_{n\in\mathbb{N}}$ and $(f \circ X_n)_{n\in\mathbb{N}}$ converge to $f \circ X$ in distribution. Now, an application of Theorem 63.6 proves the assertion. □

Let (H, B, τ) be an Abstract Wiener space and $E = (B, \mathscr{B}(B), \{P_h: h \in H\})$ the Gaussian shift where $P_h = P_0 * \varepsilon_{\tau(h)}$, $h \in H$.

83.16 Theorem. *Let $D = B$ and W_h: $x \mapsto \ell(x - \tau(h))$, $x \in B$, $h \in H$, where ℓ: $B \to [0, \infty)$ is lower semicontinuous and subconvex. Then every sequence of* *estimates* $\varrho_n \in \mathscr{R}(E_n, B)$, $n \in \mathbb{N}$, *satisfies*

$$\liminf_{n\to\infty} \sup_{h\in H_n} W_h \varrho_n P_{n,h} \geqq \int \ell \, dP_0 .$$

Proof. Combine Corollary 62.6 and Theorem 73.6. □

Similarly as in Theorem 83.11 it can be shown that even

$$\sup_{a>0} \liminf_{n\to\infty} \sup_{\|h\|\leqq a} W_h \varrho_n P_{n,h} \geqq \int \ell \, dP_0 .$$

83.17 Example (Minimax property of the empirical distribution function. Millar [1979]). Consider the case of Example 80.4. Assume that $\Omega = \mathbb{R}$ and P_0 is non-atomic. For every $P \ll P_0$ let F_P be the distribution function of P. Consider the experiment $E = (\mathbb{R}, \mathscr{B}, \{P|\mathscr{B}: P \ll P_0\})$. We are interested in the estimation of the distribution function F_P. Let $\mathscr{F}$ be the set of all continuous distribution functions on $\mathbb{R}$ and define loss functions

$$L_n: (F, P) \mapsto \sup_{\xi\in\mathbb{R}} \sqrt{n}\,|F(\xi) - F_P(\xi)|, \quad F \in \mathscr{F},\ P \ll P_0,$$

for every sample size $n \in \mathbb{N}$. We parametrize the sequence (E^n) locally around P_0 in the way of Example 80.4. Thus, we obtain the experiments

$$E_n = (\mathbb{R}^n, \mathscr{B}^n, \{P^n_{g/\sqrt{n}}: g \in H_n\}), \quad n \in \mathbb{N} .$$

Let $\sigma_n: \mathbb{R}^n \to \mathscr{F}$ be non-randomized estimates, $n \in \mathbb{N}$. The risk function of σ_n for E_n and L_n is

$$g \mapsto \int \sup_{\xi\in\mathbb{R}} \sqrt{n}\,|\sigma_n(\underline{x})(\xi) - F_{P_{g/\sqrt{n}}}(\xi)|\, P^n_{g/\sqrt{n}}(d\underline{x}), \quad g \in H_n .$$

It is easy to see that

$$F_{P_{g/\sqrt{n}}}(\xi) = F_{P_0}(\xi) + \frac{1}{\sqrt{n}} \int_{-\infty}^{\xi} g\, dP_0 + O\left(\frac{1}{n}\right),$$

uniformly for $\xi \in \mathbb{R}$. This implies that for every $F \in \mathscr{F}$

$$L_n(F, P_{g/\sqrt{n}}) = \sup_{\xi\in\mathbb{R}} \left|\sqrt{n}(F(\xi) - F_{P_0}(\xi)) - \int_{-\infty}^{\xi} g\, dP_0\right| + O\left(\frac{1}{\sqrt{n}}\right).$$

Now, define non-randomized estimates $\kappa_n: \mathbb{R}^n \to \mathscr{C}_0(\mathbb{R})$ by

$$\kappa_n: \underline{x} \mapsto \sqrt{n}(\sigma_n(\underline{x}) - F_{P_0}), \quad \underline{x} \in \mathbb{R}^n,\ n \in \mathbb{N} .$$

Letting $D = \mathscr{C}_0(\mathbb{R})$ and $W_g: x \mapsto \|x - \tau(g)\|_u$, $x \in \mathscr{C}_0(\mathbb{R})$, with $\tau(g)$: $\xi \mapsto \int_{-\infty}^{\xi} g\, dP_0$, $\xi \in \mathbb{R}$, $g \in \dot{H}$, we obtain that

$$L_n(.,P_{g/\sqrt{n}})\,\sigma_n P^n_{g/\sqrt{n}} = W_g \kappa_n P^n_{g/\sqrt{n}} + O\left(\frac{1}{\sqrt{n}}\right), \quad g \in H_n,\ n \in \mathbb{N}.$$

It follows from the remark below Theorem 83.16

$$\begin{aligned}\liminf_{n\to\infty} \sup_{P \ll P_0} & L_n(.,P)\,\sigma_n P^n \\ &\geq \sup_{a>0} \liminf_{n\to\infty} \sup_{P_0(g^2)\leq a} W_g \kappa_n P^n_{g/\sqrt{n}} \\ &\geq \int_{\mathscr{C}_0(\mathbb{R})} \|\,.\,\|_u \, dW_{P_0}\end{aligned}$$

since $(H, \mathscr{C}_0(\mathbb{R}), \tau)$ is an Abstract Wiener space, and where W_{P_0} is the probability measure constructed in Theorem 70.5.

Now, let (F_n) be the sequence of empirical distribution functions which are made continuous by linear interpolation. Thus, (F_n) is a sequence of estimates for the decision space $\mathscr{F}$. It is a well-known fact (cf. Parthasarathy [1967]) that

$$\mathscr{L}(\|\sqrt{n}(F_n - F_P)\|_u \,|\, P^n) \to \mathscr{L}(\|\,.\,\|_u \,|\, W_P) \quad \text{weakly},$$

uniformly for all non-atomic probability measures $P|\mathscr{B}$. This implies that (F_n) attains the asymptotic lower bound.

84. Characterization of central sequences

In this section we show that central sequences can be characterized as solutions of certain optimization problems. This will lead to formal statements of well-known properties of maximum likelihood and Bayes estimates.

We begin with the discussion of maximum likelihood estimation.

84.1 Discussion. Suppose that $\Theta \subseteq \mathbb{R}^k$ is an open subset. Let $(\Omega_n, \mathscr{A}_n, \{P_{n,\vartheta}: \vartheta \in \Theta\})$, $n \in \mathbb{N}$, be a sequence of dominated experiments and let $\{P_{n,\vartheta}: \vartheta \in \Theta\} \ll \nu_n|\mathscr{A}_n$, $n \in \mathbb{N}$. In the usual terminology a sequence of estimators $\hat{\vartheta}_n: \Omega_n \to \Theta$ is a sequence of *maximum likelihood estimates* if

$$\frac{dP_{n,\hat{\vartheta}_n}}{d\nu_n} = \sup_{\vartheta\in\Theta} \frac{dP_{n,\vartheta}}{d\nu_n} \quad \nu_n\text{-a.e.}, \quad n \in \mathbb{N}.$$

It is common reasoning, that such a sequence is a rather good choice of an estimator sequence and also tests based on this sequence are generally optimal in some sense. In the following we support this opinion by a local asymptotic property of the maximum likelihood method. To be more precise, fix $\vartheta \in \Theta$ and consider the localized experiments

$$E_{n,\vartheta} = (\Omega_n, \mathscr{A}_n, \{P_{n,\vartheta+\delta_n t}: t \in T_n(\vartheta)\}),$$

where $T_n(\vartheta) = \{t \in T: \vartheta + \delta_n t \in \Theta\}$, $n \in \mathbb{N}$. Assume that these experiments are asymptotically normal. We shall prove under certain conditions that the maximum likelihood property of $(\hat{\vartheta}_n)$ is equivalent to centrality of the sequence

$$\frac{1}{\delta_n}(\hat{\vartheta}_n - \vartheta), \quad n \in \mathbb{N}.$$

In view of the various optimality properties of central sequences established in the preceding sections this assertion is a strong argument in favour of the maximum likelihood method. Unfortunately, the conditions under which it can be proved are rather restrictive.

We begin with a general assertion which is based on the results of Section 64. Suppose that T is a Euclidean vector space and T_n, $n \in \mathbb{N}$, are open subsets such that $T_n \uparrow T$. Let $E_n = (\Omega_n, \mathscr{A}_n, \{P_{n,t}: t \in T_n\})$ be an asymptotically normal sequence of experiments.

84.2 Theorem. *Suppose that the likelihood processes* $\left(\frac{dP_{n,t}}{dP_{n,0}}\right)_{t \in T_n}$ *have continuous paths* $P_{n,0}$*-a.e.,* $n \in \mathbb{N}$. *Assume that the following conditions are satisfied:*

(1) *For every* $t \in T$ *and* $\varepsilon > 0$ *there exists a compact set* $K \subseteq T$ *such that*

$$\limsup_{n\to\infty} P_{n,t}\left\{\sup_{s \in T_n \setminus K} \frac{dP_{n,s}}{dP_{n,t}} \geqq \sup_{s \in T_n} \frac{dP_{n,s}}{dP_{n,t}} \cdot (1-\varepsilon)\right\} < \varepsilon.$$

(2) *The likelihood processes* $\left(\frac{dP_{n,s}}{dP_{n,t}}\right)_{s \in T_n}$, $n \in \mathbb{N}$, *are equicontinuous in* $(P_{n,t})$*-probability for every* $t \in T$.

Then a sequence of random variables (Y_n) *is central iff it is a sequence of asymptotic maximum likelihood estimates, i.e.*

$$\lim_{n\to\infty} P_{n,t}\left\{\frac{dP_{n,Y_n}}{dP_{n,t}} \geqq \sup_{s \in T_n} \frac{dP_{n,s}}{dP_{n,t}} \cdot (1-\varepsilon)\right\} = 1$$

for all $t \in T$, $\varepsilon > 0$.

Proof. Considering Example 64.1, conditions (1) and (2) are equivalent to conditions 64.6. Moreover, it is clear that conditions 64.5 are satisfied since the limit experiment is a Gaussian shift. Let X be the central random variable of the limit experiment. Then every likelihood process of the limit experiment attains its supremum exactly at X. Hence, the assumptions of Theorem 64.15 are satisfied, and by 69.11 and 80.12 every sequence of asymptotic maximum likelihood estimates is central. Conversely, by Theorem 64.8 and Corollary 64.13 every central sequence is a sequence of asymptotic maximum likelihood estimates. □

The conditions (1) and (2) of the preceding theorem can be simplified considerably. For this, let (X_n) be any central sequence of (E_n) and define the residuals $r_n(s)$, $s \in T_n$, $n \in \mathbb{N}$, of the stochastic expansion by

$$\frac{dP_{n,s}}{dP_{n,0}} = \exp(\langle s, X_n \rangle - \frac{1}{2}\|s\|^2 + r_n(s)), \quad s \in T_n,\ n \in \mathbb{N}.$$

84.3 Lemma. *Suppose that the likelihood processes* $\left(\frac{dP_{n,t}}{dP_{n,0}}\right)_{t \in T_n}$ *have continuous paths* $P_{n,0}$*-a.e.,* $n \in \mathbb{N}$. *Then condition* 84.2 (2) *holds iff*

$$\lim_{n \to \infty} P_{n,0}\{\sup_{s \in K} |r_n(s)| > \varepsilon\} = 0, \quad \varepsilon > 0,$$

for every compact $K \subseteq T$.

Proof. Assume first, that 84.2 (2), is fulfilled. Then it is clear that also the residuals $(r_n(s))_{s \in T_n}$, $n \in \mathbb{N}$, are equicontinuous in $(P_{n,0})$-probability. Since $r_n(s) \xrightarrow{P_{n,0}} 0$ for every fixed $s \in T$, equicontinuity implies the assertion.

Now, assume conversely that the residuals satisfy the uniformity condition. It is sufficient to prove equicontinuity of $\left(\log \frac{dP_{n,s}}{dP_{n,0}}\right)_{s \in T_n}$, $n \in \mathbb{N}$, in $(P_{n,0})$-probability. Since it is clear that $(\langle s, X_n \rangle - \frac{1}{2}\|s\|^2)_{s \in T_n}$, $n \in \mathbb{N}$, is equicontinuous it remains to be shown that $(r_n(s))_{s \in T_n}$, $n \in \mathbb{N}$, is equicontinuous. But this is an almost obvious consequence of the uniformity condition and of the continuity of the residuals. □

84.4 Lemma. *Suppose that the likelihood processes* $\left(\frac{dP_{n,t}}{dP_{n,0}}\right)_{t \in T_n}$ *have continuous paths* $P_{n,0}$*-a.e.,* $n \in \mathbb{N}$. *If for all* $\varepsilon > 0$, $\delta > 0$, *there exists a compact set* $K \subseteq T$ *such that*

$$\limsup_{n \to \infty} P_{n,0}\left\{\sup_{s \in T_n \setminus K} \frac{dP_{n,s}}{dP_{n,0}} \geqq \delta\right\} < \varepsilon,$$

then condition 84.2 (1), *is satisfied.*

Proof. Let $\varepsilon > 0$. Since $0 \in T_n$, $n \in \mathbb{N}$, we have

$$\sup_{s \in T_n} \frac{dP_{n,s}}{dP_{n,0}} \geqq 1.$$

This implies that for every $\eta > 0$ there exists a compact set $K \subseteq T$ such that

$$P_{n,0}\left\{\sup_{s \in T_n \setminus K} \frac{dP_{n,s}}{dP_{n,0}} \geqq \sup_{s \in T_n} \frac{dP_{n,s}}{dP_{n,0}} \cdot (1 - \varepsilon)\right\} < \eta, \quad n \in \mathbb{N}.$$

For convenience, denote

$$A_n(K, \varepsilon) = \left\{ \sup_{s \in T_n \setminus K} \frac{dP_{n,s}}{dP_{n,0}} \geqq \sup_{s \in T_n} \frac{dP_{n,s}}{dP_{n,0}} \cdot (1 - \varepsilon) \right\}.$$

Let us show that for any $t \in T$ there exists a compact set $K \subseteq T$ such that

$$\limsup_{n \to \infty} P_{n,t}(A_n(K, \varepsilon)) < \varepsilon.$$

For this, we apply $(P_{n,t}) \ll (P_{n,0})$ through Lemma 18.6. Let $\eta > 0$ be such that

$$\limsup_{n \to \infty} P_{n,0}(A_n) < \eta \quad \text{implies} \quad \limsup_{n \to \infty} P_{n,t}(A_n) < \varepsilon.$$

Now, let $K \subseteq T$ be a compact set such that

$$\limsup_{n \to \infty} P_{n,0}(A_n(K, \varepsilon)) < \eta.$$

This implies

$$\limsup_{n \to \infty} P_{n,t}(A_n(K, \varepsilon)) < \varepsilon.$$

Now the proof is finished since by contiguity

$$\lim_{n \to \infty} P_{n,t} \left\{ \frac{dP_{n,t}}{dP_{n,0}} = 0 \right\} = 0,$$

and we obtain finally that

$$\limsup_{n \to \infty} P_{n,t} \left\{ \sup_{s \in T_n \setminus K} \frac{dP_{n,s}}{dP_{n,t}} \geqq \sup_{s \in T_n} \frac{dP_{n,s}}{dP_{n,t}} \cdot (1 - \varepsilon) \right\}$$
$$\leqq \limsup_{n \to \infty} P_{n,t}(A_n(K, \varepsilon)) < \varepsilon$$

which proves the assertion. □

Usually, the assertion of Theorem 84.2 is established by verifying the assumptions of Lemmas 84.3 and 84.4.

84.5 Discussion (Maximum Likelihood estimates in the independent, identically distributed case). Consider the situation of Example 77.4. Fix some $x \in M$ and define

$$E_n = (\Omega^n, \mathscr{A}^n, \{P^n_{x+t/\sqrt{n}} \colon t \in T_n\}), \quad n \in \mathbb{N},$$

where $T_n = \{t \in T \colon x + t/\sqrt{n} \in M\}$, $n \in \mathbb{N}$. If conditions 77.4 (1)–(4), are satisfied then the experiment $(\Omega, \mathscr{A}, \{P_x \colon x \in M\})$ is differentiable. From Example

80.8, (1), it follows that (E_n) is asymptotically normal. In the present case this can also be seen from the Taylor expansion

$$\log \frac{dP^n_{x+t/\sqrt{n}}}{dP^n_x}(\underset{\sim}{\omega}) = \sum_{i=1}^{n} (\ell(\omega_i, x+t/\sqrt{n}) - \ell(\omega_i, x))$$

$$= \frac{1}{\sqrt{n}} \sum_{i=1}^{n} \ell'(\omega_i, x) \cdot t - \frac{1}{2n} \sum_{i=1}^{n} \ell''(\omega_i, \tilde{x}_n(\underset{\sim}{\omega}, t)) \cdot (t, t)$$

$$= \frac{1}{\sqrt{n}} \sum_{i=1}^{n} \ell'(\omega_i, x) \cdot t + \frac{1}{2} P_x(\ell''(.,x) \cdot (t,t)) + r_n(t)(\underset{\sim}{\omega}),$$

where

$$r_n(t)(\underset{\sim}{\omega}) = \frac{1}{2}\left(\frac{1}{n} \sum_{i=1}^{n} \ell''(\omega_i, \tilde{x}_n(\underset{\sim}{\omega}, t)) \cdot (t,t) - P_x(\ell''(.,x) \cdot (t,t))\right),$$

and

$$|x - \tilde{x}_n(\underset{\sim}{\omega}, t)| \leqq \frac{1}{\sqrt{n}} |t|, \quad n \in \mathbb{N},\ t \in T.$$

Let

$$B_x(s,t) := -P_x(\ell''(.,x) \cdot (s,t))$$

and $X_n\colon \Omega^n \to T$ be such that

$$B_x(t, X_n(\underset{\sim}{\omega})) = \frac{1}{\sqrt{n}} \sum_{i=1}^{n} \ell'(\omega_i, x) \cdot t, \quad \underset{\sim}{\omega} \in \Omega^n,\ t \in T.$$

Then B_x is the canonical covariance and (X_n) is a central sequence.

Now, we strengthen the conditions by the additional requirements

(5) $\lim_{\varepsilon \to 0} P_x(\sup_{|h| < \varepsilon} |\ell''(.,x+h) - \ell''(.,x)|) = 0$

(6) $\limsup_{n \to \infty} \sup_{|h| \geqq \delta} \frac{1}{n} \sum_{i=1}^{n} \ell(\omega_i, x+h) < P_x(\ell(.,x)) \quad P_x^{\mathbb{N}}\text{-a.e.}, \quad \delta > 0.$

Condition (5) is a stronger condition than 77.4 (4), and condition (6) is a typical "global" condition which is usually applied in order to achieve consistency of the maximum likelihood method. We shall prove the classical fact that under the conditions (1)–(6) the assertion of Theorem 84.2 is valid. For this, we verify the assumptions of Lemmas 84.3 and 84.4.

(a) Let us show that the assumption of Lemma 84.3 is valid. For this, we estimate the residuals $r_n(t)$ in the following way:

$$|r_n(t)(\underline{\omega})| \leqq \frac{1}{2}|t|^2 \left| \frac{1}{n} \sum_{i=1}^{n} \ell''(\omega_i, x_n(\underline{\omega}, t)) - P_x(\ell''(.,x)) \right|$$

$$\leqq \frac{1}{2}|t|^2 \left| \frac{1}{n} \sum_{i=1}^{n} \ell''(\omega_i, x) - P_x(\ell''(.,x)) \right|$$

$$+ \frac{1}{2}|t|^2 \cdot \frac{1}{n} \sum_{i=1}^{n} |\ell''(\omega_i, \tilde{x}_n(\underline{\omega}, t)) - \ell''(\omega_i, x)|$$

$$\leqq \frac{1}{2}|t|^2 \left| \frac{1}{n} \sum_{i=1}^{n} \ell''(\omega_i, x) - P_x(\ell''(.,x)) \right|$$

$$+ \frac{1}{2}|t|^2 \cdot \frac{1}{n} \sum_{i=1}^{n} \sup_{|h| \leqq |t|/\sqrt{n}} |\ell''(\omega_i, x+h) - \ell''(\omega_i, x)|.$$

Now, the assertion follows from the law of large numbers and condition (5).

(b) Next, we show that there is some $\delta_0 > 0$ such that

$$\lim_{n\to\infty} P_x^n \bigcap_{|t| < \delta_0 \sqrt{n}} \left\{ \frac{dP^n_{x+t/\sqrt{n}}}{dP_x^n} \leqq \exp\left(B_x(t, X_n) - \frac{1}{4} B_x(t,t)\right) \right\} = 1.$$

The estimation of the residuals under (1) shows that for every $\varepsilon > 0$ there exists $\delta(\varepsilon) > 0$ such that

$$P_x^n \bigcap_{|t| < \delta(\varepsilon)\sqrt{n}} \{|r_n(t)| < \varepsilon |t|^2\} \to 1.$$

It is clear that there exists some $\varepsilon > 0$ such that

$$\varepsilon |t|^2 \leqq \frac{1}{4} B_x(t,t), \quad t \in T.$$

Together with the expansion obtained at the beginning of this example, the assertion follows.

(c) We show that there exist $\delta_0 > 0$, $c > 0$, $C < \infty$, such that for every $a > 0$

$$\limsup_{n\to\infty} P_x^n \left\{ \sup_{a \leqq |t| \leqq \delta_0 \sqrt{n}} \frac{dP^n_{x+t/\sqrt{n}}}{dP_x^n} \geqq e^{-ca^2} \right\} \leqq \frac{C}{a^2}.$$

Choose $\delta_0 > 0$ according to part (b). Moreover, let

$$\alpha := \min_{|t|=1} B_x(t,t) > 0, \; \beta := \max_{|t|=1} B_x(t,t) < \infty.$$

Then

$$P_x^n \left\{ \sup_{a \leqq |t| \leqq \delta_0 \sqrt{n}} \frac{dP_{x+t/\sqrt{n}}}{dP_x^n} \geqq e^{-a^2\alpha/8} \right\}$$

$$\leq P_x^n\left\{\sup_{a\leq|t|\leq\delta_0\sqrt{n}}(B_x(t,X_n)-\frac{1}{4}B_x(t,t))\geq -a^2\alpha/8\right\}+o(1)$$

$$\leq P_x^n\{|X_n|\geq a\alpha/8\beta^2\}+o(1)$$

$$\leq\frac{64\cdot\beta^4}{\alpha^2a^2}\cdot P_x^n(|X_n|^2)+o(1).$$

Since $P_x^n(|X_n|^2)=\operatorname{tr}(P_x(\ell'(.,x)\otimes\ell'(.,x)))$ the assertion follows.

(d) Now, we are in a position to verify the assumption of Lemma 84.4. Let $\varepsilon>0$, $\delta>0$. In view of (c) it is clear that for sufficiently large $a>0$

$$\limsup_{n\to\infty}P_x^n\left\{\sup_{a\leq|t|\leq\delta_0\sqrt{n}}\frac{dP^n_{x+t/\sqrt{n}}}{dP_x^n}\geq\delta\right\}<\frac{\varepsilon}{2}.$$

Thus, it remains to show that

$$\limsup_{n\to\infty}P_x^n\left\{\sup_{|t|>\delta_0\sqrt{n}}\frac{dP^n_{x+t/\sqrt{n}}}{dP_x^n}\geq\delta\right\}<\frac{\varepsilon}{2}.$$

This is done by means of condition (6). Together with the strong law of large numbers this condition implies

$$\limsup_{n\to\infty}\sup_{|h|\geq\delta_0}\frac{1}{n}\sum_{i=1}^n(\ell(\omega_i,x+h)-\ell(\omega_i,x))<0\quad P_x^{\mathbb{N}}\text{-a.e.}$$

Abbreviating the left hand side by $-Z$ we have

$$P_x^{\mathbb{N}}\{Z>0\}=1,$$

and there exists a random variable $N\colon\Omega^{\mathbb{N}}\to\mathbb{N}$ such that

$$\sup_{|h|\geq\delta_0}\frac{1}{n}\sum_{i=1}^n(\ell(\omega_i,x+h)-\ell(\omega_i,x))<\frac{1}{2}Z(\underline{\omega})$$

whenever $n\geq N(\underline{\omega})$. Now, for $\varepsilon>0$ let $n(\varepsilon)\in\mathbb{N}$ and $\eta(\varepsilon)>0$ be such that

$$P_x^{\mathbb{N}}(\{N\leq n(\varepsilon)\}\cap\{Z\geq\eta(\varepsilon)\})\geq 1-\frac{\varepsilon}{2}.$$

Then $n\geq n(\varepsilon)$ implies

$$P_x^n\left\{\sup_{|h|\geq\delta_0}\frac{dP^n_{x+h}}{dP_x^n}\geq\exp(-n\cdot\eta)\right\}<\frac{\varepsilon}{2}.$$

This yields the desired

$$\limsup_{n\to\infty}P_x^n\left\{\sup_{|t|\geq a}\frac{dP^n_{x+t/\sqrt{n}}}{dP_x^n}\geq\delta\right\}<\varepsilon.$$

The following example needs less restrictive regularity conditions, but is limited to the one-dimensional case.

84.6 Discussion (LeCam [1970], Ibragimov and Has'minskii, [1972]). Consider the situation of Discussion 77.5. Fix some $x \in M$ and define $E_n = (\Omega^n, \mathscr{A}^n, \{P^n_{x+t/\sqrt{n}}: t \in T_n\})$, where $T_n = \{t \in \mathbb{R}: x + t/\sqrt{n} \in M\}$, $n \in \mathbb{N}$. If conditions 77.5 (1)–(3), are satisfied then the experiment $(\Omega, \mathscr{A}, \{P_x: x \in M\})$ is differentiable. From Example 80.8 (1), it follows that (E_n) is asymptotically normal.

(a) Let us prove that condition (2) of Theorem 84.2 is valid. For this, we have to show that for every $\varepsilon > 0$, every compact $K \subseteq \mathbb{R}$ and some $n_0 \in \mathbb{N}$

$$\lim_{\delta \to 0} \sup_{n \geqq n_0} P^n_x \left\{ \sup_{\substack{s, t \in K \\ |s-t| < \delta}} \left| \frac{dP^n_{x+s/\sqrt{n}}}{dP^n_x} - \frac{dP^n_{x+t/\sqrt{n}}}{dP^n_x} \right| > \varepsilon \right\} = 0 .$$

If this is proved for some $n_0 \in \mathbb{N}$ then it is also valid for $n_0 = 1$, since the likelihood ratios are continuous for every fixed $n \in \mathbb{N}$.

Choose an open neighborhood U_x of x where $y \mapsto I(y)$ is bounded and let $n_0 \in \mathbb{N}$ be such that $x + \dfrac{1}{\sqrt{n}} K \subseteq U_x$ for $n \geqq n_0$. From Lemma 77.2 it follows that

$$\sup_{n \geqq n_0} n\, d_2^2 (P_{x+s/\sqrt{n}}, P_{x+t/\sqrt{n}}) \leqq C \cdot |s-t|^2$$

whenever $s, t \in K$. This implies in view of Lemma 2.17

$$\int \left(\sqrt{\frac{dP^n_{x+s/\sqrt{n}}}{dP^n_x}} - \sqrt{\frac{dP^n_{x+t/\sqrt{n}}}{dP^n_x}} \right)^2 dP^n_x \leqq C \cdot |s-t|^2, \; s, t \in K, \, n \geqq n_0 .$$

Now, the theorem of Kolmogoroff and Prohoroff yields

$$\lim_{\delta \to 0} \sup_{n \geqq n_0} P^n_x \left\{ \sup_{\substack{s, t \in K \\ |s-t| < \delta}} \left| \sqrt{\frac{dP^n_{x+s/\sqrt{n}}}{dP^n_x}} - \sqrt{\frac{dP^n_{x+t/\sqrt{n}}}{dP^n_x}} \right| > \varepsilon \right\} = 0, \quad \varepsilon > 0 .$$

Moreover, inserting $t = 0$ we obtain

$$\lim_{a \to \infty} \sup_{n \geqq n_0} P^n_x \left\{ \sup_{s \in K} \sqrt{\frac{dP^n_{x+s/\sqrt{n}}}{dP^n_x}} > a \right\} = 0 .$$

This implies the assertion.

(b) Let us prove that under the additional hypothesis 84.5 (6), the assumption of Lemma 84.4 is valid. Copying the argument of 84.5 (d), we need only show that there exists $\delta_0 > 0$ and for $\varepsilon > 0$, $\delta > 0$ some constant $a > 0$ such that

$$\limsup_{n\to\infty} P_x^n \left\{ \sup_{a \leqq |t| \leqq \delta_0 \sqrt{n}} \frac{dP^n_{x+t/\sqrt{n}}}{dP^n_x} \geqq \delta \right\} < \varepsilon .$$

Choose $\delta_0 > 0$ such that $B(x, \delta/\sqrt{n}) \subseteq U_x$ and that $I(y) \geqq c^2 > 0$ for $|y-x| < \delta_0$. Then Remark 76.7 implies

$$d_2^2(P_y, P_x) \geqq \frac{c^2}{2} |y-x|^2, \; |y-x| < \delta_0 .$$

It follows that for $n \geqq n_0$, $|t| < \sqrt{n}\,\delta_0$,

$$\begin{aligned} P_x^n \left\{ \frac{dP^n_{x+t/\sqrt{n}}}{dP^n_x} \geqq \exp\left(-\frac{c^2 t^2}{4}\right) \right\} &\leqq \exp\left(\frac{c^2 t^2}{4}\right) \int \sqrt{\frac{dP^n_{x+t/\sqrt{n}}}{dP^n_x}}\, dP^n_x \\ &\leqq \exp\left(\frac{c^2 t^2}{4}\right) (1 - d_2^2(P_{x+t/\sqrt{n}}, P_x))^n \\ &\leqq \exp\left(\frac{c^2 t^2}{4}\right) \left(1 - \frac{c^2 t^2}{2n}\right)^n \\ &\leqq \exp\left(\frac{c^2 t^2}{4}\right) \exp\left(\frac{-c^2 t^2}{2}\right) = \exp\left(-\frac{c^2 t^2}{4}\right). \end{aligned}$$

In the following we denote for convenience

$$Y_{n,t} := \begin{cases} \sqrt{\dfrac{dP^n_{x+t/\sqrt{n}}}{dP^n_x}} & \text{if } \; |t| < \sqrt{n}\,\delta_0, \\ 0 & \text{if } \; |t| \geqq \sqrt{n}\,\delta_0 . \end{cases}$$

We shall prove that for every $a > 0$

$$P_x^n \left\{ \sup_{|t| \geqq a} |Y_{n,t}| \geqq \exp\left(-\frac{c^2 a^2}{16}\right) \right\} \leqq C_1 \exp\left(-\frac{c^2 a^2}{16}\right).$$

We consider only the case $t \geqq 0$. The case $t < 0$ is treated similarly.

Fix $m \in \mathbb{N}$ and define

$$r = \left[\exp\left(-\frac{3 c^2 m^2}{16} \right) \right], \; t_i = m + \frac{i}{r}, \quad 0 \leqq i \leqq r .$$

Then we have

$$P_x^n\left\{\max_{0\leqq i\leqq r}|Y_{n,t_i}|\geqq \exp\left(-\frac{c^2m^2}{4}\right)\right\}\leqq (r+1)\exp\left(-\frac{c^2m^2}{4}\right)$$

which implies

$$P_x^n\left\{\sup_{m\leqq t\leqq m+1}|Y_{n,t}|\geqq \exp\left(-\frac{c^2m^2}{16}\right)\right\}\leqq (r+1)\exp\left(-\frac{c^2m^2}{4}\right)$$
$$+P_x^n\left\{\sup_{\substack{|t_1-t_2|\leqq\frac{1}{r}\\ m\leqq t\leqq t_2\leqq m+1}}|Y_{n,t_1}-Y_{n,t_2}|\geqq \exp\left(-\frac{c^2m^2}{16}\right)-\exp\left(-\frac{c^2m^2}{4}\right)\right\}.$$

The last term can be estimated by means of the theorem of Komogoroff and Prohoroff in the same way as it is applied under (a), but making the constants explicit. This yields

$$P_x^n\left\{\sup_{\substack{|t_1-t_2|\leqq\frac{1}{r}\\ m\leqq t_1\leqq t_2\leqq m+1}}|Y_{n,t_1}-Y_{n,t_2}|\geqq \exp\left(-\frac{c^2m^2}{16}\right)-\exp\left(-\frac{c^2m^2}{4}\right)\right\}$$
$$\leqq\frac{C}{r\left(\exp\left(-\frac{c^2m^2}{16}\right)-\exp\left(-\frac{c^2m^2}{4}\right)\right)^2}.$$

Thus, we obtain

$$P_x^n\left\{\sup_{m\leqq t\leqq m+1}|Y_{n,t}|\geqq \exp\left(-\frac{c^2m^2}{16}\right)\right\}$$
$$\leqq (r+1)\exp\left(-\frac{c^2m^2}{4}\right)+\frac{C}{r\left(\exp\left(-\frac{c^2m^2}{16}\right)-\exp\left(-\frac{c^2m^2}{4}\right)\right)^2}$$
$$\leqq \exp\left(-\frac{c^2m^2}{16}\right)+\exp\left(-\frac{c^2m^2}{4}\right)+2C\exp\left(-\frac{c^2m^2}{16}\right),$$

provided that $m\in\mathbb{N}$ is sufficiently large. Hence, for $a>0$

$$P_x^n\left\{\sup_{t\geqq a}|Y_{n,t}|\geqq \exp\left(-\frac{c^2a^2}{16}\right)\right\}$$
$$\leqq \sum_{m=a}^{\infty}P_x^n\left\{\sup_{m\leqq t\leqq m+1}|Y_{n,t}|\geqq \exp\left(-\frac{c^2m^2}{16}\right)\right\}$$
$$\leqq 2(C+1)\sum_{m=a}^{\infty}\exp\left(-\frac{c^2m^2}{16}\right)\leqq C_1\exp\left(-\frac{c^2a^2}{16}\right).$$

84.7 Example. Let $\Theta = \mathbb{R}$ and $E = (\mathbb{R}, \mathscr{B}, \{P_\vartheta: \vartheta \in \Theta\})$ where $\frac{dP_\vartheta}{d\lambda} = f(. - \vartheta)$ and f is an absolutely continuous density of a probability distribution vanishing at infinity, with Fisher's information

$$I = \int \left(\frac{\dot{f}}{f}\right)^2 f d\lambda .$$

Then the assumptions of 77.5 (1)–(3), are satisfied. Assume further that $P_0(\log f) > -\infty$. In order to apply the results of the preceding discussion we need only show

$$\limsup_{n\to\infty} \sup_{|h|\geqq\delta} \frac{1}{n} \sum_{i=1}^{n} \log f(x_i - h) < \int \log f dP_0, \quad P_0^{\mathbb{N}}\text{-a.e.}, \quad \delta > 0 .$$

This is easily done as follows. We repeat a classical argument due to Wald [1949].

By strict concavity of log and Jensen's inequality we have

$$\int \log f(x-h) P_0(dx) < \int \log f dP_0 \quad \text{if} \quad h \neq 0 .$$

By continuity of f, for $h \in \mathbb{R}$, $h \neq 0$, there exists an open neighborhood W_h of h such that

$$\int \sup_{\eta \in W_h} \log f(x-\eta) P_0(dx) < \int \log f dP_0 .$$

The compact set $\bar{\mathbb{R}} \setminus U$ can be covered by a finite collection of those neighborhoods, say $W_{h_1}, \ldots, W_{h_k}$. The law of large numbers then implies that

$$\begin{aligned} &\limsup_{n\to\infty} \sup_{|h|\geqq\delta} \frac{1}{n} \sum_{i=1}^{n} \log f(x_i - h) \\ &\leqq \limsup_{n\to\infty} \max_{1\leqq j\leqq k} \frac{1}{n} \sum_{i=1}^{n} \sup_{\eta\in W_{h_j}} \log f(x_i - \eta) \\ &= \max_{1\leqq j\leqq k} \lim_{n\to\infty} \frac{1}{n} \sum_{i=1}^{n} \sup_{\eta\in W_{h_j}} \log f(x_i - \eta) \\ &= \max_{1\leqq j\leqq k} \int \sup_{\eta\in W_{h_j}} \log f(x-\eta) P_0(dx) < \int \log f dP_0 \quad P_0^{\mathbb{N}}\text{-a.e.} \end{aligned}$$

Now, we turn to the discussion of Bayes estimates.

84.8 Discussion. Suppose that $\Theta \subseteq \mathbb{R}^k$ is an open subset and let $G_n = (\Omega_n, \mathscr{A}_n, \{P_{n,\vartheta}: \vartheta \in \Theta\})$, $n \in \mathbb{N}$, be a sequence of continuous experiments. Assume, that there exists a sequence $\delta_n \downarrow 0$ such that for every fixed $\vartheta \in \Theta$ the localized experiments

$$E_{n,\vartheta} = (\Omega_n, \mathscr{A}_n, \{P_{n,\vartheta+\delta_n t}: t \in T_n(\vartheta)\}), \quad n \in \mathbb{N},$$

are asymptotically normal. Let $\mu|\mathscr{B}(\Theta)$ be a probability measure. In the usual terminology, a sequence of nonrandomized estimators $\hat{\vartheta}_n: \Omega_n \to \Theta$, is a sequence of Bayes estimators for W and μ if

$$\iint W\left(\frac{1}{\delta_n}(\hat{\vartheta}_n - \vartheta)\right) dP_{n,\vartheta}\,\mu(d\vartheta)$$

$$= \inf_{\varrho \in \mathscr{R}(G_n, \Theta)} \iiint W\left(\frac{1}{\delta_n}(\sigma - \vartheta)\right) \varrho(., d\sigma)\, dP_{n,\vartheta}\,\mu(d\vartheta), \quad n \in \mathbb{N}.$$

Recalling the results of section 37 we know that this is more or less equivalent to

$$\int W\left(\frac{1}{\delta_n}(\hat{\vartheta}_n - \vartheta)\right) F_n(d\vartheta) = \inf_{\sigma \in \Theta} \int W\left(\frac{1}{\delta_n}(\sigma - \vartheta)\right) F_n(d\vartheta)\; P_n(\mu)\text{-a.e.},$$

where (F_n) are the posterior distributions of the experiments (G_n) with respect to μ. We shall prove that under some conditions this is even equivalent to the centrality of the sequence

$$Y_n = \frac{1}{\delta_n}(\hat{\vartheta}_n - \vartheta), \quad n \in \mathbb{N},$$

for the sequence of localized experiments $(E_{n,\vartheta})_{n \in \mathbb{N}}$ for every $\vartheta \in \Theta$. The essential difference to maximum likelihood estimation is that for Bayes estimators centrality depends rather on integrability of the underlying experiments than on smoothness.

First, we establish a general result and then specialize to the independent, identically distributed case.

Let $W: T \to [0, \infty)$ be subconvex, level-compact, separating and of order $p > 0$. Given a sequence of Borel measures $\mu_n|\mathscr{B}(T_n)$, $n \in \mathbb{N}$, denote by F_n the posterior distributions of E_n and μ_n, $n \in \mathbb{N}$.

84.9 Theorem. *Suppose that (E_n) is equicontinuous, and uniformly (μ_n)-integrable of order p, where $\mu_n \to \lambda$, strongly on compacts. Then a sequence of random variables (Y_n) is central iff it is a sequence of asymptotic Bayes estimates for W and (μ_n), i.e. if*

$$\lim_{n\to\infty} P_{n,t}\{\int W(Y_n - t) F_n(dt) > \inf_{s \in T_n} \int W(s - t) F_n(dt) + \varepsilon\} = 0$$

for all $t \in T$, $\varepsilon > 0$.

Proof. This is a consequence of Corollaries 67.6 and 67.7 if we can show that the limit experiment satisfies the conditions of 67.6 (2), and if the generalized

Bayes estimate of the limit experiment coincides with the central random variable.

Let F be the posterior distribution of the limiting Gaussian shift with respect to λ and X its central random variable. Then, by Example 36.11 (1), we have $F = N_T * \varepsilon_X$. It follows from Discussion 38.24 that X is the uniquely determined Bayes estimate for the limiting Gaussian shift with respect to W and λ. □

84.10 Discussion (Generalized Bayes estimation in the independent, identically distributed case). Suppose that $\Theta \subseteq \mathbb{R}^k$ is an open set. Let $E = (\Omega, \mathscr{A}, \{P_\vartheta: \vartheta \in \Theta\})$ be a differentiable experiment whose derivatives are injective for each $\vartheta \in \Theta$, and which satisfies $P_\sigma \neq P_\tau$ if $\sigma \neq \tau$. Then the experiment satisfies the following condition:

(1) For every $\vartheta \in \Theta$ there is an open neighborhood $U(\vartheta)$ of ϑ and constants $a(\vartheta) > 0$, $b(\vartheta) < \infty$, such that

$$a(\vartheta)|\sigma - \tau| \leqq d_2(P_\sigma, P_\tau) \leqq b(\vartheta)|\sigma - \tau| \quad \text{if} \quad \sigma, \tau \in U(\vartheta).$$

Fix some $p > 0$. Let $\mu|\mathscr{B}(\Theta)$ be a σ-finite measure such that $\mu \ll \lambda_k$ and $g := \dfrac{d\mu}{d\lambda_k}$ is continuous and positive on Θ. Assume that for some $n \in \mathbb{N}$ the mixture

$$A \mapsto \int P_\sigma^n(A)|\sigma|^p \mu(d\sigma), \quad A \in \mathscr{A}^n,$$

is σ-finite. Then the consistency theory developed by Lorraine Schwartz [1964] and LeCam [1973] (see also Strasser [1981]) leads to the following assertion:

(2) For every $\vartheta \in \Theta$, $s \in \mathbb{R}^k$ and every $\varepsilon > 0$ there are a constant $a > 0$ and a sequence of critical functions $\varphi_n \in \mathscr{F}(\Omega^n, \mathscr{A}^n)$, $n \in \mathbb{N}$, such that

$$P^n_{\vartheta + s/\sqrt{n}}\varphi_n > 1 - \varepsilon \quad \text{and}$$

$$\int\limits_{\sqrt{n}|\sigma - \vartheta| \geqq a} P_\sigma^n(\varphi_n)|\sqrt{n}(\sigma - \vartheta)|^p \mu(d\sigma) < \frac{\varepsilon}{\sqrt{n}}$$

as soon as $\vartheta + s/\sqrt{n} \in \Theta$, $\{\sigma \in \Theta: \sqrt{n}|\sigma - \vartheta| < a\} \subseteq \Theta$.

Let W: $\mathbb{R}^k \to [0, \infty)$ be a function which is subconvex, level-compact, separating and of order p. Denote by F_n the posterior distribution of $(P_\sigma^n)_{\sigma \in \Theta}$ with respect to μ, $n \in \mathbb{N}$. Then $\hat{\vartheta}_n$: $\Omega^n \to \Theta$ is a (generalized) Bayes estimate for

$$W_n: (\sigma, \tau) \mapsto W(\sqrt{n}(\sigma - \tau)), (\sigma, \tau) \in \Theta^2, \quad n \in \mathbb{N},$$

and μ if

$$\int W(\sqrt{n}(\hat{\vartheta}_n - \sigma)) F_n(d\sigma) = \inf_{\vartheta \in \Theta} \int W(\sqrt{n}(\sigma - \vartheta)) F_n(d\sigma), \quad n \in \mathbb{N}.$$

In the following we discuss the local asymptotic behaviour of the sequence $(\hat{\vartheta}_n)$.

For this, fix some $\vartheta \in \Theta$ and consider the experiments

$$E_{n,\vartheta} = (\Omega^n, \mathscr{A}^n, \{P^n_{\vartheta + t/\sqrt{n}}: t \in T_n(\vartheta)\}), \quad n \in \mathbb{N}.$$

We shall prove that the sequence $Y_n := \sqrt{n}(\hat{\vartheta}_n - \vartheta)$, $n \in \mathbb{N}$, is central for $(E_{n,\vartheta})$. This is done by verifying that on the one hand (Y_n) is a sequence of Bayes estimates for $(E_{n,\vartheta})$ and on the other hand that $(E_{n,\vartheta})$ satisfies the assumptions of theorem 84.9.

Let $(\mu_{n,\vartheta})_{n\in\mathbb{N}}$ be measures on $\mathscr{B}(T_n(\vartheta))$ defined by

$$\mu_{n,\vartheta}(B) = \frac{\sqrt{n}}{g(\vartheta)}\mu(\{\sigma \in \Theta: \sqrt{n}(\sigma - \vartheta) \in B\})$$

$$= \int_B \frac{g(\vartheta + t/\sqrt{n})}{g(\vartheta)}\, dt, \quad B \in \mathscr{B}(T_n(\vartheta)),\ n \in \mathbb{N}.$$

For every $n \in \mathbb{N}$ let $F_{n,\vartheta}$ be the posterior distribution of $(P^n_{\vartheta+t/\sqrt{n}})_{t\in T_n(\vartheta)}$ and $\mu_{n,\vartheta}$. Then it is easy to see that

$$F_{n,\vartheta}(B) = F_n\{\sigma \in \Theta: \sqrt{n}(\sigma - \vartheta) \in B\}, \quad B \in \mathscr{B}(T_n(\vartheta)),\ n \in \mathbb{N},$$

and it follows that (Y_n) is a sequence of Bayes estimates for W and $(\mu_{n,\vartheta})$.

It remains to be shown that the assumptions of Theorem 84.9 are satisfied. First, it is obvious that $\mu_{n,\vartheta} \to \lambda_k$, strongly on compacts. Secondly, equicontinuity of $(E_{n,\vartheta})$ follows from (1) since

$$d_2(P^n_{\vartheta+s/\sqrt{n}}, P^n_{\vartheta+t/\sqrt{n}})$$

$$\leqq \sqrt{n}\, d_2(P_{\vartheta+s/\sqrt{n}}, P_{\vartheta+t/\sqrt{n}}) \leqq b(\vartheta)|s-t|,$$

whenever $\vartheta + s/\sqrt{n} \in U(\vartheta)$, $\vartheta + t/\sqrt{n} \in U(\vartheta)$. Finally, we have to show that $(E_{n,\vartheta})$ is uniformly $(\mu_{n,\vartheta})$-integrable of order p. This property is a consequence of (2) which can easily be seen substituting $t := \sqrt{n}(\sigma - \vartheta)$ into (2) and recalling the definition of $\mu_{n,\vartheta}$, $n \in \mathbb{N}$.

84.11 Example (Pitman estimation in the independent, identically distributed case). Let $\Theta = \mathbb{R}$ and $E = (\mathbb{R}, \mathscr{B}, \{P_\vartheta: \vartheta \in \Theta\})$ where $\dfrac{dP_\vartheta}{d\lambda} = f(.-\vartheta)$ and f is an absolutely continuous density of a probability distribution with Fisher's information

$$I = \int \left(\frac{\dot{f}}{f}\right)^2 f\, d\lambda \in (0, \infty).$$

Then, by Discussion 77.5 the experiment E is differentiable and the condition (1) of 84.10 is satisfied. Assume further that

$$\int t^2 f(t)\, dt < \infty.$$

Then, by σ-finiteness of the mixture also condition (2) of 84.10 is satisfied with

$p = 2$. Now, consider the generalized Bayes estimates $\hat{\vartheta}_n$, $n \in \mathbb{N}$, for $W(t) = t^2$, $t \in \mathbb{R}$, and $\mu = \lambda$. From Example 37.6 (1), we know that

$$\hat{\vartheta}_n(\underset{\sim}{x}) = \frac{\int t \prod_{i=1}^{n} f(x_i - t)\, dt}{\int \prod_{i=1}^{n} f(x_i - t)\, dt}, \quad \underset{\sim}{x} \in \mathbb{R}^n,\ n \in \mathbb{N}.$$

These estimates are usually known under the label Pitman estimates and the results of Section 39 identify them as the optimal equivariant estimates for the experiments E^n, $n \in \mathbb{N}$. From 84.10 it follows that $(\sqrt{n}(\hat{\vartheta}_n - \vartheta))_{n \in \mathbb{N}}$ is a central sequence for the localized experiments $(E_{n,\vartheta})$, $\vartheta \in \Theta$.

Appendix: Notation and Terminology

This part is intended to fix the mathematical terminology and some notation. It seemed to us the best way for achieving this is talking about parts of mathematics which are presumably well-known to every reader. In this way, we hope that the reader conveniently becomes acquainted with the specific terminology and the basic notation of this book. Thus, one should not be surprised that our remarks here are far from being complete or in the logical order of a textbook. Nevertheless, we have tried to give a survey of mathematical knowledge which is indispensable for understanding this book.

Sets and mappings. If X is a set then $x \in X$ means that x is an element of X. The empty set is denoted by $\emptyset$. If E is an assertion concerning the elements of X then the subset of those elements having the property E is denoted by $\{x \in X: x \text{ satisfies } E\}$. Let A, B be subsets of X, i.e. $A \subseteq X$, $B \subseteq X$. Then $A \cup B$ is the union of A and B, $A \cap B$ the intersection, $A \setminus B$ the difference and $A \triangle B$ the symmetric difference. Two sets A, B are disjoint if $A \cap B = \emptyset$. The complement of A is denoted by A'. If A is a set then $|A|$ is the cardinal number of A. The set of all subsets of X is denoted by 2^X.

Frequently used notations are $\mathbb{N}$ for the set of natural numbers, $\mathbb{N}_0 = \mathbb{N} \cup \{0\}$, $\mathbb{R}$ for the set of real numbers, $\mathbb{R}_+$ for the set of positive real numbers. $\mathbb{Q}$ denotes the set of rational numbers, $\mathbb{C}$ that of complex numbers and $\bar{\mathbb{R}} = \mathbb{R} \cup \{\infty\} \cup \{-\infty\}$. The most important subsets of $\mathbb{R}$ are intervals being denoted by

$$[a, b] = \{x \in \mathbb{R}: a \leqq x \leqq b\},\ (a, b) = \{x \in \mathbb{R}: a < x < b\},$$
$$[a, b) = \{x \in \mathbb{R}: a \leqq x < b\},\ (a, b] = \{x \in \mathbb{R}: a < x \leqq b\}.$$

Moreover, we use the notations $[a, \infty) = \{x \in \mathbb{R}: x > a\}$, $[a, \infty] = [a, \infty) \cup \{\infty\}$ and so on. Every subset $A \subseteq \mathbb{R}$ has a least upper bound and a greatest lower bound, denoted by $\sup A$ and $\inf A$.

Let $I \neq \emptyset$ be an arbitrary set. Consider a family of subsets $\mathscr{A} = (A_i)_{i \in I}$ of a set X. Then the intersection of $\mathscr{A}$ is

$$\bigcap \mathscr{A} := \bigcap_{i \in I} A_i := \{x \in X: x \in A_i \text{ for every } i \in I\},$$

and the union of $\mathscr{A}$ is

$$\bigcup \mathscr{A} := \bigcup_{i \in I} A_i := \{x \in X: x \in A_i \text{ for at least one } i \in I\}.$$

If $I = \emptyset$ then we put $\bigcap \mathscr{A} = X$ and $\bigcup \mathscr{A} = \emptyset$. A partition of X is a family $\mathscr{A}$ of subsets of X, which are pairwise disjoint and such that $\bigcup \mathscr{A} = X$. A covering of a set A is a family of sets $\mathscr{B}$ such that $\bigcup \mathscr{B} \supseteq A$. Let $\mathscr{B}_1$, $\mathscr{B}_2$ be subsets of 2^X. If $\mathscr{B}_1 \subseteq \mathscr{B}_2$ then $\mathscr{B}_1$ is coarser than $\mathscr{B}_2$, and $\mathscr{B}_2$ is finer than $\mathscr{B}_1$.

The Cartesian product of A and B is the set of all ordered pairs $\{(x, y): x \in A, y \in B\} =: A \times B$. Let $C \subseteq A \times B$. For every $x \in A$ the fibre of C at x is $C^x = \{y \in B: (x, y) \in C\}$. If $(A_i)_{i \in I}$ is a family of sets then the Cartesian product is given by

$$\prod_{i \in I} A_i = \{(x_i)_{i \in I}: x_i \in A_i \text{ if } i \in I\}.$$

If $A_i = A$, $i \in I$, then we denote $A^I := \prod_{i \in I} A_i$.

A relation R between two sets A and B is described by its graph G_R which is a subset of $A \times B$. The graph G_R is interpreted as the set of pairs which are related by R. A relation R on a set A is transitive if $(x, y) \in G_R$ and $(y, z) \in G_R$ implies $(x, z) \in G_R$. If it is transitive, reflexive (i.e. $(x, x) \in G_R$ for every $x \in A$) and symmetric (i.e. $(x, y) \in G_R$ implies $(y, x) \in G_R$), then R is an equivalence relation. An equivalence relation defines a uniquely determined partition of A into sets of equivalent elements. This partition is called the set of equivalence classes and is denoted by A/R.

A relation which is transitive and reflexive is an order relation. Let $(I, \leqq)$ be an ordered set. It is directed from above if every pair $a, b \in I$ has a least upper bound $a \cup b (= \sup(a, b))$. It is directed from below if every pair $a, b \in I$ has a greatest lower bound $a \cap b (= \inf(a, b))$. An ordered set is a lattice if it is directed from below and from above.

A relation f between X and Y is a mapping or a function from X to Y if for every $x \in X$ there exists exactly one $y \in Y$ such that $(x, y) \in G_f$. In this case we denote $y = f(x)$ or $f: x \mapsto y$. The fact that f is a mapping from X to Y is expressed by $f: X \to Y$. The set X is the domain of f and Y is the range of f. The image of f is $\operatorname{im} f = \{f(x): x \in X\}$. If $A \subseteq X$, $B \subseteq Y$ then $f(A) = \{f(x): x \in A\}$ is the image of A and $f^{-1}(B) = \{x \in X: f(x) \in B\}$ is the inverse image of B. A mapping f is surjective if $f(X) = Y$, injective if $|f^{-1}(\{y\})| = 1$ for every $y \in \operatorname{im} f$. It is bijective or one-to-one if it is both surjective and injective. If $f: X \to Y$ is bijective then there is an inverse mapping $f^{-1}: Y \to X$ satisfying $f(f^{-1}(y)) = y$, $y \in Y$, and $f^{-1}(f(x)) = x$, $x \in X$. If X, Y, Z are sets and $f: X \to Y$, $g: Y \to Z$ are mappings then their composition is $g \circ f: x \mapsto g(f(x))$, $x \in X$. If $(X, \leqq)$, $(Y, \leqq)$ are ordered sets then a mapping $f: X \to Y$ is isotonic or increasing if $x_1 \leqq x_2$ implies $f(x_1) \leqq f(x_2)$ and antitonic or decreasing if $x_1 \leqq x_2$ implies $f(x_1) \geqq f(x_2)$, $x_1, x_2 \in X$.

There are some frequently used notations for special mappings. The indicator of a set $A \subseteq X$ is

$$1_A\colon x \mapsto \begin{cases} 1 & \text{if} \quad x \in A, \\ 0 & \text{if} \quad x \notin A. \end{cases}$$

A linear combination of indicators is a simple function. The identity is $\mathrm{id}_X\colon X \to X\colon x \mapsto x$. Considering a product $X \times Y$ we define the projections $\mathrm{pr}_1\colon X \times Y \to X$ by $\mathrm{pr}_1(x, y) = x$, $(x, y) \in X \times Y$, and pr_2 similarly. The function sgn: $\mathbb{R} \to \{-1, 0, 1\}$ is called the sign function and is defined by

$$\operatorname{sgn}(x) = \begin{cases} 1 & \text{if} \quad x > 0, \\ 0 & \text{if} \quad x = 0, \quad x \in \mathbb{R}, \\ -1 & \text{if} \quad x < 0. \end{cases}$$

If $f\colon X \times Y \to Z$ is a mapping then $f(., y)$ denotes the mapping $x \mapsto f(x, y)$, $x \in X$, $y \in Y$, $f(x, .)$ has to be understood similarly, $x \in X$. If f, g are real valued functions on X then $f \cup g\colon x \mapsto \max\{f(x), g(x)\}$, $f \cap g\colon x \mapsto \min\{f(x), g(x)\}$, $x \in X$. We denote $f^+ = f \cup 0$, $f^- = (-f) \cup 0$, $|f| = f^+ + f^-$.

A sequence in a set A is a mapping $f\colon \mathbb{N} \to A$, usually written as $(x_n)_{n \in \mathbb{N}}$ where $x_n = f(n)$, $n \in \mathbb{N}$. The subsets $\{x_1, x_2, \ldots, x_n\}$, $n \in \mathbb{N}$, are called sections of the sequence. A restriction of the sequence to an infinite subset of $\mathbb{N}$ is called a subsequence. The notations $x_n \uparrow$ and $x_n \downarrow$ mean that the sequence (x_n) is increasing and decreasing, respectively.

A set is countable if it admits a bijective mapping to a subset of $\mathbb{N}$.

Let $(A_n)_{n \in \mathbb{N}} \subseteq 2^X$ be a sequence of sets. Then

$$\liminf_{n \to \infty} A_n = \bigcup_{n=1}^{\infty} \bigcap_{k=n}^{\infty} A_k,$$

$$\limsup_{n \to \infty} A_n = \bigcap_{n=1}^{\infty} \bigcup_{k=n}^{\infty} A_k.$$

The sequence converges if $\liminf A_n = \limsup A_n =: A$ and A is called the limit (i.e. $\lim\limits_{n \to \infty} A_n$). The sequence is increasing if $A_n \subseteq A_{n+1}$, $n \in \mathbb{N}$, and decreasing if $A_n \supseteq A_{n+1}$, $n \in \mathbb{N}$. It is monotone if it is increasing or decreasing. Every monotone sequence converges, and we have $\lim A_n = \bigcap\limits_{n \in \mathbb{N}} A_n$ if $(A_n)_{n \in \mathbb{N}}$ is decreasing and $\lim A_n = \bigcup\limits_{n \in \mathbb{N}} A_n$ if it is increasing.

Let $X_i \neq \emptyset$, $i \in I$, and denote by $A(I)$ the set of all finite subsets of I, denoted by $\alpha, \beta, \ldots$ The projections from $\prod\limits_{i \in \beta} X_i$ onto $\prod\limits_{i \in \alpha} X_i$, $\alpha \subseteq \beta$, are denoted by $p_{\beta\alpha}$. We abbreviate $p_{I\alpha} =: p_\alpha$, $\alpha \in A(I)$. A cylinder set in $\prod\limits_{i \in I} X_i$ with base in $\alpha \in A(I)$ is a set of the form $A \times \prod\limits_{i \in I \setminus \alpha} X_i$, $A \subseteq \prod\limits_{i \in \alpha} X_i$, i.e. any inverse image of a set in $\prod\limits_{i \in \alpha} X_i$ under p_α. If I is finite then sets of the form $\prod\limits_{i \in I} A_i$, $A_i \subseteq X_i$, $i \in I$, are called rectangles.

Linear algebra. Suppose that H is a linear space or vector space over $\mathbb{R}$. For every subset $A \subseteq H$ there is a smallest subspace L containing A, called the linear hull or the linear span of A and denoted by $L =: \operatorname{span} A$. A subset $A \subseteq H$ is linearly independent if it is not the linear hull of a proper subset of its own. It is a basis if it is linearly independent and its linear hull is X. Given a linear space H the cardinality of every basis is the same and is called dimension of H, $\dim H$ for short.

If $A, B \subseteq H$ are subsets then $A + B = \{x + y: x \in A, y \in B\}$. If $L_1, L_2 \subseteq H$ are subspaces such that $L_1 \cap L_2 = \{0\}$ and $L_1 + L_2 = H$, then H is the direct sum of L_1 and L_2, i.e. $H = L_1 \oplus L_2$. For every subspace $L_1 \subseteq H$ there are complementary subspaces $L_2 \subseteq H$ such that $H = L_1 \oplus L_2$. These complementary subspaces are all of the same dimension which is called the codimension of L_1, denoted by $\operatorname{codim} L_1$.

A set of the form $M = x + L$, where $L \subseteq H$ is a subspace, is called a linear manifold in H. The dimension of M is $\dim M := \dim L$, similarly $\operatorname{codim} M := \operatorname{codim} L$. If $\operatorname{codim} M = 1$, then M is a hyperplane in H.

Suppose that H_1 and H_2 are vector spaces and $f: H_1 \to H_2$ is a linear mapping or linear function. The kernel of f is the set $\ker f := \{x \in H_1: f(x) = 0\}$ and the rank of f is $\operatorname{rk}(f) := \dim \operatorname{im} f$. A bijective linear mapping $f: H_1 \to H_2$ is an isomorphism. Vector spaces are isomorphic if there exists an isomorphism between them. Finite dimensional vector spaces are isomorphic iff they are of the same dimension. A translation is a mapping of the form $x \mapsto x + a$, $x \in H$. The sum of a linear mapping and a translation is an affine-linear mapping.

If $\dim H < \infty$ then the set of all linear functions $f: H \to \mathbb{R}$ is the dual space of H and is denotes by H^*. If $B = (b_i)_{i \in I}$ is a basis of H let $b_i^* \in H^*$ be such that $b_i^*(b_j) = \delta_{ij}$, $i \in I$, $j \in I$. Then $B^* = (b_i^*)_{i \in I}$ is a basis of H, called the dual basis corresponding to B. Let H_1, H_2 be two vector spaces and $f: H_1 \to H_2$ a linear mapping. Then $f^*: H_2^* \to H_1^*: x_2^* \mapsto x_2^* \circ f$ is a linear mapping, too, and is called the dual or adjoint of f.

Given a fixed basis a k-dimensional vector space H is naturally isomorphic with $\mathbb{R}^k$, and so is its dual H^*. For distinction we consider $\mathbb{R}^k$ as the vector space of column vectors whereas $(\mathbb{R}^k)^*$ denotes the vector space of row vectors. Within the matrix-calculus the $*$-operation means transposition. If $f: H_1 \to H_2$ is a linear mapping between two finite dimensional vector spaces let A be the matrix corresponding to f with respect to given bases B_1 of H_1 and B_2 of H_2. Then the transpose A^* is the matrix of the adjoint f^* with respect to the bases B_1^* of H_1^* and B_2^* of H_2^*. If A is a quadratic matrix then we denote the determinant of A by $\det A$ and the trace of A by $\operatorname{tr}(A)$.

A seminorm on a vector space H is a function $\|.\|: H \to [0, \infty)$ satisfying $\|\lambda x\| = |\lambda| \cdot \|x|$, $\lambda \in \mathbb{R}$, $x \in H$, and $\|x + y\| \leqq \|x\| + \|y\|$, $x, y \in H$. It is a norm if it satisfies $\|x\| = 0$ iff $x = 0$. If $\|\cdot\|$ is a norm then $(H, \|\cdot\|)$ is a normed vector space.

Let $f: (H_1, \|.\|_1) \to (H_2, \|.\|_2)$ be a linear mapping between normed vector spaces. Then f is bounded iff

$$\|f\|_{1,2} := \sup_{x \in H} \frac{\|f(x)\|_2}{\|x\|_1} < \infty.$$

The number $\|f\|_{1,2}$ is the norm of f (with respect to $\|.\|_1$ and $\|.\|_2$). Let $(H_1, \|.\|_1)$, $(H_2, \|.\|_2)$ and $(H_3, \|.\|_3)$ be normed vector spaces and B: $H_1 \times H_2 \to H_3$ a bilinear mapping, i.e. $B(x_1, .)$ and $B(., x_2)$ are linear for all $x_1 \in H_1$, $x_2 \in H_2$. Then B is bounded if

$$\|B\|_{12,3} = \sup_{x_1 \in H_1, x_2 \in H_2} \frac{\|B(x_1, x_2)\|_3}{\|x_1\|_1 \cdot \|x_2\|_2} < \infty.$$

The number $\|B\|_{12,3}$ is the norm of B (with respect to $\|.\|_1$, $\|.\|_2$ and $\|.\|_3$).

Let H be a vector space and p: $H \to \mathbb{R}$ a seminorm. By the Hahn–Banach theorem any real-valued linear function f on a subspace $L \subseteq H$ satisfying $|f| \leqq p$ can be extended to a linear function on the whole of H such that still $|f| \leqq p$.

Let B: $H \times H \to \mathbb{R}$ be a bilinear function on a vector space. It is positive semidefinite if $B(x, x) \geqq 0$, $x \in H$, and it is symmetric if $B(x, y) = B(y, x)$, $x, y \in H$. It is an inner product if it is symmetric and positive definite, the latter meaning the $B(x, x) > 0$ iff $x \neq 0$. Inner products are usually denoted by $\langle ., . \rangle$. A vector space $(H, \langle ., . \rangle)$ endowed with an inner product is an inner product space. It is a Euclidean space if it is of finite dimension. An inner product defines a norm by $\|x\|^2 = \langle x, x \rangle$, $x \in H$.

Let us return to an arbitrary vector space H. A linear combination is a convex combination if the scalars are nonnegative and add to one. A subset $A \subseteq H$ is a convex set if it contains all convex combinations of its elements. For every set $A \subseteq H$ there is a smallest convex subset containing A, which is called the convex hull of A and denoted by co A. The convex hull of a finite set is a convex polyhedron. A cone (of vertex zero) is a subset $A \subseteq H$ such that $\lambda x \in A$ whenever $\lambda > 0$, $x \in A$. A set $A \subseteq H$ is centrally symmetric if $x \in A$ implies $-x \in A$. A convex cone is a linear space iff it is centrally symmetric.

A function f: $H \to \mathbb{R}$ is convex if $f(\alpha x + (1-\alpha) y) \leqq \alpha f(x) + (1-\alpha) f(y)$ whenever $\alpha \in [0, 1]$ and $x, y \in H$. It is strictly convex if equality for some $\alpha \in (0, 1)$ implies $x = y$. The function f is concave if $-f$ is convex. It is quasiconvex if its level-sets $\{f \leqq \alpha\}$ are convex sets for every $\alpha \in \mathbb{R}$. A centrally symmetric function f is such that $f(x) = f(-x)$, $x \in H$. Finally, a function f is positively homogeneous if $f(\lambda x) = \lambda f(x)$, $\lambda \geqq 0$, $x \in H$.

Topology (Bourbaki [1958]). Let $X \neq \emptyset$ be an arbitrary set. A subset $\mathscr{T} \subseteq 2^X$ is a topology if it is closed under finite intersections and arbitrary unions. The pair $(X, \mathscr{T})$ is a topological space, the elements of $\mathscr{T}$ are the open sets, their complements the closed sets. Every subset $A \subseteq X$ contains a greatest open set

$\mathring{A}$, called the interior, and is contained in a smallest closed set $\bar{A}$, called the closure. The difference $\partial A = \bar{A} \setminus \mathring{A}$ is the boundary of A. The topology $\mathscr{T}$ is a Hausdorff topology if any two different points are contained in disjoint open sets. A subset $A \subseteq X$ is dense if $\bar{A} = X$. The topological space $(X, \mathscr{T})$ is separable if it contains a countable dense set. A subset $\mathscr{B} \subseteq \mathscr{T}$ is a base of $\mathscr{T}$ if the system of arbitrary unions of sets in $\mathscr{B}$ coincides with $\mathscr{T}$. The topological space is an A_2-space if there is a countable base of $\mathscr{T}$. Every A_2-space is separable. A point $x \in X$ is an inner point of $A \subseteq X$ if there is a set $B \in \mathscr{T}$ such that $x \in B \subseteq A$. In this case A is called a neighborhood of x. The system of all neighborhoods of x is denoted by $\mathscr{U}(x)$.

Let $(x_n)_{n \in \mathbb{N}} \subseteq X$ be a sequence. The sequence converges to a limit $x \in X$ (i.e. $\lim\limits_{n \to \infty} x_n = x$ or $x_n \to x$) if every neigborhood of x contains the complement of a section of $(x_n)_{n \in \mathbb{N}}$. The point $x \in X$ is an accumulation point of the sequence if every neigbourhood of x contains infinitely many points of the sequence. If $(x_n)_{n \in \mathbb{N}} \subseteq \mathbb{R}$ then the greatest accumulation point is $\limsup\limits_{n \to \infty} x_n$ and the smallest is $\liminf\limits_{n \to \infty} x_n$.

Let $(X_1, \mathscr{T}_1)$ and $(X_2, \mathscr{T}_2)$ be topological spaces. A function $f: X_1 \to X_2$ is continuous at $x \in X_1$ if for every $U \in \mathscr{U}(f(x))$ there is $V \in \mathscr{U}(x)$ such that $f(V) \subseteq U$. It is continuous if it is continuous everywhere. If f is bijective, continuous and f^{-1} is continuous, too, then f is a homeomorphism, and $(X_1, \mathscr{T}_1)$ and $(X_2, \mathscr{T}_2)$ are topologically equivalent. A bijective and continuous mapping is always a homeomorphism if the domain is compact and the range is Hausdorff. The real-valued continuous functions on a topologically space are denoted by $\mathscr{C}(X)$, the subset of bounded functions by $\mathscr{C}_b(X)$. If $f \in \mathscr{C}(X)$ then the support of f is $\operatorname{supp}(f) = \overline{\{f \neq 0\}}$.

A real valued function f on a topological space $(X, \mathscr{T})$ is lower semicontinuous if it is bounded from below and its level sets $\{f \leq \alpha\}$, $\alpha \in \mathbb{R}$, are closed. It is upper semicontinuous if $-f$ is lower semicontinuous.

Let $(X_i, \mathscr{T}_i)$, $i \in I$, be a family of topological spaces. Assume that I is finite. An open rectangle is a set $\prod\limits_{i \in I} A_i \subseteq \prod\limits_{i \in I} X_i$ consisting of open factors $A_i \in \mathscr{T}_i$, $i \in I$. The open rectangles are a base of the product topology $\bigotimes\limits_{i \in I} \mathscr{T}_i$. Now, let I be arbitrary. An open cylinder set with base in $\alpha \in A(I)$ is a cylinder set $A \times \prod\limits_{i \in I \setminus \alpha} X_i$, such that $A \in \bigotimes\limits_{i \in \alpha} \mathscr{T}_i$. The open cylinder sets are a base of the product topology $\bigotimes\limits_{i \in I} \mathscr{T}_i$.

Let $(X, \mathscr{T})$ be a Hausdorff space. A subset $A \subseteq X$ is compact if every open covering of A contains a finite subfamily which still covers A. This is the case iff A has the finite intersection property. It means that every system $\mathscr{C}$ of closed subsets of X whose finite intersections have common points with A satisfies $\bigcap \mathscr{C} \cap A \neq \emptyset$. A set $A \subseteq X$ is sequentially compact if every sequence in A contains a convergent subsequence. A set $A \subseteq X$ is relatively compact if $\bar{A}$ is compact. On a compact set a lower semicontinuous function attains the infimum of its values.

X is a locally compact space if every point has a compact neighbourhood. Let $(X, \mathcal{T})$ be a locally compact space. A sequence $(x_n) \subseteq X$ tends to infinity if it finally leaves every compact set. The set of all continuous functions with compact support is denoted by $\mathscr{C}_{00}(X)$. A continuous function vanishes at infinity if it becomes arbitrarily small outside of compact sets. The set of those functions is $\mathscr{C}_0(X)$.

A pseudodistance is a function $d\colon X \times X \to [0, \infty]$ satisfying $d(x, x) = 0$, $d(x, y) = d(y, x)$ and the triangle inequality $d(x, y) \leqq d(x, z) + d(y, z)$, $x, y, z \in X$. The pair (X, d) is called a pseudometric space. If $d(x, y) = 0$ implies $x = y$ then d is a distance and (X, d) is a metric space. Sets of the form $B(x, r) = \{y \in X\colon d(x, y) < r\}$ are called open balls around x with radius $r > 0$. If $A, B \subseteq X$ then we denote $\operatorname{dist}(A, B) = \inf\{d(x, y)\colon x \in A, y \in B\}$ and $\operatorname{dist}(x, A) = \operatorname{dist}(\{x\}, A)$, $x \in X$.

On a pseudometric space (X, d) the finite intersections of open balls are the base of a topology $\mathcal{T}_d$. The topology $\mathcal{T}_d$ is Hausdorff iff (X, d) is a metric space. It is an A_2-topology iff it is separable. On metric spaces compactness and sequential compactness coincide. A set $A \subseteq X$ is bounded if it is contained in a ball, it is totally bounded or precompact if it admits finite coverings by balls of arbitrarily small radius.

A Cauchy sequence on a pseudometric space (X, d) is a sequence $(x_n)_{n \in \mathbb{N}}$ such that the complements of sufficiently long sections are contained in arbitrarily small balls. A subset $A \subseteq X$ is complete if every Cauchy sequence in A converges to a limit in A. If (X, d) is a metric space then $A \subseteq X$ is compact iff it is complete and totally bounded.

Let (X_1, d_1) and (X_2, d_2) be pseudometric spaces. A function $f\colon X_1 \to X_2$ is uniformly continuous if for every $\varepsilon > 0$ there exists $\delta > 0$ such that $d_1(x, y) < \delta$ implies $d_2(f(x), f(y)) < \varepsilon$. The set of uniformly continuous, real valued functions on a pseudometric space (X, d) is denoted by $\mathscr{C}_u(X)$. A function $f\colon X_1 \to X_2$ is Lipschitz-continuous if there exists a number $K \geqq 0$ such that $d_2(f(x), f(y)) \leqq K d_1(x, y)$, $x, y \in X_1$. Every number K with this property is a Lipschitz constant of f, the infimum of all Lipschitz constants is denoted by $\operatorname{Lip}(f)$. A family of functions $f_i\colon (X_1, d_1) \to (X_2, d_2)$, $i \in I$, is equicontinuous at $x \in X_1$, if for every $\varepsilon > 0$ there is $\delta > 0$ such that $d_1(x, y) < \delta$ implies $d_2(f_i(x), f_i(y)) < \varepsilon$ simultaneously for all $i \in I$. It is equicontinuous if it is equicontinuous everywhere. It is uniformly equicontinuous if the choice of $\delta > 0$ does not depend on $x \in X_1$.

A family of pseudodistances $(d_i)_{i \in I}$ on a set $X \neq \emptyset$ which is directed from above is a uniform structure. Then $\bigcup_{i \in I} \mathcal{T}_{d_i}$ is the base of a topology. It is called the topology of the uniform space $(X, (d_i)_{i \in I})$. A subset $A \subseteq X$ is totally bounded or precompact if it is totally bounded in (X, d_i) for every $i \in I$. If

$(X_1, (d_{1,i})_{i \in I})$ and $(X_2, (d_{2,j})_{j \in J})$ are uniform spaces then $f: X_1 \to X_2$ is uniformly continuous if $f: (X_1, d_{1,i}) \to (X_2, d_{2,j})$ is uniformly continuous for all $i \in I$, $j \in J$. The uniform spaces are uniformly equivalent if there exists $f: X_1 \to X_2$ which is bijective and such that f and f^{-1} are uniformly continuous.

A filter is a subset $\mathscr{F} \subseteq 2^X$ such that $\emptyset \notin \mathscr{F}$, $\mathscr{F} \neq \emptyset$, which is closed under finite intersections and where $F \in \mathscr{F}$, $F \subseteq F_1$ implies $F_1 \in \mathscr{F}$. For every $x \in X$ the set of neighbourhoods $\mathscr{U}(x)$ of x is a filter. Every filter is contained in a maximal one, which is called ultrafilter and which is characterized by the fact that for every $A \subseteq X$ it contains either A or A'. A filter $\mathscr{F}$ converges to a point $x \in X$ if $\mathscr{F} \supseteq \mathscr{U}(x)$. A subset of a Hausdorff space is compact iff every ultrafilter converges. An accumulation point of a filter $\mathscr{F}$ is a point $x \in X$ satisfying $x \in \bar{F}$ for every $F \in \mathscr{F}$.

Let $(I, \leqq)$ be a directed set. A family which is indexed by I is a net. If $I = \mathbb{N}$ then a net is a sequence. For every net there is a natural filter consisting of the sets which contain $\{x_i: i \geqq i_0\}$, $i_0 \in I$. This is the section filter. A net or a sequence converges if the corresponding section filter converges. An accumulation point of a net is defined similarly.

Measure and integration (Bauer [1981] and Dunford–Schwartz [1967]). Let $\Omega \neq \emptyset$ be a set. Then $\mathscr{A} \subseteq 2^\Omega$ is a field if it is closed under complementation, finite intersection and finite union. The field is a σ-field if it is even closed under countable union and intersection. A set $\mathscr{M} \subseteq 2^\Omega$ is a monotone class if it contains all limits of monotone sequences in $\mathscr{M}$. It is a Dynkin system if it contains Ω, is closed under complementation and under countable union of pairwise disjoint sets. Let $\mathscr{C} \subseteq 2^\Omega$. Then, concerning each of the structures just defined, there exists a smallest one containing $\mathscr{C}$ and denoted by $\alpha(\mathscr{C})$, $\sigma(\mathscr{C})$, $m(\mathscr{C})$ and $d(\mathscr{C})$, respectively. A field is a σ-field iff it is a monotone class. If $\mathscr{C}$ is a field then $\sigma(\mathscr{C}) = m(\mathscr{C})$. A Dynkin system is a σ-field iff it is closed under finite intersection. If $\mathscr{C}$ is closed under finite intersection then $d(\mathscr{C}) = \sigma(\mathscr{C})$. A field $\mathscr{A}$ is countably generated if there exists a countable set $\mathscr{C} \subseteq 2^\Omega$ such that $\alpha(\mathscr{C}) = \mathscr{A}$. Similarly, we define a countably generated σ-field. If $\mathscr{A}$ is a σ-field then $A \in \mathscr{A}$ is an atom whenever $B \subseteq A$, $B \in \mathscr{A}$, imply $B = A$ or $B = \emptyset$. If $\mathscr{A}$ is a countably generated σ-field then the atoms of $\mathscr{A}$ form a partition of Ω. The σ-field on $\mathbb{R}$ which is generated by the intervals is the Borel σ-field of $\mathbb{R}$ and is denoted by $\mathscr{B}_1$ or $\mathscr{B}(\mathbb{R})$.

Let $\Omega \neq \emptyset$ and $\mathscr{A}$ be a field on Ω. Then $\mu: \mathscr{A} \to \mathbb{R}$ is finitely additive set function if $\mu(\emptyset) = 0$ and $\mu(A \cup B) = \mu(A) + \mu(B)$ if $A \cap B = \emptyset$. The set of bounded, finitely additive set functions is denoted by $ba(\Omega, \mathscr{A})$. An element $\mu \in ba(\Omega, \mathscr{A})$ is countable additive or a signed measure if $\mu(\bigcup_{n=1}^{\infty} A_n) = \sum_{n=1}^{\infty} \mu(A_n)$ for every pairwise disjoint sequence $(A_n)_{n \in \mathbb{N}} \subseteq \mathscr{A}$ whose union is in $\mathscr{A}$. The set of signed measures is denoted by $ca(\Omega, \mathscr{A})$.

Let $\mathscr{A}$ be σ-field. A function $\mu: \mathscr{A} \to [0, \infty]$ is a measure if $\mu(\emptyset) = 0$ and if it is countable additive, i.e. $\mu(\bigcup_{n=1}^{\infty} A_n) = \sum_{n=1}^{\infty} \mu(A_n)$ for every pairwise disjoint sequence $(A_n)_{n\in\mathbb{N}} \subseteq \mathscr{A}$. In this case we admit $\mu(\Omega) = \infty$. If $\mu(\Omega) < \infty$ then μ bounded. If $\mu(\Omega) = 1$ then μ is a probability measure. The corresponding sets are denoted by $\mathscr{M}(\Omega, \mathscr{A})$, $\mathscr{M}_b(\Omega, \mathscr{A})$ and $\mathscr{M}_1(\Omega, \mathscr{A})$, respectively. A point measure or Dirac measure sitting at $\omega \in \Omega$ is ε_ω: $A \mapsto 1_A(\omega)$, $A \in \mathscr{A}$. A measure μ is σ-finite if there is a countable partition of Ω by sets in $\mathscr{A}$ of finite μ-measure. If $\mathscr{A}$ is a field then a nonnegative set function $\mu \in ca(\Omega, \mathscr{A})$ can be extended in a unique way to a measure $\mu \in \mathscr{M}_b(\Omega, \sigma(\mathscr{A}))$. Let $\mu_1, \mu_2 \in \mathscr{M}(\Omega, \mathscr{A})$. Then μ_2 dominates μ_1 (i.e. $\mu_1 \ll \mu_2$) if $\mu_2(A) = 0$ implies $\mu_1(A) = 0$, $A \in \mathscr{A}$. If $\mu_1 \ll \mu_2$ and $\mu_2 \ll \mu_1$ then μ_1 and μ_2 are said to be equivalent, i.e. $\mu_1 \sim \mu_2$. They are orthogonal or singular $(\mu_1 \perp \mu_2)$ if there is $A \in \mathscr{A}$ such that $\mu_1(A) = 0$ and $\mu_2(A') = 0$.

Let $\mathscr{A}$ be a field. There is a natural ordering on $ba(\Omega, \mathscr{A})$. With this ordering $ba(\Omega, \mathscr{A})$ is a lattice, i.e. for $\sigma, \tau \in ba(\Omega, \mathscr{A})$ there exist a least upper bound $\sigma \cup \tau$ and a greatest lower bound $\sigma \cap \tau$. We denote $\sigma^+ = \sigma \cup 0$, $\sigma^- = (-\sigma) \cup 0$. Then $|\sigma| = \sigma^+ + \sigma^- \in ba(\Omega, \mathscr{A})$ is the total variation and $\sigma = \sigma^+ - \sigma^-$. We denote $\|\sigma\| = |\sigma|(\Omega)$. Two elements $\sigma, \tau \in ba(\Omega, \mathscr{A})$ are orthogonal or singular $(\sigma \perp \tau)$ if $|\sigma| \cap |\tau| = 0$. In this case we have $|\sigma| + |\tau| = |\sigma + \tau|$.

A pair $(\Omega, \mathscr{A})$ consisting of $\Omega \neq \emptyset$ and a σ-field $\mathscr{A}$ on Ω, is a measurable space. Let $\mu|\mathscr{A}$ be a measure. An assertion concerning points $\omega \in \Omega$ is valid μ-almost everywhere (μ-a.e.) if the set where it is not valid is contained in some $N \in \mathscr{A}$ with $\mu(N) = 0$. Let $\mathscr{N} = \{N \in \mathscr{A}: \mu(N) = 0\}$ and let $\mathscr{A}_0 \subseteq \mathscr{A}$ be a sub-σ-field. Then $\sigma(\mathscr{A}_0 \cup \mathscr{N})$ is the μ-completion of $\mathscr{A}_0$ in $\mathscr{A}$.

Let $(\Omega_1, \mathscr{A}_1)$ and $(\Omega_2, \mathscr{A}_2)$ be measurable spaces. A function $f: \Omega_1 \to \Omega_2$ is $(\mathscr{A}_1, \mathscr{A}_2)$-measurable if $f^{-1}(\mathscr{A}_2) \subseteq \mathscr{A}_1$. A real-valued function f on a measurable space $(\Omega, \mathscr{A})$ is $\mathscr{A}$-measurable if it is $(\mathscr{A}, \mathscr{B}_1)$-measurable. Let $\mathscr{L}(\Omega, \mathscr{A})$ be the set of all $\mathscr{A}$-measurable functions and $\mathscr{L}_b(\Omega, \mathscr{A})$ the subset of bounded, $\mathscr{A}$-measurable functions. Let $\mu|\mathscr{A}$ be a measure. A sequence $(f_n)_{n\in\mathbb{N}} \subseteq \mathscr{L}(\Omega, \mathscr{A})$ converges to $f \in \mathscr{L}(\Omega, \mathscr{A})$ in μ-measure if $\lim_{n\to\infty} \mu\{|f_n - f| > \varepsilon\} = 0$ for every $\varepsilon > 0$, and μ-a.e. if $\mu\{\lim_{n\to\infty} f_n \neq f\} = 0$. On $\mathscr{L}(\Omega, \mathscr{A})$ define $f \sim g$ if $\mu\{f \neq g\} = 0$. Then we denote $\mathscr{L}_\infty(\Omega, \mathscr{A}, \mu) = \{f \in \mathscr{L}(\Omega, \mathscr{A}): |f| \leqq \alpha$ μ-a.e. for some $\alpha > 0\}$ and $L_\infty(\Omega, \mathscr{A}, \mu) := \mathscr{L}(\Omega, \mathscr{A}, \mu)/\sim$. By $\mathscr{L}_\infty^+$ and L_∞^+ we denote the nonnegative elements in $\mathscr{L}_\infty$ and L_∞. If $f \in \mathscr{L}_\infty(\Omega, \mathscr{A}, \mu)$ then

$$\|f\|_\infty = \inf\{\alpha \geqq 0: |f| \leqq \alpha \ \mu\text{-a.e.}\}.$$

This is a seminorm of $\mathscr{L}_\infty(\Omega, \mathscr{A}, \mu)$ and a norm on $L_\infty(\Omega, \mathscr{A}, \mu)$.

If $f: \Omega_1 \to \Omega_2$ is a mapping and $(\Omega_2, \mathscr{A}_2)$ is a measurable space then there is a smallest σ-field $\mathscr{A}(f)$ on Ω_1 such that f is $(\mathscr{A}(f), \mathscr{A}_2)$-measurable. If g is $\mathscr{A}(f)$-measurable then there is a factorization $g = \varphi \circ f$ such that $\varphi: \Omega_2 \to \mathbb{R}$ is $\mathscr{A}_2$-measurable. If $(\Omega_1, \mathscr{A}_1)$ and $(\Omega_2, \mathscr{A}_2)$ are measurable spaces and $\mu_1|\mathscr{A}_1$ is a measure, then an $(\mathscr{A}_1, \mathscr{A}_2)$-measurable mapping $f\colon \Omega_1 \to \Omega_2$ transforms the measure μ_1 into a measure $\mu_2|\mathscr{A}_2$, according to $\mu_2(A_2) = \mu_1(f^{-1}(A_2))$, $A_2 \in \mathscr{A}_2$. The measure μ_2 is the image of μ_1 under f and denoted by $\mu_1 \circ f^{-1}$ or, if convenient, $\mathscr{L}(f|\mu_1)$.

If $(\Omega, \mathscr{A})$ is a measurable space and $\mu|\mathscr{A}$ is a measure, then $(\Omega, \mathscr{A}, \mu)$ is called a measure space. The μ-integral of an $\mathscr{A}$-measurable function $f\colon \Omega \to \mathbb{R}$ is denoted by $\mu(f)$ or $\int f\,d\mu$. It is well-defined for all nonnegative $\mathscr{A}$-measurable functions. A function $f \in \mathscr{L}(\Omega, \mathscr{A})$ is μ-integrable if $\mu(f^+) < \infty$, $\mu(f^-) < \infty$. In this case $\mu(f) = \mu(f^+) - \mu(f^-)$. The μ-integral has the Levi-property, i.e. for every increasing sequence $(f_n) \subseteq \mathscr{L}^+(\Omega, \mathscr{A})$ we have $\mu(\sup_{n\in\mathbb{N}} f_n) = \sup_{n\in\mathbb{N}} \mu(f_n)$. If $\varphi\colon \mathbb{R} \to \mathbb{R}$ is a convex function which is bounded from below then Jensen's inequality says

$$\int \varphi \circ f\,d\mu \geqq \varphi\left(\int f\,d\mu\right),$$

whenever $\mu(f)$ is well-defined. If μ is a bounded measure then a family $(f_i)_{i\in I} \subseteq \mathscr{L}(\Omega, \mathscr{A})$ is uniformly μ-integrable if

$$\lim_{a\to\infty} \sup_{i\in I} \int_{|f_i|>a} |f_i|\,d\mu = 0.$$

The set of μ-integrable functions in $\mathscr{L}(\Omega, \mathscr{A})$ is denoted by $\mathscr{L}_1(\Omega, \mathscr{A}, \mu)$, and $L_1(\Omega, \mathscr{A}, \mu) := \mathscr{L}_1(\Omega, \mathscr{A}, \mu)/\sim$. There is a seminorm on $\mathscr{L}_1(\Omega, \mathscr{A}, \mu)$ defined by

$$\|f\|_1 = \int |f|\,d\mu,$$

which is a norm on $L_1(\Omega, \mathscr{A}, \mu)$. If μ is a bounded measure and if $(f_n)_{n\in\mathbb{N}} \subseteq \mathscr{L}_1(\Omega, \mathscr{A}, \mu)$ converges to f in μ-measure then we have $\|f_n - f\|_1 \to 0$ iff $(f_n)_{n\in\mathbb{N}}$ is uniformly μ-integrable. The set of all functions in $\mathscr{L}(\Omega, \mathscr{A})$ such that $f^2 \in \mathscr{L}_1(\Omega, \mathscr{A}, \mu)$ is denoted by $\mathscr{L}_2(\Omega, \mathscr{A}, \mu)$. If μ is a bounded measure then $\mathscr{L}_2(\Omega, \mathscr{A}, \mu) \subseteq \mathscr{L}_1(\Omega, \mathscr{A}, \mu)$. We define $L_2(\Omega, \mathscr{A}, \mu) := \mathscr{L}_2(\Omega, \mathscr{A}, \mu)/\sim$.

Let $\nu|\mathscr{A}$ be a σ-finite measure dominating $\mu|\mathscr{A}$. Then the Radon-Nikodym theorem says that there exists $f \in \mathscr{L}(\Omega, \mathscr{A})^+$ such that $\mu = f\nu$, where

$$f\nu\colon A \mapsto \int_A f\,d\nu, \quad A \in \mathscr{A}.$$

The function f is ν-integrable iff μ is bounded.

A measure space $(\Omega, \mathscr{A}, \mu)$ is said to be perfect if for any $f \in \mathscr{L}(\Omega, \mathscr{A})$ and any set $A \subseteq \mathbb{R}$ such that $f^{-1}(A) \in \mathscr{A}$ there are Borel sets $B_1, B_2 \in \mathscr{B}_1$ such that $B_1 \subseteq A \subseteq B_2$ and $\mu \circ f^{-1}(B_2 \setminus B_1) = 0$.

Topology and measure (Bauer [1981] and Billingsley [1968]). Let $(X, \mathscr{T})$ be a topological space. Then $\sigma(\mathscr{T})$ is the Borel-σ-field of X, denoted by $\mathscr{B}(X)$. The smallest σ-field $\mathscr{A}$ such that all continuous functions are $\mathscr{A}$-measurable is the Baire σ-field and is denoted by $\mathscr{B}_0(X)$. In general, we have $\mathscr{B}_0(X) \subseteq \mathscr{B}(X)$. If

(X, d) is a metric space then $\mathscr{B}_0(X) = \mathscr{B}(X)$. The Borel-$\sigma$-field of $\mathbb{R}^k$ is denoted by $\mathscr{B}_k$. If $(X, \mathscr{T})$ is a Hausdorff space then $\mathscr{B}(X)$ contains all sets consisting of single points.

Let $(X, \mathscr{T})$ be a Hausdorff space. A measure $\mu|\mathscr{B}(X)$ is a Borel measure if $\mu(K) < \infty$ for every compact $K \subseteq X$. A bounded measure is tight if for every $\varepsilon > 0$ there is a compact set $K \subseteq X$ such that $\mu(X \setminus K) < \varepsilon$. A family of bounded measures $(\mu_i)_{i \in I}$ is uniformly tight if the compact set can be chosen independently if $i \in I$. A measure $\mu|\mathscr{B}(X)$ is non-atomic if $\mu\{x\} = 0$, $x \in X$.

Let (X, d) be a separable metric space. The weak topology of $\mathscr{M}_b(X, \mathscr{B}(X))$ is the coarsest topology such that $\mu \mapsto \mu(f)$, $\mu \in \mathscr{M}_b(X, \mathscr{B}(X))$ is continuous for every $f \in \mathscr{C}_b(X)$. The weak topology is metrizable. Prohorov's theorem says that a subset of $\mathscr{M}_b(X, \mathscr{B}(X))$ is relatively compact for the weak topology iff it is uniformly tight. The theorem of Daniell-Stone says that a linear, isotonic function $L: \mathscr{C}_b(X) \to \mathbb{R}$ is of the form $L(f) = \mu(f)$ for some $\mu \in \mathscr{M}_b(X, \mathscr{B}(X))$ iff it is Daniell-continuous, i.e. if

$$f_n \downarrow 0 \quad \text{implies} \quad L(f_n) \downarrow 0.$$

If $\mu|\mathscr{B}(X)$ is a tight measure then $(X, \mathscr{B}(X), \mu)$ is a perfect measure space.

Let $(X, \mathscr{T})$ be a locally compact space. The vague topology on the set of Borel measures is the coarsest topology such that $\mu \mapsto \mu(f)$, $\mu \in \mathscr{M}_b(X, \mathscr{B}(X))$ is continuous for every $f \in \mathscr{C}_{00}(X)$. An isotonic, linear function on $\mathscr{C}_{00}(X)$ is a Radon measure. Every Radon measure is the integral of a Borel measure. A Borel measure on a locally compact space has the generalized Levi property, which says that $\mu(\sup_{i \in I} f_i) = \sup_{i \in I} \mu(f_i)$ for every family $(f_i)_{i \in I} \subseteq \mathscr{L}(\Omega, \mathscr{A})^+$ which is directed from above.

Topological vector spaces (Dunford–Schwartz [1969], Schaefer [1971 and 1974]). Let X be a vector space and $\mathscr{T}$ a topology on X. If the operations on X are continuous for $\mathscr{T}$ then $(X, \mathscr{T})$ is a topological vector space. It is a locally convex space if $\mathscr{T}$ is generated by a family of semi-norms. Obviously, X is then a uniform space. If $\mathscr{T}$ is generated by a single norm $\|.\|$, then $(X, \|.\|)$ is a normed vector space, and it is a Banach space if it is complete. A linear mapping between normed spaces is continuous iff it is bounded.

If a topological vector space is locally convex then there exist non-trivial continuous linear functions $f: X \to \mathbb{R}$. The kernels of these functions are exactly the closed hyperplanes in X. The basic separation theorem says that two non-empty, disjoint convex sets, one of which is compact and the other closed, can be separated strictly by a closed hyperplane, respectively by a continuous linear function. A a consequence, every convex function which is bounded from below is the upper envelope of continuous, affine-linear functions.

Let $X \neq \emptyset$ be an arbitrary set. Then $\mathbb{R}^X$ is a vector space. Any subspace of $\mathbb{R}^X$ is called function space. If $M \subseteq X$ and $f \in \mathbb{R}^X$ let $p_M(f) := \sup\{|f(x)|: x \in M\}$. If $H \subseteq \mathbb{R}^X$ is any function space then the family of seminorms $\{p_{\{x\}}: x \in X\}$

defines a locally convex topology which coincides with the product topology of $H \subseteq \mathbb{R}^X$ and is called the topology of pointwise convergence. If $H \subseteq \mathbb{R}^X$ is a function space containing only bounded functions then the norm $p_X = \|\,.\,\|_u$, the uniform norm, defines the uniform topology of H. Let $(X, \mathscr{T})$ be a topological space and $H \subseteq \mathbb{R}^X$ a function space whose elements are bounded on compacts. Then the family of seminorms $\{p_K: K \subseteq X \text{ compact}\}$ defines the locally convex topology of compact convergence.

If $(X, \mathscr{T})$ is a Hausdorff space then $(\mathscr{C}_b(X), \|\,.\,\|_u)$ is a Banach space. Let $(X, \mathscr{T})$ be a locally compact space and endow $\mathscr{C}(X)$ with the topology of compact convergence. By the theorem of Arzela-Ascoli a subset of $\mathscr{C}(X)$ is relatively compact iff it is equicontinuous and pointwise bounded. If (X, d) is a compact metric space then the Stone-Weierstrass theorem says that a subalgebra in $\mathscr{C}_b(X)$, which contains the constants and separates points, is dense in $\mathscr{C}_b(X)$. Let $(X, \mathscr{T})$ be a locally compact space. Then $(\mathscr{C}_0(X), \|\,.\,\|_u)$ is a Banach space and $\overline{\mathscr{C}_{00}(X)} = \mathscr{C}_0(X)$. Every subalgebra in $\mathscr{C}_0(X)$ which separates points and for every $x \in X$ contains a function g with $g(x) \neq 0$, is dense in $\mathscr{C}_0(X)$.

Let H be a locally convex space and denote by H^* the set of all continuous linear functions $f: H \to \mathbb{R}$. This is the topological dual of H. The topology of pointwise convergence of H^* is the H-topology of H^*. Similarly, the elements of H may be viewed as functions on H^* and the topology of pointwise convergence is the H^*-topology of H. Such topologies are usually called weak topologies. If $(H, \|\,.\,\|)$ is a Banach space then $(H^*, \|\,.\,\|)$ is a Banach space, too. Alaoglu's theorem says that bounded subsets of H^* are relatively compact for the H-topology of H^*. A similar assertion is valid for bilinear functions. Let $(H_1, \|\,.\,\|_1)$ and $(H_2, \|\,.\,\|_2)$ be Banach spaces. A bilinear function on $H_1 \times H_2$ is continuous iff it is bounded. The vector space $H_1^* \otimes H_2^*$ of all continuous, bilinear functions is a Banach space for the natural norm. The $H_1 \otimes H_2$-topology of $H_1^* \otimes H_2^*$ is the topology of pointwise convergence. Similar to Alaoglu's theorem, every bounded subset of $H_1^* \otimes H_2^*$ is relatively compact for the $H_1 \otimes H_2$-topology. If $f: H_1 \to H_2$ is linear and bounded then the adjoint f^* maps H_2^* into H_1^*.

If $X \neq \emptyset$ is an arbitrary set and $\mathbb{R}^X$ is endowed with the topology of pointwise convergence then $(\mathbb{R}^X)^*$ is the set of functions with finite support. If $(\Omega, \mathscr{A}, \mu)$ is a σ-finite measure space then $(L_1(\Omega, \mathscr{A}, \mu))^* = L_\infty(\Omega, \mathscr{A}, \mu)$.

A vector space H which is an ordered set is an ordered vector space if the ordering is compatible with the linear structure. Then subset $C = \{x \in H: x \geqq 0\}$ is the positive cone. It is a proper cone, i.e. it satisfies $C \cap (-C) = \{0\}$. Every proper convex cone $C \subseteq H$ defines a compatible semiordering by the definition $x \leqq y$ if $y - x \in C$. A vector lattice is an ordered vector space which is directed from above and from below. It is a Banach lattice if it is a Banach space and if the norm is compatible with the order structure. A subset A of a vector lattice is order bounded if there is an upper and a lower bound of A in H. H is order complete if every order bounded subset $A \subseteq H$ has a least upper bound $\sup A$ and a greatest lower bound $\inf A$ in H. Examples of order complete Banach lattice are $ba(\Omega, \mathscr{A})$ and $ca(\Omega, \mathscr{A})$. A linear mapping between vector lattices $f\colon H_1 \to H_2$ is a positive operator if $x \geqq 0$ implies $f(x) \geqq 0$. It is a lattice isomorphism if it is an isomorphism of the linear and the lattice structure.

If $(H, \langle .,. \rangle)$ is an inner product space then there is a natural isomorphism between H and H^*, namely $x \mapsto \langle x, . \rangle$, $x \in H$. With this identification in mind the adjoint f^* of a bounded linear mapping $f\colon H \to H$ may be viewed as mapping H into H.

Two elements x, y of an inner product space $(H, \langle .,. \rangle)$ are orthogonal (i.e. $x \perp y$) if $\langle x, y \rangle = 0$. A family $(x_i)_{i \in I} \subseteq H$ is orthogonal if its elements are pairwise orthogonal, it is an orthonormal set if it is orthogonal and its elements are of norm one. If $L \subseteq H$ is a complete subspace then there is a uniquely determined complementary subspace $L^\perp$ which is orthogonal to L, i.e. $x \perp y$ if $x \in L$ and $y \in L^\perp$. Then the sum $H = L \oplus L^\perp$ is called an orthogonal direct sum and $L^\perp$ is the orthogonal complement of L. Every $x \in H$ admits a unique decomposition as $x = y + z$ where $y \in L$, $z \in L^\perp$. We write $y = p_L(x)$ and call p_L the orthogonal projection of H onto L. It is linear, satisfies $x - p_L(x) \perp L$, $x \in H$, and $\|x - p_L(x)\| = \inf\{\|x - y\| : y \in L\}$. Moreover, $p_L \circ p_L = p_L$ and $p_L^* = p_L$.

Probability theory (Bauer [1981] and Gaenssler-Stute [1977]). In a probabilistic context a measurable space $(\Omega, \mathscr{A})$ is called sample space, probability measures are denoted by capital letters $P, Q, \ldots$, measurable functions are called random variables, also being denoted by capital letters $X, Y, \ldots$ If $P|\mathscr{A}$ is a probability measure then $(\Omega, \mathscr{A}, P)$ is called a probability space. Provided that $P(X)$ is well-defined it is called the expectation or the mean of X. The variance of X is $V(X) := P([X - P(X)]^2)$. The image $\mathscr{L}(X|P)$ of P under X is the distribution of X under P. The function $F_X\colon x \mapsto P\{X < x\}$, $x \in \mathbb{R}$, is the distribution function of X and determines the distribution uniquely. Sometimes the distribution $\mathscr{L}(X|P)$ of X under P is identified with the function $f \mapsto P(f \circ X)$, $f \in \mathscr{C}_b(\mathbb{R})$. Convergence in P-measure of random variables is called stochastic convergence, whereas weak convergence of the distributions is called convergence in distribution of the underlying random variables. If $\underline{X} = (X_1, \ldots, X_n)$ is a vector of random variables then the image $\mathscr{L}(\underline{X}|P)$ is the joint distribution of $X_1, \ldots, X_n$.

The Gaussian or normal distribution with mean $a \in \mathbb{R}$ and variance $\sigma^2 > 0$ is defined by

$$\nu_{a,\sigma^2}\colon B \mapsto \frac{1}{\sqrt{2\pi}\,\sigma} \int_B \exp\left[-\frac{1}{2} \cdot \frac{(t-a)^2}{\sigma^2}\right] dt, \quad B \in \mathscr{B}_1.$$

The particular case $\nu_{0,1}$ is the standard Gaussian distribution on $\mathbb{R}$, its distribution function is denoted by Φ, for $\alpha \in [0,1]$ the α-quantile of Φ is $N_\alpha := \Phi^{-1}(\alpha)$.

A finite system of sets $A_1, \ldots, A_n$ in $\mathscr{A}$ satisfies the multiplication rule if $P(\bigcap_{i=1}^{n} A_i) = \prod_{i=1}^{n} P(A_i)$. A family of sets $\mathscr{C} \subseteq \mathscr{A}$ is independent if every finite sub-family satisfies the multiplication rule. A family of σ-fields $\mathscr{A}_i \subseteq \mathscr{A}$, $i \in I$, is independent if every collection $(A_i)_{i\in I}$ with $A_i \in \mathscr{A}_i$, $i \in I$, is independent. A family of random variables $(X_i)_{i\in I}$ is independent if $(\mathscr{A}(X_i))_{i\in I}$ is independent.

Let $(X_i)_{i\in\mathbb{N}}$ be an independent and identically distributed (i.i.d.) sequence of random variables. If $P(|X_1|) < \infty$, then by the law of large numbers

$$\lim_{n\to\infty} \frac{1}{n} \sum_{i=1}^{n} X_i = P(X_1) \quad P\text{-a.e.}$$

Let $(X_i)_{i\in\mathbb{N}}$ be independent but not necessarily identically distributed. If $X_i \in \mathscr{L}_2(\Omega, \mathscr{A}, P)$, $i \in \mathbb{N}$, then the Lindeberg condition

$$\lim_{n\to\infty} \frac{1}{s_n^2} \sum_{i=1}^{n} \int_{|X_i - P(X_i)| \geq \varepsilon s_n} (X_i - P(X_i))^2 \, dP = 0, \quad \varepsilon > 0,$$

where $s_n^2 := \sum_{i=1}^{n} V(X_i)$, implies the central limit theorem

$$\lim_{n\to\infty} \mathscr{L}\left(\frac{1}{s_n} \sum_{i=1}^{n} (X_i - P(X_i)) \,\middle|\, P\right) = \nu_{0,1}, \quad \text{weakly}.$$

If $X_1, X_2, \ldots, X_n$ are independent random variables such that $\mathscr{L}(X_i|P) = \nu_{\delta_i, 1}$, $1 \leqq i \leqq n$, then $\mathscr{L}(\sum_{i=1}^{n} X_i^2 | P)$ is the non-central $\chi_n^2(\delta^2)$-distribution, $\delta^2 := \sum_{i=1}^{n} \delta_i^2$. The distribution function is denoted by χ^2_{n,δ^2}. In case $\delta = 0$, the distribution is called central. If $X_1, \ldots, X_{n_1}, Y_1, \ldots, Y_{n_2}$ are independent random variables such that $\mathscr{L}(X_i|P) = \nu_{\delta_i, 1}$, $1 \leqq i \leqq n_1$, and $\mathscr{L}(Y_i|P) = \nu_{0,1}$, $1 \leqq i \leqq n_2$, then

$$\mathscr{L}\left(\frac{1}{n_1} \sum_{i=1}^{n_1} X_i^2 \Big/ \frac{1}{n_2} \sum_{j=1}^{n_2} Y_j^2 \,\middle|\, P\right)$$

is the non-central $F_{n_1, n_2}(\delta^2)$-distribution. The distribution function is denoted by $F_{n_1, n_2; \delta^2}$. In case $\delta = 0$ the distribution is called central. The distribution $\Gamma_{\alpha,\nu}$ on $(\mathbb{R}, \mathscr{B})$ which is defined by

$$\Gamma_{\alpha,\nu}(B) = \frac{\alpha^\nu}{\Gamma(\nu)} \int_{B\cap(0,\infty)} \alpha^\nu t^{\nu-1} e^{-\alpha t} dt, \quad B \in \mathscr{B}_1,$$

is called the $\Gamma_{\alpha,\nu}$-distribution. Its distribution function ist also denoted by $\Gamma_{\alpha,\nu}$.

If $\mathscr{A}_0 \subseteq \mathscr{A}$ is a σ-field and $X \geqq 0$ a random variable then $\sigma: A \mapsto \int_A X dP$, $A \in \mathscr{A}_0$, is in $\mathscr{M}(\Omega, \mathscr{A}_0)$ and $\sigma \ll P|\mathscr{A}_0$. Hence, by the Radon-Nikodyn theorem there is $\frac{d\sigma}{dP} =: P(X|\mathscr{A}_0) \in \mathscr{L}(\Omega, \mathscr{A}_0)$. If X is P-integrable then $P(X|\mathscr{A}_0) := P(X^+|\mathscr{A}_0) - P(X^-|\mathscr{A}_0)$. The random variable $P(X|\mathscr{A}_0)$ is the conditional expectation of X given $\mathscr{A}_0$. If $A \in \mathscr{A}$ then $P(A|\mathscr{A}_0) := P(1_A|\mathscr{A}_0)$ is the conditional probability of A given $\mathscr{A}_0$. Let $(\mathscr{A}_n)_{n\in\mathbb{N}}$ be a sequence of sub-σ-fields of $\mathscr{A}$, increasing or decreasing, and $\mathscr{A}_0 := \sigma(\lim \mathscr{A}_n)$. Then for every P-integrable random variable X the martingale theorems imply $\lim\limits_{n\to\infty} P(X|\mathscr{A}_n) = P(X|\mathscr{A}_0)$ P-a.e.

Let $(\Omega_i, \mathscr{A}_i)$, $1 \leqq i \leqq n$, be sample spaces. The sets of the form $A_1 \times A_2 \times \ldots \times A_n$, $A_i \in \mathscr{A}_i$, $1 \leqq i \leqq n$, are called measurable rectangles. The measurable rectangles generate the product σ-field $\bigotimes\limits_{i=1}^{n} \mathscr{A}_i$. If $P_i|\mathscr{A}_i$, $1 \leqq i \leqq n$, are probability measures then there exists exactly one probability measure $P_0|\bigotimes\limits_{i=1}^{n} \mathscr{A}_i$ such that $P_0(A_1 \times \ldots \times A_n) = \prod\limits_{i=1}^{n} P_i(A_i)$ for every rectangle. This is the product measure $\bigotimes\limits_{i=1}^{n} P_i$. In case of identical components $(\Omega, \mathscr{A}, P)$ we denote $\bigotimes\limits_{i=1}^{n} \mathscr{A}_i = \mathscr{A}^n$ and $\bigotimes\limits_{i=1}^{n} P_i = P^n$.

Now, let $(\Omega_i, \mathscr{A}_i)$, $i \in I$, be a family of sample spaces. A measurable cylinder set with base in $\alpha \in A(I)$ is a cylinder set $A \times \prod\limits_{i\in I\setminus\alpha} \Omega_i$, such that $A \in \bigotimes\limits_{i\in\alpha} \mathscr{A}_i$. The measurable cylinder sets generate the product σ-field $\bigotimes\limits_{i\in I} \mathscr{A}_i$. In case of $(\Omega_i, \mathscr{A}_i) = (\Omega, \mathscr{A})$, $i \in I$, we denote $\bigotimes\limits_{i\in I} \mathscr{A}_i = \mathscr{A}^I$. A family $(P_\alpha)_{\alpha\in A(I)}$ of probability measures $P_\alpha|\bigotimes\limits_{i\in\alpha} \mathscr{A}_i$, $\alpha \in A(I)$, is projective if $\alpha \subseteq \beta$ implies $\mathscr{L}(p_{\beta\alpha}|P_\beta) = P_\alpha$. If a probability measure $P_I|\bigotimes\limits_{i\in\alpha} \mathscr{A}_i$ satisfies $\mathscr{L}(p_\alpha|P_I) = P_\alpha$, $\alpha \in A(I)$, then it is uniquely determined and is called the projective limit of $(P_\alpha)_{\alpha\in A(I)}$. In general, a projective limit need not exist. In the particular case, where $P_i|\mathscr{A}_i$, $i \in I$, are probability measures and $P_\alpha = \bigotimes\limits_{i\in I} P_i$, $\alpha \in A(I)$, the projective limit exists and is called the product of $(P_i)_{i\in I}$, denoted by $\bigotimes\limits_{i\in I} P_i$. In case $(\Omega_i, \mathscr{A}_i, P_i) = (\Omega, \mathscr{A}, P)$, $i \in I$, we denote $\bigotimes\limits_{i\in I} P_i = P^I$. If the projective system $(P_\alpha)_{\alpha\in A(I)}$ is not of the particular type considered above then additional topological properties imply the existence of the projective limit.

Let $(\Omega_1, \mathscr{A}_1)$ and $(\Omega_2, \mathscr{A}_2)$ be sample spaces. A kernel from $(\Omega_1, \mathscr{A}_1)$ to $(\Omega_2, \mathscr{A}_2)$ is a function $K\colon \Omega_1 \times \mathscr{A}_2 \to [0, \infty)$, such that $K(., A_2)$ is $\mathscr{A}_1$-measurable for every $A_2 \in \mathscr{A}_2$, and $K(\omega_1, .) \in \mathscr{M}(\Omega_2, \mathscr{A}_2)$ for every $\omega_1 \in \Omega_1$. If $K(\omega_1, \Omega_2) \leqq 1$, $\omega_1 \in \Omega_1$, then it is a substochastic kernel, if $K(\omega_1, \Omega_2) = 1$, $\omega_1 \in \Omega_1$, then it is a stochastic kernel or a transition probability. A measure $\mu|\mathscr{A}_1 \otimes \mathscr{A}_2$ admits a desintegration along Ω_1 if there is a kernel K from Ω_1 to Ω_2 such that

$$\mu(A_1 \times A_2) = \int_{A_1} K(\omega_1, A_2)\,\mu(d\omega_1, \Omega_2), \quad A_1 \in \mathscr{A}_1, A_2 \in \mathscr{A}_2.$$

If $\nu_1 \in \mathscr{A}_1$, $\nu_2 \in \mathscr{A}_2$, are σ-finite measures then every $\mu \ll \nu_1 \otimes \nu_2$ admits a desintegration which can be given in an explicit way. Otherwise, additional topological conditions imply the existence of a desintegration.

Let $(\Omega, \mathscr{A}, P)$ be a probability space and $\mathscr{A}_0 \subseteq \mathscr{A}$ a sub-σ-field. A stochastic kernel K from $(\Omega, \mathscr{A}_0)$ to $(\Omega, \mathscr{A})$ is a regular conditional probability of P given $\mathscr{A}_0$ if $K(., A) = P(A|\mathscr{A}_0)$ P-a.e., $A \in \mathscr{A}$. There are topological conditions which imply the existence of regular conditional probabilities.

Let $(\Omega, \mathscr{A}, P)$ be a probability space and $T \neq \emptyset$ an arbitrary set. A family $(X_t)_{t \in T}$ of random variables is a stochastic process. For every $\omega \in \Omega$ the function $t \mapsto X_t(\omega)$, $t \in T$, is a path of the process. Suppose that (T, d) is a metric space. The stochastic process is separable if there are $N \in \mathscr{A}$, $P(N) = 0$, and a countable set $T_0 \subseteq T$ such that for every $\omega \notin N$ and every $t \in T$ there is a sequence $t_n \to t$, $(t_n) \subseteq T_0$, satisfying $X_{t_n}(\omega) \to X_t(\omega)$. Let $T = [0,1]$ and assume that a separable process satisfies

$$P(|X_s - X_t|^\alpha) \leqq C|s-t|^{1+\beta},$$

where $\alpha > 0$, $\beta > 0$, $C > 0$. Then the theorem of Kolmogorov and Prohorov states that for arbitrary $c > 0$, $0 < \gamma < \frac{\beta}{\alpha}$, $h > 0$,

$$P\left\{\sup_{|s-t|<h} |X_s - X_t| \geqq \frac{4c}{\gamma \log 2} h^\gamma\right\} \leqq \frac{2C}{c^\alpha(\beta - \gamma\alpha)} h^{\beta - \gamma\alpha}.$$

In particular, this implies that the process has continuous paths P-a.e.

Let $(X_t)_{t \in T}$ be a stochastic process on $(\Omega, \mathscr{A}, P)$. The finite dimensional marginal distributions of the process are $\mathscr{L}((X_t)_{t \in \alpha}|P)$, $\alpha \in A(T)$. This is a projective system on $(\mathbb{R}^T, \mathscr{B}^T)$. For any projective system on $(\mathbb{R}^T, \mathscr{B}^T)$ there exists a stochastic process whose finite dimensional distributions coincide with the given projective system iff there exists a projective limit.

A stochastic process is a Gaussian process if its finite dimensional marginal distribution are Gaussian. Hence, a Gaussian process is determined by its mean value structure $t \mapsto P(X_t)$, $t \in T$, and its covariance structure $(s, t) \mapsto \mathrm{Cov}(X_s, X_t)$, $s, t \in T$. If $T = [0, \infty)$ and $P(X_t) = 0$, $\mathrm{Cov}(X_s, X_t) = \min\{s, t\}$, then the stochastic process is a Brownian motion. The distribution of a Brownian motion on $(\mathbb{R}^T, \mathscr{B}^T)$ is concentrated on $\mathscr{C}(T)$ with probability one and is called Wiener measure. If $T = [0,1]$ and $P(X_t) = 0$, $\mathrm{Cov}(X_s, X_t) = \min\{s, t\} - s.t$ then the stochastic process is a Brownian bridge.

Consider a sequence of stochastic processes $(X_{n,t})_{t \in T}$ on probability spaces $(\Omega_n, \mathscr{A}_n, P_n)$, $n \in \mathbb{N}$, where $T = [0,1]$. Suppose that the finite dimensional marginal distributions of $(X_{n,t})_{t \in T}$, $n \in \mathbb{N}$, converge weakly to the finite dimensional marginal distributions of a process $(X_t)_{t \in T}$, $t \in T$. Suppose further that there is a metric space (Y, d), $Y \subseteq \mathbb{R}^T$, such that all those processes have paths in Y with probability one. Then we say that $(X_{n,t})_{t \in T}$, $n \in \mathbb{N}$, satisfies an invariance principle if even the distributions of $(X_{n,t})_{t \in T}$, $n \in \mathbb{N}$, on (Y, d) converge weakly to the distribution of $(X_t)_{t \in T}$ on (Y, d). If $T = [0,1]$ and $(Y, d) = (\mathscr{C}_b(T), \|.\|_u)$ then the sequence satisfies an invariance principle iff it is equicontinuous and uniformly bounded in probability.

Topological groups (Nachbin [1965]). Let G be a group and $\mathscr{T}$ a topology on G. Then $(G, \mathscr{T})$ is a topological group if the group operations are compatible with the topology. A Borel measure $\lambda_\ell \in \mathscr{M}(G, \mathscr{B}(G))$ is a left Haar measure if

$$\int f(gx)\, \lambda_\ell(dx) = \int f(x)\, \lambda_\ell(dx), \quad f \in \mathscr{C}_{00}(G),\ g \in G,$$

and a Borel measure $\lambda_r \in \mathscr{M}(G, \mathscr{B}(G))$ is a right Haar measure if

$$\int f(xg)\, \lambda_r(dx) = \int f(x)\, \lambda_r(dx), \quad f \in \mathscr{C}_{00}(G),\ g \in G.$$

For the following assume that $(G, \mathscr{T})$ is locally compact group with countable base for its topology. Then there exists right and left Haar measures and each is uniquely determined up to scalar factors. The Haar measures are bounded iff $(G, \mathscr{T})$ is compact.

If λ_ℓ is a left Haar measure on G then $A \mapsto \lambda_\ell(Ag^{-1})$, $A \in \mathscr{B}(G)$, is a left Haar measure, too, and hence there is a constant $\Delta(g) > 0$ such that

$$\lambda_\ell(Ag^{-1}) = \Delta(g)\, \lambda_\ell(A), \quad A \in \mathscr{B}(G).$$

The function $\Delta\colon G \to (0, \infty)$ is called the modulus function of the group. It is a continuous homomorphism.

If $(H, \langle .,. \rangle)$ is a Euclidean space then $O(H)$ denotes the orthogonal group and $GL(H)$ the general linear group on H. Identifying H with the group of translations operating on H, we may define the semidirect product of $GL(H)$ and H. It consists of the mappings

$$(A, a)\colon x \mapsto Ax + a, \quad x \in H,\ A \in GL(H),\ a \in H,$$

and the composition is defined to be the natural composition, considering the pairs (A, a) as mappings on H.

If $(G, \mathscr{T})$ is a topological group and $\mu, \nu \in \mathscr{M}(G, \mathscr{B}(G))$ are Borel measures they can be composed to

$$\mu * \nu\colon f \mapsto \iint f(g \circ h)\, \mu(dg)\, \nu(dh), \quad f \in \mathscr{C}_{00}(G),$$

called the convolution of μ and ν.

References

Anderson, T. W. (1955): The integral of a symmetric unimodal function over a symmetric convex set and some probability inequalities. Proc. Amer. Math. Soc. **6**, 170–176.

Bahadur, R. R. (1954): Sufficiency and statistical decision functions. Ann. Math. Statistics **25**, 423–462.

(1955): Statistics and subfields. Ann. Math. Stat. **26**, 490–497.

(1957): On unbiased estimates of uniformly minimum variance. Sankhyā **18**, 211–224.

(1964): On Fisher's bound for asymptotic variances. Ann. Math. Statistics **35**, 1545–1552.

Bauer, H. (1981): Probability Theory and Elements of Measure Theory. New York: Academic Press.

Becker, C. (1982): Schwache asymptotische Normalität von statistischen Experimenten bei unabhängigen, nicht notwendig identisch verteilten Beobachtungen. Thesis. University of Bayreuth.

Berger, A. (1951): Remark on separable spaces of probability measures. Ann. Math. Statistics **22**, 119–120.

Bhattacharya, R. N. and R. R. Rao (1976): Normal Approximation and Asymptotic Expansions. New York: John Wiley & Sons.

Billingsley, P. (1968): Convergence of Probability Measures. New York: John Wiley & Sons.

Birnbaum, A. (1955): Characterizations of complete classes of tests of some multiparametric hypotheses, with applications to likelihood ratio tests. Ann. Math. Statistics **26**, 21–36.

Blackwell, D. (1947): Conditional expectation and unbiased sequential estimation. Ann. Math. Stat. **18**, 105–110.

(1951): Comparison of experiments. Proc. 2nd Berkeley Symp. Math. Statistics Prob., 93–102.

(1953): Equivalent comparisons of experiments. Ann. Math. Statistics **24**, 265–272.

Blyth, C. R. (1951): On minimax statistical decision procedures and their admissibility. Ann. Math. Statistics **22**, 22–42.

Boll, C. H. (1955): Comparison of Experiments in the Infinite Case. Ph. D. Thesis, Stanford University.

Bondar, I. V. and P. Milnes (1981): Amenability: A survey for statistical applications of Hunt-Stein and related conditions on groups. Z. Wahrscheinlichkeitstheorie verw. Geb. **57**, 103–128.

Borges, R. and J. Pfanzagl (1963): A characterization of the one-parameter exponential family of distributions by monotonicity of likelihood ratios. Z. Wahrscheinlichkeitstheorie verw. Geb. **2**, 111–117.

Bourbaki, N. (1958): Eléments de mathématique. Livre III: Topologie générale. Paris: Hermann.

Breiman, L., L. LeCam and L. Schwartz (1964): Consistent estimates and zero-one sets. Ann. Math. Statistics **35**, 157–161.

Burkholder, D. L. (1961): Sufficiency in the undominated case. Ann. Math. Statistics **32**, 1191–1200.

Chibisov, D. M. (1967): A theorem on admissible tests and its application to an asymptotic problem of testing hypothesis. Theor. Prob. and Appl. **12**, 90–103.

Choquet, G. (1969): Lectures on Analysis I–III. New York: Benjamin.

Cramer, H. (1946): Mathematical Methods of Statistics. Princeton: Princeton University Press.

Droste, W. (1985): Lokale asymptotische Normalität und asymptotische Likelihood-Schätzer. Thesis. University of Cologne.

Dunford, N. and J.T. Schwartz (1969): Linear Operators. Part I: General Theory. New York: Interscience.

Farrell, R.H. (1967): Weak limits of sequences of Bayes procedures in estimation theory. Proc. 5th Berkeley Symp. Math. Statistics Prob. **1**, 83–111.

(1985): Multivariate Calculation. Use of the Continuous Groups. New York – Berlin – Heidelberg – Tokyo: Springer.

Federer, H. (1969): Geometric Measure Theory. Berlin – Heidelberg – New York: Springer.

Feller, W. (1971): An Introduction to Probability Theory and Its Application II. New York: John Wiley & Sons.

Ferguson, T.S. (1967): Mathematical Statistics. New York: Academic Press.

Gaenssler, P. and W. Stute (1977): Wahrscheinlichkeitstheorie. Berlin – Heidelberg – New York: Springer.

Giri, N. (1976): Invariance and Minimax Statistical Tests. Selecta Statistica Canadia. Montreal: University of Montreal.

Hajek, J. (1969): A Course in Nonparametric Statistics. San Francisco: Holden-Day.

(1970): A characterization of limiting distributions of regular estimates. Z. Wahrscheinlichkeitstheorie verw. Geb. **14**, 323–330.

(1971): Limiting properties of likelihoods and inference. In: Foundations of Statistical Inference. Ed.: V.P. Godambe and D.A. Sprott. Toronto, 142–162.

(1972): Local asymptotic minimax and admissibility in estimation. Proc. 6th Berkeley Symp. Math. Stat. Prob., Vol. **1**, 175–194.

Hajek, J. and Z. Sidak (1967): Theory of Rank Tests. New York: Academic Press.

Halmos, P.R. and L.J. Savage (1949): Application of the Radon-Nikodym theorem to the theory of sufficient statistics. Ann. Math. Stat. **20**, 225–241.

Heyer, H. (1969): Erschöpftheit und Invarianz beim Vergleich von Experimenten. Z. Wahrscheinlichkeitstheorie verw. Geb. **12**, 21–55.

(1972): Zum Erschöpftheitsbegriff von D. Blackwell. Metrika **19**, 54–67.

(1982): Theory of Statistical Experiments. Berlin – Heidelberg – New York: Springer.

Ibragimov, I.A. and R.Z. Has'minskii (1972): Asymptotic behaviour of statistical estimators in the smooth case. I: Study of the likelihood ratio. Theor. Prob. Appl. **17**, 445–462.

(1973): Asymptotic behaviour of statistical estimators in the smooth case. II: Limit theorem for the a posteriori density and Bayes' estimators. Theor. Prob. Appl. **18**, 76–91.

(1981): Statistical Estimation. Berlin – Heidelberg – New York: Springer.

James, W. and Ch. Stein (1960): Estimation with quadratic loss. Proc. 4th Berkeley Symp., Vol. **2**, 361–379.

Janssen, A. (1985): The Lévy-Hinčin formula for infinitely divisible experiments. In: Infinitely Divisible Statistical Experiments. Berlin – Heidelberg – New York: Springer.

Landers, D. (1968): Existenz und Konsistenz von Maximum Likelihood Schätzern. Thesis, University of Cologne.

(1972): Sufficient and minimal sufficient σ-fields. Z. Wahrscheinlichkeitstheorie verw. Geb. **23**, 197–207.

Landers, D. and L. Rogge (1972): Characterization of the topologies used in the theory of maximum likelihood estimation. Z. Wahrscheinlichkeitstheorie verw. Geb. **21**, 197–200.

LeCam, L. (1953): On some asymptotic properties of maximum likelihood estimates and related Bayes' estimates. Univ. Calif. Publl. Statistics **1**, 277–330.
(1955): An extension of Wald's theory of statistical decision functions. Ann. Math. Statistics **26**, 69–81.
(1956): On the asymptotic theory of estimation and testing hypotheses. Proc. 3rd Berkeley Symp. Math. Stat. Prob. **1**, 129–156.
(1960): Locally asymptotically normal families of distributions. Univ. Calif. Publ. Statistics **3**, 37–98.
(1964): Sufficiency and approximate sufficiency. Ann. Math. Statistics **35**, 1419–1455.
(1969): Théorie asymptotique de la décision statistique. Les Presses de l'Université de Montreal.
(1970): On the assumptions used to prove asymptotic normality of maximum likelihood estimates. Ann. Math. Statistics **41**, 802–828.
(1972): Limits of experiments. Proc. 6th Berkeley Symp. Math. Stat. Prob., Vol. **1**, 245–261.
(1973): Convergence of estimates under dimensionality restrictions. Ann. Statistics **1**, 38–53.
(1974): Notes on Asymptotic Methods in Statistical Decision Theory. I. Publ. du Centre de Recherches Mathématiques. Université de Montréal.
(1979): On a Theorem of J. Hájek. Contributions to Statistics – Hájek Memorial Volume. Ed.: Dr. J. Jurecková, 119–135. Dordrecht: D. Reidel.
Lehmann, E. (1958): Testing Statistical Hypotheses. New York: John Wiley & Sons.
Lehmann, E.L. and H. Scheffé (1950): Completeness, similar regions and unbiased estimation: Part 1. Sankhyā **10**, 305–340.
Levit, B.Ya. (1975): On the efficiency of a class of nonparametric estimates. Theor, Prob. and Appl. **20**, 723–740.
Luschgy, H. (1984): Invariante statistische Entscheidungsprobleme. Habilitationsschrift. Universitaet Muenster.
Michel, R. and J. Pfanzagl (1970): Asymptotic Normality. Metrika **16**, 188–205.
Milbrodt, H. (1983): Global asymptotic normality Statistics and decisions **1**, 401–425.
Milbrodt, H. and H. Strasser (1983): Limits of Triangular Arrays of Experiments. In: Infinitely Divisible Statistical Experiments. Berlin – Heidelberg – New York: Springer.
Millar, P.W. (1979): Asymptotic minimax theorems for the sample distribution function. Z. Wahrscheinlichkeitstheorie verw. Geb. **48**, 233–252.
(1983): The minimax principle in asymptotic statistical theory. Lecture notes in math. **976**, 75–265. Berlin – Heidelberg – New York: Springer.
Moussatat, M.W. (1976): On the Asymptotic Theory of Statistical Experiments and Some of Its Applications. Ph.D. thesis. Berkeley: University of California.
Nachbin, L. (1965): The Haar integral. Princeton. Van Nostrand-Reinhold.
Nölle, G. (1966): Zur Theorie der bedingten Tests. Thesis. University of Münster.
(1971): Produktmeßbarkeit von Funktionen. Z. Wahrscheinlichkeitstheorie verw. Geb. **17**, 163–167.
Nölle, G. and H. Witting (1970): Angewandte Mathematische Statistik. Stuttgart: Teubner.
Oosterhoff, J. and W.R. van Zwet (1979): A Note on Contiguity and Hellinger Distance. Contributions to Statistics – Hájek Memorial Volume. Ed.: Dr. J. Jurecková, 157–166. Dordrecht: D. Reidel.
Parthasarathy, K.R. (1967): Probability Measures on Metric Spaces. New York: Academic Press.
Pfanzagl, J. (1963): Überall trennscharfe Tests und monotone Dichtequotienten. Z. Wahrscheinlichkeitstheorie verw. Geb. **1**, 109–115.
(1969): On the existence of product measurable densities. Sankhyā **31**, 13–18.

(1970a): On the asymptotic efficiency of median unbiased estimates. Ann. Math. Statistics **41**, 1500–1509.
(1970b): Median unbiased estimates for M.L.R.-families. Metrika **15**, 30–39.
(1971): On median unbiased estimates. Metrika **18**, 154–173.
(1972a): Further results on asymptotic normality I, Metrika **18**, 174–198.
(1972b): Further results on asymptotic normality II, Metrika **19**, 89–97.
(1974): A characterization of sufficiency by power functions. Metrika **21**, 197–199.
(1979): On optimal median unbiased estimors in the presence of nuisance parameters. Ann. Statistics **7**, 187–193.
(1985): Asymptotic Expansions for General Statistical Models. Berlin – Heidelberg – New York: Springer.
Pfanzagl, J. and W. Wefelmeyer (1982): Contributions to a General Asymptotic Statistical Theory. Lecture notes in statistics **13**, Berlin – Heidelberg – New York: Springer.
Rao, C.R. (1952): Some theorems of minimum variance estimation. Sankhyā **12**, 27–42.
Rogge, L. (1972): The relations between minimal sufficient statistics and minimal sufficient σ-fields. Z. Wahrscheinlichkeitstheorie verw. Geb. **23**, 208–215.
Roussas, G.C. (1972): Contiguity of Probability Measures. Cambridge University Press.
Sacksteder, R. (1967): A note on statistical equivalence. Ann. Math. Stat. **38**, 787–794.
Schaefer, H.H. (1971): Topological vector spaces. New York: Springer.
(1974): Banach Lattices and Positive Operators. Berlin – Heidelberg – New York: Springer.
Schmetterer, L. (1963): Some remarks on the power of a most powerful test. Sankhyā **25**, 207–210.
(1974): Introduction to Mathematical Statistics. Berlin – Heidelberg – New York: Springer.
(1978): Einige Resultate aus der Theorie der erwartungstreuen Schätzungen. Information theory, statistical decision functions, random processes. Trans. 7th Prague Conf., Vol. B, Prague 1974, 489–503.
Schwartz, L. (1965): On Bayes procedures. Z. Wahrscheinlichkeitstheorie verw. Geb. **4**, 10–26.
Siebert, E. (1979): Statistical experiments and their conical measures. Z. Wahrscheinlichkeitstheorie verw. Geb. **46**, 247–258.
Stein, C. (1959): The admissibility of Pitman's estimator for a single location parameter. Ann. Math. Statistics **30**, 970–979.
Strasser, H. (1981): Convergence of estimates. Part 1. Journal of Multivariate Analysis **11**, 127–151.
(1981): Convergence of estimates. Part 2. Journal of Multivariate Analysis **11**, 152–172.
(1982): Local asymptotic minimax properties of Pitman estimates. Z. Wahrscheinlichkeitstheorie verw. Geb. **60**, 223–247.
(1985): Einführung in die lokale, asymptotische Theorie der Statistik. Schriftenreihe des Mathematischen Instituts der Universität Bayreuth. University of Bayreuth.
Torgersen, E.N. (1970): Comparison of experiments when the parameter space is finite. Z. Wahrscheinlichkeitstheorie verw. Geb. **16**, 219–249.
(1972): Comparison of translation experiments. Ann. Math. Stat. **43**, 1383–1399.
(1974): Asymptotic Behaviour of Powers of Dichotomies. Statistical Research Report No. **6**, Institute of Mathematics, University of Oslo.
Wald, A. (1943): Tests of statistical hypotheses concerning several parameters when the number of observations is large. Trans. Amer. Math. Soc. **54**, 426–482.
(1947): An essentially complete class of admissible decision functions. Ann. Math. Statistics **18**, 549–555.

(1949): Note on the consistency of the maximum likelihood estimate. Ann. Math. Statistics **20**, 595–601.

(1950): Statistical Decision Functions. New York: John Wiley & Sons.

Wesler, O. (1959): Invariance theory and a modified minimax principle. Ann. Math. Stat. **30**, 1–20.

Witting, H. (1985): Mathematische Statistik I. Stuttgart: Teubner.

List of Symbols

Author Index

Subject Index